FOLKLORE,
Myths, and Legends

FOLKLORE,
Myths, and Legends
A World Perspective

Donna Rosenberg

 NTC Publishing Group
Lincolnwood, Illinois USA

The epigraph on page vii, from Pablo Neruda's "The Word," in *Pablo Neruda: Selected Poems,* Nathaniel Tarn, trans., is reprinted here with the permission of Jonathan Cape, Ltd.

Library of Congress Cataloging-in-Publication Data

Rosenberg, Donna.
Folklore, myths, and legends: a world perspective/Donna Rosenberg.
p.   cm.
Includes bibliographical references and index.
ISBN 0–8442-5763-X (hardback). —ISBN 0-8442-5784-2 (paperback).
—ISBN 0-8442-5780-X (paperback)
1. Tales.   2. Legends.   3. Folklore.   4. Mythology.   I. Title.
GR76.R665   1996
398.2—dc20   96-14501
                                                              CIP

Executive Editor: John T. Nolan
Project Manager: Nancy Liskar
Cover design and illustration: Ophelia Chamblis
Interior design: Megan Keane DeSantis
Production Manager: Rosemary Dolinski

Published by NTC Publishing Group
© 1997 NTC Publishing Group, 4255 West Touhy Avenue,
Lincolnwood (Chicago), Illinois 60646-1975 U.S.A.

6 7 8 9 ML 0 9 8 7 6 5 4 3 2 1

To David, Deborah, and Miriam,
who loved to hear the old stories
and who now share them with their children

Words give glass-quality to glass, blood to blood, and life to life itself.

—Pablo Neruda

CONTENTS

PREFACE   XVII

INTRODUCTION   XXI

PART 1   AFRICA   **1**

THE CREATION OF HUMAN BEINGS   4

ANANSI, THE CLEVER ONE   7

THE WOMAN WITH ONE HAND   17

THE ROAMER-OF-THE-PLAIN   28

THE CROCODILE AND HIS SON   43

PART 2   THE MIDDLE EAST   **63**

ENKI, LORD OF THE EARTH AND THE WATERS OF
     LIFE *AND* ADAPA   65

THE CRAFTSMAN'S WIFE   86

ROSTAM, SHIELD OF PERSIA *AND* THE TRAGEDY
     OF SOHRAB   94

PART 3   EUROPE   **159**

PROMETHEUS, THE FIRE-BRINGER   161

OISIN MAC FINN, POET OF THE FIANNA   178

SAGA OF GUNNLAUG SERPENT-TONGUE   204

AUCASSIN AND NICOLETTE   236

DOCTOR FAUST   254

PART 4   THE AMERICAS   **283**

BOTOQUE, BRINGER OF FIRE   286

THE LITTLE FROG   300

THE JOURNEY BENEATH THE EARTH   314

EL BIZARRÓN AND THE DEVIL *AND* WILEY

    AND THE HAIRY MAN   321

THE SHEPHERD WHO UNDERSTOOD ANIMAL SPEECH   347

RIP VAN WINKLE   354

GIANT, THE FIRE-BRINGER   364

PART 5   THE FAR EAST   **371**

SAVITRI   373

KUN AND THE GREAT FLOOD *AND* YU THE GREAT

    AND THE GREAT FLOOD   395

SONG OF THE WATER GODDESS   415

TARO URASHIMA, THE YOUNG FISHERMAN   421

THE TIGER'S WHISKER   432

KERTA'S SACRIFICE   442

NOTES   457

SELECTED BIBLIOGRAPHY   489

PRONUNCIATION GUIDE   505

INDEX OF TITLES   511

QUESTIONS FOR RESPONSE, DISCUSSION,

    AND ANALYSIS   513

THEMATIC
TABLE OF CONTENTS

CREATION
THE CREATION OF HUMAN BEINGS   4
ENKI, LORD OF THE EARTH AND THE WATERS
    OF LIFE   65

CULTURE HEROES AND FERTILITY GODS
THE ROAMER-OF-THE-PLAIN   28
THE CROCODILE AND HIS SON   43
ENKI, LORD OF THE EARTH AND THE WATERS
    OF LIFE   65
PROMETHEUS, THE FIRE-BRINGER   161
BOTOQUE, BRINGER OF FIRE   286
GIANT, THE FIRE-BRINGER   364
KUN AND THE GREAT FLOOD   395
YU THE GREAT AND THE GREAT FLOOD   395
SONG OF THE WATER GODDESS   415
KERTA'S SACRIFICE   442

MORTALITY AND DEATH
ANANSI, THE CLEVER ONE   7
ADAPA   65

OISIN MAC FINN, POET OF THE FIANNA   178

DOCTOR FAUST   254

BOTOQUE, BRINGER OF FIRE   286

THE JOURNEY BENEATH THE EARTH   314

EL BIZARRÓN AND THE DEVIL   321

WILEY AND THE HAIRY MAN   321

RIP VAN WINKLE   354

SAVITRI   373

TARO URASHIMA, THE YOUNG FISHERMAN   421

PARENTS AND CHILDREN

ANANSI, THE CLEVER ONE   7

THE WOMAN WITH ONE HAND   17

THE ROAMER-OF-THE-PLAIN   28

THE CROCODILE AND HIS SON   43

ADAPA   65

THE TRAGEDY OF SOHRAB   94

AUCASSIN AND NICOLETTE   236

OISIN MAC FINN, POET OF THE FIANNA   178

SAGA OF GUNNLAUG SERPENT-TONGUE   204

THE LITTLE FROG   300

WILEY AND THE HAIRY MAN   321

RIP VAN WINKLE   354

SAVITRI   373

KUN AND THE GREAT FLOOD   395

YU THE GREAT AND THE GREAT FLOOD   395

KERTA'S SACRIFICE   442

RIGHT AND WRONG

ANANSI, THE CLEVER ONE	7
THE WOMAN WITH ONE HAND	17
THE ROAMER-OF-THE-PLAIN	28
THE CROCODILE AND HIS SON	43
ADAPA	65
THE CRAFTSMAN'S WIFE	86
THE TRAGEDY OF SOHRAB	94
PROMETHEUS, THE FIRE-BRINGER	161
SAGA OF GUNNLAUG SERPENT-TONGUE	204
AUCASSIN AND NICOLETTE	236
DOCTOR FAUST	254
BOTOQUE, BRINGER OF FIRE	286
THE LITTLE FROG	300
EL BIZARRÓN AND THE DEVIL	321
WILEY AND THE HAIRY MAN	321
THE SHEPHERD WHO UNDERSTOOD ANIMAL SPEECH	347
GIANT, THE FIRE-BRINGER	364
SAVITRI	373
KUN AND THE GREAT FLOOD	395
YU THE GREAT AND THE GREAT FLOOD	395
THE TIGER'S WHISKER	432
KERTA'S SACRIFICE	442

LOVE AND FRIENDSHIP

THE WOMAN WITH ONE HAND	17
THE CRAFTSMAN'S WIFE	86

THE TRAGEDY OF SOHRAB   94

OISIN MAC FINN, POET OF THE FIANNA   178

SAGA OF GUNNLAUG SERPENT-TONGUE   204

AUCASSIN AND NICOLETTE   236

THE LITTLE FROG   300

THE JOURNEY BENEATH THE EARTH   314

THE SHEPHERD WHO UNDERSTOOD ANIMAL SPEECH   347

SAVITRI   373

TARO URASHIMA, THE YOUNG FISHERMAN   421

THE TIGER'S WHISKER   432

ANIMAL HELPERS

THE WOMAN WITH ONE HAND   17

THE ROAMER-OF-THE-PLAIN   28

THE CROCODILE AND HIS SON   43

BOTOQUE, BRINGER OF FIRE   286

THE LITTLE FROG   300

THE SHEPHERD WHO UNDERSTOOD ANIMAL SPEECH   347

GIANT, THE FIRE BRINGER   364

KUN AND THE GREAT FLOOD   395

YU THE GREAT AND THE GREAT FLOOD   395

THE TIGER'S WHISKER   432

REBELLION AND CONFORMITY

THE ROAMER-OF-THE-PLAIN   28

THE CROCODILE AND HIS SON   43

PROMETHEUS, THE FIRE-BRINGER   161

DOCTOR FAUST   254

THE SHEPHERD WHO UNDERSTOOD ANIMAL SPEECH   347

KUN AND THE GREAT FLOOD   395

YU THE GREAT AND THE GREAT FLOOD   395

KERTA'S SACRIFICE   442

HEROES AND HEROINES

THE CROCODILE AND HIS SON   43

ROSTAM, SHIELD OF PERSIA   94

THE TRAGEDY OF SOHRAB   94

PROMETHEUS, THE FIRE-BRINGER   161

OISIN MAC FINN, POET OF THE FIANNA   178

SAGA OF GUNNLAUG SERPENT-TONGUE   204

GIANT, THE FIRE-BRINGER   364

SAVITRI   373

KUN AND THE GREAT FLOOD   395

YU THE GREAT AND THE GREAT FLOOD   395

CLEVER BEINGS, WISE AND FOOLISH

ANANSI, THE CLEVER ONE   7

ADAPA   65

THE CRAFTSMAN'S WIFE   86

PROMETHEUS, THE FIRE-BRINGER   161

AUCASSIN AND NICOLETTE   236

THE LITTLE FROG   300

EL BIZARRÓN AND THE DEVIL   321

WILEY AND THE HAIRY MAN   321

THE SHEPHERD WHO UNDERSTOOD ANIMAL SPEECH   347

GIANT, THE FIRE-BRINGER   364

SAVITRI   373

THE TIGER'S WHISKER   432

PREFACE

To the Reader

Folklore, Myths, and Legends: A World Perspective is an anthology of great stories that have universal appeal. A great story satisfies our minds and hearts. Its ability to entertain us distracts us from our present concerns, and we return to our own world refreshed and renewed. Colors appear brighter, objects appear to have greater depth, and life appears to offer more possibilities.

It is appropriate and meaningful to value the stories in this anthology for what their similar themes reveal about human nature and the human condition. They examine the closest of relationships: that of wives to their husbands, children to their parents, and siblings to each other. In the process, they examine the many faces of virtue, along with human failings—such as pride, greed, jealousy, and distrust—that often wear the masks of virtue.

Many characters must weigh their own needs and wishes against their responsibility to others. They all find themselves challenged by what appear to be insurmountable obstacles and take risks in order to achieve their goals. For most of these characters, courage, integrity, determination, and perseverance enable them to use their physical and mental capabilities to enrich their own lives and those of others. Therefore, even when they are nameless, they live on in our minds and hearts as enduring testimony to the complexity and fragility of the human spirit and to the possibilities that each new day offers us.

It is also appropriate and meaningful to relate the attitudes, values, and behavior of these characters to our own personalities and our own lives. All of these stories have serious moral themes. Taken together, they strike chords deep within us that continue to resonate because they deal with profound human issues. They ask us to consider: Who am I? How do I want to define myself as an individual? From where have I come, and where do I want to go? What do I want to experience along the way? Given my destination, am I taking the best route?

In response, these stories provide us with a variety of alternatives, some more life-enhancing and appropriate than others. Many of the characters reflect what we already value in ourselves and in others. A few characters influence our attitudes and behavior by providing examples of counterproductive behavior. They can all lead us to live our lives more thoughtfully and to strive to live up to the best that is within us. These characters can remind us that as long as we are alive, we can determine who we are by how we act. Moreover, by giving us insight into ourselves, they can lead us to find similarities and to appreciate differences between ourselves and others, thereby making us feel more a part of the human family.

A fine story, well told, is a treasure—whether its rendition is oral or literary. Many of the stories in this anthology continue to inspire the creation of literature, art, and music within their own and other cultures. They inspire some students to read them in their original language. They inspire others to become scholars in archaeology, cultural anthropology, folklore, history, linguistics, psychology, and religion. A fine story, well told, lives as long as people are alive to experience its sense of wonder and celebrate their own capacity to be touched by it.

I have written these stories as you might hear them from a storyteller. Their style is designed to appeal to your ear, reflecting the cadences of speech and the repetition that characterize an oral tale. Their style is also designed to appeal to your mind's eye. An old Chinese proverb states that "one picture is worth more than ten thousand words." Poets and storytellers must agree because figurative language, which uses images to express ideas, is also characteristic of oral tales.

Despite this approach to style, I have remained faithful to my sources in the depiction of characters, plot, and themes. Wherever possible, I have worked with original versions in translation. Moreover, I have usually been able to work with at least two versions of each story.

The selections in this anthology have been arranged geographically into five major cultural groups: Africa; the Middle East; Europe; the Americas; and the Far East. In order to facilitate cross-cultural comparisons and contrasts, each cultural group contains folktales, myths, and legends that relate thematically to those in the other cultural groups. Section introductions highlight the selections that appear within each cultural group. In addition, an introduction to each selection provides you with historical, religious, and literary background, as well as my evaluation of the story's appeal.

In the back of this volume, you will find notes about my principal sources, original sources, alternative versions, and additional historical material, as well as the ways in which I may have changed the stories. A Selected Bibliography contains a detailed listing of relevant sources. Other useful features of the book include a thematic table of contents, a pronunciation guide, and an index of selection titles.

Acknowledgments

I especially want to thank my husband, Dick, for encouraging my efforts to transform a vision into a reality and for editing my first draft.

I also want to thank my editor, Nancy Liskar, for all the ways in which she has made my association with NTC a joy.

INTRODUCTION

Folktales

What Is a Folktale?

A folktale is a story that, in its plot, is pure fiction and that has no particular location in either time or space. However, despite its elements of fantasy, a folktale is actually a symbolic way of presenting the different means by which human beings cope with the world in which they live. Folktales concern people—either royalty or common folk—or animals who speak and act like people.

Folktales have different subjects. They focus on the behavior of the individual and are not usually concerned with the human being's relationship to divinity. However, some folktales were originally myths, and others function as both simultaneously. For example, human sacrifice, which takes center stage in "The Crocodile and His Son," is religious in origin and is usually a subject of myth. The origin of death, the interaction with death—personified as Death or as the Devil—and a journey into the Underworld are also usually the subjects of myth.

Many folktales, such as "The Little Frog," are told from the child's point of view and are symbolic depictions of the journey that each person makes from youth to maturity. The characters in these tales must cope with overwhelming tasks that are usually imposed upon them, not taken on willingly. The characters need help in order to succeed, and they receive it because they have befriended a helper-figure who appears in disguise. Therefore, they achieve their goals.

Other folktales, such as those with "trickster" and "clever lass" motifs, reveal the strengths or weaknesses of human character, including the ability to outsmart adversaries who have an advantage. Sometimes, however, clever characters outsmart themselves instead of their adversaries. In this anthology, for example, the craftsman's wife, Wiley, and El Bizarrón are successful, whereas Anansi is too clever for his own good.

Still other folktales are animal tales in which the animals exhibit the attitudes and behavior of people. Anansi is so human that it is

difficult to think of him as a spider. In other tales, such as "The
Woman with One Hand" and "The Shepherd Who Understood
Animal Speech," animals function as the protagonists' helpers.

All traditional folktales focus on plot rather than on character
development, and they omit descriptive passages. They occur
somewhere on Earth where the supernatural is accepted as part of
life. They present a realistic view of the world in that it is incompre-
hensible, unpredictable, and dangerous. Eventually, however, justice
always operates in the world of the folktale, and the good characters
triumph.

Folktale characters have neither a past nor a future. They have no
psychological depth and are characterized by how they treat others.
They all must deal with difficult and interesting challenges, and
they learn that they can affect much of what happens to them by
how they choose to respond. Many are vulnerable to powers who
have authority over them. For example, Aucassin is subject to the
will of his parents, and the craftsman's wife is subject to King
Solomon. Moreover, in tales like "The Little Frog," appearances are
deceiving, so Juan's brothers discover, too late, that his wife is more
than a frog.

Many tales, such as "The Woman with One Hand," reveal that
good and evil are part of human nature. They dramatize the dual
nature of the human psyche by giving good and evil traits to two
opposite characters. In other tales, such as "The Little Frog," the
characters who fail bring their fate upon themselves because their
arrogance makes them "nearsighted," or "blind."

Folktales stress the importance of relationships and the need to
make an effort to preserve them. Nothing of lasting value comes
easily. Only with determination and perseverance do the characters
achieve their goals. For example, Nicolette exhibits courage, determination, perseverance, and creativity in her efforts to become
reunited with Aucassin, and the wife in "The Tiger's Whisker"
exhibits the same qualities in her desire to heal her husband's
psychological wounds.

Contrast is the major artistic device of the folktale, where oppo-
sites are the rule. Characters are beautiful or ugly, good or bad,
industrious or lazy, and successful or ineffectual. Even repetition,
which is a hallmark of the oral tale, often functions to highlight the
contrast between different characters.

Folktales can enrich our lives. We learn that we must make a
concerted effort if we want to achieve anything of value. We learn

that people are available to help us on our journey through life. We learn that the lover's ability to recognize and appreciate inner beauty transforms the loved one, just as it transforms frogs into folktale princesses or princes. Finally, we learn that it is foolish to take to heart the negative views that others have of us because such views only reveal that they do not know who we are and who we will become.

The Function of Folktales

Folktales—which are often called fairy tales, even though fairies hardly ever appear in them—are probably the earliest stories that we remember. They were our first bedtime stories. Later, we read them on our own. We encountered some of them in literature textbooks, in a Great Books program, and in the form of J. R. R. Tolkien's tales.

Folktales are universally appealing because they are very entertaining. Trickster tales, such as "The Craftsman's Wife," emphasize the cleverness of the protagonist. Other tales, such as "The Woman with One Hand," reveal the rewards of courageously leading an ethical life. Tales of love have always captured the human heart, and, in the Middle Ages, "Aucassin and Nicolette" was the most popular love story of its time.

Folktales also have lasting appeal because of other ways in which they enrich our lives. They respond to questions that young people have always asked, such as: How can I gain control over my own life? Given the dangers of the world in which I live, how can I succeed without the help of my parents? What must I do in order to survive and, I hope, thrive as an independent person? How can I cope with those who would use their greater physical strength or their greater power against me? What is likely to be my greatest source of personal happiness, and how can I attempt to achieve it?

Taken together, folktales relate us to human beings across time and space. Psychologically, they give us the encouragement and the tools that will help us forge our own path, and they give us reason to hope that we will find happiness at some point along the way. Like myths, they are a compass that guides us along life's journey, but the compass is practical rather than spiritual. It directs our eyes down to the path before us, rather than up to the sky above us.

In the West, the function of the folktale has changed over time. The idea that folktales are a child's entertainment is a modern development. Homer included folktales in the *Iliad* and the *Odyssey*,

epics written in the eighth century B.C. that were designed to entertain and instruct warriors and other adults, as well as children, in
the cultural values of ancient Greece. The great sacred texts of both
the East and the West have treated folktales seriously, including
them as moral lessons. Religious leaders have included them in
their sermons for the same purpose.

Throughout history, the telling of folktales has also been a
popular form of entertainment among farmers and laborers, merchants, sailors and other travelers, and household servants. In the
fourteenth century, Giovanni Boccaccio and Geoffrey Chaucer
incorporated folktales into the *Decameron* and the *Canterbury Tales,*
respectively.

The literary folktale was born in France in the mid-seventeenth
century. Aristocratic women created them for their own social
gatherings and often put them into written form before presenting
them. Late in that century, the French aristocrat Charles Perrault
published his versions of certain folktales for adults in his social
circle.

In the eighteenth century, folktales that had moral themes began
to be considered appropriate material for children. However, they
did not become truly acceptable as children's literature until the
nineteenth century. In 1812 and 1815, in Germany, Jacob and
Wilhelm Grimm published their folktales, which include compos-
ites of different oral versions of the same tale as well as tales based
on written sources such as Perrault. Hans Christian Andersen's
literary tales were published in Denmark in 1835.

In Western cultures of the nineteenth and twentieth centuries,
folktales have contributed to a national sense of identity and pride,
and they often developed in response to particular political and
social needs. However, this is not unusual. In China, myths, legends, and folktales had been serving these purposes since the Han
dynasty (202 B.C.–A.D. 220).

Myths

What Is a Myth?

A myth is a *sacred* story from the past. It may explain the origin of
the universe and of life, or it may express its culture's moral values
in human terms. Myths concern the powers who control the human

world and the relationship between those powers and human beings. Although myths are religious in their origin and function, they may also be the earliest form of history, science, or philosophy.

Myths are a form of religion whenever—like the myths about Adapa, Prometheus, the Ainu Water Goddess, and Kerta and the mythic tale about the Roamer-of-the-Plain—they set forth the nature of their culture's divinities and the relationship that is expected between the members of their culture and these divinities.

Myths are an early form of history whenever—like the myth about Enki and the African myths and mythic tales about creation, death ("Anansi, the Clever One"), and human sacrifice ("The Crocodile and His Son")—they relate the way in which the universe and its various forms of life were created and the events that followed in the early periods of human existence.

Myths are an early form of science whenever they explain the origin of natural phenomena. Myths about culture heroes—such as Enki, Prometheus, Botoque, Giant, Kun, and Yu, who give human beings the knowledge and technology that they need in order to survive—often function as scientific myths.

Myths are an early form of philosophy whenever—like the myths about Savitri, Oisin Mac Finn, and Taro Urashima, and the mythic tale "The Journey beneath the Earth"—they provide a view of life, unwritten laws governing social conduct, and models of expected attitudes, moral values, and behavior.

The relationship between human beings and the divine world is so important that most myths teach proper behavior by illustrating what the gods will do to those who are so arrogant as to treat them disrespectfully, either in word or in deed. "The Roamer-of-the-Plain," "Prometheus, the Fire-Bringer," and "Kerta's Sacrifice"—each from a different culture—are all fine examples of this technique.

Such myths make their point by flooding the human heart with terror. Part of this psychological impact—the wonder and terror of myth—is caused by the fact that we recognize the ease with which we, too, can become arrogant. Myths remind us that excessive pride is a slippery slope.

Whether myths are historical, scientific, philosophical, or religious, the members of a culture consider their own myths to be factual and true. Each myth has its place in the mythology of its culture. Taken together, the myths unify the members of that culture by giving them a shared past; a meaningful, life-sustaining present; and a predictable future.

The Function of Myths

Most of us love myths from the time we first encounter them. When we are children, we take them literally and let them speak to us of the wonder that fills the universe and the joy, terror, and responsibility of being alive. When we are older, we are likely to be so involved in our technological environment that we forget our awe of life and our earlier reverence for the world of nature. We forget (or we try hard to forget) the aspects of life over which we still have no control—until natural and human disasters fill us with terror. However, if we are fortunate, we let the beauty of the world remind us that the universe is still filled with wonder, a wonder that is visible in sunrise and sunset, the rainbow, frost on a windowpane, fog and flowers, the song of a bird, and human life—with its love and laughter, and with its possibilities.

Since human beings first began to think, they have wondered about the Great Unknown, and they have asked: Who am I? What is the nature of the universe in which I live? How do I relate to both the known and unknown world? How much control do I have over my own life? What must I do to survive? How can I balance my own desires with my responsibilities to my family, my community, and the powers that control my world? How can I reconcile myself to the inevitability of death?

Myths answer these questions in terms of our relationship to the divine world and, therefore, they provide us with moral answers. They are the source of our most important attitudes and values, the principles by which we live, and the ideals for which we sacrifice our lives. They create meaning out of nothingness, sense out of nonsense, order out of chaos, and purpose out of aimlessness. Myths meet genuine psychological needs. They make a culture's spiritual beliefs and values concrete and understandable. They are a spiritual compass that guides us along life's journey.

Legends

What Is a Legend?

A legend is a story from the past about a subject that was, or is believed to have been, historical. Legends concern people, places, and events. Usually, the subject is a saint, a king, a hero, a famous person, or a war. A legend is always associated with a particular place and a particular time in history.

Every culture has its own heroic legends, which the society regards as historically accurate. Many are among the greatest stories in the world. Their heroes embody their culture's values and function as role models, depicting the attitudes and behavior that their society considers to be ideal.

Legends and myths address some of the same questions, but legends respond to them from a more self-centered perspective. The great heroes of legend determine who they are by how they act throughout their lives. Although they take their divinities seriously, they focus primarily on pleasing themselves and their society. Because the heroes' only route to immortality is the lasting fame of their deeds, heroic behavior is of principal importance. Therefore, the heroes' primary goal in life is to achieve self-esteem by earning the esteem of their peers and their community. Community service is so important that, if heroes act irresponsibly toward others in their society, their personal desires turn to dust.

The great legends perpetuate the deeds of heroes in the songs and tales that their culture's historians, bards, and poets created about them. Because a legend originates in the oral tradition, it often acquires material from myth and folklore. When legendary characters possesses superhuman or divine qualities, or when supernatural beings interact with them—as in the legends of Oisin Mac Finn, Rip Van Winkle, Taro Urashima, and Savitri—then the legend becomes a myth as well. When stories of similar people become attached to a legendary character, as they have with Doctor Faust, or when fantastic material highlights the extraordinary qualities of heroes like Rostam and Sohrab, then folktale elements have become part of the legendary biography or history.

In many ways, legendary heroes are like the heroes of both myth and folktale. For example, like characters in both myth and folktale, Rostam, Sohrab, and Gunnlaug face overwhelming tasks that, usually, are imposed on them. In legend, these tasks are imposed by the kings whom the heroes serve.

Moreover, like the gods of mythic heroes, the gods of legendary heroes often help them to succeed. Therefore, the legendary heroes achieve an unusual degree of success, which includes the immortality conferred by lasting fame. However, unlike the heroes of myth and folktale, legendary heroes usually do not emerge triumphant in the end, despite their many great deeds. Instead, they die prematurely—either through treachery, or because their excessive pride has led them to misjudge their circumstances.

Great heroes are not made of pure gold. They are always as human as they are heroic, and they make many mistakes. Although it is the arrogance of legendary heroes that often leads to their ultimate defeat, legend differs from myth in that this arrogance is not directed against divinity, and it is not their gods who punish them with death. Part of the psychological impact—the wonder and terror of legend—is caused by the fact that we recognize the complexity of our own lives, and we know that despite our best efforts, we too can become the victim of circumstances that we can neither foresee nor control.

The Function of Legends

Most of us love legends. We love to hear and to read about people who have accomplished great tasks. We often hope that a special opportunity will enter our own lives so that we can prove ourselves by acting in a way that will bring us lasting fame.

We know how we would like to respond to this great, nameless challenge because we know how our heroes would respond. We have heard about them in the bedtime stories of our childhood. We have studied their legends in school. We have read about others in comic books, magazines, and newspapers, and we have seen still others on television and movie screens. Some of us never tire of them and continue to read about them in historical fiction, drama, and epic literature.

Major Perspectives on Folklore, Myths, and Legends

Historical Background

The serious study of folktales began early in the nineteenth century with the German brothers Jacob and Wilhelm Grimm, who collected their tales from aristocrats, members of the educated middle class, and written sources. Thereafter, others—such as Sir Walter Scott in Scotland—became interested in collecting multiple versions of folktales in order to trace the tales' history back to their place of origin. At the end of the century, Sir James George Frazer, the Scottish folklorist and classical scholar, published the groundbreaking, twelve-volume comparative study of myth and folktale *The Golden Bough: The Roots of Religion and Folklore.*

In the twentieth century, scholars have brought literary, psychological, sociological, economic, religious, and structural analysis to the study of myths and folktales. These scholars' contributions are discussed briefly in the paragraphs that follow.

A Literary Perspective

Max Luthi (b. 1909) is a Swiss scholar who is recognized for his study of European folk literature. In his view, the folktale is an advanced oral form of literature that could have originated in a dream, a fantasy, during a period of delirium, or in the ecstatic experience of a shaman. Luthi analyzes the structure of the folktale in such a way that he opens the door to psychological interpretation; however, he does not attempt to make such interpretations.

In *The European Folktale: Form and Nature,* Luthi explains that the folktale "translates feelings into actions by transposing the internal world onto the level of external events," and "instead of different possible models of behavior being combined in a single person, we see them sharply separated from one another and divided among persons who stand side by side."

Psychological Perspectives

Sigmund Freud (1856–1939) was an Austrian neurologist who is recognized as the father of psychoanalysis. His work has led many people throughout the world to accept the unconscious as a factor in human thought and behavior, thus broadening how we may interpret all products of the human mind, including literature.

It is Freud's view that we do not permit troublesome feelings about family members, such as our mother and father, to become conscious because we view these feelings as forbidden. These unconscious feelings express themselves both in dreams (their private form) and in myths (their public form), and they determine the symbolic nature of the content of both forms. Dreams and myths satisfy our unconscious feelings by expressing them in an acceptable format in which they are fulfilled symbolically. Since everyone has a mother and father, myths contain universally similar images and motifs.

Géza Róheim (1891–1953) was a Hungarian anthropologist who is known for his studies in European folklore. He was the first to take Freudian psychoanalysis into the field and apply it to the study of native cultures in Australia and North America. It is Roheim's view that folktale and myth are the product of fantasies about the adult world as the child perceives it. Folktales begin as dreams and are told and retold until they become part of a people's cultural heritage.

Bruno Bettelheim (1903–1990) was a Freudian psychoanalyst who is recognized for his work with children. It is his view that folktales are beneficial for the psychological development of children because their abstract symbolism enables children to resolve their psychological crises.

Alan Dundes (b. 1934) is a contemporary American folklorist who applies a Freudian psychoanalytic approach to folklore. In his view, the content of folktales, like that of dreams, reflects the unconscious thoughts and desires of individuals in a particular culture. The child relegated these thoughts and desires to the unconscious because he or she originally considered them to be dangerous. The child is the "parent" of the adult in that unresolved childhood issues remain in the adult unconscious.

Dundes does not accept Carl Jung's theory of the collective unconscious (see below) because, after two hundred years of research into world cultures, no one myth or folktale has been found in every culture.

Emile Durkheim (1858–1917) was a French sociologist who is recognized for his theory of "the collective conscious." In his words, "The collective conscious is the highest form of the psychic life. . . . It alone can furnish the mind with the molds which are applicable to the totality of things and which make it possible to think of them." (Bierlein: *Parallel Myths*) Durkheim viewed myth as a product of the collective conscious, a shared pool of ancestral memories and images that are common to all human beings.

Carl Gustav Jung (1875–1961) was a Swiss Freudian psychoanalyst who later developed his own influential theories about the unconscious. Jung was influenced, in part, by Durkheim's theory of the collective conscious.

It was Jung's view that myths express universal aspects of the human personality that have not yet become conscious. He is known for his theory of the "collective unconscious," which is composed of innate, universal psychological characteristics that have influenced our attitudes and behavior ever since human life began. The content of the collective unconscious is divided into archetypes—patterns of thought and symbol, such as the mother, the child, the trickster, and the hero. Archetypal images are influenced by individual life experiences. The collective unconscious, as expressed in myths, reveals similar and universal motifs that have been influenced by a particular culture.

Marie-Louise von Franz (b. 1915) is a Swiss Jungian psychologist who is recognized for her application of Jungian theory to fairy tales.

Joseph Campbell (1904–1987) was a Jungian scholar in the field of comparative mythology. In his view, hero myths originate and function in order to fulfill an unrealized psychological need—the need to discover and nurture the latent, unknown, and unconscious side of a person's psyche. Like Jung, and unlike Freud, Campbell thought that the unconscious contains nothing socially or personally objectionable. Therefore, we do not purposely hide its contents; we simply do not recognize them.

An Economic Perspective

Paul Radin (1883–1959) was an anthropologist who is recognized for his economic approach to religion and mythology. In Radin's view, early peoples had no economic security and, therefore, they were emotionally insecure and felt both vulnerable and insignificant in their environment.

In *Primitive Religion: Its Nature and Origin,* he explains that "the religious formulator developed the theory that everything of value, even everything unchangeable and predictable about man and the world around him, was surrounded and immersed in danger, that these dangers could be overcome only in a specific fashion and according to a prescription devised and perfected by him." The religious leader then would often work with the political leader of the community in order to assure their mutual power and economic benefit.

A Religious Perspective

Mircea Eliade (1907–1986) is recognized for his study of the history of religion. Eliade viewed myth as the vital link between the ancient past and contemporary reality. Myth is a religious phenomenon and a sacred experience, and it is the sacredness of myth that gives it its structure and its function. Eliade's research in comparative mythology reveals numerous similarities among the myths of different cultures.

A Structural Perspective

Claude Lévi-Strauss (b. 1908) is a French social anthropologist who is recognized as the father of "structural anthropology." In his view, myths operate in the human mind unconsciously and reflect the shared aspects of human nature as they are affected by cultural differences. Human beings solve their problems in similar ways because the structure of the human mind is universal. Therefore, myths also possess a common, universal structure.

According to Strauss, a myth consists of all of its variants, and no one variant is the true version. Its meaning is not to be found in its narrative or in its symbolic interpretation, but in how its pieces are combined. The opposing factors in myths—such as male and female, good and evil, human and superhuman, and life and death—reflect primary (economic and social) conflicts in human life. The structure of myths bridges these conflicts and, in this way, creates compromises and resolutions to these problems.

Cultural Influence in Folktales, Myths, and Legends

While folktales, myths, and legends have their universal and personal aspects, we must proceed more carefully with regard to what they appear to reveal about the cultures that have produced them. It is true that because myths, legends, and folktales are all stories about human or humanlike relationships, they inevitably share certain building blocks, or motifs. It is also true that in order to build something that suits its worldview, each culture uses these building blocks in its own way. Therefore, small differences between apparently similar stories can reflect important cultural differences.

Myths and legends, in particular, can be expected to reflect significant aspects of their culture. They were created for the purpose of conveying cultural values, attitudes, and pride, and they are tied to specific locations in time and space through the historic settlement of their people and the actions of their heroes.

However, we cannot ignore the impact of the teller upon the tale. Each of the selections in this book reflects the art of individual storytellers. While they designed their versions to captivate the minds and hearts of their audience, their versions also reflect their own attitudes, values, insights, and artistic gifts. Even when we know that some of these myths and legends were written by poets and dramatists for their own people, using the oral and written materials that were available to them, we also know that these artists have shaped this material to their own taste.

Reliability is even more in question wherever a culture has lacked its own written language and, too often, this has been the situation. People—such as tourists, soldiers, historians, missionaries, and monks—have been recording the literature of other cultures since travel began. Anthropologists and folklorists have been working in this field since the nineteenth century. In these instances, outsiders have recorded the literature of a culture that is foreign to their own, and, frequently they have not understood the local language.

Consequently, either the storyteller or the translator may have been motivated or constrained to change the content of the material that a stranger was recording. Moreover, too often, the recorder—consciously or unconsciously—has brought an inherent social, religious, or political bias to the task. Finally, even with the best intentions, translating one language, with its implied cultural values, into another language, with its own implied cultural values, always presents a difficult problem.

As culture bearers, folktales present a further problem. Homer's epics and the popularity of Greek mythology have led us to expect to find myths and legends in a literary form, whereas the word "folktale" has led us to expect that this type of story appears in its original form, as told by an uneducated person. However, while most folktales originated with the common folk, others were derived from written sources that were either middle-class or aristocratic in social origin or were folktales that had been transformed into literary tales. In a literary tale, aspects of different plots may be combined, description is added, and aspects that are not politically, socially, or linguistically correct are transformed or deleted in order to meet the needs of a particular audience.

Finally, because they are so easy to tell, folktales easily pass from one person to another. Therefore, many exist in numerous versions, both within their own culture and within other cultures, where they have developed new roots and produced new blossoms. Scholars have been surprised to find that, often, the versions within a particular culture differ more significantly from the generic tale than those that have taken root in another culture.

Chronology and Folktales, Myths, and Legends

Folktales, myths, and legends arise in the oral tradition of a culture, a circumstance that makes it difficult to locate them in time. Legends can be dated by establishing the period in which the events of the legend occurred or the hero of the legend would have lived. Since legends usually include some historical or pseudohistorical information, scholars can usually make an educated guess as to when the action originally took place. Myths often cannot be dated, since their content refers to the origin of the universe; the creation of divinities, human beings, and all other forms of life; and the establishment of divine sanctions with regard to human behavior.

Although we often do not know when a particular folktale, myth, or legend originated, we are often able to discover when it was first written down. The ancient cultures of Sumer, Babylonia, Egypt, Persia, Greece, India, and China put their own material into writing, and scholars can date the material that has survived. Of course, earlier material continues to be discovered, both from established, literate, ancient cultures and from literate cultures that are currently being unearthed.

Multiple written versions that are very similar suggest that they derive from one earlier written source (which may no longer exist). Conversely, significant differences among multiple written versions suggest the existence of multiple earlier sources in the oral tradition.

AFRICA

The following myths, legends, and folktales from Africa have a double appeal. First, each is a fine story that captures the imagination of the reader. Second, taken together, these stories strike chords deep within the reader that continue to resonate because the stories deal with profound human truths. They ask: Who are we? Where have we come from? Where do we want to go? What do we want to experience along the way? Given our destination, are we taking the best route?

These African stories reflect the human condition in a way that bridges time and space. They live on in the mind, heart, and soul as enduring testimony to the complexity and fragility of the human spirit, to the kinship that exists between animals and humans, and to the possibilities that each new day offers those who are traveling along the road of life.

"The Creation of Human Beings" takes the Shilluk people back to their origins, reflecting their way of life and explaining the existence of different human races. Particularly interesting are the personality of the creator-god, his reason for creating human beings, and the attributes with which he endows them.

The Ashanti folktale and myth "Anansi, the Clever One" explains the origin of death. Here, death is not an original part of life but is caused by an error in judgment. Anansi is the principal trickster hero of his people. Although he is a spider, his characteristics are so inherent in human nature that it is difficult to think of him as just an animal. His actions reveal that natural catastrophes such as famine can bring out the worst aspects of human nature. However, he lives in a world in which morality is valued and justice operates.

The Swahili folktale "The Woman with One Hand" reveals how our values determine the choices we make and how those choices often produce consequences that we cannot anticipate. We can also interpret the tale psychologically. First, we can view it as a reflection of rivalry between a brother and sister, interpreting it both from the brother's and the sister's perspectives. In addition, we can view it as a reflection of the dual aspects of human nature that coexist within each of us. The tale highlights the existence of these good and evil inclinations by separating them and allocating each to a different character, thereby enabling us to recognize and understand them more easily.

Both the Baronga tale "The-Roamer-of-the-Plain" and the Fan tale "The Crocodile and His Son" examine the relationship between human beings and the powers upon which they depend for their survival. The power of both tales stems from the fact that they are deeply rooted in fertility myths. Both are windows into the lives of people who have not yet developed the technology that will enable them to exert greater control over their environment. Both contain elements of wonder and terror, which we, too, can feel whenever our technology leaves us with little defense against the forces of nature.

"The Roamer-of-the Plain" reflects the role of a totem animal in a culture that depends on nature for survival and prosperity. The people of the young woman's community have established a spiritual connection with their buffalo that involves an exchange of souls and mutual help and protection. The tale deals with such issues as respect for tradition and the conflict between personal desires and responsibility to community. Its roots in myth give it extraordinary power.

"The Crocodile and His Son" is a legend that reflects a different aspect of the same dependence on nature. It combines features of myth in that the crocodile functions as a nature divinity who demands human sacrifice. The crocodile's son functions as the community's culture hero, enriching the life of his community by putting an end to such sacrifice and teaching his people how to fashion their first boats. Since he rebels against and kills his father, this legend demonstrates the presence of classic psychological themes in literature from around the world.

A distinctive aspect of African tales is the importance of animals in human life. Although Anansi is a spider, he is conceived in human terms—a way of saying that animals and human beings are all members of one family. Many of these tales also reveal the friendship that exists between human beings and animals. In "The Woman with One Hand," the young woman treats a snake as if he were another human being, and the snake responds in kind. In "The Roamer-of-the-Plain" and "The Crocodile and His Son," the buffalo and the crocodile are vestiges of early fertility gods, who must be treated properly if the community is to survive.

The Creation of Human Beings

The following myth about the creation of human beings is a Shilluk myth from the area of the Sudan republic that is south of Khartoum, along the White and Blue Nile rivers. The Shilluks are a Sudanic-speaking Black people, who physically resemble the Nubians, their former neighbors who lived in southern Egypt.

This myth reflects the fact that the Shilluks were primarily a sedentary, agricultural people, who cultivated millet and other crops. Fishing was their other important occupation.

Traditionally, the king of the Shilluk people was also their high priest. He was viewed as a divine or sacred king, who had a ritual connection to the earth and to the founding culture hero of their people. The king embodied the spirit of this hero, who ruled the people through him.

Traditionally, the Shilluk people believed that their survival and prosperity depended on the power, influence, and goodwill of their culture hero. This power and goodwill was reflected in the health of their sacred king and in their own fortunes. If their sacred king became ill, or if they suffered from disease, famine, or defeat in battle, they feared that their sacred king was losing his divine power and the goodwill of their culture hero. Therefore, they would kill their sacred king, either by ambush, by strangling, or by sealing his house and leaving him to die in it. Then they would install a new sacred king. The divinity of the Shilluk king reflects one of many important similarities to the political and religious systems of ancient Egypt, which obviously influenced their culture.

The Shilluk story of the creation of human beings is appealing because of the nature of the Shilluks' divine creator, the thoughtful way in which he proceeds with the creative process, the nature of the human beings whom he creates, and his attitude toward them. Scholars think that the other peoples referred to in this myth may be the Cushite people, who lived to the east of the Shilluk people in the highlands of Ethiopia, and the Egyptian people, who lived in northern and central Egypt and who were separated from the Shilluks by the Nubians.

THE CREATION OF HUMAN BEINGS

It came to pass that Juok, creator of life on earth, wandered here and there throughout the world. And as Juok wandered, he said to himself, "The earth will be a better place if I fashion human beings, both men and women, out of the different soils that I have created. For who else will be able to speak and to shout, to sing and to dance in both joy and sorrow? Who else will be able to make the earth grow green and gold with food for those who will live on it?"

And so it came to pass that Juok, creator of life on earth, kneeled down and picked up a handful of clay. And having done this, Juok paused and said, "Now, I must think. If they are to prosper, the men and women whom I fashion must be able to stand straight and tall, to walk and to run, and to work in their fields and to fish in the shallow waters. Therefore, I will give each of them two long legs like those of the pink flamingo."

This Juok did.

And having done this, Juok paused and said, "Now, I must think. If they are to prosper, the men and women whom I fashion must be able to sow, to cultivate, and to reap their fields of millet. Therefore, I will give each of them two long, strong arms. With one arm, they can swing their hoe as monkeys swing sticks, and they can prepare the soil for sowing seeds of millet. With the other arm, they can pull out the weeds that would starve the millet."

This Juok did.

And having done this, Juok paused and said, "Now I must think. If they are to prosper, the men and women whom I fashion must be able to see their fields of millet, or they will not be able to sow, cultivate, and reap it. And they will not be able to see in order to eat it. Therefore, I will give each of them two forward-looking eyes."

This Juok did.

And having done this, Juok paused and said, "Now, I must think. If they are to prosper, the men and women whom I fashion must be able to eat the millet that they have cultivated. Therefore, I will give each of them a mouth."

This Juok did.

And having done this, Juok paused and said, "Now, I must think. If they are to prosper, the men and women whom I fashion must be able to express their joys and sorrows. They must be able to speak and to shout, and to sing and to dance. Therefore, I will give each of them a tongue."

This Juok did.

And having done this, Juok paused and said, "Now, I must think. If they are to prosper, the men and women whom I fashion must be able to hear the words of their companions and the words of the great ones, and they must be able to hear the music of their songs and dances. Therefore, I will give each of them two ears."

This Juok did.

And having done this, Juok paused and said, "Now, I must think. When I am in the northern lands, I will fashion men and women just like this from the pure white sand, and they will have white skin."

This Juok did. And Juok sent these men and women out into the world as perfect human beings.

And having done this, Juok paused and said, "Now, I must think. When I am in the lands of the Egyptian Nile, I will fashion men and women just like this from the reddish-brown mud of that river, and they will have reddish-brown skin."

This Juok did. And Juok sent these men and women out into the world as perfect human beings.

And having done this, Juok paused and said, "Now, I must think. When I am in the land of the Shilluk people, I will fashion men and women just like this from the black earth, and they will have black skin."

This Juok did. And Juok sent these men and women out into the world as perfect human beings.

And so it came to pass that Juok, creator of life on earth, wandered here and there throughout the world. And as Juok wandered, he said to himself, "The earth is now a better place because I have fashioned human beings, both men and women, out of the different soils that I have created. For they alone are able to speak and to shout, to sing and to dance in both joy and sorrow. And they alone are able to make the earth grow green and gold with food for those who live on it. The men and women whom I have fashioned are perfect human beings, and my heart is happy with all that I have created."

Anansi, the Clever One

The spider Anansi is the principal trickster-hero of the Ashanti people of Ghana, a nation in West Africa. At the time that the Anansi tales were created, an Ashanti village was governed by a chief or headman and a council of elders who represented the various families in the village.

The Anansi tales reveal their creators' keen knowledge of human nature and a cultural environment where morality and justice are important values. They also reveal that famine was a common occurrence. As is true of all oral literature, the repetitive style appeals to the ear and aids the memory of both the poet-performer, or bard, and the listener.

The Anansi tales are so popular that they have traveled throughout West Africa, southeast into the African Congo region, and across the Atlantic to the West Indies and the Americas. In Africa, Anansi may be called Kwaku (Uncle) Anansi. In the Americas, Anansi is often called Nancy, Aunt Nancy, or Sister Nancy.

Although Anansi is a spider, he possesses many human characteristics. Not only does he speak the language of the Ashanti people, but his personality is that of a human being. He may live in the world of animals, or in the world of human beings, or in both worlds. However, despite these details, to the peoples of West Africa, Anansi is always Spider.

Some Anansi tales explain aspects of the world of nature and human nature. For example, they explain how the moon came to be in the sky, why people die, why people are greedy and have debts, why snakes turn belly-up when they are killed, and why spiders weave their webs in dark corners. Other Anansi tales may lead listeners to evaluate both their own personality and their own behavior.

In world literature, the trickster symbolizes both the complexity of human nature and the creative aspect of human intelligence. The trickster's behavior reveals that deception, greed, suffering, and death are an inherent part of the human condition, and that it is part of human nature to harm others. However, the trickster's clever schemes reveal a bright side of human nature, as well, because human intelligence can often compensate for physical weakness.

The power of the following tale derives, in part, from the connection between Anansi's personality and the fact that the consequences of his actions affect all human beings from that time forward.

ANANSI, THE CLEVER ONE

In a time long past, Famine stalked the land of Ghana, causing the Ashanti people—and all who lived there—to suffer from lack of food. Uncle Anansi's wife came to him and said, "It is hard to believe that someone who is as clever as you are cannot find a way to feed his family! Either you are not as clever as you used to be, or else you have grown uncommonly lazy!"

To these words, Uncle Anansi replied, "Do my ears hear the words that my wife's tongue speaks? No husband wants to be married to a nag!

"Now, Wife, of course I am as clever as I used to be! However, Famine is a sly enemy," Uncle Anansi explained. "We can see the damage he causes, but we cannot catch him at it. Even I, as clever as I am, cannot coax food from an enemy that I cannot see! However, since your hunger has given you a sharp tongue, I will go forth in search of food. And I promise you that I will not return without it!"

And so it came to pass that Uncle Anansi went forth into the forest. His legs took him far, and then they took him farther, until he found that he was deep in the woods and in an area that he had never seen. He stopped, wondering which way to proceed. After much looking, he finally spied a path—a very narrow path, but a path nevertheless. Uncle Anansi decided to follow it.

In time, it came to pass that the path led Uncle Anansi to a small meadow. There an old man was sitting on a log and twisting vines and long grasses into a rope. The old man appeared to have no blood in his body, for he was gray from head to foot. His hair was gray, and his beard was gray. His eyes were gray, and his mouth was gray. In fact, his entire face had a gray pallor. His arms were gray, and his hands were gray. Even the cloth that he wore was gray.

If the old gray man's ears heard Uncle Anansi's arrival, the old man did nothing to show it. He just kept working away on his rope.

And so Uncle Anansi called out, "Hello, grandfather! I wish you a good day! And I hope that your life goes well with you here, deep in the forest!"

Now if the old gray man's ears heard the sound of Uncle Anansi's tongue, the old man did nothing to show it. He just kept working away on his rope.

"It may be that this old man's ears have become too worn out with age to hear the words of my tongue," Uncle Anansi thought to himself. "Therefore, I will approach him and speak again."

Uncle Anansi let his legs take him right up to the old gray man, and then he shouted, "Hello, grandfather! I wish you a good day! And I hope that your life goes well with you here, deep in the forest!"

Once again, as close as Uncle Anansi now was to him, if the old gray man's ears heard the sound of Uncle Anansi's tongue, the old man did nothing to show it. He just kept working away on his rope.

And so it came to pass that Uncle Anansi began to look around the meadow with great curiosity. And once he saw what he saw, his heart flooded with envy.

"Why, grandfather!" he exclaimed. "I see that your life here in the forest goes very well indeed! Back where I come from, Famine stalks the land, and my family and the people of my village cry out from hunger! But here I see that you have trapped hundreds of animals—large and small animals, young and old animals, fat and lean animals. You are certainly a great trapper! No wonder you have to be a rope-maker as well!

"But what are you going to do with all of these animals that you have trapped?" asked Uncle Anansi, after a brief pause. "Surely, you have too many to eat all by yourself! And some are so long dead that they are rotting! Why, they have done no one any good at all!"

When Uncle Anansi heard the words of his own tongue, a clever idea suddenly entered his head and lodged between his ears. "I am not known as Anansi the Clever One for nothing!" he exclaimed to himself, his heart flooding with pride. "Grandfather! Would you mind very much if I carry some of your freshly trapped meat back to my family?" he asked. "You have so much food here, and my wife and my children are so very hungry!"

Now if the old gray man's ears heard the sound of Uncle Anansi's tongue, the old man did nothing to show it. He just kept working away on his rope.

And so it came to pass that Uncle Anansi carefully looked over the piles and piles of animal carcasses, chose those that had been trapped most recently, and returned home with as many as he could carry.

And it came to pass that days and nights came and went with the sun and the moon while Uncle Anansi and his family ate heartily and well. Now, when they had eaten the last of the meat, once again Uncle Anansi went forth into the forest. Once again his legs took him far, and then they took him farther, until he found that he was deep in the woods. Once again he found the narrow path that led to the small meadow, and he followed it to where the old gray man was sitting on a log and twisting vines and long grasses into a rope for one of his traps.

Once again Uncle Anansi let his legs take him right up to the old gray man, and then he shouted, "Hello, grandfather! I wish you a good day! And I hope that your life continues to go well with you here, deep in the forest!"

Once again, if the old gray man's ears heard the sound of Uncle Anansi's tongue, the old man did nothing to show it. He just kept working away on his rope.

And so it came to pass that Uncle Anansi did not bother to ask the old man whether he could take some of his freshly trapped meat back to his family. Instead, he carefully looked over the piles and piles of animal carcasses, chose those that had been trapped most recently, and returned home with as many as he could carry.

However, it came to pass that, as Uncle Anansi made his way back through the forest, his heart flooded with anxiety. "How long will I be able to keep my source of food hidden from the others in my village?" he asked himself. "After all, I am the one who found it and, therefore, I am the one who should keep it!"

When Uncle Anansi heard the words of his own tongue, a clever idea suddenly entered his head and lodged between his ears. "I am not known as Anansi the Clever One for nothing!" he exclaimed to himself, his heart flooding with pride. "The time will surely come again when we need more food," he thought, "and one night the moon will make the forest bright with its light. If I return at that time, I may be able to learn how the old gray one is able to trap so many animals!"

And so it came to pass that when his family had eaten the last of the meat, Uncle Anansi chose a night when the moon would make the forest bright with its light, and again he went forth into the forest. Again his legs took him far, and then they took him farther, until he found that he was deep in the woods. Now, it was very hard to see the narrow path that led to the small meadow, but, having already found it twice, Uncle Anansi found it again and followed it.

The meadow was deserted, but Uncle Anansi heard the sounds of someone at work nearby, and he let these sounds lead him into the forest. Sure enough! There was the old gray man, busily at work emptying his old traps and setting new ones.

Uncle Anansi watched the old man and, as he watched him, he exclaimed to himself, "Why, grandfather! You may be old, and your ears may no longer hear the words of my tongue, but you certainly are one great hunter! You trap more animals than I can carry, but you easily carry all of their carcasses despite your age!"

And it came to pass that, as Uncle Anansi silently watched the old gray man at his work, a clever idea suddenly entered his head and lodged between his ears. "I am not known as Anansi the Clever One for nothing!" he exclaimed to himself, his heart flooding with pride. "I will give my daughter in marriage to this old man, and then the animals that he traps will be hers, and what is hers will be mine as well!" he thought. "After all, my daughter is young. She is beautiful. And she is accomplished. Surely, any man would be delighted to have her for his wife!"

And so it came to pass that, without a word to the old gray man, Uncle Anansi returned home. However, before leaving, he returned to the meadow. There, as before, he could see the hundreds of animals that the old man had trapped—large and small animals, young and old animals, fat and lean animals, some freshly trapped, and some so old that their flesh was rotting.

Once again, he carefully looked over the piles and piles of animal carcasses, chose those that had been trapped most recently, and returned home with as many carcasses as he could carry.

When the sun next made the day light, Uncle Anansi announced, "Come, Daughter! Take your personal belongings and your cooking pots, and come with me into the forest. I have found a husband for you! He is a great hunter, and once you marry him, you and the rest of us will surely prosper!"

And so it came to pass that Uncle Anansi's daughter dutifully obeyed her father. She said farewell to her mother and her brother, and she followed her father as he went forth into the forest. Their legs took them far, and then they took them farther, until they found that they were deep in the woods.

Uncle Anansi found the narrow path, which was becoming broader with each of his successive trips, and they followed it into the small meadow. There, just as he had expected, the old gray man was sitting on his log and twisting vines and long grasses into a rope for one of his traps.

Uncle Anansi let his legs take him right up to the old man, and then he shouted, "Hello, grandfather! I wish you a good day! See how I have brought my daughter to you to become your wife. Surely, you will agree that she is lovely, is she not? And she will be a good wife! She will take care of you and cook your meals. And then you can trap as much as you please!"

Once again, if the old gray man's ears heard the sound of Uncle Anansi's tongue, the old man did nothing to show it. He just kept working away on his rope.

And so it came to pass that Uncle Anansi proceeded as if the old gray man had accepted his daughter as a wife. Together, he and his daughter collected branches and vines and built a hut for her to live in. Then, they collected firewood so that she would be able to cook dinner for her new husband.

Having done this, Uncle Anansi once again carefully looked over the piles and piles of animal carcasses, chose a few that had been trapped most recently, and took them along with him as he left. "We do not really need more food right now," he admitted to himself. "But this old man has so many carcasses that they only rot here! If I take them, they will do someone some good!"

Then, as he was leaving, Uncle Anansi declared, "I will return tomorrow, Daughter, for I would see how you are faring in your new life!"

As he had promised, when the sun next made the day light, Uncle Anansi went forth into the forest. His legs took him far, and then they took him farther, until he found that he was deep in the woods. Now, he easily found the path that led to the small meadow, and he followed it. As always, he found that the old gray man was sitting on a log and twisting vines and long grasses into a rope for one of his traps.

Meanwhile, Uncle Anansi's daughter was sitting on a log in front of her hut, with her cooking pots at her side and a tempting, hot breakfast inside them. However, her father could see from her expression that her heart was flooded with grief.

Uncle Anansi exclaimed brightly, "Hello, Daughter! I wish you a good day! And I hope that all goes well with you here, deep in the forest! Does your new husband treat you well? And does he appreciate your cooking?"

To these words, Uncle Anansi's daughter replied, "Oh, Father! Please take me home with you right now! You have chosen a strange man to be my husband, and his ways flood my heart with terror! Since you left me here with him, he has not drunk one drop of water! He has not eaten one bite of food! His tongue has not spoken one word. He just sits on his log and twists vines and long grasses into ropes. So, I implore you, please take me home!"

Now if the old gray man's ears heard the sound of his wife's tongue, the old man did nothing to show it. He just kept working away on his rope.

And so it came to pass that Uncle Anansi replied, "Now, now, Daughter! My ears hear the words of your tongue, and this is what I would say to you in reply. Put terror from your heart! In time, it will come to pass that your husband, like all other men, will need to eat, and once he tastes your cooking, you will find that he will be delighted to have you as his wife!

"Now, I will eat this breakfast—for I know what a good cook you are!" Uncle Anansi continued. "Once the sun has gone to its rest, you should have a fresh meal ready for your husband. Then, when the sun next makes the day light, I will return to you. You will see what has come to pass, and we will discuss the matter then."

To these words, Uncle Anansi's daughter replied, "My ears hear the words of your tongue, Father, and if that is how it must be, then I will do as you say."

And so it came to pass that Uncle Anansi returned to his village. But once again, before leaving, he carefully looked over the piles and piles of animal carcasses, chose a few that had been trapped most recently, and took them along. "We do not really need more food right now," he admitted to himself. "But this old man has so many carcasses that they only rot here! If I take them, they will do someone some good!"

As he had promised, when the sun next made the day light, Uncle Anansi went forth into the forest. After a late start, his legs took him far, and then they took him farther, until he found that he was deep in the woods. Once again he easily found the path that led to the small meadow, and he followed it. By this time, the sun was mid-way in its journey. Just as he had expected, the old man was sitting on his log and twisting vines and long grasses into a rope for one of his traps.

As always, nearby, Uncle Anansi could see the hundreds of animals that the old man had trapped—large and small animals, young and old animals, fat and lean animals, some freshly trapped, and some so old that their flesh was rotting. However, he could see no sign of his daughter anywhere, either in her hut or in the meadow.

Uncle Anansi let his legs take him right up to the old gray man, and then he shouted, "Hello, grandfather! I wish you a good day! I have come to see my daughter. But I do not see her anywhere. Where is she?"

If the old gray man's ears heard the sound of Uncle Anansi's tongue, the old man did nothing to show it.

Therefore, Uncle Anansi shouted, "Grandfather! Where is my daughter? I cannot see her anywhere! She is your wife now, so surely you know where she is!"

Once again, if the old gray man's ears heard the sound of Uncle Anansi's tongue, the old man did nothing to show it.

And so it came to pass that Uncle Anansi began to look around the meadow with great curiosity. And once he saw what he saw, his heart flooded with horror. As always, the piles and piles of animal carcasses—with their fresh and rotting meat—had drawn him to them. And there Uncle Anansi found his daughter! His eyes could see that she was now as dead as every other freshly trapped animal.

Quick as the wind, Uncle Anansi turned and let his legs take him back to where the old gray man was still sitting on his log and twisting vines and long grasses into a rope for one of his traps.

"You monster!" cried Uncle Anansi. "How could you kill your wife? Have you no heart? Have you no honor? You are truly despicable!"

With these words, Uncle Anansi began to strike the old man with all of the strength that he possessed. And the anger that flooded his heart made him very strong indeed.

Suddenly, it came to pass that the old gray man looked up from his work. For the first time in all of Uncle Anansi's visits, the old man looked his visitor straight in the eye and silently stared at him. And as he stared, his eyes shone brighter and brighter, with an increasingly evil light. Finally, he stood up, and Uncle Anansi saw that the old gray man towered over him.

Now Uncle Anansi's heart overflowed with terror, and quick as the wind he turned from the old gray man. As fast as his legs could take him, Uncle Anansi then fled through the forest and all the way back to his village. And as he fled, he heard the cracking of branches and the thumping of trees as the old man followed him.

Finally, at long last, Uncle Anansi reached his village. "Help me! Help me!" he screamed. "That man has killed my daughter! And now he is after me!"

When the people of Uncle Anansi's village heard the words of his tongue, it came to pass that they left their work and their huts and came to see what was happening. Men and women, grandparents, parents, and children of all ages looked toward the forest. Meanwhile, Uncle Anansi bolted into the chief's compound and hid inside one of his huts.

Meanwhile, the old gray man reached Uncle Anansi's village. In shocked silence, he stood and stared at all of the people. "What a great supply of carcasses!" he exclaimed to himself. "And they are all in one place, too! It will be so easy to set my traps here that this will be far better than living in the forest!"

Now, while the old gray man stood staring at the people, the people were staring back at him. "Who are you?" they asked him. "Where have you come from? And what do you want with any of us?"

"My name is Death," the old gray man replied. "I have always lived deep in the forest, where I have trapped animals. But from this time forth, I will live among you!"

And so it came to pass that Death discovered human beings. And from that time forth until this, Death has set his traps for us. He has trapped piles and piles of people—tall and short people, young and old people, fat and thin people. And from that time forth until this, no one has felt safe any longer, for Death is always watching and waiting for the moment to trap another human being. He traps some people while they sleep. He traps others by making them very ill. He traps still others by causing them to have terrible accidents.

Meanwhile, it came to pass that Uncle Anansi never forgot that it was he who had given Death a new type of animal to trap. "I am not known as Anansi the Clever One for nothing!" he exclaimed to himself, his heart flooding with pride.

This time, however, as Uncle Anansi listened to his own words of self-praise, a disturbing thought pushed its way into his head and lodged firmly between his ears. "I have heard our people say, 'Only a person who has no sense will choose to drink from a pool when a stream is close by.'" He paused briefly to consider this observation. "I must not think about this," he decided, "or else my heart will flood with grief!"

The Woman with One Hand

"The Woman with One Hand" is a tale told by the Swahili, a group of Bantu-speaking peoples who live on the east coast of Africa in Somalia, Kenya, Tanzania, Mozambique, and the offshore islands, including Zanzibar. In fact, the word "Swahili" means "coast-dwellers."

Both ethnically and culturally, the Swahili are a mixture of various Black African groups and Arab peoples who first began to settle this coastal area in ancient times. Some of the Swahili people have retained their traditional beliefs, while others are Muslim or Christian.

The Swahili people have been great traders for so many centuries that their language is the language of commerce in Africa, from the east coast west to Zaire. The ancestors of the Swahili people probably began to trade with the coastal areas of southern Arabia and India in the first century A.D. They exchanged African ivory, gold, tortoiseshell, and rhinoceros horn for iron tools and weapons, cloth, pottery, and glassware. The eastern coast of Africa contained many commercially developed harbors and towns at this time. Ancient historians discuss the importance of the metropolis of Rhapta to the Romans in the first and second centuries A.D.

The Central Bantu people who became the Swahili moved up the eastern coast of Africa between the sixth and ninth centuries. They absorbed local Bantu peoples and traded with the Persians, who dominated trade with India and China until 879, when the Arabs replaced them. Archaeologists have found the remains of more than four hundred eighth-century east coast settlements. There, African ivory and gold were exchanged for products from the Mediterranean and the Far East.

When the Arabs, who were Muslim, established trading centers along the east coast of Africa in the ninth and tenth centuries, the Swahili peoples continued their African culture while adopting aspects of the Islamic culture of their partners in trade, such as their type of government and architecture and certain of their customs and vocabulary. Founded in 975, the city of Kilwa in Tanzania became the center of the Swahili culture. Kilwa was the most important east African port from the twelfth to the fifteenth centuries, with an estimated population of about twenty thousand people in the fourteenth century.

"The Woman with One Hand" leads readers to consider their own values and to decide how they wish to conduct their own lives. Another important aspect of the tale is the friendship that people and animals feel toward one another. The emphasis on a relationship between people and animals is not only a characteristic of the African folk tradition; it exists in cultures throughout the world.

THE WOMAN WITH ONE HAND

A man and his wife had two children, a young man and a young woman. It came to pass that their father contracted a fatal disease, and knowing that the remaining days of his life were few, he called his children to his side and asked each of them, "When I die, which do you want me to leave to you, my property or my blessing?"

The young man, being the older, replied first and declared, "I choose to receive your property, Father."

The young woman then replied, "Father, I choose to receive your blessing."

"It will be as you wish, then," their father replied. "To you, my dear son, I give all of my property. You will receive it when your mother's days on this earth have come to an end."

"And to you, my dear daughter, I give my blessing: for long life, good health, loving relationships, and prosperity."

It came to pass that, shortly thereafter, their father died. They had just completed the seven days of mourning when their mother suddenly became very ill. Knowing that the remaining days of her life were few, she called her children to her side and asked each of them, "My children, when I die, which do you want me to leave to you, my property or my blessing?"

The young man, being the older, again replied first and again declared, "I choose to receive your property, Mother."

The young woman then replied, "Mother, I choose to receive your blessing."

"It will be as you wish, then," their mother replied. "To you, my dear son, I give all of my property, which includes all of your father's property as well."

"And to you, my dear daughter, I give my blessing: for long life, good health, loving relationships, and prosperity."

It came to pass that shortly thereafter, their mother died. And as soon as they had completed the seven days of mourning, the brother said to his sister, "Bring every possession that belonged to our father and mother before me that I may take them as my lawful inheritance."

The sister did as her brother requested, giving him everything and keeping nothing for herself. The villagers observed this and said to the brother, "You are behaving in a cruel and shameful way toward your sister! Can you not spare a small thing or two that will make it easier for her to survive? As it is, you have left her nothing at all!"

"To each his own!" the young man replied. "I do not see why I should give my sister anything! Surely, it is no source of shame to give her what she has requested! When our parents asked us what we wanted for our inheritance, I was the one who asked to receive their property. My sister only wanted to receive their blessing! Now, I intend to let her live on our parents' blessing so that she will appreciate the value of property!

"However, to show you that my heart is not a stone," he added, "I will give my sister our mother's cooking pot and the mortar and pestle that she used for grinding corn. And with these possessions, surely my sister can find a way to eat!"

With these words, the brother then gave his sister these pieces of their mother's cooking equipment, and he left the village.

The women of the village then gathered together and said, "Our hearts flood with pity for this young woman! We must do what we can to help her, for her brother has left her with so little that, without our help, she will surely starve! So, let us agree to borrow her cooking pot and also her mortar and pestle to grind our corn. Each time we return her cooking equipment to her, we will pay her with food. In this way, we will help her survive."

The women's hearts felt as one heart, and they agreed. And it came to pass that the women of the village were as good as their word.

It then came to pass that, one day, the young woman wandered through her mother's hut, searching for anything useful that she or her brother might have overlooked. The only thing that she found was a lone pumpkin seed. Nevertheless, the young woman was delighted with her discovery. "Every pumpkin vine sprouts forth from a small seed like this one," she thought to herself. "I will plant this seed by the well, where it will receive lots of light as well as lots of

water, and, with luck, it will prosper and produce a vine that is filled
with pumpkins!"

Meanwhile, the young woman's brother wondered how his sister was faring, since he was certain that no one could survive only
on a parent's blessing. When he happened to meet a man from his
old village, he asked him, "Is my sister still alive? Does she fare well?
And how is she managing without any property?"

To these questions the villager replied, "You have no cause to
worry about your sister! She is managing well enough. The women
of our village borrow her cooking pot and also her mortar and pestle
to grind their corn. Each time they return the cooking equipment,
they pay her with food, and this enables your sister to survive."

The brother smiled when he heard this news, but his heart
flooded with rage at his sister's good fortune. And so it came to pass
that when the moon next made the night bright, he waited until the
villagers and their dogs were asleep, and he stealthily entered his old
village. He then secretly went into his mother's hut, where he took
the cooking pot and the mortar and pestle that he had given to his
sister.

"It is only fair that I take what is rightfully mine!" the young man
exclaimed to himself. "My sister was so certain that she could survive on our parents' blessing that she left all of their property to me.
If the villagers had not made me feel that I have a stone heart, I never
would have given her our mother's cooking pot and mortar and
pestle. So now, all is as it should be! To each his own! I have all of
my parents' property, and my sister has their blessing."

With these thoughts in his mind, the brother stealthily left his
mother's hut and his parents' village, being careful not to awaken
anyone.

When the sun made the next day light, the women once again
came to borrow the young woman's cooking pot and her mortar and
pestle. However, the equipment was not in its usual place. Nor could
the young woman find them anywhere else. And so it came to pass
that the women of the village returned to their huts empty-handed,
and the young woman received nothing to satisfy the craving of her
empty stomach.

The complaints of her stomach led the young woman to remember the pumpkin seed that she had planted by the well. "Maybe the
seed has sprouted, and a vine has grown," she thought to herself.
"It would be wonderful if I found a pumpkin, for I am so hungry!"

And so it came to pass that the young woman went to the well, where, sure enough, she found that her seed had produced a vine that was now filled with pumpkins. The woman laughed with delight at the sight!

Three days came and went with the sun while the young woman gathered her pumpkins and sold them to the villagers in exchange for grain. The pumpkins were so sweet that everyone wanted one! And so it came to pass that many more days came and went with the sun as the young woman supplied the villagers with pumpkins. In return, the villagers supplied the young woman with a plentiful amount of food. Finally, the time for pumpkins came to an end, and the vine rested.

It was just at this time that the wife of the young woman's brother heard about her sister-in-law's pumpkins. She gave her slave a payment of grain and ordered her to go to her sister-in-law's village, find her hut, and purchase one of her pumpkins.

When the young woman realized that it was her sister-in-law's slave who had come to buy a pumpkin, she declared, "I am so sorry! You have arrived just after the time for pumpkins has finished. However, I will give you this pumpkin of mine to take to your family. Please return their grain to them as well because I do not charge for what I give to my brother and his wife."

The young woman's sister-in-law so enjoyed the pumpkin that she sent a slave for another. This time, the slave returned empty-handed, causing the sister-in-law to declare to her husband, "Your sister sells her pumpkins to everyone but me! She told my slave that she has no pumpkins left. My heart floods with anger at this lie!"

"Push the anger from your heart, my dear," her husband replied. "When the sun makes the next day light, I myself will visit my sister, and when I leave she will no longer be able to raise pumpkins!"

And so it came to pass that the brother visited his sister and learned what his wife already knew. "My brother, I have already given your wife my own pumpkin as a gift from me to you. The time for pumpkins has passed, and now the vine rests. All those who bought my pumpkins came earlier, while pumpkins still grew upon the vine. I am sorry, but I can do nothing for you until they grow again."

"It may be that you can do nothing for me," the brother responded. But I can do something for you! If I cannot have your pumpkins, no one can! And so I will pull out the roots of this plant of yours!"

"Before you do that, you will have to cut off my right hand!" his sister exclaimed.

And so it came to pass that the brother sliced off his sister's right hand and then destroyed her pumpkin plant. "Now pack up whatever is yours and leave this house," he commanded. "This hut belonged to our parents, and therefore it now belongs to me!"

The young woman placed her maimed arm into heated water, put medicine on the wounded area, and wrapped a cloth around it. Then she took whatever was hers and entered the forest, where she wandered from place to place. And so it came to pass that one day followed another as the moon follows the sun. Meanwhile, her brother sold his parents' house and spent whatever he received from the sale.

Six days had now come and gone with the sun. When the sun made the next day light, the young woman found that she was on the outskirts of a town. Seeing a great fruit tree, she climbed up and hungrily feasted upon its fruit. Then she fell asleep among the branches.

While she was sleeping, a prince and his friends entered the forest to shoot birds. When the sun was midway in its journey, the heat from its rays tired the prince, and he and his slave took refuge in the shade beneath the tree in which the young woman was sleeping.

In time, it came to pass that the young woman awoke. Seeing the prince below, her heart overflowed with grief for her own situation, and tears fell from her eyes like rain. When they fell upon the prince, he exclaimed, "Why, it is raining!"

"It cannot be raining, master," his slave replied. "See how the sun casts its light upon the trees and the earth around us."

"Then, climb this tree and see what bird is making these drops fall on me!" the prince exclaimed.

And so it came to pass that the slave came upon the young woman. He returned to the prince and said, "The drops that you feel are not from a bird. They are the tears of a beautiful young woman! You might want to climb up and talk to her!"

Quick as the wind, the prince climbed that tree in order to see what his slave had seen. When he saw the young woman's beauty, his heart flooded with love for her.

"Why are you crying, my beauty?" he asked. "Come, let me take you to my home, for I would marry you! I am the son of a king, so with me your heart will flood with joy, not sorrow!"

"You want to marry me?" the young woman questioned. "Are you certain that this is what your heart tells you? I am a woman of no position. I have neither parents nor a home. Moreover, I have but one hand. However, if you still wish it, I will come with you, but only if you arrange it so that no one can see me!"

And so it came to pass that the young woman accompanied the prince to his home in the royal compound of the capital town. They traveled in two closed litters that were carried by four men.

When they arrived at the king's compound, the prince approached his parents and declared, "I have found the woman that my heart has chosen for my wife! She has no family, and she has only one hand, but I will marry her nevertheless!"

And so it came to pass that the prince married the young woman, and when nine moons had come and gone, the young woman gave birth to the prince's son. When the celebration ended, the prince left on a journey that would take him to the many towns in his father's kingdom.

Meanwhile, the young woman's brother was begging in one of the towns near the forest—for he had spent whatever wealth he had possessed—when he overheard that the king's son had married a young woman who had but one hand. When he asked where the prince had found this woman, and he learned that he had found her in the forest, the young man knew that the prince had married his sister.

And so it came to pass that the brother went to the king and declared, "Great King, I hear that your son has married the woman who has but one hand! You should know that this woman is a witch, and that she has killed every man who has married her!"

"Alas!" the king replied. "I can see that we had better make this woman leave the capital!"

"You would do better to kill her!" her brother replied. "The last time she killed her husband, the people cut off her right hand. You can see that even that injury has not stopped her!"

"No," the king replied. "We will not kill her. However, we will make her leave the capital!"

And so it came to pass that the young woman, with her infant son and a small pack, left the royal compound and the capital town and wandered once again in the forest. Being tired, she was resting against the trunk of a tree when she spied a snake that was gliding toward her, quick as the wind. Her heart flooded with terror, and she gave her infant son a farewell kiss.

However, the snake stopped at her feet and said, "Woman, I see that you have a clay pot with you. Open it and let me enter its darkness! I promise that if you will protect me from the sun, I will protect you from the rain!"

The young woman had hardly opened and closed the pot when she spied another snake that was gliding toward her, quick as the wind. Once again, her heart flooded with terror, and she gave her infant son a farewell kiss.

However, this snake also stopped at her feet, and he asked, "Have you seen my friend? I thought that he came this way!"

The young woman remembered the first snake's need for her protection, and so she replied, "I did see him, and he has taken the path that goes deep into the forest."

Quick as the wind, the snake glided off along that path, and when he had gone, the voice of the snake who was hiding in the young woman's clay pot commanded, "Woman, now let me out of here!"

When the snake emerged, his heart was flooded with gratitude. "Now, woman, tell me what you are doing here in the forest with your infant son and your small pack," he demanded. "Do you have no home?"

To these words, the young woman replied, "No, I have no home, and that is why I am wandering here in the forest."

"Then, come with me," the snake responded, "and I will take you to my home! My parents will want to repay your kindness to me."

And so it came to pass that the snake led the young woman deep into the forest. The sun was midway in its journey when they came upon a great lake. "Woman, we will stop here and rest a little," the snake declared. "Even in the forest, the heat from the sun's rays tires the body. So take your infant son, and bathe in the lake. The cool water will refresh both of you!"

The woman did as the snake suggested, but the current suddenly swept the infant out of her hand and out of sight. Her heart flooded with horror, and she screamed.

"Why do you scream, woman?" the snake called out.

"My child! The current has carried my child away! I cannot find him, and my heart knows that he has drowned!"

"Keep looking!" the snake advised.

The young woman looked and looked. Her hand reached under the water here and there, and it swept over the water there and here, but she could neither see nor feel her child anywhere.

"I cannot find him!" the young woman cried. Her heart flooded with grief, and tears flowed from her eyes like rain. "The current has carried my child away, and my heart knows that he has drowned!" she exclaimed.

"You are using only one of your hands, woman!" the snake responded. "You must use both hands if you wish to find your child!"

"This is no time for a laughing heart!" the young woman replied. "Surely you have seen that I have but one hand! My right arm is useless without its hand, so it will not help to submerge it in the water!"

"Put it in, woman!" the snake exclaimed. "You must use both hands if you wish to find your child!"

And so it came to pass that the young woman submerged both arms in the water. Her arms reached under the water here and there, and they swept over the water there and here.

Suddenly, the young woman felt the body of her child! She picked him up and found that he was alive and well. And she found that she had regained her right hand, and that it, too, was alive and well.

The young woman's heart flooded with delight and gratitude. "I have found my child, and he is well! And I have regained my right hand!" she exclaimed joyfully. "How can I ever thank you for your gifts?"

To these words, the snake replied, "Woman, I have not yet fully repaid your own gift, so let us now continue on our way. I still want to take you to my home, for my parents will want to repay your kindness to me."

And so it came to pass that the young woman and her infant son came to live with the snake's family, who loved and cared for them as their own.

Meanwhile, the prince returned to his parents' kingdom. When he asked for his wife and child, his parents told him that they had died and showed him their two graves. The prince's heart flooded with grief, and tears flowed from his eyes like rain. The prince also met the king's new advisor, but he did not know that this important man was his wife's brother.

It came to pass that one day followed another as the moon follows the sun. The young woman then said to the snake who had befriended her, "You and your people have been so good to me that I would happily spend the rest of my days here, but the time has come for me to take my son and go on my way."

"Sister, you are certainly free to do this," the snake replied. "However, when you say farewell to my parents before you leave, my parents will probably offer you parting gifts. Refuse everything they offer, except for my father's ring."

The snake's parents loved the young woman, and when they could not convince her to remain with them, they offered her great wealth.

"I thank you, Mother and Father, for all of these gifts!" the young woman exclaimed. "However, they are far more than I need, and I cannot carry them. If I could choose, I would ask for only one gift, and that is your ring, Father!"

"Who told you about my ring, Daughter?" the snake's father asked. "Surely you do not know how special it is! And yet, since it is our son who must have told you about it—for only he knows about it—then this is how he wants us to repay your kindness to him!"

"Therefore, my daughter, I give you my ring with my love," the snake's father declared. "Whenever you want shelter, food, and clothing, just speak to this ring, and it will give them to you—with my blessing as your father and with the blessing of the gods!"

And so it came to pass that the young woman took her child and returned to the town that was the capital of the kingdom and the home of her husband. She did not want to return to the king's compound just yet, so she asked her ring for a large house on the outskirts of the town.

A large furnished house—with slaves to attend to her needs—immediately appeared. And it came to pass that the king and his son heard about this house and went to look at it. The young woman's brother accompanied them.

When the young woman saw them at her gates, she invited the royal party to enter and to share her food. The prince's heart flooded with joy to see his wife. However, he had much wisdom between his ears, and he decided that it would be best for his tongue to remain silent and to let his eyes speak for him. His father and mother gave the young woman a puzzled look because they were amazed at the young woman's resemblance to their one-handed daughter-in-law.

Meanwhile, the heart of the young woman's brother flooded with fear. "What powerful magic does my sister possess that she won a prince for her husband, and now she has two hands and a great house with slaves to wait on her!" he exclaimed to himself. "And how is she going to punish me for the way that I have treated her?" he added, feeling his heart tremble with terror.

After the meal, the king said to the young woman, "You bear a remarkable resemblance to our one-handed daughter-in-law. Tell us, if you would, who are you? And what brings you to the capital of the kingdom?"

And so it came to pass that the young woman told the story of her life. She began with her choice of blessings, and continued with her treatment by her brother and her meeting with the prince. Finally, she related her experience with the snake who adopted her as his sister, and she concluded with her return to the capital town with her snake-father's ring.

As they heard her story, the hearts of the king, the queen, and the prince flooded now with love, now with pity, and now with joy. Meanwhile, the heart of the young woman's brother remained flooded with terror.

"I hope that you will find it in your heart to forgive me, my daughter," the king declared, as soon as the young woman had concluded her story. "Your brother's tale chased the wisdom from between my ears. However, now that I know him for the scoundrel that he is, how would you like me to punish him?"

"Treat my brother with the same kindness with which you treated me, Father," the young woman replied. "Do not kill him. Just make him leave the capital. What will be, will be."

And so it came to pass that the young woman and her husband lived to the end of their lives with joyful hearts. They never saw the young woman's brother again.

The Roamer-of-the-Plain

The Baronga (or Ronga) live in Mozambique, in southeastern Africa, and are part of the great Bantu-speaking nation that is known as the Thonga. "The Roamer-of-the-Plain" reflects both economic and social aspects of the Baronga society in which it is set. At the time that this tale was collected, agriculture was the principal occupation of the people. Women would cultivate maize (Indian corn), as well as beans, peas, pumpkins, and sweet potatoes. Men would hunt, fish, and care for the cattle, which were a source of milk and bride-price payments.

At the time, the Baronga lived in small villages, where the inhabitants were often all members of one large extended family. The villagers were governed by a hereditary leader, who was aided by an informal council of family heads. Society was patriarchal in its organization, and when a woman married, she left her own family and went to live with her husband in his village.

The cape buffalo, which takes center stage in "The Roamer-of-the-Plain," is one of Africa's most dangerous animals because of its massive, curved, pointed horns. It is most active during the morning and the evening, and it always remains near a source of water.

Understanding the concept and practice of totemism, a mystical relationship between a group of people and a specific plant or animal, is important in understanding the significance of the following tale, where a buffalo is the totem of the wife's people. Totemism developed at a time when people first began to cultivate the soil, and it reflects their dependence on the natural world. With nature's cooperation, the people could hope to survive; without it, they would inevitably experience famine and death.

The early farmers believed that animals have human emotions and that they are equal or superior to human beings in intelligence as well as in physical strength. Therefore, the farmers believed that it would be to their advantage to treat certain animals in a special way so as to gain their help, their advice, and their protection. This belief fostered respect and consideration for the totem, rather than the attitude that the totem was their servant.

28

This bond between a people and their totem animal often involved a ceremony in which the villagers and their totem exchanged souls, thereby giving the villagers the benefit of the totem's protection. By taking the villagers' souls, the totem gave the souls a physically stronger and, therefore, more secure home, and by giving the people its own soul, the totem transferred part of its own strength to them.

This concept was based on the belief that the totem animal was unusually well-equipped to survive. Consequently, it served the interests of the people only as long as their totem animal thrived. Since it now housed the souls of the people, if the totem were to become weak or ill, the souls of the people would be in peril, and if the totem were to die, then the souls of the people would die. In "The Roamer-of-the-Plain," the young woman's parents tell her that the lives of their people are inextricably connected to the life of their totem—that they will prosper as long as their buffalo prospers, but that when it dies, they will die as well.

Because it possesses a human soul, the people view their totem as being part-animal and part-human, and it functions as their teacher, advisor, and protector. In "The Roamer-of-the-Plain," the buffalo totem helps the young woman with her work. In her community, it may also have advised her people, and it may have protected them by warning them about impending danger.

"The Roamer-of-the-Plain" is a powerful tale because it combines elements that are universal and easily understood with other elements that are mystical and ambiguous. On one level, it describes the universal conflict that often occurs between the older and younger generations over the validity of tradition. However, while this tale can be interpreted as showing that parents know best and that traditions should be preserved, it can also be interpreted as showing that traditions must be evaluated and then changed if they become harmful. On another level, it explores certain psychological implications of totemism.

THE ROAMER-OF-THE-PLAIN

It was the custom among the Baronga that when a young man became old enough to marry, his family chose an appropriate wife for him. So it had always been. So it would always be.

However, it came to pass that, when a certain young man became old enough to marry and his parents offered to find him a lovely bride, the young man was not satisfied.

"Thank you, Mother and Father, but I intend to choose my own wife!" he declared. "My heart does not love any of the maidens whom you might choose. So give me the bride-price—the herd that you are offering me for this purpose—and I will venture forth by myself and find the wife who pleases me!"

"You may go your own way, if that is your wish, my son," his father replied, "but, in truth, it is your parents who know what is best for you! And we must warn you that you probably will not be as happy as you would be if you permitted us to choose your wife."

"So do not blame us if misfortune follows your footsteps as the sun follows the moon," his mother added, "for it is very likely that this is just what is going to come to pass!"

"My ears hear the words that your tongues speak," their son replied, "but my heart will not listen! A young man should be free to choose the woman whom he will marry, and my heart is happy that you will let me have my own way in this matter."

So it came to pass that the young man left his village. In his pursuit of the woman whom his heart could love, he even left his country behind him. In fact, he traveled on and on until he reached a land that was strange to him.

Finally, it came to pass that the young man entered a village at the time when its young women were busily preparing food for dinner. Some were pounding maize; others were already cooking. As he walked among them, the young man's heart found a woman whom it could love, and so the young man approached the old ones of the village and formally asked to view their daughters of marriageable age, as was the custom.

And it came to pass that the village elders were willing to assemble their maidens and let them pass before the visitor so that he might choose one of them to be his wife. When the young woman whom his heart had chosen walked before him, the young man told the elders that she was the maiden of his choice, and, quick as the wind, the young woman agreed to the marriage.

"Now, young man, return to your village, and inform your parents of your choice," the village elders declared. "We will eagerly await their arrival. When they bring the bride-price, we will give them the young woman whom you have chosen, and they will bring her home to you."

"Thank you, grandfathers, but that is not how it will be. My parents gave me permission to choose my own bride, and they gave me my bride-price as well. Therefore, if the young woman's parents agree, I will pay the price and return to my village with their daughter."

And it came to pass that the young woman's parents agreed. "Daughter, it is well that you have chosen a husband," they declared. "For the time has come for you to marry. And since you will need to care for your husband, and for his parents as well, we would like to give you a young girl to help you with your tasks."

The young woman's parents offered her one young girl after another—at least twenty of them—but the young woman refused them all. "The only servant who pleases me is our people's buffalo, the Roamer-of-the-Plain. Let him serve me, and my heart will rejoice!" she declared.

"What a rash request!" her father exclaimed. "Our lives and the lives of all our people are tied to our buffalo's life! Here, living among us, the Roamer-of-the-Plain does well, and so we, too, prosper. However, you are leaving for a strange village in a strange land, and you have before you an uncertain fate."

"We cannot take the risk that the Roamer-of-the-Plain will go thirsty or hungry there, or that he will become ill and die there," her mother added. "For if he should die, we will die as well!"

"My ears hear the words that your tongues speak," replied their daughter, "but my heart will not listen. A young woman should be free to choose her own servant, and my heart expects that you will let me have my own way in this matter. I promise you that I will give you no cause to worry about the Roamer-of-the-Plain. I will care for him in my husband's village as well as you care for him here!"

"Our ears hear the words of your tongue, Daughter," the young woman's father replied. "And, because we have confidence in your judgment, we will permit you to have your way in this matter. However, should it come to pass that the Roamer-of-the-Plain falls on hard times in your new village, we are giving you a remedy. Take with you this small pot with the packet of medicinal roots that it contains, this small knife, this horn for bleeding, and this calabash gourd filled with grease."

"Should the Roamer-of-the-Plain become injured," her mother explained, "you must first fill the small pot with water and cook the medicinal roots until the water boils and steam rushes forth from the pot. Then you must make small incisions with this knife near the buffalo's wounds. Use the bleeding horn to suck out his blood, rub the grease from the calabash into his wounds, and let the medicinal steam enter his body through your incisions."

"Now, as you steam the wounded area, you must sing the ritual chant that you have heard us sing ever since you can remember," her father concluded. "And if you have done everything correctly, then all will be well with the Roamer-of-the-Plain, and all will be well with all of us!"

"My ears hear the words that your tongues speak," their daughter replied. "Nothing will happen to the Roamer-of-the Plain, but should an unforeseen misfortune occur, know that I will remember to do just what you have advised."

The young woman then went to the Roamer-of the Plain and declared, "I want you to be my servant when I accompany my husband to his village. I have asked my parents, and they have agreed. However, my husband lives in a strange village in a strange land, and I know nothing about his people. Therefore, to assure your own safety and well-being, you must take care that I am the only person who sees you!"

"My ears hear the words of your tongue," the buffalo replied, "and I will do as you advise."

And so it came to pass that the Roamer-of-the-Plain accompanied the young couple when they left the young woman's village, always following at a safe distance behind them. Although the young woman could find him whenever she searched for him, her husband never saw him. The young woman had never told her husband about the Roamer-of-the-Plain. Therefore, her husband was unaware that the buffalo existed and that he was accompanying the young woman to her new village, where he would be her servant.

When the young couple arrived back at the young man's village, the old ones exclaimed, "So the young man who has chosen his own wife has returned! Welcome! It may be that you will be happy, and we certainly wish you well! But we think that you will not be as happy as you would have been if you had permitted your parents to choose your wife for you.

"Parents—being older and more experienced—are wiser in the ways of the world, and their judgment in matters of marriage is sound," they continued. "However, your parents let you have your own way in this, and what will be will surely come! Now, if misfortune follows your footsteps as the sun follows the moon, remember who is to blame! For it is very likely that this is just what is going to come to pass!"

"My ears hear the words that your tongues speak, grandfathers," the young man replied, "but my heart will not listen! A young man should be free to choose the woman whom he will marry! And you will see that all will be well with me!"

The young man was quick to show his young wife around the village that was to be her new home. He also showed her the fields where the women cultivated the village's crops. One field belonged to his mother, and another belonged to him. Finally, he showed her the nearby lake, where she would find water for drinking and cooking.

The young woman searched the forest for the Roamer-of-the-Plain, and as soon as she could find an opportunity to be alone with him, she declared, "My husband and I will live in the village with his parents. But you must remain here, near my husband's field. There is a lake nearby, so at least you will always be able to satisfy your thirst.

"Now, remember what I told you—for your own safety and well-being, you must take care that I am the only person who ever sees you," she continued. "You should be safe as long as you hide from the sun's rays. And once the sun makes the day light, this forest should protect you!"

"My ears hear the words of your tongue," the buffalo replied, "and I will do as you request."

And so it came to pass that one day followed the next as the sun follows the moon. The young woman performed a wife's tasks easily and well—for the Roamer-of-the-Plain was her faithful servant. He hid in the forest near her husband's field so that he would not be visible to anyone but his mistress.

Whenever the young woman needed water, the Roamer-of-the-Plain picked up her jar in his jaws, filled it at the nearby lake, and returned it to her. Whenever she needed wood, he broke off trees and branches with his great curved horns and carried them to her in his teeth. Whenever she needed to clear new land and prepare it for cultivation, he would wait until the moon cast its light upon the fields. Then, gripping a hoe between his teeth, he would work until the sun made the next day light, preparing even more land than she needed.

Because the young wife performed her tasks so quickly and so well, the villagers would always say, "What a strong young woman our young man has married! She performs every task as quick as the wind! And she has no servant to help her! Even though she is from another village and another people, she is a fine wife and daughter!"

And so it came to pass that everything went well with the young woman. Because the Roamer-of-the-Plain was such a good servant, she lacked nothing.

As for the Roamer-of-the-Plain, however, everything was not going well for him. Although the servant did everything for his mistress, his mistress did nothing for her servant. The buffalo could walk to the nearby lake and drink his fill of water, but, day after day, he had nothing to eat. The young woman would not tell her husband about her servant, and since she and her husband shared their one plate of food, she could find no way to bring food to the Roamer-of-the-Plain.

Finally, the Roamer-of-the-Plain exclaimed, "Mistress, I am so hungry that I am in great pain! Every day, I have less strength! Now, unless you begin to feed me, I will soon become too weak to serve you! Back in your village, I always had my own plate of food. Why do you withhold my plate now that you are living here?"

"Roamer-of-the-Plain, my ears hear your words, and I wish that my hands could help you!" the young woman declared. "However, my husband and I share the one plate of food that we have. Therefore, you must take whatever pleases you from the fields that these villagers cultivate. Start with my husband's field, and then move on to the others. Eat a few beans here and a few beans there! But do not eat only one family's crops. You do not want to call anyone's attention to what you are doing!"

"My ears hear the words of your tongue," the buffalo replied, "and I will do as you suggest."

And so it came to pass that the Roamer-of-the-Plain did as his mistress advised. When the moon cast its light upon the fields, he entered the cultivated area and ate his fill. He munched a few beans here and a few beans there. However, as he moved from one place to another, he could not help but trample on young plants and tear up the soil. By the time he returned to his hiding place, the fields looked as if a great beast had ravaged them.

When the sun made the next day light, the women of the village returned to their fields. At first, their eyes could not believe the scene that greeted them. "What evil has befallen us!" they cried. "What are we to do? A great beast has trampled our fields, and what it has not eaten, it has destroyed!"

Quick as the wind, they returned to their village with the news. Although everyone was upset, the young woman did not think that they would take action.

And so it came to pass that the young woman returned to the forest that bordered her husband's field in order to speak with her buffalo. "Roamer-of-the-Plain, if you are still so hungry that you are in great pain," she declared, "then, again tonight, you must take whatever pleases you from the fields that these villagers cultivate. Eat a few beans here and a few beans there! But do not eat only one family's crops. You do not want to call more attention to what you are doing!"

"My ears hear the words of your tongue," the buffalo replied, "and I will do as you suggest."

And so it came to pass that, once again, the Roamer-of-the-Plain did as his mistress advised. When the moon cast its light upon the fields, he entered the cultivated area. This time, he moved to a more distant area, where he stopped and ate his fill. Once again, he munched a few beans here and a few beans there. And once again, as he moved from one place to another, he could not help but trample on young plants and tear up the soil. When he had finished with the outlying areas, he returned to the field that belonged to the husband of his mistress and began to munch on those bean plants.

Meanwhile, the other women of the village had asked for the help of their village watchmen. Now the husband of the young woman was so good with his gun that he was one of these watchmen. And so it came to pass that he went forth to protect the fields that belonged to him and to his mother. He stealthily approached the cultivated area, and then he hid behind a group of plants in his own field. There he watched and waited to see if the predator would come forth once again. And so it came to pass that, when the Roamer-of-the-Plain returned to the field that belonged to the husband of his mistress, the young man was waiting for him, gun in hand.

At the sight of the buffalo, the young man exclaimed to himself, "What a terrifying animal! Its great curved horns flood my heart with fear! It must be a buffalo! But, how strange to see one of them here!"

With these words, the young man raised his gun and shot the

Roamer-of-the-Plain right between his eye and his ear. The bullet flew faster than a bird, straight through the buffalo's great-horned head and out again. And so it came to pass that his legs gave way beneath his great body, his terrifying head fell forward, and he crumpled upon the ground and died. The young man's heart flooded with joy and, quick as the wind, he returned to the village, where he announced his success with great pride.

The words of his tongue caused his wife's heart to flood with pain and sorrow, and she burst into tears. Quick as the wind, the young woman exclaimed to herself, "I must take care not to reveal my connection to the buffalo!" And so it came to pass that, in order to disguise the real cause of her anguish, she doubled over and cried, "Oh, my stomach! The pain! The pain!"

As she intended, the villagers believed that her stomach was the source of her agony. Quick as the wind, her husband's mother gave her medicine to relieve her pain. However, the young woman secretly tossed it away, since no medicine could cure the secret anguish that flooded her heart.

It now came to pass that the villagers prepared to go forth and take whatever they could use from the carcass of the great fallen beast. Of course, despite her apparent illness the young woman insisted upon accompanying them. And when the villagers had finished carving up the buffalo, despite her apparent illness the young woman insisted that she must be the only person to carry the buffalo's great-horned head back to the village.

And so it came to pass that the young woman secreted herself in her cooking shed with the Roamer-of-the-Plain's great-horned head. There she remained despite the concerned entreaties of her husband and his mother to return to her house and let them care for her. There she remained while the sun completed its journey and went to its home for the night. And there she remained while the villagers went to sleep.

Finally, only two people in the village were still awake—the young woman, who was still in the dark cooking shed, and her husband, who was lying awake in his bed in their house, straining to hear any sounds that came forth from his wife's tongue. In her ears, the young woman heard her parents' advice. And in her ears, she could hear the words of her own tongue as she replied, "Should an unforeseen misfortune occur, know that I will remember to do just what you have advised."

And so it came to pass that, when all was still in the village, the young woman brought the fire-starter into the dark cooking shed and built a small fire. Then, she went into the corner of the shed and found the bundle that she had brought with her from her village. She carefully unwrapped the small pot with the packet of medicinal roots that it contained, the small knife, the horn for bleeding, and the calabash that was filled with grease.

The young woman filled the small pot with water and cooked the medicinal roots until the water boiled and steam rushed forth from the pot. Then she made small cuts with her knife around the two bullet wounds in the Roamer-of-the-Plain's great-horned head. She placed the bleeding horn over these incisions and proceeded to suck out the buffalo's blood. She rubbed the grease into these wounds and directed the medicinal steam toward the incisions that she had made.

As the young woman steamed the wounded area of the Roamer-of-the-Plain's great-horned head, she sang the ritual chant that was so familiar to the people of her village. "Oh, Roamer-of-the-Plain— you who are a father to me!" she declared. "They told me that you would go through the darkest darkness and wander in all directions throughout the night! Oh, Roamer-of-the-Plain! They told me that, like a young plant, you sprout afresh from what is decayed and dead! And that you die before your time, the feast of a gnawing worm! Oh, Roamer-of-the-Plain! You made flowers and fruits fall upon your path!"

It now came to pass that, by the time her chant was finished, the Roamer-of-the-Plain had grown a new body and new legs and had begun to feel new life. He shook his great curved horns and his long ears. And he even rose and stood firmly upon his legs.

The young woman's heart flooded with joy. "Now, all will be well with me and with my people!" she exclaimed to herself.

However, the young woman's husband was still awake, and being concerned about his wife, he now left his bed and went forth from his house to the dark cooking shed. Before he could see anything, both his wife and the Roamer-of-the-Plain heard the sound of his feet. The young woman's heart flooded with anger, and she told her husband to leave.

Her husband left, but it was too late. Quick as the wind, the Roamer-of-the-Plain's life departed and his body disappeared, leaving his pierced, great-horned, and lifeless head upon the ground—

and leaving the young woman in the same sorry state that was hers before she had begun the healing ceremony.

And so it came to pass that the young woman repeated the healing ceremony. Again she filled the small pot with water and cooked the medicinal roots until the water boiled and steam rushed forth from the pot. Again she made small cuts with her knife around the two bullet wounds in the Roamer-of-the-Plain's great-horned head. Again she placed the bleeding horn over these incisions and proceeded to suck out the buffalo's blood. And again she rubbed the grease into these wounds and directed the medicinal steam toward the incisions that she had made.

Again, as the young woman steamed the wounded area of the Roamer-of-the-Plain's great-horned head, she sang the ritual chant that was so familiar to the people of her village. "Oh, Roamer-of-the-Plain—you who are a father to me!" she declared. "They told me that you would go through the darkest darkness and wander in all directions throughout the night! Oh, Roamer-of-the-Plain! They told me that, like a young plant, you sprout afresh from what is decayed and dead! And that you die before your time, the feast of a gnawing worm! Oh, Roamer-of-the-Plain! You made flowers and fruits fall upon your path!"

Again it came to pass that, by the time her chant was finished, the Roamer-of-the-Plain had grown a new body and new legs and had begun to feel new life. Again he shook his great, curved horns and his long ears. And again he even rose and stood firmly upon his legs.

Again the young woman's heart flooded with joy. "Now, all will be well with me and with my people!" she exclaimed to herself.

However, the woman's husband was still awake and very concerned about his wife. Again he left his bed and went forth from his house to the dark cooking shed. Again, before he could see anything, both his wife and the Roamer-of-the-Plain heard the sound of his feet. And again the young woman's heart flooded with anger, and she told her husband to leave.

However, again, it was too late. Quick as the wind, the Roamer-of-the-Plain's life departed and his body disappeared, leaving his pierced, great-horned, and lifeless head upon the ground—and leaving the young woman in the same sorry state that was hers before she had begun the healing ceremony.

Meanwhile, her husband asked, "My dear wife, whatever are you doing here in the cooking shed in the dark? What are you cooking on that small fire? And what words are you singing? Surely you realize that the sun will soon make the day light. The sun will be well-rested, but you have been awake the whole night long! Is this the way you cure your stomachache? Whatever you are doing here, I will keep you company!"

When the young woman's ears heard the words of her husband's tongue, she replied, "Stay here if you wish, my dear! But I am leaving this place to you! Do not let my eyes look upon your face nor my ears hear the sound of your feet or your tongue until I have finished my work!"

And so it came to pass that the young woman gathered her fire-starter, her pot with the medicine, her knife, her bleeding horn, her grease, and the head of the Roamer-of-the-Plain, and she left the cooking shed. Outside, in the dark, she gathered grass and made another small fire.

The young woman then began to repeat the healing ceremony for the third time. Once again, she filled the small pot with water and cooked the medicinal roots until the water boiled and steam rushed forth from the pot. Once again, she made small cuts with her knife around the two bullet wounds in the Roamer-of-the-Plain's great-horned head. Once again, she placed the bleeding horn over these incisions and proceeded to suck out the buffalo's blood. And, once again, she rubbed the grease into these wounds and directed the medicinal steam toward the incisions that she had made.

Once again, as the young woman steamed the wounded area of the Roamer-of-the-Plain's great-horned head, she sang the ritual chant that was so familiar to the people of her village. "Oh, Roamer-of-the-Plain—you who are a father to me!" she declared. "They told me that you would go through the darkest darkness and wander in all directions throughout the night! Oh, Roamer-of-the-Plain! They told me that, like a young plant, you sprout afresh from what is decayed and dead! And that you die before your time, the feast of a gnawing worm! Oh, Roamer-of-the-Plain! You made flowers and fruits fall upon your path!"

Once again, it now came to pass that the Roamer-of-the-Plain had grown a new body and new legs and had begun to feel new life. And, once again, he shook his great, curved horns and his long ears.

However, it had also come to pass that the well-rested sun was now beginning to make the next day light. Being very concerned about her son's wife, the young woman's mother-in-law now awoke, left her bed, and went forth from her house to find her daughter-in-law. She appeared just as her son's wife was singing the last line of the ritual chant—before the buffalo could rise and stand firmly upon his legs.

Fortunately, her mother-in-law could not see anything because both the young woman and the Roamer-of-the-Plain had heard the sound of her feet. Once again, the young woman's heart flooded with anger, and now it was her mother-in-law whom she told to leave.

However, once again, it was too late. Quick as the wind, the Roamer-of-the-Plain's life departed and his body disappeared, leaving his pierced, great-horned, and lifeless head upon the ground— and leaving the young woman in the same sorry state that was hers before she had begun the healing ceremony.

And it came to pass that, as the sun made its journey, the Roamer-of-the-Plain's wounds began to decay. The young woman knew that the time for healing and resuscitation had passed, and her heart flooded with horror. "Now the fate of the Roamer-of-the-Plain will be my fate and the fate of my people!" she exclaimed to herself.

Looking as pale as the moon, the young woman asked her husband to permit her to leave the village and go forth to the nearby lake in order to bathe herself. Hoping that the cool water would revive her, he consented.

The young woman left her husband's village and walked in the direction of the lake. She remained out of sight long enough to think of an excuse to return to her village. Then she went to her husband and announced, "As I was walking toward the lake, I met a man from my village who told me that my mother is very ill and that she will soon die. I wanted to let you know that I am now going forth to see my mother. I will return as soon as I can."

And so it came to pass that the young woman returned to her own village. As she walked, she sang the ritual chant that was so familiar to the people of her village. "Oh, Roamer-of-the-Plain—you who are a father to me!" she declared. "They told me that you would go through the darkest darkness and wander in all directions throughout the night! Oh, Roamer-of-the-Plain! They told me that, like a young plant, you sprout afresh from what is decayed and dead! And that you die before your time, the feast of a gnawing worm! Oh, Roamer-of-the-Plain! You made flowers and fruits fall upon your path!"

And it came to pass that, as she walked, everyone whom she met fell into step behind her and accompanied her to her village. As soon as she arrived, the young woman exclaimed, "The Roamer-of-the-Plain is dead! My husband shot him through the head with his gun!"

Quick as the wind, the word spread far and wide, and other people began to arrive at the village.

Meanwhile, the villagers said to the young woman, "Why did you insist on taking the Roamer-of-the-Plain as your servant when your parents offered you your choice of our young girls? Now you have destroyed us all!"

It now came to pass that the young woman's husband, who had followed his wife, arrived at her village. As soon as they noticed him, the old ones of the village shouted, "Villain! Murderer! You have destroyed us all! Because of you, our people now take leave of the sun's light!"

"What do you mean, grandfathers?" the young man asked. "I did nothing more than kill a buffalo that was eating the crops of our villagers!"

"Yes, that is all that you did, and yet that is everything!" they replied. "The buffalo that you killed was no ordinary animal. He was your wife's servant. He brought her water when she needed it; he cut her wood when she needed it; and he farmed her field when she needed it."

"Then why did my wife not tell me this?" the young man asked. "If only I had known about her buffalo, I never would have killed him!"

"Who knows why she did not tell you!" one of the elders replied. "What is important is that you did not know, and so you killed him. And what you still do not know is that the fate of that buffalo is our own fate as well. As long as the Roamer-of-the-Plain lived, we too could live! But now that he has died, we too must die! Therefore, you are about to witness the death of our people!"

The young man's ears heard these words, but his tongue could only remain silent. And it came to pass that, while he stood in the center of the village, the young woman who was his wife came forth and stood face to face with her husband. She then cried, "Oh, Roamer-of-the-Plain—you who are a father to me!" and slit her own throat.

The young woman's father then came forth and stood face to face with his daughter's husband. He cried, "They told me that you would go through the darkest darkness and wander in all directions throughout the night!" and then slit his own throat.

The young woman's mother then came forth and stood face to face with her daughter's husband. She cried, "Oh, Roamer-of-the-Plain! They told me that, like a young plant, you sprout afresh from what is decayed and dead!" and then slit her own throat.

The young woman's brothers then came forth and stood face to face with their sister's husband. They cried, "And that you die before your time, the feast of a gnawing worm!" and then slit their own throats.

Finally, the young woman's sisters came forth and stood face to face with their sister's husband. They cried, "Oh, Roamer-of-the-Plain! You made flowers and fruits fall upon your path!" and then slit their own throats.

Meanwhile, all of the other villagers were also reciting a line of the chant to the buffalo and slitting their throats. Mothers wailed as fathers killed their children—even those who were so young that they had to be carried upon their mother's back. "We cannot let them live!" they exclaimed. "They will only go mad!"

And so it came to pass that, quick as the wind, no one who had lived in the village remained alive. The young man returned to his village. "Hear what have I done!" he cried. "By killing the buffalo that was eating our crops, I am responsible for the death of my wife and her entire village! Their fate was tied to his fate! As long as the Roamer-of-the-Plain lived, they lived! And when he died, they too had to die!"

"What a shame that you had to bring such misfortune upon innocent people, my son!" his mother replied. "And we told you that this is what usually happens when a young man chooses his own wife! Misfortune follows his footsteps as the sun follows the moon!"

"You have even lost your wealth, my son," his father added, "for you gave your bride-price to your wife's parents, and the dead cannot return it to you!"

The young man's ears heard these words from the tongues of his parents, but his own tongue could only remain silent.

The Crocodile and His Son

"The Crocodile and His Son" is a Fan legend from equatorial West Africa. At the time this legend was recorded, the Fan, a Bantu-speaking people, inhabited the tropical forests of the Congo River basin. The legend reflects many aspects of the life of the Fan people. For example, their economy was based on agriculture, hunting, and fishing, with bananas, manioc (an edible root vegetable), and maize (Indian corn) as the principal crops. The people possessed goats and chickens as well as dogs. Although men cleared the land for farming, women cultivated the crops. The Fan were also a people who specialized in trade, using iron and copper as money.

As the following legend indicates, each Fan village was governed by a chief, who was helped by a village council that was composed of the older men and the heads of the village families. Because Fan society was polygamous, even the crocodile chief in the legend has many wives. Because Fan society was patriarchal, with inheritance through the male, when the great Fan chief in the legend dies, his brother is the next to rule, followed, eventually, by the great chief's grandson. The role and the power of the hero's mother in the legend may reflect an earlier matriarchal organization within the Fan culture. This is not unusual among African peoples.

"The Crocodile and His Son" is particularly interesting because of the relationship that exists between human beings and the natural world. Whenever people are not technologically advanced, they are particularly dependent on and at the mercy of their environment. Consequently, peoples who live among the great forest and water animals may view a particular animal either as their totem or protector, or as an anthropomorphic, godlike being. In the following legend, the crocodile is a godlike being that the Fan people attempt to please with sacrifices in order to gain its favor, and thus their own survival and prosperity.

Although these peoples attempt to gain some control over powerful animals by creating specific types of relationship to them, they are still vulnerable to the forces of nature—such as the sun, rain, storms, and earthquakes—all of which they believe are controlled by powerful divinities or other supernatural beings. Only the greatest of magic can control a force such as lightning. However, the forces of nature often defeat even the greatest hero, despite the fact that he possesses the greatest magical powers.

"The Crocodile and His Son" is particularly appealing because it provides a window into the life of people before they become technologically advanced enough to have some control over their environment. This is the period in every culture when powerful myths come into being and thrive, and the crocodile legend is rooted in such a myth. The role of uncontrollable forces in human survival and prosperity is inherent in the universal human condition, and "The Crocodile and His Son" reminds us of our accomplishments and of those aspects of our lives that remain beyond our control.

THE CROCODILE AND HIS SON

In a time long past—long before the people learned how to fashion boats from trees—the Fan were subject to the wishes of Ombure, the great crocodile chief, who made his home deep in the dismal depths of the great river that washed the shore of their village. And what a great crocodile he was!

Each of his eyes was larger than a young goat. His jaws were longer than one of our huts. And as for his teeth, why they could slice into human flesh as easily as your teeth can slice through a ripe banana! His great body was covered with scales that protected him from the mark of any weapon. A light spear would bounce off his hide like rain off a bird's wing. The strongest stone axe would make no more of a mark than a breeze makes upon the trunk of a tree. So you can see what a great crocodile Ombure was!

Now, it came to pass that this crocodile chief emerged from the dismal depths of the great river and crawled forth upon the shore of the Fan village. He then crawled forth to the hut of the great Fan chief.

Calling the Fan chief before him, Ombure declared, "Man Chief, let your ears listen well to these words that my tongue now speaks! I find that human flesh is far tastier than the flesh of fish.

Therefore, from this time forth, when the sun begins to make each day light, I demand that you give me a human life. One who is a slave will satisfy me, but you must please my appetite by giving me both men and women, first one, and then the other.

"And whenever the old moon makes way for the young one," Ombure continued, "you must give me one of your own young maidens. She must be dressed like a bride, with her face painted and her body well-adorned and rubbed with oil until it shines. For she will be my wife. I will take her down to my home, deep in my great river, so that she will prepare my food and take care of me.

"Now, if you leave these offerings for me on the bank of my river, all will go well with you and your people. However, should you choose to refuse me, know that I will call forth my warriors and all those spirits who rule the waters and the forests at my command. And with their help, I will feast upon all who live in your village! For I am Ombure, Chief of the Waters! And I am Ombure, Chief of the Forests!"

To these words, the great Fan chief replied, "Ombure, my ears have heard the words that the tongue of the great crocodile chief speaks. Well do I know that your power is everywhere and that, with one word from you, quick as the wind, your subjects—the spirits who rule the waters and the forests at your command—will conquer my people! Therefore, I will do all that you ask of me!"

"That is just as it should be," Ombure responded. Then the crocodile chief turned and crawled back into the dismal depths of the great river.

Although the Fan people wept and wailed, it came to pass that one day followed another as the dry season follows the rains.

Each moon was born, matured, grew old, and died, and a new moon was born once again. And, day after day, when the sun began to make the day light, the great crocodile chief, Ombure—he whose eyes were larger than a young goat, he whose jaws were longer than one of our huts, he whose teeth could slice into human flesh as if it were a ripe banana, he whose scales protected him from the mark of any weapon—this great crocodile chief emerged from the dismal depths of the great river and crawled forth upon the shore of the Fan village. There he feasted upon a Fan slave, either a man or a woman, first one and then the other.

And when the old moon made way for the young one, Ombure's jaws—those jaws that were longer than one of our huts—fastened upon a young Fan maiden. She was dressed like a bride, with her face painted and her body well-adorned and rubbed with oil until it shone.

The poor maiden had wept and wailed at the thought of her horrible wedding. Nevertheless, when the sun next made the day light, she left her mother's loving voice and her friends in the village and exchanged them for the home of the crocodile chief, deep in the dismal depths of the great river.

Ombure was pleased with his feast, and he was pleased with the Fan people who offered it. And Ombure's subjects—the spirits who ruled the waters and the forests at his command—were pleased as well. And so it came to pass that they let the Fan people prosper. They prospered in their farming. They prospered in their fishing. And they prospered in their hunting.

Ombure was pleased. And yet, as one day followed another and each moon was born, matured, grew old, and died, the heart of the great Fan chief became flooded with fear.

"I have no slaves left to offer Ombure!" the chief exclaimed to himself. "The riches from my royal storehouse have all gone to appease his greedy appetite. Only one elephant tusk and a few iron and copper pieces remain! Therefore, unless I can find a way to save my people, the crocodile chief will soon be feasting on them!"

And so it came to pass that the great Fan chief met with his council of advisors and warriors. In their discussion, they thought with one mind and felt with one heart.

"It is clear that our only acceptable choice is to move our village," the chief declared. "I have hunted far and wide, and I know the land well. If we move to the other side of the mountains, we will leave the river and Ombure far behind. My heart floods with sadness to leave our huts, our fields, and our fishing, but only by moving can we live with happy hearts.

"Therefore, tell our women to sow no more seeds," he concluded. "For as soon as the dry season is upon us, we will pack our possessions and leave our village. Then, the streams will be easy to cross, and our women and children will have an easier time of it!"

And so it came to pass that when the rainy season had passed and the waters had subsided, the great Fan chief went forth on foot with his people. Each man of the village was in charge of his wives, and each wife was in charge of her children, all of her household goods, and food for the journey. The women walked as fast as they could, their backs bent beneath the weight of their dishes, their baskets and pots, their sleeping mats, their hoes, their supply of maize and dried manioc, and their infants and young children. Their men worked at covering their tracks lest Ombure discover them.

The great Fan chief led his people through the forest in silence, his heart flooded with confidence, and his power as a great hunter revealed by his necklace of gorilla's teeth. He had left no sacrifice for Ombure, and lest his heart flood with fear when he thought about the great crocodile chief's rage and revenge, before leaving he had offered great sacrifices to the water and forest spirits.

Both groups of spirits had replied, "Great Man Chief, we are pleased with your sacrifice, and we promise you that, when Ombure asks us, we will know nothing about you and your people."

And so it came to pass that the great Fan chief led his people through the forest in silence. One day followed another as the dry season follows the rains. Each moon was born, matured, grew old, and died, and a new moon was born once again. And still the great Fan chief led his people forth to find a safe place for their new village.

And it came to pass that the great Fan chief led his people across the mountains and into a new land. The chief then asked his fetish, which possessed great magical power, "Is this a good place to build our village?"

To these words, the fetish replied, "No, Man Chief, you must not build your village here, because this is not a good place. Instead, you must continue your journey."

And so it came to pass that the great Fan chief led his people away from the mountains and across the plains into the great never ending forest. Once again the chief asked his fetish, "Is this a good place to build our village?"

To these words, the fetish again replied, "No, Man Chief, you must not build your village here, because this is not a good place. Instead, you must continue your journey."

And so it came to pass that the great Fan chief led his people through the great never ending forest until they found themselves upon a great plain and by the shore of a great lake. Once again, the chief asked his fetish, "Is this a good place to build our village?"

To these words, the fetish now replied, "Yes, Man Chief, you must build your village here, on the shore of this great lake, because this is a good place."

And so it came to pass that the Fan people built their new village by the shore of this great lake. By now, they had many strong hands to do the work, for those who had been infants and young children at the start of the journey were now boys and girls, those who had been boys and girls were now adolescents, and those who had been adolescents were now young men and women. The men cleared the land for farming and built new huts, while the women helped with the huts and planted manioc and maize.

And it came to pass that when the manioc and maize were full grown, the Fan people gathered together to celebrate their first harvest in their new village. The heart of the great Fan chief was flooded with joy as he announced, "Let us now give thanks for our great harvest, and let us also give thanks for our victory over Ombure, the great crocodile chief. In honor of our victory, from this time forth, let us call our new village Safe-from-the-Crocodile."

Now, the hearts of the great Fan chief and his people were flooded with joy. However, if they had known more than they knew, their hearts would have been flooded with terror, and not with joy. For when the great Fan chief had first set forth on his journey on foot with his people—before one day had followed another as the dry season follows the rains—as soon as the sun began to make the next day light, the great crocodile chief, Ombure—he whose eyes were larger than a young goat, he whose jaws were longer than one of our huts, he whose teeth could slice into human flesh as if it were a ripe banana, he whose scales protected him from the mark of any weapon—this great crocodile chief emerged from the dismal depths of the great river and crawled forth upon the shore of the old Fan village.

And it came to pass that when Ombure found that no human offering was waiting for him on the shore of the Fan village, he crawled forth into the village itself and called for the great Fan chief. And when the great Fan chief did not appear, Ombure crawled into the huts of the Fan people. And when Ombure saw that the Fan huts were deserted, he crawled forth into the fields of the Fan people. And when he saw that the fields of the Fan people were deserted, then his heart flooded with rage.

Quick as the wind, the great crocodile chief turned back toward the great river and returned to his home, deep in the dismal depths of the waters. There he chanted, "I, Ombure, chief of all who rule the waters, command you who rule my waters to tell me what I wish to know. For I command the mighty storm that rushes forth from the sky and bends all beneath it to its will. I command the lightning that tears apart the sky. I command the thunder that shatters all things. And I command the great storm-wind that overturns the banana tree.

"Therefore, Water Spirits," Ombure concluded, "I command you to show me the path of these people who have fled from me! Show me their path that I may follow them! For I am your chief, and you will obey my command!"

At first, all was silent. At first all was still. But then it came to pass that the water spirits came before Ombure and replied, "Master, we do not know the path of the people who have fled from you. They did not come our way, and so we have not seen them."

To these words, Ombure replied, "Then, Water Spirits, the people whom I seek have not fled upon the water, for you are my subjects, and I know that you would not dare to disobey my command. And if you have not seen them, then surely the forest spirits have seen them!"

And so it came to pass that, once again, the great crocodile chief chanted, "I, Ombure, chief of all who rule the forests, command you who rule my forests to tell me what I wish to know. For I command the mighty storm that rushes forth from the sky and bends all beneath it to its will. I command the lightning that tears apart the sky. I command the thunder that shatters all things. And I command the great storm-wind that overturns the banana tree.

"Therefore, Forest Spirits," Ombure concluded, "I command you to show me the path of the people who have fled from me! Show me their path that I may follow them! For I am your chief, and you will obey my command!"

At first, all was silent. At first all was still. But then it came to pass that the forest spirits came before Ombure and replied, "Master, we know the path of the people who have fled from you. They came our way, and we will show you the path that they have taken!"

To these words, Ombure replied, "Then, Forest Spirits, let those of you who know this now speak!"

And so it came to pass that Spirit of Night and Spirit of Day came forward. Spirit of Lightning and Spirit of Thunder came forward. Spirit of Wind and Spirit of Storm came forward. And these spirits told Ombure all that he needed to know about the path that the great Fan chief had taken with his people.

It came to pass that Ombure then called before him the fetish spirit that served the great Fan chief. And the great crocodile chief commanded, "Fetish Spirit, see to it that the great man chief whom you serve does not learn that I am your master. Whenever he asks you, 'Is this a good place to build our village?' you must reply, 'No, Man Chief, you must not build your village here, because this is not a good place. Instead, you must continue your journey.'

"You must say these words," the great crocodile chief continued, "so that the great man chief will lead his people away from the mountains, across the plains, and through the great never ending forest. Only when they have arrived upon the great plain and when they stand upon the shore of the great lake are you to reply, 'Man Chief, you must build your village here, on the shore of this great lake, because this is a good place.'"

And so it came to pass that Ombure was waiting in the great lake for the great chief of the Fan people. He was waiting close to the shore where the Fan people had built their new village, when the great Fan chief led his people in celebration of their first harvest and their victory over the great crocodile chief.

The sun had long gone to its rest, and the moon was casting its pale light upon the Fan village when Ombure—he whose eyes were larger than a young goat, he whose jaws were longer than one of our huts, he whose teeth could slice into human flesh as if it were a ripe banana, he whose scales protected him from the mark of any weapon—this great crocodile chief emerged from the dismal depths of the great lake and crawled forth upon the shore of the new Fan village.

Ombure then went forth to the hut of the great Fan chief and called, "Man Chief, come forth to greet Ombure! The words of your tongue declare that you have escaped the great crocodile chief. But, as you see, I am here to greet you!"

And so it came to pass that, as the great Fan chief stood inside his hut, his heart flooded with terror. For now he knew that the Fan people could neither hide nor flee from Ombure. And he knew that Ombure would always rule the great chief of the Fan people!

When the great Fan chief emerged from his hut, Ombure was waiting for him. "Man Chief, surely you have too much wisdom between your ears to have forgotten my power!" he exclaimed. "And surely you have not forgotten the prosperity that I have brought your people! You must know that you owe your lives to me as well, for I can kill all of you whenever I choose!"

And with these words, the great crocodile chief opened his jaws—those jaws that were longer than one of our huts—and with one bite of his teeth—those teeth that could slice into human flesh as if it were a ripe banana—he bit the great Fan chief in two. Then, the crocodile chief turned, and with the corpse of the great Fan chief stuffed between his teeth, he crawled back into the dismal depths of the great lake.

The council of advisors and warriors that had advised the great Fan chief now gathered together and chose a new chief—he who was the brother of the great chief whom Ombure had eaten.

Then the new Fan chief and the members of his council went forth to the hut of the great Fan chief, where they grabbed his widow, bound her, and placed her on the shore of the lake. They were determined that, once again, when the sun made the next day light, the great crocodile chief would have his offering of human flesh. First it had been a man; and now it would be a woman.

And so it came to pass that, when the sun made the next day light, Ombure emerged from the dismal depths of the great lake and crawled forth upon the shore of the Fan village. There he feasted upon the widow of the great Fan chief. However, his rage was still unappeased.

The sun had long gone to its rest, and the moon was casting its pale light upon the Fan village when the great crocodile chief, Ombure, emerged once again from the dismal depths of the great lake and crawled forth upon the shore of the Fan village. He then crawled forth to the hut of the new Fan chief—he who was the brother of the great chief whom Ombure had eaten.

Calling the chief before him, Ombure declared, "Man Chief, let your ears listen well to these words that my tongue now speaks! I find that human flesh is still far tastier than fish, and I am now far hungrier than I used to be. Therefore, from this time forth, as always, when the sun begins to make each day light, I demand that you give me one human life. However, now, when the sun has gone to its rest, I demand that you give me a second human life as well. One who is a slave will satisfy me, but you must appeal to my appetite by giving me both men and women, first one and then the other.

"And when the old moon makes way for the young one," he continued, "you must now give me two of your own young maidens, instead of one. They must be dressed like brides, with their faces painted and their bodies well-adorned and rubbed with oil until they shine. For they will be my wives. I will take them down to my home, deep in the lake, so that they will prepare my food and take care of me.

"As always, if you leave these offerings for me on the shore of my lake, all will go well with you and your people. However, should you choose to refuse me, know that I will call forth my warriors and all those spirits who rule the waters and the forests at my command. And with their help, I will feast upon all who live in your village! For I am Ombure, Chief of the Waters! And I am Ombure, Chief of the Forests!"

To these words, the new Fan chief—he who was the brother of the great chief whom Ombure had eaten—this chief replied, "Ombure, my ears have heard the words that the tongue of the great crocodile chief speaks. Well do I know that your power is everywhere and that, with one word from you, quick as the wind, your subjects—the spirits who rule the waters and the forests at your command—will conquer my people! Therefore, I will do all that you ask of me!"

"That is just as it should be," Ombure responded. Then, the crocodile chief turned and crawled back into the dismal depths of the great lake.

Although the Fan people wept and wailed, it came to pass that one day and night followed another as the dry season follows the rains. Each moon was born, matured, grew old, and died, and a new moon was born once again. And day after day, and night after night, when the sun began to make the day light, and again when the sun had gone to its rest, the great crocodile chief, Ombure, emerged from the dismal depths of the great lake and crawled forth upon the shore of the Fan village. There, he feasted upon two Fan slaves. He feasted upon one man by the bright light of the sun, and he feasted upon one woman by the pale light of the moon.

And when the old moon made way for the young one, Ombure's jaws—those jaws that were longer than one of our huts—fastened upon the two young Fan maidens. They were dressed like brides, with their faces painted and their bodies well-adorned and rubbed with oil until they shone.

The poor maidens had wept and wailed at the thought of their horrible wedding. Nevertheless, when the sun next made the day light, they left their mothers' loving voices and their friends in the village and exchanged them for the home of the crocodile chief, deep in the dismal depths of the great lake.

Ombure was pleased with his feast, and he was pleased with the Fan people who offered it. And Ombure's subjects—the spirits who ruled the waters and the forests at his command—were pleased as well. And so it came to pass that they let the Fan people prosper. They prospered in their farming. They prospered in their fishing. And they prospered in their hunting.

The riches from the great Fan chief's royal storehouse were long gone, having been used to purchase the slaves who appeased Ombure's greedy appetite. Therefore, the new Fan chief—he who was the brother of the great chief whom Ombure had eaten—this chief had no choice but to wage war on his neighbors, and then to wage war on his neighbors' neighbors, in order to capture more slaves to sacrifice to Ombure. The Fan warriors were always victorious because the great crocodile chief always protected those who were fighting on his behalf.

And so it came to pass that two years came and went like the dry season after the rains. Ombure was pleased. And yet, as one day followed another and each moon was born, matured, grew old, and died, the heart of the Fan chief—he who was the brother of the great chief whom Ombure had eaten—the heart of this chief became flooded with anger. And so it came to pass that the chief met with his council of advisors and warriors. In their discussion, they thought with one mind and felt with one heart.

"It is clear that we are tired of appeasing Ombure so that our people will prosper. We are tired of human sacrifice! We are tired of war! Our hearts flood with rage at the thought of Ombure's tyranny! It is clear that, once again, we must move our village," the chief declared. "After all, what more can the great crocodile chief do to us?

"My heart floods with sadness to leave our huts, our fields, and our fishing, but only by moving can we live with happy hearts! Therefore, tell our women to sow no more seeds," the Fan chief concluded. "For as soon as the dry season is upon us, we will pack our possessions and leave our village. Then, the streams will be easy to cross, and our women and children will have an easier time of it!"

And so it came to pass that when the rainy season had passed and the waters had subsided, the young men of the Fan village went forth to find a new place to settle. The warriors followed them, each in charge of his wives, and each wife in charge of her children, all of her household goods, and food for the journey. The women walked as fast as they could, their backs bent beneath the weight of their dishes, their baskets and pots, their sleeping mats, their hoes, their supply of maize and dried manioc, and their infants and young children.

Now, as soon as the sun began to make the next day light, the great crocodile chief, Ombure, emerged from the dismal depths of the great lake and crawled forth upon the shore of the Fan village. And it came to pass that, once again, when Ombure found that no human offering was waiting for him on the shore of the Fan village, he crawled forth into the village itself and called for the Fan chief.

And when the Fan chief did not appear, Ombure crawled forth into the huts of the Fan people. And when Ombure saw that the Fan huts were deserted, he crawled forth into the fields of the Fan people. And when he saw that the fields of the Fan people were deserted, then his heart flooded with rage.

Quick as the wind, the great crocodile chief turned back toward the great lake and returned to his home, deep in the dismal depths of the waters. There he chanted, "I, Ombure, chief of all who rule the forests, command you who rule my forests to stop the flight of the people who have fled from me and send them back to their village!

"I command the mighty storm that rushes forth from the sky and bends all beneath it to its will," he continued. "So, Spirit of the Storm, hear the words of my tongue, now, and be quick to act upon my command!

"I command the lightning that tears apart the sky," Ombure declared. "So, Spirit of Lightning, blind the eyes of this ungrateful chief and his people with your light!

"I command the thunder that shatters all things," Ombure declared. "So, Spirit of Thunder, shatter the ears of this ungrateful chief and his people with your drum-beats!

"And I command the great storm-wind that overturns the banana tree," Ombure declared. "So, Spirit of the Storm-wind, overturn the trees of the forest so that they will block the paths that this ungrateful chief and his people would take! For I am your chief, and you will obey my command!"

And so it came to pass that a mighty storm rushed forth from the sky and bent all beneath it to its will. It forced the Fan chief—he who was the brother of the great chief whom Ombure had eaten—and his people to come to a halt in the great forest. Spirit of Lightning tore apart the sky, blinding their eyes with his light. Spirit of Thunder shattered their ears with his drum-beats. Spirit of the Storm-wind overturned the trees, both great and small, so that the only path open to this chief and his people was the path back to their village. Their hearts flooded with despair as, together, they turned back.

And it came to pass that, as soon as they had returned to their village, they came face to face with Ombure. There the great crocodile chief lay, on the shore of the great lake, eagerly watching and waiting for the return of the Fan chief—he who was the brother of the great chief whom Ombure had eaten—and his people.

Calling the chief before him, Ombure declared, "Man Chief, surely you have too much wisdom between your ears to have forgotten my power!" he exclaimed. "And surely you have not forgotten the prosperity that I have brought your people! You must know that you owe your lives to me as well, for I can kill all of you whenever I choose!"

"And now, Man Chief, let your ears listen well to these words that my tongue now speaks," Ombure commanded. "I find that human flesh is far tastier than the flesh of fish. However, I am no longer interested in your male and female slaves. From this time forth, each night, after the sun has gone to its rest, you must give me two of your own young maidens," the crocodile chief declared. "They must be dressed like brides, with their faces painted and their bodies well-adorned and rubbed with oil until they shine. For they will be my wives. I will take them down to my home deep in the lake so that they will prepare my food and take care of me.

"As always, if you leave these offerings for me on the shore of my lake, all will go well with you and your people. However, should you choose to refuse me, know that I will call forth my warriors and all those spirits who rule the waters and the forests at my command. And with their help, I will feast upon all who live in your village! For I am Ombure, Chief of the Waters! And I am Ombure, Chief of the Forests!"

To these words, the Fan chief—he who was the brother of the great chief whom Ombure had eaten—this chief once again replied, "Ombure, my ears have heard the words that the tongue of the great crocodile chief speaks. Well do I know that your power is everywhere and that, with one word from you, quick as the wind, your subjects— the spirits who rule the waters and the forests at your command— will conquer my people! Therefore, I will do all that you ask of me!"

"That is just as it should be," Ombure responded. Then the crocodile chief turned and crawled back into the dismal depths of the great lake.

Although, once again, the Fan people wept and wailed, it came to pass that one night followed another as the dry season follows the rains. And, night after night, when the sun had gone to its rest, the great crocodile chief, Ombure, emerged from the dismal depths of the great lake and crawled forth upon the shore of the Fan village.

There, while the moon was casting its pale light upon the shore, Ombure's jaws—those jaws that were longer than one of our huts— fastened upon the two young Fan maidens. They were dressed like brides, with their faces painted and their bodies well-adorned and rubbed with oil until they shone.

The poor maidens had wept and wailed at the thought of their horrible wedding. Nevertheless, when the sun had gone to its rest, they left their mothers' loving voices and their friends in the village and exchanged them for the home of the crocodile chief, deep in the dismal depths of the great lake.

Once again, Ombure was pleased with his feast, and he was pleased with the Fan people who offered it. And once again, Ombure's subjects—the spirits who ruled the waters and the forests at his command—were pleased as well. And so it came to pass that, once again, they let the Fan people prosper. They prospered in their farming. They prospered in their fishing. And they prospered in their hunting.

That was the way that it was, and it now appeared that that was the way that it would always be. However, it came to pass that one night, one of the two young maidens chosen for the sacrifice to Ombure was the beautiful daughter of the great Fan chief—he who had been eaten by the great crocodile chief.

The poor maidens had wept and wailed at the thought of their horrible wedding. However, it came to pass that, when the sun made the next day light, the Fan people discovered that only one of the girls had exchanged her mother's loving voice and her friends in the village for the home of the crocodile chief, deep in the dismal depths of the great lake.

The other young maiden—she who was the beautiful daughter of the great Fan chief—this young maiden was still where the people had left her, and she was alive and well! For a reason as yet unknown to them, the great crocodile chief, Ombure, had decided to preserve the life of the daughter of the great Fan chief!

It then came to pass that nine moons were born, matured, grew old, and died—as always, one after the other, like the dry season after the rains. And then, with the birth of the next new moon, the beautiful daughter of the great Fan chief gave birth to a male child. The people called the grandson of their great chief Son-of-the-Crocodile.

Years then came and went—as always, one after the other, like the dry season after the rains. And as these years passed, Son-of-the-Crocodile—he who was the grandson of the great chief whom Ombure had eaten—this male child grew from an infant into a young child, from a young child into a boy, from a boy into an adolescent, and from an adolescent into a young man.

And it came to pass that the chief of the Fan people—he who was the brother of the great chief whom Ombure had eaten—this chief became too old to rule the people. Then, Son-of-the-Crocodile—he who was the grandson of the great chief whom Ombure had eaten—this young man became the new chief of the Fan people.

Son-of-the-Crocodile was known both as a great shaman and as a great warrior. And the heart of this new chief of the Fan people was flooded with two great desires. Son-of-the-Crocodile was determined to avenge the death of his grandfather—he who had been the great chief of the Fan people. And Son-of-the-Crocodile was determined to end the tyranny of the great crocodile chief, Ombure, who would emerge from the dismal depths of the great lake and crawl forth upon the shore of the Fan village in order to eat the human sacrifices that he demanded.

And it came to pass that the mother of Son-of-the-Crocodile—she who was the daughter of the great chief whom Ombure had eaten—this woman gave her son a powerful fetish stone. And the spirit of this fetish stone spoke to Son-of-the-Crocodile and told him how to make an intoxicating wine from the sap of the sacred palm tree. And the new Fan chief—he who was the grandson of the great chief whom Ombure had eaten—this chief listened to the words of his mother's fetish spirit. And Son-of-the-Crocodile used what he learned from the fetish spirit for the good of the Fan people. And he used what he learned from the fetish spirit to heal the pain that flooded his mother's heart and his own.

"Men and women of the Fan people," Son-of-the-Crocodile announced. "Collect all of your clay jars, fill them with sap from the sacred palm tree, close them, and keep them sealed until three nights have followed three days as the dry season follows the rains."

And so it came to pass that the women brought all of their clay jars—and many newly fashioned jars as well—into the forest, where the men used their knives and stone axes to cut into the trunks of the sacred palm trees and let the sap flow into the jars. When the women had carried the jars back to the village, Son-of-the-Crocodile— he who was the new chief and the grandson of the great chief whom Ombure had eaten—this chief tasted the sap every day to see how strong it had become. However, he made it taboo for any of his people to taste the fermenting liquid.

Finally, when it had come to pass that three nights had followed three days as the dry season follows the rains, Son-of-the-Crocodile— he who was the new chief and the grandson of the great chief whom Ombure had eaten—this chief gathered his people and announced, "Men and women of the Fan people, the time has come to use this palm wine. Women, I want you to fashion two great clay pans on the shore of the lake. And, men, as soon as the pans are ready, I want you to bring the jars of palm wine down to the shore and empty all of the wine into the pans."

"And now, men and women of the Fan people, let your ears listen well to these words that my tongue now speaks," Son-of-the-Crocodile commanded. "Remember that it is taboo for you to taste the wine!"

The Fan people obeyed the commands of Son-of-the-Crocodile— he who was their new chief and the grandson of the great chief whom Ombure had eaten. And once the two great clay pans were filled with wine, the people ceremonially broke the clay jars that had contained the palm wine and threw them into the great lake.

Son-of-the-Crocodile—he who was the new chief and the grandson of the great chief whom Ombure had eaten—this chief then commanded the Fan warriors to tie two slaves next to the wine-filled pans. And when this, too, had been done, Son-of-the-Crocodile ordered the rest of the Fan people to return to their huts and remain hidden there. Meanwhile, he himself hid nearby in order to observe the great crocodile chief when he emerged from the dismal depths of the great lake and crawled forth upon the shore of the Fan village.

And it came to pass that just before the sun began to make the next day light, the great crocodile chief, Ombure—he whose eyes were larger than a young goat, he whose jaws were longer than one of our huts, he whose teeth could slice into human flesh as if it were a ripe banana, he whose scales protected him from the mark of any weapon—this great crocodile chief emerged from the dismal depths of the great lake and crawled forth upon the shore of the Fan village. First, he approached the two bound slaves, and their hearts flooded with terror at the sight of him! However, when he spied the great wine-filled pans, his heart flooded with curiosity. Quick as the wind, he turned from the slaves and crawled forth to taste some of the palm wine.

"How sweet this drink is!" Ombure exclaimed. "The taste of it makes my heart sing! I will command Man Chief to have this drink here for me whenever I come for my maidens!"

And so it came to pass that the great crocodile chief, Ombure—he whose eyes were larger than a young goat, he whose jaws were longer than one of our huts, he whose teeth could slice into human flesh as if it were a ripe banana, he whose scales protected him from the mark of any weapon—this great crocodile chief drank every drop of palm wine that he could find in the two great pans.

And when he had drunk all of the palm wine, Ombure sang, "Oh, how my heart floods with joy from this wine that I have drunk! I am Ombure, Chief of the Waters! And I am Ombure, Chief of the Forests! I am that great chief whom everyone must obey! Oh, how my heart floods with joy from this wine that I have drunk!"

And then it came to pass that, with this song, Ombure fell asleep on the shore of the great lake by the Fan village. His heart was so flooded with joy that he had forgotten all about the bound slaves!

And so it came to pass that Son-of-the-Crocodile—he who was the new chief and the grandson of the great chief whom Ombure had eaten—this chief emerged from his hiding place and stealthily stole forth to where the pair of slaves were lying bound upon the shore of the great lake. Son-of-the-Crocodile freed the slaves, and together they took their strongest rope and bound the great crocodile chief to a great stake.

Then Son-of-the-Crocodile drew forth his light spear and thrust it upon Ombure's scaly hide. However, his spear bounced off the hide of the great crocodile chief like rain off a bird's wing because Ombure's scales protected him from the mark of any weapon.

The great crocodile chief just stirred in his sleep and mumbled, "What pesky insect throws itself against me?"

And so it came to pass that Son-of-the-Crocodile drew forth his great stone axe and chopped at Ombure's scaly hide. The two slaves fled in terror at the sound of it! However, his axe made no more of a mark upon the hide of the great crocodile chief than a breeze makes upon the trunk of a tree, because Ombure's scales protected him from the mark of any weapon.

Once again, the great crocodile chief just stirred in his sleep and mumbled, "What pesky insect throws itself against me?"

And so it came to pass that Son-of-the-Crocodile raised his powerful fetish toward the sky and summoned the spirit of thunder. "Spirit of Thunder!" he commanded. "With this fetish in my hand, I call upon you to hurl your darts against Ombure, the great crocodile chief!"

To these words, Spirit of Thunder responded, "Man Chief, your words flood my heart with terror! I cannot kill my master! And Ombure, the great crocodile chief, is your own father!"

These words from the tongue of Spirit of Thunder reached the ears of Son-of-the-Crocodile's mother—she who was the daughter of the great chief whom Ombure had eaten. And this woman now came forth from her hut in order to help her son and her people. In her hand she carried her own fetish stone, the fetish spirit that had the most powerful magic.

The daughter of the great chief placed this stone in Son-of-the-Crocodile's hand and declared, "My son—you who are now the great chief of our people!—my fetish spirit has helped us before. Surely, it will help us now!"

And so it came to pass that Son-of-the-Crocodile raised his mother's powerful fetish toward the sky and summoned the spirit of lightning. "Spirit of Lightning!" he commanded. "With this fetish in my hand, I call upon you to hurl your darts against Ombure, the great crocodile chief!"

To these words Spirit of Lightning responded, "Man Chief, your words flood my heart with terror! However, I cannot disobey you when you possess the power of your mother's fetish stone, even though you are commanding me to kill my master!"

And so it came to pass that Spirit of Lightning struck and killed the great crocodile chief, Ombure—he whose eyes were larger than a young goat, he whose jaws were longer than one of our huts, he whose teeth could slice into human flesh as if it were a ripe banana, and he whose scales protected him from the mark of any weapon. This great crocodile chief died from a lightning blast between his eyes while he slept on the shore of the Fan village, by the great lake where he had made his home deep in the dismal depths of the waters.

The Fan people emerged from their huts—men and women, and boys and girls—their hearts flooding with joy. For Son-of-the-Crocodile—he who was their great chief and the grandson of the great chief whom Ombure had eaten—this chief had avenged the death of his grandfather. And Son-of-the-Crocodile—he who was their great chief and the grandson of the great chief whom Ombure had eaten—this chief had brought the tyranny of Ombure, with his demands for human flesh, to an end.

And it came to pass that the Fan people danced their great funeral dance around the corpse of the great crocodile chief, Ombure—he whose eyes were larger than a young goat, he whose jaws were longer than one of our huts, he whose teeth could slice into human flesh as if it were a ripe banana, he whose scales protected him from the mark of any weapon—because this great crocodile chief had been their great protector as well as their great enemy, and they respected his spirit in death as they had respected it in life.

In time, it came to pass that Son-of-the-Crocodile—he who was their great chief and the chief who had killed Ombure—this chief taught the men of his people, the Fan, how to hollow out the trunks of trees and fashion boats so that they would be masters of the great rivers and lakes and prosper as great traders.

And so ends the legend of the crocodile and his son.

THE MIDDLE EAST

The following myths, folktales, and legends from the Middle East are among the greatest in the world. Those who recorded them lived many centuries ago, but each author was interested in the timeless connection between human psychology and the human condition. Consequently, these selections examine some of the closest human relationships: those of wives and husbands, and of sons and fathers. In addition, whether these stories focus on gods, heroes, or common folk, they reveal the many faces of virtue, along with the human failings—such as pride, greed, jealousy, and distrust—that often wear the masks of virtue.

The recorded myths about Enki (c. mid-eighteenth century B.C.) and Adapa (fifteenth or fourteenth century B.C.) are among the oldest surviving works of literature. The Persian legends "Rostam, Shield of Persia" and "The Tragedy of Sohrab," although written in their present form in A.D. 1000, derive from oral traditions that are much older. The Jewish folktale "The Craftsman's Wife" appears in the *Gesta Romanorum* (*Deeds of the Romans*), a popular Latin collection of European, oriental, and classical tales that was probably compiled in England in the late thirteenth or early fourteenth century. Today, we value these myths, legends, and tales for what they reveal about their respective cultures and for what they reveal about human nature, which remains unchanged through time and space.

"Enki, Lord of the Earth and the Waters of Life," a creation myth from Sumer, offers one explanation for the fertility of the earth and the technological progress that has made this ancient civilization famous. Enki is a divine culture hero who makes the earth livable for gods and mortals. The creation of such a divinity reflects a belief in a benign universe in which human beings are able to survive and prosper.

In contrast, "Adapa," a remarkable myth from Akkad, Babylonia, and Assyria, is darker in tone. It offers one explanation for the creation of human beings, human mortality, and the nature of the human condition. Built into this myth are the father-son relationship and the mortal-god relationship, with their psychological and religious implications. As is true with other myths throughout the world, the issue of human mortality receives special attention. Here, Adapa, who is a gifted man, brings mortality and misfortune upon himself and his people. However, the circumstances are ambiguous, and it is far from clear whether Adapa is actually to blame.

"The Craftsman's Wife" is a delightful example of the "clever wife" motif in folklore. Although King Solomon is famous for his wisdom, the craftsman's wife outwits him. In this game between two well-matched players, it is interesting to consider the factors that make it possible for the craftsman's wife to succeed against a more powerful adversary. It is also interesting to note that the story is about a woman who is never named.

"Rostam, Shield of Persia" and "The Tragedy of Sohrab" come from the remarkable Persian *Shahnameh,* one of the greatest epics in world literature. They reveal the way in which a hero's values determine the choices that he makes and how these choices lead to tragic consequences. Rostam, the ultimate traditional hero, becomes a victim of his pride and loses what he most values. Sohrab, who is Rostam's son, has an overwhelming need to prove his heroism both to himself and to his father, and, in the process, he experiences a tragic fate. These legends provoke questions about the extent to which these heroes have the power to control the course of their lives and the role that Fate plays in determining human destiny.

Enki, Lord of the Earth and the Waters of Life and **Adapa**

The myths about Enki and Adapa came from the ancient land of Mesopotamia (the term refers to the land between the Tigris and Euphrates rivers), which is now Iraq. The myth about Enki originated in the ancient land of Sumer, the oldest civilization that has left written records in a language that scholars can read. Located in southern Mesopotamia, Sumer extended from what is now Baghdad south to the Persian Gulf.

These two myths reflect important aspects of four successive civilizations that occupied ancient Mesopotamia—the Sumerians, the Akkadians, the Babylonians, and the Assyrians. The myth about Adapa may be as old as the myth about Enki. However, all four surviving versions of "Adapa" are written in Akkadian, rather than in Sumerian. Because the later peoples of Mesopotamia valued the contributions of the Sumerians so highly that they preserved Sumerian culture, it is both interesting and helpful to understand certain aspects of Sumerian history, religion, and literature.

Historical Background

By the fifth millennium (5000–4000) B.C., the Sumerians were producing enough food to permit division of labor. By c. 3500 B.C. they had invented writing, mathematics, and the wheel. By c. 2500 B.C. they were recording economic and administrative matters on clay tablets. Around 2100 B.C. they developed a written code of law. In addition, they are famous for their monumental temples, called ziggurats, which they constructed as the earthly homes for their gods, as well as for their sophisticated literature, which they inscribed in cuneiform script on clay tablets.

The complexity of Sumerian civilization in the third millennium (3000–2000) B.C. is evident in the following description of Uruk, the first Sumerian city-state. In c. 2800 B.C., its population numbered between forty thousand and fifty thousand people. Its society was composed of a social hierarchy that placed the priest and king at the top, followed by (in descending order) merchants and large landowners, craftspeople (weavers, leather-workers, metalsmiths, bricklayers, scribes, and artisans), laborers (sailors, fishermen, farmers, and water carriers), and finally slaves (who were usually female) at the bottom.

The ziggurat, now finer and larger, had changed from a purely religious structure to a secular storehouse. It was a center for the distribution of agricultural products and related goods for the inhabitants of the city and its surrounding countryside. At the start of the third millennium B.C., the priest was both the religious leader and the chief political leader of his community. However, by c. 2600 B.C., this authority had become split between the priest and the king.

Sumerian tablets dating from about 1750 B.C. reveal that Eridu was the first Sumerian temple-city. It was one of the most revered places in Sumer because it was dedicated to Enki, whose name means "Lord of the Earth" and who was also the Sumerian god of water, arts and crafts, and wisdom. The Sumerian King List—which is a composite of historical fact, legend, and fantasy—states that kingship "came down from heaven" and that the Sumerian gods chose Eridu to be the first city to be ruled by kings.

By the twentieth century, both Eridu and the fertile plain that had been nourished by the waters of the Euphrates were viewed as myth, since all that met the eye was a bleak land of barren mud. However, in 1946, the scanty remains of a ziggurat, which protruded through drifting sand at one end of a flat-topped mound, led Iraqi archaeologists to investigate the site. They named their dig Tell Abu Shahrain, and by the end of the summer of 1950, they had found the ruins of twelve temples, each built on the ruins of the preceding one, and all constructed of clay, mud bricks, and marsh reeds. The most recent temple was dated c. 4000 B.C., and the earliest c. 5900 B.C.

The earliest temple is a small, one-room shrine with an altar in the middle. The "great heaps of ashes ... thickly intermingled with vast quantities of fish bones" found on the altar are the earliest evidence of the sacrifice of fish to the god Enki. However, in sifting through the upper layers of the mound—sand and rubble from a two-thousand-year period—archaeologists have unearthed the bones of fish on collapsed altars in many of the other twelve temples. Consequently, scholars currently think that Enki's city of Eridu actually existed, that it was in fact located near the marshes of southern Sumer and the Persian Gulf, and that Tell Abu Shahrain may be the Eridu of Sumerian myth.

Sumerian culture became the foundation of three other major civilizations in Mesopotamia: Akkad, Babylonia, and Assyria. The first of these was Akkad, which took root as a separate culture in northern Mesopotamia during the fourth millennium (4000–3000) B.C. The Akkadians developed a written language that first appears on clay tablets dated c. 2400 B.C. Sargon the Great (c. 2334–2279 B.C.), the famous ruler of Akkad, united the Sumer-ian city-states of southern Mesopotamia in 2350 B.C. and absorbed them into his northern kingdom. In the process, he adopted Sumerian religion, literature, and socioeconomic organization. Akkad, the first Mesopotamian empire, thrived until the death of Sargon the Great, finally collapsing when it was invaded in about 2200 B.C.

Babylonia, the second Mesopotamian empire, was created by Hammurabi (ruled 1750–c. 1708 B.C.), who is most famous for his code of law. He made his capital the city of Babylon (which means "Gate of God" in Akkadian). He conquered the old empire of Akkad and called his own empire Babylonia. Like Sargon the Great, Hammurabi adopted the religion and literature of Sumer. He called himself "the sun of Babylon, who causes light to go forth over the lands of Sumer and Akkad." The Babylonians spoke and wrote a dialect of the Akkadian language. Their empire thrived until the death of Hammurabi, finally collapsing when the Hittites raided Babylon in c. 1600 B.C.

The Hittite empire, which thrived until c. 1200 B.C. (the approximate time of the Trojan War), cannot be called Mesopotamian, and it was not based on Sumerian culture. However, the Hittites permitted Babylonia to preserve its culture, with its Sumerian/Akkadian roots. Moreover, the Hittites themselves adopted Akkadian script and Babylonian literature and introduced them to the Aegean coastal lands and the islands off Asia Minor. These areas later became colonies of ancient Greece, and two settlements there claim to be the home of the ancient Greek poet Homer.

Assyria became the third Mesopotamian empire—and the last that was based on Sumerian culture. Except for a period of two hundred years, Assyrian kings ruled Mesopotamia from the twelfth to the end of the seventh century B.C. The Assyrians, too, preserved Babylonia's culture, with its language and its Sumerian/Akkadian roots. The Assyrian dialect was different from the Babylonian, but it was also a form of Akkadian. The last great king of Assyria, Ashurbanipal (ruled 668–627 B.C.), was a warrior, a priest, a scholar, and a patron of the arts. He made Nineveh, located on the Tigris River, an intellectual and artistic center where the contributions of Sumer, Akkad, and Babylonia were highly valued. Archaeologists' findings have made his huge library famous. Assyria thrived until Ashurbanipal's death in c. 627 B.C., finally collapsing when Babylonians and Medes united and destroyed Nineveh in 612 B.C.

A Babylonian renaissance thrived for less than a century and then was snuffed out by Cyrus the Great of Persia in 539 B.C. Akkadian continued to be the language of Mesopotamia until the end of the first millennium (1000–1) B.C. Consequently, most of the surviving tablets from this area are written in Akkadian.

Religious Background

The lives of the Sumerians were profoundly affected by the Tigris and the Euphrates rivers, which often unpredictably and radically changed courses from one season to the next, destroying whatever farms and cities lay in their paths. The Sumerians felt that they were at the mercy of awesome divine power, and they viewed most of their gods as unpredictable and terrifying.

The Sumerians worshiped a multitude of human-like divinities (numbering between three thousand and four thousand by the third millennium [3000–2000] B.C.). Later, the Akkadians, Babylonians, and Assyrians adopted many Sumerian divinities and religious views. Archaeologists have found ziggurats of a size and wealth that testify to the importance of religion in Sumerian culture.

Foremost among the Sumerian divinities were two creator-gods who are important in the following two myths. The Sumerians called them An and Enki. However, the Akkadians, Babylonians, and Assyrians called them Anu and Ea. An/Anu, the god of the sky or heaven, was the ruler and father of the gods, while Enki/Ea was his second son and the god of the sea and rivers, the earth, and wisdom.

A wealth of surviving literature from Sumer, Babylonia, Assyria, and the Hittite empire—written over a period of almost three thousand years—reveals that Enki/Ea was the most beloved male god in Mesopotamia. The Sumerians, Babylonians, and Assyrians worshiped Enki/Ea by sacrificing fish to him. Usually, they were real fish. However, King Sennacherib of Assyria (704–681 B.C.) recorded that he "cast into the sea a gold fish and a gold tortoise" as well as a "ship of gold" as offerings to Enki.

Since gods were thought to need food and water like mortals, the myth about Adapa stresses the importance of food and water with regard to the worship of Enki/Ea, along with the broader issues of immortality and death. The myth also explains the special importance of the city of Eridu, the center of Enki's worship, and its priests.

Literary Background

Sumerian myths, like all mythology, respond to the need of human beings to explain their culture's origins, the relationships among their principal divinities, the roles of these gods in both the divine and the human worlds, and the origin of their own mortality and misfortune. Although these myths were once thought to be connected to religious rituals, scholars now consider them to be secular in their purpose. They were found in the Sumerian academy of learning, the Edubba, where poets and bards were educated and trained in their art, rather than in the Sumerian temples. Like the tragedies of the ancient Greek playwrights and the traditional stories of the ancient Jewish rabbis, the themes and episodes related in the Sumerian myths are rooted in the oral traditions of their culture.

Sumerian literature continued to thrive long after Sumer was no longer a political entity. Under Sargon the Great, the Akkadians translated, adapted, and preserved Sumerian literature while they were recording their own epic literature and poetry. Under Hammurabi, Babylonian scribes translated Sumerian literature into their own Akkadian-based language and recorded it. When the Hittites conquered Babylonia, they disseminated Sumerian, Akkadian, and Babylonian literature throughout Asia Minor. The Assyrians continued to preserve Mesopotamia's Sumerian-based culture. Consequently, for a period of almost two thousand years (as long as schools existed that trained scribes to read Sumerian script), Sumerian myths were adopted, adapted, and translated by the Akkadians, the Babylonians, the Hittites, and the Assyrians.

Fortunately, Ashurbanipal, the great Assyrian king, loved learning and literature. He collected the surviving religious and literary tablets from Sumer (which had ceased to exist as a political entity fifteen hundred years earlier!) as well as from Akkad and Babylonia, and he stored them in his palace library in Nineveh. According to his inscriptions, he could "read tablets written before the Flood" (two thousand years earlier), and he had "received the revelation of the wise Adapa, the hidden treasure of the art of writing."

British archaeologists began excavating Nineveh in 1845. They unearthed twenty-five thousand tablets and fragments from Ashurbanipal's library and they sent them to the British Museum in London. Sumerian literature first became known in 1875, when "the father of Assyriology," Henry Rawlinson, published a book of bilingual Sumerian and Akkadian cuneiform texts from Ashurbanipal's collection.

Shortly thereafter, in 1877, the first major excavation of a Sumerian site took place under French leadership at Lagash (the modern Telloh, in Iraq). Unfortunately, the first forty thousand Sumerian tablets and fragments discovered at Lagash were found by local workers during the director's absence. The tablets were sold to museums throughout the Western world, and this dispersion severely impeded the process of their translation.

Eventually, the Museum of the Ancient Orient in Istanbul, Turkey, collected as many as one hundred thousand tablets and fragments from Lagash, as well as important Sumerian literary texts of myths and epics, dated at c. 1750 B.C., from Nippur (in Iraq). The American excavation of Nippur, the second major excavation of a Sumerian site, occurred between 1889 and 1900. Nippur supplied an additional thirty thousand tablets and fragments, dating from c. 2500 B.C. to c. 800 B.C., and including four-fifths of the five thousand existing Sumerian literary tablets and fragments.

Different museums often owned different parts of the same tablet, but this was of little academic interest until 1944. It was then that Samuel Noah Kramer published his *Sumerian Mythology*, which contained translations of major Sumerian literary texts and, therefore, presented earlier versions of Mesopotamian literature. This aroused great academic interest, but scholars had to wait for modern technology to provide a way for museums to publicize what they owned in a way that would not risk destroying their fragile materials.

The content of at least 90 percent of the surviving Sumerian tablets and fragments is either economic or administrative. However, the remaining six thousand are literary in subject. Poets and scribes wrote most of the literary material around 1750 B.C. Much of it probably came from older oral or written sources. It includes more than two hundred hymns, the complete texts or fragments of twenty myths, nine epics (including *Gilgamesh*), and numerous fables, essays, and proverbs. Of course, further excavation of Sumerian cities may uncover a storehouse of literary riches that are as yet unknown.

Appeal and Value

Part of the appeal and value of the Enki and Adapa myths is the fact that they were written by poets and scribes for their own people. Consequently, like the myths from ancient Greece and ancient India, they are either an authentic reflection of the cultural period in which their poets lived, or they are a reflection of an older cultural heritage, or both.

The myth about Enki reveals the accomplishments of one of the world's great creator-gods. Given the age of this myth, it is fascinating to see all that Enki accomplishes. Moreover, it is interesting to see the Sumerian view of the universe from this perspective, compared with the perspective in the myth about Adapa.

The Adapa myth is one of the most fascinating and provocative in world mythology. Adapa is a son of Enki (who here is called Ea, his Akkadian name). The myth offers the Sumerian or Babylonian explanation for human mortality and the human condition—interests and concerns that are universal. Equally striking is the extent to which the characters in this myth, both divine and mortal, resemble ourselves.

Built into this myth are the father-son relationship, the mortal-god relationship, and the psychological motivation of each of the three characters. All three are appealing figures, but each may or may not have the best intentions. What is particularly appealing about the myth is its genuine ambiguity. Scholars question the psychological motivations of the two gods and the reason for Adapa's choice.

However, the poor condition of the tablet that contains the end of this myth is partly responsible for its ambiguity. (See the notes on "Adapa" at the end of this text for a direct translation of these ambiguous passages.)

The myth about Enki presented here combines related aspects of three Sumerian myths: "Enki and Inanna: The Organization of the Earth and Its Cultural Processes" (one of the longest and best-preserved myths); "Inanna and Enki: The Transfer of the Arts of Civilization from Eridu to Erech"; and "Enki and Eridu: The Journey of the Water-God to Nippur" (one of the shortest and best-preserved myths).

The version of "Adapa" presented here is based on the four existing fragments of the Akkadian version of this myth. Archaeologists discovered three of these fragments in the library of Ashurbanipal, and it is one of these that contains the ambiguous end of the myth.

The fourth fragment—which contains the oldest and most complete version—eventually reached scholars after a local resident accidentally discovered this tablet, along with a host of others, while looking through what is now called Tell el-Amarna, the ruins of an ancient Egyptian city. In its time, the tablet was part of the royal archives of Akhenaton, the famous monotheistic pharaoh who ruled Egypt from c.1372 to c.1354 B.C. (The civilization of ancient Egypt was at its height at this time, and Egypt's major cities were great cultural centers.)

Because the myths about Enki have come down to us on tablets written in Sumerian, Enki retains his Sumerian name in the following myth about him. However, the Adapa myth has come down to us on tablets written in Akkadian, and therefore, An and Enki are here called Anu and Ea, their respective Akkadian names. ("Adapa" begins on page 74.)

ENKI, LORD OF THE EARTH
AND THE WATERS OF LIFE

Long, long ago, in the time before the Great Flood—before land rested along the Persian Gulf, before plants and herbs clothed that land, and before water cooled and nourished that land—Enki decided to build a great house for himself. He chose to build the Sea-House, the temple-city of Eridu, to be his home on Earth. For Enki was Lord of the Sweet, Life-Giving Waters and Lord of the Earth. He was the wisest and the cleverest of the great gods, the creator of life on Earth, and the master of the spoken and written word.

Enki fashioned his Sea-House of sun-dried mud bricks; of the sky-stone, lapis lazuli; and of silver that sparkled like light in the blue sky. And he decorated his Sea-House with gold that gleamed like light in the blue sky. He fashioned his Sea-House, his temple-city of Eridu, beneath the salt waters. And when he had finished his work, he raised Eridu like a mountain from the depths of those waters and made it a floating island.

Enki himself then rose up from the depths of those salt waters and rode upon the waves toward the temple-city of Eridu that would be his home on Earth. And as he rode forth upon the sea, Enki spoke words of command. And whatever he commanded came to be.

Enki called forth fish to live in the salt waters and commanded them to multiply. Many of these fish rose up from the depths of those waters, like Enki, and accompanied him as he rode forth upon the sea. He then called forth reed hedges to surround his Sea-House, his temple-city of Eridu, in order to fix its borders and confine the waters nearby.

Enki planted fruit trees in the gardens that surrounded his Sea-House, his temple-city of Eridu, and he created a multitude of birds to nest and multiply in these orchards. Then he called forth a flood of fish to frolic and multiply among the small reeds that grew in the ponds and marshlands that surrounded his Sea-House, his temple-city of Eridu. And so it came to pass that Enki's Sea-House, his temple-city of Eridu, in form and size like a mighty mountain, now rested upon land and climbed toward Heaven like a rainbow.

Enki then called forth the fresh, sweet waters of Heaven. He commanded them to float over Earth as clouds in order to nourish the land in the form of rain. And he appointed the divinity who is Lord of Storms to be in charge of them.

Next, Enki called forth fresh, sweet waters for drinking and irrigation. He filled the great Euphrates and the Tigris with these sweet, life-giving waters. And he appointed the divinity who loves to inspect canals to be in charge of them. He called forth floods of fish to frolic in these fresh, sweet waters. And he appointed the divinity who loves fish to be in charge of them.

Enki then called forth the low plains. He placed seeds of barley, chickpeas, and lentils in the fields, and he commanded the grains to sprout forth from the seeds. He ordered the grains to multiply until they had to be stacked high in heaps and in piles. And he appointed the goddess who loves grain to be in charge of them.

Next, Enki called forth the high plains. He covered them with luxurious vegetation and commanded sheep and oxen to graze upon them. He ordered the herds of sheep to increase and multiply in order to provide milk and fat. And he appointed the divinity who is Lord of the Mountains to be in charge of them.

Enki spoke words of command, and whatever he commanded came to be, for Enki was Lord of the Sweet, Life-Giving Waters and Lord of the Earth. He was the wisest and the cleverest of the great gods, the creator of life on Earth, and the master of the spoken and written word.

Then, Enki taught the gods how to be cowherds, shepherds, and farmers. He taught them how to build the stalls and the sheep pens to house the oxen and sheep. And he appointed the divinity who loves shepherds to be in charge of them. He taught the gods how to yoke the oxen and how to use the plow, so that the fields would produce more grain. And he appointed the divinity who loves farm animals to be in charge of them.

Enki now spoke the words of a teacher, and whatever he taught came to be, for Enki was Lord of the Sweet, Life-Giving Waters and

Lord of the Earth. He was the wisest and the cleverest of the great gods, the creator of arts and crafts, and the master of the spoken and written word.

Next, Enki directed the gods in the building of ditches and canals, so that the sparkling, sweet water that he had placed in the rivers could be brought to nourish these fields. And he appointed the divinity who loves to inspect canals to be in charge of them. He taught the gods how to build granaries so that grain could be stored, for he had made the land surrounding his temple-city of Eridu to be a place of abundant harvest. And he appointed the divinity who loves harvests to be in charge of them.

Enki then turned his attention to his home on Earth, his Sea-House, his temple-city of Eridu. He taught the gods to use the pickax and to make molds for brickmaking. And he appointed the divinity who loves bricks to be in charge of them. He taught the gods how to construct firm foundations for buildings and how to build the houses of mud bricks and reeds that rested upon these foundations. And he appointed the divinity who loves construction to be in charge of them.

Next, Enki taught the gods how to do leatherwork and carpentry, copperwork and reedwork, weaving and work with cloth. And he appointed the divinity who loves crafts to be in charge of them. He taught the gods how to write on clay tablets. And he appointed the divinity who loves symbols to be in charge of them. Finally, he fixed the borders of all the cities and states. And he put the divinity who is Lord of the Sun in charge of them.

Enki now spoke the words of a teacher, and whatever he taught came to be, for Enki was the Lord of the Sweet, Life-Giving Waters and Lord of the Earth. He was the wisest and the cleverest of the great gods, the creator of arts and crafts, and the master of the spoken and written word.

ADAPA

In time, it came to pass that the gods gathered in assembly and to Ea, "Son of Anu, and Lord of the Earth and the Waters of Life!

You have given us burdens that weigh too heavily upon us! We must be cowherds, and shepherds, fishermen, and farmers. We must build stalls and sheep pens. We must yoke the oxen and use the plow. We must build ditches and canals and granaries. We must use the pickax and make bricks. We must construct foundations and build houses. We must do leatherwork and carpentry, copperwork and reedwork, weaving and working with cloth. We must even write on tablets of clay! These burdens are too much for us! And we will no longer carry them!

"Now, Son of Anu, and Lord of the Earth and the Waters of Life!" they continued. "You have called forth the waters of Heaven and Earth, and fields of grains. You have planted orchards of fruit trees and created birds to nest in them. You have called forth grassy plains and the sheep and oxen to graze on them. You have filled the sweet waters with floods of fish. Now, surely, Ea, you who have done all this can create creatures who will walk the earth and do our work for us! Surely, Ea, you who have done all this can create servants who will walk the earth and take care of us!"

This is what the gods said to Ea, Lord of the Earth and the Waters of Life, when they gathered in assembly. And so it came to pass that Ea created human beings to walk the earth and serve the gods— to do their work and to take care of them.

And having done this, Ea—Lord of the Earth and the Waters of Life—said to himself, "For the gods, I have created human beings to walk the earth and serve them—to do their work and to take care of them. Now, for my own pleasure, I will create a man to be my own son. And he will be the priest of my Sea-House, my temple-city of Eridu. I will name my son "Adapa" because *adaap* means 'man,' and *adapu* means 'wise.'"

And so it came to pass that Ea—Lord of the Earth and the Waters of Life—created Adapa to be his own son. And Adapa was the wisest of all who walk the earth. In fact, his mind was godlike in its wisdom. For Ea had given his son the ability to understand and to reveal the ways of Heaven and Earth. Ea had given Adapa the knowledge that would enable him to teach all who walk the earth how to hunt and how to fish, how to gather and how to herd, how to sow and how to reap, how to build canals and how to construct buildings, how to work at arts and crafts, and how to read and write.

Adapa was the wisest of human beings, for Ea had created his son in his own image in order to enable him to protect all who walk the earth. He had fashioned Adapa to be their model. And Adapa was indeed a worthy model! He was remarkably learned and wise. And he was equally pious. Adapa taught the people of Eridu how to worship Ea, Lord of the Earth and the Waters of Life. And the people of Eridu respected Adapa and obeyed all of his commands as if he were the god Ea himself!

However, Adapa was not Ea. Although Adapa's mind was god-like in its wisdom, his body was mortal. Although Ea had given Adapa wisdom, he had not given his son everlasting life.

Adapa spent the days of his life doing a priest's work. He was a holy person, one who was pure of soul and clean of hands. He scrupulously observed all of the divine laws and all of the holy rites in connection with Ea's Sea-House, his temple-city of Eridu, and the worship of Ea, his father.

Every day, Adapa baked bread with the priestly bakers in order to supply Ea's Sea-House, his temple-city of Eridu, with fresh bread. Every day, Adapa collected fresh water with the priestly water collectors in order to supply Ea's Sea-House, his temple-city of Eridu, with water for cooking and drinking. And every day, Adapa caught fresh fish with the priestly fishermen in order to supply Ea's Sea-House, his temple-city of Eridu, with fish for the sacrificial offerings.

However, only Adapa himself—and no other—could prepare the holy table by arranging the offerings to Ea that would be placed upon it. Only Adapa himself—and no other—could clear the table at the proper time. And every day when the time came for Ea to take refuge in his home on Earth, his Sea-House, his temple-city of Eridu, and relax upon his bed, only Adapa himself—and no other—could serve him.

Time passed in this fashion, with each new moon following the old without event until once again the time of the new moon, a holy period, came to be. And now it came to pass that Adapa set sail in his little boat in order to catch fish for his father's Sea-House, for Ea's temple-city of Eridu. And Adapa's small craft was at the mercy of the wind as it drifted upon the wide sea, for Adapa had no more than an oar with which to steer it.

A brisk breeze had carried Adapa's little boat out to sea—and Adapa was happily fishing there—when it came to pass that suddenly South Wind came swooping down upon the waters. The vigorous flapping of his giant wings created a gale wind! And as his wingtips swept the surface of the sea, they created tumultuous waves.

Fear flooded Adapa's heart. "My small craft will never survive this storm!" he exclaimed to himself.

Adapa's fearful thought could just as well have been the father of the deed! For a monstrous wave suddenly capsized his little boat, tossing Adapa into the turbulent waters. And Adapa now found that he was swimming in the underwater home of the fish that he had come to catch!

As Adapa fought his way back to the storm-tossed surface of the sea, rage replaced the fear that had flooded his heart. Furious with South Wind, he angrily confronted the monster.

"What have I done to anger you that you treat me like this?" shouted Adapa. "Do the great floods that you cause no longer satisfy you, so that now you want to harass me?

"Your prank has deprived my father, Ea—Lord of the Earth and the Waters of Life—of his food! And you will live to regret what you have done to me! May your wings break because of this!" Adapa exclaimed.

South Wind would have done well to remember that Adapa was Ea's son! For it came to pass that Adapa's words were the father of this deed. As soon as Adapa spoke them, South Wind's wings broke!

The sea immediately became calm, causing Adapa's small craft to float to the surface, where it waited for him to climb back into it. Once he had regained his place, Adapa caught the fish that he needed. And then he returned to his father's Sea-House, to Ea's temple-city of Eridu.

However, South Wind withdrew to nurse his broken wings. And so it came to pass that not a breath of wind—not even the most gentle breeze—caressed land or water for seven days!

And so it came to pass that Anu, Lord of Heaven, called Winged God, his chief messenger, before him and asked, "Winged One, why is it that not a breath of wind—not even the most gentle breeze—has caressed land or water for seven days?"

To these words, Winged God replied, "My lord, not a breath of wind—not even the most gentle breeze—has caressed land or water for seven days because Adapa, the son of your son Ea, has broken South Wind's wings!"

These words caused Anu's heart to flood with rage. Rising from his throne, he commanded, "Winged One, fly down to Earth! Find Adapa and send him to me! I want to hear the reason for his crime from his own lips!"

Now Ea was Lord of Wisdom as well as Lord of the Earth and the Waters of Life. And he knew the heart of Anu—Lord of Heaven— for Anu was his father. In fact, Ea knew everything! Nothing could be hidden from him!

And so it came to pass that Ea called Adapa before him and announced: "Adapa, my son, your grandfather, Anu—Lord of Heaven— is planning to send Winged God, his chief messenger, to me. Winged God will announce that you have broken South Wind's wings. And he will relate Anu's command that you appear before him in order to explain the reason for your crime. My son, you would have done well to remember that South Wind is Anu's servant! Now, your grandfather's heart has flooded with fury toward you!

"Therefore, Adapa, if you possess a heart of wisdom, you will honor your father, respect his knowledge and judgment, and follow his advice. I know the heart of Anu, Lord of Heaven! And I know how you can win a favorable reception with him. For Anu is my father and your grandfather!

"Therefore, this is my advice, my son. You must appear before Anu, Lord of Heaven, with your hair loose and uncombed, and with ashes heaped upon your head as if you are in mourning. You must appear before him in a torn and dirty garment as if someone whom you love and respect has died," declared Ea.

"Now, when you have taken the road to Heaven, in time you will come upon the gate to Anu's kingdom—the kingdom of Heaven— where two sentries, Dumuzi and Gizzida, will be standing on guard. They are lords of fertility, but they leave Earth during the dry season. Since it is most unusual for a mortal to approach the home of the gods in the kingdom of Heaven, as soon as they see you, they will question you," declared Ea.

"They will say, 'Adapa, why does the son of Ea, Lord of the Earth and the Waters of Life, appear before Anu, Lord of Heaven, with his hair loose and uncombed and with ashes heaped upon his head as if he is in mourning? And why does he wear a torn and dirty garment as if someone whom he loves and respects has died? Tell us, now, Adapa, whom do you seek here in Anu's kingdom— the kingdom of Heaven?' This is what they will ask you, Adapa," declared Ea.

"Now, my son, you must respond to Dumuzi and Gizzida so as to win their sympathy and their affection. Therefore, this is my advice, Adapa. You must respond to Dumuzi and Gizzida's questions by saying, 'My lords, how can I not appear before Anu, Lord of Heaven, with my hair loose and uncombed and with ashes heaped upon my head as if I am in mourning? And how can I not wear a torn and dirty garment as if someone whom I love and respect has died? Two beloved gods who once lived on Earth have disappeared! My heart is flooded with longing for them! The people of my land long for them! And so I mourn for them! And I have come to plead with Anu, Lord of Heaven, for their return.' This is what you must tell them, Adapa," explained Ea.

"And then, my son, Dumuzi and Gizzida will respond to your words by asking you, 'Adapa, who are these two beloved gods who once lived on Earth but now have disappeared? For whom does your heart flood with longing? For whom do the people of your land long? For whom do you mourn? And for whose return would you plead with Anu, Lord of Heaven?' This is what they will ask you, Adapa," declared Ea.

"Then, my son, you must reply, 'My lords, Dumuzi and Gizzida are the gods for whom I mourn and for whose return I have come to plead with Anu, Lord of Heaven,'" advised Ea.

"Now, upon hearing your words, the two sentries will smile at each other, and they will speak well of you to your grandfather. Anu, Lord of Heaven, will then turn away his anger from you, and instead he will look kindly upon you," declared Ea.

"However, when your grandfather treats you with the courtesy that is due an honored guest, you must beware of his offerings, my son! When Anu, Lord of Heaven, offers you bread, you must not eat it. For it will be the bread of death! And when he offers you water, you must not drink it. For it will be the water of death! But when Anu, Lord of Heaven, offers you a fresh garment, you must put it on! And when he offers you oil, you must consecrate yourself with it!" declared Ea.

"Now, remember my advice, Adapa! For my instructions are important!" Ea concluded.

And indeed it came to pass that everything happened to Adapa just as Ea had foretold. For Ea was Lord of Wisdom as well as Lord of the Earth and the Waters of Life. And he knew the heart of Anu—Lord of Heaven—for Anu was his father. In fact, Ea knew everything! Nothing could be hidden from him!

Winged God obeyed Anu's command and took his master's message to Ea. "My lord, your son, Adapa, has broken South Wind's wings!" he exclaimed. "Now Anu, Lord of Heaven, commands that Adapa appear before him in order to explain the reason for his crime."

To these words, Ea replied, "Winged One, tell Anu, Lord of Heaven, that Adapa will appear before him as he requests."

And it came to pass that Adapa honored his father, respected his wisdom, and followed his advice. He dutifully wore his hair loose and uncombed, and he heaped ashes upon his head as if he were in mourning. He dutifully wore a torn and dirty garment as if someone whom he loved and respected had died.

And when Adapa had dutifully taken the road to Heaven, he eventually came upon the gate to Anu's kingdom—the home of the gods, in the kingdom of Heaven. There, the two sentries were standing guard.

As soon as Dumuzi and Gizzida saw Adapa, they asked him, "Adapa, why does the son of Ea—Lord of the Earth and the Waters of Life—appear before Anu—Lord of Heaven—with his hair loose and uncombed and with ashes heaped upon his head as if he is in mourning? And why does he wear a torn and dirty garment as if someone whom he loves and respects has died? Tell us now, Adapa, whom do you seek here in Anu's kingdom—the kingdom of Heaven?"

To these questions, Adapa dutifully replied, "My lords, how can I not appear before Anu, Lord of Heaven, with my hair loose and uncombed and with ashes heaped upon my head as if I am in mourning? And how can I not wear a torn and dirty garment as if someone whom I love and respect has died? Two beloved gods who once lived on Earth have disappeared! My heart is flooded with longing for them! The people of my land long for them! And so I mourn for them! And I have come to plead with Anu, Lord of Heaven, for their return."

In response to these words, the sentries asked, "Adapa, who are these two beloved gods who once lived on Earth but now have disappeared? For whom does your heart flood with longing? For whom do the people of your land long? For whom do you mourn? And for whose return would you plead with Anu, Lord of Heaven?"

Adapa then dutifully replied, "My lords, Dumuzi and Gizzida are the gods for whom I mourn and for whose return I have come to plead with Anu, Lord of Heaven."

Upon hearing Adapa's response, Dumuzi and Gizzida smiled at

each other and took Adapa before their lord, Anu, Lord of Heaven. And so it came to pass that Adapa entered the royal chamber of his grandfather, in the kingdom of Heaven.

Anu looked at his grandson and asked him, "Adapa, you would have done well to remember that South Wind is my servant! Now, tell me, why did you break South Wind's wings?"

To these words Adapa replied, "My lord—Grandfather!—this is how I came to injure South Wind. My father, Ea—Lord of the Earth and the Waters of Life, and your own son—has made me the wisest of mortals. He has told me the ways of Heaven and Earth. And in return I provide his Sea-House, his temple-city of Eridu, with food and water. And I serve him with love and respect.

"Now it came to pass that I set sail in my little boat in order to catch fish for my father's Sea-House, for his temple-city of Eridu. And my small craft was at the mercy of the wind as it drifted upon the wide sea, for I had no more than an oar with which to steer it," explained Adapa.

"A brisk breeze had carried my little boat out to sea," he continued, "and I was happily fishing there when it came to pass that, suddenly, South Wind came swooping down upon the waters. The vigorous flapping of his giant wings created a gale wind! And as his wingtips swept the surface of the sea, they created tumultuous waves. Fear flooded my heart, for I knew that my small craft could not survive this storm!

"My fearful thought could just as well have been the father of the deed!" Adapa exclaimed. "For a monstrous wave suddenly capsized my little boat, tossing me into the turbulent waters. And I found that I was swimming in the underwater home of the fish that I had come to catch!

"As I fought my way back to the storm-tossed surface of the water, rage replaced the fear that had flooded my heart," Adapa continued. "Furious with South Wind, I angrily confronted the monster. 'What have I done to anger you that you treat me like this?' I shouted. 'Do the great floods that you cause no longer satisfy you, so that now you want to harass me?'

"'Your prank has deprived my father, Ea—Lord of the Earth and the Waters of Life—of his food! And you will live to regret what you have done to me! May your wings break because of this!' I exclaimed.

"South Wind would have done well to remember that I am Ea's son! For it came to pass that my words were the father of this deed. As soon as I spoke them, South Wind's wings broke! And that, my lord, is my story," Adapa concluded.

Dumuzi and Gizzida then approached Anu, Lord of Heaven, and spoke well of Adapa. "Look with favor upon your grandson, my lord," they said, "for Adapa is the wisest of human beings. His mind is godlike in its wisdom! For your son Ea has given Adapa the ability to understand and to reveal the ways of Heaven and Earth. Ea has created his son in his own image in order to enable him to protect all who walk the earth. He has fashioned Adapa to be their model.

"And Adapa is indeed a worthy model!" they declared. "He is remarkably learned and wise. And he is equally pious. He has taught the people of Eridu how to worship Ea, Lord of the Earth and the Waters of Life. And the people of Eridu respect Adapa and obey all of his commands as if he were the god Ea himself!

"Adapa spends the days of his life doing a priest's work," they added. "He is a holy person, one who is pure of soul and clean of hands. He scrupulously observes all of the divine laws and all of the holy rites in connection with Ea's Sea-House, his temple-city of Eridu, and the worship of Ea, his father.

"Every day, Adapa bakes bread with the priestly bakers in order to supply Ea's Sea-House, his temple-city of Eridu, with fresh bread," they continued. "Every day, Adapa collects fresh water with the priestly water collectors in order to supply Ea's Sea-House, his temple-city of Eridu, with water for cooking and drinking. And every day, Adapa catches fresh fish with the priestly fishermen in order to supply Ea's Sea-House, his temple-city of Eridu, with fish for the sacrificial offerings.

"However, only Adapa himself—and no other—may prepare the holy table by arranging the offerings to Ea that will be placed upon it! Only Adapa himself—and no other—may clear the table at the proper time! And, every day, when the time comes for Ea to take refuge in his home on Earth, his Sea-House, his temple-city of Eridu, and relax upon his bed, only Adapa himself—and no other—may serve him!

"Therefore, my lord, we plead Adapa's case before you," Dumuzi and Gizzida concluded, "and we ask that you pardon him for injuring South Wind."

To these words, Anu, Lord of Heaven, replied, "Why did Ea—Lord of the Earth and the Waters of Life—make his son, and my grandson, so preeminent among those who walk the earth? And why did Ea—Lord of the Earth and the Waters of Life—disclose the ways of Heaven and Earth to a mere mortal? For compared with the gods, even the best of mortals is worthless!

"But now that Ea has given these gifts to his son," Anu continued, "what shall I do about my grandson? What should I do for Adapa? With his wisdom and his knowledge of Heaven and Earth, should he not become one of the gods?"

Anu, Lord of Heaven, then turned away his anger from Adapa. Instead, he looked kindly upon his grandson and treated him with the courtesy that is due an honored guest.

And so it came to pass that Anu—Lord of Heaven—declared, "Here, Adapa, eat this bread. For it is the bread of everlasting life!"

Adapa dutifully remembered his father's warning, and he did not eat the bread that Anu offered him.

"Here, Adapa," Anu then declared, "drink this water. For it is the water of everlasting life!"

Adapa dutifully remembered his father's warning, and he did not drink the water that Anu offered him.

"Here, Adapa," Anu then declared, "put on this fresh garment."

Adapa dutifully remembered his father's advice, and he put on the clean garment that Anu offered him.

"Here, Adapa," Anu then declared, "consecrate yourself with this oil."

Adapa dutifully remembered his father's advice, and he consecrated himself with the oil that Anu offered him. And having dutifully responded to Anu—Lord of Heaven—as his father had taught him, Adapa thought to himself, "Oh, how my heart floods with pride and pleasure! For I have remembered all of my father's advice. And I have followed it! For my father is Ea—Lord of Wisdom as well as Lord of the Earth and the Waters of Life! I honor him! I respect his wisdom! And he told me that his instructions were important!"

This is what Adapa thought to himself. Therefore, it came to pass that Anu—Lord of Heaven—surprised Adapa with his response.

"Come now, Adapa!" laughed Anu. "I hear that your father—my son Ea, Lord of Wisdom as well as Lord of the Earth and the Waters of Life—has endowed you with godlike wisdom! And I hear that, in Ea's Sea-House, in his temple-city of Eridu, you are a man of great renown! Therefore, your behavior astonishes me!

"So tell me, Grandson, why did you refuse to eat the bread that

I offered you? And why did you refuse to drink the water that I offered you? Does everlasting life mean so little to you that you reject it so easily? Truly, you are no better than any other mortal! For you are as foolish and imprudent as the rest of them! No wonder all of you are weighed down by heavy hearts!"

To these words, Adapa replied, "Grandfather! My lord! Surely I am not to blame! For I did just what my father told me to do! Before I began my journey, Ea said to me, 'Now when your grandfather treats you with the courtesy that is due an honored guest, you must beware of his offerings. When Anu, Lord of Heaven, offers you bread, you must not eat it. For it is the bread of death! And when he offers you water, you must not drink it. For it is the water of death! But, when Anu, Lord of Heaven, offers you a fresh garment, you must put it on! And when he offers you oil, you must consecrate yourself with it! Now, remember my advice,' he declared, 'for my instructions are important!'"

This is how Adapa responded to his grandfather. Therefore, it came to pass that Anu—Lord of Heaven—again surprised Adapa with his response.

"Why, Adapa, now it is your words that astonish me!" he declared, laughing heartily once again. "Of all the gods of Heaven and Earth—and both kingdoms are flooded with divinities!—only my son Ea—your own father, Adapa—would have dared to make his command more important than the command of Anu, Lord of Heaven! And it is to your father—Lord of the Earth and the Waters of Life—that I am now going to return you!

"However, Adapa," Anu continued, "before you leave, I want you to look upon the kingdom of Heaven—my kingdom!—and appreciate its breadth and its height!"

Adapa did as his grandfather—Anu, Lord of Heaven—commanded. And then Adapa replied, "Why, my lord! I am awed by the grandeur, the wonder, and the glory of your kingdom!"

To these words, Anu replied, "That is as it should be, my grandson! And you would do well to remember it when you return to Earth and perform your obligations to Ea. Your father may be Lord of the Earth and the Waters of Life, but he rules only one part of the universe!

"Now, before you leave, Adapa," Anu added, "I want you to know the decrees that I am sending down to Earth with you. First, with regard to your father, Ea—he who is Lord of the Earth and the

Waters of Life—I confer upon his Sea-House, his temple-city of Eridu, the destiny that it will have hereafter and forevermore: the special status of being exempt from all political obligations with regard to any earthly king. Moreover, I confer upon your father's priests the destiny that they will be held, hereafter and forevermore, in special honor and esteem."

Anu then continued, "However, upon you, Adapa, you who are Ea's mortal son—you who, godlike, broke South Wind's wing so that Anu, Lord of Heaven, had to summon you here in order to hear the reason for your crime—upon you, Adapa, I confer the following two-fold destiny.

"You would have done well to remember that South Wind is my servant!" Anu exclaimed. "And lest you continue to lie down in sweet sleep, I will now show you that rash and irreverent behavior has con-sequences—even for someone as blessed by the gods as you are, Adapa. Therefore, I now decree that, because of your impious act, joy must flee from every human heart so that, hereafter and forever-more, dread and dismay will live in its place. Moreover—and again because of your impious act—I now decree that, hereafter and for-evermore, misfortune will be the food and disease will be the water of all who walk the earth, attacking the bodies of all who are mortal.

"However," Anu concluded, "as proof that I do not have a heart of stone, I also decree that the goddess who loves healing will leave Heaven and spend her days and nights visiting all who are afflicted on Earth. Hereafter and forevermore, she will bring relief from the pain, suffering, and sorrow that your crime has brought upon all those who walk the earth."

And with these words, Anu, Lord of Heaven, said to Winged God, his chief messenger, "Now that Adapa has heard my judgment, take him away! Return him to Earth!

"And Adapa," Anu concluded, "you will do well to remember that Earth will sustain you—and all who share your mortality—only as long as all of you remember to honor and to serve all of the gods!"

The Craftsman's Wife

"The Craftsman's Wife" has been popular in Europe and the Middle East since the *Gesta Romanorum* (*Deeds of the Romans*) was first printed in about 1473 in Europe, not long after Johannes Gutenberg invented movable metal type. First printed in Latin, this anthology probably originated (also in Latin) in England in the late 1200s or early 1300s.

Despite its title, the *Gesta Romanorum* included many tales that originated in the oral traditions of the Middle East, the Far East, and Europe as well as ancient Greece and Rome. Therefore, it is not surprising that similar tales appear in the *Tuti Nameh* (a Persian collection of Hindu tales that was also compiled in the early 1300s) and in the *Thousand and One Nights* (an Arabic-language collection of ancient tales from Arabia, Persia, and India that was published in Egypt in about 1450).

The *Gesta Romanorum* may have been designed for religious instruction since a moral is attached to each tale. It became so popular that it was often reprinted with additions, and therefore, some editions contain as many as two hundred selections. Many of the tales were so appealing that they later reentered the oral tradition of various cultures. Consequently, as recently as the first half of the twentieth century, "The Craftsman's Wife" was part of the Jewish oral tradition in Morocco, Tunisia, Libya, and Afghanistan.

The virtuous wife has been a favorite motif in world folklore for more than 2,500 years. Throughout time and across space, audiences have admired the qualities possessed by women such as Penelope in Homer's *Odyssey* (c. 750 B.C.) and the craftsman's wife in the following folktale. The captive suitor is another popular motif in folklore around the world.

The belief that a person's fate can be connected to that of an external object is an ancient idea. For example, in "The Calydonian Boar Hunt," a myth from ancient Greece, the hero Meleager will not die unless a particular log is consumed by fire. The talisman in "The Craftsman's Wife" also has a magical connection with human events.

Although "The Craftsman's Wife" contains universal motifs, it is characteristic of Jewish folktales in that it has a Jewish setting, Jewish characters, and a Jewish message or theme. A significant characteristic of Jewish folktales is their emphasis on moral behavior, with the goal of teaching a lesson either through positive or negative role models.

The characters in this story are a Jewish couple and the historical King Solomon (ruled c. 970–931 B.C.), who was a son of King David and a king of Israel. According to the Bible, King Solomon was "wiser than all other men." He is renowned for his understanding of human nature, his ability to discern right from wrong, and his clever and sound judgment of disputes. For example, in the Bible, he discovers the true mother of a contested infant because she will give up her child rather than let the king slice him in half in order to divide the baby between the two women who claim to be his mother.

The events in "The Craftsman's Wife" take place both in Jerusalem, where King Solomon is building his great Temple, and in the master craftsman's city, which is not named. Solomon's Temple is a famous historical structure because of its great size and importance in the ancient world. Its construction took seven years. Completed in c. 952 B.C., it remained the center of Jewish life until the Babylonians destroyed it in 586 B.C.

Both the characters and the plot of "The Craftsman's Wife" are appealing. The virtuous wife is a familiar character in Jewish literature because Jewish women, from Biblical times to the present, have played an important role in Jewish culture.

An unusual aspect of this tale is King Solomon's secondary role, since he usually commands center stage in the Bible and in folklore. The fact that Solomon meets his match in the craftsman's wife creates a delightful story. The battle of wits between the sexes adds vitality and humor, and in the end, the craftsman's wife's victory is even greater because her adversary was King Solomon.

"The Craftsman's Wife" is valuable in three important ways. First, it leads readers to appreciate the attitudes and behavior of the husband and wife in terms of the time and place in which these characters lived. Second, it invites readers to analyze and evaluate the behavior of these characters in terms of their own values and their own lives. Finally, the tale encourages readers to examine the extent to which they can apply the virtuous qualities of these characters to their own lives.

THE CRAFTSMAN'S WIFE

It came to pass that King Solomon planned to build a great temple in Jerusalem, the Holy City. In preparation, he asked the kings of nearby countries to send him their most valued master craftsmen, assuring them that he would highly reward these artisans for their work. Because of the awe with which the rulers of other countries regarded King Solomon, they dutifully honored his request.

However, one master craftsman refused the lucrative offer, despite his king's command. In fact, the greatest reward could not motivate this craftsman to leave the city in which he lived. For he had such a beautiful wife that other men were captivated by her, and this craftsman lived in fear that if he were to leave his wife's side, another man would seduce her in his absence.

When the king of the craftsman's country learned of his subject's refusal to work on King Solomon's Temple, he sent for this master craftsman and announced, "Master craftsman, you must go to Jerusalem at once and do your part in building the great Temple! To refuse such a powerful king could bring war to my kingdom and, therefore, if you continue to refuse my command, you will force me to kill you!"

The master craftsman returned to his wife in despair. Seeing his despondent expression, his wife exclaimed, "Oh, my dear! What has happened? Has one of our friends died?"

"No one has died yet, dear one," her husband replied. "But the king has just cut short the days of my own life! Either I go to Jerusalem with the other master craftsmen, or the king will kill me! What an impossible choice I face! I value my life and yet I cannot possibly leave you! A married woman without her husband is as vulnerable to the advances of other men as if she were a maiden or a widow. And a woman with your beauty will be pressured to accept another man in my absence! So of course I am despondent, and of course I am dismayed! My heart is burdened with care and sorrow!"

"My dear, calm yourself!" the craftsman's wife replied. "Such care and sorrow burden your heart without cause. You have no need to fear our separation! For I will never love any man but you, no matter how handsome, or wealthy, or powerful he might be! In fact, I will give you a special talisman to take with you on your journey so that your heart will know peace while you are in the Holy City. Just wait and see!"

The craftsman's wife was true to her word. When the time came for her husband to leave on his journey, she placed a necklace around his neck that held a small glass cylinder in which she had sealed a piece of cotton wick and a glowing coal.

"Wear this talisman day and night, dear one," she commanded him. "If I should burn with desire for another man, the hot coal will ignite the cotton wick in the cylinder. However, as long as my love for you is constant, the wick will not catch fire despite the presence of the burning coal. So, dear one, put your heart at ease, trust me, and fare well on your journey and in your work!"

And so it came to pass that the master craftsman took leave of his wife and went forth to Jerusalem in order to do his part in the building of King Solomon's great Temple. He was plying his trade in the Holy City when King Solomon made one of his daily visits to the site. The mighty king happened to come upon the craftsman, and he immediately noticed the strange talisman that hung from the man's neck.

Calling the craftsman to him, King Solomon addressed him, saying, "Master craftsman, why do you wear that strange object around your neck? And what does it mean?"

To these words, the master craftsman replied, "Your Majesty, as I was leaving for the Holy City, my wife placed this talisman around my neck and said to me, 'Wear this talisman day and night. If I should burn with desire for another man, the hot coal will ignite the cotton wick in the cylinder. However, as long as my love for you is constant, the wick will not catch fire despite the presence of the burning coal.'"

King Solomon was fascinated by the craftsman's explanation. And so he said to himself, "This man must have a wife in a million—for her mind is as great as her heart! Yet, I wonder . . . Is she really as good as she appears to be? I must find out! If she is, her virtue and her wisdom will win my heart and my blessing!

"Now, I will test both the woman's virtue and the accuracy of her husband's talisman. And since I cannot be in two places at one time, I will remain here and observe the talisman. Meanwhile, I will send two handsome suitors forth to woo her!" the king concluded.

And so it came to pass that King Solomon called two handsome young men before him. "My friends, I want you to go to the master craftsman's city and find a way to live in his house until you manage to seduce his wife. I am sending you forth with ample money and tempting gifts so that your journey will not be in vain. Know that, if you are successful, I will reward you well!"

To these words, the young men replied, "It is our pleasure to do as you command, Your Majesty! And be assured that we will please this craftsman's wife and conquer her heart!"

The two young men then took their leave of the king and set forth on their journey. When they arrived at the master craftsman's house and asked to rent a room, the craftsman's wife treated them kindly, fed them a tasty dinner, and then led them into the guest bedroom, where they would retire for the night.

She explained what they needed to know about their accommodations, wished them a good night, and left the room, closing the door behind her. She then turned and locked the two young men inside the room!

The craftsman's wife kept the young men imprisoned in the guest bedroom for thirty days and nights. Her servant saw to it that they were fed and cared for every day, but they were never permitted to leave their room.

Meanwhile, day after day, King Solomon watched the wick in the master craftsman's talisman to see whether or not the burning coal had ignited it. He waited as, day after day, the wick remained untouched by the coal's heat. Thirty days came and went, and still the wick did not burn. Nor did the two young men return to the Holy City.

So it came to pass that King Solomon decided to journey to the master craftsman's home in order to see for himself what had happened. He disguised himself as a merchant, traveled to the craftsman's city, and lodged in the craftsman's house.

Now the master craftsman's wife immediately realized that her new guest must be King Solomon himself, and therefore she treated him with the greatest courtesy. As part of a delicious dinner, she set a plate of colored hard-boiled eggs before the king and said, "Please taste these eggs, Your Majesty, and tell me whether the red, the yellow, the brown, or the black egg is best."

To these words, King Solomon replied, "Why do you address an ordinary merchant as if he were a king?"

"Your Majesty, you have the bearing and the manner of one who could only be King Solomon," the craftsman's wife replied. "Therefore, I am your humble servant, and I wish to learn which egg has the finest flavor."

When the king had tasted each egg, he declared, "Woman, despite their different colored shells, all of these eggs taste the same!

After all, one hard-boiled egg is just the same as another! What reply did you expect?"

"Oh, you have said just what I expected you to say, Your Majesty!" the craftsman's wife exclaimed. "For indeed one hard-boiled egg is just the same as another! More important, however, is the fact that making love to one woman is just the same as making love to another. For women are like these colored eggs. Some are prettier to the eye than others, but inside they are all alike!

"And, of course, this fact applies to me as well," the craftsman's wife explained. "I may be more beautiful than other women, but I am different in no other way. Therefore, unless your intent was simply to admire my beauty, you have wasted your time by making this long journey!"

"Enough about eggs!" King Solomon responded. "You act as if you were not surprised to see me suddenly appear at your door! Were you actually expecting me? And if so, why? Moreover, I have heard that, thirty days ago, two young men sought lodging here in your house. Are they living here? And do you now rent rooms in your husband's absence?"

To these words the craftsman's wife smiled with delight, and she responded, "Your Majesty, I am so happy that you have asked me these questions, for now I can tell you what you would really like to know!

"When two handsome young men suddenly arrived on my doorstep asking to lodge with me," she explained, "I immediately suspected that you had sent them! After all, I knew that you might have encountered my husband one day when you made one of your daily visits to the site where the master craftsmen are building your great Temple. And if you had come upon my husband, I knew that you surely would have noticed the strange talisman that hangs from his neck. I knew that you would then have called my husband before you and asked him, 'Why do you wear that strange object around your neck? And what does it mean?'

"And I knew that to these words, my husband would have replied, 'As I was leaving for the Holy City, my wife placed this talisman around my neck and said to me, "Wear this talisman day and night. If I should burn with desire for another man, the hot coal will ignite the cotton wick in the cylinder. However, as long as my love for you is constant, the wick will not catch fire despite the presence of the burning coal."'"

The craftsman's wife continued: "I knew that you probably would have been fascinated by both the question of my fidelity and my clever solution to the problem. And I knew that if you were, then you probably would decide to test my virtue and, at the same time, observe the accuracy of the talisman. Since you could not be in two places at one time, I knew that you would have to send someone else to try to seduce me. Consequently, when two handsome young men suddenly arrived on my doorstep and asked to rent a room in my house, I knew who they must be.

"These young men have been here for thirty days and nights, and they are still living here," the craftsman's wife added. "I have had my servant see to it that they have been fed and cared for every day. Indeed, they have lacked only two things, my presence and their freedom! For from the moment they first stepped into the guest bedroom to retire for the night, I have not permitted them to step outside their room, and I have not seen them.

"Now I knew that when enough days and nights had come and gone and still the wick had not caught fire despite the presence of the burning coal in the talisman, if indeed you had sent these young men to live in my house, you would surely come after them yourself. For you would want to learn their fortune, and seeing that they had failed to seduce me, you might even want to try your own luck with me! And indeed you came! And of course I immediately knew who you must be!

"However, your own behavior toward me remains to be seen, Your Majesty," the craftsman's wife concluded. "You are the greatest of kings, whereas I am but your humble servant, powerless to defend my honor and my marriage. And therefore, you are able to do with me whatever you think is best.

"But before you decide, Your Majesty, I ask you to remember your own reputation. Remember that throughout the world, people honor you for your great wisdom! And just as surely as you know that an egg in any colored shell is simply an egg, so you must surely know that the desires and pleasures of this world are as fleeting as a bird's song! So, I ask you, what do you intend to do with me?"

King Solomon had listened, speechless, to the words of the craftsman's wife. Then he exclaimed, "Woman, God has blessed you with a wise and good heart! For, yes, I encountered your husband when I made one of my daily visits to the site where the master craftsmen are building my Temple. And I noticed the strange talisman that hangs from his neck. I called him before me and asked him, 'Why do you wear that strange object around your neck? And what does it mean?'

"And, yes, to my words your husband replied, 'As I was leaving for the Holy City, my wife placed this talisman around my neck and said to me, "Wear this talisman day and night. If I should burn with desire for another man, the hot coal will ignite the cotton wick in the cylinder. However, as long as my love for you is constant, the wick will not catch fire despite the presence of the burning coal."'"

King Solomon continued, "And, yes, I was fascinated by both the question of your fidelity and your clever solution to the problem. And I decided to test your virtue and, at the same time, observe the accuracy of the talisman. And since I could not be in two places at one time, I sent the two handsome young men to live in your house and try to seduce you. And, yes, when thirty days and nights had come and gone and still the wick had not caught fire despite the presence of the burning coal in the talisman that hangs from your husband's neck, I decided to come after them myself. For I did want to learn their fortune, and seeing that they had failed to seduce you, yes, I did want to try my own luck with you!

"But now, in return for your purity of heart and tongue, your wisdom, and your virtue," King Solomon concluded, "I promise you the love, honor, and respect in which a brother holds his sister. And I give you this gold bracelet to treasure always as a sign of my regard!"

So it came to pass that King Solomon returned to the Holy City with the two handsome young men. And the king found the master craftsman and said to him, "I have tested your wife and found that she is the most wise and virtuous of women, and I have promised her the love, honor, and respect in which a brother holds his sister."

The king then related the entire story to the husband, concluding with these words, "Now, master craftsman, because I also honor and value the man who possesses such a wife, I command you to take these wages, which are many times the amount I owe you, and return home in peace to enjoy her!"

And so it came to pass that the craftsman returned home to his wife, who proceeded to relate the same story that King Solomon had told him. The master craftsman gained a greater appreciation for his wife, whom he held in highest esteem to the end of their days. And their friendship with King Solomon was a lasting one.

Rostam, Shield of Persia and The Tragedy of Sohrab

Historical Background

Although Ferdowsi wrote the *Shahnameh* in about A.D. 1000, many aspects of the legends it contains are rooted in four ancient cultures: the Neolithic matriarchal societies; the Scythians; the Persians; and the Parthians.

The *Shahnameh's* legends of Rostam and Sohrab contain echoes of a matriarchal society. There, a woman chose her own mates and each of her children might have a different father. Children remained with their mother and were also reared by their mother's oldest brother, who was the male head of their family. Because their father returned to his own family, where he helped rear his sister's children, children and their father might not know each other.

War is a major subject in the section of the *Shahnameh* that presents the history of Persia's legendary kings, and Ferdowsi's descriptions of war gear and battle practices have a distinctly Scythian flavor. Oral tradition, the continued use of certain Scythian war gear and battle practices, and Ferdowsi's written sources are probably responsible for the survival of such details during the many centuries between the Scythian invasions and Ferdowsi's writing.

Two groups of Scythians settled the area that in time became the Persian and then the Parthian empire. In about 1400 B.C., the first group settled the southwestern part of the Persian plateau and became the ancestors of the legendary kings of Persia. They called themselves Aryans ("Iranians" in Persian), meaning "the noble ones" and called their area "Iran," meaning "the land of the Aryans." Later, in the second century B.C., related Saka tribes moved southwest from Sakestan ("the land of the Sakas") to the area that became Seistan and Zabulestan on the eastern border of Persia, where they became the ancestors of Rostam and the other legendary Saka heroes in the *Shahnameh*.

Like their Scythian ancestors, the legendary kings and heroes in the *Shahnameh* are expert horsemen and archers. They view war as a way of life and relax by going hunting. Like their Scythian ancestors, they wear leather armor and carry a metal-plated leather shield. They hang a case containing their bow and arrows from their waist at their left side, while tied to their right thigh they wear a sheath containing a long knife or a short sword of bronze or iron. They carry both a battle-ax (used with the left hand) and a javelin (used with the right hand). In battle, they be-head their enemies, and they are rewarded for their valor in battle based upon the number of heads they have taken. They make leather-bound drinking cups from the skulls of their most hated enemies, and if they are wealthy, they may line these skulls with gold.

Long before Ferdowsi was born, Persian history was a source of na-tional pride and an appropriate subject for epic material. Approximately eight hundred years after the Scythians settled in Persia, Cyrus the Great (sixth century B.C.) had turned a country of people whose ancestors were nomads into an empire that contained about ten million people and cov-ered almost two million square miles.

The Parthian kings considered themselves to be the legitimate suc-cessors to the great kings of the earlier Persian empire and to rule with the divine blessing of Ahuramazda, the chief god of Zoroastrianism, the religion of the Persians. Their empire, established in about 171 B.C., ex-tended from the Caspian Sea on the north to the Persian Gulf on the south, and from the Euphrates River on the west to India on the east, and therefore included Rostam's kingdom of Seistan and Zabulestan.

Because of their pride in their Persian heritage, the Parthian kings revived Persia's oral and written literature, which included the Rostam cycle of Saka legends. Undoubtedly, the Parthian aristocrats particularly enjoyed these ancient stories because they reflected their own interests and values. Like their Scythian ancestors and the legendary kings and he-roes who have come down to us in the *Shahnameh*, the Parthians were a warlike people who excelled as horsemen and archers and loved both war and hunting.

Political Background: The Persian King

The *Shahnameh* depicts a time in Persian legend and history when a strong Persian king means the difference between freedom and captivity. The King of Kings, or the Great King of Persia, demands total submission and obedience from his subjects, and he is served by a large group of warriors who protect and increase his power. The greatest of these warriors are usually kings or chieftains in their own right, and they lead their own warriors into battle when they defend Persia from aggressors or go on the offensive to enlarge the empire. Consequently, the plain of battle is always filled with tents, pennants, and warriors from the various Persian provinces, Persia's subject states, and its allies.

Because the Great King receives his right to rule directly from Ahuramazda (the Zoroastrian God of Light), each warrior's primary responsibility is to serve the Great King, and by so doing to serve Ahuramazda as well. The warrior's responsibility to the Great King takes precedence over his responsibility to his own kingdom, to his family, and to himself. Moreover, he is obligated to serve the Great King with the same total and sacred loyalty no matter how wise or foolish, and how just or cruel, the Great King may be.

Persia's legendary kings and heroes combat two perennial enemies: the Turanians, or Tatars (their northeastern neighbors), and the Demons (their northern neighbors). The Demons are mortals who are depicted as possessing superior intelligence and the superhuman powers of magic and sorcery. They can be giants or godlike, and they are described as having human form but with long ears, horns, and sometimes tails. Given their attributes, they are great allies and formidable foes.

Cultural Background

The Persian Hero

Like other authors of major epics from around the world, Ferdowsi wrote the *Shahnameh* for an audience of aristocrats. Consequently, the heroes of the *Shahnameh* are also aristocrats. They spend their time with family and friends who are their companions-in-arms, defending their country in times of war and hunting in times of peace. Like all epic heroes, the heroes of the *Shahnameh* need exceptional courage, strength, and skill on the plain of battle.

The Persian hero, like his Scythian ancestors, takes pride in his ability to ride a horse, to draw his bow, and to use his lariat. Wars are bloody affairs in which each warrior aims to behead his foe with one stroke of his sword. The best warriors enjoy the challenge of single combat, where they also use such weapons as the war club or the ox-headed mace (a sign of kingship), the spear, and the dagger.

Each warrior's fate, like that of everyone else in his society, is written in the stars for the king's wise men (his astrologers) to read. What is written there comes to pass, no matter how one tries to avoid it. Since death comes to everyone sooner or later, the Persian hero aims to perform valiant deeds on the plain of battle in order to gain the immortality of lasting fame.

The Religion of Zoroaster

Ferdowsi brushes his entire epic canvas with an overlay of Zoroastrianism, even though he reveals that it was a later legendary king who became a convert to the new religion. In Zoroastrianism, the human condition reflects the struggle between Ahuramazda (Urmazd) and Ahriman to control the universe. Ahuramazda is the god of wisdom, goodness, and light, and the constructive force in the universe, whereas Ahriman is the evil spirit, who represents deception, darkness, and the destructive force in the universe.

Ahriman is always busily using deception as a lure in his attempt to harm human beings and destroy the world of truth. Consequently, Zoroastrianism contributes an additional moral dimension to the *Shahnameh*, where a war between Persia and Turan becomes a war between good and evil, and where Ferdowsi reveals his characters' conflicts between the claims of their political and social selves and the demands of their moral selves.

Patriarchy and Matriarchy in the *Shahnameh*

Once patriarchal supremacy became established, myth and legend glorified male gods and warrior-heroes. The loving mother either lost her original significance and became transformed into an evil monster or witch whom a hero destroys, or she was relegated to the background, or she was no longer present at all. Because epic poets often had no interest in reconciling every strand in their materials, matriarchal fragments often remain as inconsistencies in patriarchal myths and legends.

Because the *Shahnameh* is clearly patriarchal in its values and its focus, Ferdowsi includes only those aspects of family relationships that are important to kingship and heroism. Just as the king rules his country, so the father rules his home. His expectations of his son and how his son reacts to them may develop into tragic situations.

Given its patriarchal focus, women play a very small role in the *Shahnameh*. Yet the women who have a role in the lives of the legendary kings and heroes are surprisingly independent despite their dependent and secluded position in their families. For example, three non-Persian princesses choose to marry Persian kings or princes despite the fact that

Persia is an enemy of their country. It is possible that these marriage patterns reflect an earlier matriarchal society where women had the power to select their own mates.

Moreover, despite Persia's patriarchal warrior culture, one woman is a superb warrior, although she fights in male attire. In contrast, the fact that Demons often transform themselves into lovely women in their attempt to capture a warrior-hero reveals the continued importance of women, even when their role has been transformed into one that is evil. Finally, both the love affair between Rostam and Tahmineh, and the resulting battle between Rostam and Sohrab, make the most sense when viewed as having roots in an older matriarchal culture.

Literary Background

Ferdowsi

Mansur ibn Ahmad, later known as Ferdowsi, was born into a family of landowners in about A.D. 935. His place of birth was the city of Tus in the province of Khurasan, in what is now northeastern Iran. However, at that time, Khurasan extended into what are now Afghanistan and parts of former Soviet Central Asian republics.

At the time of Ferdowsi's birth, Khurasan was under Turkish control and was relatively independent of the Arab Muslim caliph (spiritual leader) of Baghdad. Khurasan and the other eastern provinces of Persia could be called "the cradle of Persian civilization," for much of Persia's significant history had occurred in this area. Consequently, it was also here that the landowning class had become responsible for preserving Persian oral and written literature as a way of perpetuating the Persian values and traditions that had existed before the Arab Muslim conquest in the seventh century. Living during a time when the language, cultural traditions, and religion had changed, these Muslims prided themselves on being the historians of their Persian heritage.

By Ferdowsi's time, a Persian cultural renaissance had occurred, with the result that the language spoken in the king's court was Persian rather than Arabic, and the court poetry was written in Persian. Ferdowsi was in his thirties when Sultan Mahmud, ruler of the Turkish Muslim kingdom of Ghazni, received an old prose version of the history of Persia, also called the *Shahnameh,* and decided to commission a poetic version of the work.

According to the legend, Sultan Mahmud selected seven stories from the prose version of the *Shahnameh* and gave one to each of seven esteemed poets to versify for a competition. Meanwhile, Ferdowsi had matured in the ideal environment for a poet and had been working independently, in Tus, on a poetic rendition of parts of the *Shahnameh*. On a trip to the capital of Khurasan, he happened to meet the poets who were participating in this competition. They appreciated his genius and recommended him to Mahmud.

Sultan Mahmud awarded the project to Ferdowsi and offered him a thousand gold pieces for every thousand verses. He also gave him the name of Ferdowsi (which means "Paradise"), since Ferdowsi had brought the delights of Paradise to his court. Ferdowsi announced that he preferred to be paid the total amount at the end of the project because he intended to rebuild the dikes in Tus with the money.

Ferdowsi worked on the *Shahnameh* for at least thirty years, being about seventy years old when he finished it in A.D. 1010. A favorite courtier of the sultan charged that the poem contained heretical views. Sultan Mahmud had agreed to pay Ferdowsi sixty thousand gold coins, one for each of the poem's couplets, but the courtier secretly substituted sixty thousand silver coins. Ferdowsi was in the public baths when the courtier's servant delivered the sultan's payment. Finding the coins to be silver rather than gold, Ferdowsi gave them all away, distributing them among the keeper of the baths, the person who sold refreshments, and the slave who had brought him the coins. When the courtier learned of this, he told Sultan Mahmud what Ferdowsi had done with his patron's payment, and Mah-mud sentenced the poet to die by being trampled beneath the feet of an elephant.

Friends of Ferdowsi heard the news and immediately informed the poet of his impending fate. Ferdowsi wrote a satire about Sultan Mahmud on a copy of the *Shahnameh*, left it for the sultan to read, and fled from Khurasan. Wanted by the authorities and with his life at stake, Ferdowsi spent most of the ten remaining years of his life moving from place to place. Finally he returned to his home in Tus.

Meanwhile, the kings who had sheltered Ferdowsi were attempting to get Sultan Mahmud to appreciate Ferdowsi's genius. When Mahmud finally learned the truth about his favorite courtier, he had him either banished or killed. Then, in about A.D. 1020, Sultan Mahmud sent sixty thousand gold pieces by caravan to Ferdowsi in Tus, who by this time was about eighty-five years old.

The legend concludes on a tragic note. One day, while the caravan was en route, Ferdowsi heard a child in the street chanting his satiric verses about Sultan Mahmud. The verses caused the poet to remember the past, and he dropped dead in the street from a heart attack. Just as the caravan bearing Ferdowsi's gold pieces was entering Tus through the east gate, Ferdowsi's funeral procession was leaving the city through the west gate. His family later accepted the money and used it as Ferdowsi had intended, to build stone dikes in Tus.

It is interesting to consider the relationship between Ferdowsi's fortunes with regard to the *Shahnameh* and the epic's content. Since Ferdowsi's patron was a Turkish ruler of a Muslim kingdom, he may have wanted, and expected, something quite different from Ferdowsi's poetic version.

Ferdowsi wrote a work that glorifies the mythological, legendary, and historical past of an old, non-Muslim empire, with its Zoroastrian religion and its condemnation of the Turanians, or Tartars, as Persia's greatest enemy. Moreover, Ferdowsi transformed Persia's history into literature, creating memorable human heroes out of pasteboard figures, thereby reviving cultural values and national issues that, for many people, had been long dead and forgotten.

Steeped as Ferdowsi was in his Persian heritage, the process of writing such a book for so many years of his life could not help but create a fusion between the writer and the work. Inevitably, the *Shahnameh* would reflect Ferdowsi's social values, and the principles that governed the lives of Persia's legendary heroes would influence Ferdowsi's own life. As a result, the *Shahnameh* is a captivating work of genius, infused with genuine emotions and attitudes that a Turk could find offensive. Whether for personal or for political reasons, the courtier who complained about the work was able to convince Sultan Mahmud to share his point of view.

The Nature of the *Shahnameh*

The *Shahnameh* covers a period of 3600 years, from the creation of the world and the first Persian king (the first two-thirds of the book) to the Arab Muslim conquest of Persia by the Saracens in A.D. 636 (the last third). It provides a history of four dynasties and fifty Persian kings. The kings in the earliest dynasty are mythical; those in the second dynasty, the Kayanids, are legendary; and those in the third and fourth dynasties (c. 150 B.C.–A.D. 632) are historical. Kay Kobad, the first king of the great dynasty of Kayanids is said to have ruled from 700 to 600 B.C., followed by Kay Kavus, and then by Kay Khosrow.

Ferdowsi deftly intertwines the legends of the Kayanid kings with the Rostam legends from Seistan by having Rostam lead the king of Persia's army into battle. Rostam's family is not related to the kings of Persia, either in fact or in fiction. His ancestors were Saka kings of Seistan, which in the *Shahnameh* is an independent ally on the eastern border of Persia.

Ferdowsi was a compiler and editor as well as an author and poet. He used a combination of written and oral sources for his version of the *Shahnameh*, choosing his content from many competing versions. The titles to some of his written sources still exist, as does the introduction to the *Shahnameh* that he used. The age of Ferdowsi's oral sources—legends passed down from generation to generation for hundreds of years—is reflected by their preservation of Scythian battle procedures and by their depiction of women.

Ferdowsi retained the repetitive devices that are the hallmark of oral literature. Throughout the epic he used particular epithets to describe Sam, Zal, and Rostam; certain descriptions of the sun to signify particular times of day; and set passages to describe scenes of war. These have the stylistic function of unifying the epic, the dramatic function of expressing one or more important themes, and finally, the practical function of making it easier for both the performer and the listener to remember the long text.

The Appeal and Value of the *Shahnameh*

The *Shahnameh* contains a series of legends that take their place among the greatest stories in world literature. These heroes, and the kings for whom they perform their deeds, are unforgettable characters who live forever in the reader's mind and heart. In the course of their adventures, the heroes encounter the magic of demons, the power of monsters, and the skill of other valiant warriors. They experience the joys of friendship and the passions of love, jealousy, and hatred. They courageously encounter the challenges of danger, treachery, and death.

The *Shahnameh* bears approximately the same relation to Persian culture (prior to the 1979 Islamic Revolution) that the *Iliad* bears to ancient Greek culture and the *Ramayana* and the *Mahabharata* bear to ancient Indian culture. Like them, it aims to preserve and, in fact, to immortalize some aspect of its country's history. Like them, it defines, symbolizes, and perpetuates the values of its particular culture, thereby providing a sense of national and ethnic identity that enhances the self-esteem and dignity of its people.

Like the great epics from ancient Greece and India, the *Shahnameh* is a world treasure as well as a national jewel. The legends of Persia's heroes reach across time and space to touch the lives of modern readers and listeners just as they have touched the lives of countless others throughout Persia's long history.

Ferdowsi possessed the gift of being able to create characters who are truly human and who display a tragic nobility as they come to grips with their soul-rending conflicts. He composed all of his characters' speeches and their letters, turning history into literature and names into human beings who think and feel in ways that we can understand and appreciate.

Ferdowsi had an instinct for psychological high drama, and his genius illuminates both the bright and dark sides of human attitudes and behavior. He saw the potential for great good and great evil that exists in each human being. He saw the danger of excessive pride, the slippery slope that leads to rash and imprudent actions, and the inevitable retribution that follows. Moreover, he saw that basically good people can succumb to this pattern of attitudes and behaviors. Ferdowsi also saw that people who perform deeds that harm others are not necessarily evil people. They may fail to consider the consequences of their actions, or they may be ruled by temporary passions, or they may simply behave differently in different situations.

Ferdowsi is fascinated by the human aspect of history—by the people who both shape the events and are shaped by them. In the legends that he recounts, he focuses on the personalities of kings and heroes, whose attitudes and behavior reveal their motivations, their goals, and their internal and external conflicts.

The Appeal of the Persian Hero

Rostam and Sohrab are unforgettable individuals. In their speeches and actions, they advocate the universal principles of love, honor, loyalty, wisdom, justice, and freedom, along with such qualities as courage, strength, skill, and creative intelligence on the plain of battle. They are majestic figures because of their virtues and their valiant deeds.

However, they live on in the minds of those who come to know them because of the age-old conflicts between their obligation to themselves—given their own needs, desires, and values—and their obligations to their family and their society. The fact that each of these heroes must choose between important competing values—knowing that neither choice is satisfactory—heightens his stature while creating his personal tragedy.

Tragedy abounds in the lives of the legendary kings and heroes of Persia. These human beings play out their lives on a dark stage, often acting like puppets. Given the frailties that are inherent in the human personality, the transitory nature of human life, and the inevitability of

Fate that is integral to the Persian worldview, it cannot be otherwise.

In such an environment, Rostam and Sohrab strive to make their own lives worthwhile, recognizing that noble deeds are their only source of immortality. However, they are not duplicates of some generic Persian hero. Each is unique in his personality and in his goals.

Rostam is one of the world's greatest traditional heroes. Like the others, his fame resides in his many great deeds that make his society a better place in which to live. He is not only Persia's greatest hero, but he is the greatest hero of his time, and he takes pride in his greatness. Rostam embraces heroism solely for its satisfaction and its joy. Having no ambition beyond heroism, he is the friend of the just king and the enemy of all tyrants. Doing his best to serve Persia's kings and preserve Persia's autonomy gives him self-esteem and also earns the respect and admiration of these kings, his own family, and his peers. His success in combat—whether against monsters, demons, or warriors—earns him the epithets Rostam the Mighty and Shield of Persia. His courage, strength, and skill make him as great as his reputation. His pride makes him very human.

Like the world's greatest heroes, Rostam is born into a family marked by its nobility of birth and deeds. Like them, tragedy blemishes the golden luster of his life. Finally, like many heroes, Rostam dies the victim of a treacherous deed. Rostam's life, which lasts over three hundred years and encompasses the reign of many kings, becomes inextricably bound up with Persia's other great legendary heroes of the *Shahnameh*, including Sohrab.

Sohrab is probably the most poignant hero in world literature. He is born with the mark of a hero upon him, and he has an extraordinary youth. However, Sohrab needs his father, whom he has never met, and knowing that he is Rostam's son is not enough. Because his father is Persia's greatest hero, Sohrab wants to establish a heroic identity in his own right and then to impress Rostam with that identity. Unfortunately, Sohrab's personality and the circumstances under which he chooses to meet his father combine to create a tragedy that leads readers to question whether Sohrab to any extent brings his fate upon himself.

The legends of Rostam and Sohrab can function independently as great hero stories. However, each hero makes a greater impact on the reader because of the existence of the other. Taken together, they form a multifaceted portrait of the hero, both in ancient Persia and in any culture today. Like Rostam, people still choose to become heroes in order to help the society in which they live and to give meaning to their own lives through deeds that others will remember. Like Sohrab, people still choose to become heroes in order to create an identity that others will recognize and value.

Today, we can take these heroes into our hearts because we, too, know what it is to have to choose between our own personal desires and our responsibilities to our families, friends, and society. Often, we too must choose between what others would like us to do—and even what we might wish to do—and our own moral and ethical values. We understand the temptation, we understand the torment of internal conflict, and sometimes we lose the battle against the external and internal forces that lead us to exercise bad judgment. In our own environment, we too must make our own lives worthwhile, and we too must recognize the importance of our good deeds in whatever type of immortality we hope to achieve.

The Later History of the *Shahnameh*

The subject of the *Shahnameh* was so appealing that at least eight other important epics about the heroes of Seistan followed. The first was written fifty years after Ferdowsi completed the *Shahnameh*. These include epics devoted to Sam the Hero and to Rostam's son Faramarz. However, by the time the last of these epics was written, in the late thirteenth or early fourteenth century, the stories had become much more romantic. Their heroes can defeat the foe—no matter how numerous, how strong, or how supernatural—and these heroes must contend against the spells of evil wizards and an array of greater demons and monsters.

The earliest existing manuscript of the *Shahnameh*, written in 1216 and containing only the first of two volumes, was recently discovered in Florence. The earliest complete manuscript, written in 1276–1277, is owned by the British Museum in London. The two manuscripts clearly relate the same story, but each contains incidents that the other omits, and the arrangement differs. Many other manuscripts exist that date from the 1300s and later.

Over the centuries, the kings of Iran had the *Shahnameh* copied and illustrated by the greatest artists of the period. The most famous edition of the *Shahnameh* was commissioned by King Tahmasp in the 1520s. It is considered to be one of the most beautiful books ever created—so beautiful and prized that at one point in its recent international history, the manuscript was taken apart so that individual paintings could be sold to museums and private art investors. Iran, which once again owns the remnant of the manuscript, is currently in the process of trying to recover the missing pages of its national treasure.

Characters in the Legends of Rostam and Sohrab

Rostam, His Family, and Friends

SAM: Called "Sam the Hero"; son of Nariman; father of Dastan/Zal; grandfather of Rostam; lives during the reign of Manuchehr

DASTAN/ZAL: (DASTAN means "tricked"; ZAL means "ancient") Called "White-Haired Zal"; son of Sam the Hero; husband of Rudabeh; father of Rostam and Zavareh; king of Seistan and Zabul/ Zabulestan; lives from the reign of Manuchehr through the reign of Bahman

RUDABEH: Daughter of the king of Kabul; wife of Dastan/Zal; mother of Rostam; queen of Seistan and Zabul/Zabulestan

ROSTAM/TAHAMTAN: (ROSTAM means "delivered"; TAHAMTAN means "giant-body") Called "Rostam the Mighty"; son of Dastan/Zal; grandson of Sam the Hero; fourth and greatest hero from the royal family of Seistan; husband of Tahmineh; father of Sohrab Faramarz; lives from the reign of Manuchehr into the reign of Goshtasp

ZAVAREH: Son of Dastan/Zal and Rudabeh; Rostam's brother and loyal companion

FARAMARZ: Son of Rostam; grandson of Dastan/Zal and Rudabeh

SHAGHAD: Son of Dastan/Zal and one of his slaves; half-brother of Rostam; son-in-law of a king of Kabul

GUDARZ: Old hero and wise counselor; father of Giv

HOJIR: One of Gudarz's eighty sons; Persian commander of the White Fortress

GIV: Greatest son of Gudarz; warrior-friend of Rostam

The Persian Kings and Their Families
(in chronological order)

MANUCHEHR: King of Persia for whom Sam the Hero and young Rostam perform heroic deeds

KAY KOBAD: Father of Kay Kavus; a king for whom Rostam performs heroic deeds

KAY KAVUS: Son of Kay Kobad; a king for whom Rostam performs heroic deeds

KAY KHOSROW: King of Persia following Kay Kavus; greatest of the legendary Kings of Persia; king for whom Rostam performs heroic deeds

The Turanians and Their Allies

TAHMINEH: Daughter of the king of Samengan, an ally of Afrasyab; wife of Rostam; mother of Sohrab

ZHENDE: Brother of Tahmineh

SOHRAB: ("Sunshine") Son of Rostam and Tahmineh

AFRASYAB: Commander-in-chief of the armies of Turan; later, king of Turan

HUMAN: Turanian commander under King Afrasyab

Divinities and Demons

URMAZD: (Or Ahuramazda, "Wise Lord"); the holy spirit who represents truth and light and operates as a constructive force in the universe; supreme divinity in Zoroastrianism; God of wisdom, goodness, and light; creator of the world; great foe of Ahriman

AHRIMAN: ("Maker of Evil") The evil spirit who represents deception and darkness and operates as a destructive force in the universe; uses deception to lure people into choosing evil; the greatest Demon, who lives in the dark lands of the North, which are populated by Demon peoples; Ahriman can change his shape, often into a youth or a snake; the great foe of Ahuramazda

DEMONS: ("Divs") Mortal beings who are human in shape, but possess horns, long ears, and sometimes a tail; are enchanters and sorcerers; can appear to be giants or weather spirits; can change shape or vanish; are great allies and formidable enemies, usually the enemy of the Persians; the most powerful live in the kingdom of Mazanderan, which is thought to be controlled by Ahriman

("The Tragedy of Sohrab" begins on page 131.)

ROSTAM, SHIELD OF PERSIA

Prologue

Listen and learn about life for those of us who are mortal, and mourn for us! For both rich and poor, both old and young, death is our destiny. For both wise and foolish, both kind and cruel, death is our destiny. For both hero and coward, both conqueror and defeated, death is our destiny. Time sweeps over us and our achievements, sooner or later bringing death to us all!

Hope is a deception, and certainty and safety are but dreams that beguile the dreamer into false trust. Those who are wise know that the world is not to be trusted, for passions rule life. Happiness and love, family and friendship, fame and wealth are but fleeting pleasures, for jealousy and unchecked desires lurk in mortal hearts. No one is safe, since treachery knows no limits and cares nothing for friends and relatives. Those who sow the seeds of strife, and those who are pure of heart, together reap sorrow and misery for their lot.

Who among mortals can escape Fate? Who among us can use our wisdom, or our courage, or our strength, or our skill to this end? No one. What is written in the stars in the heavens is sure to come! So it was with Rostam. So it is with all who walk the earth!

Zal is reared by the simurgh. Later, the king's wise men declare that his son will be the world's greatest hero.

In a time long past, in the province of Seistan, White-Haired Zal was born to Persia's greatest warrior, Sam the Hero. Zal was as fair to look upon as a summer garden, and he was formed as straight as a cypress tree. However, he was born with hair as white as a goose's wing, like that of an old man.

Sam the Hero, who was commander-in-chief of King Manuchehr's armies, was shocked and embarrassed at the sight of his infant son. Fear flooded his heart, and he listened to the voice of Rumor, who exclaimed, "This ill-fated infant cannot be Sam the Hero's child! Surely he is the Demon-child of Ahriman, the Evil One! He shames his noble family, and he disgraces the great kingdom of Persia!"

So it came to pass that Sam the Hero directed his servants to take White-Haired Zal into the wilds far to the north, and to abandon the infant on a slope of Mount Elburz. They dutifully exposed him there, on a cold bed of rocks and thorns, with neither food to sustain him nor clothing or shelter to protect him, expecting that, alive or dead, he would soon become food for birds and beasts of prey.

However, Urmazd, Creator of the World, called to the simurgh, the Bird of Marvel, as it sat upon its nest on a cliff near the summit of Mount Elburz, whose peak touches the stars in the heavens. "Look down from your nest," he commanded, "and see the infant who has been abandoned on the mountainside far below you. The poor child shivers with cold and tearfully sucks his fingers in hunger! Rescue this infant—nourish, protect, and rear him with paternal care—for he is destined to become the father of the champion of the world, one who will bring honor to his people and lasting fame to your name."

So it came to pass that White-Haired Zal was reared in the Bird of Marvel's nest and loved the simurgh as his mother and father.

After many summers had passed, Sam the Hero had a terrifying dream in which a wise man approached him and said, "How long will you let your white-haired son be nursed by a mountain bird? Although you are the cruelest of fathers—for even the savage lion and crocodile protect their offspring—Urmazd has blessed and protected your son."

Sam the Hero awoke and called upon his wise men to explain his dream. When their reading of the stars in the heavens confirmed its truth, he prayed to Urmazd for forgiveness, and he went to Mount Elburz to discover the son whom he had long thought to be dead.

So it came to pass that the simurgh looked down and spied Sam the Hero on the slope far below. The Bird of Marvel then said to White-Haired Zal, "Oh, child, whom I have reared as my own son! Your true father is the noble warrior, Sam, son of Nariman, and he is the greatest of heroes! Manuchehr, king of Persia, values him above all other nobles! I must now return you to him and his kingdom, where you will earn glory at his side.

"I give you the name of Dastan, which means 'tricked,' for your father tricked you when he abandoned you on this mountainside to die," the simurgh declared. "From this time forth and for as long as you live, retain it as your formal name."

Zal's eyes overflowed with tears, and his heart flooded with sorrow. "Do I really have to leave you?" he asked the simurgh. "Your loving wings are the only parent I have ever known! And your nest is the only home I have ever had! You are my only friend! Surely you can find a way to keep me with you!"

"So great is my love for you that I would do that if I could," the simurgh replied, "but you have a great destiny, and I must bow to that and restore you to your father and your rightful home. However, as a token of my lasting love and concern for you, take this golden breast feather as my parting gift. Should you ever find yourself in danger or in need, just toss it onto a fire, and quick as dust in the wind, I will come to your aid."

The Bird of Marvel then descended with Dastan and said to Sam the Hero, "Rejoice that you have a son who will bring honor, glory, and fame to your family and your kingdom!"

Sam's wise men looked into the heavens and confirmed this statement, for it was written in the stars that Dastan, the son of Sam the Hero and grandson of Nariman, would outshine every warrior of his time, that he would outlive everyone in his age, and that he would defend Persia for hundreds of years.

It came to pass that, while Sam the Hero yet lived, Dastan inherited the crown and throne of his father's kingdoms of Seistan and Zabulestan and that he fell in love with Rudabeh, the daughter of the king of Kabul. Because her father, although a good man, was a descendant of an evil king who had been the enemy of an earlier king of Persia, Rudabeh and Zal were forced to meet and to pledge their love secretly. They knew that the kings of Seistan and Kabul did not dare to displease the king of Persia, and consequently they were not surprised when their fathers greeted their desire to wed with the fury of two wolves.

Predictably, King Manuchehr reacted like an enraged elephant. However, his wise men looked into the heavens and read in the stars that Manuchehr should encourage this marriage. They announced: "The love between the king of Kabul's daughter and the son of Sam the Hero shines like the sun's bright shield! These two will have a son who will be the greatest hero in the world. As long as he lives, he will uproot the wicked from the earth. His courage, strength, and skill will shield Persia in her times of greatest danger. Persia will rejoice, for her glory will ascend to the heavens, and the world will bow to her might!"

After their marriage in Kabul, Zal brought Rudabeh to Seistan, where she wore a golden crown and sat beside her husband on the throne.

Rostam has a remarkable birth and youth.

When nine moons had come and gone, the time for the arrival of Rudabeh's child's drew near, and it appeared that the mother would die before giving birth. The best doctors in Seistan could do nothing to help her, and Zal was beside himself with grief. Suddenly he remembered the simurgh's golden feather, and he tossed it on the fire. Quick as dust in the wind, a dark cloud wafted into Rudabeh's room, and Zal found himself looking into the eyes of the simurgh.

"Why do I see tears in my lion's eyes?" the Bird of Marvel asked Dastan. "Rudabeh is about to give birth to your son! He is destined to be fair of face and tall of limb, as strong as an elephant and like his father in wisdom and judgment. His power will cause the world to wonder at his might. The lion will worship him, and the leopard will panic upon hearing his voice. Yet your son is so large that he cannot be born in the usual way; instead, he must be cut from his mother's womb."

Plucking a golden feather from its wing, the simurgh commanded Dastan, "Wave this feather over your wife and child, and all will be well with you." With these parting words, it returned, quick as dust in the wind, to its mountain nest.

So it came to pass that Zal and Rudabeh's child was born. He was as beautiful to behold as a wreath of spring flowers and so strong that it was clear that no mortal would be his equal. His parents named him Rostam, which means "delivered," since it was his destiny always to deliver Persia from her enemies. His birth was celebrated with great charitable donations to the poor and with feasting in the streets of Seistan, Zabul, and Kabul.

When the sun next raised his shining shield, scattering the armies of night and brightening the earth with its brilliant light, Rostam had become as large and strong as a child whose eyes had seen one summer, and he was so hungry that he needed ten nurses to provide him with milk. Soon he ate as much solid food as five grown men. By the time his eyes had seen three summers, he was wrestling, riding, hunting, and using the lariat, the bow, the war club, and the spear.

When Rostam had seen eight summers, he was as large and strong as the great heroes of his time, and it was then that he first met his grandfather, Sam the Hero. The great warrior greeted him with delight, saying, "My eyes have seen more than a hundred summers since I became chief of the Persian princes, and many honors have made my heart sing. But never have I been as happy as I am to see you, my young hero! Tell me, what would you like to receive from your grandfather as a special gift?"

Rostam replied, "I have no interest in the toys my friends enjoy! I like to use my spear and my bow. But I have no horse and no armor or helmet to call my own! To me, adventure and combat taste as sweet as honey on my tongue! And as soon as my father permits, I will destroy all your enemies and throw their heads at your feet!"

To these words, Sam the Hero replied, "It will be my pleasure to give these to you as soon as your father tells me that in combat you have the courage of the lion, the strength of the elephant, the skill of the fiery-tongued dragon, and the fury of the crocodile."

Rostam performs his first heroic deeds.

It came to pass that, by the time Rostam's eyes had seen ten summers, he had become as straight as a young cypress tree and as tall and strong as eight men. He had the chest of a lion, the limbs of an elephant, and the feet of a stag.

One night a great roaring noise, the strong vibration of his sleeping quarters, and fearful shouts awakened him. Rostam immediately jumped up, grabbed his grandfather's great war club, the ox-headed mace, and commanded the guards to let him leave the palace. Fearing for the life of the young prince, and for their own lives as well if they disobeyed the king's orders to protect him, the guards hastened to bar Rostam's path.

Rostam angrily struck the guard who faced him with Sam the Hero's mace, splitting his head in two. He then pushed his way through the heavily chained gates, where he was amazed to see that King Manuchehr's white elephant had suddenly gone mad, had broken its chains, and was trampling everyone it encountered on its rampage. He was equally amazed to see that his father's warriors were fleeing in panic from the rampaging monster as if they were sheep at the mercy of a ravenous wolf. The Persian king's elephant was the size of a mountain, but Rostam cried, "Warriors of Seistan! You shame your name! What is the life of one man if he can save the lives of a hundred!"

Then, shouting his lion's battle cry with a roar that made the mountains tremble in terror, Rostam charged the king's elephant, which raged toward him like the spring waters of the Nile. As the elephant raised its trunk to seize and crush the young prince, Sam the Hero's mace smashed into its head with a mighty blow, causing the beast to fall dead upon the earth. Rostam went back to sleep, but the fame of his deed soared like an eagle through Seistan, Zabul, Persia, Kabul, and Turan, soon reaching the ears of Sam the Hero and King Manuchehr.

When the sun next raised his shining shield, scattering the armies of night and brightening the earth with its brilliant light, Zal said to his son, "Although you are still a child, no one can match your stature, your courage, and your strength. Therefore, I think the time has come for you to test your skill. If you succeed with the task I am going to give you, your grandfather will reward you with your own horse and armor and the rank of a young warrior!

"Long ago, your great-grandfather, Nariman, died attempting to conquer the great fortress atop Mount Sepand, with its fabled treasure-house," Zal explained. "No warrior has been able to attack it, and no siege has been successful. The city is surrounded by a barren desert with a steep ascent of three miles. The only way to enter it appears to be by invitation of the people who live there. And they do not welcome foreign warriors!

"However, since you are too young to be known to them, you have a chance to win by guile what your great-grandfather could not win by force," Zal declared. "If I send you disguised as a salt merchant, the people will surely welcome you, and once you are inside their walled city, you should destroy them—root, branch, and leaf—for the air will smell far sweeter without them!"

So it came to pass that Rostam led a caravan of camels to the fortress, with weapons hidden within some of the storage containers and salt placed obviously within others. His ruse was successful. Having gained admittance, he and his warrior-merchants traded salt for clothes, jewels, and gold until the sun's bright shield sank from sight. Then, with Sam the Hero's ox-headed war club in one hand and a sword in the other, Rostam led his warriors in an assault upon the occupants of the fortified city. He avenged Nariman's death by splitting the head of one mighty warrior after another.

When the sun next raised his shining shield over the city, scattering the armies of night and brightening the earth with its brilliant light, no man, woman, or child was there to see it. Those who were still alive had fled. Sam the Hero's great war club smashed the iron gates to the treasure-house, with its fabled jewels and gold. Rostam and his warriors loaded their caravan with all the treasure their camels could carry, and then they burned the fortress to ashes so that not a trace of the city remained.

Rostam returned to Seistan filled with the joy of battle. "Now, Father, surely I am ready to choose my own horse and become a warrior!" he exclaimed.

Once again, the fame of Rostam's deed soared like an eagle through Seistan, Zabul, Persia, Kabul, and Turan, soon reaching the ears of Sam the Hero and King Manuchehr. However, while Seistan was celebrating its new hero, the Persian king's wise men revealed that it was written in the stars in the heavens that Manuchehr, having seen one hundred twenty summers, was about to die. It came to pass that Sam the Hero also died.

Rostam chooses his horse and restores Persia's autonomy.

The king of Turan soon learned that Manuchehr's young and inexperienced son had inherited the throne of Persia and that Sam, son of Nariman, had died. Ambition flooded his heart. He put his son, Afrasyab, who was a formidable foe, in charge of a Tatar army so large and so strong that it crossed the Oxus River and covered Persian soil like ants and locusts. No Persian warrior could stop its progress, and so it came to pass that Afrasyab beheaded Manuchehr's son and put himself on the throne as king of Persia.

Rostam pleaded with his father for permission to rescue Persia, but Zal was reluctant to send his young son against such a seasoned warrior. "I do not want to listen to the tales of heroes," Rostam proclaimed. "I want to be the hero of those tales! Sam the Hero's war club makes men's blood explode into such showers that you would think the clouds were raining blood! My spear shines like the bright blade of the sun, and it can draw forth a river of blood from a rock! All I need is my grandfather's great war club and a great horse!"

So it came to pass that Rostam tested the horses of Zabul and Kabul for one of such stature and strength that it could bear his weight when he rode it armed for combat. Not one, however, could withstand the pressure of his hand upon its back.

Finally, Rostam spied a colt whose hide shone like the sun's bright shield. It was clear from watching him that he possessed the height and speed of a racing camel, the strength of an elephant, and the courage of a lion. His eyes blazed with the fire of intelligence, and his hooves were like iron.

"To whom does that wonderful colt belong?" Rostam asked the old herdsman. "And what can you tell me about him?"

"I have no idea who owns him, for he and his mare have not been branded," the old herdsman replied. "The two of them have been following our horses, but the best warriors have been unable to lasso the colt without encountering the mare, and she can tear the skin from a leopard and the heart from a lion! We call the colt Rakhsh (Lightning) because his hide flashes like the sun's bright rays in water, and he is as swift as fire. He is the perfect match for Prince Rostam!"

Rostam silently agreed. As swiftly as an arrow flies forth from a warrior's bow, he lassoed the colt. The mare charged madly upon him and was preparing to seize his head between her teeth and crush him to death with her hooves when Rostam shouted his lion's battle cry with a roar that made the mountains tremble in terror. The mare stopped in surprise and fear, and swift as fire in a gale-wind, Rostam hit her on the head with his clenched fist, causing her to retreat.

"What price are you asking for this colt?" he asked the old herdsman, "for I must have him!"

"Your actions reveal that you must be Prince Rostam, and if indeed you are he, then Rakhsh's price is the land of Persia!" the old herdsman declared. "Wipe away our tears by destroying the Turanian evil which has descended upon us. Together, the two of you will surely save us!"

"Yes, Rakhsh!" Rostam exclaimed. "You will be my throne, and together, we will accomplish great deeds!" Then, to the old herdsman he said, "May Urmazd bless you, old man, and may he bless us as well! With his help, we will pay your price!"

So it came to pass that Dastan, son of Sam the Hero, put Rostam in command of a great Persian army. While Afrasyab feasted complacently, fearing neither a boy warrior nor his old father, Rostam rescued the wise and courageous young Kay Kobad from his obscure home on Mount Elburz. Then, together with Dastan and the other great Persian warriors, Kobad and Rostam set out to restore Persia to the Persians and reclaim the Persian throne and crown for King Kobad.

War flared up like fire in a gale-wind. The Turanian warriors fled from Rostam on the battle-plain as sheep flee in panic from the ravenous wolf. Wielding his lariat, his sword, and Sam the Hero's great war club, Rostam swept across the plain like a fiery-tongued dragon whose breath scorched the earth to ashes. Each time he attacked the Tatars, his sword severed more than a thousand heads, which fell upon the battle-plain like dry old leaves in the winds of autumn and dyed the earth blood-red. And just as these autumn winds blow the leaves off the willow tree, so battle-axes battered both helmets and heads off the warriors. The battle-plain soon became a sea of blood, with waves of arrows, spears, and swords. Like ships, horses floated until they sank. The Persian warriors began to call their young chieftain Rostam the Mighty, or "Tahamtan," because of his gigantic stature and strength.

Secure in his strength and skill, Tahamtan now begged Zal to point out Afrasyab, for he longed to meet him in single combat. However, despite his amazement and delight at his son's prowess, Zal feared for his young lion-cub.

"Be as wise as you are courageous, my son!" Zal advised. "Afrasyab is as strong as ten of the mightiest warriors, and he is as quick as a racing camel! He fights from his saddle like a fiery-tongued dragon, with the fury of the lion and the crocodile. In terror, mountains formed of rock or iron melt into water upon hearing his name! When you see him, you will know him! For his banner is as black as night, and his iron helmet and armor are as black as Death!"

"Do not fear for my life, Father!" Rostam exclaimed, undaunted. "Urmazd smiles upon me! Afrasyab would not dare to meet me in combat, for even if he were a fiery-tongued dragon or a Demon, he would fall beneath my arm!"

So it came to pass that Rostam the Mighty, whom men call Tahamtan, went in search of Afrasyab and attacked him with the power of a thousand Demons. He grasped the Tatar chieftain by the waist and flung him from his horse, intending to drag him to Kay Kobad, but Afrasyab's belt broke, enabling his warriors to rescue him.

The Turanian forces then retreated from Persian soil, and Afrasyab pledged that his forces would remain on the Turanian side of the Oxus River. King Kobad rewarded Rostam the Mighty with a golden crown and throne and the title "Champion of the World."

Rostam performs "The Seven Stages."

Kay Kobad's eyes had seen a hundred summers as the king of Persia when his death put his son, Kay Kavus, upon the Persian throne. The new king determined to conquer the Demon kingdom of Mazanderan even though the Demons possessed great powers of magic and sorcery. All weapons, wisdom, and even gifts of wealth were useless against this people. And the wisdom of White-Haired Zal, son of Sam the Hero, was unable to dissuade the Persian king.

Kavus told Zal, "Pillar of Persia, I am braver of heart and more powerful than the Persian kings of old. You and Rostam stay here and protect my kingdom. I want only warriors whose hearts are set upon winning glory to accompany me, and the best warriors among the Persians have already volunteered!"

So it came to pass that Kay Kavus's warriors destroyed the enchanted city of Mazanderan, changing a flowering land into a desert and slaughtering its inhabitants. Meanwhile Kavus himself watched from a safe distance.

However, it also came to pass that the great White Demon—the most powerful and dreaded of the master magicians, and the one who could charm the stars in the heavens—heard of the Persian invasion, and his heart flooded with fury. Swift as clouds before a storm, and with the roar of the River Nile and the strength of a snow-capped mountain, he wrapped Kay Kavus and his warriors in a heavy black cloud. He then descended upon them in the form of a great hailstorm, which pelted the helpless Persians to death with knifelike stones. Those who survived—including wise old Gudarz, his son Giv, other warrior-chiefs, and Kay Kavus himself—had become blind and were now imprisoned in Mazanderan.

In time it came to pass that news of the Persian king's desperate position reached Seistan. "If my eyes had not seen two hundred summers, I would go forth myself and rescue Kay Kavus from the dragon's den! But this is not the task for an old warrior! Therefore, you must go in my place, Rostam!" Zal declared. "Wrap your leopard-skin armor around your chest, take your grandfather's great war club and your sword, and with Rakhsh win lasting honor and fame by delivering the king of Persia from the White Demon!

"Two roads lead to that enchanted land," Zal explained. "Both are difficult and dangerous. The longer way is safer, but vengeance is successful only if it is as swift as an arrow sent forth from a warrior's bow. Therefore, I must advise you to take the shorter route. It is a journey of only seven days, but the path is paved with peril. You must defeat seven successive foes—among them, lions, Demons, and sorcerers—and they destroy everyone who dares to choose that route!

"May Urmazd bring you safely back to me," Zal concluded. "But if it is written in the stars in the heavens that you are destined to be killed by the great White Demon, you can do nothing to change your fate. Sooner or later, Death's door swings wide for everyone who breathes the wind of life, and he who leaves behind him a trail of honor and glory is most blessed!"

"Do not fear for my life, Father!" Rostam exclaimed, undaunted. "Urmazd smiles upon the warrior whose goal is to free his king! If the great White Demon dares to meet me in combat, he will surely fall beneath my arm!"

So it came to pass that Rostam the Mighty, whom men call Tahamtan, set out alone with Rakhsh upon this perilous journey.

The First Stage

Rostam traveled until the sun's bright shield sank from sight. Then he camped upon a plain where he could hunt and feast upon the wild donkey. Exhausted, he removed his leopard-skin armor from his chest, set Rakhsh to pasture, and lay down to sleep with his head upon his shield and with his helmet, sword, lariat, and Sam the Hero's war club at his side.

It soon came to pass that a huge, fierce lion returned to his nearby den. Attracted to Rostam by the smell of roasted flesh, the lion came upon Rakhsh and attacked him. Rakhsh fought back with his hooves and his teeth. The noise of their struggle belatedly awakened Rostam, whose eyes opened to find that Rakhsh was stomping on the lion's lifeless body.

"Oh, Rakhsh!" he exclaimed. "I know that your heart and fear are strangers, but do not be so foolish as to fight my foes alone! You might be killed! Instead, alert me to whatever dangers I face! It is far better that we should risk our lives together, for I cannot reach Mazanderan without you!"

The Second Stage

When the sun next raised his shining shield, scattering the armies of night and brightening the earth with its brilliant light, Rostam and Rakhsh had to cross a vast, barren desert with neither trees for protection nor water for sustenance. Even birds fled the sun's bright blade on this perilous route.

Knowing that Rakhsh was faring no better than he was, Rostam the Mighty finally succumbed to the heat and his parching thirst. He prayed to Urmazd for his blessing and divine protection, since he was on his way to rescue King Kavus and his great warriors. Then, fearing that he was going to be food for wolves despite his prayers, in despair Tahamtan lay down to die.

Suddenly he heard footsteps. He opened his eyes to see a fat ram wandering across his path. He and Rakhsh got to their feet and followed the ram to an oasis, only to find that, quick as dust in the wind, the ram had disappeared. Rostam thanked Urmazd for the miracle, and then he and Rakhsh refreshed themselves with water and food.

The Third Stage

When the sun's bright shield sank from sight, Rostam, exhausted from the day's adventure, removed his leopard-skin armor from his chest, set Rakhsh to pasture, and lay down to sleep with his head upon his shield and with his helmet, sword, lariat, and Sam the Hero's war club at his side.

He then said to Rakhsh, "Now remember what I told you! I know that your heart and fear are strangers, but do not be so foolish as to fight my foes alone! You might be killed! Instead, alert me to whatever dangers I face! It is far better that we should risk our lives together, for I cannot reach Mazanderan without you!"

However, Rostam did not know how soon Rakhsh would need to remember these words. Rostam had inadvertently chosen to sleep near the den of a monstrous dragon, eighty yards long, which guarded the desert path so fiercely that no elephant, lion, or even Demon dared to approach its den. Even the birds chose a different route, for the fiery-tongued dragon's poison could snare an eagle high in the heavens.

Twice Rakhsh smelled the dragon's fiery breath in the darkness, and twice he noisily neighed and stamped his feet in an attempt to awaken his master, but each time his noise caused the dragon to withdraw from sight before Tahamtan awakened. The first time Rostam thought that Rakhsh had needlessly awakened him, he flared up like fire in a gale-wind. The second time roused him to fury like a wolf.

"You are awakening me without cause, Rakhsh!" he exclaimed. "And I need my sleep! I neither see nor hear any danger! If you do this to me again, I fear I will have to kill you! And I do not want to go alone to Mazanderan!"

Once again, Tahamtan went back to sleep, and once again Rakhsh smelled the dragon's fiery breath in the darkness. Rakhsh risked

Rostam's uncontrollable rage and once again noisily neighed and stamped his feet in an attempt to awaken his master. Tahamtan awakened with fury in his heart against his friend, but fortunately, this time Urmazd awakened the sun who, quick as the flames of fire, raised his shining shield, scattering the armies of night and brightening the earth with its brilliant light.

So it came to pass that Tahamtan suddenly spied the huge monster lurking in the shadows. Quick as clouds before a storm, he put on his armor, unsheathed his sword, and rushed to the attack, shouting the battle cry of the lion with a roar that made the mountains tremble in terror.

The dragon opened its fiery mouth and said, "Whoever you are, prepare to have your name removed from the lists of the living! For nothing can withstand my fire!" Undaunted, Rostam continued to approach, exclaiming, "Your words and your fire do not frighten me!"

The two met in dreadful combat, and it came to pass that the dragon curled its body around the hero and prepared to crush him to death. Seeing that Rostam was in mortal danger, Rakhsh attacked the monster from the rear and, with his teeth, tore its scaly hide from its flesh. Swift as the wind, Rostam then raised his sword and sliced off the dragon's head, flooding the earth with its boiling blood.

The hero apologized to Rakhsh for misunderstanding his warnings. He then thanked Urmazd for permitting him to rid the earth of such a scourge. "A lion's strength, a dragon's rage, and the terrors of a dry and burning desert are nothing against your protecting arm!" he declared. "You alone are the source of my strength and skill!"

The Fourth Stage

The sun's bright shield was sinking from sight when Rostam the Mighty and Rakhsh arrived in the beautiful land of the magicians. There, they suddenly came upon a table set up in a cool, shaded area, which contained tropical fruits, roasted venison, bread, salt, and wine. Rostam ate and drank without questioning the source of his good fortune, and joy so filled his heart that he picked up the lyre that also lay upon the table and played it. His singing attracted a beautiful maiden to his side. Perfumed like a spring flower garden, she possessed soft, dark eyes, skin of shell-tinted ivory, and a form appealingly hidden within a misty oriental robe.

Rostam placed a glass of wine in her hand, raised his own glass, and thanked the Creator of the World for what they were about to drink. Hearing Rostam address Urmazd, the lovely maiden immediately turned into an old hag, for a Demon's magical powers cannot withstand Urmazd's power. Then, as swiftly as an arrow flies forth from a warrior's bow, Rostam the Mighty lassoed the Demon-woman and sliced her in two with one stroke of his sword.

The Fifth Stage

When the sun next raised his shining shield, scattering the armies of night and brightening the earth with its brilliant light, Tahamtan and Rakhsh were not there to see it. They had arrived in the land of eternal darkness, where even the stars did not shine. Trusting that Urmazd would guide and protect them, Rostam continued blindly forward on Rakhsh, ever on the alert for dangers that he could not see.

Finally, they reached a beautiful land, brilliant under the sun's bright shield, with fields of golden corn waving in the cool wind. Exhausted, Rostam dismounted, removed his leopard-skin armor from his chest, set Rakhsh to pasture, and lay down to sleep with his head upon his shield and with his helmet, sword, lariat, and Sam the Hero's war club at his side.

While Tahamtan slept, the farmer became enraged to see that a strange horse was trampling and eating his corn. Beating Rostam the Mighty upon the feet with a stick, he roused the hero and ordered him to leave. Rostam responded by seizing the farmer by his ears, thus tearing them from his head. The mutilated man, ears in hand, ran to complain to his master, Aulad, who owned this fertile land. Aulad flared up like fire in a gale-wind, gathered a group of warriors, and prepared to avenge his servant. Despite Rostam's stature, Aulad remained undaunted, outraged, and roused to fury like a wolf.

"You would do well to know whom you challenge!" Rostam the Mighty declared. "The sound of my name will turn your blood to ice and stop your heart in terror! You and your warriors will fall beneath my sword like leaves in autumn winds, dyeing the earth blood-red!"

Tahamtan was as good as his word, and so it came to pass that Aulad became Rostam's prisoner. Rostam the Mighty then said to him, "Captive, I need to find the caves of the great White Demon and his warrior-chiefs, and also the place where he has imprisoned the king of Persia and his warriors. Therefore, I have a proposal for you. If you agree to show me the caves of the Demons, and if you tell me the best way to kill them and to free my people, I will reward you by making you king of Mazanderan! However, if you make any attempt to deceive me, quick as clouds before a storm, the earth will feed on your blood!"

"I accept your proposal," Aulad replied. "The home of the great White Demon lies between two dark, tall mountains in a region known as the Seven Mountains. There, the White Demon and his warriors live deep within two hundred caves, and there, lions and twelve hundred Demons guard the mountain passes every night.

"Moreover, the way to these passes is filled with danger," he added. "You must cross both a rocky desert and a great river, which is patrolled by an army of Demon warriors who guard the passage into Mazanderan.

"Mighty as you are in battle, with your huge arms, your swift sword, and your great war club, you will find the White Demon to be a formidable enemy!" Aulad exclaimed. "The very sound of his voice makes the mountains tremble like reeds in a summer breeze! And even if Urmazd helps you conquer the Terrible One, his Demon warriors number in the thousands, with no coward among them. The Demons fight with the courage of the lion, the strength of the elephant, the skill of the fiery-tongued dragon, and the fury of the crocodile. I do not see how you, alone, can hope to overcome such an enemy!"

To these words Rostam the Mighty replied, "Fearful one, just show me the way, and I will show you what one man who has the support of Urmazd can do!"

So it came to pass that Rostam the Mighty and Rakhsh set off toward their sixth adventure, following Aulad both day and night without rest. They finally stopped at midnight, just outside Mazanderan, where Kay Kavus had been conquered. Blazing fires brightened the night sky, and they could hear the clamor that announced the arrival of Arzhang, the great White Demon's most powerful chieftain.

When the sun next raised his shining shield, scattering the armies of night and brightening the earth with its brilliant light, Rostam the Mighty wrapped his leopard-skin armor around his chest and rode toward Mazanderan. As he approached Arzhang's camp, he shouted his lion's battle cry with a roar that made the mountains tremble in terror. When the Demon-chief charged out of his tent, Tahamtan seized him by his arms and ears, tore his head from his body, and tossed it among the terrified Demon warriors, who panicked and fled in terror like sheep from a ravenous wolf.

The Sixth Stage

Rostam now had Aulad take him to the city of Mazanderan, where Kay Kavus and his men were imprisoned. Once Rostam the Mighty had freed them, the blind king said to him, "Beloved of Urmazd! Go as swiftly as fire in a gale-wind to the Seven Mountains and capture the great White Demon before that hideous monster receives word of you or Rakhsh and seeks revenge for the death of Arzhang.

"If you succeed in destroying the Demon warriors who guard the passes to the Seven Mountains, you will then come to a deep and dark mountain cave," he explained. "Terrifying monsters guard its entrance, for the great White Demon lives within its depths. Those who are wise about cures have told me that three drops of warm blood from his heart placed in our eyes is the only cure for our blindness.

"And so, Beloved of Urmazd, go forth and rescue us!" he concluded. "Destroy the White Demon, and put an end to our dark world. For then the tree of happiness will bloom once again in Persia, and your name will shine like the sun's bright shield among the stars in the heavens!"

So it came to pass that Rostam the Mighty and Rakhsh, led by Aulad, sped forth like arrows shot from a warrior's bow, mastering all difficulties until they arrived at the Seven Mountains. There, Demon warriors milled about the mouth of a huge cavern from which flickered a fiery red light.

Rostam now asked his guide, "What is the best way to conquer these Demon hordes?"

"Wait until the sun's bright shield is high in the heavens," Aulad replied, "for that is when all but a few of the Demons sleep, and then you can surprise them."

Rostam the Mighty followed Aulad's advice, and when the sun's bright blade blazed overhead, he stealthily approached the slumbering Demons and shouted his mighty lion's battle cry with a roar that made the mountains tremble in terror. Tahamtan was roused to fury like a wolf, and his speed, strength, and skill with his sword were so great that he killed the Demons before any of the evil creatures had time to warn the others. Those who escaped with their heads panicked and fled in terror like sheep from a ravenous wolf.

The Seventh Stage

So it came to pass that Rostam the Mighty came upon a great black hole, which he knew to be the cave of the great White Demon.

Although it was forbiddingly dark and dismal, he was not afraid, either of its black depths or of the great magical powers of its occupant. As fearless as a lion when it stalks its prey, he entered the cave, advancing blindly in the total darkness and rubbing his eyes to sharpen his sight.

Suddenly, Tahamtan heard a thunderous sound of snoring, and he sensed that the entire darkness was moving before his eyes. It came to pass that he could see a mountainous, hairy mass lying deep in slumber at the end of the cave. Shouting his lion's battle cry with a roar that made the mountains tremble in terror, Tahamtan caused the sleeping Demon to awaken shaking with fright. Swift as clouds before a storm, the monster jumped to his feet and chased the hero back into the light, where the great White Demon now became a shimmering white form.

Quick as the flames of fire and with a blood-curdling shriek, the Demon grabbed a boulder the size of a small mountain and asked, "Are you so foolish and tired of life that you dare to invade my cave? Tell me who you are so that I may know who it is I am about to destroy!"

To these words, Rostam replied, "I am Rostam the Mighty, whom men call Tahamtan! My father, Dastan, the son of Sam the Hero, has sent me here to avenge your imprisonment of the king of Persia and his valiant warriors."

The White Demon fought off a shiver of fear and hurled his boulder at Tahamtan's head. Quick as the wind, Tahamtan dodged the blow, but facing the monster's fiery eyes and foaming mouth, he knew terror for the first time in his life. Forcing himself to think only of the task at hand, and rousing himself to the fury of the wolf, Rostam wielded his sword with such strength that he sliced off one of the White Demon's feet. Out of his mind with pain, the Demon jumped upon Rostam like a mad elephant, and even the mountains trembled in terror as they watched the wrestling match. The monster and the hero tore huge hunks of flesh from each other, making the earth slimy with their blood.

Tahamtan thought to himself, "If I survive this combat, surely I will never die!" However, he forced himself to think only of the task at hand, and wrestled so well that the great White Demon feared for his own life. With renewed strength, the monster put forth one last effort, causing Tahamtan to pray to Urmazd for divine protection, renewed strength, and victory. Then, summoning all of his remaining strength, Tahamtan clasped the great White Demon in his arms, raised the Demon high above his head, and hurled him to the ground with such force that the wind of life fled from the Demon's battered body. Tahamtan beheaded the monster and tied the head to his saddle as a trophy of his victory. Then he tore the Demon's heart from his crushed and mangled body.

Before returning to the city of Mazanderan, Rostam cleansed himself and thanked Urmazd for his victory. "Without your divine blessing, a man is nothing!" he exclaimed. "And with it, he cannot be conquered!"

He then returned with Aulad to the Persian captives and restored their sight. So it came to pass that Rostam the Mighty, having completed the Seven Stages, won lasting fame among all who walk the earth.

Rostam conquers Mazanderan and rescues Kay Kavus.

Aulad was ready to ascend the throne of Mazanderan, but the last of the great magicians, the Demon-king of Mazanderan, still lived. Although the Persian king and his warriors had burned the city of Mazanderan to ashes, the Demon-king was not intimidated. He responded to Kay Kavus's demand for homage and tribute by declaring war.

"I have no reason to fear an empire that is weaker than my own!" the Demon-king exclaimed. "My valiant warriors will level the hills of Persia!"

So it came to pass that war flared up like fire in a gale-wind. For seven days, the air was dark with dust, and swords flashed like lightning in a stormy sky. Just as autumn winds blow the leaves off the willow tree, so battle-axes battered both helmets and heads off the warriors. The battle-plain soon became a sea of blood, with waves of arrows, spears, and swords. Like ships, horses floated until they sank. Yet, neither side could claim a victory. So on the eighth day, Tahamtan challenged the Demon-king to single combat, and he accepted.

The Demon-king was a frightful-looking adversary, with the neck and tusks of a wild boar. However, Tahamtan was undaunted. Fighting with spear and sword, he gained the advantage and dealt the Demon-king what should have been a mortal blow. However, quick as dust in the wind, the Demon-king of Mazanderan escaped death by turning himself into a gigantic boulder.

King Kavus commanded his warriors to drag the boulder into his tent and set it before his throne. However, the combined effort of the strongest Persian warriors, even with the aid of ropes, could not budge it.

Finally, Tahamtan bent over, grasped the boulder in his great hands, and strode, swift as the flames of fire, across the hills to the entrance to the Persian king's tent. There, he threw it down upon the earth and exclaimed, "Cowardly magician, if you do not come forth from this rock as swiftly as fire in a gale-wind, I will pound you and your hiding place into dust with my war club, and I will scatter that dust to the four winds!"

At these words, the Demon-king's heart trembled with terror. And so it came to pass that he emerged and stood before Tahamtan who, as quickly as an arrow flies forth from a warrior's bow, lassoed him and took him before the Persian king. Kay Kavus ordered his warriors to behead the evil creature and then chop his body into a thousand pieces.

The death of the Demon-king brought the war against Mazanderan to an end. King Kavus rewarded every Persian warrior for his heroic deeds and gave the throne of Mazanderan to Aulad. Rostam the Mighty returned home to Seistan with the highest honors and priceless treasures.

Before long, it came to pass that Kay Kavus went to war against the king of Hamaveran. The Persian king not only won the war, but he won the defeated king's beautiful daughter, who insisted on marrying Kay Kavus despite her father's wishes.

The king of Hamaveran, having lost his daughter, who was the pearl of his heart, and his kingdom, which was the pride of his heart, plotted revenge. He invited Kay Kavus to return to Hamaveran as his guest, and despite his wife's warnings, Kavus accepted.

Kavus's visit ended with his imprisonment in a remote fortress located on a high mountain and defended by a thousand warriors. When the daughter of the king of Hamaveran remained loyal to her husband, her father imprisoned her in the same dungeon. Tahamtan, always the Shield of Persia, invaded Hamaveran with an army, defeated the king and his allies, and rescued Kavus and his wife.

Then it came to pass that King Kavus listened to Ahriman's wicked whisperings. "Why should I be satisfied when I rule only all things on earth?" he asked himself. "If I could learn the secrets of the sun, the moon, the stars—and even Urmazd's secrets!—why then

I would be king of heaven as well as earth! One difficulty, only, stands in my way. I will have to find a way to fly!"

The Persian king's craftsmen created a special type of throne, which would be carried aloft by four bound eagles. First, a protruding spear would be attached to each of the four corners of the throne. An eagle would then be bound to each spear in such a way that it would still be able to have full use of its wings. Finally, goat flesh for the eagles to eat would be attached to the point of each spear, but placed beyond each eagle's reach. If the device worked, in straining to reach the meat, the eagles would have to flap their wings, and that motion would transport the chariot high into the heavens.

The marvelous device worked as planned and carried King Kavus high into the clouds. However, it came to pass that the eagles became famished, and when they had become exhausted with their attempt to grab their food, they fell to earth. The throne bearing the Persian king fell with them, landing in a desert in the province of Cathay, in China. Tahamtan, always the Shield of Persia, rescued the physically uninjured but very embarrassed Kay Kavus.

Rostam kills the Demon Akvan and rescues Giv's son.

Many years later, during the time when Kay Khosrow was king of Persia, it came to pass that the king asked Rostam the Mighty—whom men still called Tahamtan—to destroy the powerful Demon Akvan. Akvan would transform himself into a wild donkey and invade inhabited areas, where he would destroy crops and kill people as well as animals. Then, before anyone could capture him, he would become invisible and vanish from the scene.

At first Tahamtan, too, was unsuccessful. For three days and nights, he chased after the Demon Akvan. However, his lariat, bow, sword, and spear were useless, for the Demon always disappeared at the point when Tahamtan expected that, this time, he would surely capture him. Finally, exhausted from his continuous effort, Rostam gave up the chase. He removed his leopard-skin armor from his chest, set Rakhsh to pasture, and lay down to sleep with his head upon his shield and with his helmet, sword, lariat, and war club at his side.

While Tahamtan slept, the Demon Akvan quickly changed himself into a great wind and, swift as the flames of fire, dug up the earth on which Rostam slept, placed Rostam and his earthen bed upon his head, and flew off with Rostam as his prisoner. When Tahamtan awakened to find himself on the wind's shoulders, the Demon Akvan asked him to choose his death—either by being plunged into the sea or by being dropped upon a mountainside.

Realizing that Akvan would choose the opposite of what he requested, Tahamtan replied, "The people of China say that he who dies at sea will lose his soul to the ocean and be denied entrance into heaven. So toss me upon a mountainside. I would rather be food for lions and leopards!"

Just as Tahamtan had anticipated, Akvan tossed him to the crocodiles in the sea. Tahamtan swam toward shore for hours before he finally reached land, beheading one blood-thirsty crocodile after another with his sword. Arriving safely, he thanked Urmazd for his survival and set off to search for Rakhsh. When he had found him, the Demon Akvan reappeared and challenged Tahamtan to single combat, expecting that he would be too exhausted to save himself.

"Unless you are made of stone, brass, or iron, you cannot conquer a Demon!" Akvan exclaimed. "So prepare to leave the world of light for lasting darkness!"

However, Tahamtan shouted his lion's battle cry with a roar that made the mountains tremble in terror and, as swiftly as an arrow flies forth from a warrior's bow, he lassoed the Demon Akvan. Then, before Akvan could use his magic to vanish, Tahamtan beheaded him with a mighty blow of his sword. Once again, Tahamtan thanked Urmazd for his victory, and then he took the Demon Akvan's head back to Kay Khosrow.

In time, it then came to pass that King Khosrow called upon Rostam the Mighty to rescue Bizhan, the young hero who was the son of Giv, Rostam's warrior-friend. Manizha, one of Afrasyab's daughters, had met Bizhan and, choosing the young Persian prince for her husband, the Tatar princess had drugged him and had brought him with her to her father's palace in Turan.

Afrasyab's heart had flooded with fury and shame when he heard of this and, listening to Ahriman's wicked whisperings, the king of Turan had decided to imprison Bizhan, head-first and in chains, in a deep pit. He had commanded his warriors to use their war elephants to bring, from the forests of China, the great boulder that had belonged to Akvan the Demon. Once they had imprisoned Bizhan in the pit, they had covered the opening with this boulder. Afrasyab had then cast off his daughter, condemning her to remain by the boulder as her lover's sole companion and to find a way, if she could, to supply him with food and drink.

Rostam realized that he would need to be cunning as well as courageous in order to rescue Bizhan. He left a thousand warriors to wait at the border between Persia and Turan, while he and seven hand-picked warriors, all disguised as merchants, led a camel caravan containing luxurious clothing, jewels, and carpets into Turan.

It came to pass that Manizha heard about the caravan and told the Persian merchants what had happened to Giv's son. After the disguised Rostam learned her identity, Manizha took him and his seven warriors to the pit where Bizhan was imprisoned. However, the warriors could not move Akvan the Demon's boulder from the opening of the pit. Therefore, Tahamtan prayed to Urmazd for youthful strength and, swift as the wind, he lifted the boulder himself. Then, quick as an arrow shot forth from a warrior's bow, he tossed it back into the forests of China, causing the earth to tremble far and wide from that mighty blow.

Bizhan and Manizha returned to Persia with the caravan, while Tahamtan, who had become roused to fury like a wolf, avenged Bizhan's imprisonment by breaking into Afrasyab's palace with his seven warriors, killing everyone in sight, and taking its treasures. Once again, Afrasyab panicked and fled from Rostam like a sheep from a ravenous wolf. And once again, war flared up between Iran and Turan like fire in a gale-wind.

First, Rostam led the Persian attack; then Gudarz led a similar attack; and finally, King Khosrow led the last and greatest attack. Just as autumn winds blow the leaves off the willow tree, so battle-axes battered both helmets and heads off the warriors. The battle-plain soon became a sea of blood, with waves of arrows, spears, and swords. Like ships, horses floated until they sank. Finally, the Persian warriors emerged victorious. The Turanian warriors panicked and fled from Kay Khosrow like sheep from a ravenous wolf. Afrasyab was captured and brought before King Khosrow, who beheaded the king of Turan. However, then Khosrow gave Persia's great enemy an honorable burial.

Rostam's half brother plots his death.

It came to pass that, in his old age, Rostam's father loved a slave in his house who bore him a son whom he named Shaghad. However, the wise men of Seistan revealed that it was written in the stars in the heavens that Shaghad would live a short, evil life, that he would destroy the house of Nariman in Seistan, and that he would bring trouble to Persia.

Zal was fearful of this prophecy, but he kept the infant and reared him carefully, doing his best to be certain that the child learned to be honest and loyal toward his family and the king of Persia.

When Shaghad had grown to become a young man, he married the princess of Kabul, whose father had to pay Rostam the annual tribute of a bull's hide as a token of his subservience to the house of Nariman. The king of Kabul hoped that the marriage of his daughter to Dastan's son would have the political advantage of removing any tribute, with its stain upon his own sovereignty. However, when that did not occur, the king listened to Ahriman's wicked whisperings and found a willing listener and a welcome heart in Shaghad, who had no love for his half brother. Shaghad invited the king to become famous by joining him in plotting Tahamtan's death.

So it came to pass that as part of this plot, it appeared that the king of Kabul offended Shaghad at a great feast. With the pretense of great outrage, Shaghad then returned to Seistan and complained to Rostam. Because Rostam was fond of his half brother and considered the king of Kabul to be arrogant, he was very willing to confront the king and avenge the king's verbal attack on Shaghad's honor.

When Tahamtan arrived in Kabul with his brother Zavareh and a group of warriors from Seistan, the king prostrated himself before him in sorrow and repentance. Pleased with such humility, Rostam did not suspect that treachery lurked beneath the king's honeyed tongue. He and Zavareh agreed on behalf of the entire company to become the king's guests and to join their hosts on a hunting expedition.

So it came to pass that when the group from Seistan set out on the day's entertainment, Shaghad accompanied Rostam on foot in order to show him the way. Suddenly, Rakhsh smelled freshly turned earth and reared in protest, unwilling to proceed. Rostam, seeing only a forest floor of earth and greenery, thought that Rakhsh had become afraid and commanded him to move forward. When Rakhsh refused, fury flooded Rostam's heart. Quick as the flames of fire, and for the first time in his life, Rostam struck his steed sharply with his whip.

Leaping forward in surprise and anger, Rakhsh fell with Rostam into one of many cleverly disguised deep pits, which were lined with protruding sharp edges and points of daggers, swords, and spears.

The bodies of both Rakhsh and Tahamtan were stabbed, slashed, and torn with fatal wounds as they found themselves impaled on this bed of barbs. Their struggle to escape increased their injuries, and only Tahamtan was able to drag his body up to the edge of the pit, where the world turned black before his eyes.

Tahamtan opened his eyes to see Shaghad triumphantly smiling down at him. "So you are responsible for this evil deed!" Rostam exclaimed. "And what was written in the stars has come to pass!"

"Do not blame me!" Shaghad replied. "Urmazd is punishing you for all the warriors you have killed!"

"Why, what has happened here?" the king of Kabul asked, coming upon the dying Rostam as if he were surprised. "I am ashamed that Tahamtan should die such a degrading death when he is my guest! I will send for my physicians!" he exclaimed reassuringly. "I am sure that they can heal your wounds!"

To these words, Rostam replied, "Most clever king! Death will now come to you as swiftly as an arrow flies forth from a warrior's bow! When my son, Faramarz the Brave, learns of your treachery, quick as the flames of fire he will avenge my death!"

Then, weary and weak with his impending death, Rostam turned his head toward Shaghad and said, "I see Death standing by, ready to claim my spirit. I ask only one favor of you. Prepare my bow and give me one or two arrows so that, as I die, I can kill any wolf or vulture that would feast on my still-living flesh. Do this, my brother, for the sake of the father we share!"

So it came to pass that Shaghad removed Rostam's great bow from its case, strung it, fitted an arrow to the string, and with a smile, placed the weapon in his dying brother's hands. Suddenly, he saw Tahamtan's eyes sharpen and his hands tighten on his bow. Terrified, Shaghad fled in panic, as swiftly as clouds before a storm, to hide behind a great dead tree.

Tahamtan summoned all of his remaining strength and sight to raise his bow, draw its string to his chest, and aim his arrow at the figure who stood cowering behind the great trunk. The arrow flew, swift as the flames of fire, and with such force that it pierced the tree's trunk from one side to the other and lodged in the treacherous heart of the man who hid behind it.

So it came to pass that Rostam met Death with joy and contentment in his heart. He spent his last living moments in prayer to the Creator of the World, saying, "Thank you, Urmazd, for giving me enough life and power to avenge my own death!"

Zavareh and all but one of the other warriors who had accompanied Rostam perished in the other pits. That one warrior fled, quick as the wind, to Seistan, where he told the tale to White-Haired Zal. Rostam's aged father tore his clothes and covered his head with ashes as he mourned the loss of his two sons. "Would that I had died in Rostam's place!" he exclaimed.

It then came to pass that Zal sent his grandson Faramarz with Seistan's warriors to Kabul. Faramarz the Brave and his warriors killed the king of Kabul and his entire family and burned the capital city to the ground, leaving a desert in its place. Then they retrieved the skeletons of Rostam, Zavareh, and Rakhsh—birds and beasts already having devoured their flesh—and they transported their remains back to Seistan.

White-Haired Zal and Faramarz built a great tomb to house Rostam's and Rakhsh's remains so that the name and fame of Rostam the Mighty, whom men called Tahamtan, and his horse Rakhsh would live as long as those who walk the earth could see it. And a great wail arose from the lands of Seistan, Zabul, Kabul, and Persia, soaring to the sun, moon, and stars in the heavens and to Urmazd above all. For the Champion of the World and the Shield of Persia breathed no more. Death had claimed the last and greatest of Persia's valiant heroes and had brought an end to Persia's glory for years to come.

Who among mortals can escape Fate? Who among us can use our wisdom, or our courage, or our strength, or our skill to this end? No one. What is written in the stars in the heavens is sure to come! So it was with Rostam. So it is with all who walk the earth!

THE TRAGEDY OF SOHRAB

Tahmineh wins a Persian hero for a husband.

In a time long past, in the small Tatar kingdom of Samengan, in Turan, Princess Tahmineh longed to marry Rostam the Mighty, whom men call Tahamtan. It was a dream that could only remain a fantasy—for Rostam was Persia's greatest hero, while Tahmineh's father owed allegiance to Persia's great enemy, the king of Turan.

Although Tahmineh's dream was a fantasy, she was content to live in the world of dreams. No suitor for her hand in marriage pleased her. Instead, she fed her hungry heart with Rostam's adventures. She collected every tale of Tahamtan's courage, strength, and skill. And she reconstructed them in her mind until she knew them so well that she herself could have been present when the feats occurred.

The king of Samengan treasured his daughter, and he knew the ways of her mind and her heart as well as he knew his own. When it came to pass that Tahmineh turned down yet another fine suitor, her father said to her, "Dear one, you are the fairest flower in a king's garden! I only wish that I could find a way for Rostam the Mighty to meet you, for to know you is to love you! However, you know as well as I that Persian fruit does not grow on Samengan's trees!

"And what if, by some chance, Rostam were to meet you and love you? What then?" the king asked his daughter. "Surely, Tahmineh, you do not expect that Tahamtan would remain here in Samengan! And surely you do not expect that he would take an ally of Turan back with him to Seistan! I fear that you have no choice but to put aside this dream and find another prince—a real one—who will make your heart sing!"

"No, Father! I am not yet ready to give up my dream!" responded Tahmineh. "Urmazd may hear my prayers and bring Rostam to Samengan! And if that comes to pass, I am certain that Rostam will love me! Then, Father, despite our obligations to the king of Turan, Rostam may take me back to Seistan with him! After all, it may be written in the stars that I will give birth to Rostam's child! If so, what a joy that would be! Just imagine how heroic the son of the world's greatest hero would be!"

"Tahmineh, flower of my heart! Beware! You are letting dreams flood your mind and drown all common sense! I fear that this will only cause your heart to flood with pain!" the king exclaimed.

"No, Father!" Tahmineh responded. "These are not just dreams! Such things really happen! You know as well as I that Rostam's father loved Rudabeh against the will of the Persian king—until it was written in the stars that the world's greatest hero would come from their marriage! Now, if Urmazd could smile upon Rudabeh, then he can also smile upon me!" declared Tahmineh. "And, Father, if Rostam loved me and yet he returned to Seistan without me, it would be enough for me to have received his love!"

"All right, Daughter! I will leave you to your dreams!" Tahmineh's father replied. "And maybe it will come to pass that you will meet Tahamtan after all! If it is written in the stars in the heavens, then it will surely come! And if it is not written there, then in time another fine hero will surely make your heart sing!"

This exchange of words was still fresh in the minds of the king of Samengan and his daughter when it came to pass that Rostam the Mighty—whom men call Tahamtan—went hunting wild donkeys in the wilderness near the border between Persia and Samengan, in Turan. At the end of each day, when the sun's bright shield sank from sight, he would roast his catch for his dinner. Then, he would remove his leopard-skin armor from his chest, set his horse Rakhsh (Lightning) to pasture, and lie down to sleep with his head upon his shield. He would put his helmet, sword, lariat, and his grandfather Sam the Hero's war club within reach at his side.

Now, hearing that Tahamtan was in the area, swift as fire in a gale-wind, Rumor spread the news that the Persian sun was shining on the kingdom of Samengan. Consequently, it came to pass that one night while Rostam slept, seven of the king's warriors set about to earn a fine reward by capturing Rakhsh and bringing him to the royal stables, where the king's grooms wanted him to sire a colt.

Rakhsh gave these Turanian warriors a fight for their money. Warned by the sound of a lariat, he avoided its noose and, swift as fire, sprang upon his foe like a lion, killing two warriors with a swipe of his forefeet and a third by biting off the man's head. However, the remaining warriors managed to rope, blindfold, and gag him, and so it came to pass that Rakhsh entered the royal stables of Samengan.

Rostam awoke, amazed and dismayed when even his thunderous voice drew no response from Rakhsh. "How humiliating!" he thought. "I can see the Tatars' amusement when I enter Samengan on foot, wearing my helmet and armor, and carrying my spear, sword, and Sam the Hero's great war club. 'Look at the mighty Tahamtan now!' they will jeer. 'The Champion of the World cannot even protect his own horse!'"

Rostam, his heart flooded with fury, followed Rakhsh's tracks into the city and went straight to the palace of the king. The king of Samengan, who knew nothing about Rakhsh's disappearance, did his best to reassure Rostam and allay his anger. "We will soon find him," he said consolingly, "for Rakhsh cannot remain hidden any more than you, in combat, could become lost to men's sight! And when we discover the thief, we will place him in your hands to do whatever you choose with him! Meanwhile, please accept our hospitality as our honored guest!"

And so it came to pass that the king placated Rostam, entertained him royally at dinner, and gave him luxurious quarters in which to sleep. Later that night, Rostam was awakened by the sound of women's voices. He opened his eyes upon the loveliest maiden he had ever seen, surely the fairest flower in a king's garden.

"Am I dreaming, or are you real?" Rostam asked. "And if you are real, who are you? And what do you want from me that you have come here in the middle of the night? Lovely vision, speak!"

To these words, the maiden replied, "Oh, hero of matchless fame! I am Tahmineh, daughter of the king of Samengan. Lions and leopards are my ancestral relatives.

"Pity me!" she exclaimed, "for my love for you has conquered my good breeding and my good judgment! You are the first man—except for the men in my family—who has ever seen me unveiled, or who has even heard my voice!

"I have long heard of your great deeds," she declared. "I know that your arm is as swift as the wind and as strong as the elephant! I know that the earth trembles in terror beneath your feet! And I know that a hungry eagle, hovering over its prey, will forgo its food in fright at the sight of your sword!

"I know that you and fear are strangers," she added. "I have heard how you traveled to Mazanderan alone and conquered a monstrous dragon and the great White Demon! I know that you are the Shield of Persia! I have heard how you rescued King Kavus from both Mazanderan and from Hamaveran, and how you found the king when his flight into the heavens ended in disaster.

"I have been enchanted by the tales of your heroic deeds," she explained, "and your glory and fame have won my love! Every maiden longs to meet the hero of her dreams! And so I have longed to meet you, to see your face and your form.

"I would search Samengan on foot in order to lead Rakhsh before you," she exclaimed, "but he is close at hand. When I learned that you were hunting near our city—and, here, word of your actions travels as swiftly as the wind!—it seemed to me that Urmazd had heard my prayers and had brought you here just for me. It was easy for me to accomplish the rest. My servants arranged for our warriors to capture Rakhsh in order to mate him with one of the royal horses. Knowing how important Rakhsh is to you, I knew that you would follow him here!

"You are the only hero in the world for me!" Tahmineh concluded. "And if you will marry me I am yours! I have promised Urmazd that, of all the princes in the world, I will marry none but you! In the morning, if you ask my father's consent, he will surely bless our marriage. And perhaps I will bear you a son who will be like you in strength and courage and who, one day, will rule the world!"

Rostam's heart flooded with joy to hear that Rakhsh was near, and that he had won the love of a beautiful maiden—particularly one who possessed the qualities he admired in himself: courage, determination, and spirit. And so it came to pass that Rostam married Tahmineh, for the king of Samengan felt honored by an alliance with Rostam the Mighty, whom men call Tahamtan, one who was the son of Dastan, the grandson of Sam the Hero, and the great-grandson of Nariman.

Soon after the marriage, the king located Rakhsh, and Rostam, anxious to return to his life in Seistan, took a loving farewell of his wife. Before he departed, he removed his signet arm ring. The arm ring contained a gem—an onyx—that had been engraved with the form of a simurgh, the Bird of Marvel.

Giving his arm ring to Tahmineh, Rostam said, "Dear one, keep this ring for our child. If Urmazd gives us a daughter, fasten it around her curls that joy and honor may be hers. However, if we are so fortunate as to have a son, fasten it as a band around his arm as I have worn it, for this onyx is the seal of Dastan and Rostam.

"Tell our son that it is my special gift to him," Rostam explained, "and that I give it with the hope that it will give him the strength of Sam the Hero, the temperament of Dastan, and the courage of Rostam the Mighty, so that he will become a valiant warrior and perform virtuous deeds, thereby winning lasting fame."

With these words, Rostam embraced his wife, kissed her eyes and face, and departed for Seistan as swiftly as an arrow flies from a warrior's bow. Many times he would remember his joyous hours in Samengan, but his eyes would see eleven more summers before it would come to pass that he would mention his marriage.

Sohrab is born a hero's son.

When nine moons had come and gone, Tahmineh gave birth to a son whose face was as bright as the sun's shield, and whose stature resembled that of his father and Sam the Hero. Because her son smiled upon the world, Tahmineh named him Sohrab (Sunshine). Rostam was delighted with the news and sent his son jewels and gold as a birth gift.

At the age of one month, Sohrab possessed the stature of a child whose eyes had seen one summer. When he had seen three summers, he began instruction in wrestling, riding, hunting, and the use of the lariat, the bow, the war club, and the spear. By the time he had seen five summers, he displayed the courage of a lion and the strength of an elephant.

For as long as he could remember, Sohrab had gone to sleep each night to his mother's tales of the legendary heroes of Persia and of Tahamtan, that hero of heroes who always rode forth to greet adventure and combat seated upon Rakhsh, his fabulous warhorse. Night after night, the boy dreamed of his own mighty exploits in adventure and in combat. He, like Tahamtan, would become the Champion of the World, bringing glory and fame to his name, and pride to his mother and Samengan.

When Sohrab's eyes had seen ten summers, he had gained the skill of the fiery-tongued dragon. He now could outrun the fastest horse and surpass every Turanian hero in wrestling and in combat skills. He had already become as straight and tall as a young cypress tree, with the chest of a lion, the limbs of an elephant, the feet of a stag, and the voice of thunder.

So it came to pass that one day Sohrab asked Tahmineh, "Mother, who is my father that I tower over my friends and surpass even Samengan's greatest warriors in feats of strength and skill? When a friend or foe asks me to name my father, how should I reply? To remain silent proclaims my shame!

"So answer me truthfully, now," he commanded her, "for my heart bursts with fury at your long delay! And hesitate no longer! For as much as I love you, if you try to deceive me, I am prepared to kill you!" he declared.

Tahmineh smiled to hear these words. "I see that your heart burns with your father's fire!" she exclaimed. "Now let joy put out its flames! Sohrab, you are the young branch of a mighty tree, whose shadow covers the earth, and whose fame will be sung as long as mortals walk the earth to sing of it! For your father is none other than the greatest hero that the world has ever known—Rostam the Mighty, whom men call Tahamtan, the son of Dastan, and the grandson of Sam the Hero!

"When you were born," she explained, "Rostam sent you a letter and three gifts: three rubies, three gold pieces and, to adorn your arm, his own signet arm ring, which is engraved with his family's seal. All these I was to give you at the proper time. Now, they are yours!

"But you must promise to keep your identity a secret!" she continued. "And make no effort to become a hero! We look to Turan for our safety, and we owe loyalty to its mighty king. Yet Afrasyab is your father's bitter enemy, and he is a heartless foe! If he were to know who you are, he would do everything in his power to kill you as a way of punishing your father."

"I cannot keep such a secret, Mother!" Sohrab exclaimed. "Just look at my stature. I tower over any Tatar! And look at my youthful strength and skill. No seasoned warrior is my equal with weapons of war! Tell me where Tahamtan is, for I would fight at his side!"

"That I will not do, Sohrab," Tahmineh replied, "for I have lost my husband, and it would break my heart to lose you as well! Your father thinks of you as a lion cub. If he hears of your strength and skill, he will take you into his heart and home, and I cannot live without you!"

"My heart weeps with sorrow for you, Mother," Sohrab responded, "but my heart, like my father's, also longs for the glory and fame won in battle! And my fate, like my father's, is surely written in the stars in the heavens! Your most clever devices cannot change my destiny! I, too, will win glory with valiant deeds in battle! And my fame, too, will be sung as long as mortals walk the earth to sing of it!

"I will lead a great Turanian army against the foolish King Kavus, and I will put my father in his place upon the throne of Persia," Sohrab declared. "Then you, Mother, will be the Persian queen! My father and I will join forces against King Afrasyab, and I will take the throne of Turan from him. Together, Tahamtan and I will destroy every foolish or evil king. And we alone will rule the world, for when the sun and the moon light the heavens, there is no need for starlight!"

Thus it came to pass that Sohrab put his childhood behind him and set forth to make his name and place in the world. "Prepare me for Persia, Grandfather!" he exclaimed. "For I would see my father, the great hero Tahamtan!"

The king of Samengan's heart flooded with pride and joy in his grandson, so he gave Sohrab the finest helmet, armor, and weapons, plus an army of warriors, camels, and horses. In the royal stables, Sohrab found a horse to withstand his own prodigious strength, one bred from Rakhsh. This colt had the chest of a stag, the strength of an elephant, and the speed of the warrior's arrow, the eagle's flight, and the storm's lightning.

"What a horse!" Sohrab exclaimed after he had observed him. "The Persian king reigns no more! Now, Sohrab and Tahamtan rule the world!"

Meanwhile, Rumor rushed as swiftly as fire in a gale-wind to King Afrasyab of Turan with the news that Sohrab, a child-warrior from Samengan, had gathered a great army and was preparing to set out to attack Kay Kavus. Afrasyab summoned his two greatest chieftains and explained, "I am putting twelve thousand warriors under your joint command. Enjoy what a sweet opportunity this is for Turan— It tastes like honey on my tongue! Sohrab, this child-warrior from Samengan, must be Tahamtan's son, for his stature, strength, and skill, his courage, determination, and ambition are much greater than the royal house of Samengan—or any kingdom in Turan—could produce! And surely no one else could lead an army to war at the age of ten!

"But you must guard this secret well!" Afrasyab commanded. "Two lions, father and cub, go forth to battle, neither knowing the identity of the other. May it always be so! Your goal must be to advise Sohrab, to bring the cub against the lion in single combat, and yet to keep the lion cub ignorant of his father's presence on the battle-plain, lest he greet him with love and loyalty.

"Once the combat between father and son occurs, the lion cub's strength and skill will surely surpass that of the old lion, and Sohrab will kill Tahamtan for us. Then, we can easily create a plan to kill Sohrab, and Persia will be ours!

"However, if it is written in the stars in the heavens that Tahamtan will kill his son, the father will no longer be a threat to us. The mighty Rostam's heart will be so filled with grief that he will rush to his grave as swiftly as an arrow flies forth from a warrior's bow!

"Therefore, at all costs," Afrasyab concluded, "you must keep this secret locked in your hearts. For, if you do, the world can now be ours!"

In search of his father, Sohrab attacks Persia.

It came to pass that, as Sohrab led the Turanian armies toward King Kavus, they came upon the White Fortress, which guarded the Persian border across the Oxus River. Hojir, a son of wise old Gudarz, challenged the youthful leader, rousing him to fury like a wolf. Strong and swift single combat followed, with Sohrab the easy victor over the great Persian warrior. He then bound Hojir and sent him to Human, who was one of Afrasyab's two commanders and Sohrab's counselor.

Suddenly, quick as the flames of fire, the warrior Gordafarid came forth to do battle with Sohrab. At first, Sohrab had no defense against his opponent's arrows, and then his foe's sword sliced his own spear in two. Victorious, Gordafarid was racing back toward the fortress when Sohrab charged after the warrior and struck off his foe's helmet with his sword. To his amazement, Sohrab discovered that the warrior who had defeated him in battle was a beautiful maiden. As swiftly as an arrow flies forth from a warrior's bow, he lassoed her.

Gordafarid, fearing the worst, used her one remaining weapon. Turning her charming smile upon Sohrab, she said, "Brave warrior! Save your honor! Surely you cannot boast to the Turanian warriors that you fought a maiden in single combat and conquered her! Your name will fare far better if you keep my identity a secret and instead take the fort, its commander, and its treasure!"

With love and admiration flooding his heart, Sohrab followed Gordafarid to the fortress. However, she passed through the gate as swiftly as clouds before a storm and, to his shame and fury, she locked him out.

Human turned Sohrab's thoughts back to his task. "Young as you are," he advised Sohrab, "beware of love, for it brings neither glory nor lasting fame to a warrior's name. Love instead your sword and spear, for it is through victory in battle that you will win a maiden's love. To linger here is to bring Tahamtan, Gudarz, Giv, and the other great Persian warriors to the king's aid!"

So it came to pass that quick as the flames of fire, Gordafarid's father, the commander of the White Fortress, sent a messenger to Kay

Kavus with the dreadful news. The message informed the Persian king that Turanian warriors were invading Persia like a plague of locusts, that they had taken Hojir captive and had put the White Fortress under siege, and finally, that an unknown child-chieftain, who possessed matchless stature and skill, was leading the Turanian armies.

"His head towers above the other warriors like a great cypress tree," the message declared. "He has the chest of a lion, the limbs of an elephant, the feet of a stag, and the voice of thunder. His skill puts the lion, the dragon, and the crocodile to shame! The sun shines on him! Yet his eyes have only seen ten summers! He is called Sohrab and is a prince of the house of Samengan, but to see him in action is to see Sam the Hero once again, or Tahamtan himself!"

Kay Kavus summons Rostam to Persia.

"Only Tahamtan can deliver Persia from this assault!" King Kavus exclaimed upon hearing the message. So it came to pass that he ordered Giv, the son of Gudarz who was Rostam's warrior-friend and one of Persia's greatest champions, to take the message to Seistan. "Leave immediately," he commanded. "for, more swiftly than an arrow flies forth from a warrior's bow, my eyes want to see Rostam standing here before me!"

When Rostam the Mighty heard the news, he could not believe the description of Sohrab. "Such a great warrior could be Persian, but never a Tatar!" he exclaimed to Giv. How can a hero of Turan so resemble the heroes of the house of Nariman? I myself have a son in Samengan, the child of the Tatar king's daughter, Princess Tahmineh. But my son is a mere babe, one who plays the warrior like a child! In time, he will probably become a hero, but he is much too young to lead an army. In fact, no child can do what this Sohrab is doing!

"And, as for you, Giv, I want you stay here and enjoy yourself for a few days," he encouraged his friend. "Kavus has nothing to fear, for I will come with you when I am ready. Even if this young Tatar is the hero of heroes whom the world has yet to see, in time he will come face to face with me in single combat. And even if he is as strong as Sam the Hero is or as I myself am, he will surely fall to his death beneath my arm!"

So it came to pass that Rostam delayed their departure for four days. By the time he greeted Kay Kavus, the king exploded with the fury of a mad elephant or crocodile.

"So, you have finally decided to come, insolent one!" he exclaimed. "Who do you think you are that you may defy my power and scorn my commands! If I had my sword, I would slice your head from your body! As it is, I will have you impaled alive upon a stake! And Giv as well!"

Quick as the flames of fire, Rostam responded with the dragon's fiery tongue. "You weak, despotic, vain man!" he exclaimed. "How dare you attack me! Your own actions are a chain of foolish deeds, each worse than the last. You led your army into Mazanderan and Hamaveran, twice inviting your own capture. Then you tried to fly up to the heavens! You bring nothing but trouble and sorrow to your people and shame to your title and your throne! Surely Persia deserves better!

"You ungrateful man!" Rostam added. "Just what would you be without me? But for your father, you would not be king of Persia, and Kay Kobad owed his title to me! I have been your shield! My sword and spear have kept you on your throne. Who rescued you from Mazanderan, Hamaveran, and China? Who killed the White Demon and restored sight to your eyes? My great deeds shine like golden strands upon your chest. Without me, you are nobody!

"And as for me," Rostam declared, "I am a free man, and not your slave! Why should I fear your wrath? I serve only Urmazd, and it is he who gives me my courage and my strength. I am the Champion of the World and its king! My crown is my helmet; my robe is my armor; and my throne is Rakhsh. My seal is my spear and sword; and my scepter is Sam the Hero's great war club.

"Many times I have risked my life to rescue you from the results of your vanity," Tahamtan declared. "But no more! I am tired of your foolishness! Sohrab is your enemy—go kill him! When this Tatar child-chief appears, meet him yourself in single combat—you who are so brave, so strong, so skillful, and so wise! Save your spear or your sword, your stake or your lariat for him! As for me, I am returning to Seistan. And if Sohrab grinds you to dust beneath his feet, I will neither know nor care! In my eyes, you are nothing but a worthless clump of dirt!"

Then, turning to Giv, Gudarz, and the other nobles who were standing around King Kavus, Tahamtan exclaimed, "My friends, be wise and leave while you can! A conqueror has battered Persia's gates! What he leaves will be food for vultures!" And with these words, Tahamtan turned from the king, mounted Rakhsh, and rode away.

Like sheep without their shepherd when they see that a ravenous wolf is running toward their pen, the Persian nobles stood paralyzed with terror. They asked Gudarz, the wise old warrior, to come forth as a peacemaker. Gudarz convinced Kay Kavus that he had been unjust and unwise, and so it came to pass that Kavus sent Gudarz to Tahamtan bearing his apology.

When Gudarz found Tahamtan, he declared, "Oh hero of heroes, listen to the words of an old warrior who loves both you and Persia. You were right to be angry with Kavus, but he now regrets that he addressed you with the dragon's fiery tongue. Shame and sorrow flood his heart. He still must learn judgment and discretion, but these qualities are already yours! Do not confuse Persia with its king. Persia has done nothing to incur your wrath, and without you, it will surely fall to the Tatars!"

To these words, Tahamtan replied, "Gudarz, do not talk to me about cowardly Kavus! He blows hot and cold like the wind! Let him say and do what he will! I do not care about his anger, and I do not care about his change of heart!"

The old warrior, wise with age, knew well the ways of the human heart and mind. And so he fanned the flames of pride and patriotic fire in Tahamtan's heart by saying, "Greatest of warriors, you truly see the man who wears the king of Persia's crown! But what will the Persians and the Tatars think when the Champion of the World runs from a beardless boy?

"Surely they will say, 'Alas! How quickly heroism flees when age grows heavy on a warrior's shoulders! Just as strong new leaves replace the dry old ones each spring, so a new champion always takes the old one's place!'" he continued.

"Now, surely you are not ready to forfeit your glory and fame to this beardless boy! And surely you do not want the destruction of Persia to rest on your own shoulders! So do not turn your back on King Kavus, to whom you owe allegiance," he declared.

"Instead, forget his foolish anger, and lead Persia into battle against Turan. For if the Persians think you fear the Tatars, they will panic and flee from them in terror like sheep from a ravenous wolf, and Turan will destroy Persia!" he concluded.

Tahamtan lassoed his anger at these words and replied, "Gudarz, you well know that pride, and not fear, is the issue here! Fear and I are strangers! I do not dread facing Sohrab in battle—I look forward to putting that lion cub in his place! However, you speak well to my pride as a warrior. I will forget Kavus's insults to my honor for the good of Persia!"

And so it came to pass that Rostam returned with Gudarz to King Kavus, who welcomed him with contrite apologies.

Rostam apologized as well, saying, "Ruler of the world, you had the right to demand my obedience to your wishes. May you always have such power! Know that, as long as I live, I will be your shield!"

When the sun next raised his shining shield, scattering the armies of night and brightening the earth with its brilliant light, more than one hundred thousand Persian warriors responded to the call to arms. Sprouting like blades of grass upon the ground, they marched toward the White Fortress. Their horses' hooves shook the earth and darkened the sky with dust. Lightning bolts flashed from their gold-emblazoned shields as if the clouds were raining drops of sparkling amber.

Rostam spies on Sohrab.

It had come to pass that Sohrab and the Turanian troops were now lodged within the White Fortress. Looking out upon the Persian encampment, Sohrab could not see anyone who could be Tahamtan. Confident that no Persian would be his match, he decided to give a banquet on this night before the battle.

When the sun's bright shield had sunk from sight, the Persian camp became illuminated by torchlight. It looked as if Demon magic had caused a huge shimmering city suddenly to appear upon the plain by the Oxus River. It was then that Rostam disguised himself in Tatar attire and stole like a lion into the White Fortress in order to learn what he could about the Tatar chieftains, particularly Sohrab, since King Kavus was so terrified of him. And just as the lion stealthily stalks a herd of antelope and silently becomes one of them before launching his attack, so Tahamtan stood in the shadow of the doorway to the banquet hall, observing Sohrab as he sat surrounded by a large and impressive group of Tatar chieftains.

Rostam exclaimed to himself, "Why, that boy-chieftain could be Sam the Hero himself! His head towers above the other warriors like a great cypress tree. He has the chest of a lion, the limbs of an elephant, and the voice of thunder. Although his eyes have only seen ten summers, the sun's bright shield shines on him! Kavus is right to be terrified of this lion cub, for Sohrab has no equal among either Tatars or Persians!"

It had come to pass that Princess Tahmineh, being concerned that father and son might inadvertently meet each other in combat and fearing that her brother Zhende might be the only Tatar who would recognize Rostam, had asked Zhende to accompany Sohrab in order to identify Rostam. Upon leaving the banquet hall, Zhende saw the shadow of a man who was as tall as a cypress tree hiding in the doorway. "What Persian spy hides beneath the cloak of night?" he cried. "Come forth into the light, and show your face! Your stature tells me that you are no Tatar!"

Zhende's words roused Tahamtan to fury like a wolf. And just as the ravenous wolf silently sneaks into the sheep pen, kills the best of the flock while the shepherds and their dogs stand guard, and then springs over the fence and runs away, so Tahamtan, quick as the flames of fire, silently struck his brother-in-law a mortal blow across the back of his neck and returned to the Persian camp, leaving the bloody corpse for the unsuspecting Tatars to mourn. Thus it came to pass that Rostam set into motion the events that would bring his own tragedy upon him. For what is written in the stars in the heavens is sure to come!

The festivities in the White Fortress continued until Sohrab missed Zhende, and his warriors discovered his uncle's beheaded body. Recognizing an enemy trick and vowing revenge, Sohrab used this tragedy to fan the flames of battle in his warriors.

After the banquet, thoughts of Rostam kept Sohrab awake. "I must avenge Zhende's death," he thought to himself. "Now, if I challenge the best Persian warriors to single combat, my father will surely hear about it, and he may introduce himself to me."

Sohrab attempts to identify his father.

When the sun next raised his shining shield, scattering the armies of night and brightening the earth with its brilliant light, Sohrab looked out upon the Persian camp and commanded that Hojir be brought to him. Then he said to the Persian captive, "Answer my questions truthfully, Hojir, and I will give you your freedom and reward you with honors and wealth. Deceive me, however, and you will die a prisoner in chains!"

Hojir replied, "I will tell you whatever I know."

"To whom does the gold brocade tent bearing the pennant with golden suns on it, and with a hundred war elephants surrounding it, belong?" Sohrab asked.

"That tent belongs to Kay Kavus, the king of Persia," Hojir responded.

"And to whom does the tent bearing the golden pennant with a lion on it belong?" Sohrab asked.

"That tent belongs to Gudarz, an old warrior who is as brave as he is wise," Hojir answered. "And the men in armor who surround him are most of his eighty sons and grandsons."

"Then to whom does the tent bearing the pennant with wolves on it belong? Heroes, horses, and slaves surround a great chieftain there!" Sohrab exclaimed.

Hojir replied, "That tent belongs to Giv, who is a son of Gudarz and one of the greatest Persian champions. Giv even surpasses his father in strength, skill, and fame!"

"And to whom does the green tent bearing the pennant with a lion and dragon on it belong?" Sohrab asked. "The head of that noble warrior must touch the stars in the heavens! And next to him stands a horse as tall and noble in stature as he is! What chieftain is he? I have never seen a warrior to match him!" Sohrab exclaimed.

At these words, Hojir, quick as the wind, thought to himself, "If I reveal Tahamtan to Sohrab, surely the cub will try to kill the lion, for Sohrab is a mighty foe, even if he is just a child!"

And so it came to pass that Hojir responded, "I think that warrior comes from China, but I do not know his name."

At these words, Sohrab's heart flooded with fury and despair. Despite Hojir's denial, he recognized Rostam's banner and horse from his mother's descriptions. However, he lassoed his anger and craftily continued to question his prisoner about the tents of other Persian warriors.

Finally, without revealing the secret of his birth to Hojir, Sohrab asked, "Then, where is Tahamtan's tent? How can it be that he who leads the Persians in battle would be unmarked and, therefore, unknown upon this plain? Identify Rostam's tent for me, and I will richly reward you!"

"I do not see it," Hojir answered. "He must not have arrived from Seistan yet."

To these words, Sohrab replied, "You are very clever, Hojir, but your wiles will not work with me! I know that you are trying to conceal Tahamtan from me, but Kay Kavus would never go to battle without his strongest shield, and Rostam would never shun a battle! Therefore, identify Rostam's banner right now or, with one stroke of my sword, I will slice your head from your body!"

At these words, Hojir, quick as the wind, thought to himself, "I fear that this child, with his great shoulders, chest, and arms, may be Tahamtan's equal, and he has the strength of youth on his side as well. What is my life worth compared with the welfare of Persia? It is better to die a thousand deaths than to give glory and fame to a foe! And it is far better to die with honor than to lie shamed in the grave, having dishonored my father's name as well as my own. An honorable death lives on in the minds of men and the tales they tell! And surely my brothers will avenge my death!"

So it came to pass that Hojir responded, "Why are you so interested in Tahamtan? You will know him soon enough, Sohrab, should you choose to meet him in battle! He is a towering adversary, stronger than a hundred warriors! On the battle-plain, he possesses the courage of the lion, the strength of the elephant, the skill of the fiery-tongued dragon, and the fury of the crocodile!"

"No one—no warrior, no lion, no dragon, no Demon—can face Tahamtan in combat and survive!" Hojir declared. "Surely your eyes have not already tired of seeing the sun's bright blade! And surely you do not already long for the hard, cold bed of Death! Go ahead and fight Tahamtan, if you must! But I will not point him out to you!"

"Do not brag about Tahamtan's strength to me!" Sohrab exclaimed. "In battle, I too have the heart of the lion, the strength of the elephant, the skill of the dragon, and the fury of the crocodile! And I am young! If Tahamtan breathes fire, I will snuff it out! And just as the sun's bright blade routs the raven of night, so I will chase Rostam from the battle-plain!"

Then, true to his word, Sohrab raised his sword and killed Hojir with one great blow. For what is written in the stars in the heavens is sure to come!

So it came to pass that Sohrab led the Turanian warriors in battle against the Persians. War flared up like fire in a gale-wind. Just as autumn winds blow the leaves off the willow tree, so battle-axes battered both helmets and heads off the warriors. The battle-plain soon became a sea of blood, with waves of arrows, spears, and swords.

Like ships, horses floated until they sank. Yet neither side could claim a victory.

Sohrab and Rostam meet in single combat.

The Morning of the First Day

When the sun next raised his shining shield, scattering the armies of night and brightening the earth with its brilliant light, Sohrab, roused to fury like a wolf and elated at the prospect of earning glory and lasting fame, galloped out upon the battle-plain and charged toward the Persian warriors. He shouted in his voice of thunder, "I have sworn to avenge the murder of Zhende, the great Tatar warrior who was treacherously slain within the White Fortress. Therefore, I call upon you, King Kavus, if you are a man of honor, to meet me in single combat!"

Kay Kavus did not respond. Not one Persian warrior responded. They all stood, silent and still, looking at the Tatar version of their own Tahamtan while fear chased honor and courage from their hearts. Then, just as the wild donkey flees from the fierce lion that hungers for its prey, so King Kavus and the Persian warriors fled in panic from Sohrab's charge.

As they fled, Sohrab continued to charge after them, shouting, "Kay Kavus! You shame the crown of the Persian king! My spear hungers to feed on your cowardly flesh! Surely an honorable king does not, like a fox, slink away from battle with a lion! Who then will you send to combat with me? Where are your great warriors when you need them? Where is Rostam the Mighty—the warrior whom men call Tahamtan? The best of the Persians must be cowards, one and all!"

Seeing the best of the Persian chieftains running like the wild donkey from battle, Tahamtan wrapped his leopard-skin armor around his chest, put his iron helmet upon his head, mounted Rakhsh, and collected his weapons. "Surely Ahriman, and not Sohrab, is leading the Turanian warriors!" he exclaimed to his brother Zavareh, who accompanied him holding the banner with the lion and the dragon.

As soon as Rostam saw Sohrab, so like Sam the Hero in his stature, he called out, "Young hero! Let us choose a good place for combat!"

To these words, Sohrab replied, "And let us fight each other alone, in single combat, without the aid of our warriors!" Then, coming face to face with Tahamtan, he asked, "Valiant old warrior, are you sure that you want to fight a young lion like me? You are tall, with the shoulders and chest of the lion and the limbs of the elephant, but age has surely taken its toll on your strength and skill. No warrior can withstand the might of my arm! And you will never survive single combat with me!"

"On the contrary, young hero!" Rostam replied softly, his heart flooding with sudden sorrow and pity for this bright young warrior. "You are but a child and still too young to know what war is really like! Reconsider your own challenge. If we fight, I will surely send you to your death, for I am iron-clad and seasoned in the blood of battle. The stars in the heavens and the mountains and seas on earth can bear witness to my courage and skill in battle. No enemy has ever conquered me, be he warrior, lion, dragon, or Demon. So I urge you! Do not rush, as swift as fire in a gale-wind, to your early death! The grave is cold and dark, and your eyes should enjoy many summers of life in the sun!

"I find myself strangely loathe to kill you!" Rostam continued softly. "Instead, let us part. The battle-plain is filled with other warriors for us to fight! You are too bright a star to be snuffed out before you have barely begun to shine! No Tatar warrior—or even a Persian—can match your stature and your strength!"

These words flooded Sohrab's heart with hope, for surely here was the father whom he longed to meet! Kneeling before Rostam, and wrapping his arms about his knees, Sohrab responded, "Valiant old warrior! It appears to me—from how you look and from what you say—that surely you are Rostam the Mighty, whom men call Tahamtan, the son of Dastan, and the grandson of Sam the Hero! For if you are not that greatest of heroes, then who else could you be? Tell me that you are he, and my heart will flood with joy!"

To these words, Rostam replied, "No, young hero, I am not Rostam, and I am not related to Dastan and Sam the Hero. They are nobles, whereas I am much lower in station, having no rank and no crown, throne, or palace.

"And who are you, young hero, that only Rostam the Mighty, whom men call Tahamtan, is good enough to fight with you?" Rostam asked. "If I were he, you would not be kneeling here, trying to conquer me with honeyed words. You would have turned and fled from Tahamtan as a sheep panics and flees from a ravenous wolf!

"So either surrender," Rostam commanded, "or, for the last time, feast your eyes upon the sun's bright blade! But I warn you! Choose combat, and your bones will lie here upon the Oxus riverbank until the sun and wind have bleached them or the spring floods have washed them away!"

Thus did Rostam crush Sohrab's hopes and darken the day that had dawned so bright for him. Sohrab wondered at the disparity between what he saw and what he heard but, swift as an arrow sent forth from a bow, the blood of a warrior conquered the blood of a son, and fury flooded his own heart.

"You may be a common warrior, as you say, but you have a dragon's tongue!" Sohrab declared. "Yet you will have to do more than breathe fire to frighten me! I am not a babe that I tremble at your threats! If you were Tahamtan, I would refuse this combat. But since you are not, let our skill with weapons now speak for us! You are more battle-hardened than I, but time and the stars in the heavens will choose the victor!"

So it came to pass that father and son mounted their warhorses and began their duel. They hurled their spears until the heads and bindings were broken. They sparred with their Indian swords until these had become hacked into sawlike blades. They pounded their war clubs against each other until the armor fell from their horses, and their own chain mail littered the earth. The two armies watched in stunned silence, broken only by inadvertent shouts and groans as each warrior made his mark. Finally, with their throats choked with dust, their bodies dripping with sweat, their arms too worn to lift a weapon, and their horses exhausted, Tahamtan and Sohrab stopped for a short respite.

Rostam then said to Zavareh, "What a dragon this young lion cub is in battle! I marvel at his courage, strength, and skill! In summers he is but a child, yet his head touches the stars in the heavens like a cypress, and the earth trembles in terror beneath his feet.

"Sohrab makes my battle with the White Demon look like a child's game!" Rostam added. "His strength and skill make my heart long for my own youthful vigor! And both Persia and Turan are watching while this child, who has yet to earn a hero's fame, tarnishes the golden glory of the world's champion! My eyes would weep with the shame of it!"

The Afternoon of the First Day

It came to pass that when father and son had rested, they resumed their battle. They showered each other with arrows, which darkened the sky like a rain of hailstones, but their armor and leopard skins protected them. They wrestled as each warrior tried to unseat the other from his horse, but just as mighty mountains withstand the blows of winter winds, so each warrior remained firmly planted on his horse. Then they battered each other with their war clubs. With Sam the Hero's ox-headed mace, Tahamtan could make a mountain tumble and turn a rock into wax, but it was Sohrab who gave Tahamtan such a blow that he lost his balance and cringed with pain.

Sohrab laughed and exclaimed, "I have punished you enough for now, valiant old warrior! The wounded old lion fights with courage even as his strength fails him! But his days of glory have come and gone! Age must bow to youth on the battle-plain! So let us stop this unequal contest! Turan has many old warriors for you to combat. Go fight with one of them!"

Fighting to keep fear at bay, and feeling overwhelmed by the shame and rage that flooded his heart, Rostam responded by turning from Sohrab and attacking the Turanian warriors like a leopard lunging at its prey. Then Sohrab, in turn, attacked the Persian warriors as a wolf slaughters a flock of sheep.

The child-warrior dealt such death and destruction that Rostam feared for the life of King Kavus. Charging after Sohrab, he exclaimed, "Young hero! It is enough that we fight each other! But since the sun's bright shield now sinks from sight, let our swords meet again in single combat tomorrow, and then we will see how Urmazd ends our combat."

The First Night

Rostam then returned to his tent, disturbed, discouraged, and depressed. Fearing the combat to come, he prayed to Urmazd for youthful strength, and he prepared both for battle and for death.

"Sohrab is made of iron, not flesh!" he exclaimed to Zavareh. "If it is written in the stars in the heavens that this is how I am to die, then tomorrow I will meet Death! But sooner or later Death claims us all! Surely it is best for a Persian warrior to face Death valiantly in battle, defending his king and his country!"

Meanwhile, Sohrab returned to the White Fortress, where he said to Human, "I am fighting a warrior who is so like me in form and stature—and in courage, strength, and skill—that he surely must be the father whom my mother described to me. For who else could be so like Rostam the Mighty? He shows me all the proofs my heart demands, causing my heart to reach out to him! And if he really is my father, then I cannot continue to fight him as if I were blind to our ties of blood and love! Having offended the laws of nature, I would live with lifelong shame!"

To these words, Human replied, "Push such thoughts from your mind and heart, Sohrab. Do not let your imagination make you soft on that Persian! I have seen Tahamtan and Rakhsh in combat," he lied, "and you are not contesting against them!"

The Second Day

When the sun next raised his shining shield, scattering the armies of night and brightening the earth with its brilliant light, father and son rose to resume their combat. Sohrab galloped toward Rostam and, smiling with affection, he cried, "Valiant old warrior! Did you sleep well? Are you ready to continue? What weapons have you chosen for today's battle?"

And without waiting for Rostam's reply, he added, "Let us put aside our contest and our weapons! Instead, let us call a truce between us and pledge lasting friendship! Love has pushed anger from my heart, and I cannot fight a warrior whom I so respect! Sit with me and tell me about yourself and your family, for surely you must be the son of Dastan and the grandson of Sam the Hero! Now tell me, is it not true that you are Rostam the Mighty, whom men call Tahamtan?"

To these words, Rostam responded, "Young hero, you are a wily child, indeed, to keep asking this of me! We have come together to fight, not to talk! Do you think that I am a fool that you can tame me with honeyed words? You have shamed me enough before the warriors of Persia and Turan! So eat your talk of truce and love, and fight like a warrior, hand to hand in battle!"

To these words, Sohrab replied, "My heart weeps that my words have fallen on ears too old to hear them! I had hoped to spare you a warrior's death, but since your heart loves only combat, let us begin!"

And so it came to pass that father and son hitched their warhorses to nearby rocks and wrestled like enraged lions until the sand along the Oxus was slippery with their sweat and blood. As long as the sun's bright blade blazed overhead, the lion and his cub fought one another. Suddenly, with the speed of fire's flames in a gale-wind and the strength of a mad elephant, Sohrab seized Tahamtan by the waist, threw him backward upon the earth, and sat upon his chest. Just as a lion who is prowling through the forest springs upon a wild donkey and pants for his blood, so Sohrab drew his sword and prepared to behead his foe.

Rostam, now desperately fighting for his life, tried a trick. "Stop, young hero!" he commanded. "You must not know our rules of combat! In Persia, the code of honor decrees that a warrior must conquer his foe twice before he has the right to behead him!"

Hearing these words and proud of his victory, Sohrab went off to hunt wild animals, giving no more thought to the valiant old warrior and the war with Persia.

The Second Night

When the sun's bright shield had sunk from sight, Sohrab returned to the White Fortress. There he told Human how he had conquered the old warrior and then released him.

Afrasyab's commander then said to Sohrab, "Alas, young hero! You have acted like a foolish child! Conquerors obey no such custom! You must be ready to welcome Death! The lion has tricked the cub into letting him escape from a deadly trap! You have freed him to devour you!"

"I am not afraid of that!" Sohrab exclaimed. "My youth is my advantage, for old age has stolen the old warrior's strength and skill. Therefore, I will surely defeat him tomorrow as I defeated him today!"

"Now you speak like a foolish child!" Human replied. "Most warriors are fortunate if they can prevail over an enemy once. You have given victory away twice! The wise warrior never judges his foe to be weak or unworthy of his best efforts! Remember that tomorrow you could be the one who meets Death!"

Meanwhile, back at his tent, Rostam cleansed himself and once again prayed to Urmazd for youthful strength. For he knew that, when the sun's shining blade next brightened the earth, it was written in the stars in the heavens that either he or Sohrab would meet Death.

The Third Day

When the sun next raised his shining shield, scattering the armies of night and brightening the earth with its brilliant light, Rostam returned to the battle-plain refreshed and renewed, but with concern on his face and fear in his heart. For he did not know what the stars in the heavens had decreed for him.

Sohrab returned like a mad elephant! As he galloped toward Rostam, he shouted in his thunderous voice, "Old coward, why do you still choose to fight? Twice the lion-killer has pitied your age and let you escape! Is it that you were ashamed to win our combat through guile? Or are you anxious to meet Death? Try no more tricks with me, old warrior! I am wise to your wiles!"

So it came to pass that father and son once again hitched their warhorses to the nearby rocks and wrestled like enraged lions until the sand along the Oxus was slippery with their sweat and blood. As long as the sun's bright blade blazed overhead, the lion and his cub fought each other. Suddenly, with the speed of flames of fire and the strength of a mad elephant, Tahamtan seized Sohrab by the waist, threw him backward upon the earth, and sat upon his chest. Then, fearing that he lacked the strength to constrain his foe from renewing their contest, Rostam the Mighty withdrew his dagger from its sheath and, quick as the wind, tore into Sohrab's chest.

Sohrab writhed in agony and said, "Do not boast of your victory, old warrior, for I have brought my death upon myself! You are but the arm of Fate. I chose combat, not for glory and fame, but to find my father. My only wish was to see him, and I have died for it! I am only sorry that I have given up so much for so little! I die at an age when war should still be but a harmless game, and I still do not know my father's face!

"Yet, just as you have thirsted for my blood, Fate is hungry for yours!" Sohrab declared. "She will turn the hairs on your body to daggers so that, quick as fire in a gale-wind, you will meet Death! For my father will surely hear that the cold earth has become my bed. Some Persian hero will bring Tahamtan his signet arm ring and word of his son's death and will tell him that Sohrab's only wish was to find his father. Then, even the fish in the sea or the stars in the heavens or total darkness will not conceal you! Wherever you may be, Rostam the Mighty will find you, and he will avenge my death as swiftly as an arrow flies forth from a warrior's bow!"

With these words, Rostam's heart froze like ice from a winter storm. An uncontrollable shudder shook his body, and the world turned black before his eyes. When he recovered, his bleeding heart sent bloody tears to his eyes, and he asked in a voice shaking with sadness, "Let me see the signet arm ring that you say belongs to Rostam, for I am that most unfortunate son of Dastan! May my name be wiped from the list of heroes, and may the house of Nariman soon mourn my death!"

To these words, Sohrab replied, "Why, if you really are Rostam, then your dagger is bathed in your son's lifeblood! And we meet in that blood to bewail your fatal blow! We have lost the love we could have had. And you are to blame, stubborn dragon that you are! For your angry pride has killed me! How often I searched for you, only to be disappointed when you denied your family and your name. Why did your heart remain closed to my love?

"Now, open my armor," Sohrab commanded, "and see how your signet ring encircles my arm! My mother tied it there to be the token by which you would know me," Sohrab explained. "It helps too late! And her other plan failed as well, for a spy killed her brother Zhende before he could identify you to me. My uncle's death surely heralded my own!"

When his trembling fingers opened Sohrab's armor, and Rostam discovered his own signet ring upon Sohrab's arm, he wept bloody tears, covered his head with ashes, and tore his clothes. "Oh, my son! How I wish that I had met Death in battle before I could hurt you!" he exclaimed. "Having found you, I cannot bear to lose you! And I cannot live, knowing that my own hand has caused your death!"

"Your tears are useless, Father," Sohrab responded. "They cannot restore life as rain nourishes a dying plant. And you must not let your grief ruin your life! It must be written in the stars in the heavens that this was meant to be, and what will be is sure to come!"

Now it came to pass that when the sun's bright shield was sinking from sight and yet Tahamtan had not returned to his tent, Kay Kavus sent Zavareh and Gudarz to find him. And seeing Rakhsh alone, they wailed in sorrow, thinking that Rostam had died.

Sohrab, seeing them in the distance, said to his father, "Do not let Kay Kavus blame Turan for my attack. The Turanian warriors came here to support me, intending to reap glory from my dream. So when I die, let them return to Turan in peace.

"For I chose to find you through war," he explained to Rostam. "You were to be my treasured prize, and with you by my side, I dreamed of victories against all tyrants! Now those flowers will never bloom for me, but will wither as buds in my grave! For I came like a flash of lightning, and I vanish like the empty wind!"

When Zavareh found his brother, Rostam told him his dreadful tale. "I have lived to kill my son, that great child-warrior who earned praise from Turan and Persia for his courage, strength, and skill in battle!" he exclaimed. "What father has ever done such a deed! What a curse upon a parent's head!"

Rostam told Zavareh Sohrab's wishes about the Tatar army and asked him to relay the message to Kay Kavus. He also asked him to send a message to Human that said, "My sword of vengeance sleeps in its scabbard, for I am no longer a warrior! But know that I blame you for Sohrab's death, for you refused to reveal the father to the son, and your evil intent led him to his tragic death!"

"Not only will I do that," Zavareh replied, "but I will ask Kavus to let me lead the Turanian warriors safely across the Oxus and leave them on their own soil."

Then, seeing Sohrab's agony, Rostam would have beheaded himself, but Zavareh and Gudarz stopped him. "Stay your hand, dear friend and Champion of Persia!" Gudarz exclaimed. "If you were to give yourself a thousand wounds, your death would not heal Sohrab! It would only enable Afrasyab to conquer our land and destroy our people! If it is written in the stars that Sohrab's wound was destined to be fatal, then you must make your peace with the sorrowful lot of all who walk the earth. Fate offers glory with one hand and steals life with the other. The living have no weapon against this foe. Death comes to all, kings and slaves alike!"

"Wise old hero," Rostam said, "it occurs to me that Kavus has a salve that heals all wounds. Please, go to him, tell him of my plight, and plead for that salve. For Kavus has it within his power to cure my son, and Sohrab, alive and well, will honor him as I do!"

So it came to pass that, as swiftly as clouds before a storm, Gudarz rode to the king with Rostam's request. However, Kay Kavus replied, "Although I honor Rostam, I will not heal Sohrab! I remember too well that child's insolent tongue! He ridiculed me before the warriors of Persia and Turan! And he sought to destroy me, intending, I am sure, to put my crown on his father's head! Why should I preserve the life of my enemy? My charity now would only invite future strife. If he lives, Sohrab will join Tahamtan, and I am not strong enough to withstand their combined might! At best, they would ignore my authority and power because Seistan and the other kingdoms under Dastan's control can be independent of Persia. At worst, they might even kill me!"

Gudarz brought the bad news to Rostam, saying, "The king's evil heart is like a bitter seed; it always becomes a bitter fruit! But maybe, with honeyed words, you can sweeten it!"

So it came to pass that Sohrab died without his father's presence. For, while Rostam was racing to plead with Kavus, Zavareh overtook him, saying, "Alas, Rostam! Sohrab has died! He cried, 'Father!' and went, weeping, from life!"

Rostam mourns Sohrab's death.

Seeing Rostam's tears, Urmazd wept for him. The sun mourned Sohrab's death as his bright shield sank from sight. The moon and the stars mourned Sohrab's death and could not shine. Instead, a weeping fog settled upon the Oxus plain, shrouding the sobbing warrior who sat bowed over the still and silent body of his son. "Oh, my son!" Rostam cried. "Most noble child, and hero of heroes! The sun, the moon, and the stars in the heavens will never shine upon another like you!

"And what is to become of me, a father who, in his old age, has killed his own innocent child?" he asked Zavareh. "I have turned my honor and glory into dust, without excuse and without pardon! If only I had thought that I could have had such a mighty young son— so tall, so strong, so skillful, and a leader of heroes! What can I tell Tahmineh? How will she bear the loss of her son? And how will I?"

Then, Rostam asked Zavareh to help him build a great fire, and it came to pass that he tossed his tent, his leopard-skin armor, his helmet and armor, Sam the Hero's great war club, Rakhsh's saddle, and all that he prized upon the raging flames. And, having done this, Rostam the Mighty, whom men call Tahamtan, sat in silence, watching all the symbols of his pride crumble, until nothing was left but ashes and dust.

Kay Kavus came to sit by Rostam and Zavareh, and he tried to soothe Tahamtan's grief. "Death is our lot in life, and no one who lives escapes sorrow!" he declared. "Sohrab fought, and it was his destiny to die. You can do nothing to restore his life. What is past is past, and too much grieving cannot help you. But, out of respect for your wishes, I will permit Persia's greatest enemy to retreat in peace! And I will permit Zavareh to lead them."

And then it came to pass that the warriors of Persia and Turan mourned the death of the young hero, who was a child in age, but another Tahamtan in battle. The Persian heroes wept, covered their heads with ashes, and tore their clothes to see the child of the house of Nariman dead before his prime. At the front of the Turanian warriors, Human led Sohrab's horse, riderless, with its shorn mane and tail and the hero's armor hanging from its reversed saddle, back to

Samengan and Princess Tahmineh. Rostam bled a thousand horses and scattered torn drums upon the Oxus plain. Then he and Zavareh joined their warriors as the funeral procession made its way back to Seistan. Rostam walked alone in front of the bier.

Once the funeral procession arrived in the capital city, old and young, husbands and wives, masters and servants, family and friends all joined Rostam and Zavareh, the warriors of Seistan and Zabulestan, and Dastan and Rudabeh in weeping for the heroic youth who had died so young. And it came to pass that Rostam built a tomb shaped like a horse's hoof for Sohrab, so that the young hero's name and fame would live as long as those who walk the earth could see it.

And, in Samengan, it came to pass that when Tahmineh heard about Sohrab's death, she tore her hair and clothing and rolled in the dirt. Day after day, and night after night, she kissed Sohrab's horse, his clothing, his armor, and his weapons, bemoaning his death and her own loss. For her, Sohrab's death dimmed the sun's shield, clouded the moon, and extinguished the stars. For her, the flowers no longer bloomed. For her, nothing but empty days and lonely nights stretched in a funeral procession without end. And so it came to pass that, at the year's end, Tahmineh followed Sohrab to the grave.

Who among mortals can escape Fate? Who among us can use our wisdom, or our courage, or our strength, or our skill to this end? No one. What is written in the stars in the heavens is sure to come! So it was with Sohrab. So it is with all who walk the earth!

EUROPE

3

The following myths, legends, and tales from Europe are among the best known in Western culture. They include two of the world's most famous rebels and one of the world's most famous pairs of lovers. The myth of a hero who attains immortality and the legend of a love triangle and blood feud are famous within their respective cultures. Each of the five selections is remarkable in terms of its plot, the nature of its characters, its themes, and the point of view of its author. Moreover, each involves a character who is an independent thinker and who acts in a way that breaks with the socially acceptable behavior of the time.

"Prometheus, the Fire-Bringer," often considered to be the greatest Greek myth, is also remarkable in world mythology. It depicts a conflict between human beings and their god and supports the importance of human beings. Although Prometheus is an immortal culture hero, he possesses the most admirable human qualities: creative intelligence combined with the determination and perseverance to defend his values. He is a fascinating character because he can be viewed both as a hero and as a rebel. Readers must evaluate his motives and then balance them against his defiance of the established order. The myth has provided the inspiration for literary works by Giovanni Boccaccio, George Gordon Lord Byron, Pedro Calderón de la Barca, Johann Wolfgang von Goethe, Victor Hugo, and Percy Bysshe Shelley.

"Oisin Mac Finn, Poet of the Fianna," the beautiful Celtic myth from Ireland and Scotland, examines illusion and reality in terms of the human wish to become immortal and the price that one would pay for it. This myth is remarkable in its depiction of the divine world, with its magic, its mystery, and its irresistible appeal to the human mind and heart. To read it is to understand why it inspired Ireland's greatest poet, William Butler Yeats, to write "The Wanderings of Oisin."

The "Saga of Gunnlaug Serpent-Tongue," one of the most popular Icelandic sagas, is the legend of a great Icelandic hero who suffers misfortune in love because of his personality and Fate. Although the legend depicts a famous rivalry between two men that develops into a tragic love triangle, the character of the woman is interesting as well. Readers are left to consider whether Helga the Fair has options that she does not exercise, or whether she is a pawn in her society.

"Aucassin and Nicolette," a gem of a love story from thirteenth-century France, was the most popular tale of its period. The tale deals with thwarted adolescent love and the trials and tribulations of the lovers. The anonymous author, who appears to have been a minstrel, playfully reverses the traditional roles of the hero and heroine and the traditional values of the Age of Chivalry. Although hundreds of years have passed, the tale has retained its charm and humor.

"Doctor Faust," often considered to be the greatest German legend, explores one of the most popular themes in the Western tradition, namely, the human desire for unrestricted knowledge and power, and the price that one is willing to pay for it. Although the original Faust rebels against his Christian teachings and pledges allegiance to Lucifer, some later writers, such as Johann Wolfgang von Goethe, have viewed Faust's quest for knowledge as heroic. In the early version of the legend that is presented here, the attitudes of the devils toward their plight and toward human beings, as well as Faust's character, are particularly thought-provoking. In addition to Goethe, the Faust legend has provided the inspiration for literary works by Honoré de Balzac, Robert Browning, George Gordon Lord Byron, Nathaniel Hawthorne, Christopher Marlowe, and Thomas Mann.

Prometheus, the Fire-Bringer

Historical Background

Greek mythology is known and valued throughout the world because of its exciting tales and the universal psychological relevance of its themes. The myths themselves reflect a cultural enrichment that began with the invasion of the Mycenaeans, Indo-European peoples from the Caucasus and the grassland steppes of Eurasia. They entered Macedonia around 2600 B.C. and moved south into mainland Greece and the Peloponnesus between c. 1900 and c. 1600 B.C. In Greece, the Mycenaeans, who were pa-triarchal in their social and religious organization, encountered local communities that were sedentary, agrarian, and matriarchal, and that worshiped the Great Goddess.

Archaeologists have discovered the ruins of many important Mycenaean palace-states as well as major centers of the Minoan, goddess-oriented culture on the islands of Crete and Santorini. Surviving artifacts reveal much about the attitudes and values of the two cultures.

With their dead, the Mycenaeans buried a wealth of pottery, jewelry, and war gear in the form of metal helmets, shields, and a variety of weapons. The fact that they decorated their possessions with scenes of hunting, raiding, and warfare testifies to their love of these pursuits. They built fortified palaces that were the political, economic, and social centers of their kingdoms and that had walls as thick as twenty-three feet. Greeks living in the fifth century B.C. thought that giants had constructed these walls in a bygone Age of Heroes.

Minoan burials included pottery and jewelry as well, but they were remarkably lacking in war gear. Their decorations emphasized the beauty of nature and joyful pursuits.

The Mycenaean golden age occurred between c. 1450 B.C., when the Mycenaeans conquered the island of Crete with its fabulous Minoan civilization, and c. 1200 B.C., when civil wars throughout the Mediterranean brought their civilization to an end. After the conquest of Crete, the Mycenaean written language, known as Linear B, and Mycenaean gods became part of Minoan culture as well. For example, a clay tablet from the palace at Pylos in the Peloponnesus dated c. 1316 B.C., mentions Zeus,

Poseidon, Ares, Hera, and Athena. Surviving tablets from the same period, but found at the palace of Knossos on Crete, mention Zeus,
Poseidon, Ares, and Athena, but not Hera.

Although tablets from both locations mention many earth divinities,
the names of the Titans do not appear on tablets from either location.
Despite the lack of this type of evidence, the role of the Titans in the
myths and legends told by Homer, Hesiod, and the ancient Greek poets
who followed them testifies to their earlier importance. For example, in
the following myth Cronus rules the Titans; Helius and Selene are, respectively, god of the sun and goddess of the moon; and the oracle at
Delphi belongs to Themis.

The Mycenaeans were a seafaring people who appreciated, adopted,
and transformed the accomplishments of the older Mediterranean civilizations. The Minoans and Egyptians introduced them to painting and sculpture, the Phoenicians to the alphabet, the Babylonians to mathematics,
and the Hittites to the use of iron. However, given the nature of the
oral tradition, Mycenaean literature (including their mythology) reflects
aspects of all of these cultures and, fortunately, it survived the dark age
that followed the collapse of their civilization.

Appeal and Value

Greek mythology is particularly interesting because it was recorded as
early as c. 775 B.C. by Homer, and then by later Greek poets, bards, and
dramatists, all of whom were educated in the oral literature of their culture and trained to perpetuate it through their art. Consequently, Greek
myths reflect the authentic perspective of the insider, and any particular
version combines the author's cultural heritage with his or her personal
attitudes and values.

The myth of Prometheus is the most important myth from ancient
Greece. It is remarkable in that it asserts that divinity must respect the
needs of human beings, and it depicts complex personality traits that are
universal and timeless. Because Greek gods and heroes resemble modern human beings, and because the Greek view of the human condition
resembles our own, the myth of Prometheus has influenced ideas and
attitudes in the Western world through the centuries.

The myth reflects the view of the ancient Greeks toward human beings and their gods. The Greek divinities—both the earlier family of Titans and the later family of Olympians—are reflections of ancient Greek
aristocrats. They look, think, speak, and act like human beings, with the
same needs, the same desires, and the same imperfections.

In this myth, both the lives of human beings and the lives of their gods are in the early stages of transition. Human society is changing from one that is sedentary, agricultural, and generally peaceful to one that is multidimensional in its economy and more acquisitive and aggressive in its pursuits. Divine life is changing from the rule of the Titans, led by Cronus, to the rule of the younger and more civilized Olympians, led by Zeus.

We owe the appeal and value of the Prometheus myth to the vision of two great writers from ancient Greece: first, Hesiod; and, later, Aeschylus.

Hesiod's Contribution

The earliest existing version of the myth of Prometheus is related by the ancient Greek poet Hesiod, who explains the origin of gods and mortals as well as particular aspects of human life. In his *Theogony* (written c. 725 B.C.), he tells of the time when the power of Zeus is new and the religious practices of human beings are changing. He relates how Prometheus, the clever Titan, creates a deceptive sacrifice to Zeus and later steals fire from the gods, thereby bringing the wrath of Zeus upon himself and mortal men.

Hesiod also relates the myth of Prometheus in order to explain the source of the many evils that are part of the human condition. Anyone who attempts to trick Zeus, including another divinity, brings dire consequences upon himself and those he loves. (Other Greek myths share this perspective.)

Consequently, Zeus not only punishes Prometheus for his rebellious behavior, but he also levies two severe punishments against mortal men. First, he deprives them of the use of fire. Then he causes the creation of the first mortal woman, Pandora (whose name means "all gifts"), and makes her the source of all of the evils and consequent suffering that from that time forth will afflict human beings. (Hesiod himself created Pandora to be an evil transformation of the Great Goddess, who always provides the life-giving gifts that sustain human beings.)

Aeschylus's Contribution

Approximately two hundred fifty years after Hesiod, the great Greek dramatist Aeschylus, in his *Prometheus Bound* (written c. 450 B.C.), developed the Prometheus myth that Hesiod relates. However, Aeschylus focused on the part of the myth that Hesiod barely mentioned, Prometheus's bondage. Aeschylus lived at a different time from Hesiod, and he was interested in different issues. Given the loss of so much of the Greek literature that was available to Aeschylus, we cannot know which parts of the Prometheus myth he developed from other sources and which parts he created. However, his *Prometheus Bound* is the first (and the only existing) play of a trilogy. Presumably, the issues that he raises in the first play were brought to their resolution in the third play of the trilogy.

It is possible that an earlier form of this myth may have offered an explanation for the origin of earthquakes. Certain myths and folktales that are indigenous to the Caucasus region explain earthquakes as being caused by the efforts of a giant to free himself from a divinity's punishment. Depending upon the version, this giant thrashes about while he is either imprisoned in a mountain cave or tied to a great pillar.

It is Aeschylus, not Hesiod, who relates the tale of Prometheus's gifts to mortal men. Aeschylus explains how human beings were created; acquired the ability to reason; learned how to farm, hunt, and make tools and weapons; build ships and chariots; read and write; and make medicines. It is Aeschylus who develops the relationship between Prometheus and Zeus and, in the process, develops the myth's political, religious, and psychological themes.

In political terms, the Athenians of Aeschylus's generation could look back to a period when Athens was ruled by tyrants. Consequently, given the potentially volatile nature of politics in Athens, one of Aeschylus's goals may have been to keep the specter of the tyrant, here in the form of Zeus, before the Athenian people in order to kindle memories of their own history of tyranny and thus help them value and preserve their current democracy.

In religious terms, Aeschylus chooses to examine the relationship between human beings and their gods, and he questions religious views that prevailed not only throughout the Mediterranean but throughout the world. The study of world mythology reveals how early religious behavior was based on the belief that a reciprocal relationship existed between human beings and their gods. If the gods were pleased with sacred offerings of humans, animals, or plants, they would help those who had sacrificed to them. Consequently, it is Aeschylus's treatment of this subject, rather than the subject itself, that is remarkable for its time.

In psychological terms, Aeschylus examines a pattern of attitudes and behavior that is typical of the characters in Greek myth and legend, from its earliest appearance in Homer through its development by the Greek tragedians—a pattern still exhibited by people today. The foundation of this four-stage pattern is the possession of *aretē,* or excellence. Titans, gods, and mortals all strive for *aretē,* in their endeavors. The *aretē,* of gods or heroes is often their renowned leadership, their unusual cleverness, their tremendous strength, or their great skill in battle.

Those who possess *aretē*, are likely to slide into the second stage of the pattern, which the ancient Greeks called *hubris*, or excessive pride. If *hubris* remains hidden in the mind and does not reveal itself in words or deeds, it is harmless.

However, those who possess *hubris* usually fall into the third stage of the pattern, *atē*, where they believe that, given who they are and what they already have accomplished, they can do whatever they want to do, no matter what it is. Therefore, they usually speak and act arrogantly, with what the ancient Greeks called *atē*, or "blind recklessness." Without stopping to consider the consequences of their behavior (hence the Greek emphasis on "blind"), they imprudently overstep their boundaries and commit a rash act.

Those who succumb to *atē*, inevitably experience the final stage of this pattern, which is a type of punishment that the ancient Greeks called *nemesis*. *Nemesis* is always a form of retribution that results in personal tragedy.

It is possible to find this four-stage pattern in Prometheus's attitudes and behavior, and in Zeus's as well. Consequently, beyond the significant political and religious impact of this myth, Prometheus's personality and his ability to endure the consequences of his actions combine to make him one of the greatest figures in world mythology. For Zeus, the pattern is incomplete, both in *Prometheus Bound* and in the following version of the Prometheus myth. However, both versions imply that in order to avoid his *nemesis*, Zeus will eventually free Prometheus.

PROMETHEUS, THE FIRE-BRINGER

In a time long past, when the world was young and the Olympian gods first ruled the universe, Prometheus, the clever Titan, created mortal men out of clay and water. At first, these men were frail and helpless. They lived like ants in dark shelters within the earth. Because they did not understand the cycle of the seasons, they enjoyed the beauty of spring flowers and the taste of summer and autumn fruits, but they did not prepare for the barren winter that would inevitably follow. Peaceful by nature and agrarian by pursuit, they were prey to disease, to flood and drought, and to famine.

Prometheus's heart flooded with pity for the fragile creatures whom he had created. Just as when reapers cut barley and wheat in a rich man's field, the grains fall thick and fast upon the ground, so Prometheus quickly did everything in his power to enrich the lives of his poor mortals. First, he gave them intelligence and the ability to reason. And then he gave them the knowledge and skills in every art and craft that they would need in order to survive and prosper.

The clever Titan taught his frail creatures how to build houses of wood and brick that would face the path of Lord Helius's chariot so that they would receive the warmth and light of the sun's fiery rays. He taught them how to understand the cycle of the seasons by observing Night's robe of brightly shining stars. And he also taught them how to tame wild beasts, and then how to train them to carry burdens.

The clever Titan taught his frail creatures how to find fire in the ash tree—how to keep it alive by covering it with ashes, how to tame it, and how to make it work for them—because he knew that the use of fire leads to greatness in every art and craft. He taught them how to find copper, silver, and gold beneath the earth's surface. He also taught them how to use fire in order to make bronze from copper and tin. And he taught them how to form bronze into tools and weapons.

The clever Titan taught his frail creatures how to build seaworthy ships that could travel the sea-roads so that they might gain goods by trading and raiding. And he also taught them how to build wheeled chariots and how to harness their horses to them so that, with this device, they could both show off their wealth and excel in battle.

The clever Titan taught his frail creatures how to read, how to write, and how to calculate with numbers. He taught them how to use plants to make healing foods, drinks, and salves. And he also taught them to read the future through dreams, oracles, bird-signs, and the flames in a blazing fire.

However, being mortal, the men whom Prometheus had created were still vulnerable. Although they possessed medicines, they were still prey to disease. They suffered from floods and drought and famine. Consequently, despite the gifts that the clever Titan had given them, Prometheus's frail creatures often died before they had had a chance to live.

And, being aware of their own vulnerability, they offered Zeus, Greatest of the Immortals, the best of their food. In solemn rites, the flames of their sacrificial fires consumed their offerings of entire animals, even though they themselves often lived in hunger.

Now, Zeus Who Reigns on High—he who gathers the clouds and delights in thunder—had only recently become Lord of Olympus and Father of Gods and Men. Zeus had led the Olympian gods in revolt against his father, Cronus, who was Lord of the Titans. Prometheus had chosen to side with Zeus in the great war between the two generations of gods, offering the rebellious god his wise counsel. And it was with the help of Prometheus that the Loud-Thunderer had forcibly seized the throne of his father, whom he had then hurled into the darkest depths of black Tartarus—that sunless land that lies far below the surface of the earth. Thus it had come to pass that Zeus now reigned supreme in place of Cronus.

Now, however, it came to pass that Prometheus learned that Zeus wished to destroy his fragile creatures and to create a new race of mortals in their place. The heart of the clever Titan flooded first with pity, then with wrath, and finally, with cunning resolve.

"Zeus Who Delights in Thunder will not have his way in this matter!" Prometheus declared to himself. "I will protect my frail mortals from the evil designs of the Mighty Lord of Olympus! For I alone possess the courage and intelligence to outwit Zeus!"

And so it came to pass that the clever Titan used his favored position with Zeus to argue on behalf of the mortal men who now walked the earth. He approached the Loud-Thunderer and declared, "Father of Gods and Men! Greatest of the Immortals! Let pity flood your heart for the frailty of the men whom I have created! As if it were not enough that they are doomed from their birth to die, they are buffeted by a flood of ills!

"Storms and drought rob them of the food that would sustain them," the Titan explained. "Therefore, in order to attempt to win the goodwill of the Great Cloud-Gatherer, they offer you the meat that they themselves need in order to survive! And so I have come to ask for your help. In your infinite kindness, will you not permit my poor creatures to cast but part of their sacrificial victim into the flames so that they can have the rest for their own nourishment?"

To these words Zeus Who Delights in Thunder responded, "Prometheus, you are not the only immortal who has a kind heart! You will see that Zeus Who Reigns on High can match your nobility! As long as your helpless creatures honor the Mighty Lord of

Olympus with an appropriate offering, I hereby decree that they may keep for themselves what remains!

"The only issue will be to decide which part of the ox will be for the Lord of Olympus and which part for mortal men," Zeus declared. "And, of course, the appropriate offering for the Greatest of the Immortals is the rich ox meat!"

"Father of Gods and Men, your kind heart is surely the equal of your greatness!" Prometheus declared. "And, as proof of our gratitude, on behalf of my fragile creatures I now invite you to join us in order to choose which part of the sacrifice will be yours and which you will leave for those who walk the earth. The mortal men whom I have created long to do their best to please you. Therefore, it is only fair for you to tell them how they may best accomplish this!"

With these words, the clever Titan returned to earth and began to prepare the sacred sacrifice to Zeus. First, he killed and skinned a huge ox. Then he cut up and separated the rich red meat from the animal's white bones. He divided the sacrifice into two separate offerings, placing both on the altar dedicated to the Cloud-Gatherer. First, the clever Titan hid all of the rich ox meat together with the ox's fatty inner parts within and beneath the animal's foul-smelling stomach. Then, he carefully hid all of the ox's barren white bones within and beneath layer upon layer of the animal's shining fat. Finally, he ignited the sacred sacrificial fire.

When it came to pass that Zeus Who Reigns on High smelled the smoke from the sacred fire, he came down from Mount Olympus in order to determine which part of the sacrificial ox would become his. The Cloud-Gatherer was quick to see that the Titan had indeed prepared two sacrifices instead of one. And he was quick to see how unequal these two sacrifices appeared to be.

Just as the flames of a shepherd's campfire darken and look benign when they have become most searing, so the eyes of the Loud-Thunderer now smoldered with hidden fury. "Most clever Titan, it will now be my pleasure to choose between these two offerings!" Zeus exclaimed. "However, I expected that you and I would fight over this sacrifice even as a mountain lion and a boar fight over the right to drink from a small spring high in the mountains. Instead, I see that you have divided the portions so unfairly that you have given me a gift rather than a choice!

"I fear that this does not bode well for our friendship!" the Cloud-Gatherer declared. "Surely you know which of these offerings will please the Mighty Lord of Olympus! And I know that the great benefactor of mortal men will never starve the frail creatures whom he so dearly loves!

"Now, if you are as wise as you are clever, Prometheus, you will have treated me with the respect that I deserve! However, if you are so foolish as to think that you are outwitting me, beware of the consequences of my wrath!" Zeus warned.

To these words, the clever Titan smiled gently and responded, "Father of Gods and Men! Greatest of the Immortals! It may not appear to be so, but I have truly given you a choice rather than a gift! The men whom I have created wish to do their best to please you! And so it is only fair for you to tell them how they may best accomplish this! You must choose whichever of the two offerings will bring joy to your heart!"

And so it came to pass that Zeus—he who gathers the clouds and delights in thunder—declared, "In honor of the Mighty Lord of Olympus, I hereby choose the offering that includes all of this shining fat! From this time forth and forever, those who walk the earth must offer to Zeus Who Reigns on High this sacrifice that I myself have chosen—this sacrifice and none other! And, from this time forth and forever, the other offering—the ox's foul-smelling stomach and whatever else lies in that pile—mortal men may keep for themselves!"

Just as the sight of land is welcome to shipwrecked swimmers whose swift ship Poseidon destroyed by sending towering waves and mighty winds to attack its strong frame, and with hearts overflowing with relief and joy, they finally set foot upon the small rocks that line the shore of the wine-dark sea, so a smile of delight quickly crossed Prometheus's face while Zeus attended to his offering. However, the clever Titan stood silent and still, his eyes attentive but inscrutable, as Zeus picked up layer upon layer of the ox's shining fat and discovered that one barren white bone after another had been hidden within and beneath its folds. And he stood silent and still, his eyes attentive but inscrutable, as Zeus picked up the foul-smelling stomach and discovered that all of the rich ox meat, together with the ox's fatty inner parts, had been hidden within and beneath it.

Meanwhile, Zeus Who Delights in Thunder stood silent and still before the barren white ox bones that he had chosen for his portion of the sacrifice. Then, just as the waves of the winter sea come bursting upon the shore and then rush forth wildly to flatten the walls of rich vineyards, so Zeus's heart flooded with a rage that now burst upon Prometheus.

Turning to face his adversary, the Loud-Thunderer shouted, "Why, you crafty trickster! How dare you deceive the Greatest of the Immortals! Thanks to your wily devices, from this time forth and forever, the Mighty Lord of Olympus has chosen barren white ox bones as his part of the sacrifice!

"But tell me, Prometheus—old friend!—why have you flooded my heart with wrath for such a trivial cause? Have you not done enough for these frail creatures of yours? Is there no end to the pity that your heart feels for them?" Zeus asked.

"Why, you have honored mortal men far more than they deserve! You have already given them intelligence and the ability to reason. You have already given them the knowledge and skills in every art and craft that they need in order to survive and prosper! I have seen you do this, and I have permitted you to do it!" the Cloud-Gatherer declared.

"It would have been enough if you had just taught your frail creatures how to build houses of wood and brick that face the path of Helius's chariot in order to receive warmth and light from the sun's rays! But you have taught them how to understand the cycle of the seasons by observing Night's robe of brightly shining stars. And you have also taught them how to tame wild beasts, and then how to train them to carry their burdens. I have seen you do all this, and I have permitted you to do it!" the Cloud-Gatherer declared.

"It would have been more than enough if you had just taught your frail creatures how to find fire in the ash tree—how to keep it alive by covering it with ashes, how to tame it, and how to make it work for them—because the use of fire leads to greatness in every art and craft! But you have taught them how to find copper, silver, and gold beneath the earth's surface. You have also taught them how to use fire in order to make bronze from copper and tin. And you have taught them how to form bronze into tools and weapons. This, too, I have observed, and yet I have permitted you to do it!" the Cloud-Gatherer declared.

"Then, as if all this still were not enough, you have taught your frail creatures how to build seaworthy ships that can travel the sea-roads so that they might gain goods by trading and raiding. And you have also taught them how to build wheeled chariots and how to harness horses to them so that, with this device, they can show off their wealth and excel in battle. I have seen you do all this, as well, and still I have permitted you to do it!" the Cloud-Gatherer declared.

"And, finally—as if, for you, nothing is ever enough!—you have taught your frail creatures how to read, how to write, and how to calculate with numbers! Why, you have even taught them how to use plants to make healing foods, drinks, and salves! And you have taught them to read the future through dreams, oracles, bird-signs, and the flames in a blazing fire! I have observed all this, and yet I have still permitted you to do it!" the Cloud-Gatherer declared.

Zeus's eyes suddenly became so bright that they outshone the sun in their brilliance. "But now, Prometheus, you have been too clever for your own good!" he exclaimed. "You have made your frail creatures more important than the Lord of Olympus!"

And just as a great storm suddenly sweeps in on the wings of the wind, causing the sun to flee from its power, so, quick as the storm-wind, dark clouds of rage chased the brilliance from Zeus's eyes. "Know your place, Prometheus!" the Loud-Thunderer declared. "It is Zeus who is Greatest of the Immortals! It is Zeus who is Lord of Gods and Men! Therefore, you and your frail creatures will respect Zeus's power! And you and your frail creatures will fear Zeus's wrath!"

To these words, Prometheus responded, "Why, Zeus, what is the power of mortal men compared with the power wielded by the Lord of Olympus? It is not as if my frail creatures are Titans or gods that you should fear them! They are weak, and they live but a day in the eternity that belongs to those of us who are immortal!

"Now, I should not have to remind the mighty son of Cronus that he should look with favor upon mortal men for my sake, if not for theirs," the clever Titan added. "But for the wise counsels that I offered you, Zeus, it is your father—and not you—who would now be Lord of Gods and Men! Surely, you know as well as I that your power—even with all of the gods united behind you in the great battle—could not have defeated Cronus and the Titans!"

"Most clever Titan! The fault lies with you, not with me!" the Loud-Thunderer roared. "Your heart floods with pride in your own wiles! And I have been waiting for you to devise a crafty scheme against me, knowing that it would be just a matter of time before you committed a rash deed! For I have known—as surely as Helius will drive forth the chariot of the sun at the start of each day—that your pride would destroy you! And now what was sure to be has come! You have behaved recklessly, and your pride has blinded you to the consequences!

"As for me, I welcome your deception!" the Cloud-Gatherer declared. "For now you will know which of us is subject to the will of the other! Now sorrow and suffering will chase all pride from your heart!

"Therefore, Prometheus, you may have saved the best of my sacrifice for your frail creatures—but from this time forth, they are going to have to eat their meat raw!" Zeus declared. "And they will have to fashion and build without the forge! Because I forbid mortal men the use of fire!" Zeus declared. "From this time forth, the ash tree will no longer have the power to house fire's flames! When I return to Olympus, I will have removed all existing fires and all sources of fire from the earth!"

To these words, Prometheus responded, "Can it be that the son is as quick to anger and as merciless as his father was before him? Zeus, if you are nothing more than the son of Cronus, then I fear that I have only helped one tyrant replace another!"

"Your words fall upon deaf ears, Prometheus! Instead of criticizing me, you would fare far better if you aimed to soothe and to please the Mighty Lord of Olympus!" Zeus exclaimed.

And with these words, Zeus turned on his heels and left the clever Titan with his sacrificial offerings. True to his word, the Great Cloud-Gatherer wandered the earth, collecting all existing fires and all sources of fire. Finally, with a satisfied smile, he returned to his home on Mount Olympus.

Prometheus's proud heart flooded with rage, and the clever Titan now prepared to go forth to the home of the gods on Mount Olympus in order to steal fire for his frail creatures. He waited until Helius had completed his journey across the sky, and then, while he was driving the chariot of the sun back to Mount Olympus, Prometheus climbed up the mountain to the home of the gods. The clever Titan was carrying a giant fennel stalk in his hand.

Just as a wildcat waits, silent and still in the darkness, for the farmer and his family to go to sleep so that it can safely pounce upon a young sheep in the sheepfold and quickly carry the lamb off to the wildcat's den in order to feed its cubs, so Prometheus waited in the shadows of Helius's palace until he had returned with his chariot. Then, the clever Titan stealthily crept into the enclosure. He quickly approached Helius's chariot and put the tip of his fennel stalk into the sun's untiring flames.

As soon as the blazing sun stretched forth its ravenous tongue and tasted the fennel's pith, Prometheus's heart flooded with joy. The clever Titan knew that the dry white pith within the fennel stalk would not melt easily upon the fire's tongue, and that the fire would not like the taste of the rind that enclosed the pith. He also knew that the fennel's rind would protect the flaming pith from the wind's overpowering breath. Therefore, he hid an untiring flame from the blazing sun in his fennel stalk and returned to earth as quickly as if his feet had sprouted wings. And so it came to pass that the clever Titan once again gave untiring fire to his beloved creatures.

Not long thereafter, it came to pass that Zeus Who Reigns on High looked down from his home high on Mount Olympus and saw that smoke was rising from untiring flames here and there upon the earth. His heart flooded with rage to see that mortal men once again possessed fire.

Zeus found Prometheus and exclaimed, "Most crafty rebel! How dare you steal fire for your frail creatures after I have forbidden them to use it! I see that I must teach you how much more powerful I am than you are! And your fate will teach Titans and Olympians alike that no one may treat me as an equal and disobey my commands!

"First, hear what I intend to do to your beloved creatures," Zeus Who Delights in Thunder announced. "You know my son Hephaestus, do you not? He is the strong-armed Lame God and a gifted creator like yourself. At my command, Hephaestus will fashion my special gift for mortal men—the first mortal woman.

"The Lame God will mold her out of clay and water, the same materials from which you yourself created mortal men," he explained. "And once he has completed her, the other Olympians will heap their own special gifts upon her. They will endow her with beauty, charm, and skill with handiwork. And they will endow her with deceit as well—because, of course, I intend her to be an evil gift! I will call her Pandora in honor of all of the gifts that the gods will have given her."

Zeus then added, "Finally, I will give Pandora my own special gift. I will send her down to earth with a sealed jar that contains a multitude of evils. Given Pandora's inherently evil nature, in time she will open this jar. And, as soon as she removes the lid, all of its contents—except for Hope—will fly forth, never to be confined again! They will bring upon your frail creatures all of the troubles that hereafter will afflict them.

"Therefore, despite her beauty and her appealing ways, Pandora will be no blessing to anyone!" the Loud-Thunderer declared. "For I hereby decree that, from this time forth and forever, Pandora and her female descendants will be the cause of mortal men's misfortune as well as their joy!"

The Loud-Thunderer looked Prometheus in the eye, challenging him to respond to the fate of his frail creatures. However, the clever Titan only stood silent and still, his eyes attentive but inscrutable.

When Prometheus remained silent, Zeus spoke once more. "Now, crafty rebel, hear what I intend to do to you!" he exclaimed. "Because you are immortal, you and I both know that I cannot kill you any more than I could kill my father. However, I can make you wish for death every waking moment of your life! I do not have to tell you that, like the other deathless gods, you can experience physical pain and mental anguish. And, therefore, I have designed a special set of tortures that are just for you!

"First, I am sending you far to the north, to the barren and desolate land of Scythia—untrodden, pathless, and at the world's end. My son Hephaestus, the Lame God, will accompany you," Zeus explained. "There, he will bind you with inescapable bronze chains and shackle you with bronze spikes to a cliff high on Mount Caucasus. Your arms and your legs, your hands and your feet will be nailed to the cliff, and one great wedge through your chest will nail your body so that you cannot turn it. You will find no refuge, either in shelter or in sleep. For the sun will play with you by day, roasting you with its blazing rays, and the wind will play with you by night, battering you with its icy blasts.

"And there you will remain until I hurl my lightning and thunder-bolts against Mount Caucasus, shattering the rock and hurling you far beneath the earth into darkest Tartarus, where you will spend sunless days and nights beyond count shackled to the fallen boulders in the gloomy region saved for the greatest criminals!" Zeus exclaimed.

"But that will be the least of your agonies," the Mighty Lord of Olympus declared. "For, in time, the sunless days and nights beyond count will again give way to an eternity upon the heights of Mount Caucasus. Once again, Hephaestus will bind you with inescapable bronze chains and shackle you with bronze spikes to the cliff. Once again, your arms and your legs, your hands and your feet will be nailed to the cliff, and one great wedge through your chest will nail your body so that you cannot turn it. And, once again, you will find no refuge, either in shelter or in sleep. For, once again, the sun will play with you by day, roasting you with its blazing rays, and the wind will play with you by night, battering you with its icy blasts.

"Then, however, a new torture will await you," the Mighty Lord of Olympus announced. "Hephaestus will fashion a great-winged, shining eagle for me, and I will give this bird the breath of life. Just as a hungry mountain lion who has had no meat for days breaks into a sheepfold—where it pounces upon the flock, carries off a lamb, and then ravenously tears into its living flesh with its sharp teeth— so my great-winged eagle, ravenous for the taste of meat, will swoop down from the heights of Mount Caucasus and pounce upon you.

"And just as the great waves of the salt sea pound the shore one after another when the dread blast of the north wind drives them up from the deep, so every day—uninvited and unwelcome—my great-winged, shining eagle will greedily tear into your flesh," explained the Mighty Lord of Olympus. "He will savagely gnaw upon your liver until he has devoured it, and his feast will take as long as it takes Helius to transport the chariot of the sun across the sky.

"Meanwhile, every night, your liver will restore itself and your body will heal. Therefore, when Helius next drives forth his chariot, once again my great-winged, shining eagle, ravenous for the taste of meat, will swoop down from the heights of Mount Caucasus. Once again, he will savagely tear into your flesh, and once again he will feast upon your liver," added the Mighty Lord of Olympus.

"Just think of it, Prometheus! Excruciating physical pain and mental anguish, day and night, again and again! Either you will be experiencing the greatest physical agony, or you will be dreading its return! Surely, the plan that I have for you, crafty rebel, is a match for your own clever schemes! And your punishment will teach the deathless ones and mortals alike that Zeus Who Reigns on High is, indeed, Greatest of the Immortals, and he is to be honored and feared above all others!" the Mighty Lord of Olympus concluded.

Once again, the Loud-Thunderer looked Prometheus in the eye, this time challenging him to respond to his own fate. However, the clever Titan only stood silent and still, his eyes attentive but inscrutable.

Finally, the clever Titan looked his enemy in the eye and declared, "Zeus, you may be Mighty Lord of Olympus now, but you are also a tyrant! The Olympians are quietly judging you, and, if you continue to be unjust, they will unite and revolt against you!

"Whether or not that comes to pass, the time will come when, if you wish to remain in power, you will need to know a secret that my mother Themis has told me!" Prometheus added. "Now, I will tell you this much, but no more. You have a fondness for women—

lovely immortal women, and, in time to come, lovely mortal women as well. You will become the father of great gods and great heroes!

"Now, my mother has told me that you will marry a goddess whose son will be greater than his father!" Prometheus declared. "You may have forgotten—or you may no longer appreciate—that you reign supreme in your father's place because my advice enabled you to overpower Cronus and seize his throne. However, you cannot afford to forget that unless I choose to help you by revealing the identity of this goddess, this son of yours will seize your throne and reign supreme in your place! And this will come to pass, Zeus, as surely as Selene follows Helius, driving forth the chariot of the moon!"

To these words Zeus Who Thunders on High responded, "Your threats fall upon deaf ears, Prometheus! Once you are chained to Mount Caucasus, and my great-winged, shining eagle happily feasts upon your liver each day, you will do anything I ask of you!"

Prometheus then replied, "Mighty Lord of Olympus, you do not have the wisdom to rule the deathless gods and mortal men if you think that I am a frail creature who will help you while you keep me subjected to your torture! Just as I have yet to feel the pain of your punishment, you have yet to feel the torment of my own strength of will! In time, you will learn that I will remain silent until you release me from the agony of my bondage.

"So, proceed with my punishment, Zeus!" declared Prometheus. "Chain me to the cliffs of Mount Caucasus, and torture me! Hurl your mighty storm-winds, your lightning, and your thunder-bolts against me! Enlist the aid of your great brother, Poseidon, the Earth-Shaker. Let his great arms wrench the earth loose from the roots that hold it firm, and let his mighty trident send the waves of the sea soaring into the sky to splash Night's robe of brightly shining stars! Hurl me deep into the sunless gloom of Tartarus!

"Then, nail me high upon the cliff of Mount Caucasus once again, and set your great-winged, shining eagle upon me that he may feast upon my liver! I still will not reveal the name of the goddess whose marriage you should fear! You can tear my body to shreds, but you will never break my spirit! My will to survive your tortures is far stronger than the strongest fetters!" exclaimed Prometheus. "Sooner or later, when none of your tortures have been successful, you will release me in order to learn my secret!"

And so it came to pass that Prometheus remained chained to Mount Caucasus, where he was tortured—above and below the earth—for thirty thousand years. Early in his bondage, he warned his son Deucalion about the great flood that Zeus was sending to destroy the entire human race. The clever Titan told Deucalion how to build a chest that would hold his wife, himself, and provisions to sustain them for a long sea journey. And it came to pass that Deucalion and his wife, alone of all mortals, survived the great flood. They floated for nine days and nights before the rain finally stopped, and their chest landed on a slope of Mount Parnassus. There, with the help of Themis, they brought a new race of mortals into the world.

And, finally, it came to pass that, when these thirty thousand years had come and gone, Zeus needed to know Prometheus's secret. In order to give even greater glory to his great mortal son, Heracles, who was busily performing his famous labors, the Father of Gods and Men permitted Heracles to kill the ravaging eagle and to free Prometheus from his bonds.

However, as a symbol of Prometheus's bondage and his subordination to the Lord of Olympus, Zeus—Greatest of the Immortals—ordered Prometheus to bind his fingers with two rings, one of stone and one of bronze. The stone ring was in memory of the cliffs of Mount Caucasus, while the bronze ring was in memory of Prometheus's unbreakable bronze bonds. And from that time to this, mortals too have worn rings on their fingers in memory of the suffering that their great creator and benefactor endured for their sake, in that time long past, when the world was young.

Oisin Mac Finn,
Poet of the Fianna

Historical and Literary Background

The Celts

Irish tradition reflects Celtic roots in Ireland and Scotland. The Celts were Indo-Europeans who dominated Iron Age Europe and were known for their use of iron tools, weapons, and wagons. They arrived in the British Isles from the fifth to the third centuries B.C. and controlled Britain until A.D. 43, when Rome conquered the southern part of the island. They controlled Ireland until it became Christian in the fifth century A.D. Their language and the oral tradition of their myths and legends continued to thrive for centuries thereafter.

The Celts never united to form a nation, and they never developed their own written language. Consequently, our information is based primarily on the reports of others: sixth- and fifth-century B.C. Greeks, who called them *Keltoi*; Julius Caesar's *Commentarii de bello Gallico* (a seven-volume commentary on the Gallic Wars); the oral literature of the Celts as Christian monks recorded it; and the results of archaeological investigation.

The Celtic peoples worshiped the Tuatha De Danaan (People of Danaan). Danaan, or Danu, was the Great Goddess or Mother Goddess and the mother of all the Celtic gods (her "people"). These were nature gods, who lived in the Otherworld, called Tir na nOg (Land of Youth), and brought life, light, warmth, and civilization to the Celtic people. Queens of the Tuatha De Danaan were also Great Goddesses. In the following myth, both Sadbh (Finn's wife and Oisin's mother) and Niamh (Oisin's wife) are members of the Tuatha De Danaan.

The religious leaders of the Celts, called druids, were the scientists, doctors, priests, prophets, magicians, poets, and musicians of their society. They were so important that they ranked next to the Celtic chieftain-kings in prestige.

Mediterranean peoples were living in Ireland when the Celts arrived. In Celtic myth, the gods of this non-Celtic people are called the Fomor. They are skilled in the use of magic, and they are the formidable enemy of the Celtic gods. Although they bring death, darkness, and cold, they also possess the power to make the land fertile. In the following myth, the tale of the queen whom Oisin rescues on his journey with Niamh to the Land of Youth reflects the enmity between the Fomor and the Tuatha De Danaan. In this way, Celtic myth reflects actual religious, social, and political differences within Celtic Ireland.

In Irish tradition, as in many others, mythology and ancient history are the same, which is to say that the authors of these myths treated them as if the events had actually occurred. However, Irish tradition is complicated by the fact that the ancient history and legends of Celtic Ireland were transformed by the Irish and Scottish monks who recorded them, beginning in the eighth century A.D.

While these monks recorded old and authentic myths and legends in the *Lebor Gabala Erenn (Book of the Taking of Ireland)*, they rewrote them in a manner that reflects both their fascination and their discomfort with this non-Christian material. They were too concerned with the issue of preserving it in a way that would be compatible with their own spiritual beliefs to attempt to understand anything about its underlying spiritual significance for the Celts. Consequently, the following history has been "Christianized" and contrasts with more authentic Celtic belief.

Irish history, set forth in the *Lebor Gabala Erenn*, records the settlement of Ireland by six successive races of peoples. Some of these people are divine, while others are human. The divine races possess great powers but inhabit the land like human beings.

The most important of the ancient races (the fifth race to occupy Ireland) is the Tuatha De Danaan, called the People of the Gods of Dana, or the Men of Dea, and composed of both gods and humans. The gods are the powerful and talented members of the race, such as the craftspeople, artists, poets, musicians, doctors, and aristocratic warriors, and they are all known for their skill in the use of magic. The humans are the farmers and the common laborers who work in the fields. In time, the Tuatha De Danaan are conquered by the sixth and last race, the children of the Gael, led by the Sons of Miled (a human race from Spain).

Since their defeat, the divine members of the Tuatha De Danaan no longer inhabit the land like human beings. Instead, they have made themselves invisible to the human eye, and they have retreated into the most beautiful valleys, hills, and mountains of Ireland, where they have hidden their sites behind invisible walls. They also live on islands, in lakes, under the sea, and in ancient burial mounds. In the following myth, the Land of Youth (Tir na nOg) is far beyond the western sea.

The enemy of the invading races, the Fomor, is a race of divine, monstrous giants who have one eye, one hand, and óne foot. They are a sea people who inhabit the islands off the coast of Ireland and take slaves as tribute.

The Irish Cultural Renaissance

Toward the end of the nineteenth century, Lady Isabella Augusta Gregory and William Butler Yeats led the Irish Cultural Renaissance by reviving Celtic mythology and Irish folktales. Lady Gregory visited countless Gaelic storytellers—who lived in the Irish countryside and in the Scottish Highlands and spoke a modern form of the language of the ancient Gaels or Celts—in order to record and publish their renditions of the old Celtic myths, legends, and folktales.

Lady Gregory's *Gods and Fighting Men: The Story of the Tuatha De Danaan and of the Fianna of Ireland* (1904) became the first popular literary version of the great Celtic hero cycle of Finn Mac Cumhal, his son Oisin, and his company of warrior-heroes, called the Fianna Erin (Gaelic), or the Fenians (Troops) of Ireland. Meanwhile, Yeats chose Oisin's journey to the Land of Youth as the subject of his famous poem, "The Wanderings of Oisin," featured in the title of his first collection of poetry (1889).

The Fenian Cycle of Finn, Oisin, and the Fianna

When Lady Gregory and others investigated the contemporary Gaelic oral tradition, they found that the content of the Fenian cycle was far older than the existing manuscripts indicate. Because it was loved in Scotland as well as in Ireland, initially it was probably the folk literature of a pre-Celtic people who occupied first Ireland and then Scotland.

Finn Mac Cumhal and the Fianna were common folk, rather than aristocrats and, therefore, they later became the heroes of the Celtic common people of both countries, who continued to develop stories about them. Even later, the aristocratic Celts adopted and adapted some of the Fenian material. Finally, Finn and the Fianna acquired historical significance, and the Fenian cycle became part of the written literature of Ireland and Scotland.

The Fenian cycle reveals its ancient roots in that its content concerns the activities of heroes who are not aristocrats themselves, but who serve the High Kings of Ireland by keeping order. It is interesting that the laws of ancient Ireland recognized the existence of the Fianna and that they fought on foot rather than on horseback (a fact that distinguishes the common people from aristocrats).

Although the members of the Fianna were warriors on occasion, they spent most of their time hunting and enjoying other outdoor activities in the southern and eastern Irish countryside. The poems about them, most of which are attributed to Oisin, celebrate the joys of sharing these active pursuits with good friends and the appreciation of Ireland's rocky coast and beautiful wilderness.

Finn and Oisin in Written Literature

Although Irish historians from the eleventh century to the seventeenth century have treated Finn Mac Cumhal and his son Oisin as real people, according to Lady Gregory's research, Finn and the Fianna are mythical rather than legendary because neither the existing, older written texts nor the contemporary Gaelic oral tradition confirm a particular period in which these heroes lived.

The manuscripts place Finn and the Fianna in the third century, during the reign of King Cormac Mac Art. According to legend, Cormac appointed Finn to be the commander of his professional army early in the third century, and the famous battle of Gabhra, which marked the end of the Fianna's power, occurred at the end of that century.

However, many other events in the lives of Finn, Oisin, and their companions reflect either much later occurrences, such as the Norse invasions in the eighth and early ninth centuries, or the supernatural environment that exists only in myths and ancient legends. Although Finn and Oisin live in the world of ordinary mortals, they and their companions possess superhuman size and strength, and the supernatural is an active presence in their lives. Oisin, for example, is a demigod in that his mother is a divinity who has been magically transformed into an animal. He relates to the gods as if he is their equal, and he even becomes king of their country. He defeats a giant who is the enemy of the gods, and he lives a miraculously long life.

Oisin lives long enough to be able to meet Saint Patrick (c. A.D. 385–462), the patron saint of Ireland. Saint Patrick is credited with introducing Christianity, European ideas, and writing to Celtic Ireland in the fifth century, and he is the author of the two oldest Irish documents.

Poets and official bards continued to transmit literature orally until at least the middle of the seventh century, and the Celtic oral tradition was strong enough to preserve heroic cycles for seven hundred or eight hundred years. The first manuscripts apparently were written from the seventh to the ninth centuries, but these were destroyed by the Norse invaders, who had no use for them. Consequently, the oldest existing manuscripts are twelfth-century copies of earlier manuscripts.

The earliest existing manuscript about Finn, "The Boyish Exploits of Finn Mac Cumhal," is a copy from the year 1453. The "Colloquy of the Old Men" (also known as the "Dialogue between Oisin and Patrick") was probably composed toward the end of the twelfth century, but the existing manuscripts are fourteenth- and fifteenth-century copies and present different versions of the event. Usually, Oisin remains determined to die a pagan; however, in a few versions, Saint Patrick succeeds in converting him to Christianity.

The myths in which Oisin enters a cave, a rock, or Tir na nOg appear in eighteenth-century poems. In one version, which may reveal matriarchal roots, Niamh's father condemns her to wear a pig's head in a futile attempt to avoid the prophecy that his son-in-law will win the contest for his throne and succeed him as king of Tir na nOg. The most famous version of Oisin in Tir na nOg appears in the last Gaelic work of literature, the "Lay of Oisin in the Land of Youth," written by the poet Michael Comyn in the 1750s, during the period that Yeats called "the Celtic twilight."

Appeal and Value

The myth of Oisin treats the issue of illusion on two levels, style and subject. It is evident that those who created this myth felt the presence of magic in nature because the aura and power of that magic found its way into their worldview and into their oral literature. The style of the myth conveys the mysterious atmosphere and mood that mark the world beyond the human world. It succeeds in the difficult task of creating the essence of illusion, which is intangible, in the tangible form of a poet's words, first heard in the oral tradition, and later, read. To the extent that illusions are fantasy—images that appear and disappear in the mists, or worlds that human beings cannot experience—this myth successfully captures them and makes them appear to be real. At their best, Oisin's experiences shimmer and captivate the reader's imagination just as Niamh captivates Oisin.

The myth also deals with the illusion of the value of immortality. Oisin's choice addresses the human need to remain eternally alive and young, and the fantasy that these would be blessings. It supplies an answer to the question, "How would I feel if I could find a way to live forever?" Oisin's experience leads readers to reconsider the value of love and friendship, shared human joys and sorrows, and the unexpected challenges and surprises in their lives. Consequently, this myth has the power to influence how we view our own life experiences.

In the following myth and the culture from which it comes, a son is known in connection with his father, and in Gaelic "Mac" means "son of." Consequently, Oisin is known as Oisin Mac Finn, and his father Finn is known as Finn Mac Cumhal. Although the father-son relationship may no longer exist, the old structure is present in surnames that are common in our own culture. For example, the original "son of Donald" has become the surname McDonald, MacDonald, Mac Donald, or Macdonald.

OISIN MAC FINN, POET OF THE FIANNA

Prologue

When the heroes of Erin walked the earth in times long past, Finn Mac Cumhal was renowned among them. With the Fianna—his great warrior clan that numbered three thousand in time of peace and more in time of war—Finn protected the High King and defended Erin from all who invaded its inviting green shores. Mortal mind and tongue lack words to praise the king of the Fianna. Finn possessed the qualities that make a man the respected leader of men. He possessed uncommon wisdom and the gifts of prophecy and magic. He possessed a kind and generous heart, distributing gold as if it were as plentiful as autumn leaves in the woods and silver as if it were as plentiful as the foamy waves of the sea. And he was like a father to the Fianna, helping anyone who was in pain or in trouble through contest, or battle, or payment of silver or gold.

Like all the Fianna, Finn was the creator and singer of tales. However, Finn fathered a son who was an even greater poet. And it is because of this son—wise Oisin of the fierce deeds—that tales of Finn and the Fianna have lived from their time to ours. So listen now to Oisin's story, and learn how it came to pass that we, who live in a much later age, can hear of times long past and rejoice in the renowned heroes of Erin.

Finn Mac Cumhal marries Sadbh of the Tuatha De Danaan.

One day, Finn and his companions among the Fianna were returning from the hunt when a lovely fawn suddenly crossed their path
and ran toward their walled compound on the Hill of Almhuin, located on the broad green plains of Leinster. All of the deerhounds
were quick to begin the chase, but the fawn was so fleet and so
nimble of foot that she outran all but Finn's pair of hounds.

Finn ran behind his hounds, listening for their cries and waiting to give them encouragement. However, only their silence reached
his ears. Finn ran faster. Suddenly, an amazing sight greeted his eyes.
The fawn was lying fearlessly on the grass while his own deerhounds
licked her face and leaped playfully over her.

Now Finn's hounds had a special place in his heart. He treasured
them because, as deerhounds, none could surpass them. He respected
them because they were actually his own cousins, and their nature
was human rather than bestial. A goddess, who had fallen in love
with Finn's uncle, had jealously transformed his aunt into a deer-
hound, and in time it had come to pass that Finn's unfortunate aunt,
in her changed form, had given birth to these two hounds.

Therefore, when Finn saw how his deerhounds were treating the
fawn, he commanded his companions to respect her life and call off
their own hounds. Finn and the Fianna resumed their journey toward the Hill of Almhuin, and Finn's hounds and the fawn followed
them, merrily frolicking along the way.

That night, it came to pass that while he slept, Finn sensed that
someone had entered his room and was watching him. When he
opened his eyes, an extraordinarily beautiful young woman was
standing next to his bed.

Finn was the first to speak. "Maiden or vision," he began, "you
are no one I have ever seen, for having seen you, I would never forget you! So if you would, please tell me who you are and why you
have chosen to come to me."

"Finn Mac Cumhal, you may call me Saba," the woman replied,
"but my name is Sadbh, and I am the fawn that your hounds chased
today. I am one of the Tuatha De Danaan, the People of the Mother
Goddess. We live far beyond the western sea, in the Land of Youth.
My grandfather is the Dagda, ruler of the earth. He was our king until
his oldest son, my father, became our new king. We bring life and
light and warmth to your land."

"Then what brings you from your land to ours?" Finn asked. "Has
your husband left you, or has another disaster befallen you?"

To these words, Sadbh replied, "Husband I have not, nor have I ever been engaged to marry, although many a prince among my own people has asked for my hand. The Dark Druid of the Gods—you might know him as the Black Magician of the Tuatha De Danaan—wanted my love, and when I rejected him, he punished me by transforming me into a fawn.

"I have traveled long and far to find you," Sadbh continued, "because just as you have earned power and respect among your own people, you have earned power and respect among my people as well. I have learned that only with you will my natural form return to me! And only with you will I be safe from another enchantment! Therefore, I have come to ask for your protection and, if you will have me, I will be your loving wife!"

"Put fear from your heart, Sadbh," Finn responded. "My heart has already claimed you for my own! No one—from my world, or from yours—will take you from me! You will be my Saba, and not only will I protect you, but the Fianna will defend you as well!"

So it came to pass that Finn and Sadbh became husband and wife, and Finn's love for his Saba flooded his heart and conquered his soul. Finn felt as if the sun did not begin to shine until he met his Saba. With her by his side, the stars shone brighter, the grass grew greener, and even the woodland streams bubbled more happily.

Gone was Finn's joy in nature. He no longer loved to hear the scolding of the blackbird, the scream of the seagull, the screech of the raven, the whistle of the otter and the eagle. He had no interest in the quacking of the ducks and the bellowing of the wild oxen. To his ears, the sound of Saba's voice put the sweet song of the lark to shame.

Gone was Finn's joy in the hunt. He no longer wished to follow the deer through the green wooded valleys, and the cry of the deerhounds could not entice him to leave his Saba. He had no interest in the badger, the hare, the great wild boar, or the wolf. One deer alone had captured his heart, and she was already his.

Gone was Finn's desire for battle and the spoils of victory. He no longer cared to contest against heroes, conquer kingdoms, and earn broad fame. The poets' rousing songs of war could not entice him to leave his Saba.

Finn was content only when his wife was by his side, and as long as she was his companion, his life was complete. So it came to pass that, when the Fianna went hunting, Finn was not among them. And when the Fianna offered or accepted challenges of skill, Finn was not among them.

However, in time it came to pass that ships bearing the Northmen of Denmark entered the Bay of Dublin, and then the High King commanded Finn and the Fianna to leave the Hill of Almhuin and defend Dublin and Erin in this time of great crisis. Reluctantly, Finn left Sadbh to the protection of those who would remain behind and guard his fortress, while he and the Fianna set out for Dublin. Under Finn's leadership, the Fianna of Erin soon sent the Northmen back across the sea. And by the time seven days and nights had come and gone, Finn was joyfully approaching the Hill of Almhuin and anticipating the welcome of his beloved wife.

However, it now came to pass that, much to his surprise, Finn's servants did not seem to be pleased to see him. And he was even more disappointed when his Saba did not come forth to welcome him.

"What is the matter?" he asked. "Why do you greet me with such solemn faces? And where is Sadbh that she has not come forth with you to greet me?"

To these words, his chief servant replied, "Finn Mac Cumhal, my dear master, you were wise to remain within our compound and to keep Lady Sadbh by your side! We tried to do as you would have us do in your absence. However, one day, someone who looked just like you—and who was even accompanied by your own deerhounds—came to the gate of our fortress, stretched forth his arms, and called in your voice, 'Oh Saba! My dear Saba! I have returned! Come forth to greet me!'

"We tried our best to prevail upon our mistress to wait a moment, and to let us go forth in her place to be certain that it was indeed you who were calling to her. For it seemed to us that, skilled as you are, you could not have arrived in Dublin, fought a great battle against the Danes, and returned to the Hill of Almhuin in so short a time. But we could not convince Lady Sadbh. We could not constrain her. And we could not delay her. With greater strength than all of us together possessed, our mistress cried, 'Let me go! I say, let me go forth to meet my Finn!' And with these words, your lady tore herself free from our grasp and joyfully rushed forth to the gate of the compound.

"As soon as Lady Sadbh came within reach," the servant continued, "the figure who resembled you raised a hazel wand and struck her with it. Suddenly—and you would have to have seen this to believe it!—Lady Sadbh vanished, and a fawn stood in the place where she had been! The fawn tried to run back into the compound, but the magician's hounds drove her back toward their master. Our hearts flooded with terror but, of course, we did our best to rush after the fawn. However, our best was not good enough—and I intend no disrespect when I tell you that I fear that your best would not have been a match for that magician either!

"We arrived too late to rescue her," the servant concluded, "for the fawn, her enchanter, and his hounds suddenly disappeared into the air, and although we tracked them through the woods by following the cries of the two hounds, they proceeded with such speed that eventually we could no longer hear them, and we were forced to give up the chase."

Finn discovers Oisin, his son, and trains him for the Fianna.

It came to pass that Finn never forgot his love for Sadbh. For seven long years, whenever he was not defending the high king and Erin, Finn and his pair of hounds would search one part of the land or another for his wife. Finn even prohibited the Fianna from hunting deer unless he and his hounds accompanied them. If he was present, he hoped to find Sadbh, and if he was not, he feared that the deerhounds of the Fianna might mistake Sadbh for an ordinary fawn and kill her. Nevertheless, despite Finn's best efforts, Sadbh remained beyond his reach. Finally, he gave up the search and returned to his former leisure pursuits.

It then came to pass that one day, as Finn and his companions were enjoying the hunt, the angry cries of their deerhounds ripped into the serene forest air and ominously rustled the leaves on the trees about them. Finn immediately rushed to the scene, with the others in close pursuit. To their amazement, they found that Finn's two hounds were angrily holding all the other deerhounds at bay, apparently protecting a naked young boy who was calmly standing with his back against the trunk of a great old tree.

"Call off your hounds, my friends!" Finn shouted. "Let me see what gift my hounds have found for me!"

Seeing that their task was over, Finn's hounds immediately turned and approached the young boy. They lovingly licked his hands and feet while Finn and his companions watched in silent amazement—for Finn's hounds were known to show affection only to Finn himself and to Sadbh.

Finn stared at the boy. The youth was tall, and he had the stature and the bearing of a young hero. However, what was most remarkable about him was his head. The gentle eyes of a deer stared out at Finn from a face that was surrounded by a mass of beautiful, long hair and, at the side of his face, a patch of deer's fur rested on his temple, as if a deer had licked him there.

Finn could not tear his own eyes away from the eyes of the boy, for his Saba appeared to be looking at him, causing his heart to cry out in fresh anguish. Suddenly, a boundless love welled up alongside the pain, overwhelming and conquering it, for Finn's heart knew that he had found Sadbh's child and his own son.

"My son!" Finn exclaimed joyfully. "I shall call you Oisin, or Little Fawn, for surely your fawn-mother is none other than Sadbh, my fawn-wife!"

The boy responded by giving Finn a questioning look, for he could not understand a word of what Finn had just said. Having taken Oisin into his heart, Finn now gathered him in his arms and hugged him. As the two walked home together, hand in hand, Finn's great hand surrounded the small hand tucked inside his own with the love that he would always feel for this child of his heart, and the woods echoed with Finn's merry laughter.

It came to pass that when Oisin learned to understand and to speak the Gaelic language, he told his father all that he could remember of his earlier life. "I lived in a cave in a beautiful land," he said, "with hills and valleys and woods and streams that are very much like those in your land, except that my land was enclosed by towering cliffs. I never did learn how one entered or left it. Summer provided me with fruits and roots, and autumn with seeds and nuts; but every winter someone whom I never saw left food for me in my cave."

"Did you have no mother or father?" Finn asked Oisin.

"The only mother whom I remember was a gentle deer. I never saw anyone who could have been my father," Oisin replied. "It is true that a tall, dark man would visit my mother, but he terrified her, and he ignored me. So great was my mother's hatred of him that his sweetest words could never find a way into her heart, and he always left her with a fury that promised to become violent. Of course, my mother, being a deer, could not speak, and therefore I have no idea who that man was."

"I have heard tales of him," Finn replied. "Your mother called him the Dark Druid of the Gods, and she said that he is the Dark Magician of the Tuatha De Danaan. He always wanted her love, and she always refused to give it to him. With his hazel wand, he could transform her into a deer and force her to obey his wishes."

"Then you are describing that tall, dark man," Oisin responded. "For it came to pass that, one day, he became so angry with my mother that he struck her with his hazel wand, causing her to leave me and to follow him. It is clear that my mother did not want to leave me, for she would walk a few steps, stop, and turn back toward me. And although she was just a deer, I remember that, as she looked at me for the last time, her eyes flooded with tears.

"I tried to follow her, but suddenly I could not move either my legs or my arms. My heart flooded with loneliness—and with anger toward the tall, dark man who was taking my mother away from me! The world outside my cave spun before my eyes, and then everything became black. I remember nothing else until I awoke and found myself far from my valley. I searched and searched for it," Oisin concluded, "but I was not able to find it. And then you found me," he said to Finn, and his gentle eyes brightened with his smile.

To these words, Finn replied, "My heart aches for you, my son! For I too have loved your mother and have lost her! But, Oisin— Little Fawn—you are my child as well as hers. You will not be lonely, because in losing your mother you have gained your father! And I will treasure you as I treasured your mother! I will teach you to become a great warrior and a valued member of the Fianna. But as great as your skills as a warrior will be, your lasting fame will come from your songs and your stories about your father and the Fianna. And in times to come—when the heroes of Erin no longer walk the earth—those who come after us will know the bard Oisin, son of Finn Mac Cumhal and Sadbh of the Tuatha De Danaan."

Years waxed and waned like the leaves on the trees in the forest. Finn trained Oisin in the values that governed the behavior of members of the Fianna. Oisin learned to be polite, kind, gentle, hospitable, and generous to women and children and to the common folk. He learned not to brag, not to lie, not to start a fight, and not to take a bribe. He learned to be loyal to his king, to value his weapons, to excel in battle, and never to retreat.

Finn also trained Oisin to perform the tasks that those who would join the Fianna must perform successfully. Oisin learned to recite the Twelve Books of Poetry and to create poetry of his own. He learned to ward off the spears of nine warriors of the Fianna and to remain unwounded while being buried up to his waist in an earthen pit and using only his arms for a shield and a hazel wand for his weapon.

Oisin learned to win a race against members of the Fianna while running through the forest with so light a foot that dry sticks remained silent beneath his feet and branches remained unbroken, and while running with such ease that his braided hair did not loosen and his weapons did not tremble in his hands as he won the race. He learned to leap over a branch as high as his forehead, to stoop under a branch as low as his knee, and to pluck a thorn from his heel—all while running at full speed.

So it came to pass that Finn, Oisin, and members of the Fianna— often a group of only fifteen heroes—defeated the king of the Saxons, the king of Britain, the king of Greece, and the king of India. And tributes in gold poured into Finn's generous hands. Finn, Oisin, and members of the Fianna fought nine battles in Spain and one hundred eighty battles in noble Erin. And tributes in gold poured into Finn's generous hands.

More years waxed and waned like the leaves on the trees in the forest. Finn became an old man, and Oisin became the father of the generous Osgar—hero of the sharp blade, the strongest warrior among the Fianna, and the source of their greatest pride after Finn and Oisin.

And it came to pass that the High King of Erin resented the power and pride of the Fianna, and he prepared to contest against them to the death. And the great battle at the hill of Gabhra took place— that last, great battle that felled the High King as well as Osgar and most of the youth of the Fianna as if they were but autumn leaves caught in a strong crosswind, that last great battle that marked the end of the Fianna as a power in Erin.

Niamh of the Golden Hair comes in search of Oisin.

Not long thereafter, early one misty spring morning, Finn, Oisin, and the surviving leaders of the Fianna took to the hunt. They hoped that their excursion into the forest at the time when all of nature was rejoicing at being alive would lighten their own heavy hearts. They were pursuing a hornless deer near Lake Lein when suddenly a royal maiden on a snow-white horse emerged from the mists of the western sea. The Fianna stopped in their tracks and stared at her.

Clearly the maiden was more than human, and except for those who remembered Finn's Sadbh, no one had ever seen such a beautiful woman. Her long, dark brown, silk cloak sparkled with stars of red and gold and was fastened in front with a gold brooch. She wore a slender gold crown upon her head, and her long golden hair was adorned with gold rings that hung from each of her curls. Her eyes were as blue as the cloudless summer sky, and they sparkled like dewdrops on the early morning grass. Her cheeks were the color of the rose, while her chalk-white skin was like a swan upon the waves. Her lips were the color of berries, and her mouth looked as sweet as the taste of honeyed wine.

The maiden sat upon a snow-white horse that was more beautiful than any horse in Erin. He carried her in a saddle of red-gold upon his back. He wore a crown of silver and a bit and reins of gold, and he was shod with four gold shoes.

The maiden was the first to speak. "Finn Mac Cumhal—noble king of the Fianna—I am delighted to see you here, for I have traveled long and far to find you!"

To these words Finn replied, "Lovely maiden or divine vision, you are no one I have ever seen, for having seen you, I would never forget you! So if you would, please tell me who you are and from what land you have come."

"I am called Niamh of the Golden Hair," the woman replied. "I am one of the Tuatha De Danaan, the People of the Mother Goddess. We live far beyond the western sea, in the Land of Youth, where my father is king. We bring life and light and warmth to your land."

"Then what brings you from your land to ours?" Finn asked. "And why do we see you here traveling alone? Where are your noble companions? Has your husband left you, or has another disaster befallen you? And why are you looking for me?"

To these words, Niamh replied, "Husband I have not, nor have I ever been engaged to marry, although many a prince among my own people has asked for my hand. I have traveled all this way in order to find your son, Oisin. And I wish to marry him, if he is willing."

"Now, fair Niamh, surely men far more suitable than my Oisin live in your own land!" Finn exclaimed.

"No, noble king," Niamh replied. "From what I have heard the poets sing of Oisin's beauty and his wisdom, his gentle nature at home, his courage in battle, and his skill in weaving tales, he alone has earned my love."

Meanwhile, Oisin was looking at this most beautiful of women and listening to her gentle, sweet voice, and he fell in love with her then and there. So it came to pass that Oisin approached her, took her hand in his, and said to her, "Niamh of the Golden Hair, your name suits you, for you are as bright and beautiful as the most brilliant stars in the heavens! Of all the maidens who live to speak my name, you alone will I marry. And for you I will fashion a thousand songs so that all the world will know of you, both now and in times to come!"

"Oisin Mac Finn," Niamh replied, "if you love me with the love of a true hero, you will not resist the obligation that I herewith place upon you. I ask you to accompany me to the Land of Youth. Do you love me enough to come with me to my father's kingdom?"

"My dearest Niamh! I will accompany you to the end of the world, if that is your wish!" Oisin exclaimed.

"Then, Oisin Mac Finn, climb upon my horse and come with me! In the Land of Youth, Life reigns supreme and has cast out Death, who would woo folk to his dreary land with the sweet music of his song and his harp. In the Land of Youth, Time reigns beyond all desires and has cast out Change, with its Disease, Decline, and Decay. In the Land of Youth, Delight reigns beyond all dreams and has cast out Care, Pain, and Sorrow.

"In the Land of Youth, Summer reigns perpetually and has cast out Darkness, Cold, and Hunger. In the Land of Youth, Beauty reigns beyond all visions, while Plenty reigns beyond all needs. Flowers bloom in every field, while fruit hangs heavily on the branches of every tree. Silver, gold, and jewels, shining beyond all splendors, fall like leaves in a wood, while wild honey and wine, flowing beyond all measure, feed all who would eat and drink.

"In the Land of Youth, feasting never overfills, hunting never tires, and the music of the harp never ceases. In the Land of Youth, Love and Honor reign eternally.

"Climb upon my horse, Oisin Mac Finn, and come with me to the Land of Youth," Niamh continued, "and I will give you a hundred swift horses that outrun the wind, a hundred keen-scenting deerhounds, a hundred swords, a hundred bows, and a hundred coats of armor. Come with me to the Land of Youth, and I will give you a hundred cows, a hundred calves, and a hundred sheep with golden fleeces.

"Come with me to the Land of Youth, and I will give you a hundred shirts of satin, a hundred cloaks of silk, and a hundred jewels that are found only in the Land of Youth. Come with me to the Land of Youth, and I will give you a suit of mail that weapons cannot pierce and a gold-hilted sword that always finds its mark, bringing death to whomever it strikes.

"Come with me to the Land of Youth, Oisin Mac Finn, and a hundred mighty heroes, attired in armor and armed for battle, will await the command of your horn. The music of a hundred harpers will delight your ears, and the songs of a hundred maidens—sweeter by far than the music of birds—will lull you to sleep.

"You will be Lord of the Land of Youth, for you will be the first to wear my father's crown. And it will protect you, both night and day, against any danger. You will be forever young, with beauty, strength, and power that will never fade. And you will be Lord of Niamh of the Golden Hair, as well, for I will be your wife. I promise you all of this, Oisin Mac Finn—and more as well—if you will come with me to the Land of Youth."

Oisin leaves Erin and travels with Niamh to the Land of Youth.

To these words, Oisin replied, "My dear Niamh, princess of the golden rings, you have charmed me! I cannot resist your love! Of course I will marry you. And I will accompany you to the Land of Youth—or anywhere else, if you wish it! Wherever you turn, I too will turn, and wherever you lead, I will follow!"

Finn Mac Cumhal then said to Oisin, "Oh, Oisin, my son! Showers of tears fill my eyes with sorrow, and my heart floods with grief to know that you would leave us! Think of your old father, who has lost his dear grandson Osgar, and feel for him! Think of your companions among the Fianna, who have lost dear friends, and feel for them! Do not be so quick to leave the love of your father and the companionship of your friends! Do not be so quick to leave this world, with its pleasures, its challenges and its adventures, and with everything that you know and value!"

To these words, Oisin replied, "Dearest Father! Dear friends! Showers of tears fill my eyes with sorrow as I leave you! With love I remember all the times I have shared with you, my father, and with you, my friends! I remember the battles we fought so well together against great heroes, and I remember our pride in our power! I remember the hunting of deer together in the wooded valleys with our hounds, and I remember our joy in our success! I remember our chess games, our music, and our stories!"

As he gently and sweetly kissed Finn's cheek, he exclaimed, "Put grief from your heart, Father! It is true that I am leaving you and the Fianna, but I promise you that I will return!"

And with these words, Oisin mounted Niamh's princely steed and placed his arms around Niamh's waist. As they set out through the forest, Oisin did not look back.

More quickly than a beam of light flies across the earth when clouds ride across the sun, Niamh's snow-white horse carried his riders west to the great sea. As soon as his gold-shod hooves touched the waves, he neighed three times and immediately cantered forward over the surface of the clear green water with the speed of a winter wind on a mountain summit.

Finn and the Fianna heard Niamh's horse and gave three shouts of grief and mourning. The last human voice Oisin heard was his father's as he cried, "Oh, Oisin! Woe is mine, my son! For you are leaving me, and my heart knows that I will never see you again!"

The wind overtook the waves, and Niamh's horse overtook the wind. They traveled through a golden mist, which obscured all but the waves beneath them. However, it came to pass that fabulous sights would appear and disappear in the golden mist.

Oisin saw islands, cities, and white palaces. He saw a hornless fawn who was running from a pearly-white hound that had one red ear. He saw a beautiful young maiden who had a golden apple in her right hand as she rode upon a brown horse. The wind carried her on its wings as she fled from a noble young warrior who had a gold-hilted sword in his right hand as he rode upon a snow-white horse.

"My dear Niamh, are these your people, or are they mortals like me?" Oisin asked.

To these words, Niamh replied, "Pay no attention to the sights that you may see, Oisin. The sights in the Land of Youth will surpass them all!"

It came to pass that Niamh's snow-white horse carried them within sight of a beautiful fortress that rose above the waves at the end of the sea. It sparkled like the morning sun.

"Where are we now, and to whom does that fortress belong?" Oisin asked Niamh.

"That is the Land of Virtues, and that fortress belongs to the giant-king called Fomor of the Hard Blows. He captured the daughter of the lord of the Land of Life against her will, and he has brought her there to be his queen," replied Niamh.

"Although she is imprisoned in Fomor's fortress, she has told him that if he loves her with the love of a true hero, he will not resist the obligation that she has placed upon him," Niamh continued. "And she has prohibited him from asking for her hand in marriage until she can find a hero who will agree to fight him hand to hand in single combat. As yet, no hero who has passed this way has possessed the courage to do battle with the giant-king."

"My dear Niamh," Oisin replied, "surely this task has been waiting for me! I will bravely confront the giant and, if it is his fate to die, he will fall by my hand, and the queen will be free!"

So it came to pass that Niamh's snow-white horse brought its riders to the Land of Virtues and to Fomor's fortress. The young queen, a woman whose beauty equaled that of the sun, greeted them and hospitably offered them food and drink.

As they sat together on chairs of gold, she tearfully told them the tale of how she had become Fomor's prisoner. "I know that I will never be able to return to my own land as long as this great giant still lives!" she concluded.

To these words, Oisin replied, "The time has come when you can put aside your sorrow, Queen, for I will be your champion and rescue you! I will batter your captor by raining blows upon him. I promise you that either I will be successful and kill him or I will give up my life on your behalf!"

The queen responded by saying, "Oisin Mac Finn, do not be so quick with your confidence and courage! The greatest hero beneath the sun has not come forth to do what you have promised to do. I advise you to flee this land while you still can!"

The queen would have said more, but the giant-king suddenly appeared, carrying a great iron club in his right hand and a load of deerskins on his back. As soon as he saw Oisin, he looked into the face of his young queen and, without greeting his guests, he threw his pelts upon the floor and challenged Oisin to single combat.

Oisin's heart and fear were strangers. Nevertheless, this was the most powerful and valiant adversary that he had ever encountered.

Fomor was greater than any foreign invaders or wild boars that the Fianna had ever encountered. The hero and the giant fought for three days and three nights, without pausing to drink, to eat, or to rest. Bruised and bleeding, Oisin was beginning to fight a second battle against weariness, and seeing his fatigue, the two women began to weep with fear.

It came to pass that suddenly a vision appeared to Oisin in which he saw his father, Finn Mac Cumhal, as he performed his great deeds on the plain of battle. The sight flooded Oisin's limbs with renewed strength. With a mighty blow, like the blast of a winter wind upon a mountaintop, Oisin knocked the giant upon the floor, and then he quickly cut off his head.

The two young women gave three joyful cries upon seeing the defeat of the giant-king. Because Oisin was weak from his wounds, he and Niamh remained in the Land of Virtues for the night. They buried the giant in a deep earthen grave, which Oisin marked, and the queen applied healing herbs to Oisin's wounds. They quickly worked their magic, and the next morning Niamh and Oisin continued their journey to the Land of Youth.

As soon as the gold-shod hooves of Niamh's horse touched the waves, he neighed three times and immediately cantered forward over the surface of the clear green sea with the speed of a winter wind on a mountain summit.

The wind overtook the waves, and Niamh's horse overtook the wind. They traveled through a golden mist, which obscured all but the waves beneath them. However, once again, it came to pass that fabulous sights would appear and disappear in the golden mist.

Oisin saw islands, cities, and white palaces. He saw the hornless fawn who was still running from the pearly-white hound that had one red ear. He saw the beautiful young maiden who had a golden apple in her right hand as she rode upon her brown horse. The wind still carried her on its wings as she fled from the noble young warrior who had a gold-hilted sword in his right hand as he rode upon his snow-white horse.

In time it came to pass that black storm clouds suddenly arose and overtook the sun. Thunder roared and flashes of lightning angrily illuminated the sea. Wind-tossed waves became mountains that crashed down around Niamh and Oisin, but Niamh's snow-white horse continued steadfastly on his journey, single-minded in his purpose and unswerving in his direction.

Oisin weds Niamh of the Golden Hair.

When the storm clouds finally fled from the sun's rays, a land of flowers and green plains, with blue hills, sparkling lakes and waterfalls, and a great palace came into view. The palace was covered with gold and colorful gems. The surrounding summer houses shone with precious stones as well.

"Where are we now, and to whom does that palace belong?" Oisin asked Niamh.

"That is the Land of Youth, and that palace belongs to my father, who is lord of that land," Niamh replied. "You will see that my land is all that I said it would be—and more!"

Niamh and Oisin were welcomed by a hundred warriors in colorful attire, followed by the king and queen with their attendants. The king of the Land of Youth kissed his daughter, took Oisin's hand, and then announced to the assembled group:

"We hereby greet brave Oisin, gentle son of the hero Finn Mac Cumhal, whom my daughter, Princess Niamh of the Golden Hair, has chosen for her husband. A hundred thousand welcomes, my son! You will be forever young in our happy land! So enjoy yourself here with my lovely daughter, who is about to become your wife!"

Oisin thanked the king, bowed to the queen, and entered the palace with Niamh, where they feasted for ten days and ten nights. On the final day, Oisin married gentle Niamh of the Golden Hair.

Niamh and Oisin had three children—two noble young sons, named for Finn and Osgar, and a lovely daughter—when it came to pass that Oisin's thoughts turned back to Erin. His heart told him that three years had passed since he had left his father and the Fianna, and it flooded with longing to see them once again.

"My dear Niamh!" he said to his wife. "The time has come when I must return to Erin—if only for a few hours or for one day—for I must see my father and my friends!"

To these words, Niamh of the Golden Hair replied, "Poor Oisin, my beloved husband! Showers of tears fill my eyes with sorrow, and my heart floods with grief to know that you would leave me! My heart floods with despair to know that not all the joys of this land— not all my love for you—can loosen your ties to your own people, even though they are burdened by Time and by Change, and we are not. Disease, Decline, Decay, and Death are their fate, and yet you choose to leave me and return to them.

"Do not be so quick to leave the love of your wife! Do not be so quick to leave the Land of Youth, with its beauty and its peace, and with the youth, beauty, strength, and power that it has given you! Of course, if you wish, you may leave. But weep for me! Weep for yourself! Weep for our love and our life together! My heart floods with sorrow, for I know that you will never return to me!"

Oisin gently and sweetly kissed his wife and exclaimed, "Put grief from your heart, dearest Niamh! It is true that I am leaving you and the Land of Youth, but I promise you that I will return! Your horse knows the way between your land and mine, and he is sure to carry me safely to Erin and safely back again to this joyful land!"

Niamh of the Golden Hair then replied, "Oisin, my love, if you are determined to leave, then listen well to my words. I must warn you that Erin is no longer the land that you remember. Your father, Finn Mac Cumhal, and your friends, the Fianna, are there no longer. You will never find them because Death is the fate of all mortals who live in your green Erin. Instead, upon your return, you will find Saint Patrick and many priests.

"But if you must make the journey in order to learn this for yourself, then, my beloved, you must take care to believe and to remember what I am about to tell you." Niamh then declared, "If you wish to return to me, Oisin, then you must remain seated on my horse no matter what befalls you in the land of Erin. For, if you dismount from his saddle—or if just one of your feet touches the earth of Erin—you will never be able to return to the Land of Youth!

"Moreover, once your foot touches the earth of Erin, you will wither like a leaf in autumn! Sight will flee from your eyes on the wings of the wind. Strength, too, will flee from your limbs on the wings of the wind. Then you will weep with grief for your lost past and your lost future, and tears will fall from your blind eyes like berries from a tree. So remember my words, my darling!" Niamh concluded. "Remain seated on my horse no matter what befalls you upon your return to green Erin!"

To these words, Oisin exclaimed, "Do not worry, my beloved! I promise you that I will remember your warning and that I will return to you!"

Oisin's heart flooded with pain to see the beautiful faces of his wife, his sons, and his daughter marred by their grief, but his longing for Erin pushed away his anguish.

Oisin returns to Erin.

So it came to pass that Oisin mounted Niamh's princely snow-white steed and placed his hands on its gold reins. As they set out, Oisin heard Niamh cry, "Oh, Oisin! Woe is mine, my loving husband! For you are leaving me, and my heart knows that you will never return to the Land of Youth and that I will never see you again!"

However, Oisin did not look back. More quickly than a beam of light flies across the earth when clouds ride across the sun, Niamh's snow-white horse carried his rider eastward toward the great sea. As soon as his gold-shod hooves touched the waves, he neighed three times and immediately cantered forward over the surface of the clear green water with the speed of a winter wind on a mountain summit.

The wind overtook the waves, and Niamh's horse overtook the wind. Oisin traveled through a golden mist, which obscured all but the waves beneath him. However, once again, it came to pass that fabulous sights would appear and disappear in the golden mist.

Oisin saw islands, cities, and white palaces. He saw the hornless fawn who was still running from the pearly-white hound that had one red ear. He saw the beautiful young maiden who had a golden apple in her right hand as she rode upon her brown horse. The wind still carried her on its wings as she fled from the noble young warrior who had a gold-hilted sword in his right hand as he rode upon his snow-white horse.

In time it came to pass that Niamh's snow-white horse brought Oisin to the green wooded shores of Erin. Despite the years that had passed, Oisin was returning younger and stronger than when he had left.

The green wooded shores had not changed, but everything else was different. No matter where Oisin looked, nothing looked the same! He searched for signs of Finn and the Fianna, but in vain. His eyes found only what appeared to be little men, little women, and little horses. Finally, he approached a group of these little folk and asked, "Tell me, please, are Finn Mac Cumhal and the Fianna still alive, or has some terrible event destroyed them?"

The little folk regarded Oisin with wonder, amazed at his great size, his heroic strength, his unusual beauty, and his extraordinary question. After moments of silence, a little old man replied: "Long ago, when I was just a child, old bards would sing about Finn Mac Cumhal. As I recall, he was a great hero who ruled an army of warriors called the Fianna of Erin—but that was over three hundred years ago! From that day to this, no one has ever matched his wisdom, his courage, and his character."

The old man paused, as if to prod his memory. Then he added, "The old bards also sang about Oisin, Finn's noble son, who went off with a beautiful maiden from the Land of Youth. According to the old songs, Oisin's father and his friends among the Fianna searched for him to the end of their days, their hearts flooded with sorrow. However, Oisin never returned to Erin."

These words caused Oisin's own heart to flood with sorrow. He directed Niamh's snow-white horse to the Hill of Almhuin on the broad green plains of Leinster, home of Finn of the mighty deeds, home of many leaders of the Fianna, and his own home as well. He remembered the fortress as well as if it were his own face: the earthen, defensive walls that surrounded the compound; Finn's white, seven-sided palace; the white-walled houses of the lesser chiefs of the Fianna; the guest houses; and the great feasting hall that towered high above the others in the center.

However, it came to pass that, when Oisin arrived, only greater sorrow greeted his eyes. For the Hill of Almhuin was now deserted and lonely. The bright white fortress lay in ruins beneath grassy mounds and a luxurious growth of weeds and nettles, which provided grazing for a farmer's cows.

Oisin called out to Finn. But only the beating of the wind's wings reached his ears.

Oisin then called out to his father's deerhounds, for he knew that their hearing surpassed that of mortal men. But only the cows greeted his voice with their vacant eyes. And, once again, only the beating of the wind's wings reached his ears.

Oisin looked upon the decay of the home that he had known, and his heart flooded with horror. "Surely I have come under Niamh's spell, and this is but a terrifying dream that she has designed in order to punish me for returning to Erin!" he exclaimed to the wind.

And so it came to pass that Oisin traveled throughout Erin in order to find the home of every member of the Fianna. However, like Finn's fortress on the Hill of Almhuin, these strongholds also lay ruined, deserted, and lonely—buried beneath grassy mounds and a luxurious growth of weeds and nettles.

Oisin traveled throughout Erin in search of a friend. However, he only found more of the little folk, who were amazed at his great size, his heroic strength, and his unusual beauty, and who regarded him with wonder.

"Can I find no escape from this terrifying dream?" Oisin asked the wind. But the beating of the wind's wings was the only reply that reached his ears.

And so it came to pass that Niamh's snow-white horse carried Oisin from shore to shore in Erin. However, his search was fruitless. Wherever he went, Finn and the Fianna were names from an irretrievable past.

Sorrow, horror, and loneliness flooded Oisin's heart. In this Erin of the present, Oisin alone had lived in the past. In this Erin of little folk, Oisin alone was a giant among men. In this Erin of the weak, Oisin alone was truly strong. In this Erin of mortal men, Oisin alone had the power to conquer Disease, Decline, Decay, and Death.

"I have everything that mortals have always wished to possess!" Oisin exclaimed, "and yet, without the love of my father and the companionship of my friends, I have nothing at all!"

In time it came to pass that Oisin was passing through the Glen of the Thrushes—in time of old, one of the Fianna's favorite hunting places near Dublin and the eastern sea—when he saw that more than three hundred of the little folk had gathered there. Oisin directed Niamh's snow-white horse in their direction, hoping beyond hope for better news of Finn and the Fianna.

Seeing him approach, one of the little folk called out to him, "By your size and bearing, sir, you are surely some king's champion! Would you be so kind as to be our hero as well? Try as we might, we labor in vain to lift this great marble slab, for it now crushes those who were attempting to move it. And without your help, I fear that this marble slab will become their eternal grave marker!"

Oisin, from his perch on Niamh's snow-white horse, appraised the assembled throng with a mixture of curiosity, disdain, and pity. "What has the earth of Erin now produced that a group of more than three hundred men lacks the strength to lift this marble slab with ease from its bed?" he asked himself.

"These are poor, puny folk indeed—worn out from overwork and other troubles—if they cannot make their six hundred arms do what one strong arm of a member of the Fianna could do with ease! Why, if my son Osgar were alive, he would pick up this slab with his right hand, toss it above the heads of those gathered here, and let it come to rest on a far field," he thought to himself.

And so it came to pass that Oisin chose to help them. He bent forward over his saddle, grabbed the slab of marble with his right hand, and flung it up from the imprisoned men and over a thousand feet away from the assembled group.

However, the weight of the marble in Oisin's hand strained and broke the golden saddle strap on Niamh's horse. The saddle slipped, and Oisin instinctively landed safely on the earth of Erin, first on his right foot, and then on his left foot as well.

More quickly than a beam of light flies across the earth when clouds ride across the sun, Niamh's snow-white horse, frightened by the event and suddenly free of Oisin's weight, shook himself, neighed three times, and cantered off toward the west with the speed of a winter wind on a mountain summit.

As Oisin watched him depart, blindness flooded his eyes. His heart then froze with horror. "Niamh's warning!" he exclaimed in a feeble, trembling voice.

Meanwhile, Oisin could hear shouts of terror and the sound of scurrying feet, at first close at hand, and then quickly receding into the distance. "I have terrified them!" he said to himself. "Poor little folk! They have witnessed their hero change from a beautiful, strong, and powerful youth into a wrinkled, withered, and feeble old man, and they must fear that what has happened to me will also happen to them."

Oisin passed his trembling hands over his face and down his body. "My skin is dry and wrinkled, and I now have a long beard," he noted. "Even my clothes have changed. A coarse homespun fabric has replaced the yellow silk in my tunic, and my sash has become a hemp rope. My gold-hilted sword is gone as well," he added, as his fingers examined the support on which he was leaning. "Dressed as I am, and carrying this oakwood staff, I must look like the old men who wander from one farmhouse to another, dependent on others for their next meal. How humiliating!"

It came to pass that, finding that they did not share their hero's fate, the local little folk returned to Oisin, hoping that they now could help the man who had been so willing to help them. "Tell us who you are and where you are from, so that we can do our best to help you," they said.

To these words, Oisin replied, "I am Oisin, the son of Finn Mac Cumhal, king of the Fianna in Erin. I have been searching Erin from sea to sea for my father, since his fortress on the Hill of Almhuin lies deserted and in ruins, and weeds and nettles rule local cattle where once Finn ruled the Fianna."

"Old man! Your wits must have fled along with your youth!" a voice exclaimed. "Surely, in the course of your wanderings, someone has told you that Finn Mac Cumhal has been dead for over three hundred years! Patrick now rules our land, and he preaches to us about the one God and Christ, His Son. Gone are the old ways of feasting and hunting, and gone are the old songs of love and war. So we will take you to Patrick," the voice concluded, "for only Patrick will know what to do with you, and surely he will want to hear your tale."

So it came to pass that Oisin told his story to Patrick, who commanded his scribes to record Oisin's words. For Patrick wanted those who walk the earth to remember the hero Finn Mac Cumhal and his companions among the Fianna, even though he believed that their life in their pagan age had condemned them to an eternity of torment in Hell.

It also came to pass that Patrick tried to convince Oisin to reject the Fianna's values and their way of life for those of the new religion of Ireland. However, Oisin preferred the old ways to the new, and he argued with Patrick over the fate of his father and friends.

Finally, Oisin told Patrick, "I will die as I have lived, and I will join the Fianna—whether to share bowls of barley, honey, and wine, to hunt the fleet deer, to sing rousing songs of war, and to fight bravely in battle—or to burn in the flames or the ice of your Hell. Wherever the Fianna are, there I too will be, for wherever they are, the joy of life floods the human heart! Without them, I am a tree without a leaf, a nut without a seed, a horse without a bridle, and a man without a home! I am the last of the Fianna, and I cry because Finn and the Fianna are no longer alive!"

Epilogue

It came to pass that Oisin was true to his word. To the end of his days, he missed the food, the music, and the generous old ways of times long past. To the end of his days, he missed the hunting, the learning of new skills, the fighting, and the great deeds of those times as well. And to the end of his days, he longed for his lost father, his lost friends, and his lost years.

Oisin never again heard the sweet voice of his gentle wife or the neigh of her snow-white horse. And he never regained his sight, or the beauty, strength, and power of his youth, or the joy of life.

Saga of Gunnlaug
Serpent-Tongue

Iceland is renowned for its sagas, which are works of historical fiction that depict the lives of famous Icelanders and their families who lived between 930 and 1030. These sagas reveal much about the lives of these aristocrats. However, in order to understand the world in which Gunnlaug Serpent-Tongue and the other saga characters lived, it is helpful to understand certain aspects of early Icelandic history and culture.

Historical Background

When the first Norwegian settlers arrived in Iceland in the year 874, this isolated far-northern island was inhabited only by a few Celtic monks. By the year 930, settlements had become established throughout most of the island. In order to make laws for the entire community, local chieftains met each summer in a general assembly called the Althing. This form of government continued until 1262, when Iceland lost its independence and became the feudal estate of the king of Norway. The principal male characters in the "Saga of Gunnlaug Serpent-Tongue" are two chieftains who are members of the Althing and two of their sons.

The Althing was Iceland's intellectual, cultural, and social center. Besides handling matters related to government, those who attended the Althing both entertained and were entertained by other poets and saga-narrators, enjoyed competitive sports—such as swimming, ballgames, and wrestling—and heard news of other parts of Iceland and other northern countries. Travelers were the newspapers, radio, and television of their time, and the only way to reach or to leave Iceland was by sea. Therefore, seafaring merchants and their shipmasters, as well as the sons of wealthy landowners who had recently returned from visits to foreign courts, always found a large, interested audience at the Althing.

The Althing adopted Christianity as Iceland's religion in the year 1000. From the eleventh to the thirteenth century (often called the "Age of Peace"), the Church built monasteries and religious schools, where the sons of chieftains received an education along with those who were studying to become priests. By the end of the twelfth century, a majority of the aristocrats in Iceland could both read and write, making them one of the most literate groups of aristocrats in medieval Europe.

It is clear from historical records—such as annals, chronicles, and other sagas—that Gunnlaug Serpent-Tongue and the other principal characters in the saga, including the rulers whom Gunnlaug visits, are all historical figures. The historical Gunnlaug, who was born in about 994 and therefore was a child when Iceland became Christian, later became a famous court poet and warrior. Earl Hakon the Great, who ruled Norway from the year 970 to 995, was in fact murdered by one of his slaves in 995. His son, Earl Eirik Hakonarson, ruled Norway from the year 1000 to about 1015. King Ethelred ("the Unready") ruled England from the year 978 to 1016. King Sigtrygg Silk-Beard ruled Dublin from the year 980 to 1014. King Olaf Skötkonung ("the Swedish") ruled Sweden from about the year 995 to 1021.

Scholars think that some, and possibly many, of the court poems included in the "Saga of Gunnlaug Serpent-Tongue" were written by the historical Gunnlaug and are in themselves very reliable historical sources of the saga material.

Social Background

The Role of Family

Family relationships were of great importance in Iceland during the period depicted by the sagas. The Althing was a legislative body, but it could not enforce the laws that it established. Therefore, a man needed influential relatives who could help protect him and his property, help him carry out retributive justice, and in other ways help him apply the laws of the country to his own life. A man who had no relatives to act on his behalf was a man who could not enforce his political, economic, and social rights.

The importance of an Icelander's father was evident in the construction of each Icelander's surname. A male's last name revealed that he was his father's son, while a female's last name revealed that she was her father's daughter. Consequently, if a man named Egil had a son named Grim and a daughter named Thora, these children were known to the world as Grim Egilsson and Thora Egilsdottir.

Women were viewed as a type of property. Their fathers chose their husbands, and their husbands expected to make the important decisions in their lives.

The Saga Hero

Early in the eleventh century, the period in which both the historical Gunnlaug Serpent-Tongue and his saga-counterpart live, it was customary for a young aristocrat to leave Iceland and spend an extended period of time in the courts of other northern European countries in order to make a name for himself. The historical Gunnlaug—and the other young men in his social and economic position—joined trading or raiding expeditions and took positions in foreign courts in order to win honor, wealth, and fame. Similarly, the saga hero often establishes his reputation abroad, both as a poet and as a warrior, in the court of a king or an earl.

The saga hero lives in a culture that believes that an unalterable Fate determines the course of everyone's life. Yet the hero is not a puppet. True to the human condition, the hero's personality will contribute as much to his fate as the unpredictable and uncontrollable circumstances that he will encounter in the course of his life.

In the saga hero's life, death and the unexpected are the greatest certainties, and the only immortality available to a hero is lasting fame. Consequently, the saga hero's principal goal is to achieve an honorable reputation. He will fight to the death to preserve his own honor and that of his family. Then he can take pride in his accomplishments, and his family, his peers, and those who come after him will remember his great deeds and value his good name.

The saga hero knows that, although his death is inevitable, he can attempt to control how he lives and how he dies. He may be rash in his behavior and have no mercy toward his opponent in battle. However, he knows that he must be loyal to his family, his friends, and the king or earl whom he serves; he must be brave in battle and in his acceptance of Fate; and he must be generous in his dealings with those who deserve his respect. Moreover, he knows that his deeds must reveal his intelligence and that his words must reveal his education in the arts of poetry and narrative.

Since each person in the saga hero's society is responsible for executing the law as it affects his own life, retributive justice is accepted practice. Thus, revenge—by retaliating in kind—is the means through which the saga hero achieves justice in his own life.

Saga characters believe that their dreams symbolically predict the future. However, these dreams do not reveal how or when actual events will occur. The saga hero accepts his fate without being intimidated by it. He lives his life as best he can, and he views his situation as being an inevitable part of the human condition.

Literary Background

Prior to the advent of writing, Iceland developed an elaborate oral tradition. Storytelling was a principal form of entertainment, and every aristocrat was trained to be a poet as part of his education. The Icelandic word for "amusement" means "that which shortens the time," and during their long, dark winters, the Icelanders loved to listen to their myths and heroic legends.

The "Saga Age" includes the years between 930 and 1030, when most events mentioned in the sagas occurred. However, more than a hundred years passed between these events and their preservation in written saga form. Iceland's written saga tradition began in about 1150, when its first monastery developed a school of historical writing. The three earliest complete and extant sagas were written sometime after the year 1180. Although the first subjects were saints—such as the Norwegian king who was responsible for Christianizing Iceland—the family history of renowned Icelanders soon became the saga writers' focus.

The greatest Icelandic sagas were composed during the first half of the thirteenth century, before Iceland lost its independence in 1262. This period has come to be known as the Age of Writing.

The saga writers had three sources of historical material available to them: first, the late-eleventh-century *Book of Settlements,* which contains information about Icelandic families and their traditions; second, the early-twelfth-century *Book of Icelanders*, which contains miniature sagas and anecdotes about renowned Icelandic families; and finally, the poetry composed by the Icelandic court poets who served various Scandinavian kings. It is interesting that five of the seven Icelandic sagas that were written by the year 1230 are about poets and contain incidents that are taken from their poetry.

Scholars think that the "Saga of Gunnlaug Serpent-Tongue" was written sometime during the second half of the thirteenth century. It contains references and similarities to material that appears in sagas that were written during the first half of that century, and it is also more romantic in subject than earlier sagas.

Like the other Icelandic sagas, the "Saga of Gunnlaug Serpent-Tongue" exists in later manuscripts that clearly do not record the original version. One extant manuscript was written toward the end of the fourteenth century, and the other was written in the fifteenth century. Discrepancies between these two complete versions of the saga make it impossible to know the nature of the original manuscript.

Scholars disagree about the role of the oral tradition in the saga writers' work. Whether or not stories about Gunnlaug Serpent-Tongue and his blood feud with Poet-Hrafn over Helga the Fair existed in Iceland's oral tradition at the time when the saga writer lived, the saga writer clearly turned a historical subject into an art form through his selection and organization of the material, his integration of themes, his symbolic use of dreams, and his detailed depictions of character.

Scholars also disagree about the authorship of the poems in the saga. Some were probably written by the historical Gunnlaug and the historical Hrafn. Others were probably composed by the saga writer, possibly from stories in the oral tradition.

The "Saga of Gunnlaug Serpent-Tongue" reflects the saga writer's knowledge of Icelandic literary conventions. These dictated that the saga would have a male focus, a male point of view, and a concealed, objective narrator. A character's fate would be revealed through earlier dreams. His personality and values would be depicted through his actions and, often, the comments that reliable characters would make to or about him. Male characters would express their emotions only in highly complex, metaphorical, and alliterative poetry. Female characters, even when important to the plot, would often be relegated to the background and depicted as more passive personalities.

The "Saga of Gunnlaug Serpent-Tongue" also reflects the interest of the saga writers in the importance of moral and ethical conduct in Icelandic society. These writers lived in a later, less stable age, and they chose historic tales and legends about violent behavior—with their motives, consequences, and futility—in order to show Icelanders that their society prospers when they follow the laws established by the Althing, whereas lawlessness always endangers the community.

The Icelandic sagas were first translated into other languages for the enjoyment of the general reader in the nineteenth century. From that time to this, the "Saga of Gunnlaug Serpent-Tongue," with its stark, violent passions, has been one of the most popular and widely translated of these sagas. It is famous for its love triangle and its tragic blood feud. Moreover, the saga writer's interest in characterization creates a realistic interplay between Fate and the human personality. Therefore, the story leaves an indelible mark on the reader's imagination.

SAGA OF GUNNLAUG SERPENT-TONGUE

Prologue

Now, listen! For I have a tale from a place far north and from a time long past. The place is at once a fire-land and an ice-land, a place where the passions of men and women may, like the world in which they live, remain frozen until they suddenly erupt, leaving destruction and death in their wake.

There, in that land of fire and ice, long, dark winters give birth to famine and disease, the implacable enemies of all who are mortal. There, human life is but a candle-flame, burning brightly and bravely in the darkness for its brief life-span—unless a random brush of the wind's wings or an angry act from a mortal's hand suddenly snuffs it out.

There, Death hovers over those who walk the earth, waiting and watching, and patiently biding his time—time that will surely come—until he can claim another valiant spirit and drag it down with him into the depths of his dark and dismal kingdom, where it will languish for eternity.

And yet, in that fire-land and ice-land, all is not dark and joyless. In the brief summer of the year, the warmth of the sun-light lifts the human spirit and makes the human heart sing.

Thorstein Egilsson has a disturbing dream.

It came to pass that a wealthy land-owner and wise chieftain by the name of Thorstein Egilsson traveled some distance from his farm at Borg in order to repair the building that sheltered him during the period when the Althing convened each summer. A Norwegian ship-master, who was currently Master Thorstein's guest-friend—and who was also known to be a wise man—accompanied him.

Summer flowers had followed the spring snow, and a hot sun watched the two men perform the necessary tasks on Master Thorstein's structure. As soon as they finished their work, the shade within the enclosure beckoned them with its welcome offer of relief from the heat. There Thorstein soon fell into an uneasy sleep.

When Thorstein Egilsson awoke, his guest-friend said to him, "Thorstein, my friend, what did you dream that was so troubling to you?"

To these words, Thorstein replied, "I dreamed of events so strange that, while I know that they mean nothing, yet my heart is now flooded with foreboding and fear. In my dream, I was standing in front of my farm-house when I spied my beautiful swan upon my house-top. And as I watched, a great eagle—with peat-black eyes, iron-clad claws, and the bearing of a great predator—flew down from the north and came upon my swan. He alighted at her side, and spoke gently and quietly to her in his bird-voice while she listened with heart-love.

"Then," Thorstein continued, "a second great eagle flew up from the south and he, too, came upon my swan. He, too, had peat-black eyes, iron-clad claws, and the bearing of a great predator. And he, too, alighted at her side and spoke gently and sweetly to her in his bird-voice. This outraged the first eagle, who provoked a fight with his rival, and the two eagles fought with such blood-thirsty battle-joy that they killed each other, leaving my swan to cower between their two corpses in heart-shock.

"However," Thorstein continued, "before long, a third bird flew in from the west. He was not an eagle, but a hawk. He alighted in front of my swan and he, too, spoke gently and sweetly to her in his bird-voice. My swan was still quivering with heart-grief. However, in time, when the hawk rose from my house-top and flew away, my swan rose with him and accompanied him.

"It was then that I awakened from my dream," Thorstein concluded.

To these words, the Norwegian ship-master replied, "I must tell you, my host-friend, that dreams are heavy with meaning. And therefore it is with good reason that your dream has flooded your heart with foreboding and fear.

"As I read your dream," he continued, "the two eagles, the hawk, and the swan are the spirits of three men and a woman, who, in your dream, have appeared to you in their animal form. And in time you will see that what has passed among these birds in your dream will surely come to pass among them when you meet them in their human forms in your life.

"As I see it," the ship-master continued, "your wife, Mistress Jofrid—who is shortly due to give birth—will bring forth a beautiful daughter whom you will love with all your heart. Her beauty and her gentle ways will bring you a choice of marriage-suits, and you will have to choose between two great life-mates for her hand. These two strong-hearted, valiant men will fight a death-duel because of their heart-love for her and, in the end, you will give your daughter to a third life-mate, who also will feel heart-love for her."

To these words, Thorstein replied, "My host-friend, a wise man does not walk upon slick rock. A man's dreams, too, are slippery stuff, and you have fallen on your face by trying to be a dream-reader. You are sea-skilled. You know the ways of the crest-gliders. You know the wave-road. Take my advice and deal only with what you know well. That becomes you far better!"

That is what Thorstein Egilsson said. However, his heart remained flooded with foreboding as he and his guest-friend returned to the farm at Borg. Shortly thereafter, the ship-master boarded his sea-ready trade-ship, left Borgarfjord, and took the wave-road to Norway.

It soon came to pass that Thorstein prepared to attend the Althing. As he took leave of his wife, he said to her, "My dear, it will probably come to pass that you will give birth while I am away at the Althing. If we have a son, all will be well and good. However, if we have a daughter, then you must give her to a servant immediately—before you feed her, before you name her, and before I see her. Tell our servant to take her into the hills and abandon her there. Comfort yourself in the knowledge that, without food, her period of suffering will be brief!"

To these words, Mistress Jofrid replied, "What trouble has hardened your heart, Thorstein, that you demand such a deed from your wife? We are not poor people who have more children than we can feed! And you are renowned in our district for being a wise and a moderate man! You are loving of others and much loved by them in return. Therefore, I know that you cannot mean what you say!"

"Jofrid, I have said exactly what I mean to say," Thorstein replied, "and I expect you to be my good and loving wife and to obey me!"

Thorstein Egilsson then left for the Althing, and it came to pass that Mistress Jofrid gave birth to a girl. Even as an infant, she possessed remarkable beauty.

And it came to pass that, instead of taking the infant into her arms, Jofrid called for her shepherd. "Take my newborn daughter to Master Thorstein's sister," she commanded. "Tell her to rear the child secretly as her own daughter—and to take care that my husband never learns that she is really his!

"As for you, my husband's sister will find work for you on a farm far from here, so that you will never have to reveal what you have done. Here is payment for what I am asking of you," Jofrid concluded. "Now go with good fortune!"

Six summers came and went like flowers after the spring snow. The Althing adopted Christianity for all of Iceland, and all the folk agreed to renounce their old gods and their ancient religious practices. Thorstein Egilsson still believed that his daughter had been exposed to die and that the shepherd had run away.

It came to pass that, when new summer flowers had followed the spring snow, Master Thorstein visited his sister's family. There he saw a little girl who was far more beautiful than her two sisters. "That beautiful child of yours has the best of her father's beauty and our own!" he exclaimed to his sister.

"Indeed, she has the beauty of our kin-folk," his sister replied, "but she does not have my husband's beauty, for she is not his daughter, my brother. She happens to be your own! When you ordered Jofrid to expose her—and six summers have come and gone since then—your wife gave her to me to rear in secrecy. Now I hope that you will find it in your heart to forgive both of us for defying your will and preserving your child's life!"

"Fate will roll where it must!" Thorstein responded. "I do not blame either of you for ignoring my bad judgment. I can see that I am the most fortunate of men to have such a beautiful daughter! Now she will know her own parents, and Jofrid and I will treasure her! What have you named her?"

"We have named her Helga, after Jofrid's mother," his sister replied.

So it came to pass that Helga the Fair came to live with her parents. And six more summers came and went like flowers after the spring snow.

Gunnlaug Serpent-Tongue sets his heart on Helga the Fair.

Illugi the Black—a land-owner and chieftain who was second only to Thorstein Egilsson in wealth and prominence in their district—had a son whom he had named Gunnlaug Serpent-Tongue after his own maternal grandfather.

It came to pass that Gunnlaug Serpent-Tongue, who was now twelve years old, approached Master Illugi and said, "Father, you know that it is the custom for the son of a chieftain to board a sea-ready trade-ship and to travel the wave-road to other lands. That is what I now wish to do! So I ask you to permit me to make such a sea-journey, and I ask you to give me the trade-goods that I will need to take with me. A sea-ready trade-ship now lies waiting at Borgarfjord!"

To these words, Master Illugi replied, "Gunnlaug, when you reach the age when you can be considered a man in our district, then—and only then—will I consider your petition. However, I want you to know that, unless your personality improves, you will only win enemies and not friends in other lands. These days, I personally find it very difficult to deal with you! And I am your father, and I know your talents. I fear that even those who will come to recognize your talents are not likely to appreciate your ways!"

Gunnlaug Illugason, who was unusually mature in size, in accomplishments, and in ambition—and who was equally stubborn—refused to bow to his father's will. Instead he rode to the farm of Master Thorstein at Borg and told the land-owner about his disagreement with his father. Thorstein invited him to live with his family for as long as he wished, and Gunnlaug accepted.

The summer flowers became the frost-white stalks of winter while Thorstein taught Gunnlaug Illugason the laws of the land. And it came to pass that Gunnlaug and Helga became heart-friends. Helga the Fair was Gunnlaug's equal in age, and those who knew about such matters said that Helga Thorsteinsdottir was the most beautiful young woman who had ever been born in Iceland. Her hair, as luminous as beaten gold, fell to her feet and could cover her like a robe of heavy silk. Folk wondered who in Iceland—or even in Norway—would ever be her match.

Gunnlaug Illugason, however, did not wonder. He knew who would be the ideal match for Helga Thorsteinsdottir, and it came to pass that, in the presence of other men, he said to her father, "Master Thorstein, I am the son of Master Illugi, and despite my age, I am already the most accomplished of men and a poet of distinction. Therefore, I would have you now tell me what the law requires if I wish to give a woman my marriage-pledge."

When Thorstein had informed him, Gunnlaug replied, "Now let me practice, to be certain that I understand the procedure. I will ask you for the hand of your daughter, Helga the Fair, in marriage."

"If you insist, Gunnlaug," Thorstein replied, "but I hereby make it clear to the folk who are present that this is but a lesson and not an agreement."

And so it came to pass that Gunnlaug Illugason named his witnesses and pledged himself in marriage to Helga Thorsteinsdottir. Everyone who was present laughed at the idea.

It came to pass that six more summers came and went like flowers after the spring snow. Gunnlaug spent these years both with Thorstein Egilsson and with his father, with whom he was now on good terms.

Gunnlaug Illugason was now eighteen, and he still longed to travel the wave-road to other lands. A new summer of flowers had followed the spring snow and had long been in bloom, when he once again asked his father for trade-goods and for his permission to board a sea-ready trade-ship that lay waiting at Borgarfjord. This time, Master Illugi agreed to his son's request.

While the supplies and trade-goods were being put aboard the trade-ship, Gunnlaug stayed with Master Thorstein and his family at Borg. For Gunnlaug preferred to be with Helga Thorsteinsdottir than to be involved in the final preparations for the trade-ship's journey.

It came to pass that Thorstein Egilsson offered Gunnlaug Illugason some of his finest horses. In response, Gunnlaug declared, "Because I am about to travel the sea-road to other lands, I have no need for even the best horses. However, if you were to offer me your daughter, Helga the Fair, then I would accept her! So, tell me, Master Thorstein, how do you regard my marriage-suit?"

To these words, Thorstein replied, "Gunnlaug, I cannot take your marriage-suit seriously! You are already committed to travel the wave-road to other lands, and you are about to leave Iceland. How then can you commit to marry anyone at this time? Until you know what you really want, you are no match for any maiden!"

"Surely you cannot object to my desire to go abroad so that I can make a name for myself!" Gunnlaug exclaimed. "You know as well as I do, Master Thorstein, that it is the custom for the high-born young men of Iceland to win honor and wealth in over-sea lands—whether in the court of the earl of Norway, or in battle, or through trade. You would want no less from one who deserves the hand of Helga the Fair in marriage! And you know that I am the best suitor for her! Now, if you reject one of my father's sons, then who will you accept?"

"I would accept you, Gunnlaug, if you were the man that your father is!" Thorstein exclaimed. "However, I must tell you that such excessive pride in yourself does not become you! I assure you that you are far from the only good man in our district!"

"You insult me, Master Thorstein!" Gunnlaug replied, "And it is only because of our friendship that you can refuse my marriage-suit without suffering the consequences!"

"Curb your tongue, young man!" Master Thorstein retorted. "You may be able to push around your hill-folk, but down here among the marsh-men, we do not look with favor upon hot words and rash threats!"

And so it came to pass that Gunnlaug Illugason returned to his father. "You must accompany me to Master Thorstein, Father, and help me in my suit for the hand of Helga the Fair," he demanded.

"Come now, Gunnlaug," Master Illugi replied. "You are eighteen years old and still you do not know what you want! You bend this way and that like a young tree in a storm-wind. First you ask my permission to travel the wave-road to over-sea lands. Now you ask my help with a marriage-suit. Your frivolity does not become you! And I know that my hearth-friend, Master Thorstein, will not look with favor upon your proposal."

"I do intend to travel, Father," Gunnlaug replied. "But if you love me, you will give me the help that I need with my marriage-suit!"

And so it came to pass that Gunnlaug, his father, and eleven chosen witnesses rode to Borg. There Master Illugi and Gunnlaug Serpent-Tongue met privately with Master Thorstein.

"Thorstein," Illugi the Black began, "my son, Gunnlaug, tells me that he has asked you for your daughter Helga's hand in marriage. You know us well. Although it is my son, Hermund, who has the bearing and disposition of a chieftain, it bodes well that he and Gunnlaug are the best of friends! And I assure you that I will give Gunnlaug a place to live and a position of authority. Therefore, does this enable you to accept my son's marriage-suit for the hand of your Helga?"

"Illugi, I know your son, Gunnlaug Serpent-Tongue, well. And I like him!" Thorstein replied. "And if only he were like you in temperament, I would happily accept his marriage-suit. But this son of yours does not know his own mind! You are a father. Tell me, how can I give my daughter to a young man like Gunnlaug?"

To these words, Illugi the Black replied, "We have been hearth-friends for many years, Thorstein. But I cannot permit you to refuse my son! I will not give folk reason to say that a son of mine is not an equal match for your daughter! So if you value our friendship you will accept my son Gunnlaug's marriage-suit—like it or not!"

"Then, Illugi, I offer you this proposal," Thorstein replied. "And if you agree, let our witnesses confirm the following agreement between us. I will promise my daughter, Helga, to your son, Gunnlaug Serpent-Tongue. However, for the period of three years, Helga will not be formally engaged to Gunnlaug.

"During this time," Thorstein continued, "let Gunnlaug travel the wave-road to other lands and become more noble in his attitudes and in his behavior. When these three years have come and gone, if he returns to Helga—and if he has become a worthy husband—then the marriage between your son and my daughter will take place with my blessing.

"However, if Gunnlaug does not return by the end of this period, or if he has returned but I do not like what he has made of himself, then I will no longer be legally obligated to accept his marriage-suit," Thorstein concluded.

"That is a fair agreement between us, Thorstein," Illugi replied.

And so it came to pass that Gunnlaug Illugason boarded a sea-ready trade-ship and set off upon the wave-road for over-sea lands.

Gunnlaug travels to Norway, England, Dublin, and Orkney.

First, Gunnlaug Illugason took a trade-ship to Norway, which, at that time, was a feudal estate of King Svein of Denmark. Earl Eirik Hakonarson welcomed Gunnlaug because of Illugi the Black's fine reputation. However, the earl's favor was as short-lived as summer flowers.

When a Norwegian nobleman commented admiringly that Gunnlaug was able to walk without limping despite a great foot-sore, Gunnlaug Serpent-Tongue lived up to his name and unlocked a word-hoard of battle-thrusts. Faster than the wings of the wind, he replied, "Any man whose legs are equal in length should walk without a limp!"

These words caused one of Earl Eirik's noblemen to reply, "This youth is most impressed with himself! We should see if he is as good as he says he is!"

Gunnlaug responded to this nobleman in poetry, saying, "You

have an evil temper, sir! The Devil would find you to be good company!"

The nobleman reached for his battle-axe, but Earl Eirik advised, "Ignore the hot-headed Icelander! He is but a youth and not worth your anger."

The earl then turned to Gunnlaug and asked, "Icelander, how old are you?"

"Eighteen, my lord," Gunnlaug announced.

"Take care then, Icelander, if you wish to live another eighteen years!" Earl Eirik exclaimed. "Personally, I do not foresee that you will have such good fortune!"

"Save your curses for someone else, Eirik Hakonarson!" Gunnlaug softly replied. "And worry instead about your own future!"

"What do you mean by that, Icelander?" Earl Eirik asked.

"My lord, you know as well as I do that you rule this land at the pleasure of your brother, the Danish king. So I think that you should take care that you do not die as your own father did! Everyone knows that Earl Hakon the Great was killed by one of his own slaves, who cut short his master's life with a slash of his blood-hungry blade!"

Earl Eirik's heart flooded with fury, and he would have felled Gunnlaug Illugason then and there, but one of his nobles, who happened to be one of Thorstein Egilsson's sons, interceded on Gunnlaug's behalf.

"All right! The Icelander can leave as long as he never again sets foot in Norway!" Earl Eirik declared.

Now, under the rule of King Ethelred, the English spoke a language that the folk of Iceland could understand. And so it came to pass that Gunnlaug Illugason boarded a sea-ready trade-ship and took the wave-road to London. The English king was a great treasure-giver! He scattered gold like sunlight on sea-ways, and he showered silver like snowflakes in winter.

The summer flowers would soon become the frost-white stalks of winter when Gunnlaug Illugason arrived on English soil and sought the royal house of England's great king. He came before King Ethelred with a well-designed poem of praise. In return, King Ethelred gave the young poet a scarlet, fur-lined cloak as a king's-gift, and he made him a member of his royal body-guard. And so it came to pass that Gunnlaug spent the first winter of his travels in London with the English king.

In time, Gunnlaug loaned money to a stranger who was well known to the English king as a bully and a thief.

"Do not deal with one such as he," King Ethelred advised Gunnlaug. "I will pay you the debt that the scoundrel owes you."

"Nonsense, my lord!" Gunnlaug exclaimed. "I cannot let one who is innocent take on the debt of one who is a thief!"

So it came to pass that Gunnlaug insisted on attempting to collect his own money, and the thief refused to pay his debt. Gunnlaug therefore created a poem for the situation in which he announced to the thief, "I give you three days in which to pay your debt to me, or else you must agree to meet me in single combat!"

"You are the first to challenge me to single combat—despite problems that others, too, have had with me!" the thief exclaimed, laughing. "However, I am prepared to fight, if you insist."

When Gunnlaug repeated this conversation to King Ethelred, the English king replied, "Gunnlaug Serpent-Tongue, your thief possesses magical powers and a superior sword. Ordinary weapons have proved to be useless against such men. Therefore, when you meet him in combat, show him your ordinary sword, but use mine, King's-Gift, which I now bestow upon you. Know that it will be to your advantage to conceal King's-Gift from your foe until the proper time."

So it came to pass that Gunnlaug Illugason fought in single combat against the thief. Seeing Gunnlaug's ordinary sword, the thief quickly sliced off a great part of Gunnlaug's strong shield with one sword-blow from his own superior weapon. However, Gunnlaug swiftly drew forth King's-Gift and, faster than the wings of the wind, plunged that blazing battle-blade into the heart of the unsuspecting thief. The thief gave up his breath and his life together.

King Ethelred appreciated Gunnlaug's courage and battle-skill, and with this deed, the young Icelandic poet earned great fame throughout England as a keen-witted shield-bearer and a valiant warrior.

When summer flowers soon would follow the spring snow and sea-ready trade-ships once again could travel upon the wave-road, Gunnlaug asked King Ethelred for his permission to continue his travels.

Gunnlaug then added in poetry, "My lord, I have promised myself that I would be the court-guest of three great kings and two earls. You, of course, are the first of these kings. However, I shall also visit King Sigtrygg Silk-Beard and King Olaf the Swedish. And I shall visit Earl Sigurd Hlodvisson and Earl Sigurd of Gautland, as well. Nevertheless, I promise to return to your service whenever you send me a gold ring as your royal sign."

To these words, King Ethelred replied, "Gunnlaug Serpent-Tongue, I give you this heavy gold ring as my token that you have my permission to take a limited leave of absence. However, when you see that the summer flowers will soon become the frost-white stalks of winter for the second time, I expect to see you back in my court. For Svein—that blood-thirsty king of the Spear-Danes—is my bane! He will not be satisfied until he takes my life and my crown! You are a member of my royal body-guard, and you are too keen-witted a shield-bearer and too battle-brave for me to part with you for too long!"

So it came to pass that Gunnlaug Illugason left London on a sea-ready trade-ship and traveled the wave-road to Dublin. The kingdom of Ireland was ruled by Sigtrygg Silk-Beard and, once again, Gunnlaug introduced himself to the king by offering him a poem of praise. King Sigtrygg Silk-Beard was a great treasure-giver! He scattered gold like sunlight on sea-ways, and he showered silver like snowflakes in winter. In return for Gunnlaug's poem, the gold-giving king gave the young poet the king's-gifts of a fur-lined cloak, an embroidered tunic, and a heavy gold ring.

It came to pass that Gunnlaug's time in Dublin was as short-lived as summer flowers. It was still the first summer of his travels when he boarded a sea-ready trade-ship and traveled the wave road north to Orkney. This island group off the northern sea-coast of Scotland was ruled by Earl Sigurd Hlodvisson. There Gunnlaug introduced himself by offering the earl a fine ballad. In return, this royal treasure-giver gave Gunnlaug the earl's-gift of an axe that was inlaid with silver.

It came to pass that Gunnlaug's time in Orkney was also as short-lived as summer flowers. He soon boarded a sea-ready trade-ship and traveled the wave-road east to Norway. From there he made his way toward Sweden, first reaching West Gautland and the court of Earl Sigurd with the help of a guide. There Gunnlaug introduced himself by offering the earl a fine ballad. In return, this royal treasure-giver gave Gunnlaug an earl's-gift.

By this time, the summer flowers were becoming the frost-white stalks of winter, and the earl invited Gunnlaug to remain as his court-guest throughout the winter. So it came to pass that Gunnlaug spent the second winter of his travels in West Gautland with Earl Sigurd.

Earl Sigurd's Yule feast was attended by a dozen noblemen from the Norwegian court, who came bearing gifts from Earl Eirik

Hakonarson. They boasted that the earl of Norway was superior to the earl of Gautland. Both groups asked Gunnlaug Serpent-Tongue to judge their arguments. The poet praised both rulers in verse, and it came to pass that the Norwegian noblemen repeated Gunnlaug's praise of Eirik Hakonarson to their earl upon their return. Earl Eirik's heart smiled when he heard their tale. He forgave Gunnlaug for his earlier rash word-thrusts, and he sent word to the young poet in Gautland, welcoming him to return to Norway as his court-guest.

It came to pass that, when summer flowers soon would follow the spring snow, Earl Sigurd sent Gunnlaug Illugason on his way to Sweden, accompanied by a guide.

Gunnlaug Serpent-Tongue meets Poet-Hrafn in Sweden.

Gunnlaug Illugason arrived at the court of King Olaf Skötkonung, who was known as "Olaf the Swedish," to find that a fellow Icelander by the name of Hrafn Onundarson was already a king's-guest there. Poet-Hrafn was the son of Master Onund, the wealthy land-owner and chieftain of the southern headlands district in Iceland. Like Gunnlaug, Hrafn was a young man of size, strength, and skill, and like Gunnlaug, he was also a good poet. Moreover, Hrafn was handsome, well-traveled, and well-regarded by all who met him.

"Tell me about this Icelander who wishes to be a king's-guest in my court," King Olaf commanded Poet-Hrafn.

"My lord," Hrafn replied, "your new guest is from the noblest Icelandic family, and he is the most valiant of men."

The two Icelanders—being of similar age and birth-right and currently spending a period of travel away from home—became court-friends. In time, however, it came to pass that Gunnlaug Serpent-Tongue announced to King Olaf that he had a poem to recite for him. As soon as the king agreed to Gunnlaug's request, Poet-Hrafn requested that the king hear his own poem as well, and the king agreed.

"My lord, I ask you to hear my poem before you hear Hrafn Onundarson's," Gunnlaug declared.

"My lord, permit me to present my poem first, since I arrived at your court before Gunnlaug Illugason did!" exclaimed Hrafn.

"That is not proper, Hrafn Onundarson," Gunnlaug declared. "Your father is second to mine, and you will be second to me!"

"Gunnlaug Illugason, let us permit King Olaf to decide between us," Hrafn responded. "That is the courteous way."

"Then I command that Gunnlaug Serpent-Tongue recite his poem first," King Olaf responded, "since he insists on having his own way."

And so it came to pass that Gunnlaug recited a complex narrative poem, one that he thought was appropriate for the ears of a generous king who was a powerful protector of his people.

When Gunnlaug had finished, King Olaf said, "Now, Poet-Hrafn, you have the reputation of being a fine poet. So tell me, what is your opinion of Gunnlaug Illugason's poem?"

To this question, Hrafn replied, "My lord, the poem is just like its poet. Both are pompous and unrefined!"

After Poet-Hrafn had recited his ballad, King Olaf said, "Now, Gunnlaug Serpent-Tongue, since you, too, have the reputation of being a fine poet, tell me, what is your opinion of Hrafn Onundarson's poem?"

To this question, Gunnlaug replied, "My lord, the poem is just like its poet. Both are handsome in appearance but not impressive in substance!"

Gunnlaug then turned to Hrafn and asked, "Hrafn Onundarson, do tell me why you chose to compose a ballad rather than a more formal narrative poem for this occasion? Do you think so little of King Olaf?"

To these words, Hrafn responded, "Gunnlaug Serpent-Tongue, I will discuss this matter with you at some other time."

It then came to pass that King Olaf made Hrafn Onundarson a member of his personal body-guard. When summer flowers soon would follow the spring snow, Poet-Hrafn requested a leave of absence to return to Iceland, which the king granted.

As Hrafn was about to depart, he said to Gunnlaug, "Serpent-Tongue, since you have tried to dishonor me with King Olaf, we can no longer be friends. And know this as well—the day will come when I shall repay you in kind."

"You speak empty words, Hrafn Onundarson," Gunnlaug replied. "Know who and what you are. And then you will know that I will always be more honored than you are!"

So it came to pass that Hrafn Onundarson boarded a sea-ready trade-ship and traveled the wave-road to Iceland, while Gunnlaug Illugason spent the second summer of his travels in Sweden, where he was on good terms with King Olaf.

Gunnlaug and Hrafn become rivals for Helga the Fair.

By the time that the summer flowers would soon become the frost-white stalks of winter, Poet-Hrafn was back in Iceland with his father Master Onund and his kin-folk. Meanwhile, Gunnlaug Serpent-Tongue had boarded a sea-ready trade-ship and had traveled the wave-road to London in order to keep his promise to Ethelred, the English king.

King Ethelred was delighted to have Gunnlaug Illugason in London with him once again. "Gunnlaug, you certainly chose a good time to leave the English king!" Ethelred exclaimed, referring to himself. "For Fate rolls where it must!

"Surely you have heard," he continued, "that Svein—that blood-thirsty king of the Spear-Danes!—brought his stout-hearted son, Knut, with him, and together they and their battle-hungry warriors conquered most of England. Of course, they could not conquer London! Still, I thought it best that we cross the English sea and visit the queen's brother, the duke of Normandy. And then, suddenly, Svein died! England must have been too rich a meal for him to digest! He died, and here we are—back in London!"

And so it came to pass that Gunnlaug spent the third winter of his travels in London with Ethelred, the English king. When it came to pass that summer flowers soon would follow the spring snow, permitting sea-ready trade-ships to travel the wave-road once again, Gunnlaug approached King Ethelred.

"My lord, the time has come when I must return to Iceland," he declared. "I have promised to remain in over-sea lands for no more than three years, and three winters have already come and gone. I must arrive home while this summer's flowers are still in bloom."

Gunnlaug went on to explain, "Travel to Iceland takes months of days and nights, for the trade-ship spends time in many sea-ports, and the sea-ways often are unfriendly to broad-beamed boats. Therefore, may I have your leave to depart?"

"I am sorry, Gunnlaug Serpent-Tongue, but I cannot honor your request right now," King Ethelred replied. "Surely you realize that Svein's son—they now call him Knut Sveinsson the Great!—now rules the Spear-Danes. And he will surely be my bane! For he has vowed that he will continue to attack us until he conquers London and puts my crown upon his head! You are a member of my bodyguard, and I cannot spare you at this time!"

"My lord, I will abide by your response," Gunnlaug replied, "but permit me to leave as soon as the summer flowers bloom, if the Spear-Danes have not invaded by then."

"You may be assured that, when I see summer flowers in bloom, I will reconsider your suit," King Ethelred replied.

It came to pass that the Spear-Danes rattled their battle-blades, but Knut Sveinsson the Great did not attack London.

It then came to pass that summer flowers followed the spring snow, and still Knut Sveinsson did not attack. But Ethelred still did not permit Gunnlaug to depart for Iceland.

Meanwhile, in Iceland, when new summer flowers had followed the spring snow and the time of the Althing was close at hand, Poet-Hrafn approached his cousin and prominent relative, Skapti the Law-Speaker.

Hrafn declared, "Skapti, I need your help with Thorstein Egilsson, for I intend to ask him for the hand of his daughter, Helga the Fair, in marriage."

"Hrafn, is it not true that Helga Thorsteinsdottir is promised to Gunnlaug Illugason?" Skapti asked.

"I think that the period of three years has come to an end," Hrafn replied. "Three winters have come and gone since Gunnlaug left Iceland. And knowing Gunnlaug Serpent-Tongue as I do, he probably will neither remember nor value his agreement with Thorstein Egilsson."

And so it came to pass that Skapti the Law-Speaker, accompanied by Hrafn Onundarson, Master Onund, and a group of other witnesses, approached Thorstein Egilsson at the Althing. Skapti spoke to Thorstein about his cousin's fine reputation and the wealth and social status of his kin-folk, and he asked Thorstein to consider Poet-Hrafn's marriage-suit for the hand of Helga the Fair.

However, Thorstein replied, "Skapti, three winters may indeed have come and gone since Gunnlaug Serpent-Tongue left Iceland to travel to over-sea lands. But Gunnlaug departed at a time when our summer flowers had long been in bloom. Consequently, my daughter is promised to him for as long as these summer flowers keep their bloom. Now, I intend to keep my agreement with Illugi Onundarson, and therefore, this matter must rest as it is until the Althing meets again next summer."

Meanwhile, in London, it came to pass that the Spear-Danes still rattled their battle-blades, but Knut Sveinsson the Great did not attack London. Still Ethelred would not permit Gunnlaug to depart for Iceland. And so it came to pass that Gunnlaug spent the third summer of his travels in London with the English king.

It then came to pass that the summer flowers would soon become the frost-white stalks of winter, but still Knut Sveinsson did not attack. And still Ethelred would not permit Gunnlaug to depart for Iceland. And so it came to pass that Gunnlaug spent a second winter in London with the English king, and this was the fourth winter of his travels.

When a new summer of flowers soon would follow the spring snow, permitting sea-ready trade-ships to travel the wave-road once again, Gunnlaug once again asked King Ethelred for permission to return to Iceland.

However, as always, King Ethelred replied, "I cannot honor your request right now, Gunnlaug Serpent-Tongue. Surely you realize that Knut Sveinsson the Great still lusts after my crown—and that the Spear-Danes again stand ready to attack London! You are a member of my body-guard, and I cannot spare you at this time!"

Once again, Gunnlaug declared, "My lord, I will abide by your response, but permit me to leave as soon as the summer flowers bloom, if the Spear-Danes have not invaded by then."

"Be assured that, when I see summer flowers in bloom, I will reconsider your suit," King Ethelred replied.

It came to pass that the Spear-Danes rattled their battle-blades, but Knut Sveinsson the Great still did not attack London. It then came to pass that summer flowers followed the spring snow, and still Knut Sveinsson did not attack. But King Ethelred still did not permit Gunnlaug to depart for Iceland.

Meanwhile, when new summer flowers had followed the spring snow in Iceland, the Althing met once again, and once again Hrafn Onundarson, his cousin Skapti the Law-Speaker, and Master Onund pressed Thorstein Egilsson to accept Poet-Hrafn's marriage-suit for the hand of Helga the Fair.

Skapti declared, "Thorstein, surely without question the period of your agreement will Illugi Onundarson has now ended. Three full summers and four winters have come and gone, and still Gunnlaug Illugason has not returned to Iceland. Therefore, you are now free to honor my cousin's marriage-suit!"

To these words, Thorstein replied, "Skapti, my agreement is with Master Illugi, so that I am not free to make this decision independently. However, I agree to consult with Gunnlaug's father, and I will let you know the outcome of our discussion."

And so it came to pass that Thorstein Egilsson approached Illugi the Black and asked, "Illugi, what news do you have of your son, Gunnlaug? Three full summers and four winters have come and gone, and he has yet to return to Iceland! Therefore, does his behavior not free me of any obligation toward you?"

To these words, Illugi replied, "Thorstein, I cannot hold you to our agreement any longer if you wish to make other arrangements for your daughter, Helga. Unfortunately, I cannot speak for my son, Gunnlaug. I do not know what thoughts live in his head, and I do not know what feelings flood his heart. I do not even know what keeps him from returning to Iceland!"

And so it came to pass that Thorstein Egilsson met with Skapti the Law-Speaker and formally accepted Hrafn Onundarson's marriage-suit for the hand of Helga the Fair. It was agreed that Helga would marry Poet-Hrafn on Winter's Eve—unless Gunnlaug Illugason returned before then, still determined to marry his betrothed. However, knowing that Gunnlaug might not return, Thorstein began to prepare to give his daughter in marriage to a man for whom she had no heart-love.

Meanwhile, in London, it came to pass that the Spear-Danes still rattled their battle-blades, but Knut Sveinsson the Great still did not attack London. Yet Ethelred still would not permit Gunnlaug to depart for Iceland.

So it came to pass that Gunnlaug Illugason once again approached the English king. "My lord, the time has come when I must depart for Iceland!" he declared. "Summer flowers have long been in bloom, and still Knut Sveinsson has not attacked London. I have done my best to honor my obligation to you by remaining with you for a full year beyond the time when I had promised to return to my own land. Now I can delay no longer! I would like to have your permission, but even without it, I must take my leave of you!"

So it came to pass that King Ethelred finally permitted Gunnlaug Serpent-Tongue to leave London. Gunnlaug boarded a sea-ready trade-ship and traveled the wave-road to Norway, where Earl Eirik Hakonarson welcomed him and invited him to be his court-guest.

Gunnlaug replied, "Thank you, my lord. I regret that I must decline your kind invitation, but I must now return to Iceland and the woman to whom I am betrothed."

So it came to pass that Gunnlaug Illugason finally boarded the sea-ready trade-ship that would travel the wave-road west to Iceland. However, the summer flowers would soon become the frost-white stalks of winter.

As the crest-rider rode the waves, the ship-master announced to the young poet, "You have been away for too many summers, Gunnlaug Illugason!—four of them, I have heard! You should know that Thorstein Egilsson's daughter, Helga the Fair, is now betrothed to Hrafn Onundarson, whom many folk think is as valiant a young man as you are!"

"As long as we travel on the wings of the east wind, I do not fear Hrafn's marriage, but I fear to hear him valued as my equal!" Gunnlaug replied in poetry.

To these words, the sea-captain replied, "Gunnlaug Serpent-Tongue, you must have reason to think that you will fare better with Hrafn Onundarson than I have! I once owed his house-man a half-mark of silver and did not repay him. So Hrafn gathered a force of sixty men, and they cut my trade-ship loose from its moorings. Thanks to them, it ran aground, and the rocks almost made a ship-wreck of it! And, as if that were not enough to have to bear, in the end, I had to pay Hrafn a full mark of silver! So I advise you to think twice before you dare to interfere with whatever belongs to Hrafn Onundarson! He is a hard-minded man with angry blood in his proud heart!"

The trade-ship docked only two weeks before Winter's Eve. A lo-cal farm-youth challenged each of the trade-ship's ship-men to a wrestling contest.

"You will see that Thor, the great Hammer-Hurler, will give me the strength to overcome you, one and all!" he bragged.

The god did indeed smile upon this farm-youth, for it came to pass that his deeds confirmed the words of his tongue. And when the youth challenged Gunnlaug Illugason, the poet-warrior imme-diately accepted. Gunnlaug overpowered the youth and forced him to fall upon the ground. However, in the process, he disjointed his own leg, lost his balance, and fell to the ground as well.

The farm-youth then said to his opponent, "Gunnlaug Illugason, know that you also may not win your next contest! For Thorstein Egilsson's daughter, Helga the Fair, will marry Hrafn Onundarson on Winter's Eve. Master Thorstein and Master Onund formally reached this agreement when the Althing met this summer. And I know this for a fact, because I was present!"

It came to pass that Gunnlaug reached his father's farm just as the marriage feast was beginning at Thorstein Egilsson's farm at Borg. Gunnlaug wished to continue on to Borg, but Master Illugi advised against it. Although Gunnlaug disagreed, he had to admit that his bound leg had become so swollen that another horse-back ride would have been unbearably painful.

And so it came to pass that Helga Thorsteinsdottir, that fair gold-wearer, married Hrafn Onundarson instead of Gunnlaug Illugason. However, Helga was heart-cold toward her husband, for Gunnlaug Serpent-Tongue was her first and lasting heart-love.

Soon thereafter, Master Hrafn said to Mistress Helga in poetry, "My dear, I am troubled. I dreamed that I received my death's blow from a sword-thrust while I lay in bed, with you at my side."

"Do you look to me for sympathy, Hrafn?" Helga Thorsteinsdottir responded. "Know that I will not weep a tear should that be your fate! And know that, as far as I am concerned, you cannot die too soon—for I have been forced to marry the wrong man! My heart tells me that Gunnlaug Illugason has returned, and that you have hidden the news so that I would have to marry you.

"So I have no tears of woe to weep for you, my husband!" Helga repeated. "My heart floods with bitter tears—tears of anguish, tears of anger, tears of sorrow—for Gunnlaug Serpent-Tongue, and for myself, and for the life that we will never share!"

It came to pass that Helga Thorsteinsdottir soon learned that Gunnlaug Illugason had indeed returned. Then her heart blazed with ill will, and her tongue froze. Poet-Hrafn decided that it would be better for them to live on Master Thorstein's property. They moved to Borg, but their marriage still brought them no joy.

Helga's marriage to Hrafn causes a blood-feud.

It soon came to pass that a winter feast brought Helga Thorsteinsdottir and Gunnlaug Illugason together for the first time since Gunnlaug had left Borg in order to travel to over-sea lands. Gunnlaug had returned to Iceland with the strength and stature of a hero, the fine clothes of a nobleman, and a handsome face. Helga the Fair could not take her eyes from him, and all of the folk at the feast could see her love for Gunnlaug Serpent-Tongue in the way that she gazed at his face.

The feelings of the fair gold-wearer for the returning hero sat uncomfortably upon her recent marriage to his rival. And the love-loss of these three young people—the heart-pain of these who were the pride of all Iceland—lodged uncomfortably within the hearts of all who were present at the feast. Fear and foreboding rushed into the fire-hall, quelling all feelings of joy and merriment as surely as the wings of the winter north-wind snuff out a candle-flame.

It came to pass that, when all of the folk were busily preparing to depart, Gunnlaug Serpent-Tongue found an opportunity to talk with Helga the Fair.

"Good day, Mistress Helga! I see that, in my absence, my betrothed has become a married woman!" Gunnlaug exclaimed. "It is a cause for pity and for shame that Thorstein Egilsson has never taken my heart-love for you seriously. And now I see that Master Thorstein has sold his fair gold-wearer for too little too soon!"

To these words, Helga Thorsteinsdottir replied, "Gunnlaug Illugason, do you really blame my father for my marriage to Hrafn Onundarson? As I recall, you professed to regard me with a heart-love that was ever-lasting. And yet you forgot the terms of our marriage-contract! And so, as I see it, you have only yourself to blame for the fact that I am now married to another man!

"Tell me," she continued, "why did you not honor our fathers' agreement? And why did you not, at least, send word to your father about your intentions?"

To these words, Gunnlaug responded, "Helga, Fate will roll where it must! I was on a trade-ship in crossed sea-currents. I intended to honor our marriage-contract, but I also owed allegiance to Ethelred, the great English king. He had made me a member of his royal body-guard and, therefore, he held my life in his hands. As long as he feared an invasion of the Spear-Danes, he refused to give me leave to leave him.

"But, dear heart-friend, I tell you this," he added in poetry, "I have not had one happy day since you married Hrafn Onundarson!"

"Oh, Gunnlaug!" Helga replied. "I know that, for you, three years must have come and gone like winter sunlight. But, for me, each day of those three years was as long as a winter-night! Indeed, Fate rolls where it must, Gunnlaug, and we are caught on its wheel!"

In parting, Gunnlaug gave Helga the scarlet, fur-lined cloak that the English king had given to him as a king's-gift, and Helga's heart flooded with love for Ethelred's-Gift—this greatest of treasures—and for the man who gave it to her.

Gunnlaug Illugason then leaped upon his horse and galloped across the field to where he saw that Hrafn Onundarson was standing. He rode straight at him so that his horse forced Poet-Hrafn to jump aside. "You fear me too soon, Hrafn Onundarson!" Gunnlaug exclaimed. "Instead, fear the day when I will repay you for what you have done to me!"

Poet-Hrafn answered Gunnlaug's words with a poem in which he declared, "Gunnlaug Serpent-Tongue, it is not appropriate for the two of us to fight over one woman. You will find women as good as Helga the Fair—and many of them—in regions to the south!"

"You may be right, Hrafn, that many other women are the equal of Helga the Fair," Gunnlaug replied. "But for me, no one can compare with my fair gold-wearer! She alone brings me heart-joy!"

It came to pass that, when summer flowers had followed the spring snow, the Althing met once again. Gunnlaug Illugason took this opportunity to stand before the assembled Icelanders and recite a poem that he had prepared for the occasion.

"For a payment of gold, Hrafn Onundarson—whom some boast is my equal—has been given my fair Helga, while, east of the sea, my host, Ethelred, the English king, prevented my leaving. Therefore, I was silent when I would have claimed my bride," he declared.

Gunnlaug then called Poet-Hrafn before him and announced, "Hrafn Onundarson, because you have wed the woman who was betrothed to me, we are enemies. Therefore, I challenge you to single combat three days from today. If you accept my challenge, we will put on our sword-belts, and the island in the Axe River will become our battle-field. There we will let our battle-blades decide whose cause is just!"

To these words, Poet-Hrafn replied, "You are entitled to challenge me, Gunnlaug Illugason. I have been expecting it, and I am ready to meet you in single combat."

The families of both men were heart-heavy with anxiety as they set out together for the combat. However, they were helpless, for the law said that anyone who thought that he had a wrong to redress had the right to demand a duel.

Gunnlaug Illugason, who was accompanied by his father, Master Illugi, and his brother, Hermund Illugason, recited a poem in which he declared, "Burning for battle, I depart in order to fight Hrafn Onundarson with my unsheathed sword this day. May God favor me in my fight and enable me to slice Hrafn's head from his shoulders with my blood-thirsty battle-blade!"

Hrafn Onundarson—who was accompanied by his cousin, Skapti the Law-Speaker, and his father, Master Onund, replied in poetry as well. He declared, "Once our strong-thrusting swords are unsheathed, no one knows which poet will win the combat, so battle-eager are we both to sever each other's bones!"

Both Gunnlaug and Hrafn knew what Icelandic law dictated about single combat. Poet-Hrafn had the right to the first sword-thrust, since Gunnlaug Serpent-Tongue had challenged him to this duel. They would alternate sword-thrusts until one of them shed first-blood. Then the combat could cease if the wounded man agreed to pay the winner three marks of silver in order to redeem himself from the duel.

However, Fate continued to roll where it must, caring not at all about the rules for single combat. As the two sword-belted warriors faced each other, both were battle-brave and blood-thirsty, and each was eager to turn the other into a cold corpse. It came to pass that Poet-Hrafn's first sword-thrust struck the top of Gunnlaug Serpent-Tongue's shield with a mighty blow. His sword shattered at the hilt, and his severed battle-blade jumped up and grazed Gunnlaug's cheek.

As their fathers rushed in to prevent further combat, Gunnlaug exclaimed, "I have defeated you, Hrafn, since you no longer have a weapon!"

To these words, Poet-Hrafn responded, "Serpent-Tongue, it is you who are defeated, since my sword-blade has wounded you!"

Gunnlaug's heart flooded with rage. A duel without a death-wound was unacceptable. He hated Fate for favoring Hrafn Onundarson and permitting his broken battle-blade to drink first-blood fortuitously. And he hated both of their fathers for stopping their duel.

The wheel of Fate then rolled into the Althing as well. When the sun made the new day light, the Legislative Council met and legally abolished single combat as a permissible way to solve an argument between men.

Soon thereafter, it came to pass that Gunnlaug and his brother, Hermund, saw Helga Thorsteinsdottir on the opposite bank of the Axe River. In poetry, Gunnlaug told Hermund, "Helga the Fair was born to be a bone of contention between two men. I burn to possess this woman who is the goddess of gold, but it does me no good to gaze upon her swan-fair face, since she is Hrafn Onundarson's wife."

Nevertheless, Gunnlaug crossed the river in order to talk with Mistress Helga. When they separated, Helga the Fair followed his retreating figure with her eyes. Gunnlaug looked back at her and saw that, through her eyes, her heart was speaking to him of her love and her longing.

Gunnlaug Serpent-Tongue then said to Hermund in poetry, "My heart floods with feelings that roll in and out like the tide—the fire of my love for Helga Thorsteinsdottir, and the ice of my loathing for Hrafn Onundarson! Day and night, fire and ice! Month after month, fire and ice! Over and over, fire and ice! And now, the eyes of my fair gold-wearer send me a message that I cannot resist! But it will bring misfortune upon both of us!"

The Althing had concluded its work, and the men had long since retuned to their homes, when Gunnlaug Illugason awoke one morning to find that Hrafn Onundarson and eleven sword-belted companions were facing him in battle-dress.

Faster than the wings of the wind, Gunnlaug grabbed his own weapons, but Hrafn Onundarson announced, "I intend to do you no harm this day, Serpent-Tongue, but I have come to give you this message. You were not satisfied with our combat last summer when our battle-field was the island on the Axe River. Therefore, I propose that, when trade-ships next take the wave-road to Norway, we plan to meet again in single combat, this time on Norwegian land. There our kin-folk cannot prevent us from dueling to the death."

"You are indeed a man of honor, Hrafn Onundarson," Gunnlaug replied. "I accept your challenge with heart-joy, and I welcome you as my house-guest here."

To these words, Hrafn Onundarson replied, "Thank you, Serpent-Tongue, but no thank you. We will continue on our journey."

As always, summer flowers followed the spring snow, and Fate rolled where it must. When Poet-Hrafn's kin-folk tried to dissuade him from taking the wave-road to Norway, Hrafn told them, "I have no choice but to challenge Gunnlaug Illugason. As long as he lives, he is my Helga's heart-love, and her heart only floods with hatred at the sight of me. I have nothing to lose! If I kill Serpent-Tongue, Helga's heart-joy will be mine. On the other hand, if Serpent-Tongue kills me, I will lose a life that I no longer value."

It came to pass that, soon thereafter, Hrafn Onundarson boarded a sea-ready trade-ship that was bound for Norway. However, Gunnlaug Illugason was apparently in no hurry to leave Iceland. When the time came that the summer flowers would soon become the frost-white stalks of winter, he finally boarded a sea-ready trade-ship. And then he chose to travel the wave-road to Orkney, rather than to Norway.

Once again, Gunnlaug Illugason became the court-guest of Earl Sigurd Hlodvisson. And when the time came that summer flowers would soon follow the spring snow, Gunnlaug accompanied that battle-brave warrior-earl in his raids upon the Southern Isles to the west of Scotland. In every battle, Gunnlaug Serpent-Tongue earned fame as a keen-witted shield-bearer and the most valiant of warriors.

When the summer flowers would soon become the frost-white stalks of winter, Gunnlaug Illugason at last boarded a sea-ready trade-ship and took the wave-road to Norway. There he once again became the court-guest of Earl Eirik Hakonarson. Earl Eirik had heard about the blood-feud between the two Icelanders, and he knew the reason for Gunnlaug Serpent-Tongue's visit. He immediately announced that he would not permit his court-guest to fight Hrafn Onundarson on Norwegian soil.

Meanwhile, Hrafn Onundarson, who was still in Norway, had received no word about Gunnlaug Illugason. And so it came to pass that the two blood-rivals spent the winter in the same country, but each was ignorant of the other's presence.

The time came when summer flowers would soon follow the spring snow. It came to pass that Gunnlaug was on a stroll when a gathering of Norwegian folk attracted his attention. They were watching two youths who were dueling for sport. The opponents were calling themselves Serpent-Tongue and Poet-Hrafn, whom they were busily mocking for the amusement of their audience.

Gunnlaug's heart flooded with fury at the sight. He returned to the Norwegian court and announced to Earl Eirik, "My lord, the time has come when I must meet Hrafn Onundarson in single combat! Your protection—although well-intended—has made me the object of jest, and my blood is boiling with the shame of it!"

So it came to pass that Earl Eirik learned that Hrafn Onundarson had left Norway and was in Sweden. The earl sent Gunnlaug on his way with two guides to accompany him. However, Gunnlaug arrived at one place after another in the evening, only to learn that Poet-Hrafn had departed that morning.

Finally, Gunnlaug decided to forego sleep and travel on through-out the moon-lit night. And it came to pass that, just as the sun was beginning to make the new day light, he came upon a meadow that was washed by two lakes. There Gunnlaug Illugason came face to face with his enemy, who apparently was waiting and watching for him.

"It is well, Hrafn Onundarson, that we finally meet," Gunnlaug announced. "And now, we can let our battle-blades decide whose cause is just!"

"I agree, Gunnlaug Illugason. It is well," Poet Hrafn replied. "Fate will roll where it must!"

Then Gunnlaug turned to Earl Eirik's guides and said, "You may remain here, but you must agree to take neither side in our duel, no matter what comes to pass! Your task is to observe every detail. I want you to be able to return to Earl Eirik with an accurate report of our combat."

And so it came to pass that Gunnlaug Illugason and Hrafn Onundarson met once again in blood-angry battle. And once again, Fate continued to roll where it must, caring not at all about the rules for single combat. Once again, as the two sword-belted warriors faced each other, both were battle-brave and blood-thirsty, and each was eager to turn the other into a cold corpse. Gunnlaug Serpent-Tongue had the right to the first sword-thrust, since Poet-Hrafn had chal-lenged him to this duel.

It came to pass that Gunnlaug mightily wielded Ethelred's sword, King's-Gift, and sliced off Poet-Hrafn's leg. "Our duel is over!" he cried, "for I will not fight a crippled man!"

To these words, Poet-Hrafn replied, "If I could have a drink of water, Gunnlaug Serpent-Tongue, I would still be a match for you!"

"Then I will use my helmet as a bowl and bring you some wa-ter," Gunnlaug responded. "But I do not want my act to entrap me! I want no tricks from you!"

"Put guile from your mind," Poet-Hrafn replied. "This is not a ruse!"

And so it came to pass that Gunnlaug Illugason filled his hel-met with water from the nearby stream and handed it to Hrafn Onundarson. However, as Hrafn reached for Gunnlaug's helmet with his left hand, that wily weapon-wielder grabbed his war-weapon in his right hand and, with a blood-hungry sword-flash, he struck Gunnlaug Serpent-Tongue upon the head, giving him a mighty death-wound.

"So that is how you repay my trust!" Gunnlaug exclaimed.

"Since I can never have Helga's heart-love, I had to be certain that you could never become her husband!" Poet-Hrafn exclaimed.

Despite his battle-bloody death-wound, Gunnlaug fought Poet-Hrafn until he finally gained the advantage over his rival. Then, faster than the wings of the wind, he swiftly struck the evil-doer upon the head with King's-Gift, dealing a mighty death-wound with that blazing battle-blade. That wily weapon-wielder gave up his breath and his life together. However, by the time that three days had come and gone, Gunnlaug Serpent-Tongue had given up his breath and his life as well.

Before trade-ships would travel the wave-road and bring the news to Iceland, Master Illugi dreamed that his son, Gunnlaug Serpent-Tongue, appeared before him—battle-bloody—and that he recited a poem.

Gunnlaug declared, "Both battle-hungry, Ethelred's King's-Gift and I sliced off one of Hrafn Onundarson's legs. But then, Hrafn, corpse-eager, sliced into my head with his own war-weapon, giving me my death-wound as I tried to quench his thirst with my helmet-bowl of stream-water. However, King's-Gift and I—both burning for battle—repaid that wily weapon-wielder in kind. We cut short Hrafn's life-span then and there with a blood-thirsty blow to his head, and that wily weapon-wielder gave up his life with his blood!"

Meanwhile, in the southern headlands district, Master Onund dreamed that his son, Hrafn, appeared before him—battle-bloody— and that he recited a poem.

Hrafn declared, "My battle-hungry sword was blood-red with Serpent-Tongue's death-wound when his own blood-red war-weapon, gift from a great king—or else the sword-god!—sliced into my head and released this river of gore!"

Epilogue

It came to pass that the summer flowers became the frost-white stalks of winter. Then new summer flowers followed the spring snow, and the Althing met once again. Master Illugi met Master Onund at the Law Rock and said, "Onund, since your son, Hrafn, killed my son, Gunnlaug Serpent-Tongue, through guile, you owe me a blood-price for my son's death."

"Illugi, I will neither give you a blood-price for the life-loss of your son, nor will I demand a blood-price from you for the life-loss of my own son," Onund replied.

"Then know that one of your kin-folk will become my son's blood-price," Illugi the Black responded.

And so it came to pass that Master Illugi took thirty men and rode into the southern headlands district near Master Onund's farm, where they killed one of Poet-Hrafn's kin-folk. Master Onund accepted the blood-price without protest.

However, Hermund Illugason, Gunnlaug's brother and friend, was not satisfied with this blood-price. He rode alone to the trade-ship of Hrafn Onundarson's cousin and, faster than the wings of the wind, he swiftly killed the ship-master with one mighty spear-thrust while the ship-master's companions stood by in stunned silence. Again, Master Onund accepted this blood-price without protest.

And with this deed, the blood-feud between the kin-folk of Gunnlaug Illugason and the kin-folk of Hrafn Onundarson came to an end. However, it came to pass that Master Illugi and Master Onund chose to have no further dealings with each other.

It also came to pass that, in time, Thorstein Egilsson gave Helga the Fair in marriage to Thorkel Hallkelsson, a wealthy farmer who was a good man and a good poet. Like a storm-bowed young tree, Helga still sorrowed for Gunnlaug Serpent-Tongue, her lost heart-love, but she appreciated this husband and gave him children.

However, one thing alone could make Helga's heart smile. She would spread out Ethelred's scarlet fur-lined cloak—the king's-gift that Gunnlaug Serpent-Tongue had given to her—and she would fasten her eyes upon it. Then she would feast upon thoughts of her lost heart-love.

It then came to pass that, in time, Death came to live at Thorkel Hallkelsson's farm. Helga Thorsteinsdottir, too, became ill. She was sitting by the fire-place in the fire-hall of the farm-house, with her head on her husband's knee, when once again she called for Ethelred's scarlet fur-lined cloak—the king's-gift that Gunnlaug Serpent-Tongue had given to her. Once again, Helga's heart smiled as she fastened her eyes upon it. Then she collapsed in her husband's arms and died.

Thorkel Hallkelsson created a poem in which he said, "God alone has taken my wife's life, and without her it will be hard for me to continue to live."

Thorkel Hallkelsson continued to grieve, but he also continued to live.

And so ends this saga of Gunnlaug Serpent-Tongue.

Aucassin
and Nicolette

"Aucassin and Nicolette," put into writing by an anonymous author early in the thirteenth century, is a famous love story that is clearly influenced by the oral and written traditions of medieval France during the Age of Chivalry. The tale may have been influenced by "Floire et Blancheflor," the most popular love story in France during the preceding century, as well as by earlier Greek, Byzantine, and Moorish tales.

The sole manuscript of "Aucassin and Nicolette" was written in northeastern France, probably by a professional minstrel for his or her own use, since its style lends itself to performance. It contains alternating sections of prose (for recitation) and poetry (for singing). Moreover, repetition is an important part of its style.

In the Middle Ages, storytelling was an important form of entertainment in all levels of society, and wandering minstrels formed a professional class of their own. They often recited the great old tales and legends because of the stories' popularity. Minstrels performed for common folk on the village green as well as for aristocrats in palaces. They traveled alone or were accompanied by boys who sang, girls who danced, and bears that performed tricks. These minstrels were free to shape their tales to their own taste, and in time, gifted writers such as the author of "Aucassin and Nicolette" would often put their favorite tale into writing.

The manuscript copy of "Aucassin and Nicolette" is a medieval "romance," a literary form that originated in France in the mid-twelfth century. The romance was always set in the world of the aristocrats who were its patrons, and the attitudes and actions of the characters in these tales could influence real knights and ladies. The major focus of the typical medieval romance is chivalric adventures and heroic deeds, and love is usually secondary and nonessential. However, "Aucassin and Nicolette" focuses solely on love.

A favorite theme in medieval literature about courtly love is the idea that the course of true love is not smooth. According to the rules of courtly love set forth by Andreas Capellanus in the twelfth century:

> Love is a certain inborn suffering derived from the sight of and excessive meditation upon the beauty of the opposite sex, which causes each one to wish above all things the embraces of the other and by common desire to carry out all of love's precepts in the other's embrace . . . . The easy attainment of love makes it of little value; (whereas) difficulty of attainment makes it prized.

The typical plot of a medieval love story may involve any combination of the following themes: the love of a young knight for a foreign slave, unsympathetic parents who prohibit their child's love, the consequent forced separation of the young lovers, the often dangerous adventures that mark their struggle to be reunited, and their eventual success. "Aucassin and Nicolette" reflects this complex view of love. Not only do such themes create an exciting plot, but listeners and readers, from that day to this, may identify with the struggles of the lovers.

AUCASSIN AND NICOLETTE

Long ago, a particular count repeatedly attacked the castle of Count Garin of Beaucaire, in southern France. And because Garin was an old man, his enemy continued to burn his land and kill his knights.

Count Garin's only heir was Aucassin, a handsome youth with laughing blue eyes. From head to toe, Aucassin was so filled with goodness that he and evil were strangers. However, love had conquered Aucassin's heart and soul and, therefore, he had no interest in the war and his father's misfortunes, even though these were his misfortunes as well.

Aucassin's father would often summon him and declare, "Come now, Aucassin, dear son! It is your responsibility to put on your armor, gather your weapons, mount your horse, and defend our castle. Our knights need your moral support!"

And to these words, Aucassin would always reply, "Father, you cannot bend me to your will unless, first, you give me my dear friend, Nicolette, whom I love!"

"I will never do that, my son!" Count Garin would reply. "Nicolette is sweet, but you must put her from your mind and heart! She is a slave from Carthage, purchased from Saracen merchants! When you wish to marry, we will find you a maiden who is appropriate for you—one of royal blood, who is the daughter of a king or a count. As for Nicolette, the viscount has christened her and reared her as his daughter, and he will find a suitable young man for her."

"Father, you would think that you had never been in love!" Aucassin would declare. "Nicolette makes my heart sing! She is so courteous, gentle, and good that she could be queen of France or empress of Germany! Nothing you can say will turn my mind and heart away from her! Love does not bow to family and wealth!"

Finally, seeing that he could not dampen his son's love for Nicolette, Count Garin summoned the viscount, who owed allegiance to him, and announced, "Captain, because my son loves your godchild, he will not obey me and perform his duties as a knight. Therefore, you must send Nicolette away immediately! If you refuse, I will have her burned at the stake!"

"It will be as you wish, sire. I will send my daughter away to a distant land, where your son will never find her!" declared the viscount.

However, this is not what the viscount did. He imprisoned Nicolette in a room high in his great palace and gave her an old servant as a companion. Meanwhile, he sent Rumor throughout the land to tell everyone that Nicolette had disappeared. Some heard that she had fled the country. Others heard that Count Garin had put her to death.

Aucassin heard these tales and went directly to the viscount. "Sire, tell me, if you will, what has really happened to Nicolette? She is my dear friend and the person I love most in the world! My heart longs for her, and if I die because of it, you will have killed me by taking her from me!"

"Young sire," responded the viscount, "Nicolette should be no concern of yours! She is but a captive maiden from a distant Saracen land! Some day I will give her in marriage to a suitable young man, but you are not he! You have been born and bred to marry the daughter of a king or a count! And if you choose to love Nicolette outside the bonds of marriage, your soul will suffer the eternal torments of Hell instead of the heavenly bliss of Paradise!"

"Paradise, sire!" Aucassin exclaimed. "I only want to be with my dear friend, Nicolette, whom I love! What do I care about Paradise unless Nicolette is there! Only old priests and those who are crippled or starving go to Paradise! All of the interesting people—worthy knights who have lost their lives in tournaments and great wars, lovely ladies, good clerks, and fine minstrels—go to Hell! But, wherever Nicolette is, that is where I want to be!"

"You speak empty and foolish words, Aucassin! Put Nicolette from your mind and heart for, truly, you will never see her again! Speak to her, and your father will burn her at the stake! Who knows what he would do to you!"

And so it came to pass that Aucassin returned to his palace, his heart flooded with grief. "Oh, Nicolette!" he declared. "How sweet your laughter and your face! How sweet your kiss and your embrace! But now our parents have taken you from me! And I feel as if they have taken my life, dear friend—my love!"

Meanwhile, war pressed against the gates of Count Garin's castle once again. "Come now, Aucassin, dear son!" the count exclaimed. "It is your responsibility to put on your armor, gather your weapons and your horse, and defend our castle. Our knights need your moral support! You need not kill or be killed. Just be present on the field of battle!"

To these words, Aucassin replied, "Father, we have had this conversation many times. And I have told you that you cannot bend me to your will unless, first, you give me my dear friend, Nicolette, whom I love!"

"Son, I will not give you Nicolette! In fact, I would willingly lose all that is mine before I would see you have any relationship with that slave-girl!"

"Then consider this proposal, Father. I will go forth to defend our castle on one condition. If I return safely, you must let me talk with Nicolette and give her one kiss. For I would rather have Nicolette's kiss than a hundred thousand gold marks!"

"All right, Son," responded Count Garin. "I give you my word that if you go forth to battle, I will permit you to have a brief visit with Nicolette."

And so it came to pass that Aucassin's squire helped him put on his chain-mail tunic and his helmet, and then buckle on his sword. Once Aucassin had mounted his great warhorse, his squire handed him his shield and his spear. Thus armed, Aucassin fearlessly rode forth through the castle gates and into battle.

However, as he rode, Aucassin gave no thought either to killing or to being killed. Instead, his mind was flooded with love for Nicolette. And so, as he rode, his reins dropped from his hands, and the enemy easily grabbed him and took him prisoner, taking his shield and his spear from him as if he had generously offered them. His captors were discussing how best to kill him when Aucassin finally paid attention to what they were saying.

"Why, I am being led to my death!" he exclaimed to himself. "And if these knights behead me, I will never be able to speak with Nicolette again! I see that they have taken my spear and my shield. Fortunately, I still have my sword and my horse! I must defend myself for Nicolette's sake, or I am not worthy of her love!"

These thoughts flooded Aucassin's heart with the will to fight. Swiftly drawing forth his sword, he slashed the knights who surrounded him—here, slicing through a helmet, and there, slicing through an arm or a glove—as if he were an enraged wild boar who found himself beset with attacking hounds. And so it came to pass that Aucassin killed ten knights and seriously wounded seven more.

Meanwhile, the count who was Garin's enemy was riding toward Aucassin, having been informed that he had been captured. However, when the count came within range, Aucassin quickly sliced his sword into the count's helmet, splitting it and causing the stunned count to fall from his horse. Aucassin then grabbed the nose-piece of the count's helmet and led him as his prisoner to his father.

"Here is your great enemy, Father!" he exclaimed. "For twenty years, he has been defeating you because no one has been brave enough or skilled enough to stop him!"

"Your own courage and skill become you, my son!" his father replied. "And they certainly become you far better than your dream of marrying some slave-girl!"

"That may or may not be true, Father," Aucassin responded. "But now is not the time for such words. You, too, have deeds to perform! You must remember your promise to me!"

"What promise?" asked Count Garin.

"Come now, Father! You promised that, if I returned safely from battle, you would let me talk with Nicolette and give her one kiss! I expect that you will keep your word, just as I have kept mine!"

"God knows that I would never keep such a promise, Aucassin!" Count Garin replied. "If Nicolette were here, I would condemn her to be burned at the stake, and you would have cause to fear for your own life!"

"Shame upon your old head, Father!" Aucassin declared. And turning to his prisoner, he said, "Sire, my father is a man who does not keep his word. So give me your hand and your word that, as long as you live, you will take any opportunity to dishonor him!"

"You cannot be serious, Aucassin!" the count replied. "Free me, and I will give you whatever you wish. You have only to name your price: gold, silver, horses, hound, or hawk."

"Make no mistake, sire," responded Aucassin. "I will slice your head from your shoulders with one stroke of my sword unless you swear to do just what I have asked of you!"

"Then, Aucassin, in God's name, I promise to act as you wish."

And with these words, Aucassin let his father's enemy mount a horse, and he led him safely back to his own knights.

It was the month of May, the time of gentle weather and sweet thoughts. However, Count Garin's heart had turned to stone. Seeing that Aucassin would never give up his love for Nicolette, he imprisoned his son in a dungeon deep beneath the earth.

"Oh, Nicolette!" Aucassin wailed. "How sweet your laughter and your face! How sweet your kiss and your embrace! Surely everyone loves you as I do! But because I love you, my father has imprisoned me in this dungeon! And here I must now die for you, dear friend— my love!"

Now, while Aucassin was languishing in the dungeon, Nicolette lay on her bed, wide awake in her secluded room. The sight of the moon and the song of the nightingale turned her thoughts to her dear friend, Aucassin, whom she loved with all her heart. Then she thought of Aucassin's father, whose heart flooded with hatred at the sound of her name. "If Count Garin discovers where my godfather has hidden me, he will either hang me or burn me at the stake! Therefore, I must leave here while I can!"

Seeing that her old companion was asleep, Nicolette tightly knotted her sheets and towels into a long rope, which she tied to her window frame and then tossed out the window. Putting on her best cloak, she then climbed down to the garden below. As she made her way toward the back gate, she was a vision of loveliness, with her curly golden hair, her blue smiling eyes, her lips as red as the summer rose, and her waist so tiny that two hands could encompass it. It was no wonder that Aucassin loved her!

Nicolette opened the back gate and moved on silent feet through the streets of Beaucaire, staying within the shadows on this moonlit night. Finally, she came to the tower where she had heard that her lover was imprisoned. Putting her head into an old crevice, to her surprise and delight, she heard Aucassin's declaration of love.

"Aucassin, my dear and fearless knight!" she called. "I share the sorrows of you heart! However, your tears are useless! You may never marry me! Your parents hate me! And so, I have no choice but to cross the sea and seek refuge in some distant land. I leave you with this curl that I now cut for you. May it find its way through this crevice into your dungeon, and may it remind you of how much I love you! Farewell, my dear one!"

"Stay but a moment, Nicolette!" Aucassin replied. "I have kissed your curl and placed it on my heart. But you cannot leave me! Without you, I will die! And you must never love anyone but me."

Now, while Aucassin and Nicolette were speaking together, it came to pass that the town's guards were approaching. Their swords were unsheathed beneath their cloaks because Count Garin had charged them to find Nicolette and kill her. Nicolette was too engaged with Aucassin to hear their approach. However, the watchman high in the tower saw them and could hear them as they spoke of killing Nicolette.

"What a pity that such a lovely maiden should lose her life!" he thought to himself. "I must warn her in time, for if she should die, then my lord Aucassin will die also. And that too, would be a pity!"

And so it came to pass that the clever watchman suddenly broke forth into a loud song. He sang about a gentle, loyal maiden who spoke with her lord and lover, unaware of her need to flee the danger from cloaked men who had been charged to take her life with their swords.

Nicolette heard the watchman's song and withdrew deep into the shadows, pulling her cloak over her face. As soon as the guards had passed, she bid Aucassin a hasty farewell and went forth amidst the shadows of the streets until she came to the castle wall. Its poor condition enabled her to climb it without difficulty. However, once she reached the top, her heart flooded with terror at the sight of the deep, dry moat that loomed below her.

"What dare I do now?" Nicolette asked herself. "If I try to descend into the moat, I will surely die! And if I do not, Count Garin's men will surely discover me before tomorrow's sun sets, and then I will be burned at the stake! I face death either way! Therefore, it is better to die here, alone, than to burn in the square and entertain everyone who comes to watch!"

And so it came to pass that Nicolette slid down the wall of the castle and then down the wall of the moat. As the flesh on her hands and feet became torn and bloody, she said to herself, "Ignore the pain, Nicolette! Think only of staying alive!"

At the bottom of the moat, Nicolette looked through the debris to see if anything could help her climb up the steep, far side. Finding a sharp stake, she cut footholds in the far wall and slowly climbed out of the moat.

Now she faced the dark, fearsome forest. "Dare I enter these dark woods?" she asked herself. "Surely, there is no way to avoid them—for they extend more than a hundred miles in every direction! I know not where to flee or how to go! If I enter the forest, surely wolves or boars or snakes will kill me! And if I wait in the hope of finding some other way, surely Count Garin's men will capture me and burn me alive in the town square. I face death either way! Therefore, it is better to die alone in the forest as food for hungry beasts than to amuse the folk in town as food for hungry flames!"

And so it came to pass that Nicolette entered the forest and found a secluded place to sleep. Early the next morning, she came upon a group of young shepherds who were enjoying their breakfast.

"Good boys, do you know the youth named Aucassin who is the son of Count Garin of Beaucaire?"

"Yes, we know him," one of the boys replied.

"Then, take these five sols, if you will, and give him this message for me. Tell Aucassin that a beast roams through this forest—and that, if he were to catch it, he would not sell one limb of it for five hundred marks of gold! Now, if Aucassin tells you that no beast in these woods—no stag, no wolf, no boar—is worth even one gold mark, then tell him that this beast—should he find it—will cure his great wound. But tell him that he must find it within three days—or else his wound will never heal!"

"We will remember your message," the boy responded. "And we will give it to Aucassin should we see him. But I must tell you that we will make no effort to look for him."

"I thank you for whatever you will do," Nicolette replied.

And with these words, the maiden made her way into the forest.

She trod an old overgrown path until she came to a place where seven paths split off from her own. There she wove leafy branches into a lovely bower, which she then decorated with white lilies.

"If Aucassin comes upon this rustic shelter, surely he will know that I fashioned it. If he truly loves me as he says, then he will rest here. However, if he does not rest here, he does not love me! And then, I certainly do not love him!" Nicolette declared to herself. "Meanwhile, I will conceal myself near this crossway and wait for him. It is a good time to put your heart to the test, Aucassin—my dear friend, my love!"

Now, back in the town of Beaucaire, everyone knew for a fact that Nicolette had disappeared. Some thought that she had fled the country. Others thought that Aucassin's father had put her to death. Count Garin was delighted that he could now restore Aucassin to his rightful position in Beaucaire, and he gave a great feast in order to flood his son's heart with joy.

Aucassin's heart remained flooded with grief. However, during the celebration, a knight saw his grief and approached him with a remedy. "I, too, have been lovesick like you, Aucassin. But a ride into the forest—with the sight of its beautiful flowers and the sound of its birds' lovely songs—brought cheer to my heart. Maybe such a ride would lighten your own sorrow as well. And you might even hear some word that will bring joy back into your heart!"

And so it came to pass that Aucassin rode into the forest and encountered the shepherd boys. Now they were singing about Aucassin and a golden-haired maiden who had rewarded them for some deed. "Surely, you are singing about Nicolette!" he exclaimed. "If you will tell me what you know about her, I will give you ten sols for your pains!"

The spokesman for the boys responded by saying, "Thank you, sire. We know that you are Aucassin, the son of Count Garin. And we have been waiting to see if you, too, would come this way! You see, we were sitting here at our breakfast when a beautiful maiden came upon us and asked us to give you the following message.

"'A beast roams through this forest—and, if you were to catch it, you would not sell one limb of it for five hundred marks of gold!' she announced. Now, sire, if you tell us that no beast in these woods—no stag, no wolf, no boar—is worth even one gold mark, then the maiden said to tell you that this beast—should you find it—will cure your great wound. But you must find it within three days—or else your wound will never heal!

"With these words, we have kept the promise we made to that fair maiden! Now whether you hunt this beast—or whether you do not—is for you to decide!"

Nicolette's message flooded Aucassin's heart with joy. He thanked the shepherd boys, rewarded them as he had promised, and quickly went forth in search of his love. And as he rode deep into the woods, he declared, "Oh, Nicolette! Neither boar nor deer—but you alone!—bring me into this forest! I want to hear your sweet laughter and see your sweet face! I want to feel your sweet kiss and your sweet embrace! Oh, may God help me to find you, dear friend—my love!"

Now so quickly did Aucassin ride through the forest that thorns and briars tore his clothes to shreds and ripped his flesh into a multitude of bloody wounds. If he had been a boar or a deer, a hunter could easily have followed his bloody trail. However, Aucassin felt no pain because love for Nicolette flooded his heart, and thoughts of Nicolette flooded his mind.

Aucassin rode on and on through the woods. In time, it came to pass that day turned to dusk. As yet, he had found no sign of Nicolette, and so his heart flooded with despair, and his eyes flooded with tears.

Aucassin was riding down an old, overgrown path when suddenly he came face to face with a monstrous-looking young man. His thoughts of Nicolette had blinded him to his presence—until now, when it was too late! Just the sight of him caused Aucassin's heart to flood with terror!

The youth's huge head was covered with a thick mop of charcoal-black hair. His broad and ugly nose hovered over lips that were redder than raw meat. And when his lips parted, they displayed large yellow teeth. The youth wore leather stockings and shoes that had been fashioned from a bull's hide, and his shoes were tied to his legs with bark laces that extended above his knees. A long, full cloak concealed his body and, as he faced Aucassin, he leaned upon his great club.

"May God bless you, my fair brother!" Aucassin declared. "What are you doing so deep in these woods?"

"May God bless you as well, sire," the ugly youth responded, "But why should you care what I am doing here?"

"I mean no offense," Aucassin replied. "I was simply making polite conversation."

"And I mean no offense, sire, when I now ask you, why are you weeping as if your heart is flooded with sorrow? Surely, if I were as rich as you are, nothing in the world could make me weep like that!"

"How do you know how rich I am?" Aucassin asked. "Do you know who I am?"

"Certainly, I know who you are!" responded the ugly youth. "You are Aucassin, the son of Count Garin of Beaucaire, and if you will tell me why you weep, then I will tell you why I am here."

"Then I will tell you," Aucassin replied. "Early this morning, I went forth with my white hound to hunt in these woods. And my hound—the best hunting dog in the world!—has disappeared! I weep because I have lost him!"

"Sire, no one could listen to your tale of woe and still respect you!" the ugly youth declared. "Do you feel such sorrow for a mere dog? Why, any rich man in Beaucaire would happily give you twenty dogs if your father asked it of him! It is I—not you—who have real cause to weep!

"I worked for a rich farmer, plowing his fields with his team of four oxen. However, three days ago, the best of the four wandered off, and I have been searching for him—tasting neither food nor drink—from that time to this! I dare not enter the town because—when they see that I have no money to pay for the ox that I have lost—they will throw me into prison! I know it must seem strange to you, but I am wearing all that I own in the world! And I weep even more for my poor mother who must sleep upon a bed of straw! Therefore, I have no regard for a rich man who weeps over his lost dog!"

Aucassin listened to this tale in silence. Then he said, "My heart floods with sorrow for you, brother! What is the worth of the missing ox?"

"Sire, I would have to pay twenty sols for him! And I do not have a single penny!"

"Then take these twenty sols from me," Aucassin declared. "Use them to pay for your lost ox. And may God be with you!"

"I thank you, sire! And may God help you find what you are seeking!"

Aucassin then continued on his way down the old overgrown path. The May night was moonlit and still. Suddenly, he came upon a place where seven paths split off from his own. And there, to his surprise, he found a lovely bower woven of leafy branches. It had been decorated with white lilies that now glistened in the moonlight.

"Why, surely my fair Nicolette has fashioned this lovely shelter!" Aucassin exclaimed, his heart flooding with love for her. "Therefore, I will rest here tonight!"

And it came to pass that—with his mind flooded with thoughts of Nicolette—Aucassin slipped and fell on a rock as he dismounted from his horse, thereby dislocating his shoulder. Sorely wounded, he tied his horse to a thornbush with his one good hand, and then he lay down on his good side and slowly pushed his body into the leafy shelter. Through an opening between the branches, he could gaze upon Night's starry robe.

"Star light, star bright, Nicolette must surely live in the heavens with you! For God would want to keep her near Him!" he exclaimed. "Oh, how I wish that I were a king's son that I, too, might be worthy enough to live with my sweet love. For then I would embrace and kiss Nicolette, my dear friend—my love!"

Now as soon as Nicolette heard Aucassin's words, she quickly came forth from her hiding place, entered the bower that she had fashioned, and embraced her wounded lover.

"Dear friend! My love! My heart floods with joy to see you here!"

"As does my own, to find you here!" Aucassin responded. "With you at my side, my shoulder—which I have sorely wounded—no longer pains me!"

"I will heal your wound, my love!" Nicolette replied. And with these words, the maiden slipped Aucassin's shoulder into its rightful place with her healing hands. Then she placed healing herbs upon it and bound it fast with a strip from her gown.

Having done this, Nicolette declared, "Aucassin, dear friend—my love! Think about what we must do! Surely, as soon as the sun makes the day light, your father's men will search this forest! I know not what they will do to you, but if they find me, they will burn me at the stake!"

"You are right, Nicolette! But with God's help, I will see that that does not happen! So climb upon my horse and, together, let us leave this forest and head for the sea! Surely, we can no longer live here. But as long as you are with me, we can live in some distant land!"

And so it came to pass that Aucassin and Nicolette safely made their way to the sea, where they found a trading ship that gave them passage. A mighty storm-wind drove their ship from one land to another until, finally, it reached the country of Torelore. There the young lovers disembarked.

They learned that Torelore was ruled by a mighty king and that the land was beset by a great war. Then and there, Aucassin buckled on his sword, and he and Nicolette set forth on his horse for the great castle. When they arrived, the guards told them an amazing tale—that the king was in bed, recovering from childbirth, while the queen had led Torelore's knights into battle.

Aucassin left his horse with Nicolette, unsheathed his sword, and then went forth into the castle in order to find the king. Sure enough, he found the king in bed!

"Sire, you are not a king, but a fool!" Aucassin declared. "Why are you lying in this bed?"

"Why not?" the king responded. "I have just given birth to a son, and in a month's time, when I have recovered, I will go forth and drive our enemy from my land."

At these words, Aucassin's heart flooded with disgust and disdain. With his sword, he lifted the king's sheet from his body and tossed it on the floor. Then he grabbed a club that rested against the wall and proceeded to beat the king with it until Death came forth and hovered near the monarch.

"Fair sire!" the king exclaimed. "Why are you assaulting the king of Torelore in his own castle? What do you want from me?"

"Sire, I want you to swear that no man in your land will ever again take refuge in childbirth!" Aucassin declared. "And I want you to take me to your queen!"

"Fair sire, I will do both with good will!" the king replied.

And so it came to pass that Nicolette remained behind in the queen's room while Aucassin and the king of Torelore rode forth to battle. And what a battle it was! Aucassin's heart flooded with wonder as he watched the opposing forces. Knights were pelting each other fast and furiously—but with baked apples, fresh cheeses, mushrooms, and eggs!

"Sire, would you like me to fight here on your behalf?" Aucassin asked the king.

"I would appreciate your help, fair sire, since you willingly offer it!" the king replied. "If you are a knight of courage and skill, your actions on the field of battle will surely cause the hearts of our foe to flood with terror. And it will be my pleasure to watch their legs follow their hearts!"

And so it came to pass that Aucassin went forth to do battle in the name of the king of Torelore. And with his sword, he fought nobly and well, bringing swift death upon many among the king's foe.

However, when the king saw that his enemies were losing their lives, he rode forth to Aucassin, grabbed his horse's bridle, and declared, "Stop, fair sire! You know not what you do here! You are killing many good men!"

To these words, Aucassin replied, "On the contrary, sire! I know exactly what I am doing! I have won your battle for you!"

"Indeed you have, fair sire!" the king replied. "In fact, you have been too zealous in my defense! It is not the custom here to kill one's enemies!"

By now, the foe had run in panic from the field of battle. Therefore, Aucassin accompanied the king back to the castle of Torelore, where the king and his nobles celebrated Aucassin's great victory.

And it came to pass that three years came and went while Aucassin and Nicolette remained in the castle of Torelore as guests of the king and queen. Their hearts were flooded with love for each other, and now each day dawned more brightly, each bird sang more sweetly, and each flower bloomed more radiantly than any had in Beaucaire.

However, the joy of Aucassin and Nicolette was short-lived, for warlike Saracens suddenly arrived by sea. They lay siege to the castle, conquered it, and carried off both captives and treasure. Bound hand and foot, Aucassin found himself tossed into one ship, while Nicolette found herself tossed into another. One misfortune gave birth to another as these ships encountered a great storm at sea. Fierce winds blew the waves into mighty mountains and separated the ships from each other.

The ship on which Aucassin lay bound suffered such damage that it became the sea's captive, sailing now here and now there, at the whim of waves and currents. Finally, it came to pass that the sea drove the ship toward land.

Fortune now smiled upon Aucassin, for the land held none other than his own castle of Beaucaire! The folk who ventured forth to investigate the shipwreck were amazed to find that their own Aucassin was bound and imprisoned on board the foundering Saracen ship. And so it came to pass that the hearts of all flooded with joy! Their count and countess—Aucassin's parents—had died during Aucassin's absence. And now the people of Beaucaire welcomed home their new count, knowing that he would rule their land in peace.

As for Aucassin, his heart remained flooded with grief for his lost Nicolette. For him, the sun shone dimly, the birds sang sadly, and the flowers bloomed without radiance. "Oh, Nicolette!" he wailed. "How sweet your laughter and your face! How sweet your kiss and your embrace! If only I knew where to find you—no matter how distant, or how difficult to reach—your land would not be too far or too hard for me, dear friend—my love!"

Meanwhile, it came to pass that the Saracen ship that carried Nicolette belonged to the king of Carthage. The king's sons knew by Nicolette's appearance that she was a maiden of noble birth.

Time and again, they would ask her, "Who are you, fair maiden? Surely, with your beauty and you bearing, your father is a king or count!"

And time and again, Nicolette would always reply, "Sires, would that I could tell you who I am! But, in truth, I myself do not know. I was but a child when men took me secretly from my parents and sold me as merchandise in the marketplace."

Meanwhile, the ship sailed on to its destination, the city of Carthage. And it came to pass that when Nicolette saw the countryside and the walls of that great castle, they awakened her memory of her childhood. And then Nicolette knew that Carthage was her home—the place where she had been loved and reared.

"Why, this is my father's kingdom! I remember the houses that still stand within these walls!" she exclaimed to herself. "And I am really a princess, since I once called the king of Carthage Father!"

"Oh, Aucassin, my brave knight! My heart still floods with love at the sound of your name! Would that God would lead you to me, so that I could clasp you in a sweet embrace and feel your kisses on my face, dear friend—my love!"

The seafaring sons of the king of Carthage brought Nicolette before their father and declared, "Father, look what jewel we found on foreign shores! We have tried to learn her identity, but she tells us that she does not know who she is! Apparently, men secretly took her from her parents when she was but a child and then sold her as merchandise in the marketplace!"

With these words, the king studied Nicolette in silence. Then he said, "Fair, sweet guest, gaze upon my face without fear. Now, can you tell me who you are? For if my eyes do not deceive me, you are no stranger to Carthage!"

And to these words, Nicolette replied, "Sire, I think that this was once my home! Fifteen years have come and gone since I was stolen from my parents, the king and queen of Carthage. I was but a child then, but I remember this countryside, these houses, these palaces, and these walls! And your face calls forth love, not fear—for I have seen you in many a dream from the past!"

"Your memory rings true, my daughter! For indeed you are my child!" the king replied. "I remember well how you were taken from us! So welcome home, my beauty and my darling! Your return floods my heart with joy!"

And so it came to pass that Nicolette received a royal welcome in Carthage. Her parents prepared to marry her to a great Saracen king of Spain, but Nicolette's heart silently protested.

"Aucassin is my one and only love!" she declared to herself. "Now that I have found my true home, I must find a way to flee and find him! For no home is home to me unless Aucassin is there to share it!"

And so it came to pass that Nicolette learned to play the viol. And when the day of her marriage was close at hand, she secretly stole forth from the palace one night and sought refuge in some simple house by the sea. A poor woman took her in, and there Nicolette transformed her appearance. An herb stained her head, hair, and face brown. Then she made herself an outfit that a minstrel would wear.

And it came to pass that, in this attire, and with her viol in hand, Nicolette approached the captain of a ship bound for Provence and persuaded him to take her aboard. When the ship reached its destination, she thanked the captain and went forth into the countryside, where she performed as a minstrel for the people in the small towns and villages that served the great castles.

In time it came to pass that Nicolette reached the castle of Beaucaire, where Aucassin now ruled. Summer was in full bloom. The day was bright with sunshine, bird songs, and the perfume of radiant flowers. As Aucassin sat talking and laughing with his barons, the beauty of nature suddenly reminded him of Nicolette. His heart flooded with love for her, and his longing caused his eyes to flood with tears of grief.

"Oh, Nicolette!" he cried. "How sweet your laughter and your face! How sweet your kiss and your embrace! But now the sea has taken you from me! And I feel as if it has taken my life, dear friend—my love!"

And it came to pass that—just as if his heart had summoned

her!—Nicolette entered the castle of Beaucaire and prepared to entertain the noble folk who were gathered there with her songs.

"My lords and ladies," she announced, placing her bow upon the
strings of her viol, "hear now my song of the brave knight Aucassin
and the fair Nicolette. Hear of their great love—both sad and true!
Hear how the hatred of Aucassin's father sent Nicolette fleeing into
the woods, with Aucassin after her. Hear how the lovers finally
reached the sea, where a ship took them to the country of Torelore.
Hear how happily they lived in Torelore until the Saracens captured
and separated them.

"Of Aucassin, I can sing no more. But hear how the fair Nicolette
now lives in Carthage with her father, who is king of that great land.
Soon, he plans to give her in marriage to one of the greatest kings
of Spain! But hear how Nicolette refuses every mate but Aucassin,
saying that if she cannot be his bride, then she will belong to no
one! What great love my song reveals!—What great love, both sad
and true!"

Aucassin's heart flooded with joy when he heard the minstrel's
song. He quickly withdrew from his companions and came forth to
greet her. "Tell me, fair friend, do you actually know this Nicolette
of whom you sing?" he asked. "And can you tell me anything else
about her!"

"Why, yes, sire, I know her well!" the minstrel declared. "She is
the most lovely and loyal maiden whom you would ever hope to
know! She is gentle, modest, and kind. The men who captured her
brought her to Carthage. And finding that she is his own lost daughter, the king's heart has flooded with joy. Now he looks forward to
giving her in marriage to a great king. However, Nicolette says that
she will hang or burn at the stake before she marries anyone but
Aucassin—no matter how great a king he might be!"

To these words, Aucassin replied, "Oh, fair friend! I have a favor
to ask of you! If only you would return to Carthage, find Nicolette,
and persuade her to come here and speak with me, why I would give
you more wealth that you would ever accept! Because of my love
for Nicolette, I will not marry another—no matter how noble and
beautiful she might be!"

"Sire, if you will promise me that you love Nicolette enough to
marry her, then I will bring her to you—for your sake, and for hers
as well! For that is how much I love Nicolette!" responded the
minstrel.

And so it came to pass that Aucassin gave his word to the

minstrel, with money to cover the costs of her journey. And as the minstrel took her leave of him, tears again flooded his eyes because of his sweet memories of Nicolette.

When the minstrel saw Aucassin's tears, she said, "Sire, put grief from your heart! Before long, you will be able to feast your eyes on your dear Nicolette!"

And so it came to pass that Nicolette left the castle and returned to the town of Beaucaire, where she sought the house of the viscount who had reared her. He had died, but his wife knew her adopted child—despite her disguise—and, as always, she loved her! And so, for eight days, Nicolette remained in the palace she knew so well. She took off her minstrel's attire and applied an herb that washed off the stain from her head, her face, and her hair. She emerged more beautiful than she had ever been! She then dressed in a heavy silk robe, seated herself on a silk-covered chair, and asked the woman who had been her mother to bring Aucassin to her.

When the viscount's wife found Aucassin within his castle, she saw that his eyes were flooded with tears. "Why, sire, does your heart flood with grief? Have you lost someone who is very dear to you?"

"That I have, madam!" responded Aucassin. "I have lost your daughter, my fair Nicolette!" he cried. "How sweet her laughter and her face! How sweet her kiss and her embrace! But now, Carthage has taken her from me! And I feel as if it has taken my life, my dear friend, and my love!"

"Sire, if this is as you say, then dry your tears, and put grief from your heart! Let me show you what you love best in the world! For Nicolette—your dear friend—has come from that far land in search of you!" declared the viscount's wife.

When Aucassin heard that his true love was in Beaucaire, he went to the viscount's palace on winged feet. As soon as they came face to face, Nicolette welcomed Aucassin's embrace and his kisses that covered her face.

And it came to pass that, the very next morning, Aucassin married Nicolette—his dear friend, and his love—in a festive ceremony. Reunited at long last, the lovers lived in Beaucaire—in married bliss—to the end of their days!

Doctor Faust

Historical Background

The Earliest, Anatolian Legend

The Faust legend in its various forms involves a man who pledges his soul to the Devil in return for pleasure, knowledge, and power. The oldest version appears to have originated in Anatolia (now western Turkey), where it was recorded in Greek in the sixth century. It was translated into Latin in the ninth century, and influential versions appeared throughout Europe from the tenth through the thirteenth centuries.

According to this legend, a clergyman in Asia Minor named Theophilus rejected the opportunity to become bishop and then lost his own position. In anger, he consulted a magician, who enabled him to meet Lucifer. Theophilus agreed to become Lucifer's servant in return for regaining his lost power. He pledged allegiance to Lucifer, renounced his relationship with God, and promised to lead a life of lust, pride, and contempt for Christianity. Then, in his own blood, he signed a sealed parchment contract that confirmed this agreement.

Lucifer kept his part of the contract. However, seven years later, when he sent one of his servants to take Theophilus to Hell, Theophilus fasted for forty days and nights and put himself at the mercy of the Virgin Mary. She went down to Hell, seized the contract from Lucifer, and placed it on her suppliant's chest as he lay asleep in church. When Theophilus awoke, he destroyed the contract, and God pardoned him.

The Later, German Legend

The more famous version of the Faust legend is based on a man who lived in Germany at the time of the Protestant Reformation. A Georgius Faustus was mentioned in 1507, but it is more likely that the legend was based on Johann Faust, who was first mentioned in 1509. Since *faustus* means "fortunate" in Latin, the man may have adopted his surname. According to a professor of theology at the University of Wittenberg, Johann Faust was born in Knittlingen, Württemberg, in about 1480, and he died in the village of Staufen in about 1539.

Faust was a traveling scholar. One of Martin Luther's friends claimed that Faust studied magic at the University of Kraków, in Poland, where he is also said to have given public instruction in necromancy (the art of calling forth the spirits of the dead). Faust is also said to have lectured on the classics at the Universities of Wittenberg (the leading Lutheran institution) and Erfurt (the leading humanist institution). While at the University of Erfurt, Faust called himself "the half-god of Heidelberg," and he may have received a degree in divinity from the University of Heidelberg in 1509.

Like Doctor Faust in the following legend, the real Faust was also known as an astrologer, who earned money by predicting future events and creating horoscopes. Like him, the real Faust traveled throughout Europe and was also fond of practical jokes that could be humorous or cruel. For example, a contemporary of Faust's reported that, in return for wine, Faust agreed to remove a man's beard without using a razor. He received the wine and rubbed the man's face with an arsenic salve that removed the man's skin as well as his facial hair.

Another contemporary of Faust's reported that, like Doctor Faust in the following legend, the real Faust summoned the spirits of famous ancient heroes for his students. Greek heroes—such as Hector, Odysseus, Aeneas, and Heracles—as well as Biblical heroes such as Samson and David, all "came forth with fierce bearing and earnest countenance and disappeared again."

Still another contemporary of Faust's reported that, in a lecture hall at the University of Erfurt that was filled to capacity for the occasion, Faust caused apparitions of the heroes of Homer's *Iliad*, both Greek (Achilles, Ajax, Agamemnon, Menelaus, and Odysseus) and Trojan (Paris, Hector, and Priam), to appear in their armor. Then, to the horror of the assembled students, the Cyclops Polyphemus appeared, in the process of eating one of Odysseus's men. When Faust ordered the figures to leave, the heroes obeyed. However, Polyphemus refused to depart and began to look intently at the student audience as if he were thinking of eating more human flesh.

Because the real Faust was a scholar, he became a celebrated example of an intellectual's rebellion against God. The first mention of Faust's bargain with the Devil occurred while Faust was at Erfurt. When a famous Franciscan monk told him that his soul would be eternally damned unless he returned to God, Faust is said to have replied:

> I have pledged myself to the devil with my own blood,
> to be his in eternity, body and soul. . . . My agreement

ties me down irrevocably. . . . Nor would it be honest
or honorable if it had to be said about me that I had
gone against my letter and seal, which after all I signed
with my own blood. The devil has kept faithfully what he
promised me; so I, too, want to keep faithfully what I
have promised and pledged to him.

The monk reported these remarks to university officials, and they
dismissed Faust from their faculty.

Literary Background

Legends about Johann Faust developed during the course of his life and
continued to multiply. After his death, earlier legends about famous
magicians became attached to his name. His first biography, known as
the German *Faust-Book,* appeared about fifty years after his death, when
an anonymous Lutheran author compiled a collection of legends about
him, which Johann Spiess published in Frankfurt, Germany, in 1587. Mephistopheles, whose name means "he who is not a lover of light," makes
his first literary appearance in this volume. Its title page reads as follows:

Historia of Dr. Johann Faust, the notorious magician and
necromancer . . . how he pledged himself to the devil
for a certain time, what strange adventures he saw meanwhile, brought about and pursued, until he finally received
his well-deserved wages. Compiled and prepared for the
printer in several parts out of his own literary remains,
as a horrible example and sincere warning for all con-
ceited, clever, and godless people. James 4: Submit to
God, resist the devil, and he will flee from you.

Possibly because the German *Faust-Book* contains fascinating descriptions of Lucifer, his servants, and Hell, as well as the adventures of Doctor Faust, it was translated into other European languages within the first
few months of its appearance. Despite the publication of other, independent "Faust-books," the Spiess version became the standard version of
the legend.

The earliest mention of Faust in English appears in 1572 in *Of
Ghostes and Spirites*. The sole remaining copy of the English *Faust-Book* of
1592 (written by an anonymous author and owned by the British Museum) alludes to an earlier (lost) English edition, which presumably was
a translation of the German *Faust-Book* of 1587. The earlier translation

was obviously the source of Christopher Marlowe's play *The Tragicall History of Doctor Faustus*, which was probably performed by 1589.

Thereafter, "Faust-books" continued to appear throughout the seventeenth and eighteenth centuries. Some were magic handbooks that appeared under Faust's name and instructed people how to avoid making pacts with the Devil or how to break such a pact if they had made one. A second version of *Doctor Faust* appears in *Early English Prose Romances*, published by Thoms, in 1700. Faust also became the subject of pantomimes and farces. Two centuries later, Goethe developed the character of Faust to glorify the human mind and intellectual ambition.

Appeal and Value

Because Doctor Faust chooses to trade his soul to the Devil in return for unlimited knowledge, power, and earthly pleasure, this is one of the most important and provocative legends in world literature. It asks readers to consider whether these goals—or any goals—are worth pursuing regardless of the consequences. Moreover, the legend invites readers to evaluate their own goals and the extent to which they are willing to sacrifice other goals and values in order to attain them. In the process, it causes readers to evaluate their attitudes and behavior in moral terms, and to consider their responsibility to themselves, to others, and to their society.

Since the sixteenth century, the legend of Doctor Faust has inspired plays and poems and, later, operas, novels, and films. The legend has also inspired a variety of interpretations. German writers in the late eighteenth and nineteenth centuries (most notably Johann Wolfgang von Goethe) were likely to view Faust as a heroic figure who was determined to gain knowledge, and because they identified with him, they arranged to have God pardon him.

However, Faust is more than a German symbol. Faust lives wherever people pursue their goals single-mindedly and selfishly, with short-sighted regard for their own future, and with no concern for the consequences to other members of the human family.

DOCTOR FAUST

Johann Faust summons the Devil.

Long ago, it came to pass that a babe, christened Johann Faust, was born to a poor man and his wife who lived in the town of Rhode, in the province of Weimar, in Germany. Fortune smiled upon little Johann. His wealthy uncle, having no child of his own, adopted him and made him his heir. And so it came to pass that he grew to manhood in his uncle's city of Wittenberg.

In time, it became clear that Johann Faust would become a great scholar. He attended the great Lutheran university in Wittenberg, where he applied himself to the study of divinity so that he would become well-versed in the knowledge of God and His law. And so profound was Faust's mastery of his field of study that he surpassed his professors, and they unanimously conferred upon him the degree of Doctor of Divinity.

Johann Faust also became learned in the arts of medicine. And it came to pass that, as a physician, he used his remarkable talent to improve the quality of human life. Because of his prescriptions, entire cities escaped the plague, and he cured a thousand terrible diseases.

However, Johann Faust was not satisfied. He wanted to know all that there was to know. And so it came to pass that he contrived to enter the supernatural world in order to gain its mysterious and secret knowledge. He turned away from God and the godly way of life. He studied not only mathematics and astrology, but also witchcraft and magic, with their accompanying charms and incantations.

And it came to pass that, in this field of study, too, Johann Faust became so proficient that no one could equal him. And his heart so flooded with love for the devilish arts that he developed a loathing for his title, Doctor of Divinity. Instead, he preferred to be known as a physician, a mathematician, or an astrologer.

However, Johann Faust still was not satisfied. He still did not know all that there was to know. He could not make human beings immortal, and he could not restore the dead to life. And so it came to pass that his mind and heart flooded with disdain for the future of his soul and the joy after death that a godly life would bring. Instead, he became determined to acquire as much knowledge, power, and earthly pleasure as he could.

It was with this in mind that, early one evening, Johann Faust left Wittenberg for the great forest that lay outside the town. He set forth with the sole intention of summoning the Devil!

Upon reaching a crossway, Faust took a stick in hand and made a series of circles within circles. Then he used the special figures, charms, and incantations that would reach the ears of the devilish powers. The hours of the early evening came and went while Johann Faust occupied himself in this way.

Finally, Faust stood in the center of the circles that he had drawn and called out, "I, Johann Faust, command the swift-flying spirit, Mephistopheles—he who serves the Prince of Darkness—to appear in person before me!"

Now, as soon as Johann Faust spoke these words, the forest knew that the Devil was coming! A great wind roared through the trees, causing them to moan and groan and bend to the ground as if they were blades of grass. And hearing the trees shiver and shake right down to their roots would have caused an ordinary human heart and soul to tremble with terror. However, Johann Faust possessed no ordinary heart and soul. He and fear were strangers. And, therefore, he remained calm as he patiently waited for what he hoped was to come.

Finally, Faust thought that his hopes were fulfilled. First, the Devil suddenly appeared and ran around the circles that Faust had drawn, accompanied by the noise of a thousand wagons rumbling together down a cobblestone street. Next, the air was filled with great claps of thunder and sizzling bolts of lightning that were so strong and so bright that Faust wondered if the entire forest would ignite into one great fire.

It was then that the heart and soul of Johann Faust flooded— not with fear, but with dismay. He realized that these were but horrifying visions, and not a real Devil and a real event. And so he began to give up hope that the Devil would ever appear in person before him.

However, as soon as the question of leaving the forest entered the mind of Johann Faust, a great dragon suddenly appeared in the air above him and hovered right over his head. Then the forest echoed with a monstrous cry, and a flame fell like a lightning bolt, landing at his feet in the form of a fiery globe. Once again, an ordinary human heart and soul would have trembled with terror. However, Faust possessed no ordinary heart and soul. He and fear were strangers. And, therefore, once again he remained calm as he patiently waited for what he hoped would come.

And it came to pass that, once again, Johann Faust walked into the center of the circles that he had drawn and called out, "I, Johann Faust, command the swift-flying spirit, Mephistopheles—he who serves the Prince of Darkness—to appear in person before me!"

Suddenly, the fiery globe grew to a man's height and split open, permitting a man clothed in fire to step forth. This man ran around and around the circles that Faust had drawn until, finally, he stopped right in front of Johann Faust.

"Why have you summoned me, Doctor Faust?" he asked.

"I will answer your question if you will first tell me who you are," Johann Faust replied.

"I am Mephistopheles, the swift-flying spirit whom you summoned. I serve my lord, Lucifer, the Prince of Darkness. However, in Hell, I am a king in my own right. There I rule Lucifer's central kingdoms."

"I am impressed and delighted that I have been able to summon such a great prince!" Faust exclaimed. "I would like to speak with you tomorrow, if you will appear at my house at noon."

"As you wish, Doctor Faust, so it will be," the swift-flying spirit declared. And, quick as thought, he disappeared into the air.

Faust makes a bargain with the Devil.

So it came to pass that the swift-flying spirit, Mephistopheles—he who serves the Prince of Darkness—reappeared before Johann Faust at noon on the following day. "You have summoned me, Doctor Faust, and here I am," declared the spirit. "Now, how may I serve you?"

To these words, Johann Faust declared, "Mephistopheles, I want to become a spirit just like you—either a Devil or a servant of the Devil. Therefore, I want you to live in my house as my servant and companion, being invisible to everyone but me. Moreover, I want you to serve me obediently from this time forth until my death, giving me whatever I wish and truthfully answering every question that I ask.

"What I want is knowledge," Faust explained. "Surely, with your help, I can fly across the world with the wings of an eagle—soaring high into the heavens and swooping low upon the earth—in order to learn all there is to know. For I would discover all the secrets known to Heaven and Earth! And only when I possess such knowledge will I be satisfied! Now, will you fulfill my wishes, Mephistopheles?"

To these words, the swift-flying spirit replied, "I am not my own master, Doctor Faust. I serve the Prince of Darkness, and if he permits me to serve you as you wish, then I will do so. But you should be aware that the Prince of Darkness does not give his gifts and knowledge to any human being without receiving something of equal value in return. In order to receive them, you must promise to belong to my lord Lucifer! You must contract to give both your body and your soul to the Prince of Darkness so that he can enlarge his kingdom!"

"I will not accept such terms, Mephistopheles!" declared Faust. "I expect you to do as I wish without exacting such a price!"

"You do not have to pay our price, Doctor Faust. And you do not have to get your wish, either!" responded the swift-flying spirit. "However, you should be aware, Doctor Faust, that your ungodly pursuits have already made you Lucifer's man! The Prince of Darkness already owns both your body and your soul! And, one day, the kingdom of Hell will be your home!"

"As you have said, Mephistopheles, you have to talk with Lucifer before you can fulfill my wishes," replied Faust. "Therefore, consult with him, and bring me his answer tonight, at the stroke of midnight. I will have my own answer ready for you at that time."

"As you wish, Doctor Faust, so it will be," the swift-flying spirit declared. And, quick as thought, he disappeared into the air.

As soon as Johann Faust was left with his own thoughts, he said to himself, "Surely, if I have no other choice, this bargain with Lucifer is worth the price of my soul! In fact, if I had as many souls as there are stars in the heavens, I would surely give them all for Mephistopheles! Knowledge is power, and with his help, I can achieve ultimate power! Emperors and kings will be powerless compared to me!

"Why, with Lucifer's knowledge, the world will be my toy!" Faust mused. "I may choose to make a bridge of the sky and so cross the ocean! I may decide to move the continents wherever I choose! I may make the moon fall from the heavens, or I may cause the oceans to flood the earth! Moreover, I can have the best of what the world provides: gold and jewels, silks and satins, rare wines and exotic fruits!

"Who on earth could resist this opportunity? Surely, the Prince of Darkness cannot be as evil as people say he is! And Hell cannot be as horrible, either!" Faust concluded.

That night, at the stroke of midnight, Mephistopheles reappeared before Johann Faust. And it came to pass that the swift-flying spirit declared, "Doctor Faust, my lord Lucifer will permit me to serve you in every way, but only on the condition that you agree to give him both your body and your soul so that he can enlarge his kingdom.

"However, in order for an agreement to exist between the two of you, my lord requires even more from you, Doctor Faust," Mephistopheles continued. "You must deny your Christian belief and become the enemy of all who are Christian. Moreover, you must remain steadfast in your anti-Christian convictions, no matter how persuasively someone may attempt to convince you to return to God.

"Now, Doctor Faust, if you agree to Lucifer's conditions, you must confirm this agreement with a statement written in your own blood that I will give to my lord. Then you will indeed become a devilish spirit. You will have twenty-four more years of life, good health, and whatever knowledge, power, and earthly pleasures we can give you. Then—when your time on earth comes to an end—I will destroy your body and take your soul down to my lord Lucifer in the kingdom of Hell."

"Now, Doctor Faust, are you willing to accept these terms?" Mephistopheles asked.

To this question, Faust replied, "I am delighted that you can fulfill my wishes, Mephistopheles! And since you give me no other choice, I agree to all of Lucifer's terms. I agree to exchange both my body and my soul for the knowledge, power, and earthly pleasure that you can give me!"

"As you wish, Doctor Faust, so it will be," the swift flying spirit declared. "Just write up the contract, and give it to me!" And with these words, quick as thought, Mephistopheles disappeared into the air.

So it came to pass that Johann Faust took his pen knife, pricked a vein in his left hand, and, with his right hand, wrote his contract with Lucifer in his own blood. He declared:

> I, Johann Faust, Doctor, assert that all my learning
> and wisdom have been unable to give me what I de-
> sire, and that no mortal men can help me achieve my

goal. Therefore, Lucifer, the Prince of Darkness and his servant, Mephistopheles, will teach me whatever I want to know, and they will fulfill my every wish.

In return for their help, at the end of twenty-four years, I agree to give Lucifer and Mephistopheles permission to take my body and soul to their habitation—wherever it happens to be—where they will remain with the Prince of Darkness for eternity. I also hereby renounce God, the host of Heaven, and all creatures whom God has formed in His image.

All this I declare in writing with my own hand and my own blood, being in sound mind and body.

Johann Faust, Doctor

As Johann Faust signed this contract, quick as thought, Mephistopheles appeared before him, clothed in fire and with flames blazing forth from his mouth. Meanwhile, Faust's ears flooded with the sound of charging warriors and galloping horses.

While Faust watched, the fiery man became a dancing bull. Then the dancing bull became a pack of deerhounds that chased a great stag around Faust's study and felled it. Then the deerhounds became a dragon and a lion who fought so fiercely that Faust wondered if they would cause the walls of his house to collapse. However, he stood by and patiently waited for what was yet to come.

Finally, the dragon defeated the lion, and they disappeared. They were hardly out of sight before a raging bull appeared and charged Faust. However, once again, he stood his ground and patiently waited for what was yet to come.

Suddenly, Johann Faust's study became flooded with a fog that transformed light into darkness. When the fog lifted, two huge sacks, one of silver and one of gold, leaned against his desk. However, as soon as Faust tried to take one, he found that they were too hot to handle, and at his touch, they disappeared.

"I am delighted with your magic, Mephistopheles!" exclaimed Faust.

"This is nothing compared with what I am prepared to do for you, Doctor Faust!" responded the swift-flying spirit.

And so it came to pass that—hoping to gain his every wish—Johann Faust happily handed his contract to Mephistopheles, who, quick as thought, disappeared into the air.

Faust is granted some wishes, but not all of them.

So it also came to pass that Johann Faust renounced his own human self and viewed himself as a devilish spirit. He continued to
live in the house in Wittenberg that his uncle had bequeathed to him,
and he continued to teach his students. He continued to enliven his
classes on Homer by summoning the characters in the *Iliad* to appear before his students. And when he called them, they would indeed come! However, Doctor Faust never told anyone—even his
students—about his contract with the Prince of Darkness.

Johann Faust now possessed the best of food and wines, and the
best of clothing as well—for Mephistopheles stole everything from
the best German suppliers. Moreover, whenever Faust wished for a
rare bird to eat, quick as thought, that bird would fly through his
window! Delighted with such earthly pleasures, Faust gave no
thought to the fate of his body and his soul after his death. For him,
God did not exist; Lucifer did not exist; and Heaven and Hell did
not exist. Only the present mattered, where Mephistopheles grati-
fied his every wish.

In time, it came to pass that Johann Faust said to his swift-
flying servant, "Mephistopheles, I have everything that I could wish
for, except a woman. Therefore, I have decided that I want to get married! And I want you to help me find the most beautiful wife!"

"Marry, Doctor Faust? Why in the world would you want to
marry? A wife would only bring you a life of endless argument and
anger! Besides, this is one wish I cannot give you!" responded
Mephistopheles. "Marriage is an institution ordained by God. And
you have sworn in your contract with my lord Lucifer that you no
longer serve God! In fact, you have sworn that you are God's enemy!
Now, break this contract with the Prince of Darkness, Doctor Faust,
and I will rip you into thousands of pieces—until dust is all that remains of you!"

The swift-flying spirit had hardly spoken these words when a
great wind suddenly blew through Faust's house, knocking every door
off its hinges. Then billows of smoke flooded the house, strewing
ashes thickly upon all of the floors. Johann Faust found himself
thrown to the floor and confined there with invisible bonds. Meanwhile, a circle of fire blazed all around him, burning his body.

"Good grief!" Faust exclaimed. "I will burn to death before I have
lived my appointed time on earth! Mephistopheles! Save me from
these flames!"

However, the swift-flying spirit did not respond to Faust's summons. Instead, a monstrous-looking Devil appeared before Johann Faust and asked, "Now, Doctor Faust, do you still wish to marry?"

To this question, Faust replied, "Certainly not! I will hold to my contract with the Prince of Darkness!"

And with these words, it came to pass that Mephistopheles finally appeared before his human master. "My lord Lucifer is serious about his contract with you, Doctor Faust," he declared. "And you would be wise to be equally serious about it! Whatever beautiful woman you would like to have—whether she is alive or dead, and whether she is from Wittenberg or from any other place and time in the history of the world—I will bring her to you! Moreover, you are free to enjoy her for as long as you wish. However, she cannot become your wife.

"Here is a book that deals with the devilish arts. It is from my lord Lucifer who loves you as his own child! The Prince of Darkness takes pride in how closely the bent of your mind and your ambition resemble his own! This book will help you obtain whatever your heart wishes to have!" concluded Mephistopheles.

Mephistopheles tells Faust about Hell.

Eight of the appointed twenty-four years had gone from Johann Faust's life as if they were sifted sands in an hourglass. Now, it came to pass that he summoned his swift-flying servant and declared, "Mephistopheles, I want you to tell me about the Prince of Darkness."

"As you wish, Doctor Faust, so it will be," the swift-flying spirit declared. "My lord Lucifer was originally an angel of God. He was so gifted and so worthy that he far exceeded all of God's other angels, and he shone more brightly than the sun! He had great power in his own right, and he always sat next to God.

"However, my lord Lucifer was so gifted and so powerful that he became arrogant and overly ambitious. He determined to place himself upon God's throne and take God's power for himself," Mephistopheles explained.

"However, instead—because of his presumption—God banished my lord Lucifer from Heaven and condemned him to live apart from the host of Heaven—like a fiery stone that must burn until the world's end since no water can quench its flames."

These words, spoken by Mephistopheles, seared themselves upon the heart and soul of Johann Faust, causing them to flood with anguish. "Oh, how I wish that I had never been born!" Faust cried silently. "What have I done to myself?

"Like Lucifer, I also am one of God's creatures!" Faust declared to himself. "Like the Prince of Darkness, I am a victim of my own excessive pride. And it has blinded me so that I, too, have forgotten my creator! My arrogant mind, my greedy stomach, and my lustful flesh have all led me to banish God from my mind, from my heart, and from my soul! Like Lucifer, I will not humble myself to glorify God as being superior to me. And like the Prince of Darkness, my ambition will bring eternal damnation upon my soul! For I have willingly agreed to spend eternity in the raging flames of Hell, in return for boundless knowledge, power, and earthly pleasure!"

It should come as no surprise that, that very night, it came to pass that Johann Faust dreamed about Hell. And, therefore, as soon as the sun began to make the next day light, he summoned his servant, the swift-flying Mephistopheles, and commanded, "Tell me all about Hell, Mephistopheles. Where is it? What is it like? Who is condemned to live there? Do those who are damned suffer? Do they ever regain favor in the eyes of God?"

"As you wish, Doctor Faust, so it will be," the swift-flying spirit declared. "Hell is where God is not, and where Lucifer and we who are his servants must always be! Hell is the absence of all that is good, and the home of all that is poisonous. Hell is eternal darkness and foggy mist. Hell is fiery and filthy, and it stinks of sulfur. And yet, Hell has neither bottom, nor end, nor any substance at all. Hell is to the breath of God what a bubble of water is to the wind! And just as flint burns in fire's flames and yet is not consumed in the blaze, so the souls of the damned burn in Hell's fires and yet their agony remains."

"I would like to see Hell with my own eyes, Mephistopheles," Faust declared. "Can you take me there?"

"As you know, I am not my own master, Doctor Faust," replied Mephistopheles. "However, if you wish, I will inform the Prince of Darkness of your interest. If he agrees to your visit, he will send one of his servants to fetch you tonight, at the stroke of midnight.

"However, Doctor Faust, I must warn you that I do not favor such a visit," declared the swift-flying spirit. "The sights in Hell will sear themselves upon your mind, your heart, and your soul! Once you have seen them, you will never be able to forget them! They will interrupt you when you go to sleep and when you awaken, when you are at home and when you are away, when you work and when you relax. Believe me, Doctor Faust, they are truly terrifying!"

"Mephistopheles, my heart and soul are stronger than you think!" responded Faust. "Therefore, if you must confer with Lucifer before you can fulfill my wishes, then consult with him. Meanwhile, I will prepare to make the journey."

"As you wish, Doctor Faust, so it will be," the swift-flying spirit declared. And, quick as thought, he disappeared into the air.

Lucifer introduces Faust to Hell.

That night, it came to pass that Johann Faust awoke just before midnight, shaking from the cold. "Why, I am going to freeze to death while I am lying in my own bed!" he exclaimed to himself.

Faust jumped from his bed and reached the open window just at the stroke of midnight. A sudden wind blew a cloud of black smoke right into his room. While he was choking and gasping for breath, his ears flooded with the sound of a great clap of thunder. Suddenly, through the smoke, Faust spied a great bear standing near him. Its fur was black and curly, and it carried a gold seat upon its back.

"Doctor Faust, at your request, I have come for you," announced the bear.

"Bear or Devil, I would go anywhere with you just to get away from this smoke!" Faust declared. "But I want you to take me to Hell."

And so it came to pass that Johann Faust climbed into the gold chair, and the bear leaped out of the window with its passenger. As they traveled, the warm night air was so comfortable that Faust fell asleep.

Johann Faust was suddenly awakened by a great clap of thunder. When he opened his eyes, he saw that fiery flames flashed about him and yet did not illuminate the overwhelming darkness. Meanwhile, invisible musicians were welcoming him with the sweet sounds of music.

Suddenly, Faust saw a bull leap out the darkness and through the flames. It charged the bear, knocking it down and tossing Faust from his seat. Then a gigantic ape emerged from the darkness, walked through the flames, and said, "Climb on my back, Doctor Faust."

As soon as Faust obeyed the ape, two great, winged dragons

appeared and landed right next to him. They were harnessed to a wagon that was burning brightly, without being consumed by its flames. The ape placed Faust in the wagon and climbed in behind him. The dragons then soared into the darkness with their passengers.

What a journey this was! As the dragons carried the wagon aloft, its fiery flames streamed out from all sides. Although they were soaring into the air, the wagon's four wheels sounded as if they were rolling over a street that was paved with cobblestones.

Johann Faust gazed into the darkness around him, fascinated and amazed. The black curtain of eternal night was torn here and there by flashes of lightning and great claps of thunder. And whenever the thunder paused, Faust's ears flooded with the cries and wails of the souls of the damned, who were somewhere below him.

Finally, the dragons descended and came to rest beside a huge rock. As soon as the ape lifted Faust out of the wagon, the dragons flew away. And Johann Faust found himself face to face with the Prince of Darkness—Lucifer himself!—the Devil to whom he had promised his body and his soul.

Lucifer was sitting as a man sits. However, his face and his body were completely covered with brown, curly hair; he had paws instead of hands and feet; and a furry squirrel's tail curved upward and outward from his lower back.

"Welcome, Doctor Faust!" exclaimed Lucifer. "I understand from my servant, Mephistopheles, that you want to see my kingdom! I am happy to oblige you! However, first you should know that Hell is divided into ten kingdoms that are ruled by five kings. I rule the two eastern kingdoms as well as the kings of the other kingdoms."

To these words, Johann Faust replied, "I never realized that Hell is so large, sire! Why, you rule an empire!"

"It is good that you are suitably impressed, Doctor Faust," Lucifer replied, "given the nature of our contract."

Johann Faust now looked about him and saw that Lucifer was surrounded by Devils who, like their lord, also appeared in the form of strange beasts.

"Sire, I am here because I want to learn all there is to know about Hell," Faust declared. "So tell me, if you will, who is the Devil who looks like an upright bear? His face and his body are covered with black hair that is very long and curly. He has a wing behind each arm—and a tail that is longer than two men placed head to toe! Fiery flames are shooting forth from his two ears, and he has very long, snow-white teeth."

"Why, Doctor Faust, that is my servant Belial!" Lucifer replied. "He rules the two southern kingdoms of Hell."

"Now tell me, if you will, sire, who is the Devil who has the head of a bull—with two long ears that touch the ground and a pair of huge horns?" asked Faust. "His head and his body are covered with curly hair that is the color of horse flesh, and his tail looks like that of a cow. He has two wings on his back that are on fire, and they appear to be covered with prickly, thornlike protuberances."

"Why, Doctor Faust, that is my servant Beelzebub," Lucifer replied. "He rules the two northern kingdoms of Hell."

"Now tell me, if you will, sire, who is the Devil who looks like a huge worm that stands upright and moves on his tail?" asked Faust. "He has two short hands, but no feet. His belly is the color of gold, while the back of him is coal black. And his back has bristles on it like those of a hedgehog."

"Why, Doctor Faust, that is my servant Astaroth," Lucifer replied. "He rules the two western kingdoms of Hell."

"Now tell me, if you will, sire, what about those two Devils that are standing over there?" asked Faust. "One has a donkey's head, a cat's tail, and the hooves of an ox. The other has a dog's head, ears that hang to the ground, a pig's body, and two feet—one beneath his neck, and one beneath his tail."

"Why, Doctor Faust, they too are my servants," Lucifer replied. "However, they are not kings."

"Now tell me, if you will, sire, what about all of these other animals—these pigs and goats, stags and antelope, bears, buffalo, and elephants that I see? When your eyes meet theirs, they bow to you. Are they Devils too?"

"Yes, Doctor Faust, that is exactly what they are," Lucifer replied. "They serve the kings of each kingdom of Hell."

"Now tell me, if you will, sire, what about those horses, donkeys, and apes—and those wolves that I see? And what about those lions and cats? They also bow when your eyes meet theirs. Are they Devils as well?" asked Faust.

"Yes, Doctor Faust, that is exactly what they are," Lucifer replied. "They also serve the kings of each kingdom of Hell."

"Now tell me, if you will, sire, what about those dragons, serpents, worms, and toads that I see? Each seems to know its place here, and each of them bows to you. Are they Devils like the other animals?" asked Faust.

"Yes, Doctor Faust, that is exactly what they are," Lucifer replied.

"And like the other animals, they too serve the kings of each kingdom of Hell."

"Do all Devils have these hellish forms, sire?" asked Faust.

"Yes, Doctor Faust, they do," Lucifer replied. "Moreover, no Devil can really change his form. What he can do is blind the human eye so that he may appear to take on other forms, even a human form. But that is just appearance, not reality."

"Sire, I have been looking for Mephistopheles, but I have not seen him since he brought me here," Faust declared. "He has told me that he rules the central kingdoms of Hell. What form does he take when he is here with you?"

No sooner had Johann Faust asked this of Lucifer than a fierce, fire-breathing dragon flew around and around Faust's head. The winged serpent then landed right at Faust's feet, bowed to his lord Lucifer, and changed into the form that Faust knew.

"Doctor Faust, what would you like me to do for you?" asked Mephistopheles.

To these words, Johann Faust replied, "Mephistopheles, I would like you to teach me how to transform myself into different animal forms so that I can look like the other Devils."

"I myself will give you this gift, Doctor Faust!" Lucifer exclaimed. The Prince of Darkness then held out a book to Faust with his paws and said, "Just hold this book, Doctor Faust, and you will be able to transform yourself into whatever form you wish!"

And so it came to pass that Johann Faust changed himself, first, into a hog, then into a huge dragon, and, finally, into a lowly worm. "I like this gift!" he exclaimed, feeling very pleased with himself. "Thank you, sire!"

Faust tours Hell.

"Now it is time for your tour of Hell, Doctor Faust," Mephistopheles declared. "You wanted to know who is condemned to live here, and I will show you some of our damned souls. To you they will look just like living people, but they are the shades of the dead. Despite their appearance, they have no substance. However, they possess living souls, along with the power to think and to feel."

And so it came to pass that the swift-flying spirit began to lead Johann Faust through part of Hell. Dreadful claps of thunder and terrifying bolts of lightning made Faust jump. However, even in Hell,

Faust possessed no ordinary heart and soul. Even as Lucifer's guest in Hell, Johann Faust and fear were strangers.

"My word, Mephistopheles!" Faust suddenly exclaimed. "Who are those shades that are writhing around in that dark pit? They are clutching their stomachs, and their cries flood my ears. Why do some shriek in terror, while others wail in agony?"

To these words, the swift-flying spirit responded, "While they were alive, Doctor Faust, they pretended to be physicians. However, they poisoned their patients. Therefore, they are now condemned to spend eternity in that pit, where they must continuously take their own poisons and suffer the consequences. Unfortunately, since they are already dead, they cannot experience the relief that death brings to the living under these circumstances. Instead, they are condemned to live in constant, total misery!"

"Now tell me, Mephistopheles, who are all of those shades who are milling about over there in that long, crowded hall?" asked Faust.

"Those are all pickpockets, Doctor Faust!" the swift-flying spirit replied. "They did their best work on earth under very crowded conditions. Therefore, they are condemned to live in Hell in a very overcrowded area, where they must continuously pick each other's pockets!"

"Now tell me, Mephistopheles, who are all of those shades over there?" asked Faust. "Shades or people, I have never seen so many in one place! It looks as if many thousands are carrying wine bottles, while millions of others all have threaded needles stuck into their jackets or shirts."

"They are all either wine merchants or tailors, Doctor Faust," replied the swift-flying spirit.

"Why, Mephistopheles!" exclaimed Faust. "How did so many of those people become condemned to spend eternity in Hell?"

"The answer is simple!" Mephistopheles responded. "They cheated their customers!

"And now, Doctor Faust, I want you to look down here," commanded the swift-flying spirit, as he opened something that looked like a cellar door.

Billows of heavy smoke, with flashes of fiery flames, immediately issued forth from the subterranean area, causing Johann Faust to cough and choke. Recoiling from the broiling steam, and being unable to speak, Faust could only look at Mephistopheles with tearful eyes that asked his question.

"Witches are fighting each other down there," the swift-flying spirit explained. "While they were alive, they pretended to be saintly. But here, no one pretends to be anything!"

As soon as some of the heavy smoke had dissipated, Johann Faust peered into the interior of the cellar. "Mephistopheles, tell me, why are so many shades covered with a white, powdery substance?" Faust asked. "And who are all of those other shades—the ones who are carrying different types of objects as they wander about the cellar?"

"That white substance is flour, Doctor Faust," replied Mephistopheles. "Those are the shades of millers and bakers who—when they were alive—cheated their customers! And all of the other shades whom you see with them are the thousands of shopkeepers, who—when they were alive—also cheated their customers! You can see from their huge numbers that most people lead dishonest lives while they are alive!

"And now, Doctor Faust, I want you to look inside this fiery hole," commanded the swift-flying spirit.

Faust peered inside, and asked, "Who are those shades, Mephistopheles? And why are they running back and forth between fire and water?"

"They are lords, dukes, kings, and emperors, Doctor Faust. And they are condemned to spend eternity being tortured by fire and ice. Whenever they are scorched, they yearn to freeze. And as soon as they freeze, they yearn to be scorched. Therefore, they spend their time in Hell choosing either to warm themselves in fiery flames or to cool themselves in icy waters."

Finally, having seen all of these sights, it came to pass that Faust declared, "If you do not mind, Mephistopheles, I have now seen as much of Hell as I care to see! I will know it better all too soon! So please take me home."

To these words, the swift-flying spirit replied, "I have but one more sight to show you, Doctor Faust. And then the bear that transported you here will return you to your home. Now tell me, do you see that ladder over there?"

"Yes, Mephistopheles, I see it," Faust replied. "However, it extends farther than my eye can see. Where does it go? And who climbs it?"

"The answers to these questions will be important to you, Doctor Faust," the swift-flying spirit replied. "That ladder extends from Hell to Heaven. The damned are always climbing it in the hope of receiving God's blessing. However, as soon as the top is in sight, they lose their footing and fall back into Hell, where they are more miserable than ever!

"Somehow, the damned never learn that their time in Hell will never end," Mephistopheles explained. "If the waters of all the oceans and seas were to be emptied one drop at a time—and if a great mountain of sand reached from the earth to the heavens, and a bird were to remove one grain each day—when the time came that neither those waters nor those sands existed, the souls of the damned would still be in Hell! For it is easier to remove all the mountains, to empty all the oceans and seas, and to count all the raindrops, than it is for a damned soul to be forgiven by God!"

"I understand what you are saying," Faust responded. "And now, please permit me to leave!"

Faust tours the heavens.

No sooner had Johann Faust spoken these words than the black bear that carried the gold seat on its back appeared before him. Faust once again climbed into the seat, and the bear took off into the darkness with its passenger. Sweet music played by invisible musicians lulled Faust to sleep, and when he awoke, he was back in his own bed.

Johann Faust believed all that Mephistopheles had told him. Therefore, now more than ever, Faust had neither faith nor hope. And he was still excessively proud. Having seen Hell, he was now very sorry for the life that he had led. However, he would not consider making an attempt to earn God's favor by repenting. Even if he had believed in the possibility of forgiveness, he preferred future torment to submission.

And so it came to pass that Johann Faust continued to pursue his ungodly way of life in that he ate the best food, drank the best wines, and enjoyed the most beautiful women—from near or far, and from the present or the past. He also continued to meet with his students. Now, however, he gave up the practice of medicine, and with it his only deeds that were of benefit to society.

As you may remember, Johann Faust was a mathematician. In fact, he was one of the most famous mathematicians of his time. Now he proceeded to win equal fame for his calendars and almanacs because of the accuracy of his predictions. He possessed the marvelous ability to know exactly where and when it would become cold or hot, and stormy or sunny. Moreover, he could predict exactly where, when, and why people would experience famine, plague, war, and death.

And so it came to pass that one night, while Johann Faust lay awake thinking about his calendars and almanacs, he said to himself, "I wonder whether my knowledge of the heavens is actually correct, or whether what I consider to be facts are really no more than suppositions or blind opinions?"

Faust had no sooner asked himself this question than he heard such a great noise that he wondered if his roof had collapsed. All of his chest drawers and doors suddenly flew open.

Then Johann Faust heard a voice that moaned like the wind call out, "Doctor Faust, get up and prepare to see for yourself whether what your mind has been questioning is, indeed, fact or fancy! Go to the window, and you will see that everything is ready for your journey!"

Sure enough, when Faust walked to his window, he saw that a familiar wagon was sitting in midair, waiting for him to climb into it. The wagon was burning brightly without being consumed by its flames, and two great, winged dragons were harnessed to the front of it.

Faust seated himself in the wagon and then looked around for his servant, Mephistopheles. Quick as thought, the swift-flying spirit appeared and seated himself behind him.

What a journey this was! As the dragons carried the wagon aloft, its fiery flames streamed out from all sides. Although they were soaring higher and higher into the air, the wagon's four wheels sounded as if they were rolling over a street that was paved with cobblestones.

Faust gazed at the world around him, fascinated and amazed. The higher the dragons carried him, the darker the earth below him appeared. Mephistopheles made Faust invisible to human eyes, and the dragons carried them through the heavens for eight days.

Faust found so much to see that he never once closed his eyes in sleep. When he gazed at the earth from a height of 120 miles, he marveled at his view of Europe, Africa, and Asia.

When the dragons had transported him more than two hundred miles above the earth, Johann Faust turned his attention to the sun and its relationship to the earth. At this distance, the sun's rays were so hot that he exclaimed, "Mephistopheles! I am roasting like a bird on a spit! Unless you do something quickly, I will not live to finish this journey!"

"As you wish, Doctor Faust, so it will be," the swift-flying spirit declared. "You see, quick as thought, I have covered you with a cloud so the sun's rays will not burn you. And yet, you can see clearly through the—"

"Look, Mephistopheles!" interrupted Faust. "The sun is as large as the earth! And it does not move! It only appears to move when we observe it from the earth's surface. In fact, it is fixed in the heavens! And see how the earth floats within the heavens as an egg yolk floats within the whites inside an eggshell!"

Faust tours the earth and performs feats of magic.

When Johann Faust returned to earth at the end of this journey, fifteen of the appointed twenty-four years had gone from his life as if they were sifted sands in an hourglass. Now it came to pass that Faust summoned his swift-flying servant and declared, "Mephistopheles, I want to visit the whole face of the earth at closer range, and I want you to make me invisible whenever I choose."

"As you wish, Doctor Faust, so it will be," the swift-flying spirit declared. And, quick as thought, Mephistopheles transformed himself into a winged horse.

"I am ready, Doctor Faust!" Mephistopheles announced. "Just climb upon my back, and I will take you wherever you wish to go!"

And so it came to pass that Johann Faust galloped forth just above the surface of the earth, where he noted the many kingdoms and seacoasts. He visited Hungary, the Netherlands, and the British Isles. He visited Scythia, Egypt, Persia, and India. He even visited New Spain. Faust also toured the most famous cities in Germany, France, and Italy. Meanwhile, he continued to pursue his ungodly ways in that he ate the best food, drank the best wines, and enjoyed the most beautiful women.

During this journey, Johann Faust amused himself and awed others by performing a series of magic tricks. While in Germany, he uttered a magical incantation that summoned Alexander the Great to appear before the emperor. Faust knew that he could only conjure the shades of the dead—who had no substance and could not speak. And therefore he performed this magic only after the emperor agreed that he would make no attempt to speak to Alexander or to touch him. The famous Greek general responded to the summons, appearing to the eye as if he were still alive.

Then, to the dismay of a certain knight, Faust caused a huge pair of stag's horns to sprout forth from the knight's head while he was asleep. However, after he had made a clown of the knight, Faust caused the horns to disappear.

Faust also sold a man a particular horse, telling the buyer that he could ride this horse anywhere on land—even over hedges and dikes—but that he should not, under any circumstances, ride it through water. Then, when the buyer proceeded to do just what Faust had warned him not to do, the horse suddenly became a bundle of straw, causing the buyer to come close to drowning.

The buyer tracked Faust to the local inn, entered his room, and found him apparently sound asleep on his bed. However, when the buyer pulled Faust by the leg in order to awaken him, Faust's leg came off in his hand. Faust then awakened and cried, "Help! Help! This man has murdered me!" Meanwhile, the buyer ran away, having lost both his horse and his money.

Another day, Faust came upon a farmer who was driving his pigs to market. Faust suddenly made each pig dance upon its hind legs while it played a fiddle with its forelegs. Then he just as suddenly made the fiddles disappear. When the farmer arrived at the market, he sold his pigs. However, before the purchaser could collect them, Faust caused them to disappear. The purchaser demanded that the farmer return his money, and the sad farmer returned home only to find that every pig was back in its pen.

In still another adventure, Faust miraculously produced a dish full of fruits from distant countries so that a duchess, who was pregnant and had a taste for summer fruits, could eat apples, grapes, and pears in January. He then caused a great castle to appear, where wild beasts that were not to be found in Germany—such as the ape, antelope, buffalo, and bear—wandered in an open court within the castle's walls. Finally, after their tour of the castle and a great banquet within it, the duke and duchess watched it burst into flames and disappear.

Faust also played Cupid by causing a young woman to fall in love with a student at the University of Heidelberg, whom she hated. The young man had loved this young woman in vain, and it appeared that he would die of grief because of her rejection. However, Faust gave him a magic ring and told him to place it in his beloved's hand. The young man followed Faust's advice and, as soon as the ring touched her skin, the young woman's heart flooded with love for her suitor. The two married and lived happily ever after.

Faust refuses to repent.

Seventeen of the appointed twenty-four years had gone from Johann Faust's life as if they were sifted sands in an hourglass. Now it came to pass that a virtuous Christian neighbor, who suspected that Johann Faust had given his soul to the Devil, tried to persuade him to repent.

"Now is the time to turn from your ungodly ways, Doctor Faust!" he declared. "Repent! Truly regret how you have been living! Then call upon God for mercy! Do these things, and God will save your soul! Remember that He loves sinners who turn from their ways and place their faith in Him!"

This neighbor was so persuasive that Faust turned his thoughts to repentance and to denying his contract with Lucifer. Quick as thought, Faust's thoughts about Heaven were interrupted by the stings of a roomful of wasps, bees, and scorpions, as well as by the arrival of his servant, Mephistopheles.

"Doctor Faust! Apparently you have forgotten what your contract with the Prince of Darkness requires of you!" the swift-flying spirit exclaimed angrily. "The terms are that you must deny your Christian belief and become the enemy of all who are Christian. Moreover, you must remain steadfast in these convictions no matter who attempts to convince you to return to God. Therefore, you must now write and sign another contract with your own blood!"

And so it came to pass that Johann Faust wrote a second contract with the Prince of Darkness, again with his own blood. Then he returned to his ungodly ways in that he ate the best food, drank the best wines, and enjoyed the most beautiful women.

Helen of Troy comes to live with Faust.

Twenty-two of the appointed twenty-four years had gone from Johann Faust's life as if they were sifted sands in an hourglass. Now it came to pass that Faust decided that he wished to have the world-renowned Helen of Troy as his mistress. He had briefly conjured her for the pleasure of his students, just as he had earlier conjured Alexander the Great for the German emperor. However, Johann Faust knew that he could only conjure the shades of the dead—who had no substance and could not speak.

And so it came to pass that now Faust summoned his swift-flying servant and declared, "Mephistopheles, for over twenty years you have brought me the most beautiful women—from near or far, and from the present or the past. Now I ask you to bring me the most famous beauty the world has ever known! I want to have Helen of Troy—queen of Sparta and the cause of the Trojan War! I ask you because your powers are greater than mine, and if I choose, I want to be able to live with Helen!"

"As you wish, Doctor Faust, so it will be," the swift-flying spirit declared. And, quick as thought, Helen of Troy appeared in the study of Johann Faust!

One look at the real Helen, and the heart of Johann Faust flooded with love for the great beauty! "Oh, Helen! Now I know why your face launched a thousand ships and caused Troy's tall towers to burn to dust!" he exclaimed. "Sweet Helen, make me immortal with your kiss! I will be your Paris in great-walled Troy. I will wear your colors on my plumed helmet-crest! I will fight Menelaus—your weak husband—in single combat! And then I will return to you for your kiss! I will give the great Achilles a mortal wound in his heel! And then I will return to you for your kiss! For Helen, you are more beautiful than Night, when she is dressed in the beauty of a thousand stars!"

And so it came to pass that Helen of Troy lived with Faust until the time of his death. Helen bore him a son, whom they named Justus Faust. Meanwhile, Johann Faust continued to eat the best food, drink the best wines, and wear the best clothes. And the twenty-third year and eleven months of the appointed twenty-fourth year happily passed in this manner.

Faust faces his death.

Eleven months of the twenty-fourth year had gone from Johann Faust's life as if they were sifted sands in an hourglass. Now it came to pass that Faust suddenly thought to himself, "Why, I have only one more month to live! And then Lucifer will take both my body and my soul!"

The heart of Johann Faust flooded with anguish at the thought of his eternal life in Hell. And so it came to pass that he gave up eating, drinking, and all of his merry pursuits. Instead, he spent his time sighing, sobbing, and wringing his hands in dismay.

And it now came to pass that Johann Faust summoned his swift-flying servant for the last time and declared, "Mephistopheles, from now until the moment of my death, I do not want to look upon your face or hear your voice! My fate is so close at hand that I can almost touch it! And it has caused all desire for earthly pleasures to flee from my mind and my heart! Now the sight of you disgusts me! And the sound of your voice terrifies me! For you remind me of my contract with Lucifer and my future life in Hell! So go away! And leave me alone!"

"As you wish, Doctor Faust, so it will be," the swift-flying spirit declared. And, quick as thought, he disappeared into the air.

"Oh, how I wish that I had never been born!" cried Johann Faust. "Why, I have destroyed myself! Because of my envy and my disdain, my ambition and my stubborn will—I now face eternal damnation! My eternal companions must be other damned souls and the Devils who rule Hell! I must live in an eternal darkness that is illuminated only by eternal fires. And I must endure all of the physical torments of Hell—freezing cold and burning heat, gnawing hunger and parching thirst!

"And I must endure the torment of my mental anguish as well!" wept Johann Faust. "I can never forget that I was so foolish and so blind that I willingly traded the immortality of my soul—with its blessings of restful peace!—in return for boundless knowledge, power, and earthly pleasure! What important knowledge did I really gain? What power did it give me? And what value, now, does it have for me? What comfort to me, now, are all those earthly pleasures?

"Oh, where can I escape from my fate? Who on earth—or who in the heavens—will protect me?" wailed Johann Faust on this last day of his life. "Oh, Earth! Transform me into particles of dust, and let me be scattered by the wind! Oh, Ocean! Transform me into droplets of water, and let me disappear into your depths! Oh, Hills and Mountains! Fall upon me, and crush me beneath your rocks! Oh, Sun! Cast your fiery rays upon me, and burn me to dust! Oh, Clouds! Gather me into your mists, and conceal me within your towers!"

"Oh, Sands! Stop sifting so that time will stop! Oh, Stars! Stand still so that midnight will never come!" sobbed Johann Faust. "Oh, God! Do not hide Your face from me forever! If, now, You will not let my soul fly up to Heaven, then place some limit on my endless torment in Hell! Let me live there a thousand years! Or even a hundred thousand years! But save my soul at last! Oh, how I curse Lucifer! And how I curse myself! For together, we have made Your kingdom and Heaven's joys forbidden fruits for me!"

And it came to pass that when he had but a few hours to live, Johann Faust gathered his students to him. "Dear friends, the time has come for the Devil to claim me—body and soul," he declared. "For I promised him this in return for twenty-four years of every earthly pleasure!"

Faust paused while his students gasped in horror. They loved their professor, and he had never given them any reason to suspect his bargain with the Devil.

"Forgive me for any ill I have brought you," Faust declared. "And let my sad end live on in your own lives as a warning. Do not let the evil fellowship of wicked companions mislead you! Always remember to keep God in your mind and in your heart. And pray that He will deliver you from the temptations of the Devil!

"As for me," Faust concluded, "I die both a good and a bad Christian—good because my heart and my soul are filled with sorrow and regret for the life that I chose to live; bad because I have promised my body and my soul to the Devil! But, oh, how I wish that Lucifer would take my body, but leave my soul to God!

"Now that I have having said all that I wished to say, you must leave me to my fate," Faust commanded.

The students of Johann Faust now arose and took leave of their professor. "We will pray for you!" they exclaimed. Then they turned and went, weeping, from his study. However, they remained in his house.

And it came to pass that, at the stroke of midnight, a mighty storm-wind began to batter the house of Johann Faust as if it were determined to destroy it. Then the rooms within the house resounded with a dreadful hissing as if they were now inhabited by deadly serpents.

Faust's students heard the door to their professor's study fly open with a bang, and then they heard Faust cry, "Help! Help! Murder! Murder!" However, their hearts were flooded with terror; their limbs shook like trees in a storm-wind; and they remained frozen in their places as if they were blocks of ice. Finally, all was quiet.

As soon as the sun made the next day light, Faust's students came in search of their professor. When he did not respond to their call, they entered his study. What grisly sights met their eyes! Blood and flesh were spattered everywhere. Faust's brains were sticking to one wall. His eyes were in one corner of the study, while his teeth were in another. However, the rest of Faust's body was not in the room.

At last, after searching the house, Faust's students found their professor's body in the yard behind his house. It lay upon horse dung, with its limbs torn to pieces and its head turned from front to back.

"What a dreadful end for this learned man! What wondrous knowledge he possessed!" exclaimed Faust's students. "We must collect the pieces and bury him!"

And so it came to pass that Faust's students buried their professor's earthly remains. Then they returned to his study, where they found his autobiography. Faust had completed it up to the moment of his death. It revealed that, as soon as Mephistopheles came for him—quick as thought!—Helen of Troy and Justus, their son, disappeared into the air. Faust's final remark was his exclamation that they had not been real, after all!

And so we remember the learned Faust—that great but crooked bough that could have grown tall and straight. His Fall is a lesson to all who are truly wise. We should honor God all the days of our lives with all our heart, all our soul, and all our strength. We should respect the limits of human knowledge. And we should stand apart from all immoral pursuits and all who would mislead us.

THE AMERICAS 4

The following myths and folktales from the Americas contain a collection of characters who appeal to the human heart. Most of them are ordinary folk, rather than aristocrats, and, lacking power, they must cope by using their creative intellect. The tricksters among them, instead of being intimidated by power, turn the arrogance of their adversaries against them. Many of these selections depict how our values determine the choices we make and how these choices often have unforeseen consequences. Although they have serious moral themes, humor is often the means by which they communicate their message.

"Botoque, Bringer of Fire," a myth of the Kayapo people from the forest lands of central Brazil, explains how human beings came to possess both fire and mortality. Botoque is a young and inexperienced culture hero, who is as likely to be at the mercy of his environment as to be in control of it. He brings mortality into human life because of his own physical limitations, rather than because of his pride or greed. However, other aspects of his personality are more complex, and readers may find the end of the myth quite thought-provoking.

The role of the godlike Jaguar in this myth reveals both the close ties that exist between humans and animals in their common world of the jungle and the veneration that powerful animals receive from the weaker human species. Moreover, like other myths and folktales from around the world, this myth teaches that animals may help human beings who treat them with respect.

"The Little Frog" reveals such profound truths about human relationships that it crossed the sea from Spain and is now part of the folklore of Chile, Argentina, Brazil, and Mexico. The tale examines the nature of appearance and reality, and it reveals the blessings that love confers upon those who permit themselves to take the risks involved in loving another.

"The Journey beneath the Earth" combines two versions of one myth, one from Haiti and the other from the Mbundu people of Angola, Africa. The similarity between the plots of the two versions reveals the myth's origin and its journey across the Atlantic. Although told in the form of a folktale, the story is a myth because of its subject—death and the world of the dead. Despite its subject, the myth is gratifying because its theme emphasizes the joys of being alive.

"El Bizarron and the Devil," from Cuba, and "Wiley and the Hairy Man," from Alabama, are among the world's most delightful trickster tales. They both overflow with humor as their respective protagonists succeed in outwitting the Devil. Moreover, every character in both folktales has an interesting personality. Although the female characters are not mentioned in the title, the role of the woman in each tale is very important. The relationship between the Devil and his wife in "El Bizarron" contributes to the characterization of the Devil, while the relationship between Wiley and his mother is instrumental in Wiley's success.

"The Shepherd Who Understood Animal Speech," a Hispanic folktale from New Mexico, has a long history in world folklore. However, the end of this version, which uses humor to make its point about the ideal relationship between a husband and his wife, may be limited to this particular version. Like other folktales, this tale emphasizes the congenial relationship that potentially exists between human beings and animals, and, here, a serpent generously reciprocates when the shepherd helps it.

Washington Irving's version of "Rip Van Winkle," which is derived from a German legend, is presented here as it might have been told as part of the oral tradition of the Hudson River valley. Irving's version of the legend is humorous because it combines such stock characters as the henpecked husband and the nagging wife with the common motif of the magical drink.

However, Rip exhibits aspects of human nature that have made him a symbol in our society for almost two hundred years. While his attitudes and behavior both prior to and following his long sleep are humorous, they can also be viewed on a serious level. Therefore, this enjoyable legend can make us more insightful about ourselves and others.

"Giant, the Fire-Bringer," a myth of the Tsimshian people from British Columbia, explains how human beings came to possess fish, fruits, and fire. Giant is the great culture hero of his people, and his gifts reflect the life-supporting earth in this part of the world. Giant is also one of the world's great trickster-heroes, and his solutions to his problems are both fascinating and humorous. Giant's relationship to other living creatures reflects the kinship that exists between human beings and animals in his culture. He wears a Raven blanket as a cloak in order to fly; his companions are birds; and, when it is useful, he transforms himself into a deer.

Botoque,
Bringer of Fire

The Kayapo myth about the culture hero Botoque comes from the forest lands of central Brazil. At the time that it was collected, the Kayapo people hunted, gathered, fished, and raised crops. Aspects of this myth reflect aspects of their life. The Kayapo had no domesticated animals. They utilized the foliage that surrounded them to weave baskets by hand and to weave bark cloth on looms.

The birds and animals in the myth are important in both the physical and spiritual lives of the Kayapo people. Wherever the flaming red–feathered macaw and the yellow, fiery-eyed jaguar make their home in South America, including the forest lands of central Brazil, their traditional role in myth is connected with fire and its original source, the sun. In the myths of many South American cultures, macaws carry the sun high enough above the earth to make its fire benevolent. At its highest point in the sky, the sun rests in the House of Fire, which is constructed of the macaw's flaming red feathers.

The jaguar is also directly connected with the sun in that either the sun creates the jaguar or the jaguar gives birth to the sun. Often, the jaguar goes up to the sun and brings the sun's fire back to earth. It is through the jaguar that, in one way or another, human beings receive the sun's great gift of fire. The jaguar's eyes symbolize the sun and the fire that is associated with the sun. In fact, when the Kayapo people first received flashlights, they called them "jaguar eyes."

A special aspect of the myth of Botoque is the essence of the world that it conveys. The world of the jungle is not a safe place. It is a land of flickering shadows—where both appearance and reality change rapidly and spirits inhabit the human world. Trees and rocks speak, and an ogre can be hiding behind any tree. Jaguar is a predator to be feared, and yet he speaks and acts like a man and has a human wife. Because of Botoque's mistake, death becomes part of the human condition. Fire, as always, is of critical importance, and if it is not freely given, some brave hero must steal it.

BOTOQUE, BRINGER OF FIRE

In times of old—long before Botoque was born—two other heroes lived among our people and gave them fire. However, when they left, they took fire with them. For many, many years thereafter, our people did not know how to make fire. And they did not know the secret of the bow and arrow. So they ate the fruits and seeds of trees and shrubs. They ate caterpillars, termites—and fungus and rotten wood after the sun's rays had heated them. And they ate sun-dried meat. When their hunters returned with the animals they had trapped, our people would strip these animals of their hides, cut their meat into thin strips, and then lay these strips on stones to dry in the sun before they ate them. The meat was crisp, but it was also tough and unpleasant.

Our people were still living in this manner when Botoque was born. And they were still living in this manner once he had become a youth. And this is where the story of Botoque begins.

It now came to pass that one day, the husband of Botoque's sister was checking his traps when he saw two macaws fly out of a cleft in the rock at the top of a cliff. "Those macaws must have built their nest in that crevice," he said to himself. "I would like to have their chicks! But this cliff is too high and too steep for me! Now, if I return to the village and ask Botoque to get them for me, he will view this as an adventure!"

That is what the husband of Botoque's sister said to himself, and that is just what he did. Botoque was delighted with the idea, so they returned to the cliff. They chopped down a tall tree, cut footholds into its trunk, and propped the trunk against the rock wall in such a way that the nest that lay sheltered within the crevice at the top of the cliff was now accessible.

"I will have quite a tale to tell when I return to the village!" Botoque thought to himself as he nimbly climbed up the tree trunk.

However, Botoque did not realize that his words hit their mark with the precision of a well-aimed arrow. He would have quite a tale, indeed, when he returned to his village. But it would be different than Botoque thought. And he would return to tell it after many days had come and gone with the sun.

Botoque nimbly climbed all the way up the tree trunk, reached the top of the cliff, and walked over to the crevice. He then called down to his brother-in-law, "You are right! There is a nest up here all right, and there are two chicks in it!"

"Good, Botoque!" his brother-in-law responded. "Just grab them, and bring them down!"

However, the threatened chicks did not wait for Botoque to touch them. At the sight of his strange figure and the sound of his strange voice, they screamed menacingly at him. Their terror warned their parents, who quick as an arrow sent forth from a hunter's bow, swooped down with mad fury upon the boy who would rob them of their young. Now it was Botoque's heart that flooded with terror.

"Just grab the chicks and flee!" Botoque's brother-in-law called up to him. But Botoque just knelt at the top of the cliff, his face covered by his arms, his body shaking with sobs, his voice still.

"Botoque, listen to me! Just grab the chicks and flee!" his brother-in-law repeated. But, Botoque continued to kneel at the top of the cliff, his face covered by his arms, his body shaking with sobs, his voice still.

"Botoque, hurry up!" his brother-in-law shouted angrily. "Grab those birds, and get down here—*now!*"

However, Botoque appeared to be deaf to these words. He just knelt at the top of the cliff, his face covered by his arms, his body shaking with sobs, his voice still.

The heart of Botoque's brother-in-law flooded with fury. "Why, you are nothing but a coward!" he yelled. "And since you will not come down, you can just stay up there with the macaws!"

So it came to pass that Botoque's brother-in-law walked to the side of the tree trunk, pushed against it with all of his might, and sent it toppling to the floor of the forest.

He then returned to the village and told his wife, "I am very upset! While we were hunting in the forest, Botoque wandered off! I have searched and searched, but I have been unable to find him! I will go forth and try to find him once again. However, if I am still unsuccessful, we can only hope that he is alive and well and that he finds his way back here!"

Botoque's brother-in-law then returned to the forest. But, of course, he returned to the village without Botoque. And so, when seven days had come and gone, and still the boy had not returned, the entire village mourned his death.

Meanwhile, Botoque had no choice but to sit beside the macaws' nest while the first five days came and went with the sun. He could find no food at the top of the cliff and, since it did not rain, he could find no water either. Therefore, he became weaker and weaker.

As for the macaws, in time they became accustomed to Botoque's presence. And as he sat by their nest, his hair became covered with their droppings, which became a good home for insects.

Botoque had been reduced to skin and bones when it came to pass that Jaguar walked by the base of the cliff. Now Jaguar was returning home from a successful hunt. He was carrying his bow and arrows and the game that he had killed, as well.

Fortunately, despite his weakened condition, Botoque was still very alert. As soon as he spied Jaguar, he wanted to call down to him. But the very sight of the fearsome beast once again flooded his heart with terror, and he remained silent.

Meanwhile, as the boy stood at the top of the cliff, the sun was at his back. And quick as an arrow sent forth from his bow, Jaguar spotted the boy's great shadow as it stretched forth upon the earth that lay in front of him. Thinking that the shadow was real, Jaguar pounced on it. Seeing him pounce, Botoque moved away. When he returned to the edge of the cliff, Jaguar pounced again. Finally, it became clear to Jaguar that what he was attacking was only a shadow.

Perplexed, Jaguar stopped and looked about him. Then he looked up at the top of the cliff. There he saw Botoque.

"What are you doing at the top of the cliff, boy?" he asked.

To these words, Botoque replied, "I came here with my brother-in-law to rob a macaws' nest. But then the screams of the two chicks and their parents flooded my heart with such terror that I could not do it! My cowardice caused my brother-in-law's heart to flood with rage! He threw the tree trunk that I had climbed to the ground, and I have been stranded here from that time to this!"

"Well, boy, your bad luck is my good luck!" Jaguar exclaimed. "Toss those chicks down to me, and jump down before you die up there! As it is, you're nothing but skin and bones! And have no fear! I will catch you when you jump!"

"I am certain that you will catch me, Jaguar!" Botoque exclaimed. "I may be skin and bones—but I am not ready to be your next meal! So I think that I will just stay up here, instead."

"Nonsense, boy! Those young macaws will be my next meal. As for you, why, I will take you home with me and make you my son. I will satisfy your thirst with water, and I will fatten you up with grilled meat. Then I will teach you the secret of the bow and arrow so that you can come hunting with me! Now, toss those chicks down to me, and jump down before you die up there!"

Botoque said to himself, "Now I must choose whether I die sooner or later! Certainly, it will be less painful to end my life quickly!"

With these words, quick as an arrow sent forth from a hunter's bow, Botoque grabbed a macaw chick around the neck with each hand and, one by one, tossed them down to Jaguar. Jaguar waited for each one with an open mouth, grabbed it, and devoured it.

Botoque felt that his terror was spilling out of his heart and that it was about to paralyze his mind and body. And so, before he could think another thought, he took a deep breath and jumped down from the top of the cliff.

Jaguar waited for him at the base of the cliff with an open mouth—just as if the boy were one of the macaws. However, he caught the boy gently and, true to his word, he did not eat him.

"Now, my son, climb upon my back, and I will take you home," Jaguar commanded.

Botoque's heart quaked with fear, but realizing that Jaguar had not eaten him, he obeyed. Their route through the forest took them by three creeks. When they came to the first creek, Jaguar declared, "I can wash your head clean here, but I cannot permit you to drink from this creek, my son, because the vulture owns it!" When they came to the second creek, Jaguar declared, "I can wash your body clean here, but I cannot permit you to drink from this creek, my son, because little birds own it!" However, when they reached the third creek, Jaguar said, "Now, my son, you may drink your fill from this creek! The alligator owns it, and he's no friend of mine!" So it came to pass that Botoque drank his fill of the water from the third creek and left the creek-bed dry.

When Botoque reached Jaguar's home, the first thing he spied was smoke. It appeared to be coming from the end of a large tree trunk that extended across the floor of Jaguar's house. "What is happening there, Jaguar?" Botoque asked.

"That is smoke from a fire, my son," Jaguar replied, "The meat that I am about to give you has been grilled on stones like those that you see piled next to that fire. And when the sun has gone to its rest, you will see how good it feels to have the warmth of that fire near your skin."

Botoque greedily ate the grilled meat that Jaguar gave him. "Why, this is truly a wonder!" he exclaimed. "I never knew that meat could taste so good!"

And so it came to pass that Botoque ate his first cooked meat and spent his first night in Jaguar's house. When the sun began to make the next day light, Botoque opened his eyes and spied a woman. She was sitting and spinning cotton into string. As Botoque watched her fingers fly, he could tell that she possessed great skill.

The woman soon glanced up from her work and looked over toward Botoque to see if he was awake. Noticing that his eyes were open and staring at her, she declared, "Make no mistake about it, boy. You are here because my husband longs to have a son! Jaguar wants someone to keep him company when he goes hunting. However, to me, you are another woman's cast-off child—and, I must add, you are as skinny and ugly a one as I have ever seen! So take heed! Know that I would just as soon be rid of you! And the sooner the better!"

Jaguar's wife had just finished this welcome when her husband appeared. "I am off on a hunt, Wife. Now, I want you to be sure to feed my son while I'm away! We need to put some flesh back on those bones of his so that he can go hunting with me!"

With these words, Jaguar picked up his bow and arrow and left the house. Botoque had no wish to remain at home with the woman, so he found a good climbing tree and decided to wait there until Jaguar returned home. It was a good idea, but the boy's stomach began to clamor for more food. Finally, his stomach was in such pain that it forced the boy to return to Jaguar's wife and ask for something to eat.

"How dare you come here and ask me for anything to eat, boy!" she exclaimed, baring her teeth at Botoque. "If anyone is going to eat, it will be me—and if you pester me, I may just decide to grill and eat *you*!"

Poor Botoque! The sight of the woman's teeth flooded his heart with terror, and he ran back to his tree.

As soon as Jaguar returned, Botoque ran up to him and declared, "Please keep me with you, Jaguar! Your wife hates me! And she refuses to give me anything to eat! The very sight of her teeth floods my heart with terror!"

"Now, now, my son!" Jaguar declared. My wife's bark is worse than her bite. Just give her some time to get used to you! She is used to having her own way about the house!"

So it came to pass that days came and went with the sun. And each day, when the sun began to make the day light, Jaguar picked up his bow and arrow and declared, "I am off on a hunt, Wife. Now, I want you to be sure to feed my son while I am away! We need to put some flesh back on those bones of his so that he can go hunting with me!"

And each day, hatred for Botoque grew in the heart of Jaguar's wife. Therefore, each day, Botoque took refuge in the forest until his hunger drove him into Jaguar's house. Whenever the boy appeared and asked for something to eat, the woman would say, "I am feeding you only because I have to please my husband! But do not think that I have to give you grilled tapir meat! Leaves and dried venison are the only food that you will get from me! And even they are much too good for the likes of you!"

If Botoque dared to complain, the woman would claw his face with her fingernails. Jaguar was sure to notice the scratches when he returned, and he would say, "Now, my dear, I have adopted Botoque as my son! Therefore, you must stop mistreating him!"

"Mistreating him?" his wife would reply. "Why, I am not mistreating him. See for yourself how flesh is beginning to clothe his bones! If your son wishes to spend his day in the forest and get his face scratched, I am not to blame for his foolishness!"

Day after day came and went with the sun, and day after day, Jaguar and his wife repeated these words. Finally, one day, when the sun began to make the day light, it came to pass that Jaguar approached Botoque and said, "I have a surprise for you today, my son. I have made a new bow and arrow that are just for you. Come with me, and before I go hunting, I will teach you how to use them! You can practice by aiming at a termite's nest. You will find that it is an excellent skill to have. Once you become accurate, you can accompany me on my hunting excursions. And you will be able to defend yourself if you find that your life is ever threatened."

Now, day after day still came and went with the sun, and day after day Jaguar's wife still hated Botoque, but the boy ignored her nasty remarks and devoted himself instead to acquiring great skill with his bow and arrow.

Finally, one day, when the sun began to make the day light, it came to pass that Jaguar approached Botoque and said, "You have been away from your village now for many days. And the day may come when I am out hunting, and you suddenly long to see your family again. Should that happen, I want you to be able to pay them a visit. Just follow the creek, and it will lead you straight to your village.

"However, as you travel, you must remember what I am about to tell you," declared Jaguar. "While you are making your way along the creek, one of the ancient trees of the forest may call out to you. If you hear its voice, then be sure to answer it. Later, a great rock may call out to you. If you hear its voice, then be sure to answer it as well. However, if it comes to pass that the voice of a rotten tree calls out to you, no matter how sweetly it addresses you, you must remember *not* to answer it. Remember my words, and all will go well with you and your people. Forget them, and you will live to regret it!"

"Have no fear, Jaguar. Should the time come that I miss my family and choose to visit them, I will remember your advice," Botoque declared. "However, I think that such a time will not come before many days have come and gone with the sun! I am enjoying my life here with you, and I am sure you still have much to teach me!"

"That is good, my son," Jaguar replied. And with these words, he picked up his bow and arrow and went off on a hunt. He did not know, and Botoque did not know, how soon his words would be important to Botoque.

Soon thereafter, Botoque was chewing a piece of dried venison that Jaguar's wife had just given him when it came to pass that the woman's heart suddenly flooded with rage. "Why is it that I always have to hear your chewing while I spin my cotton into string?" she complained.

"You have to listen to my chewing because your dried venison is not tender like grilled tapir meat!" Botoque declared. "The venison is very crisp, and it crunches when I chew it. Give me grilled meat instead, and my chewing will no longer bother you!"

"You should have learned by now to curb your tongue when you speak to me, boy!" Jaguar's wife exclaimed, baring her teeth at Botoque. "I have put up with your presence in this house long enough!"

"I am hardly in this house!" Botoque replied, with a quick glance toward his bow and arrow to be sure that they were within reach of his fingertips. "I spend my days in the forest!"

"You will wish you had stayed in the forest, boy!" the woman declared. "Because now I am going to give you a lesson that you will never forget!"

With these words, the woman rushed toward Botoque. The boy's heart flooded with terror. He quickly grabbed his bow and arrow, took aim with the speed of a practiced bowman, and shot his arrow right into the woman's chest. It hit its mark just as she came within arm's reach.

Now Botoque knew even greater terror. "What will Jaguar do when he returns home and finds that I have killed his wife?" he asked himself. "I cannot afford to take the chance that he will misunderstand!"

And so it came to pass that Botoque looked around the house and gathered up some of the woman's cotton string, a piece of grilled tapir meat, and a burning ember. Although he worked quickly, he took care to wrap each item so that it would travel well. Then he picked up his bow and arrow and fled with them into the forest. Fortunately, Jaguar had told him which creek would lead straight to his village.

Botoque ran as fast as his feet would take him. He was making his way along the creek when one of the ancient trees of the forest called out, "Are you all right, Botoque?"

As soon as he heard its voice, Botoque remembered Jaguar's advice, and without pausing in his flight, he replied, "Yes, I am fine, thank you!"

Botoque kept running. Time passed, and then a great rock called out, "Are you still all right, Botoque? You have been running a long time now!"

As soon as he heard this voice, too, Botoque remembered Jaguar's advice, and, again without pausing in his flight, he replied, "Yes, I am fine, thank you!"

That was what Botoque told the rock, but that was not how he felt. By now, he was so tired that he longed to stop and rest. However, he feared that Jaguar was pursuing him. "Surely he has come home by now, and he's after me! And I will never be able to hear his steps until it's too late!" he exclaimed anxiously to himself.

And so Botoque kept running. As time passed, the boy became so tired that he feared that he would start to drag his feet, trip on some root, and fall flat on his face. But then the sight of Jaguar—as quick in pursuit as the arrow from his bow!—would take form in his mind. Terror would flare up in his heart, and Botoque would force himself to push forward.

Botoque was still running when the calm, sweet voice of a rotten tree called out, "You look exhausted, Botoque! You really have nothing to fear, you know!" it declared reassuringly. "Jaguar is not your enemy. You are his adopted son! So why not stop and rest a bit? Then, if you wish, you will be able to run even faster!"

As quick as an arrow sent forth from his bow, Botoque replied, "I can't stop now no matter how tired I am! I can't be sure about Jaguar! He may be following right on my heels!"

That is what Botoque said. And then Jaguar's words came flooding into his mind. He had said, "If it comes to pass that the voice of a rotten tree calls out to you, no matter how sweetly it addresses you, you must remember *not* to answer it. Remember my words, and all will go well with you and your people. Forget them, and you will live to regret it!"

"Now I am surely destroyed!" Botoque exclaimed aloud. "I have answered the rotten tree! How could I be so terrified of Jaguar that I forgot to remember what I was not to forget?"

No sooner had Botoque uttered these words when he found himself face to face with a man who bore a distinct resemblance to his own father. At his side, he was holding a big carrying basket.

The man beckoned invitingly to Botoque, and said, "Come with me, my son!"

To these words Botoque replied, "No, I will not come with you! With your long hair, you look like my father. But something about you is just not right!"

Then, right before the boy's eyes, the man's form changed. He still resembled Botoque's father, but in a different way.

Again, the man beckoned invitingly to Botoque and said, "Come with me, my son!"

To these words Botoque replied, "No, I will not come with you! With those earrings, you look like my father. But something about you is still not right!"

Then, before the boy's eyes, the man's form changed once again. "Who in the world are you?" Botoque now asked. "You look as if you are made of human flesh and blood, yet you can transform yourself as no human can! And why do you have a carrying basket with you?"

"You are right in what you say, Botoque," the form replied. My body was once as flooded with life as your own, but now it is dead! Until you came along, I had wandered in the spirit world with a troubled soul. For I once loved life, and I have yet to make my peace with death!

"But, thanks to you, I can now take vengeance on the living! Thanks to you, I am now free to return to your world—to steal your souls and take them to my world! No longer will I have to be jealous that you are alive while I am dead! Now you will all be dead soon as well!" the form joyfully exclaimed.

To these words, Botoque replied, "What in the world are you talking about? What have I done for you that you thank me? And why did you come before me looking like my father? And you have yet to tell me why you are holding a carrying basket!"

"What you did, Botoque, was to speak to the rotten tree when it spoke to you. When you spoke to the ancient tree, that tree gave you—and all mortals who are alive like you—the gift of its own eternal life. And then, when you spoke to the rock, that rock gave you—and all mortals who are alive like you—the gift of its own eternal life as well," explained the form.

"However, when you responded to the calm, sweet voice of the rotten tree, you accepted that tree's gift, and you forfeited the gifts that the ancient tree and the rock had given you earlier. And that rotten tree has given you—and all mortals who are alive like you—the gift of its own, short life!" declared the form.

With these words, dismay and despair flooded Botoque's heart. "So that is what Jaguar meant when he told me, 'Remember my words, and all will go well with you and your people. Forget them, and you will live to regret it!'"

"That is, indeed, what Jaguar meant!" the form declared. "And now you have brought joy to my dead soul! You have freed me to walk among you and shorten not only your life, but the lives of all who are alive like you!

"With glee, I will appear among you and steal your souls!" the form repeated. "I will steal them while you eat and while you sleep! I will steal them while you work and while you play! I will steal them when you are well and when you are sick! I will steal them when you lead good lives and when you are evil! I will steal them when you are young and when you are old! I will steal them when you see me and when you do not! But I will always steal them!"

"Why, you are nothing but an ogre!" Botoque exclaimed.

"You may call me an ogre, if you wish, Botoque!" the form replied. "But do not attempt to rob me of my power by belittling me! I will flood the living human heart with fear! So, be on guard! I have come to steal your soul, and steal it I will! That is why I have this carrying basket with me!"

With these words, the ogre leapt upon Botoque. He ripped the bag of Jaguar's possessions out of Botoque's hand and tossed it aside. Then the two wrestled for Botoque's soul. Try as he might, Botoque could not free himself to use his bow and arrow, and finally the ogre pinned the exhausted youth upon the ground.

To Botoque's surprise, the ogre did not attempt to kill him. Instead, he tossed Botoque into his carrying basket, tossed the bag of Jaguar's possessions on top of him, and proceeded on his way. On his way home, the ogre stopped to hunt raccoons.

From his place inside the basket, Botoque said to him, "Ogre, the forest growth has been tearing the fibers of this basket apart! At this rate, it will never hold both your catch and me! You might want to take the time to make a path through the forest before you do your hunting. A wider path will spare both your basket and your strength!"

"Good idea, Botoque!" the ogre exclaimed. And with these words, he put down his basket and set off to create a path.

Botoque listened carefully until the ogre's sounds no longer reached his ears. Then, as quick as an arrow sent forth from a hunter's bow, Botoque climbed out of the basket, found a large stone that weighed about as much as he himself did, and put it into the basket in his place. He grabbed his bow and arrow and the bag of Jaguar's possessions, and he set out to find his village.

The ogre, having widened his path, went hunting raccoons. When he had caught as many as he could carry, he returned to his basket, dumped the animals into it without looking inside, and headed for home. He greeted his friends with the promise of a tasty living human soul, but when he opened his bag, all he had to offer them were the raccoons and the large stone.

As for Botoque, long after the sun had gone to its rest, he finally reached his village. Everyone was asleep. In the dark, he made his way to his mother's house and awakened her. Before she welcomed him, he had to prove to her that it was he who had returned, because she told him that Botoque had died long ago. He then shared some of his grilled tapir with her and told her that he had brought her the gift of fire.

When the sun began to make the next day light, Botoque publicly announced his return. The important men of the village invited him to join them in the Men's House so that they could hear all about his adventures. They were delighted to taste the grilled meat and to know that they could make their own fire. They examined Botoque's bow and arrow in silence and watched him carefully as he demonstrated how to attach the cotton string and how to use it.

Then they decided that Botoque should lead them back to Jaguar's house so that they could bring more fire, more grilled meat, and more bows and arrows back to their village. Botoque agreed to do it.

Botoque declared, "Before we leave, we must consider two problems. First, how can we avoid arousing Jaguar's suspicions when he sees all of us in his house? And second, how can we transport Jaguar's fire safely through the forest?"

The men of the village talked it over. "Let's transform ourselves into helpful animals and birds," their leader suggested. "Then we will not call Jaguar's attention to our presence, and we can each use our special skills to transport Jaguar's possessions back to our village."

And so it came to pass that one man transformed himself into a tapir so that he would be strong enough to carry the burning tree trunk that supplied Jaguar with fire. Another transformed himself into a deer so that he could transport the meat. The third transformed himself into a pig so that he could carry the spun cotton string that was needed to string the bow. Another transformed himself into a yao bird so that he could pick up any burning embers that might fall from the tree trunk as the tapir carried it. And finally, the fifth man transformed himself into a toad so that he could extinguish any burning embers that the yao bird missed.

To Botoque's surprise, when he and his group of animals reached Jaguar's house, it was deserted. They found day-old game on the floor, but Jaguar had not grilled it. Therefore, Botoque grilled the meat for the journey. He then gave the burning log to the tapir, the grilled meat to the deer, and the cotton string to the pig. He himself carried Jaguar's bows and arrows. Accompanied by the yao bird and the toad, the group made its way back to their village.

Despite the best efforts of the yao bird and the toad, sparks flew into the air as the group made its way through the forest. Other birds caught these sparks so that they would not create a forest fire. Unfortunately, in the process, many of these birds burned themselves, and from that time to this, their beaks, legs, and feet have been the color of fire's flames.

Botoque and the animals safely returned to their village with Jaguar's possessions. Everyone was delighted to eat grilled meat. They loved being able to warm themselves by the fire when the nights became cool. And they liked having the village fires provide light in the darkness and protection from wild animals.

As for Jaguar, when he returned home and found that he had

been robbed of his special possessions, his heart flooded with fury. "So this is how Botoque has repaid me for adopting him as my son and teaching him the secret of the bow and arrow!" he exclaimed. "Why, he did not even leave me fire! Well, no matter! In memory of Botoque's theft, from this time forth and forevermore, I will hunt with my fangs and my claws, and I will eat my catch raw! This will keep the memory of my adopted son before my eyes and my hatred for him—and all who walk the earth as he does—alive in my heart!"

And so it has been with Jaguar, from that day to this. The flame in his eyes reflects the fire that Botoque stole, and it reminds us to run for our lives! And yet, each day that we live to see the sun, we thank Botoque for his gifts! Because of him, we hunt with bows and arrows, we eat grilled meat, and we sleep in safety and comfort!

The Little Frog

Most of Chile's folktales are Spanish in origin. Spanish soldiers brought them from Spain during the sixteenth, seventeenth, and eighteenth centuries, the period when Spain conquered and colonized Chile. The Araucanian Indians of Chile fought so long and hard against their invaders that it took a large number of Spanish regiments to conquer them. Eventually, many of these soldiers married Araucanian women and remained in Chile. Because their local oral tradition was not strong, these women readily adopted their husband's oral literature, either in its Spanish form or in adaptations that blended well with their own beliefs and oral traditions.

From that time to this, storytelling in Chile has remained a favorite form of entertainment for adults as well as for children. It makes household chores, community work projects, and the traditional night-long vigil that precedes a funeral more pleasant. The Chilean people prefer tales of romance, magic, and religion above all others. Because it is the custom for many people to move from place to place in Chile as they pursue their line of work, Chile's folk literature is remarkably uniform.

"The Little Frog" contains many characteristics of the European folktale, such as its point of view, three brothers, a helpful frog, and an enchanted person. Scholars have found thirty versions of this Spanish tale. In Chile, it is one of the most popular folktales, with eight different published versions as well as a beautiful Araucanian version. The Spanish version of this tale has also become part of the folktale tradition of Argentina, Mexico, and Brazil. The enchanted animal can be a monkey, toad, or rat.

In other versions, this folktale is found in Ireland, Scandinavia, central Europe, Portugal, north Africa, Turkey, and Russia. It has even been found in the Philippines. The French version also appears in Canada.

"The Little Frog" is an important folktale in that it reveals profound truths that readers can relate to their own lives. The importance of the point of view, the depiction of all of the characters, the value of the little frog, and what the frog needs in order to become transformed are highlights of the tale.

THE LITTLE FROG

A wealthy king once had three sons named Pedro, Diego, and Juan, whom he assigned to administer the affairs of his kingdom. It came to pass that the three brothers resented their task, and together they planned a way to change their lives. Prince Pedro, being the eldest, agreed to be their spokesman, and so, when the three sons gathered before their father and king, it was Pedro who announced, "Father, we ask your leave to go into the world and learn the ways of others who are less fortunate than we are."

"What a strange idea!" the king exclaimed. "I cannot imagine why you need to know more than you have learned here in my kingdom. However, if you insist on leaving me, I will give you my permission and my blessing as long as you agree to two conditions: First, each of you must appear before me one year from this day. And second, when you return, each of you must bring me the gift of a bar of silver."

"We can easily agree to your first condition," Pedro replied, "but as to the second, we can only give you the silver if our fortunes enable us to acquire it. And so, as to that, we cannot promise you a bar of silver, but we do agree to bring you the best gift that we can afford!"

The king was satisfied, and so it came to pass that when the sun made the next day light, Prince Pedro was the first of the king's three sons to leave home with his father's blessing and go off to seek his fortune. He rode on and on until, in time, he came to the cottage of what had to be a very poor man.

As the prince approached, he could hear a most lovely female voice singing a beautiful song inside that small, simple house. The prince was captivated by the sound, and so he stopped by the gate to listen.

"What a voice! And what a song!" Pedro declared to himself. "They truly make my heart sing! And if it is a maiden who is singing, and if she is as beautiful as her voice, then I must surely make her my wife!"

So it came to pass that Prince Pedro dismounted from his horse, tied the reins to the fence, walked up to the door, and knocked on it.

When an old man opened the door, Pedro greeted him with great courtesy. "Good day, father," he began. "If it is your daughter whose voice I hear, and if she is a maiden who is as beautiful as her voice, then I would like to make her my wife!"

To these words the old man replied, "Young man, my daughter is not available to marry anyone, even one who is as noble in bearing as you are. Her home is here with me, and it is here with me that she will surely stay!"

"You may be right, and you may be wrong, father," Pedro responded. "And if you will permit me to see your daughter, I will tell you if I agree with you."

"So be it," replied the old man. "You may enter my house and meet my daughter."

Prince Pedro stepped inside and watched while the old man went to the table, picked up a pottery jug, and then said to it, "Come out, my child. A visitor of noble bearing would like to meet you!"

A little frog then jumped out of the jug and onto the table. From there it jumped down to the floor, where it hopped to the feet of the prince and silently fastened its bulging eyes on his face.

Prince Pedro stared at the little frog in horror and disgust, and he exclaimed, "Father, this ugly little creature surely cannot be your daughter!"

"Oh, how wrong you are, sir!" the old man replied. "This little frog—whom you find so ugly—is indeed my daughter!"

"Well then, old man, she certainly is not going to marry me!" Prince Pedro exclaimed. "Her home is here with you, and it is here with you that she will surely stay!"

And with these words, Prince Pedro kicked the little frog out of his way and then quickly strode from the house. Without further thought, he untied his horse's reins, mounted the steed, and galloped away.

Meanwhile, back in the cottage, the little frog picked itself up and hopped back to the table, where it jumped up to the tabletop and then hopped back into its pottery jug.

It came to pass that when the sun made the next day light, the middle son, Prince Diego, was the second of the king's three sons to leave home with his father's blessing and go off to seek his fortune. Diego took the same road that Pedro had taken, and so it came to pass that he rode on and on until, in time, he came to the cottage of what had to be a very poor man.

Of course, this was the same cottage that his brother had visited and, therefore, as this prince approached, he could hear a most lovely female voice singing a beautiful song inside that small, simple house. Like his brother, this prince was captivated by the sound, and so he stopped by the gate to listen.

"What a voice! And what a song!" Diego declared to himself. "They truly make my heart sing! And if it is a maiden who is singing, and if she is as beautiful as her voice, then I must surely make her my wife!"

And so it came to pass that Prince Diego, like his brother before him, dismounted from his horse, tied the reins to the fence, walked up to the door, and knocked on it.

When an old man opened the door, Diego greeted him with great courtesy. "Good day, father," he began. "If it is your daughter whose voice I hear, and if she is a maiden who is as beautiful as her voice, then I would like to make her my wife!"

To these words the old man replied, "Young man, my daughter is not available to marry anyone, even one who is as noble in bearing as you are. Her home is here with me, and it is here with me that she will surely stay!"

"You may be right, and you may be wrong, father," Diego responded. "And if you will permit me to see your daughter, I will tell you if I agree with you."

"So be it," replied the old man. "You may enter my house and meet my daughter."

Prince Diego stepped inside and watched while the old man went to the table, picked up a pottery jug, and then said to it, "Come out, my child. A visitor of noble bearing would like to meet you!"

Once again, a little frog jumped out of the jug and onto the table. From there it jumped down to the floor, where it hopped to the feet of the prince and silently fastened its bulging eyes on his face.

Now, I must tell you that Prince Pedro had seen a frog of luminous beauty compared with the frog that now appeared before Prince Diego. This frog was so covered with wrinkles and so covered with warts that its eyes were simply two more bulges on its body.

Prince Diego stared at the little frog in terror and loathing, and he exclaimed, "Father, this repulsive little creature surely cannot be your daughter!"

"Oh, how wrong you are, sir!" the old man replied. "This little frog—whom you find so repulsive—is indeed my daughter!"

"Well then, old man, she certainly is not going to marry me!" Diego exclaimed. "Her home is here with you, and it is here with you that she will surely stay!"

And with these words, Prince Diego gave the little frog a vicious kick, pushing it out of his way and sending it crashing against the wall of the cottage. He quickly strode from the house, and, without further thought, he untied his horse's reins, mounted the steed, and galloped away.

Meanwhile, back in the cottage, the little frog slowly and painfully picked itself up and then slowly and painfully hopped back to the table. After resting on the floor for a while, it jumped up to the tabletop. Then, before hopping back into its pottery jug, it turned toward the old man and croaked, "Please stop showing me to your visitors, Father! My appearance so offends them that they hurt me! Just let me be, for I need not marry any man. I am happy enough here with you, for you love and care for me."

It came to pass that when the sun made the next day light, the youngest son, Prince Juan, was the last of the king's three sons to leave home with his father's blessing and go off to seek his fortune. Juan took the same road that Pedro and Diego had taken, and so it came to pass that he rode on and on until, in time, he came to the cottage of what had to be a very poor man.

Of course, this was the same cottage that his brothers had visited and, therefore, as this prince approached, he could hear a most lovely female voice singing a beautiful song inside that small, simple house. Like his brothers, this prince was captivated by the sound, and so he stopped by the gate to listen.

"What a voice! And what a song!" Juan declared to himself. "They truly make my heart sing! And if it is a maiden who is singing, then I must surely make her my wife!"

Like his brothers before him, Prince Juan dismounted from his horse, tied the reins to the fence, walked up to the door, and knocked on it.

When an old man opened the door, Juan greeted him with great courtesy. "Good day, father," he began. "If it is your daughter whose voice I hear, and if she is a maiden, then I would like to make her my wife!"

To these words the old man replied, "Young man, my daughter is not available to marry anyone, even one who is as noble in bearing as you are. Her home is here with me, and it is here with me that she will surely stay!"

"You may be right, and you may be wrong, father," Juan responded. "And if you will permit me to see your daughter, I will tell you if I agree with you."

"Now, listen well, young man, for it is just as I have told you," the old man answered. "My daughter is not available to marry any-one, even one who is as noble in bearing as you are. Her home is here with me, and it is here with me that she will surely stay!"

"With all respect, it is you, father, who do not appear to be lis-tening to me!" Juan exclaimed. "If your daughter is unmarried, I in-tend to marry her. Her voice and her song make my heart sing! Therefore, I do not need to know anything else about her, for noth-ing else is important!"

"Then so be it," replied the old man. "You may enter my house and meet my daughter, for she surely is unmarried!"

Prince Juan stepped inside and watched while the old man went to the table, picked up a pottery jug, and then said to it, "Come out, my child. A visitor of noble bearing would like to meet you!"

Once again, a little frog jumped out of the jug and onto the table. From there it jumped down to the floor, where it hopped to the feet of the prince and silently fastened its bulging eyes on his face.

Now, I must tell you that Prince Diego had seen a frog of lumi-nous beauty compared with the frog that now appeared before Prince Juan. This frog was so covered with bulging warts that to look at it, you could not discern eyes or a mouth or even a pair of legs.

Prince Juan stared at the little frog with interest, and then he asked the old man, "Father, is this little creature your daughter? And is it her voice and her song that I heard and that made my heart sing? For if it is, then I want her to become my wife!"

"Yes, this little frog is indeed my daughter," the old man replied. "And it is her voice and her song that brought you to my door!"

"Well then, father," Juan responded, "with your permission, your daughter's home will now be with you and me, and it is with you and me that she will surely stay!"

Prince Juan married the little frog then and there, but after the ceremony, he had to admit to himself that he was sorry that he had married a frog.

The little frog noticed the regret in Juan's eyes, and so it croaked, "Do not look so sad, my love. Let me sing you to sleep, and you will forget that I am a frog."

And so it came to pass that the months of the year came and went like leaves on the trees in the forest. Finally, it was time for the king's three sons to reappear before their father, each with his gift of a bar of silver or the best gift that he could afford. Prince Pedro joined Prince Diego, and together they rode by the cottage of the poor old man. When they looked within and spied their youngest brother inside that house, they looked at each other in amazement and exclaimed, "Can you believe it? Juanito must have married that frog! How disgusting!"

Then they called out to their brother, saying, "Juanito, today's the day that we all must return to the palace. Now, come along!"

Prince Juan came to the door of the cottage and announced, "I will come, but you two should go ahead without me. When you arrive, tell Father that I, too, will be there."

Poor Juan! Once he saw that his brothers were continuing on their way, his heart flooded with fear and grief so that tears fell from his eyes like rain. He turned to the little frog, which was sitting in its favorite place—a tub of water—and he exclaimed, "Today I am supposed to return to my father with a gift of a bar of silver or the best gift that I can afford! How can I keep my promise when I have done no work to earn it?"

"Do not look so sad, my love," the little frog croaked. "Just take what I give you and do as I say, and all will go well with you! First, you must find the sack that is lying in the coal corner by the fireplace, and you must fill it with coal. Then you must take a wood chip from the wood pile in the other corner and put it into the sack with the coal. Close the sack, and keep it well tied until the time comes when it must be opened. Put on the clothes that you were wearing when you arrived here a year ago, take your horse, and return to your father's palace. When your brothers give him their silver, just give him your bag."

Prince Juan's heart was still flooded with fear and grief, but he carefully followed all of the little frog's instructions. When he reached his father's palace, he went directly to the throne room. The king was in high spirits, for his two eldest sons had done well in their year abroad, and each had returned to the palace with a bar of silver as a gift for him.

Silently, Juan joined them, his heart still flooded with fear and grief. Silently, he walked up to his father's scales, untied his bag, and began to pour out his coal. To the amazement of everyone, including Juan himself, every piece that fell from the bag was a piece of silver, except for the wood chip, which had become a chip of gold.

"Well done, Juanito!" exclaimed the king. "Compared to your gift, your brothers have brought me nothing!"

"Clearly Juanito has surpassed us today," Pedro announced. "But,

Father, you and Mother should see what skillful wives we have married! My wife embroiders cloth so that it is fit for a king! And Diego's wife can embroider cloth that is surely fit for a queen! However, if you choose to test the skill of our wives, you will see that Juanito's wife cannot do anything of value!" he exclaimed. And, with these words, he and Diego looked at each other and laughed at their private joke.

"Well then, I will give each of you a ten-meter roll of linen," the queen announced. "Let us meet here one week from today, and we will see how beautiful a table covering each of your wives has been able to fashion between now and then."

So it came to pass that the three princes prepared to return to their wives with the cloth for the contest. As they mounted their horses, Juan's brothers were quick to exclaim, "Well, Juanito, see what you get for marrying a frog? Your wife will only be able to jump on your cloth and make it filthy with her footprints! Just think of how Mother and Father will regard your choice of a mate!"

Prince Juan fared no better when he arrived home. As usual, he found that the little frog was sitting in its favorite place—a tub of water. Poor Juan! His heart once again flooded with fear and grief so that tears fell from his eyes like rain.

"Dear one, I love you, and I appreciate your gift of the silver and gold," he announced. "But now my mother has given you a task that you surely cannot perform. She has given each of her sons a ten-meter piece of linen, and she expects our wives to embroider a table covering that will be fit for a queen. As if that is not enough of a challenge, she has given the three of you only a week of days in which to do it!"

"Let me see the cloth, my dear," the little frog croaked.

When Prince Juan showed the frog the linen, it quickly grabbed it out of his hands with its mouth and tore it into pieces. "So much for your mother's request!" it exclaimed with a croak.

Prince Juan's heart now exploded with distress.

"Do not look so sad, my love," the little frog croaked. "Just let me sing you to sleep, and you will forget that I am a frog. When the day comes, you will take what I give you and do as I say, and then all will go well with you!"

So it came to pass that the days of the week came and went with the sun and the moon, until the time came for the three brothers to reappear before their mother the queen, each with the table covering that his wife had embroidered. Once again, Prince Pedro joined

Prince Diego, and together they rode by the cottage of the poor old man.

When they looked within and spied their youngest brother inside that house, they looked at each other in amusement and exclaimed, "Can you imagine what that repulsive frog did with Mother's linen? It must look truly disgusting! And surely, now Juanito regrets the day that he chose to marry such a wife!"

Then they called out to their brother, saying, "Juanito, today is the day that we all must return to the palace. Now, come along!"

Prince Juan came to the door of the cottage and announced, "I will come, but you two should go ahead without me. When you arrive, tell Mother that I, too, will be there."

Poor Juan! Once he saw that his brothers were continuing on their way, his heart again flooded with fear and grief so that tears fell from his eyes like rain. He turned to the little frog and exclaimed, "Dear one, the day has come when I am supposed to return to my mother with the embroidered table covering! What should I do?"

"Do not look so sad, my love," the little frog croaked. "Just take what I give you and do as I say, and all will go well with you! Take this little box and little key. Keep the box locked until the time comes when it must be opened. Take your horse and return to your father's palace. When each of your brothers gives your mother the embroidered table covering that his wife has embroidered for her, just give your mother your box and key."

Prince Juan's heart was still flooded with fear and grief, but he carefully followed all of the little frog's instructions. When he reached his father's palace, he went directly to the throne room. The queen was in high spirits, for the wives of her two eldest sons had done well with their embroidery, and each son had returned to the palace with a beautiful table covering as a gift for her.

Silently, Juan joined them, his heart still flooded with fear and grief. Silently, he walked up to his mother and handed her the little box and its key. To the amazement of everyone, including Juan himself, when the queen opened the box, she found a magnificently embroidered table covering of the sheerest, most delicate fabric.

"Well done, Juanito!" exclaimed the queen. "Convey my gratitude and pleasure to your skillful wife. Compared to your table covering, the cloths that your brothers' wives embroidered are nothing! I will give their cloths to our servants, and I will keep the one that your wife made for ourselves.

"Now it happens that my little dog has just given birth to three puppies," she concluded. "And so, my sons, I want each of you to choose a puppy for your wife to train. And let us meet here one week from today, so that we can see how well each of the puppies performs for us."

When Prince Juan arrived home, as usual, he found that the little frog was sitting in its favorite place—a tub of water. Poor Juan! His heart once again flooded with fear and grief so that tears fell from his eyes like rain.

"Dear one, I love you, and I appreciate your gift of the beautifully embroidered table covering," Juan announced. "But now my mother has given you a task that you surely cannot perform. She has given each of her sons a puppy, and she expects our wives to train it. As if that is not enough of a challenge, she has given the three of you only a week of days in which to do it!"

To these words, the little frog once again croaked, "Do not look so sad, my love. Just let me sing you to sleep, and you will forget that I am a frog. When the day comes, you will take what I give you and do as I say, and then all will go well with you!"

And so it came to pass that once again the little frog sent Prince Juan back to his mother with the most captivating gift, the most elaborately trained puppy.

"Now that we know how gifted your wives are," the king announced, "it is only proper that each of them should meet her husband's parents, the king and queen of the kingdom. So let us meet here one week from today, and we will enjoy a festive banquet and each other's company!"

So it came to pass that the three princes prepared to return to their wives with the king's invitation. As they mounted their horses, Juan's brothers were quick to exclaim, "Well, Juanito, see what you get for marrying a frog? Now you truly will regret your choice! And we can hardly wait to see what Mother and Father will think of your wife!"

Prince Juan fared no better when he arrived home. As usual, he found that the little frog was sitting in its favorite place—a tub of water. Poor Juan! His heart once again flooded with fear and grief so that tears fell from his eyes like rain.

"Dear one, I love you, and I appreciate your gift of the best-trained puppy," he announced. "But now my mother and father have given you an invitation that you surely cannot accept. They have asked each of their sons to bring his wife to meet them at the palace a week from today so that we can all enjoy a festive banquet and each other's company. But I cannot possibly take you!"

"Do not look so sad, my love," the little frog croaked. "Just let me sing you to sleep, and you will forget that I am a frog. When the day comes, of course you will take me with you! I would like to see your brothers again, and it will be my pleasure to meet your parents, the king and queen. As always, you will take what I give you and do as I say, and then all will go well with you!"

So it came to pass that five days of the week came and went with the sun and the moon. When the sun made the sixth day light, the little frog croaked to the old man, "Father, I want you to bring me a tub of clean water, your best pair of oxen, and a long twig for a whip."

The old man obeyed his frog-daughter's commands.

When the sun made the seventh day light, the time had come for the three brothers to reappear with their wives before their parents, the king and queen. The little frog now croaked to the old man, "Father, I want you to yoke your oxen to your wagon, place my tub of clean water inside the wagon, and then lift me into the wagon so that I can hop into the water."

The old man obeyed his frog-daughter's commands.

It came to pass that, once again, Prince Pedro joined Prince Diego, and together they rode by the cottage of the poor old man. However, this time each prince was sitting in a splendid horse-drawn carriage. When they saw that the old man's wagon was already hitched to a team of oxen, and they saw that the little frog was already sitting in a tub of water inside the wagon, they reached across their carriages, poked each other, and howled with laughter.

"Can you imagine what Father and Mother will say when Juanito appears with his disgusting frog-wife?" Pedro asked.

"Surely then Juanito will regret the day that he married her, and we will be the favorite sons!" Diego replied.

Then the brothers called out to Prince Juan, saying, "Juanito, today's the day that we all must return to the palace. Now, come along! We are already on our way, and we each have a fast horse to transport our carriage!"

Prince Juan came to the door of the cottage and announced, "I will come, but you two should go ahead without me. When you arrive, tell Father and Mother that I, too, will be there."

It came to pass that the little frog's father now approached Juan and announced, "Everything is ready, Juanito. So climb into the wagon and sit next to the tub of water in which your wife is sitting. Then I will drive the oxen, and we will be on our way."

Prince Juan walked to the wagon, looked inside, and saw that the little frog was indeed going to accompany him on this most important journey. As usual, it was sitting in its favorite place—a tub of water. Poor Juan! His heart once again flooded with fear and grief so that tears fell from his eyes like rain.

"Do not look so sad, my love," the little frog croaked to Juan. "See that I am bringing this little box as my gift for your parents. Just let me sing you to sleep while we make this journey, and you will forget that I am a frog."

Prince Juan's heart was still flooded with fear and grief, but he took his place in the wagon next to the little frog, and they all set out to meet the king and queen.

Juan slept until their journey was about to end. When he awoke, he found that he was riding in a magnificent gold-fringed coach drawn by a team of royal horses. A royal coachman held the reins. And sitting by his side was the most beautiful of all princesses! She was holding a little guitar case in her lap.

At first, Juan was speechless. And then he had no time to say a word because he saw that his two elder brothers and his parents were already waiting for them at the gates to the palace.

Now I must tell you that Prince Pedro and Prince Diego were responsible for this. They wanted to see how Juan would appear with his frog-wife, and they wanted to be certain that the king and queen were present to observe the same sight. Therefore, you can imagine their surprise when, instead of seeing an ox-drawn wagon approaching, they beheld a strange royal coach traveling up the royal road. They stared in awe at the sight and asked each other, "What prince is coming to visit us?"

"Why, it is our own Juanito!" the queen was the first to exclaim. "And just look at his beautiful wife! Our other sons' wives cannot bloom in her shade!"

When the carriage reached the royal family, Prince Juan introduced his wife and her father to his parents. The king and queen then invited everyone to enter the palace and enjoy a rich banquet.

After the meal, Juan's wife collected all of her fish-bones and stuck them into the front of her husband's jacket. Her sisters-in-law were highly amused by her bad taste, but they were afraid to be different, so each of the other two wives quickly collected all of her own fish-bones and stuck them into the front of her own husband's jacket.

Then the king announced, "Let the entertainment now begin! My sons, I assume that your wives know how to sing and play a musical instrument. So let Pedro's wife sing and play while we watch Juanito and his wife dance together."

So it came to pass that the frog-princess danced the waltz with Prince Juan, and with each turn, she picked some bones from her husband's jacket and scattered diamonds, pearls, and fragrant flowers upon the floor of the ballroom.

"What beauty! What grace! What charm!" exclaimed the king and queen. "Now let Diego's wife sing and play while we watch Pedro and his wife dance together!" commanded the king.

So it came to pass that the second couple took their turn. However, when Prince Pedro's wife picked the bones from her husband's jacket, she scattered horse-dung—and not jewels and fragrant flowers—upon the ballroom floor.

"Oh! Oh!" cried the king and queen. "Stop the dance! Servants! Be quick to clean the floor! The stench is appalling!"

Once the servants had scraped and washed the ballroom floor, the king announced, "Now let Juanito's wife sing and play while we watch Diego and his wife take their turn at the dance."

And it came to pass that Diego and his wife fared as poorly as Pedro and his wife had fared before them, for when Diego's wife picked the bones from her husband's jacket, she, too, scattered horse-dung—and not jewels and fragrant flowers—upon the ballroom floor.

"Oh! Oh!" cried the king and queen once again. "Stop the dance! Servants! Be quick to clean the floor! The stench is appalling!"

When the servants had once again scraped and washed the ballroom floor, the king announced, "Let us now repeat the first dance. I want Pedro's wife to sing and play while Juanito dances with his wife."

And so it came to pass that Prince Juan and the frog-princess danced another waltz, and with each turn, the princess picked the bones from her husband's jacket and scattered diamonds, pearls, and fragrant flowers upon the ballroom floor.

"This is the way that it should be!" the king exclaimed joyfully. "What beauty! What grace! What charm!"

Prince Pedro and Prince Diego stood together and watched their younger brother, their hearts flooded with remorse and envy. "She could have been my wife!" Pedro exclaimed softly to his brother. "But I could not imagine marrying a frog!"

"She could have been my wife, as well," Diego admitted. "But I was repulsed by her appearance. I am afraid that we have to give praise where praise is due. Juanito has not deserved our ridicule. He has found the most beautiful and talented wife of all!"

Meanwhile, the old man stood apart from everyone, silently watching the ever changing ballroom scene. The miracle and the magic were more than his mind could absorb, for his daughter had been born a little frog and not a princess.

The royal celebration continued for three days. When the sun made the fourth day light, the king announced, "The time has come for everyone to return home. The queen and I will accompany Juanito, his wife, and her father in their coach."

It came to pass that when Prince Juan's coach returned to the old man's farm, they found that a jewel of a castle now stood in place of the small, simple cottage.

"Why, Juanito's palace is far more beautiful than my own!" the king exclaimed. "Therefore, the queen and I will live here with Juanito and his wife from this time forth and for as long as we shall live. And every day, our daughter will sing for all of us, and the sound of her voice will make our hearts sing!"

And that is just what came to pass. The princess never again became a frog, and she, her husband, her father, and her husband's parents lived happily together forever after.

The Journey
beneath the Earth

"The Journey beneath the Earth" is a Mbundu myth from northern Angola that probably traveled from West Africa to Haiti between the middle of the seventeenth and the end of the eighteenth centuries, a time when French colonists purchased African slaves to work on their sugar and coffee plantations. In 1801, Toussaint L'Ouverture, a former slave, conquered Haiti and abolished slavery on the island. In 1804, Haiti became independent, thereby making it the second colony in the Western Hemisphere (after the United States) to gain such freedom.

In the Angolan version of this myth, this community in which the action occurs is governed by King Kitamba, a sacred king, who lives in the capital town of Kasanji and is assisted and influenced by the council of elders who chose him to be the people's king. Within the limitations set forth by the traditions and laws of his community, King Kitamba has absolute power over the lives and the property of his subjects.

Queen Muhongo, Kitamba's head wife and head queen, had enjoyed special status and great power while she lived. It was expected that, from the moment the queen died, her passage into the Land of the Dead would be marked by wailing. For months following her death, this wailing would be repeated at specific times throughout each day. Her closest relatives were expected to remain silent, except for their wailing, until the period of mourning concluded.

Being her husband, King Kitamba was expected to spend these months in Queen Muhongo's house, sleeping in her bed and not engaging in any activities that would cause him to have to dress and leave the house. The conclusion of this period of mourning would be a festival marked by feasting, music, and dancing and attended by all of Queen Muhongo's relatives and friends. It is clear from the similarity of the Haitian version of this myth that many of these traditions crossed the Atlantic with the Mbundu people.

The Mbundu land of the dead was called Kalunga. It was located beneath the surface of the earth, and all of the deceased lived there as if they were still living on earth. In the following myth, after Queen Muhongo's death the shaman finds that she is busily weaving a basket because the weaving of grasses into baskets and mats was an important occupation among the Mbundu people.

The Haitian version closely follows the Angolan myth in characterization, plot, and theme. However, in the Haitian version, the mourner is a wealthy country man, and it is a Vodoun priest who goes beneath the water to the Land of the Dead in order to find the man's wife. Any body of fresh water, including a waterfall, is a road to the Underworld, and in other Haitian myths, other living human beings travel there by way of a river or spring. In the Haitian version, the man's wife is found selling coffee beans in the marketplace, reflecting its Haitian location.

The following myth combines aspects of the Haitian and the more detailed Mbundu versions. In both Angola and Haiti, a trained storyteller would have told the myth in a dramatic fashion, with voice impersonation and appropriate action.

THE JOURNEY BENEATH THE EARTH

King Kitamba had built the village at Kasanji, where he, his wives, and his people lived. Years came and went with the sun and the moon. The village became a town, and its people prospered. They prospered until it came to pass that Queen Muhongo, their king's head wife, died. The people buried her and mourned her for weeks and months, as it was done.

Now King Kitamba had other wives, but he loved none of them as he loved Queen Muhongo, for she was his first and most-favored wife. And when the mourning period was about to end, King Kitamba was not ready to put aside his own mourning, for his heart was still flooded with grief. Therefore, he sat in his house in his compound, silent and still. He did not talk with his other wives or with his children. He did not talk with the elders on his council or with his friends. He did not speak or laugh. To him, the sun and the moon were the same, and day was the same as the night, silent and still.

And so it came to pass that the council elders approached their king and announced, "King Kitamba, when the sun goes to its rest, the period of wailing will be over. It will be time for dancing, singing, and the chanting of final prayers."

"My ears hear the words that your tongues speak," the king responded. "However, my heart still floods with grief for Queen Muhongo, my beloved head wife. Therefore, I will mourn her still! I will not think of life. And I will not speak or laugh."

"So, call the people before you," King Kitamba commanded, "and repeat the words that my tongue has spoken. Tell them that I have commanded that everyone who lives in my town will continue to mourn Queen Muhongo. Tell them that no one may say a word! No one may sing or dance. The women may not pound their food. The children may not shout with joy. Tell them that no one may make a sound!"

To these words, the elders on the council replied, "King Kitamba, our ears hear the words that your tongue speaks. Yet your tongue speaks words that are strange to our ears. We know that your head queen has died, but we have already mourned her as it is done. And as it is done is enough! Lord Kalunga-ngombe takes everyone—now here, now there, now sooner, now later—to the Village of the Ancestors. Therefore, life must continue for all who are yet alive!"

"My ears hear the words that your tongues speak, and my own tongue has an answer for you," King Kitamba responded. "If you want me to speak and to laugh—and if you want the people of our town to be able to speak and laugh and make other sounds—then you will bring Queen Muhongo, my beloved head wife, back to me!"

"But that is impossible, King Kitamba!" responded the chief of the council of elders. "No one can bring back someone who has died! The dead remain with Kalunga-ngombe, who has taken them to his village. There they live with their ancestors and yours. You cannot grieve and mourn forever! Death is a part of life! And life must continue!"

To these words, King Kitamba then replied, "If it is just as you say, then I will continue to mourn for Queen Muhongo, and no one in this town will make a sound! And if the town dies because of it, then let it die!"

And so it came to pass that the council of elders came together without their king and discussed what they could do. The words of their tongues all seemed to come from one head, and they decided to consult a famous shaman.

When the shaman arrived, the chief of the council of elders declared, "King Kitamba's head wife has died, and he continues to mourn her even though the period of mourning will be finished as soon as the sun goes to its rest. Now King Kitamba has declared, 'As long as I mourn, no one in this town may make a sound. Therefore, if you want to talk and laugh and make other sounds, you will have to bring Queen Muhongo back to me!'

"And so, Doctor," the council chief continued, "we have brought you here so that you will go down to Kalunga-ngombe's Village of the Ancestors in the Land of the Dead and bring King Kitamba's head wife, Queen Muhongo, back to him!"

"My ears hear the words of your tongue," the shaman replied, "and I will do what you ask of me."

The shaman then asked the council elders to dig a grave in the fireplace in his guest hut. When it was finished, the shaman commanded his wife, "I want you to dress in mourning for me. And I want you to water the earthen floor of this fireplace—which will be the top of my grave—so that it remains wet. You must perform both of these tasks every day that I am gone!"

"My ears hear the words of your tongue, and my hands will do as you wish," his wife replied.

And so it came to pass that the shaman climbed into the newly dug grave. "Now, fill up this hole so that it is just as it was," the shaman commanded his wife. "And be sure to water the earthen floor that is its cover so that it remains wet!"

With these words, the shaman's wife buried her husband as if he were dead. As soon as the top of his grave was closed, the bottom opened, revealing a large road that led from the grave into the Land of the Dead. The shaman, quick as the wind, left his grave and walked down this road. He walked through the forest. He walked up and down the hills. Before long, it came to pass that he arrived at Kalunga-ngombe's Village of the Ancestors.

The village was teeming with those who had died! Everyone who had once been alive appeared to be somewhere! Grandmothers and grandfathers, mothers and fathers, and even children who had died before their expected time were there.

The shaman looked here and he looked there while he continued to walk forth into the village. He saw King Kitamba's grandfather, and his mother and father as well. And he saw his own mother and father. Finally, he spied Queen Muhongo. She was sitting in the center of the village, where she was weaving a basket.

When the shaman approached her, King Kitamba's head wife looked up and asked, "Who are you? And why are you here?"

To these words, the shaman replied, "I have come to the Village of the Ancestors in order to take you with me. For since your death, King Kitamba will not think of life! He will not speak or laugh! And he will not let anyone in his town make a sound! The women may not pound their food; the young ones may not shout with joy; and no one may say a word. Your husband has declared that his heart has flooded with grief and that it will remain flooded with grief until you return to him. So, come! Let us leave this place and return to the Land of the Living."

"My ears hear the words that your tongue speaks," Queen Muhongo responded, "and it is good for a wife's ears to hear that her husband's heart floods with grief because she has died.

"However, tell me, do you know who it is who sits near me?" she asked the shaman. "You do not? Well, he is Lord Kalunga-ngombe! He rules the Village of the Ancestors. Now, can you tell me who is sitting in chains over there?"

"I did not know Lord Kalunga-ngombe, but that man looks just like King Kitamba!" the shaman exclaimed. "However, it cannot be he because I just left him in the Land of the Living!"

"I know that you left my husband in the Land of the Living, but, nevertheless, that chained man is he!" Queen Muhongo exclaimed. "My husband is destined to die before many more years have come and gone in the Land of the Living, and when that time comes, he, too, will be here in the Village of the Ancestors!

"Now, Doctor," Queen Muhongo continued, "although you have come to take me back to the Land of the Living, surely you must know that once the dead come to Kalunga-ngombe's village, they never leave the Land of the Dead. And so my husband must push grief from his heart. He must think of life! He must speak and laugh! And he must sing and dance! For those who are still alive must rejoice! Death will come to them—now here, now there, now sooner, now later—as it has come to all whom you see here in Kalunga-ngombe's village.

"However, I will give you this arm-ring," Queen Muhongo declared. "I was buried with it on my arm. Take it, now, to my husband. He will recognize that it is my arm-ring, and he will know that you found me here in the Village of the Ancestors. But take care that you do not tell my husband that you found him here as well!

"And now, Doctor, you must leave this place," Queen Muhongo concluded. "I would be hospitable and offer you something to eat, but if you eat any food in the Village of the Ancestors, you can never again return to the Land of the Living!"

And so it came to pass that the shaman turned and went back along the road that he had traveled. Three days in the Land of the Living had come and gone with the sun when the shaman reentered his grave.

His wife, who was keeping watch over her husband's grave, noticed that the earthen floor of the fireplace—which she had remembered to keep wet—was cracking apart. And as she watched, first her husband's head emerged and then his arms. Finally, the shaman pulled himself out of his grave!

When the sun made the next day light, the shaman summoned the council of elders and said, "Headmen of King Kitamba's town, I have returned from Kalunga-ngombe's Village of the Ancestors in the Land of the Dead. There I met with Queen Muhongo, your king's head wife.

"And I said to her, 'I have come to take you with me,'" the shaman continued. "'Since your death, King Kitamba will not think of life! He will not speak or laugh! And he will not let anyone in the town make a sound! Your husband has declared that this period of mourning will continue until you return to him. So let us now leave this place and return to the Land of the Living!'

"And the ears of Queen Muhongo heard the words of my tongue," the shaman continued, "and she replied, 'It is good for a wife's ears to hear that her husband's heart floods with grief because she has died. However, once the dead come to Kalunga-ngombe's village, they never leave the Land of the Dead. And so my husband must push grief from his heart! He must think of life! He must speak and laugh! And he must sing and dance! For those who are still alive must rejoice! Death will come to them—now here, now there, now sooner, now later—as it has come to all whom you see here in Kalunga-ngombe's village.'"

The shaman continued, "And then Queen Muhongo declared, 'I will give you this arm-ring. Take it, now, to my husband. He will recognize that it is my arm-ring, and he will know that you found me here in the Village of the Ancestors.'

"So, here is Queen Muhongo's arm-ring. Take it to King Kitamba along with the words that have come from his head queen's tongue," the shaman concluded. "And, now that I have done what you asked of me, you must pay me for my efforts and give me leave to return to my own hut."

The council elders gave the shaman the gift of two servants, and he and his wife then returned to their home. Then the elders went forth to meet with their king.

"King Kitamba, we sent for the famous shaman, and at our request he has visited Queen Muhongo in the Village of the Ancestors," the chief of the council announced. "There your head queen gave him this arm-ring that I now give to you. She was certain that you would know that it is hers.

"The shaman told Queen Muhongo that you will not speak or laugh until she returns to you. And your head queen responded that she was pleased to hear that your heart floods with grief because she has died," he reported.

"However, Queen Muhongo told the shaman to remind you that once the dead come to Kalunga-ngombe's Village of the Ancestors, they never return to the Land of the Living," the council chief added. "And so, King Kitamba, you must push grief from your heart! You must think of life! You must speak and laugh! And you must sing and dance! For Queen Muhongo reminds you that death will come to all who live, just as it has come to all who have died. And, therefore, the living must rejoice that they are alive!"

"My ears hear the words that your tongue speaks," King Kitamba responded. "The arm-ring that you have given me indeed belongs to my head wife—she was buried with it. Therefore, I will take my beloved's words into my heart. We who are alive will live!

"So let the food be prepared!" King Kitamba commanded. "Let the drummers appear with their drums! Let the singing and dancing and the chanting of the final prayers bring this period of mourning to an end! When the people sing, I too will sing! And when the drum beats, I too will dance!"

And so it came to pass that in King Kitamba's town, once again the king spoke and laughed. And once again the town resounded with the happy sounds of the living. The women pounded their food. The young ones shouted with joy. And everyone could be heard talking and laughing.

A few more years came and went with the sun and the moon, and it then came to pass that King Kitamba died. The people buried their king and mourned him for weeks and months as it was done.

And King Kitamba has left you this story.

El Bizarrón and the Devil
and
Wiley and the Hairy Man

Stories in which a human being outwits the Devil are very popular in folklore, and they can be found wherever people have believed in the Devil. For example, "El Bizarrón and the Devil" is Cuban, whereas "Wiley and the Hairy Man" is African American. Both are versions of the traditional trickster tale, and they have much in common.

Belief in the Devil is one way of explaining the existence of all forms of evil in the universe, including every sin, every disease, and death. The Devil in his many forms is more than rebellious; he is totally and unrepentingly malicious—the manifestation of the Evil Spirit. He is known under many names and has probably existed in one form or another since the human race was young. In ancient Persia, the Zoroastrians associated him with darkness and called him Ahriman. The Muslims know him as Iblis or Shaytan, while to Jews and Christians, in his early form, he is known as the Satan.

In Hebrew, the word *Satan* means "opponent," "adversary," or "accuser." "Satan" is always preceded by the article "the," because it is a title, rather than a personal name. In the Bible and in rabbinic lore, the conception of the Satan varies. In some instances (such as that involving Job), the Satan is a courtier in God's royal court who functions as "the eye and the ear of God." Here, God has given the Satan permission to wander about on earth in order to spy on the ways of human beings, make note of their immoral behavior, and then report back with his discoveries. Therefore, from the point of view of the human community, the Satan is the opponent, adversary, or accuser of humankind.

However, the Satan can also be equated with "the evil inclination" or "the evil impulse" that is part of human nature. In addition, he can function, externally, as the one who tempts human beings to give in to an evil inclination or impulse. In both of these roles, the Satan can appear either in his own form or in symbolic form. Where he appears in the form of a serpent, his role is a pejorative transformation of the serpent's beneficent role in the matriarchal religion of ancient Middle

Eastern agricultural societies and in ancient cults that worshiped serpents.

The Satan developed into a specific immortal being with the coming of Christianity, and by the Middle Ages he was well-known as Lucifer, or the Devil. Being the embodiment of evil, the Devil was always the antithesis of God and, therefore, he was God's enemy. Because the Devil was viewed as the enemy of Christianity, he acquired the characteristics of ancient agricultural deities—such as the snake or dragon, the cow, and the goat—that, being non-Christian, were no longer accepted and that were therefore equated with evil.

Consequently, in the art and folklore of the Middle Ages, the Devil possesses one or more of the following physical characteristics: a hairy face and body, fiery eyes, pointed ears, horns protruding from his forehead, a tail, and either one or two cloven hooves. In medieval folklore, the Devil is often called the Hairy One (Old Hairy). He can be lame; he can carry a pitchfork; and he can be depicted as a serpent (or dragon) that has a human head. His bestial characteristics separate him from human beings because these attributes are external symbols of his defective and dangerous internal nature. Many people believed that one of his roles is to tempt people to join him in his evil ways.

Folktales often depict the Devil as a hunter who stalks human beings, catches their souls, and collects them in his hunter's bag. The folktale hero is likely to meet this form of the Devil in locations that are isolated from human society, such as a forest or a swamp. Unlike the heroes of myth, folktale heroes are ordinary people who both follow the advice of someone who wishes to help them and rely on their own clever intelligence. If the Devil is performing the role of tempter, the isolated location of their encounter may symbolize the human subconscious, and their contest may symbolize the folktale hero's internal psychological conflict.

Both "El Bizarrón and the Devil" and "Wiley and the Hairy Man" humanize the Devil, thereby making him less terrifying. In these tales, the Devil is good-natured, and his inability to recognize his opponent's manipulation makes him an object of humor and ridicule. "El Bizarrón and the Devil" combines the Devil's traditional reputation with aspects of modern life, whereas the Devil's depiction in "Wiley and the Hairy Man" reflects medieval origins or influence.

"El Bizarrón and the Devil" and "Wiley and the Hairy Man" celebrate the powers of the human mind. Therefore, whether these tales are heard or read, they entertain their audience. Human beings often must cope with people who are more powerful than they are. In literature as in life, they succeed by using their creative intelligence. Since listeners and readers identify with the ordinary person, they enjoy watching El Bizarrón and Wiley outwit their powerful adversary through a series of clever tricks.

Although the women in these folktales have not found their way into the titles of their tales, their roles are both very important and very appealing. The Devil's wife is far more intelligent than her husband, and Wiley could not succeed if it were not for his mother's guidance. Consequently, as much as we admire El Bizarrón and Wiley, it is the women who steal the show. ("Wiley and the Hairy Man" begins on page 332.)

EL BIZARRÓN AND THE DEVIL

A man by the name of El Bizarrón made his living by doing odd jobs here and there in our town. If you wanted to find him, all you would need to do is ask around. Someone would surely have seen him not very long ago as he walked from door to door in search of work.

It came to pass that one of the townspeople met El Bizarrón and said to him, "I hear that the Devil himself needs a servant in his house. But take care! He has already killed two other servants. In fact, I have heard that everyone who works for him dies in the process! So you should stay clear of the Devil's house unless you are in desperate need of work."

To these words, El Bizarrón replied, "Why, I thank you kindly for the news. I am just the man for the Devil! And he will find that he cannot get the better of me!"

And so it came to pass that El Bizarrón walked to the Devil's house, knocked on the door, and came face to face with the Devil himself. He knew him at once, for who else has horns protruding from his forehead, fiery bright eyes, ears reaching up in points through his heavy head of hair, and such a great mustache and beard that they conceal his face from his nose right down past his chin?

"Good afternoon, master! I have heard that you are in need of a servant. If the work is tough, I am the man for the job because I am very strong!" El Bizarrón declared.

The Devil examined El Bizarrón carefully with his fiery-bright eyes, pulling on his beard as he did so. "If you want hard work, do I have work for you!" he exclaimed. "I think you will need five more strong men to help you, but we will see about that later. Until then, come inside. Let me show you to your room, and sleep well. You will need all the rest that you can get because tomorrow you will begin!"

With these words, the Devil turned on his one good heel and slowly led El Bizarrón to the room that would be his. And as he walked, he clumped with his left foot and dragged his right foot behind him.

As for El Bizarrón, he loved nothing better than a good rest! Therefore, that night he lay down on his bed, and before he could count five sheep, he fell fast asleep. Despite the fact that his employer was the Devil himself, El Bizarrón slept soundly and did not awaken until the next morning.

When the sun next began to brighten the world with its light, El Bizarrón awakened to the sound of clumping and dragging feet. This sound became progressively louder as it approached his room. Then the noise stopped, and El Bizarrón heard someone knocking on his door.

The Devil's voice called out, "Servant, it's time to rise and earn your pay! Your first task is to bring me some water."

"I am at your service, master!" El Bizarrón replied. "But I will need both a shovel and a pick for the job!"

"Whatever you need, I will surely give you," the Devil replied, and he handed El Bizarrón the tools that he had requested.

And so it came to pass that El Bizarrón walked down to the river. With his pick and his shovel, he began to dig a ditch that would lead from the river to the Devil's house. He put his whole heart into his work—and both arms, too!—toiling away with the energy and strength of at least three men. Come to think of it, he worked more like four men!

Now when the sun had climbed high into the sky, the Devil's wife came to her husband and asked, "My dear, where is our water?"

"Where is it, indeed!" replied the Devil.

His wife then declared, "My dear, your new servant looks strong enough, and he certainly talks a good game. But it is now six hours since you sent him on his way, and he still has not returned with our water! I wonder what could have happened to him? Is he hard at work? Or is he dreaming the day away?"

To these words, the Devil replied, "Now, calm yourself, my dear! I am the master of our household affairs because I know best how to manage them. You are but a bystander! Just leave my servant to me! As I always try to tell you, if anyone knows what evil lurks in the human heart, I do! But since you are concerned, I will look into the matter!"

So it came to pass that the Devil walked down to the river. And as he walked, he clumped with his left foot and dragged his right foot behind him. Now when he reached the river, he saw that his servant was hard at work, digging away with his shovel and his pick.

"What in the world are you doing here, servant?" the Devil asked.

"What does it look like I am doing here, master?" El Bizarrón replied.

"Now look here, servant! I did not ask you to dig a ditch! All I wanted was water from the river!"

"You asked me for water, master, and I am getting you water! A man of your prestige and power should have water inside his house! He should not have to send his servant to fetch it from the river as the common folk do. So I am building you a ditch that will carry water from the river directly into your house!"

The Devil tilted his head to the right, put his right hand on his right horn, and thought about the situation. "What should I make of this?" he asked himself. "It is good that my servant likes hard work. I can see that he has already dug a hole that is as deep as my pitchfork—and that is surely a very deep hole! On the other hand, my servant has a mind of his own! I don't think that I like this at all, but I will worry about it tomorrow!"

This is what the Devil thought, but what he said was nothing at all. He just turned on his one good heel and walked all the way back to his house. And as he walked, he clumped with his left foot and dragged his right foot behind him.

As for El Bizarrón, he returned as well. And, as you know, he loved nothing better than a good rest! Therefore, that night he lay down on his bed, and before he could count five sheep, he fell fast asleep. Despite the fact that his employer was the Devil himself, El Bizarrón slept soundly and did not awaken until the next morning.

When the sun next began to brighten the world with its light, El Bizarrón awakened to the sound of clumping and dragging feet. This sound became progressively louder as it approached his room. Then the noise stopped, and El Bizarrón heard someone knocking on his door.

The Devil's voice called out, "Servant, it's time to rise and earn your pay! Leave the river and its water where they are today. Instead, bring me a load of wood from the mountain forest."

"As always, I am at your service, master!" El Bizarrón replied. "But I will need a rope—a very long rope!—for the job."

"Whatever you need, I will surely give you," the Devil replied, and he handed El Bizarrón the rope that he had requested.

And so it came to pass that El Bizarrón walked off toward the mountain forest. With his rope, he began to walk around the base of the mountain in order to enclose all of the trees in the forest. Round and round the edge of the forest he walked, winding and winding his rope. Fortunately, the rope was going to be long enough for the job!

El Bizarrón put his whole heart into his work—and both arms, too!—toiling away with the energy and strength of at least three men. Come to think of it, he worked more like four men! In fact, El Bizarrón circled the base of the mountain so many times that he wore down the heels and put holes into the soles of his shoes!

Now when the sun had climbed high into the sky, the Devil's wife came to her husband and asked, "My dear, where is our wood?"

"Where is it, indeed!" replied the Devil.

His wife then declared, "My dear, your new servant looks strong enough, and he certainly talks a good game. But it is now six hours since you sent him on his way, and he still has not returned with our wood! I wonder what could have happened to him? Is he hard at work? Or is he dreaming the day away?"

To these words, the Devil replied, "Now, calm yourself, my dear! I am the master of our household affairs because I know best how to manage them. You are but a bystander! Just leave my servant to me! As I always try to tell you, if anyone knows what evil lurks in the human heart, I do! But since you are concerned, once again I will look into the matter!"

So it came to pass that the Devil walked off toward the mountain forest. And as he walked, he clumped with his left foot and dragged his right foot behind him. Now when he reached the forest, he saw that his servant was hard at work, winding his rope around the base of the mountain in the way that you would wrap a scarf around your neck.

"What in the world are you doing here, servant?" the Devil asked.

"What does it look like I am doing here, master?" El Bizarrón replied.

"Now look here, servant! I did not ask you to rope the mountain! All I wanted was wood from its forest!"

"You asked me for wood, master, and I am collecting wood for you! A man of your prestige and power certainly needs a great amount of wood! I am roping this forest so that I can load it on my back and make just one trip of it!"

The Devil tilted his head to the left, put his left hand on his left horn, and thought about the situation. "What should I make of this?" he asked himself. "It is good that my servant likes hard work. And I can see that he has already worn out his shoes trudging around the mountain. On the other hand, my servant has a mind of his own—clearly the mind of a fool! I don't think that I like this at all, but I will worry about it tomorrow!"

This is what the Devil thought, but what he said was, "Servant, stop what you are doing, and just return to my house! I cannot use the mountain. And I can get along well enough for the present without the wood!"

With these words, the Devil turned on his one good heel and walked all the way back to his house. And as he walked, he clumped with his left foot and dragged his right foot behind him.

As for El Bizarrón, he returned as well. And, as you know, he loved nothing better than a good rest! Therefore, that night he lay down on his bed, and before he could count five sheep, he fell fast asleep. Despite the fact that his employer was the Devil himself, El Bizarrón slept soundly and did not awaken until the next morning.

Now when the sun next began to brighten the world with its light, El Bizarrón once again awakened to the sound of clumping and dragging feet. This sound became progressively louder as it approached his room. Then the noise stopped, and El Bizarrón heard someone knocking on his door.

The Devil's voice called out, "Servant, it's time to rise and earn your pay! Leave the forest and its trees where they are today. Instead, I want you to participate in a bar-throwing contest that is being held on the beach. With your strength, you will surely win a prize for me!"

"As always, I am at your service, master!" El Bizarrón replied. "Just give me the bar, lead the way, and I will win the contest for you!"

"Whatever you need, I will surely give you," the Devil replied, and he handed El Bizarrón the bar that he had requested.

And so it came to pass that the Devil led El Bizarrón down to the beach. The Devil's wife accompanied them. Now when they arrived at the seashore, all of the contestants were busily practicing for the contest.

However, El Bizarrón just lay down upon the sand and went to sleep. He loved nothing better than a good rest! The sun climbed higher into the sky, and the contest began. When the sun had climbed much higher, it was time for El Bizarrón to take his turn at tossing the bar.

"Sound your horns!" El Bizarrón commanded. "Shout through your megaphones! Order those boats on the horizon to move farther out to sea! For if they remain where they are, I will surely sink them with my first throw!"

"We cannot do that!" the judges declared. "And we cannot permit you to endanger the lives of innocent people! Therefore, we are very sorry, but we must disqualify you from participating in this contest!"

Everyone was disappointed. El Bizarrón hung his head and drooped both of his shoulders because he could not show off his prodigious strength. The Devil hung his head and drooped both of his horns because he could not win the prize.

And as for the Devil's wife, she said quietly to her husband, "I think the judges should have let your servant toss the bar! How do they know that he is as strong as he says he is?"

To these words, the Devil replied, "Now calm yourself, my dear! Judges judge because they know judging. You are but a bystander! Just leave my servant to me! As I always try to tell you, if anyone knows what evil lurks in the human heart, I do!"

However, the Devil once again tilted his head to the right, put his right hand on his right horn, and thought about the situation. "What should I make of this?" he asked himself. "It is good that my servant is very strong—much too strong, in fact, to participate in the bar-throwing contest! On the other hand, my servant has a mind of his own—clearly the mind of a fox in the body of an ox! I don't think that I like this at all, so I had better find a way to do away with him before he finds a way to get the better of me!"

This is what the Devil thought, but what he said was nothing at all. He just turned on his one good heel and walked all the way back to his house. And as he walked, he clumped with his left foot and dragged his right foot behind him.

So it came to pass that when the Devil, his wife, and El Bizarrón returned home, the Devil turned to his servant and announced, "To-night, I am going to sleep on the iron grill of my barbecue. And I want you to sleep on the ground beneath the grill."

"As always, I am at your service, master!" El Bizarrón replied. "I will sleep wherever you wish me to sleep!"

It came to pass that when the Devil climbed on the grill and lay down that night, he had two huge and heavy rocks concealed beneath his pajamas.

Now, as you know, El Bizarrón loved nothing better than a good rest! Therefore, you have every reason to expect that, when he lay down beneath the grill, he once again fell fast asleep before he could count five sheep. However, that night, El Bizarrón was not sleeping in his bed. He was sleeping on the ground beneath his employer, and his employer was the Devil himself!

Therefore, when El Bizarrón lay down beneath the grill, he saw the body of his master before his eyes instead of sheep. And as he stared up at his master, he thought to himself, "It seems to me that my master's body has a puffed-up look. Since he has chosen this new sleeping arrangement, he may not have my best interests at heart. Therefore, I had better be on my guard and prepare for some Devil-ish deed!"

And so it came to pass that El Bizarrón waited quietly until the Devil was fast asleep, and then he crept stealthily away from the grill to a place where he could watch his employer from a safe distance. Hours passed with only the sounds of the night for company and, despite his best intentions, El Bizarrón fell fast asleep.

Suddenly, El Bizarrón was awakened by the sound of huge and heavy rocks striking the ground. Even the earth was trembling beneath him. He left his sleeping place and stealthily approached the grill. Then he exclaimed, "Ouch! I've been bitten by a nasty mosquito!"

Upon hearing these words from the mouth of his servant, the Devil thought to himself, "Nothing can hurt this servant of mine! I drop two huge and heavy rocks upon him—when one of them is more than enough to crush any man alive!—and to him, they are no more than the bite of a mosquito!"

"My servant is a powerhouse, and I must remember that this ox has the mind of a fox!" the Devil declared to himself. The very thought of the fox within the ox led the Devil to climb down from the grill so that he could examine his servant for himself.

Sure enough, the Devil found that El Bizarrón was sitting calmly beneath the grill where he had been told to sleep. Now, however, he was surrounded by large chunks of broken rocks. The Devil examined El Bizarrón carefully with his fiery-bright eyes, pulling on his beard as he did so. He couldn't see the sign of one bruise on his servant! In fact, he couldn't even see a scratch on him!

When the Devil had examined his servant from head to toe, El Bizarrón looked at his employer and innocently asked, "Where did all of these rock chunks come from, master? At first, I thought that a mosquito had bitten me, but now I see that one of these rocks must have hit me!"

When the Devil's pointed ears heard his servant's words, both of his horns trembled with terror! Hastening to cover this embarrassment with both hands, the Devil replied, "Ox, fox, or whoever you are, you are fired! I will give you as much silver as my donkey can carry if you will agree to leave my house right now—before the sun next brightens the world with its light! Go anywhere—as long as it is far from here! And see to it that you never return!"

To this offer, El Bizarrón replied, "As always, I am at your service, master! Just bring me your silver and your donkey, and I promise that you will never have to look upon my face again!"

So it came to pass that the Devil gave El Bizarrón a donkey— and two bulging, silver-filled saddlebags besides. El Bizarrón now said to himself, "I had better leave quickly before the Devil changes his mind!" And that is just what he did.

El Bizarrón left none too soon! For as soon as the sun began to brighten the world with its light, the Devil's wife came to him and asked, "Husband, where is your servant? I see that his room is empty!"

"I have sent him packing, my dear," the Devil replied. "I gave him a donkey loaded with two saddlebags of silver, and I told him never to show his face here again!"

"Husband, you cannot have done this!" his wife exclaimed. "You are the man who is always telling me, 'Leave my servant to me! If anyone knows what evil lurks in the human heart, I do!' Well, I say, this servant has made a fool of you! And I am willing to bet that he is laughing his way into town with your silver and your donkey!"

To these words, the Devil replied, "Now, calm yourself, my dear. I am the master of our household affairs because I know best how to manage them. You are but a bystander! Just leave my servant to me! I always try to tell you that if anyone knows what evil lurks in the human heart, I do—because I do and you do not! But, since you are concerned, I will look into the matter!"

This is what the Devil told his wife, but having said this, he once again tilted his head to the left, put his left hand on his left horn, and thought about the situation. "What should I make of this?" he asked himself. "What midnight madness to have given that fox of an ox a treasure trove of silver and my donkey as well! However, I will now outfox him! I will surprise him by riding after him on my horse and reclaiming what is rightfully mine!"

With these thoughts in mind, the Devil turned on his one good heel and walked to his barn. And as he walked, he clumped with his left foot and dragged his right foot behind him.

So it came to pass that, before very long, El Bizarrón heard a clatter of hooves far behind him on the road. When he looked back and spied the Devil, he quickly hid his donkey in a sugarcane field. Then he lay down on his back—right in the middle of the road!—and raised both of his arms and his legs into the air, where he waved them about like flags in a gale-wind.

The Devil rode up to El Bizarrón and asked, "What in the world are you doing here, servant? And where's the donkey that I gave you?"

"What does it look like I am doing here, master?" El Bizarrón replied. "Your donkey—stubborn as a mule, that fellow is!—got tired of walking and just sat down right here in the middle of the road. No amount of coaxing could move him! I pleaded. I cajoled. I shouted. I whipped him. Finally, I just gave him one good kick into the sky!"

When the Devil's pointed ears heard his servant's words, he knew that both of his horns were trembling with terror again. Hastening to cover this embarrassment with his hands, he interrupted El Bizarrón and demanded, "Enough about my donkey! Just tell me why *you* are lying on your back in the middle of the road and creating a gale-wind by waving your arms and legs about in the air!"

"Because that donkey still carries the saddlebags you gave me, and they are bulging with silver!" El Bizarrón exclaimed. "When he falls from the clouds—and, of course, he will fall back to earth!—I want him to have a soft landing! That way, the bags of silver will stay closed, the donkey will stay alive, and I can continue on my way with the goods that you gave me."

When the Devil's pointed ears heard his servant's words, he tilted his head to the right, put his right hand on his right horn, and thought about the situation. "What should I make of this?" he asked himself. "It is good that I can turn around, leave this ox to his journey, and never have to set eyes on him again! On the other hand, if I wait around for the donkey's fall so that I can reclaim what is mine, this fox of an ox will probably kick *me* into the clouds—and I know what's up there—*heaven*! Now that is surely no place for the Devil!"

And so it came to pass that the Devil quickly turned his horse around and rode back home, leaving El Bizarrón to his journey.

Seeing that her husband had returned empty-handed, the Devil's wife exclaimed, "So your servant got the best of you after all!" And she gave her husband a scornful smile.

To these words the Devil replied, "Calm yourself, my dear! I am the master of our household affairs because I know best how to manage them. You are but a bystander! I have looked into the matter, so just leave my servant to me! As I always try to tell you, if anyone knows what evil lurks in the human heart, I do!"

WILEY AND THE HAIRY MAN

My daddy was no source of pride to his family or to anyone else. He was so lazy he'd sleep while the weeds grew taller than our cotton! And when there was no moon, he'd go off hereabouts and steal a watermelon right off someone's vine! Why, I've even heard folks say that one time he robbed a dead man! Used to be, you'd just say my daddy's name, and folks 'round here would shake their heads and say, "That man will never see heaven 'cause the Hairy Man's goin' to get him first!"

Those folks sure knew what they were talkin' about! For one day, my daddy fell off the ferry while it was crossin' the river—right where the water's always in a hurry to get where it's goin'. And that hurryin' water went and swallowed my daddy up before anyone could get him out!

Folks looked everywhere for my daddy. They looked in the calm pools 'tween the sandbanks—you know, where the swimmin's so good!—and they looked far downstream. They never found him, but they just kept right on lookin' for him anyway.

Then, one day, those folks heard laughin' comin' all the way from across the river. They couldn't see who was doin' all that laughin', but they sure knew who it was all right! "The Hairy Man's laughin' at us!" they cried. And so they gave up lookin' for my daddy.

That's when my mama said, "Wiley, you'd better watch out, Son! That old Hairy Man has gone and caught your daddy! So you'd better be careful, or he'll catch you too!"

"What does he look like, Mama?" I asked. "Will I know him if I see him? No way do I want him to sneak up on me and surprise me 'cause I don't know who he is!"

"You'll know him sure enough if you see him, Son," Mama said. "He's covered with hair from head to toe! And he has the ugliest face you ever did see! His eyes are two fires—and their flames reach out for you through the hairs on his face. When he wants to catch you, he gives you his great big smile. And that mouth of his is enough to send you runnin'! His grin spreads all the way up to his nose and shows his big white teeth swimmin' in a river of spit! So don't you worry about knowin' him, Son! If you ever see the Hairy Man, you'll know him all right!"

"Then that's all I need to know, Mama. So don't you go worryin' about me!" I said. "I'll go nowhere without my hound-dogs, and I'll watch out for that old man. You did say the Hairy Man's scared of hound-dogs, didn't you?"

"That's what I told you, Son!" Mama said. "And I know what I know 'cause I know magic!"

Days came and went as they do, and nothin' happened. But I remembered what Mama told me. Then, one day, when we needed to fix our hen-roost, I took my axe and went into the swamp for wood. Naturally, I took my hound-dogs with me. Not that they were much good! They spied a young pig and took off! They ran far and farther—I don't know how far they ran—but no way could I hear 'em yappin'.

I looked 'round at all the great trees, and I listened to the great silence. I usually liked bein' alone with the trees and the silence in the swamp. But now that the Hairy Man had caught my daddy, it wasn't the same anymore. "I sure hope that old Hairy Man's busy catchin' someone else!" I said to myself. Then I took a deep breath, grabbed my axe, and set to work.

Now, wouldn't you know it! While I was doin' my cuttin', I looked up—and there he was! I couldn't believe my eyes! The Hairy Man was walkin' through the trees—and he was comin' right toward me! The very sight of him made my heart stop still!

I knew it was *him* all right 'cause he looked just like Mama said. He was covered with hair from head to toe! And he had the ugliest face I ever did see! I could see his two fiery eyes reachin' out for me through the hairs on his face. And he was givin' me his great big smile. His grin spread all the way up to his nose, and his teeth were swimmin' in spit!

"Hairy Man, now you just stop grinnin' at me!" I hollered.

But the Hairy Man did not seem to hear me. He just kept grinnin' and walkin' toward me. He was carryin' a big frog-catchin' bag—all tied up with rope—over his shoulder. So quick as a wink, I dropped my axe and climbed the biggest tree I could find. The tree was no way big enough!

Once the Hairy Man walked out of the mud, I could see that he had the feet of a cow, not a man. "Mama told me nothin' about his feet," I said to myself. "I wonder if she knows he has hooves! As for me, I sure am glad he does! 'Cause no way can a cow make it up this tree!"

But I've said enough about his feet, 'cause the Hairy Man, he just kept on comin' toward me. And as he came, he just kept on grinnin' at me. He was after me, sure enough, 'cause he stopped right at the foot of my tree! He put down his bag, and he untied it.

"Why, Wiley, why are you sittin' way up there in this tree, boy?" he asked.

"I'm sittin' here, Hairy Man, 'cause you caught my daddy, and Mama told me to be sure you didn't catch me! But tell me, Hairy Man, what're you carryin' in that big bag of yours?"

"I'm not carryin' anythin' in it just yet," said the Hairy Man.

"Then why was your bag all tied up with rope?" I asked.

"That's for me to know, and for you to find out!" he declared.

And then, guess what he did? Why, the Hairy Man picked up my axe and began to chop down my tree—with me still sittin' in it!

"Nothin's in that bag of his, 'cause he's goin' to put *me* in it!" I said to myself. So I hollered, "Come, dogs! Come!"

I clutched at the trunk of my tree and hung on for dear life! And

I thought to use some of Mama's magic, too. "Go home, wood chips, go home!" I cried.

Mama's charm worked, 'cause the wood chips went right back to their places. But that didn't put out the Hairy Man one bit! He just kept choppin' and choppin' at the trunk of my tree. There was nothin' I could do but keep tellin' those wood chips to go home. So I did my thing and the Hairy Man did his. My voice gave out, but that Hairy Man, he just kept on choppin' and choppin' at the trunk of my tree.

I knew that I must come up with somethin' better and be quick about it! So I said, "If you know magic, Hairy Man, then you can make this tree trunk twice as big. And if you'll do that, then I'll climb down a bit! But I know you can't do it!"

"Wiley, you don't know what I can do and what I can't. But I'll tell you this—I'm not goin' to work my magic on your tree trunk, so you can just stay right where you are."

So I went back to doin' my thing, and the Hairy Man went back to doin' his. Finally, I could hear my hound-dogs barkin' in the distance. And I knew that the Hairy Man must be hearin' 'em too. So I took a great breath and I hollered, "Come, dogs! Come!"

"Wiley, you can holler for your dogs, and you can just keep hollerin' for 'em! But it won't do you any good, boy," declared the Hairy Man. "They ran after the young pig I set out for 'em, and they're long gone by now!"

That's what the Hairy Man said. But I kept on hollerin', "Come dogs! Come!"

By now, I knew that my dogs were hearin' me. For their yappin' was growin' louder and louder. And I knew that the Hairy Man must be hearin' 'em too.

"Now, Wiley," said the Hairy Man, "you just climb down from your tree, boy, and I'll show you some magic!"

"No way will you ever get me out of this tree!" I declared. "My mama knows magic. And she will teach me all I want to know!"

Now I could hear my hound-dogs yappin' very close by. And I knew that the Hairy Man must be hearin' 'em too, for, quick as a wink, he dropped my axe like a hot potato, grabbed his bag and the rope, and ran back into the swamp. He just missed seein' my dogs!

As for me, I ran all the way home so I could tell Mama all about the Hairy Man.

Now when I told Mama my tale, she said, "The Hairy Man usually carries a big frog-catchin' bag, Son. Did he have it with him?"

"He did, sure enough! And it was all tied up with rope. He untied it when he put it down by my tree," I declared. "But when I asked him what was in his bag, Mama, he said nothin' was in it!"

"Well then, the next time you see the Hairy Man, Son, don't you go climbin' any tree—even a great big one! Just listen to me, now," Mama said, "and I'll tell you how you can get the best of him."

"How do you know I'm goin' to see the Hairy Man again, Mama? Maybe he'll go after somebody else next time!"

Mama said, "Maybe he will, and maybe he won't, Wiley. But, Son, it's best to be prepared for the Hairy Man, don't you think?"

"Yes, Mama," I said. "So tell me what to do. I'll listen to you."

"First, Son, you must stand your ground and say, 'Hello, Hairy Man!' Now, Wiley, can you do that?"

"No way will you get me to do any such thing, Mama!" I declared. "If I try to get the best of the Hairy Man, he'll sure enough get the best of me first! And that means he'll carry me off in that big bag of his, and you'll never see me again!"

"Now, Wiley, you shouldn't be scared of the Hairy Man, Son," Mama declared. "I'll tell you just how to handle him!"

"No you won't, Mama!" I declared. "If I listen to you, I'll end up in the Hairy Man's bag, sure enough!"

"No you won't, Wiley," Mama declared. And before I could stop her, she kept right on talkin'. "Now after you say, 'Hello, Hairy Man,' the Hairy Man will say 'Hello, Wiley.' Then you must say, 'Hairy Man, I hear that you know the best magic!' And the Hairy Man will say, 'That I do, boy.'

"Then, Wiley, you must say, 'Well, if you're really good, you can turn yourself into a giraffe!' And the Hairy Man will say, "I can do that, boy!' Then you must tell him, 'I don't believe you, Hairy Man, and what's more, I bet you won't show me!' Say these things to the Hairy Man, Son, and you'll get him to turn himself into a giraffe."

"Sure enough, Mama?" I asked.

"Sure enough, Son," Mama said. "But you still have a way to go, Wiley, if you're goin' to handle the Hairy Man! You must look at the giraffe and say, 'Well that shows pretty good magic, Hairy Man, but I bet you can't turn yourself into a 'gator!' And when the Hairy Man says, 'I can do that, too, boy!' then you must say, 'I don't believe you, Hairy Man, and what's more, I bet you won't show me!' Say these things to the Hairy Man, Son, and you'll get him to turn himself into a 'gator."

"Sure enough, Mama?" I asked.

"Sure enough, Son," Mama said. "But you still have a way to go, Wiley, if you're goin' to handle the Hairy Man! You must look at the 'gator and say, 'Well that shows pretty good magic, Hairy Man, but anyone who knows magic can turn himself into somethin' big! I bet you can't turn yourself into somethin' as small as a 'possum!' And when the Hairy Man says, 'Boy, I can do that, too!' then you must say, 'I don't believe you, Hairy Man, and what's more, I bet you won't show me!' Say these things to the Hairy Man, Son, and you'll get him to turn himself into a 'possum."

"Sure enough, Mama?" I asked.

"Sure enough, Son," Mama said. "Now, once you see the 'possum, Wiley, then quick as a wink, you must grab him by his long tail and toss him into the Hairy Man's bag! Then tie it tight with the rope, take it to the river, and toss it in!"

"If I do this, Mama, will that be the end of the Hairy Man?" I asked.

"No way, Son, but it'll help, sure enough!" Mama said.

"All right, then, Mama. I'll try it if you say so," I said.

Days came and went as they do, and nothin' happened. But I remembered what Mama told me. Then, the next time I had to go into the swamp, I left my hound-dogs tied up at home. I told myself, "After all, if I'm goin' to handle the Hairy Man, I shouldn't scare him off first!"

So I went into the swamp without my dogs, and the time came—as it always does for me in the swamp—when I looked 'round at all the great trees and listened to the great silence. I liked bein' alone with the trees and the silence in the swamp. But now that the Hairy Man had caught my daddy, and now that I'd seen *him* here in the swamp, it wasn't the same anymore.

"I sure hope that old Hairy Man's busy catchin' someone else!" I said to myself, knowin' all the time that he was probably plannin' to catch me! And wouldn't you know it! Before I could even take a deep breath, I spied the Hairy Man walkin' through the trees. And, just as I knew he would, he was comin' right toward me!

I knew it was *him* all right! Who else would be covered with hair from head to toe? Who else would have fiery eyes reachin' out for me through the hairs on his face? And who else would be givin' me that great big smile—the one that spreads all the way up to his nose—showin' his teeth swimmin' in spit? Even though I'd seen him before, the very sight of him made my heart stop still!

"Hairy Man, now you just stop grinnin' at me!" I hollered.

But the Hairy Man didn't seem to hear me. He just kept grinnin' and walkin' toward me. He was carryin' that big frog-catchin' bag of his—all tied up with rope—over his shoulder.

"Nothin's in that bag of his, 'cause he's goin' to put *me* in it!" I said to myself. So quick as a wink, I looked for the biggest tree I could find to climb. And then I remembered Mama's words—and I knew that no way could I do that this time!

I saw the Hairy Man lookin' 'round for somethin'. "I don't see those hound-dogs of yours, Wiley!" he said. And then he laughed his great laugh.

It was all I could do to keep my two feet stuck to the ground. Even my legs wanted to run! And every tree seemed to be callin' me to climb it!

"Hello, Hairy Man," I said.

"Hello, Wiley," he said. And then he bent down and untied that bag of his.

Now was no time to be scared! I knew I must work fast or, quick as a wink, I'd be in that bag of his! "Hairy Man," I said, "I hear you know the best magic!"

"That I do, boy," he declared.

"Well, if you're really good, you can turn yourself into a giraffe!" I said.

"I can do that, boy!" he declared.

"I don't believe you, Hairy Man, and what's more, I bet you won't show me!" I said.

"You don't say," he declared. And quick as a wink, he turned himself into a giraffe—right before my eyes!

I didn't have time to be impressed with his magic. So I just blinked and swallowed. Then I said, "Well that shows pretty good magic, Hairy Man, but I bet you can't turn yourself into a 'gator!"

"I can do that, too, boy!" he declared.

"I don't believe you, Hairy Man, and what's more, I bet you won't show me!" I said.

"You don't say," he declared. And quick as a wink, he turned himself into a 'gator—right before my eyes!

I didn't have time to be impressed with this magic either. So I blinked, swallowed hard, and told my heart to keep beatin'. Then I said, "Well that shows pretty good magic, Hairy Man, but anyone who knows magic can turn himself into somethin' big! I bet you can't turn yourself into somethin' small—like a 'possum!"

"Boy, I can do that, too!" he declared.

"I don't believe you, Hairy Man, and what's more, I bet you won't show me!"

"You don't say," he said, and quick as a wink, the Hairy Man turned himself into a 'possum—right before my eyes!

As soon as I saw the 'possum, I didn't think about magic at all! Quick as a wink, I just grabbed him by his long tail and tossed him into the Hairy Man's bag! Then I tied the bag tight, carried it to the river, and tossed it in—just like Mama said to do.

As for me, I began to run all the way home so I could tell Mama all about the Hairy Man. Of course, my way took me back through the swamp. And wouldn't you know it! Suddenly, I spied the Hairy Man walkin' through the trees. And just as I knew he would, he was comin' right toward me! The very sight of him made my heart stop still!

I knew it was *him* all right! Who else would be covered with hair from head to toe? Who else would have fiery eyes reachin' out for me through the hairs on his face? And who else would be givin' me that great big smile—the one that spreads all the way up to his nose—showin' his teeth swimmin' in spit? So I knew it was *him* all right—but he wasn't wet!

"Hairy Man, now you just stop grinnin' at me!" I hollered.

But the Hairy Man didn't seem to hear me. He just kept grinnin' and walkin' toward me. And can you believe it? He was carryin' that big frog-catchin' bag of his—all tied up with rope—over his shoulder.

"Nothin's in that bag of his, 'cause this time he's gonna put *me* in it, sure enough!" I said to myself. So quick as a wink, I looked for the biggest tree I could find to climb. And I climbed it—but it was no way big enough!

"I sure am glad the Hairy Man has hooves for feet!" I reminded myself, "'cause no way can a cow make it up this tree!"

Now, the Hairy Man, he just kept on comin' toward me. And, as he came, he just kept on grinnin' at me. He was after me, sure enough—'cause he stopped right at the foot of my tree! He put down his bag, and he untied it.

"Why, Wiley, why are you sittin' way up there, boy?" he asked. "You must like to climb trees! Is that why you left your hound-dogs home today?" And he laughed his great laugh.

"I'm sittin' here, Hairy Man, 'cause you caught my daddy, and Mama told me to be sure you didn't catch me! But tell me, how did you ever get out of the bag I tossed into the river?"

The Hairy Man just looked at me and laughed his great laugh all over again. "Now, Wiley, you really didn't think you could drown me, did you, boy?" he asked. "Why, I just turned myself into the wind and blew myself right out of my bag! And so here I am—just as you see me—without a drop of water on me!"

"Now I'll just sit under your tree, Wiley, 'til your stomach cries out for food," he said. "You can't stay up there forever, you know! Or, if you'd like, you just climb down from your tree, boy, and I'll show you some magic!"

"No way will you ever get me out of this tree!" I declared. "I already told you my mama knows magic. And she will teach me all I want to know!"

I didn't know what to do next, so I just sat in my tree and thought about it. No way could my hound-dogs help me. And no way could Mama help me. I was too far from home for that!

And so I said, "Hairy Man, you're a good magician! I know, 'cause I've seen you turn yourself into a giraffe. I've seen you turn yourself into a 'gator. And I've even seen you turn yourself into a 'possum. And—since here you are again—I know you can turn yourself into the wind.

"But tell me, Hairy Man," I said, "are you good enough at magic to make somethin' really disappear? If you can do that, then you're a great magician—and not just a good one!"

"Boy, I can do that, too!" he declared.

"I don't believe you, Hairy Man, and what's more, I bet you won't show me!" I said.

"You don't say," he declared. "Now Wiley, do you see that bird's nest above your head?"

"I saw it when I was climbin' the tree," I said.

Quick as a wink, the Hairy Man gave a high-pitched whistle through his teeth. "Then where is it now, boy?" he asked.

I looked and looked—but, sure enough, the nest was gone! This was really great magic! But I didn't let the Hairy Man know it! Instead, I declared, "That's not real magic, Hairy Man! Why, even the wind can make a bird's nest disappear!"

Quick as a wink, the Hairy Man gave another high-pitched

whistle through his teeth and asked, "Now, Wiley, where is your shirt?"

I looked down, and—sure enough—my shirt was gone! This was really great magic, all right! But I didn't let the Hairy Man know it! Instead, I declared, "It's true you can make some things disappear, Hairy Man. But take my rope belt now—why, this belt of mine has magic power of its own! And your magic just can't be strong enough to make it disappear!"

"Oh, but it is, boy!" the Hairy Man declared. "In fact, with one great whistle from me, all the ropes 'round here will disappear!"

"I don't believe you, Hairy Man, and what's more, I bet you won't show me!" I said. "But you're sure good at braggin'!"

"You don't say," he declared. "Now, Wiley, look down at that magical belt of yours."

Before I could do it, quick as a wink, the Hairy Man took a deep breath and gave a great high-pitched whistle through his teeth.

"Now where's that belt you were tellin' me about, boy?" he asked. "In fact, I bet you can't find a rope anywhere!"

I looked down, and—sure enough—my rope belt was gone! And I saw the other rope was gone, too—the rope that ties the Hairy Man's bag! This was just the magic I'd hoped for. But I didn't let the Hairy Man know it! Instead, I declared, "Well, Hairy Man, my stomach tells me I'd best be gettin' home now."

"That's fine with me, Wiley! You just climb down from your tree, boy, and I'll show you some magic before you go home to your mama!"

I never looked to see what the Hairy Man did when my feet hit the ground. I probably could tell you, though, for I heard him swearin' like the Devil in that great voice of his! I know the trees were shakin' 'cause they're so scared of him! As for me, I ran all the way home so I could tell Mama all about the Hairy Man.

Now when I told Mama my tale, she said, "Well, Son, you've fooled the Hairy Man twice, and that's all to the good. First, you got him tied into his own frog-catchin' bag! And then you got him to make the rope that ties his bag disappear! Now, if we can fool him one more time, then he'll have to stop tryin' to catch you!"

"That would be real good, Mama! I sure hope you can find a way for me to do that!" I said.

"It isn't goin' to be easy, Son! But just leave me to my thinkin', and I'm sure a way will come to me," she declared.

While Mama was doin' her thinkin', I did my own thinkin'. "What if the Hairy Man busts into our house? What then?" I asked myself.

"I don't know what to do about that," I thought. "But I know what I can do—I can make sure he does no such thing!"

So I set to work. First, I tied one of my hound-dogs by our front door. Then I tied my other dog by our back door. Now I had only two more things to worry about. The Hairy Man could come in through the window, or he could climb up to our roof and come down the chimney.

The window took some thinkin'. I walked 'round the house lookin' for a way to block it up. I decided to use Mama's broom and my axe. The axe fit just so in the window, and once I sawed off part of Mama's broom handle, it fit too. I fixed 'em so they made a big X there. And I fixed 'em so they were good and tight—too tight for the Hairy Man to move 'em.

After the window, the chimney was easy. I just carried some big logs in from the woodpile and filled the wood bin. Then I built a great roarin' fire in the fireplace. "I hear the Hairy Man's used to fire, but I think he's too smart to roast himself!" I thought. I almost laughed at the idea, but I was too scared to do it. "I'd better not laugh 'til I have somethin' to laugh about!" I told myself.

I was lightin' the fire in the fireplace when Mama came to me and said, "Son, when you have your fire, bring me our piglet. He'll sleep in your bed, and you'll sleep in the loft."

"Good for you, Mama!" I declared. "I asked myself, 'What if the Hairy Man busts into our house? What then?' But I didn't know what to do about it!"

Any other time and I'd've hollered about such a thing as a pig in my bed! But not now! So I went out to our sow, took her piglet, and brought him inside so Mama could do her thing. She even covered him with my blanket! And now we were ready for the Hairy Man!

Mama sat next to the fireplace so she could keep the fire good and hot. As for me, I climbed up to the loft.

"Mama doesn't really think I'm gonna sleep on a night like this, does she?" I asked myself. "I wish I could stay downstairs with her! Up here, I'm sure I'll miss everythin'!"

That set me to thinkin' again! I decided I'd have to find a way to see out of the loft! So I walked 'round and 'round the place. I was lookin' for chinks or knotholes in the boards so I could look out and not miss anythin'.

Sure enough, I found good knotholes in boards facin' the front and back of the house. Now I could keep an eye on my hound-dogs! Then I even found a chink in one of the floorboards. And when I stretched out and put my eye to it, I could see Mama sittin' by the fire!

"Now I don't have to stay downstairs with Mama after all!" I told myself. "Besides, now that I think of it, I've really seen as much as I ever want to see of that old Hairy Man!"

Soon the wind began to howl, and the trees began to moan. "He must be comin' now!" I thought. So I walked to the front of the loft and looked down at our front door through the knothole. I could see my hound-dog all right! His fur was standin' straight up on his back just like a porky! His lips were drawn back from his teeth, and he was snarlin' like a mad dog!

Then I walked to the other end of the loft and looked down at our back door through the other good knothole. Sure enough, I could see my other hound-dog! His fur was standin' straight up on his back just like another porky! His lips were drawn back from his teeth, and he too was snarlin' like a mad dog! "Yes, the Hairy Man's comin' out of the swamp right now!" I said to myself.

So I walked back to the front of the loft and looked outside. I saw somethin' out front all right, but it was not the Hairy Man I saw! It was a critter like a mule—except he had horns on his head. He ran out of the swamp and past our house. "He's scared of the Hairy Man!" I said out loud. "The Hairy Man must be chasin' him!"

My dog tried to break loose and run after him, but I'd tied him too tight for that. "Stay here, dog!" I hollered. "You have to scare the Hairy Man! And he's comin' out of the swamp—*now*!"

But it was not the Hairy Man I saw next. I saw another critter. This one was smaller than a mule but bigger than a dog. He had a long snout and large, pointed teeth. He ran out of the swamp and past our house, snarlin' like a mad dog as he ran. "He's scared of the Hairy Man!" I said out loud. "The Hairy Man must be chasin' him, too!"

My dog tried to break loose and run after him. And this time, he did it! He ran after the second critter and chased him back into the swamp.

"Come, dog! Come," I hollered. "You have to scare the Hairy Man! And he is comin' out of the swamp—*now*!" But my dog did not come when I hollered.

"Now I'd better see what's goin' on out back," I thought. So I crossed to the back of the loft—and I got there just in time! My other hound-dog had broken loose, too, and he was chasin' after a critter that looked like a 'possum. I didn't know what it was, but I could see it was no 'possum he was chasin'!

"Come, dog! Come," I hollered. "You have to scare the Hairy Man! And he is comin' out of the swamp—*now*!" But my dog did not come when I hollered.

The wind was now howlin' even louder, and the trees were moanin' in a scary way. "The Hairy Man must be comin' *now*—sure enough!" I said to myself.

But I didn't see the Hairy Man. I heard him! He was clompin' on the roof right over my head—clompin' like a cow with those hooves of his! I couldn't see him 'cause I never did find a chink in the roof! He must've tried to come down the chimney and burned himself! When I heard him swearin' like the Devil in that great voice of his—why, I knew for sure it was no cow on our roof!

Next thing I heard—and even up here in the loft, I heard it!— the Hairy Man was poundin' on our front door. "Well, I was right about one thing," I thought. "The Hairy Man's too smart to roast himself!" I almost laughed at the idea, but I was still too scared to do it. "I'd better not laugh 'til I have somethin' to laugh about!" I told myself.

I rushed to the front of the loft and looked out through the knot-hole. I wanted to holler, "Come, dog! Come!" But it was too late for that! Sure enough—there was the Hairy Man! And he was standin' right at our front door!

Even through the knothole I could see it was *him* all right! For who else is covered with hair from head to toe? Of course, from where I was standin' in the loft—I couldn't see his fiery eyes, and I couldn't see his broad grin and his big white teeth that are always swimmin' in spit. But I knew they were there all right!

"Open your door, Mama!" I heard the Hairy Man holler. "I've come for your baby!"

"You just try and get him, Hairy Man!" Mama hollered back. (She was hollerin' at him through the closed door.)

"Mama, now you just give your baby to me, or I'll bite you! And my bite is poison!" hollered the Hairy Man.

"You bite me, Hairy Man, and I'll take a great big bite out of you! And my bite is poison too!" Mama hollered back.

"Mama, now you just give your baby to me, or I'll have lightnin' strike your house! And you'll have only a pile of ashes left once that fire dies out!" hollered the Hairy Man.

"You just try that, Hairy Man!" Mama hollered back. "I can fight fire with milk!"

"Mama, now you just give your baby to me, or I'll starve you to death!" hollered the Hairy Man. "I'll have the sun drink up the water in your spring! I'll dry up the milk in your cow! And I'll send an army of hungry boll weevils to eat all your cotton!"

"Now, Hairy Man, I know you can't be that mean!" Mama hollered back.

"Oh, yes I can, Mama!" the Hairy Man hollered. "You keep your baby from me, and you'll know I'm the meanest man you've ever heard of!"

"All right then, Hairy Man," Mama hollered back. "If I promise to give you my baby, will you promise to leave everythin' else that belongs to me alone? And will you promise to go away from here and never come back?"

"You have my promises, and you have my word that I'll keep 'em!" hollered the Hairy Man. "And even the Devil keeps his word!"

Finally, Mama must have opened the door. For I had to listen hard to hear her say, "Then you can have my baby, Hairy Man! So come right on in and take him!"

I saw the Hairy Man step inside our house. So I quickly stretched out on the floor and put my eye to the chink in the floorboards. Now I could see Mama and the Hairy Man right below me!

Mama said, "Hairy Man, my baby is right over there! You can go and get him yourself!"

Mama was pointin' to my bed! I held my breath! My heart stopped still! "My mama is really somethin' to see!" I said to myself. "There's not another one of her anywhere about! And as for me—why, I'm sure glad I'm up here and *he's* down there!"

The Hairy Man looked at my bed and laughed his great laugh. Then he walked right up to it, threw back the blanket, and stopped laughin'. "Why, Mama, your baby is nothin' but a piglet!" he cried.

"Why, of course he's a piglet!" Mama declared. "I never told you it was anythin' else, did I? But this piglet was my baby, and now he's all yours! So take him, and be off with you! As you told me, 'even the Devil keeps his word!'"

Now, the Hairy Man got so mad at Mama he almost popped!

He stomped 'round the room—pokin' here and pokin' there—and hollerin' so loud I'm sure he woke the dead! Mama knew and I knew he hoped to find me hidin' in a corner or under a piece of furniture. Why, he even poked 'round in the wood bin! The more he stomped, the less he found. And the less he found, the more he hollered. I began to fear for our house! The roof and the walls were shakin' mightily, and I feared they would come down in a great heap. "If the Hairy Man doesn't get out of here, it will be the end of Mama and me!" I said to myself.

The Hairy Man was still stompin' and hollerin' when he went back to my bed, grabbed the piglet, and ran out the door. I ran to the front of the loft and looked outside. It was the last I saw of him! He was stompin' through the swamp with such fury that he was knockin' down everythin' in his path. And he was still hollerin' so loud I could hear him clear as day.

I watched the great trees fall before him, and a great sadness fell upon me. Suddenly, I thought of how many times I've looked 'round at all the great trees and listened to the great silence in the swamp. And I thought of how I've liked bein' alone there, alone with the trees and the silence.

"I don't want to think about that old Hairy Man!" I said to myself. So I turned my back to the wall, and I sat down to wait 'til I could no longer hear him hollerin'.

At last, all was quiet, so I climbed down from the loft.

"Did we fool the Hairy Man three times, Mama?" I asked.

"Sure enough, Son," she declared. "We did just that! So don't you go worryin' about that old Hairy Man, Wiley! He can't ever catch you, so he'll never bother you again!"

Didn't I tell you? My mama is really somethin'! There's not another one of her anywhere about!

And when I thought about what Mama did to the Hairy Man—and what I did to him—I laughed out loud! I knew I could laugh now, 'cause I really had somethin' to laugh about!

The Shepherd Who Understood Animal Speech

Hispanic folklore was brought to New Mexico and southern Colorado by Spanish explorers and later Spanish and Mexican settlers. The wilderness environment helped them preserve their oral literature, because they lived in cultural isolation for centuries. With no radio or television to entertain them and with few books, they depended on the stories of their childhood, enhanced by their own creative imagination, for their entertainment.

"The Shepherd Who Understood Animal Speech" was collected from a Hispanic storyteller in New Mexico. The tale is one of the most popular in folklore. Geza Roheim, in *Fire in the Dragon*, relates a Hungarian version that is almost identical to the following version, until the concluding material.

Stith Thompson, who relates the skeleton version in *The Folktale*, states that the tale originated in India, where it can be found in the *Ramayana* (200 B.C.–A.D. 200). Other sources include both the Indian and the Chinese versions of the *Jataka* (Buddhist tales published c. A.D. 400–599); the Persian *Tuti-Nameh* (Hindu tales from the early 1300s); *A Thousand and One Nights* (*Arabian Nights,* ancient tales from Arabia, Persia, and India, published in Egypt in about 1450); the *Gesta Romanorum* (collected in England early in the 1300s and published in Germany late in the 1400s); and the Brothers Grimm's *Kinder-und Hausmärchen* (*Folk Tales for Children and the Home,* published in Germany in 1857).

Oral versions have been found throughout both Europe and Africa as well as in India and the Middle East. The tale traveled with those who loved to tell and to read it, reaching Spain and crossing the Atlantic to enter Mexico and the other countries of Latin America. The ending of the following version of this tale may be a relatively late addition.

The theme of the wife's role in her marriage has probably been popular as long as tales have been told about married couples. Most of these tales concern either the wife's fidelity or her intelligence. However, the following tale examines the nature of the relationship between a husband and his wife, explaining—with delightful humor—who should be the dominant partner. The tale is interesting because, while this issue is universal, the nature of its resolution reflects the values of a particular culture at a particular time. The tale is appealing because today this issue is important in our own culture.

THE SHEPHERD
WHO UNDERSTOOD ANIMAL SPEECH

A young man lived alone with his mother until he reached the age when he could set out on his own in order to make his way in the world. He traveled on and on until he came to a prosperous ranch. He wondered if he could find work there.

When he approached the owner of the ranch, the man said, "Young man, you look like just the type of person who will care for my sheep as I would care for them myself! Therefore, if you will agree to my terms, I will be delighted to employ you as my shepherd. You will have a thousand sheep under your supervision. If they do well, many lambs will be born, and I will give you eighty percent of those lambs as your own property. Now, tell me, what do you think of my proposition?"

To these words, the young man replied, "Your terms bring joy to my heart, and I will be happy to be your shepherd. My mother lives alone and, until now, she has had me to help her. The money that I can earn from my own flock of sheep will make her life easier!"

So it came to pass that the young man began work as a shepherd. Spring passed into summer, and summer was turning into autumn when, one day, the shepherd noticed a forest fire burning at the edge of his pastureland. He was close enough to hear a strange hissing sound, so he walked over to the burning trees to see if he could find the source of the sound. He discovered that a small snake had taken refuge in a tree that had now begun to burn. The hissing was the snake's call for help.

The shepherd quickly found a stick and held it out for the snake to climb upon, which it did. However, the snake then proceeded to coil itself around the arm of the shepherd. Frightened, the shepherd tried to pry it loose, but the more he tugged at it, the tighter it wrapped itself around him.

Finally, the shepherd headed back toward the ranch buildings in order to get help. It was then that the snake spoke to him.

"Young man, do not be afraid of me! You have saved my life! And for that greatest of gifts, I will give you a gift in return! So come with me to visit my mother, that she may give you your reward! We will find her at home, in her cave. It lies nestled among the hills, and I will take you there."

From her position on his arm, the snake directed the shepherd's steps by pointing her head. And so it came to pass that the young man came to a great cave. As he faced the black space that yawned before him, the young man shuddered with fear.

"Young man, do not be afraid of this cave. And when you see my mother, do not be afraid of her either! I must warn you that she will look very large and threatening to you because, after all, she is the mother of all snakes. However, she will not harm you!

"Now, when I tell my mother how you saved my life, she will offer you money as your reward. However, you must reject this offer," declared the snake. "Instead, you must ask her to give you the ability to understand the speech of animals. This is a far greater gift, and you will profit from it! Now, my mother will be reluctant to give you such a great gift, but if you hold to your request, your good deed will bring you this reward!

"The time has come when I must let go of your arm. Hold on to my tail as we go into the recesses of the cave," commanded the snake, "and I will bring you to my mother."

And so it came to pass that the shepherd followed the snake into the dark recesses of the cave where, as soon as his eyes became accustomed to the dim light, he saw a great snake. Her head was resting quietly among her great coils.

When the little snake explained how the shepherd had saved her life, the mother snake said to him, "Young man, you have saved my daughter's life! Money is of greatest value among those who walk the earth on two legs. Ask for as much as you wish, and it is yours!"

To these words, the shepherd replied, "Thank you for your generous gift, Mother! However, I do not place such great value on money. What I ask for is the gift of being able to understand the speech of animals!"

"You ask for the one gift I would choose not to give you!" the mother snake replied. "However, you would not know that I possessed such a gift to give if my daughter had not told you. Therefore, I give you this gift with all my heart!

"But you should know what you are receiving, lest you change your mind! This is a gift for those who have the courage and wisdom to possess it! You have shown that you have courage by rescuing my daughter from the fiery flame's tongue. As for wisdom, time will tell whether you possess that as well! Now, are you willing to take the risk that you are as wise as you are courageous?" asked the mother snake.

"I am!" the shepherd responded.

"Then open your mouth and touch your tongue to mine so that I may pass my gift along to you!"

The young man thought to himself, "Touching that great snake's forked tongue will take more courage than rescuing her daughter from the fire's flame!" However, he kept his mind on acquiring the special gift and did what the mother snake required of him.

"Now, young man, you possess this greatest of all gifts!" declared the mother snake. "I have told you that you will be called upon to be as wise as you are courageous. Before you leave, I should tell you why. If you tell anyone about this gift, you will die! Now go with my blessing!"

So it came to pass that the shepherd left the cave that was nestled in the hills and made his way back to the pasture where he had left his flocks. Now he could understood their bleating, and he heard how annoyed they were that he had abandoned them.

Time passed. One day, when the shepherd was letting his flocks graze in a wild area, it came to pass that he heard the conversation of two crows that were cawing away in a nearby tree.

"That shepherd would not have to watch sheep if he knew what we know!" the first crow cawed.

"Why, you can be sure of that!" the second crow cawed. "As I recall, long ago we observed a thief dig a hole in the earth where that black ram is sleeping and bury his hoard of treasure in it!"

"Certainly, we have never seen him come back for it!" the first crow cawed. "Therefore, unless we are mistaken, it is all still there, right where he left it!"

With these words, the two crows flew out of the tree. As for the shepherd, he looked around for a way to mark the spot where the black ram was sleeping. As luck would have it, the pastureland had rocks scattered here and there. And so it came to pass that the shepherd found a distinctive-looking rock, which he now picked up and put to this use.

When the sun next made the day light, the shepherd returned to this pasture with his flocks. This time, he had a pick and a spade with him. While his animals grazed, he dug away at the earth. Sure enough, at the base of a deep hole he found an old metal trunk! With his pick, he pried open the lid, and there—to his amazement and joy!—he found as many gold coins as the trunk could hold.

The shepherd filled his pockets with coins and then carefully concealed the hole so that his treasure would be there for him when he returned. When the day came to an end, he returned to the ranch with his flocks. He approached his employer and said, "I have enjoyed working for you, but the time has come for me to return to my mother. Therefore, I would appreciate it if you would now give me the wages you owe me."

To these words, his employer replied, "I will be sorry to lose you, young man, for you have cared well for my many flocks! However, I know that your mother will be happy to have you back with her, and what you have earned here will enrich her life. Therefore, farewell and good luck to you!"

The young man traveled on and on until he finally returned home. Of course, he brought her the coins that filled his pockets.

When the sun next brightened the earth, the young man took two of his mother's grain sacks and told her that he was going back to the ranch for grain. In the village, he bought a donkey. He traveled on and on until he came to the pasture where the thief had buried the treasure. He reopened the hole, filled the grain bags with as many of the gold coins as they would hold, concealed the hole once again, and made his way back to his mother's house. He then dug a hole in the dirt floor of their kitchen and buried the coins in it.

Each day, when the sun began to brighten the earth, the young man would repeat his journey to the pasture. Each day, he would fill the grain bags with as many of the gold coins as they would hold. He would then conceal the hole once again and make his way back to his mother's house, where he would bury the coins in the hole that he had dug in the kitchen floor. Finally, it came to pass that the young man had removed all of the thief's treasure to his mother's house.

Once his mother asked him, "Tell me, my son, how is it that you have acquired all of this gold?"

"If I could tell you, Mother, I would do so. However, I cannot reveal to anyone how I happened to come upon it. And I must ask you to seal your lips when anyone asks you about our new wealth. However, you have my word that the coins really do belong to me! I did not steal them!"

His mother did not ask him again, and whenever she went into the village, she kept her lips sealed.

So it came to pass that the shepherd became one of the wealthiest men in his part of the state. He now owned large herds of cattle, many flocks of sheep, and all of the land on which they grazed. He cared for his mother until she died, and then he married.

In time, the man's lovely wife became pregnant. Nevertheless, she still liked to accompany her husband whenever he would ride out to check on his animals. The day came when the man noticed that his wife and her mare were lagging far behind him. When he rode back to her, his horse neighed to hers, saying, "Why do you not keep up with me? Is it because you will soon give birth?"

"Yes," the wife's mare neighed in reply. "But it is more than that. I have to transport the four of us, while you only have the two of you to worry about!"

The man heard the response of his wife's mare and could not help but burst into laughter.

"Why are you laughing, dear one?" his wife asked him.

The man suddenly stopped laughing as he remembered the mother snake's warning. "Believe me, my dear, if I could tell you, I would do so. But I cannot."

"That answer may be good enough for you, dear one," his wife responded, "but I assure you that it is not good enough for me! If you love me, of course you will tell me. And if you still refuse to tell me, then of course you no longer love me! So think about it, and let me know what you decide."

Soon it came to pass that the man went off with his dog in order to consider what he should do. "I love my wife so much," he confided to his dog, "that if she continues to pester me about my laughter, I will have no choice but to tell her my secret! I will die because of it. But at least I will have proved that my love for her is so great that I was willing to pay this price!"

The man's dog heard his master's words, and his heart flooded with sorrow. When they returned to the ranch house, they came upon the family's rooster.

The rooster was strutting about in the yard with his hens in tow, and he looked at the dog and said, "What in the world has happened to you? You look as if you have lost your best friend!"

"Not yet—but I am about to!" the dog replied. "My mistress wants to know why my master laughed one day when they were out riding together. And if my master tells her, he will die! My mistress insists that if my master loves her, he will tell her. And so he has no choice!"

"That's rubbish, pure and simple!" the rooster replied. "I am surprised that your master puts up with his wife's nonsense! He has but one wife and, apparently, he lacks the wisdom to handle her! As for me, I have fifteen hens to call my own, and I can handle every one of them! When they raise a ruckus, why, I just stand my ground! And, believe me, my hens do whatever I tell them to do!"

Now the man as well as his dog heard what his rooster had to say. And so it came to pass that the man went into the ranch house in order to find his wife. He then took off his overalls and said, "I have thought about my laughter and my love for you, and this is what I have decided. I want you to take off your dress and put on my pants!"

"Why in the world should I do such a thing?" his wife asked. "I have no wish to wear your pants! In our family, the man wears the pants, and his wife wears a dress! That's the sign of who really runs the home!"

"It is true that up until now, that is the way we have handled things in our marriage. However, if you want to know why I laughed—even after I have said that I cannot tell you—then you are in charge of our home. And then it is only fitting and proper that you should wear the pants in our family. As for me, why, I will wear your dress!"

To these words, the man's wife laughed and said, "All right, dear one. If it comes to that, you do not have to tell me why you laughed! I really know how much you love me! And I much prefer you to wear the pants in our family!"

So it came to pass that the man never had to reveal his secret. And he and his wife lived happily together to the end of their days!

Rip Van Winkle

Washington Irving was the first great American author. He was born in New York City in 1783, shortly after the end of the War of Independence, and he was named after George Washington. Irving began his career as a writer in 1802, with "Letters of Jonathan Oldstyle, Gent(leman)," a satire that appeared in the *Morning Chronicle* newspaper. He was admired by Hawthorne and Poe, who used his work as the model from which they fashioned the genre of the short story, and in England by Scott, Coleridge, Byron, and Dickens. Although Irving wrote poems, plays, and shorter fiction, his fascination with the past is evident in his popular works of legend and biography, including *The Alhambra: A Series of Tales and Sketches of the Moors and Spaniards* (1832) and a five-volume *Life of George Washington* (1855–1859). Irving's most famous work, *The Sketch Book of Geoffrey Crayon, Gent(leman),* which includes his two most famous stories, "Rip Van Winkle" and "The Legend of Sleepy Hollow," was published in England in 1820.

Irving's tales show the influence of Sir Walter Scott, his literary mentor, both in their subject (old legends depicted in a local setting) and in their style (emphasis on realistic, painterly detail). In his most famous tales, such as "Rip Van Winkle," Irving takes German folktales and legends and transplants them into his own region, the Hudson River valley.

Legends and folktales about people who go to sleep and wake up years later are popular in folklore. "Sleeping Beauty," in the form of Brunhild's story in *Sigurd the Volsung,* is one of the oldest recorded legends in Western literature. In Germany, other legends involve a group of dead soldiers who reside in a cave or inside a hill and periodically haunt the battlefield on which they died.

A medieval version of the sleeping king legend has become attached to King Frederick I (Barbarossa) of Prussia (1657–1713), who was said to slumber with his men inside the Kyffhäuser, a mountain southeast of the Hartz Mountains in Saxony. If the time came when his people would be in desperate need of him, Barbarossa and his men would return and rescue them. Irving's source for the idea of "Rip Van Winkle" is a version of this German *volkssage* (folk-legend), recorded by Johann Carl Cristoph Nachtigall and entitled "Peter Klaus the Goatherd."

Irving's "Rip Van Winkle" has amused readers for more than 175 years. The husband who is dominated by a nagging wife is a favorite comic figure in world folklore. Rip's attitude toward the loss of twenty years of his life is also comic in its irony, and it stands in marked contrast to the attitudes of other famous characters in folklore who lose many years of their lives.

However, Rip is more than a comic figure. He symbolizes people who ignore important situations in order to avoid dealing with them. Therefore, while we laugh at Rip, he can help us gain important insights into our own attitudes and behavior.

The magical drink, most often seen in the form of a love potion, is a popular motif in folklore and in literature. Because it enables characters to behave as they wish instead of as they should, it symbolizes subconscious, and therefore uncontrolled, behavior.

The following version is a retelling of Irving's tale as it could have been told in the oral tradition of the Hudson River valley.

RIP VAN WINKLE

Long ago, in a timeworn, weather-beaten house of yellow brick in an old Dutch village at the foot of the Catskill Mountains in New York, there lived a man by the name of Rip Van Winkle. Rip was a meek and pleasant man who was a loyal husband to his wife and a good neighbor to those who lived in his village. All of the village children loved him and followed him wherever he went, for he made himself part of their world. He made their toys, taught them the great children's games, played ball with them, and told them exciting stories about witches, ghosts, and Indians.

Only one thing was wrong with Rip Van Winkle's personality. He refused to do any job that would bring money to his family. It was not that he was lazy, for he would hike for hours with his shotgun, trudging through woodland and swampland, just to shoot a few wild pigeons or squirrels. It was not that he was weak of limb, for he was the first to help others with the most difficult or tiring labors, such as building stone fences or husking corn. It was not that he was impatient, for he would sit and fish all day without a bite. It was not that he was selfish, for he would help the women of his village by doing the odd jobs and running the errands that their husbands avoided by postponing them. It was just that Rip found everyone else's responsibilities to be more pleasing than his own.

Rip had no interest in his own farm, and consequently, weeds made their home in his fields; his cow made its home everywhere but where it was wanted, and the stones in his fences refused to stick together and perform their function. In fact, Rip's farm was a mere patch of what it had been when it had belonged to his father. It had become a patch of corn here and a patch of potatoes there—and that was the end of it!

Rip was happy to live from hand to mouth and from day to day. The future meant nothing to him. He lived in the present, spending his time as he chose and loving the pleasure of each minute.

Only one thing was wrong with Rip Van Winkle's life. His wife refused to accept his personality. She complained for ten minutes of every hour about his laziness. She complained for the next ten minutes of every hour about his idleness. She complained for the next ten minutes of every hour about his carelessness. And she complained for the last thirty minutes of every hour about the disaster that he was bringing upon their children and her.

Rip could do little to cope with his wife. He usually shrugged his shoulders, shook his head, and looked up at the ceiling, as if asking some invisible soul sitting in the rafters to sympathize with his sorry plight. Then he would leave the house with his one constant companion, his dog Wolf.

What was bad became worse with time, and Rip could only find peace in the woods with his shotgun and his dog. There, he would either hunt squirrels or sit beneath a tree and converse with Wolf.

It came to pass that, toward the end of a beautiful autumn day, Rip found himself high in the Catskills, on a grassy knoll far above the woods and farther above the great Hudson River. He was preparing to descend, and he was thinking about how dark it would be as he made his way back to his village and his nagging wife when, suddenly, he heard a voice call, "Rip Van Winkle! Oh, Rip Van Winkle!"

Rip, suddenly aware of the loneliness of his location, asked Wolf, "Did you hear someone call my name? Surely, I imagined it! For who would be up here at this time of day?"

Once again, Rip was preparing to descend when he heard the voice call, "Rip Van Winkle! Oh, Rip Van Winkle!" This time, Wolf also heard the voice and responded by bristling the fur on his back and giving a low growl.

As Rip looked around apprehensively, he noticed that a strange figure was slowly making his way over the rocks. His body was bent low from the weight that he carried upon his back.

"One of the villagers must be coming after us!" Rip told Wolf. "Let us see why he has come so far so late in the day."

So it came to pass that Rip and Wolf went to greet the man. However, when they came face to face with him, he was no one whom they had ever seen before. In fact, the man was like no one who lived in their own time.

The stranger appeared to be a bearded Dutchman from long, long ago. He was dressed in antique Dutch clothing, and it was a keg that he was carrying on his back. As soon as Rip came up to him, he motioned for Rip to help him with his load and to follow him up the narrow, dry, and rocky streambed.

Rip viewed the stranger with some distrust, but nevertheless he was his usual helpful self to one in need. And it came to pass that, as the two men silently clambered up the streambed, Rip heard the rumble of what sounded like distant thunder.

Finally, Rip and his companion reached what must have been the old Dutchman's destination, a small amphitheater carved by nature from the rocky mountainsides. There, a group of similarly ancient and bearded Dutchmen, also dressed in antique clothing, were playing a type of bowling game with great seriousness of purpose. And Rip discovered that the sound that he had heard was the rumble of their bowling balls as it echoed off the mountain cliffs like thunder.

The ancient men stopped their play when they saw Rip, and they gazed at him with such coldness that his heart flooded with fear. Meanwhile, Rip's companion distributed some kind of liquid from the keg, and the men drank it before returning to their game. Once the men ignored him, Rip relaxed and even ventured to take a taste of their beverage. It was so delicious that he returned for repeated drinks until the drink eventually put him into a deep sleep.

It came to pass that, when Rip awoke, he found that he was back down on the grassy knoll where he had first seen the ancient Dutchman. However, now it was a beautiful, bright morning.

"Surely, I have not spent the night up here!" Rip exclaimed to himself. "That must have been a powerful potion to have done this to me," he added, with an unusual prick of shame. "How will I ever explain this situation to my wife?"

Rip looked around for his shotgun, but all he could see was a rusted old gun nearby. As for Wolf, Rip's trusty dog was nowhere in sight.

"Those wily old Dutchmen certainly got a good bargain!" Rip exclaimed. "Their potion for my shotgun! But surely Wolf refused to go with them!" he added with dawning apprehension.

And with these words, Rip whistled for Wolf—but Wolf did not appear. Then Rip shouted for Wolf—but Wolf still did not appear. The mountains helped Rip by repeating his whistles and his shouts, but still Wolf did not appear.

Rip now became determined to return to the amphitheater in the hope of finding the ancient Dutchmen and recovering his dog and his shotgun. However, as soon as he began to rise to his feet, he found that he could hardly move. "This will teach me never to spend the night in the mountains!" he exclaimed to himself. "My body is so stiff at every joint that I feel like a rusty tin man!"

And so it came to pass that Rip, slowly and painfully, made his way back toward the narrow, dry, and rocky streambed. However, to his surprise, a tumultuous mountain stream now blocked his ascent.

Nevertheless, Rip was still intent upon returning to the amphitheater in the hope of finding the ancient Dutchmen and recovering his dog and his shotgun. He therefore proceeded, very slowly and very painfully, to wend his way up through the thicket of undergrowth that lined the sides of the stream.

Rip reached the top only to find that, where yesterday's opening into the amphitheater had been, today there was a deep mountain lake. He could see that the stream that had blocked his ascent cascaded down a high, broad, and solid expanse of rocky cliff, flooding this basin before it continued down the mountainside.

At a loss as to how to proceed, once again Rip whistled for Wolf. But Wolf did not appear. Then Rip shouted for Wolf—but Wolf still did not appear. The mountains helped Rip by repeating his whistles and his shouts—but still Wolf did not appear.

Then it came to pass that Rip said to himself, "My stomach is so empty that I feel as if I have not eaten in years! The sun is already high overhead. As much as I would like to reclaim my dog and my shotgun, I must now make my way back to the village! But how will I ever explain this situation to my wife?"

Rip picked up the rusty shotgun, rested it on his sore shoulder, and with anxiety flooding his heart, began his mountain descent.

On the outskirts of the village, he encountered many people whom he had never seen before. He was surprised at this, since he knew everyone who lived in his small village. He was even more surprised to see that everyone whom he met was dressed in a fashion that he had never seen.

However, Rip was most surprised by how these strangers reacted to him. They were as surprised by the sight of him as he was by the sight of them. They would stand and stare at him and stroke their chins. Finally, annoyance flooded Rip's heart, so that he stood and stared back at them, stroking his own chin. And so it came to pass that Rip discovered the greatest surprise of all. To his amazement, he found that his beard was now a foot longer than it had been yesterday!

As Rip entered his village, his situation became even more strange. Everywhere he looked, more houses lined broader streets than had been there yesterday, and new houses had replaced those that had been old. Everywhere he looked, more people walked to and fro than had walked there yesterday, and new faces had replaced those that were familiar. Finally, everywhere he looked, new names had replaced the old names that had been there yesterday and that he knew.

Rip's heart now overflowed with anxiety. "Where am I?" he asked himself. "This is not my village, and yet it is just where my village ought to be! The Catskill Mountains are standing just where they ought to be. The Hudson River is flowing just where it ought to be. But what has happened to the world I know? And what has happened to *me*?

"That must have been a powerful potion to have done this to me," Rip thought, with an unusual prick of shame. "How will I ever explain this situation to my wife?"

The thought of Dame Van Winkle led Rip to search for his own house. His heart flooded with relief when he found that it was just where it ought to have been. However, it looked as if no one had lived in it for many years. The roof had collapsed; the glass in the windows was broken; and the doors hung loose from their hinges. Rip entered his house only to find that the interior was no better than the exterior. It was abandoned and empty. A mangy dog that looked like Wolf was wandering about. However, when Rip called to him by name, the dog snarled and walked away.

"How could you already have forgotten me?" Rip asked the retreating animal.

Rip now hastened to the village inn. However, he found a hotel where the inn had stood. He found a flagpole where the great maple tree had stood. And he saw a sign that displayed the picture of a man labeled "General Washington" where the sign that had displayed the picture of His Majesty George the Third had stood. Moreover, he found that, where his friends had gathered yesterday, today a man was distributing handouts about the heroes of 1776 and forthcoming elections.

"What has happened to the world I know? And what has happened to *me*?" Rip asked himself once again.

Meanwhile, Rip's unusual appearance was causing a crowd to gather around him. "Are you a Federal or a Democrat?" asked some of the townsfolk. "Are you here with your shotgun in order to incite a riot?" others asked.

"Oh no, gentlemen!" Rip exclaimed. "I intend no harm. I live here, and I am a loyal subject of King George the Third! I have come here in search of my friends."

Some of the townsfolk angrily shouted, "The man is a Tory! The man is a spy!" However, others asked Rip, "For whom are you looking? Tell us who your friends are!"

Rip thought for a moment and then replied, "Where is the man who owns the inn that should be where this hotel now stands? Find him for me, and he will tell you who I am!"

"You will find him in the graveyard!" a voice exclaimed. "He has been living there for the past eighteen years! Even the wooden tombstone that once marked his grave has disintegrated."

"And where is the schoolmaster, for he was his friend and mine?" Rip asked.

"He was a general in the war," someone replied, "and he is now a member of Congress."

Rip desperately fought the feeling of loneliness that was flooding his heart. "Do any of you know Rip Van Winkle?" he asked the assembled townsfolk.

To these words, a number of voices called out, "Of course we do! There he is, leaning against that tree!"

Rip turned and spied a man whom he viewed as his mirror image, a man who looked as lazy and ragged as he knew himself to be. And seeing that Rip Van Winkle was leaning against the tree, Rip no longer knew who he himself could be.

Before he could ask another question, someone asked, "Now, stranger, tell us your name!"

"I cannot do that!" Rip exclaimed. "I no longer know who I am! I see myself leaning against that tree, and if he is I, then I have no idea who I am!"

Unsettled by Rip's reply, the townsfolk began to murmur among themselves about how to go about protecting themselves and their loved ones from this strange old man with his decrepit shotgun. Fortunately, it came to pass that a young woman, carrying a child in her arms, pushed through the crowd in order to get a look at the stranger. When her child screamed in terror at the stranger's face, his mother replied, "Hush, Rip! Do not be afraid of the old man! He will not hurt you!"

Hearing the name of the child, Rip said to the young woman, "Young mother, please tell me your name and the name of your father."

"My name is Judith," the young woman replied, "and my father was Rip Van Winkle, that most unfortunate man! He went off with his shotgun and his dog twenty years ago—when I was just a little girl—and he has never been seen from that time to this! His dog returned home without him."

To these words, Rip replied, "Tell me, then, young mother, where is your own mother?"

"Oh, she died in a fit of anger at a peddler!" the young woman replied.

"Ah, my dear child!" Rip exclaimed. "I am your long-lost father! I was young when I left, and I am old as I return. But, then and now, I am still Rip Van Winkle!"

At the sound of these words, an old woman limped forth from the assembled group, studied Rip's face, and exclaimed, "So you are! You are Rip himself! Welcome home, stranger! Welcome home, old neighbor! Where in the world have you been for twenty years?"

Rip could tell his short tale in only a few words, since twenty years had passed as one night to him. Meanwhile, the townsfolk listened to his tale in silent disbelief. Fortunately, it came to pass that they spied the village elder making his way down the street.

"Come here!" they called. "Tell us who this man is! And tell us if his tale makes any sense!"

The respected old gentleman approached Rip, studied his face, and then exclaimed, "Why you are Rip himself! Welcome home, stranger! Welcome home, old neighbor! Where in the world have you been for twenty years?"

When Rip had repeated his tale, the village elder replied, "Of course, that is exactly what happened! Long ago, my father, who kept the history of our village, told me that the Catskill Mountains are haunted by Hendrick Hudson and his crew of the *Half Moon*. Once every twenty years, they return here because it is they who discovered the great river that bears Hudson's name as well as the country that lines its banks—and so they take a paternal interest in it!

"In fact, my father once hiked into a small amphitheater carved by nature from the rocky mountainsides and suddenly came upon these ancient, bearded Dutchmen as they played a type of bowling game. Even I myself heard the rumble of their bowling balls one bright summer afternoon. The sound echoed off the mountain cliffs like thunder," the village elder declared.

Satisfied with this explanation, the townsfolk returned to their other interests. As for Rip, his daughter took him home to live with her on her farm, where she employed her brother. Rip saw that his son was more than the mirror image of his own young self. His son's attitude toward the farm chores was that of Rip himself when he was his son's age.

It now came to pass that Rip returned to his old pursuits. Since the sight of his timeworn, weather-beaten friends made his heart flood with sadness, he made new friends among the younger generation. And now that he was old enough to be genuinely free of responsibility, he spent much of his time in the center of town, where he came to be respected as one of the town fathers. However, if you were to ask him, Rip would tell you that he was less impressed with his freedom from King George the Third's tyranny than he was with his freedom from Dame Van Winkle's tyranny! In fact, whenever anyone mentioned her name, Rip would automatically shrug his shoulders, shake his head, and look up at the ceiling, as if thanking some invisible soul sitting in the rafters for his deliverance.

So it came to pass that, in this fashion, Rip Van Winkle lived happily to the natural end of his days. To the end of time, some of the townsfolk doubted the reality of his story. However, the old Dutch inhabitants of the town came to think of Hendrick Hudson, his crew of the *Half Moon*, and the rumble of their bowling balls whenever the rolling sound of thunder would accompany a summer rainstorm.

And, from that day to this, many a husband and many a wife have wished that they, too, could steal a drink of Hendrick Hudson's potion!

Giant,
the Fire-Bringer

The Tsimshian people, who tell the following myth, live in Canada along the coast of British Columbia and on its coastal islands. They have always lived in a richly endowed environment, with their climate moderated by the Japan Current and their food readily available in nearby forests, meadows, and waters. Therefore, they have had leisure time in which to develop an elaborate religious and social system, accompanied by beautiful arts and crafts.

With a ready supply of cedar, spruce, and pine, the Tsimshian have been a people of house-builders, canoe-makers, and wood-carvers. These skills have been handed down from fathers and uncles to their sons and nephews. Knowledge of their tribal heritage has always been an integral part of the Tsimshian people's arts and crafts, so that their myths speak out from their totem poles, their doorposts, and their decorated storage boxes, as well as from their masks, rattles, pipes, and serving dishes.

The following myth reflects many aspects of traditional Tsimshian life. For example, like other Pacific Northwest coastal peoples, the Tsimshian have traditionally had a stratified society. Their chief has been at the top of their economic and social ladder, having earned this prestigious position through his wealth. Traditionally, the chief's wealth was inherited, although it might also have been accumulated through the efforts of his extended family. It was measured in terms of goods, such as woven baskets and blankets, animal pelts, decorative copper shields, dried fish, and fish oil.

Traditionally, the chief owned the great house in which many others lived as well as the fishing areas and the great war canoes. Therefore, he provided work and protection, and people chose to live in his community.

In addition, like other Pacific Northwest coastal peoples, the Tsimshian loved to have large gatherings that featured feasting, dancing, and singing. Historically, the Tsimshian gained as much renown for their great potlatch feasts as they did for their totem poles. The fame of these feasts rests on the host's distribution of gifts to all of his guests. A man could spend years amassing the goods that he gave away at a potlatch, and he might only give two or three potlatches during the course of his life.

Fortunately, the potlatches rotated from one wealthy man to another in the community, so that much of what a man gave away in one potlatch he would receive, in equivalent value, in others.

Raven is the greatest figure in the mythology of the Pacific Northwest coastal peoples. Different peoples have given Raven different names and different forms. For example, he is called "Giant" by the Tsimshian; "He Whose Voice Is Obeyed" by the Haida; and "Raven" by the Tlingit. Among the Kwakiutl peoples, he is called "Chief" by the Omeatl; "Real Chief" by the Hemaskas; "Great Inventor" by the Kwekwaxawe; and "Greedy One" by the Meskwa. In Haida and Tlingit myths, Raven actually has the form of a raven. However, in Tsimshian and Kwakiutl myths, Raven is a being who is able to fly whenever he wears his Raven blanket as a cloak.

Giant is both a culture hero and a trickster. Like his counterpart in other cultures throughout the world, he confronts an adversary who is more powerful than he is, and he wins by using his creative intelligence. Like many other culture heroes, he can look like an animal and yet have human thoughts, speech, and actions. This close relationship between human beings and animals, their ability to transform themselves into the other, and the consequent blurred distinction between them reflects an important aspect of the worldview of these cultures.

"Giant, the Fire-Bringer" reveals the importance of fire to human beings. Even with an ample supply of food, people prefer to eat much of it cooked. They want light in the darkness and heat when it is cold. Moreover, fire is never easily available, so that people have to work in order to get it and to keep it. Therefore, everyone who possesses fire treasures it.

The Tsimshian people value Giant because he made it possible for them to survive and prosper. However, the particular way in which Giant outwits his adversary appeals to everyone who admires human intelligence.

GIANT, THE FIRE-BRINGER

G iant was the shining son of a great chief and his wife. They lived in the Village of the Animals, located at the southern tip of the

Queen Charlotte Islands. It came to pass that Giant became afflicted with an endless appetite. First, he ate everything that his father possessed. And then, when that supply was gone, he went from house to house and ate everything that his father's people possessed.

The great chief heard about Giant's forages, and he said to his wife, "My dear, surely you, too, have heard that Giant is eating his way through our village! He is taking food from the mouth of every one of our people! If this continues, our people will starve, and our son will still be hungry! Now, I cannot permit Giant to do this! Although it makes my heart flood with grief, we must send our son away!"

And so the great chief called his son to him and said, "Giant, my son, because of your great appetite, I find that I have no choice but to send you forth to live on the mainland! My heart overflows with grief at the thought of it! And your mother's heart overflows with grief as well! However, as I have said, I have no choice! As chief, I am responsible for the welfare of my people!

"Now, my son, I want to make sure that your journey to the East is a safe one! And I want to make sure that you will always find enough to eat in the world!" declared the chief. "Therefore, I am giving you these three things to take with you: first, this Raven blanket; second, this little round stone; and, finally, this bag made from a dried sea-lion bladder.

"Now listen to what you are to do with them, my son. First, with regard to your Raven blanket—whenever you wrap it around you like a cloak, it will enable you to fly through the air just like a raven! Therefore, if you choose to wear it, you will be able to cross the sea to the mainland with ease!" the chief exclaimed. "However, as you fly across the sea, you will find that it is a long journey. And you will surely become tired along the way! Therefore, when you need to rest, just drop your small stone into the water below you. It will become a great rock! And you will be able to rest safely upon it for as long as you wish.

"Now, once you reach the mainland," the chief continued, "you will not know where you will want to live. And you may even wish to travel from place to place. Therefore, before you settle down, I want you to fly here and there over the land. As you fly over the rivers and the streams, reach into your bag and drop the salmon eggs and the trout eggs that it contains into their waters. As you fly over the mountains and the valleys, the hills and the plains, and the forests and the meadows, reach into your bag once again, and drop the berries that it contains upon them."

These were the great chief's parting words to Giant, his son. And Giant did all that his father wished.

In the form of Raven, Giant flew eastward over the sea. It was a very long journey! Fortunately, when he became tired, he was able to drop the small stone that his father had given him into the water below. And, just as his father had said, the stone became a great rock. Therefore, Giant was able to rest safely upon it until he was ready to continue his journey.

Then when he reached the mainland, Giant flew over the mouth of the Skeena River in the form of Raven. There he scattered the salmon eggs and the trout eggs. And as he scattered them, he said, "Now, let all kinds of fish live in every river and stream!"

Then, in the form of Raven, Giant flew over the mountains and the valleys, the hills and the plains, and the forests and the meadows. There he scattered the berries. And as he scattered them, he said, "Now let all kinds of fruit grow in every part of the land!"

And so it came to pass that when people came to walk upon the mainland, they found all the food that the great chief had provided for Giant, his son. However, these people had no fire. Whenever their raw meats tasted bloody and strong, they longed for a way to improve them. Whenever Moon was very young or old, and whenever clouds covered Moon like a blanket, they longed for a light that would brighten the darkness around them. And whenever the cold made them shiver and shake—even when they took refuge in their houses—they longed for a source of heat that would warm them.

Now, as soon as Giant became aware of their problem, he came to the aid of these people. He remembered that the people who lived in his father's village, the Village of the Animals, had possessed fire. Therefore, Giant once again put on his Raven blanket, and in the form of Raven he flew westward across the sea to his father's old village.

It was still a very long journey! Fortunately, when he became tired, Giant noticed that the great rock was still visible in the water below him. Once again he rested upon it, and then he continued on his way.

Giant hoped that his father's people would give him some of their fire. However, no matter what he said, he could not convince the people to give up even the smallest burning ember! Finally, the people became tired of Giant's arguments, and they told him to leave.

Now, Giant was accustomed to having what he wanted—one way or another! And so it came to pass that, as he flew back to the mainland, he said to himself, "I will get fire from my father's village yet! Those people only think that they have seen the last of me! I can tell that they will never choose to give me fire! So now I must think of a way to take it from them! I think that I am going to have a lot of fun with them!"

And so it came to pass that Giant called Sea Gull, who was one of his attendants, before him and declared, "Sea Gull, I want you to fly westward across the sea to my father's old village, the Village of the Animals. Tell the people that a handsome young chief will soon come to dance for them in their chief's great house. Tell them that this young chief will arrive when Moon is mature. And tell them that he will arrive by sea, in a great war canoe!"

These were Giant's words to Sea Gull, his attendant. And Sea Gull did all that Giant commanded. He flew westward across the sea to the Village of the Animals. And he delivered Giant's message to the people. Then he flew eastward across the sea to the mainland and returned to Giant.

As soon as Sea Gull left their village, the people began to prepare for the visit of the young chief. There would have to be dancing and singing around the great fire in the chief's house. And there would have to be food for all. It would take time and effort to make the occasion a special one!

Meanwhile, Giant began to make his own preparations. He searched the various trees in the nearby evergreen forest until he found a piece of wood that was well filled with resin. Once he had just what he needed, he caught and skinned a deer. Now, in those days, deer did not have the short tails that they have now. They had long tails like the wolf. And so it came to pass that Giant cut his piece of wood to fit the deer's long tail. And then he tied it on.

Just before Moon became mature, Giant made his final preparations. He remembered that Sea Gull had told the people that the handsome young chief would arrive in a great war canoe. Now, great Shark, who was his friend, was quick to lend him his own great sea-going craft. And what a great canoe it was! Why, at least twelve men could lie down head-to-foot along the bottom of it!

A group of crows and sea gulls immediately descended and prepared to paddle the canoe. Meanwhile, other crows and sea gulls—

cormorants and cranes, other sea birds, and some land birds, as well—descended and prepared to be passengers.

As soon as Giant saw that Shark's great war canoe was overflowing with birds and ready to depart, he climbed aboard and seated himself in the middle of the craft. Of course, he was dressed in the deerskin that he had carefully fashioned. This time, he would not appear in the Village of the Animals in his own form. And he would not appear in the form of Raven. This time, he would appear in the form of Deer!

By the time that Deer's war canoe came into sight, the people who lived in the Village of the Animals were ready and waiting for the great celebration to begin. They greeted their guests joyfully. And then everyone headed for the great chief's house, where the festivities would take place.

In honor of the celebration, a huge, flaming fire was already burning brightly in the center of the great room. The people seated themselves on one side of the fire, while their visitors seated themselves on the other. Then the festivities formally began.

The chief was the first to dance. And as he danced, his people kept time with their sticks. One person beat upon his drum. Following the dance of their chief, the people sang. And while they sang, all of the visitors kept time by clapping their hands. Then everyone— hosts and guests alike—joined together in the singing.

Suddenly, the moment that everyone had been anticipating arrived. Quick as the wind, Deer entered the chief's house with a great leap and began to dance around the central fire. Everyone—hosts and guests alike—watched him with delight!

Then—as if it were part of his dance—quick as the wind, Deer whipped his long tail over the flames of the great fire. And just as Giant had planned, the flames rushed forth to eat the pitch-filled, wooden piece that he had attached to Deer's tail.

Quick as the wind, Deer now ran from the great chief's house, dragging his burning tail and the attached piece of burning wood behind him. Upon reaching the shore, quick as the wind, he swam out to sea. And as he made his way through the water, his burning tail and the attached piece of burning wood floated behind him. However, he was swimming so rapidly that they barely skimmed the surface of the sea!

Meanwhile, all of Deer's companions flew from the great chief's house. The crows and sea gulls who had paddled Shark's war canoe to the island returned to their places and prepared to set the huge craft in motion. Other birds—cranes, crows, and land birds—flew into their places, and Shark's canoe sped off on its journey across the sea. However, even a great war canoe such as this one could not catch up with Deer!

The people who lived in the Village of the Animals also rushed to their own war canoe and jumped aboard in order to pursue Deer. The people had welcomed Deer into their village, but as soon as Deer ignited his tail and ran off with their fire, they knew that he was really Giant! Now they were so angry that Giant had tricked them that they could not wait to get their hands on him and kill him! However, when they looked out over the water and saw that Deer's horns were now only two specks on the horizon, they gave up before they even started!

And so it came to pass that Deer swam on and on. And the resin-filled wood burned on and on as it skimmed over the water behind him. Finally, Deer reached one of the forested islands where those who walk the earth made their home. Quick as the wind, he swam ashore. Then he walked to the nearest tree, struck it with his burning tail, and declared, "Fir tree, you will continue to burn from this time forth until the end of time!"

And from that time to this, the fir tree has provided those who walk the earth with the fire that they need—for cooking, for warmth, and for all the other uses that they have since developed.

As for Deer's long tail, why, it burned up, of course! And that is why, from that time to this, Deer has had a short black tail!

THE FAR EAST

5

The myths, legends, and folktales from the Far East contain unforgettable characters and profound themes. These characters, whether divinities, aristocrats, or common folk, possess extraordinary courage and determination. Many also possess great creative intelligence. Ultimately, they must weigh their own needs and wishes against their responsibility to others. Most of them choose to act unselfishly, and they enrich both their own lives and the lives of others. Those who are self-centered learn painful lessons. They can all lead us to live our lives more thoughtfully.

Savitri, whose tale is told in the *Mahabharata*, the great epic from ancient India, is one of the greatest wives in world literature. Like the typical trickster, Savitri must gain through intelligent manipulation what, lacking power and status, she cannot gain in any other way. Her virtue, wisdom, and creative intelligence convince Yama, Lord of Death, to confer a series of blessings on her husband, herself, and their families. Yama's response to Savitri reflects the Hindu values of the culture that produced the *Mahabharata*.

Kun and Yu, who are among the greatest heroes of ancient China, combat a great flood. Kun is a culture hero who rebels against the established order. Although he succeeds in his task, he is punished because of his defiance, and his accomplishment is destroyed. In contrast, Kun's son, Yu the Great, is China's greatest legendary hero, and his attitudes and behavior epitomize the Confucian ideal.

"Song of the Water Goddess," an Ainu myth from Japan, reveals the relationship between gods and mortals that is necessary in order for the earth to be a fertile source of food. The myth teaches that divinities in charge of fertility must be treated properly if the community is to survive. Although the theme is universal, the plot relates to the life-view of the Ainu people.

Taro Urashima is the protagonist of a poignant Japanese myth that has become a legend. The myth examines the human wish to become immortal. Whether Taro finds that a goddess-wife, everlasting youth, and eternal life can compensate for what he has lost is an important question. The myth reminds us that it is important to consider the price we might have to pay in order to get what we think we want.

"The Tiger's Whisker," a folktale from Korea, conveys a profound truth that is relevant to the life of every reader. The young wife exhibits courage, patience, and creativity in order to gain a magic potion, only to find that she already possesses that for which she is searching.

"Kerta's Sacrifice," from Java, is a powerful fertility myth that has acquired aspects of a folktale in that it involves child-parent issues. Viewed as myth, it examines the relationship between human beings and the powers upon which they depend for their survival, and it contains elements of wonder and terror that we, too, can feel whenever our technology leaves us with little defense against the forces of nature. Whether viewed as myth or folktale, the fact that Kerta's selfishness brings disaster on himself and others reminds us that our values determine the choices that we make, and that these choices often produce consequences that we cannot anticipate.

Savitri

Historical Background

Ancient India, in the area that is now Pakistan, was the home of one of the oldest major civilizations in the world—the Harappan, or Indus Valley, civilization. This civilization thrived from about 2500 B.C. until about 1500 B.C., after which it declined and died. At its peak, its members built cities and conducted a lively sea trade with the civilized peoples of Mesopotamia. They lived in brick houses that had sanitation facilities; they possessed a pictographic system of writing; and they fashioned beautiful ceramics on the potter's wheel. Natural disasters may have caused Mohenjo Daro, their southwestern capital, suddenly to collapse. Invading Indo-Europeans, who called themselves Aryans ("the noble ones"), probably conquered Harappa, their northeastern capital.

The Aryans were nomadic peoples who left the grassy plains of central Asia beginning in about 1500 B.C. and settled Persia, Turkey, and Greece as well as India. In time, other waves of invasion occurred, so that India's new settlers included Persians, Arabs, Greeks, Turks, and Scythians. Meanwhile, Huns and Mongols arrived from central Asia. By about 300 B.C., one hundred million people called India their home.

The Aryan peoples dominated India for about two thousand years (c. 1500 B.C.–c. A.D. 500), and today the peoples of northern India are still predominantly of Aryan descent. During the first thousand-year period, the Aryans left nothing tangible for archaeologists to study except for four major religious texts, created by Aryan priests and perpetuated through the oral tradition until they were finally written down. These texts, called the Vedas, are the foundation of Hinduism and have led scholars to call the early Aryan period in India (c. 1500 B.C. to c. 500 B.C.) the Vedic Age.

India's caste system may have originated with the division of Aryan society into three social classes. Hereditary nobles ranked at the top, followed by the priests, and finally, by the other tribespeople. (Non-Aryans were at the bottom of the social ladder, beneath all Aryans.) Later in the Vedic Age, the priests came to take precedence over the nobles, and the third rung of the Aryan social ladder came to include Aryan farmers, craftspeople, and tradespeople.

India has never become a "melting pot." More than fifteen hundred languages and dialects are spoken in modern India, and many groups have kept their special customs.

Religious Background

Hinduism became established in India during the early Aryan period (the Vedic Age) and blossomed during the late Aryan period (c. 500 B.C.–c. A.D. 500). It arose as a combination of the religious beliefs and practices of both the Aryans and the people who were indigenous to India. Today, most people in India are Hindu, and Hinduism is the basis of Indian culture.

Hinduism is a way of life as well as a religion in that its principles teach how its adherents should lead their daily lives. The righteous life requires knowledge of Hinduism, devotion to its principles, and unselfish behavior toward others.

Hinduism embraces at least four principal concepts:

1. *dharma*, the idea that all Hindus have a sacred obligation or religious duty to live their lives in a virtuous way, which is determined by their particular social circumstances (their caste and their stage in life);

2. *karma*, the idea that every good action will cause good consequences and that, conversely, every evil action will cause evil consequences;

3. reincarnation, the idea that each person's soul is continually reborn into a new life on earth by entering a body that inhabits a higher or lower status, depending on the extent to which it has lived in accordance with its *dharma* and has therefore achieved a good *karma*;

4. the idea that time is composed of four different ages that eternally repeat themselves like a revolving wheel.

The first age in the cycle, called the Krita Yuga, is the golden age of virtue and *dharma* (moral perfection). Human beings are naturally good, and they live happy, unselfish, and beautiful lives. They are devoted to meditation, which is the highest virtue, and they are loyal to *dharma*.

In the second age, called the Treta Yuga, virtue and *dharma* have declined by one-fourth. Human beings are now devoted to the pursuit of knowledge, which has become the highest virtue. They have become more passionate and greedy; however, they work hard.

In the third age, called the Dvapara Yuga, virtue and *dharma* have declined by one-half, and religious doctrines have been developed in an attempt to guide human behavior toward *dharma*. Human beings are now devoted to sacrifice, which has become the highest virtue. Meanwhile, disease, misfortune, suffering, and death have become an inherent part of the human condition.

Finally, in the fourth age, called the Kali Yuga, virtue and *dharma* have declined by three-fourths. Human beings are now devoted to charity, which has become the sole remaining virtue. Human life is short, and behavior is governed by materialism and sexual passion. Only those who are poor are honest.

The oldest of the sacred Hindu texts are the four Vedas. These were written in Sanskrit, which is an Indo-European language—like Persian, Greek, Latin, German, and Celtic. The Vedas reflect Aryan religious beliefs and social structure. Two of the gods who are mentioned in the following myth are Aryan in origin. First, Indra is the Aryan god of war, and therefore the god of heroes. Like Zeus or Jupiter, his weapon is the thunderbolt. Later, he becomes king of the Hindu gods. Second, Agni is the Aryan god of fire. Later, he becomes god of the Hindu sacred fire.

The other gods mentioned in the following myth are Hindu in origin. Brahma, the creator of the universe and the grandfather of all who live, is one of the three highest Hindu gods. It is he who determines the life span of each mortal. When the day of death arrives, Yama, God of Death, sends his messengers to take the soul of the deceased to his own city, where it is judged as being either righteous or sinful and given the appropriate reward. Narada is a sage and prophet who is a son of Brahma and is therefore semidivine.

Literary Background

The following myth of Savitri is part of the *Mahabharata*, a Sanskrit epic that was composed over a long period of time by a variety of poets. The oldest parts were composed as early as 400 B.C. and are attributed to the poet Vyasa. Vyasa's version, entitled *Jaya* ("Triumph" or "Victory"), contained 24,000 couplets.

In the north, the epic was written down on loose-leaf, birch-bark pages that were placed between two boards and tied together with string. Because the birch bark was fragile, pages frequently became damaged and had to be recopied. Given the loose-leaf format, other pages often became lost. Moreover, since poets were free to alter the content and style of their material, still other pages were added. Consequently, the epic continued to expand.

A poet who had listened to Vyasa's performance created a second version that contained 50,000 couplets. He added mythological material and the title *Bharata* ("War").

Later, a poet by the name of Sauti created a third version, which he based on the second version but to which he added Hindu instructive material. He also amended the title by adding the prefix *Maha* ("Great"). The present version, containing 100,000 couplets, is substantially his, since the text finally became closed to revision after about A.D. 400. With its eighteen books, the *Mahabharata* is one of the longest poems in world literature, and it reveals much about the civilization of Hindu India.

The *Mahabharata* ("Great War") depicts a culture dominated by males, and it was performed by male bards for a male audience. Like all oral epics, it contains repetition, proceeds at a leisurely pace, and incorporates independent myths and legends that the epic characters use for illustration, elaboration, or instruction. Like all oral epics, it preserves the heroic past of its culture. The principal story is an extraordinarily complex account of a legendary rivalry and war that occurred in connection with the invasion of an Aryan people, probably between 1000 B.C. and 900 B.C., to the north of Delhi, in the area of the Upper Ganges and Yamuna rivers.

Appeal and Value

The *Mahabharata* presents the tales of great heroes from ancient times—heroes who are as human as they are heroic—and it dramatizes the violence, intrigue, and revenge that accompany war and affect the lives of victors and vanquished alike. Its greatness as literature resides in the ability of its authors to understand the universality of the human condition and to depict it with great sympathy and power.

However, the *Mahabharata* also contains many independent selections —including myths, legends, and fables—that teach religious philosophy and morality. Because ethical behavior is a major Hindu value, the teaching of moral lessons is an important focus of the epic.

For Hindus, the *Mahabharata* is more than one of the world's great adventure stories. It has the religious importance that the Bible has for Jews and Christians. In fact, it contains the *Bhagavad Gita* ("Lord's Song"), an independent treatise on Hinduism and the religion's most important text, which appears as a sermon in the epic.

Westerners view the epic as the *Iliad* of India, and it surely is one of the greatest epic poems in the world. The *Mahabharata* continues to supply the inspiration for movies, television programs, and stories, both in India and in the West.

The myth of Savitri appears as part of the *Mahabharata* in "The Book of the Forest," where it functions as an example of ideal Hindu female behavior. Given its self-contained nature, its minor relevance to the principal plot of the *Mahabharata*, and its universal appeal, it has long been studied and enjoyed as a separate story by Hindus and non-Hindus alike. The myth conveys the drama of conflict between a human being and a divinity as well as the power of love and virtue to conquer adversity. Savitri herself is an unforgettable character who can serve as a model for males and females of every time and place.

SAVITRI

Asvapati, king of Madra, was renowned for his courage, his knowledge of the Law, his piety, and his concern for the happiness and well-being of his subjects. Being the ideal king, he ruled happily in every respect but one. He had no child.

And so it came to pass that, every day of every month of every year for eighteen years, King Asvapati devoted himself to the ascetic practices of the great hermits. He offered daily sacrifices to Agni, the god of fire; he recited hymns to Brahma's wife, the goddess Savitri; and he practiced austere penances.

Finally, Savitri descended to earth, where she appeared before the king from within the flames of his sacrificial fire. She declared, "King Asvapati, the self-restraint of your asceticism, your pious regard for your religious vows, and your devotion to me have pleased me. Therefore, I now give you the right to request a favor of me that is consistent with the Law. Ask any favor of me, and I will grant it."

To these words, Asvapati replied, "Under the Law, Great Goddess, children are held in highest regard. Therefore, I ask you to give my wife and me many sons so that my line will prosper."

"King Asvapati, I have known that this is your wish," the goddess replied, "and therefore I have discussed it with Brahma. He has decided to reward you for your piety and devotion by granting you and your wife a wonderful daughter! And, therefore, this is the gift that I now bestow upon you."

"What will be, will be, and I am grateful for your blessing!" Asvapati declared. He bowed his head in submission and prayer, and the goddess vanished within the flames.

And so it came to pass that Asvapati's queen gave birth to a beautiful daughter, with eyes as beautiful as lotus leaves, the graceful form and beauty of a goddess, and the sweetness of honey. Asvapati and his wife named the infant Savitri, in honor of the great goddess.

Savitri grew up to be beautiful, accomplished, and wise—more like a goddess than a mortal. In fact, when the time came for Asvapati to give her in marriage, Savitri had no suitors! No eligible young man would come forth to ask the king for his daughter's hand in marriage because no one would dare to ask a goddess to be his wife!

And so it came to pass that Asvapati said to Savitri, "My dear one, it is time for me to choose a husband for you, and yet you have no suitors! The father who does not give his daughter in marriage loses favor in the eyes of the gods. Therefore, I now give you permission to find your own husband. You must choose one who is as virtuous as you yourself are, and one whom you value as much as I value you!"

"I will do as you wish, Father," Savitri responded.

And so Asvapati sent his daughter forth in search of a mate, accompanied by one of his trusted ministers. "Let my daughter lead you, and give her free rein in all of her choices," he commanded.

And so it came to pass that Savitri visited the palaces of other kingdoms and, being as pious as she was virtuous, she also visited the hermitages of the religious sages who lived apart from society in the forestlands.

When Savitri returned home and came to her father to report on her travels, Asvapati was entertaining the wise and all-knowing sage, the godlike Narada himself.

As soon as the princess entered the room, the divine seer declared, "Asvapati, how is it that one who knows the Law as well as you do, and who is as pious as you are, has not yet given your daughter in marriage?"

To these words, Asvapati replied, "Your visit is well-timed, Narada! Savitri has just returned from this quest, and she has come to announce her choice. So, welcome, Daughter! We are eager to learn about your travels."

"I did just as you requested, Father," Savitri declared. "On my travels in search of a mate, I visited the palaces of kings. However, I also chose to visit the hermitages of the ascetics who have made their home in the forestlands. Given the bent of my mind, I must say that I felt more comfortable in the hermitages than in the palaces! And in one of them, I found the man whom my heart has chosen to marry!"

At these words, both Asvapati and Narada looked at Savitri with special interest. "And who is this young man who has won your heart?" Asvapati asked his daughter. "Is he, in fact, as virtuous as you yourself are, and do you value him as much as I value you?"

To these words, Savitri replied, "The answer to both of your questions is yes, Father! I have learned that the kingdom of Shalwa was once ruled by a wise and virtuous king named Dyumatsena, who suddenly became blind when his son was born. A neighboring enemy had been biding his time until he could conquer Shalwa, and he soon took advantage of the blind king and wrested his kingdom from him. And so Dyumatsena took his faithful wife and his young son into the forest wilderness, where they have lived the virtuous life of the hermit from that day until this.

"My heart has chosen Prince Satyavan the Truthful, King Dyumatsena's son, as my lord," Savitri concluded. "It is he whom I choose to marry! He is a loving son to his parents, and he will be a devoted husband to his wife!"

As they listened to her words, King Asvapati smiled with pleasure, and his heart flooded with joy. However, Narada's eyes darkened, and his face became serious.

"Alas, Asvapati!" Narada declared. "Savitri has made a very poor choice of a mate in Satyavan, even though he is the most virtuous of men! Knowing the future as I do, I must tell you what Savitri does not know about this prince. In fact, even Satyavan's parents do not know what I will reveal about him!"

"What is the matter with him, Narada?" Asvapati asked. "Is he not the loving son that Savitri thinks he is? Is he not courageous, or strong, or brilliant? Is he not patient or forgiving?"

"Oh, no, Asvapati! Satyavan's fault is not one of these!" Narada exclaimed. "Dyumatsena's son is as courageous and strong as Indra [King of the Gods] himself, and he is as wise as the seer Brhaspati [Brahma's grandson]! Satyavan is as brilliant as Vivasvat [the sun], and as patient and forgiving as Mother Earth!"

"Then, what could be the matter with him? Is Satyavan not generous? Is he not modest? Does his appearance not please the eye?"

"Oh, no, Asvapati! Satyavan's fault is not one of these!" Narada exclaimed. "Dyumatsena's son possesses every virtue! He is certainly most generous. Moreover, he is handsome and yet modest, friendly and yet prudent. Honor adorns his forehead like a divine crown!"

To these words, Asvapati replied, "Godlike Narada, you are describing a mortal who appears to possess no flaws! Surely, Satyavan is not perfectly endowed!"

"You are correct, Asvapati," Narada responded. "Satyavan is not perfectly endowed. He possesses one mighty flaw—one that he cannot remedy! He is destined to have an unnaturally short life. One year from this day, Yama, Destroyer of Human Life and Lord of the Dead, will come for Satyavan and take his soul!"

As he listened to Narada's words, all signs of pleasure drained from Asvapati's face, and dread flooded his heart. He now turned to his daughter and said, "Savitri, you have heard what Narada, the seer who is honored by the gods, has told us. Surely you agree that Satyavan's dire destiny casts a deep shadow upon his many virtues.

"And therefore, my daughter, I must advise you to go forth once again and find another man to marry!" Asvapati declared. "Others besides Satyavan possess great virtue, and surely you can make a happier choice!"

To these words, Savitri replied, "No, Father, I will not do that! The greatest events in life, like birth and death, occur only once. And marriage, too, is a singular event. You know as well as I that a father can give his daughter in marriage only once. I have chosen my lord—for better or worse, for whatever life brings, and whether his life is full or cut short! My heart has chosen him. It has informed my mind. And I have informed you. I will marry Satyavan and no other!"

Narada now said, "Asvapati, you are a great king and a wise father. It is clear that Savitri will not make another choice. Her mind is firm; her heart is steadfast. It is as it should be!

"And so," the godlike seer continued, "I tell you to push fear and foreboding from your heart, my friend! Savitri has chosen the most virtuous of men to become her husband. And, in time, you will see that she has the love and the will to face up to her husband's death. I approve of Savitri's choice, and I encourage you to proceed with her marriage."

"I will do as you advise, Narada," Asvapati responded. "For you are my teacher and my guide in the Law."

"Then I now take my leave of you. May you have a life of peace and blessing until we meet again!" Narada replied. And with these words, he left the earth and returned to the home of the gods.

And so it came to pass that King Asvapati took Savitri and went into the forest to the hermitage of Dyumatsena, the blind, dethroned king of Shalwa. He found the holy hermit seated beneath a tree, deep in thought.

"King Dyumatsena," he announced, "I have brought Savitri, my lovely daughter, to you so that she may become your daughter-in-law and the wife of your son Satyavan in accordance with the Law."

To these words, Dyumatsena replied, "King Asvapati, I am honored by your visit, and I am honored by your choice of my son as a husband for your daughter. However, have you and Savitri given sufficient thought to your choice of Satyavan as Savitri's mate?

"Surely you realize that I am not the man that I once was," Dyumatsena continued. "I am a king without a kingdom—a man of no estate, who lives a simple, pious life in the forest. It is difficult to be as righteous as our piety demands—the austerities that we practice are rigorous!—and it is difficult to live as we do, away from the companionship and entertainments that conventional society offers. Are you and your daughter certain that she can thrive in this situation? Surely, Savitri deserves a more comfortable life!"

To these words, Asvapati responded, "Dyumatsena, your situation does not give me pause for second thoughts! You are a king and a righteous man—my peer as well as my good friend—whether you are seated on your throne, or whether you make your home as a hermit in the forest! And my daughter knows as well as I do that happiness and sorrow come and go like the wind! Savitri knows her own mind and heart, and my own mind and heart confirm her good judgment. So please give my offer your serious consideration."

"All right, then," Dyumatsena replied. "It is my pleasure to accept Savitri as my daughter-in-law and my son's wife. This union between your house and mine is one that I would have sought myself if I had not lost my kingdom!"

And so it came to pass that the wedding of Savitri to Satyavan took place in the hermitage and with the blessings of the forest sages. Satyavan prized his virtuous and accomplished bride as much as

Savitri prized her heart's choice of a mate. She enthusiastically exchanged her royal robes and jewels for those of unadorned reddish-brown cloth and bark.

And it came to pass that Savitri was the ideal daughter-in-law and wife. She honored Satyavan's father and mother as her own, and she adapted easily and well to the life of her new family. She loved her new responsibilities and cheerfully greeted each new day. Her words were sweeter than the songs of the forest birds and brought joy to the ear. Her hands were helpful and skilled at their tasks and brought joy to the heart. She willingly lived the life of an ascetic, and she devotedly practiced every austerity. Her husband and lord, Satyavan, was the joy of her life and the center and support of her world!

And so it came to pass that one day and night followed another as the moon follows the sun and the sun follows the moon. Savitri treasured every waking moment of these fleeting days and nights even more than Satyavan and his parents treasured them, because she alone knew that these days were destined to end all too soon. Savitri never forgot what the godlike sage, Narada, had revealed about Satyavan's fate, and she counted each day so that she would know exactly when the appointed day would arrive that would bring the death of her beloved husband and lord.

Four days before that fatal day, Savitri made a solemn vow in which she pledged to remain standing for a period of three days and nights, during which she would abstain from food, drink, and sleep.

When her father-in-law, Dyumatsena, learned of her vow, he became very worried about her, and he declared, "Savitri, I see no need for you to impose such a rigorous austerity upon yourself, and I fear that your body will not survive what you are demanding of it! Nevertheless, if your secret sorrow or your need to repent is so great that my words cannot deter you, then I pray that this act brings you whatever you need."

Three days and nights came and went with the sun and the moon, while Savitri stood as straight and strong as a sturdy tree. However, by the time the sun made the fourth day light, the pallor of Savitri's face revealed the severity of her penance and the anguish that flooded her heart.

The righteous sages of the forest had heard of Savitri's vigil, and they came to support her as she performed the final rites. Now they blessed her, saying, "Savitri, dear child, may you never have to live without your husband and lord!"

To these words, Savitri replied in her heart, "May Yama, Lord of Death, hear your blessing!"

"Now, Savitri, surely you will eat!" Dyumatsena pleaded.

"I will eat when the sun no longer shines upon this day," Savitri replied. "Until then, I have the strength to endure."

Meanwhile, Satyavan prepared to journey into the forest in search of fruits and herbs, and wood for the sacrificial fires.

As soon as he picked up his axe, Savitri ran up to him and exclaimed, "Oh, my beloved, please take me with you today! My heart cannot bear the thought of our separation!"

To these words, Satyavan replied, "Why, Savitri! What is the matter, my beloved? You have never asked to accompany me before today! And surely this is not a good time for you to make such a journey! My tasks must take me deep into the forest and along a narrow, rutted path. On any other day, I would tell you that this journey is too difficult for you. Today, after you have concluded such a penance, I do not see how I can consider it!"

"Do not worry about me, Satyavan!" Savitri exclaimed. "I will be able to do what I have chosen to do! I am neither tired nor weak, and I will need neither rest nor food as long as I am with you. So please let my heart have its way!"

"All right, Savitri," Satyavan replied. "I will permit you to accompany me, but only if my father gives his permission as well. I do not want him to criticize me for taking you on a journey that may prove to be too difficult for you!"

And so it came to pass that Savitri went to Dyumatsena and said, "Father, I ask you to permit me to accompany Satyavan on his journey into the forest. He goes in search of fruits and herbs for me and to collect wood for the sacrificial fires, and my heart cannot bear to be separated from him today! Besides, I have never left the hermitage since the day that I arrived here, and I would love to see the woods now that they are in bloom!"

To these words, Dyumatsena replied, "If you are certain that this will not be too much for you to bear, Savitri, then I give you my permission. My wife tells me that you look too wan and wasted to make such a difficult journey. However, since the day one year ago that your father brought you to me to become my son's wife, you have never asked me for anything, and I will not deny your first request! Therefore, my daughter, I give you your heart's wish! Go and enjoy yourself, Savitri! But take care that you do not distract Satyavan from his tasks! Collecting wood for the sacrificial fires is a sacred obligation!"

And so it came to pass that Savitri accompanied Satyavan on his forest journey. Because her husband did not possess her secret knowledge, Savitri pretended to be lighthearted for his sake. As they gathered the fruits and herbs, she exclaimed with feigned joy as she discovered new forest flowers and hidden streams. Her face was wreathed in smiles, but her heart was frozen with dread! Her ears took in the sound of her beloved husband's voice and etched it deep within her heart, for she did not know when each word would be his last! And Savitri kept close to Satyavan as she gathered her fruits and herbs, for she was determined to be at his side when Yama's messengers came for him.

Once Satyavan had filled his own basket with fruits and herbs, he set about collecting the wood for the sacrificial fires. By now, the sun looked down upon the forest from the heights of the sky, and the air had become hot and still.

Satyavan was busily lopping off branches with his axe when he suddenly announced, "I must lie down now, Savitri! My head feels as if a hundred darts have ripped into it, and my limbs are shaking like a young tree in a storm wind! If I can just rest for a short while, I will awaken refreshed, and then I will surely be able to continue my work!"

Terror now flooded Savitri's heart. She ran over to Satyavan, embraced his trembling body, and helped him to rest comfortably on the grass, with his head in her lap.

While Narada's dire prophecy echoed in Savitri's ears, the sun—as if in fear of what was about to occur—suddenly took refuge behind a flood of storm clouds. A storm wind came tearing into the forest, moaning with grief as it ripped through the frightened, trembling leaves of the trees. The forest world, including the watchful Savitri and the sleeping Satyavan, now lay huddled in gloom beneath the shuddering, groaning branches of the great trees. Savitri knew that Nature was already mourning Satyavan's death and that his dreadful fate was about to envelop him.

And so it came to pass that, as Savitri sat with her beloved husband, caressing his pale forehead and kissing his cold lips, an awesome form stepped out of the gloom and glided forth into the small clearing. His size alone was enough to make Savitri's heart flood with fear. But that was not all that sent terror rushing into her heart! A pair of dark, blood-red eyes glittered beneath the sparkling red-and-black-jeweled crown that adorned the form's head, giving a flickering, ruddy cast to his face. And a pair of long-fingered hands extended from the sleeves of the form's blood-red robe. One hand grasped a staff, while a noose dangled from the other.

The form glided up to Savitri and stood quietly looking down upon the sleeping form of Satyavan. Savitri gathered her courage, placed Satyavan's head upon the grass, and then stood up and faced the fearsome form.

"Who are you?" she asked respectfully. "I can tell that you are more than human! What god are you, and why have you come here?"

To these words, the form replied, "Savitri, only because of your love for your husband and your virtue as a wife do I choose to speak to you! Good woman, I am Yama, Lord of the Law. I am also Lord of Death because I destroy all who live! Your husband's time on earth has come to an end, and I have come to remove Prince Satyavan's soul. I will bind the essence of life that forms his mind and his heart tightly with my noose, and I will carry it off to my kingdom."

"Why, good Yama, I never expected to see you here!" Savitri exclaimed. "I know that it is your messengers who come to gather the souls of those who die."

"What you know is indeed the way it usually is, good princess," Yama responded. "However, Satyavan is too worthy a mortal for me to delegate the task of collecting his soul to one of my messengers! He is so righteous that I myself have come for him! His heart is as pure as a young blossom! His virtues are as many as the stars in the night sky! And his accomplishments outnumber the fish in the great sea! Your beloved husband and lord has earned my respect and my admiration!"

Savitri watched as, with these words, Yama tossed his noose upon Satyavan's body and tore the prince's soul—a tiny person the size of a man's thumb—out of him. Yama then tightened his noose around the soul, bringing it totally under his power. Then, without another word, the Lord of Death turned south, in the direction of his kingdom, and silently glided out of the clearing.

Meanwhile, the body that lay upon the grass—all that was left of Satyavan—died. Satyavan's form had lost the power to breathe and to move, and it now became cold and hard.

Savitri's heart flooded with grief, and it came to pass that she could not bear to leave her husband, even though he now was dead.

Therefore, she followed along behind Yama as the Lord of Death took Satyavan's soul to his kingdom.

Yama finally turned toward Savitri and exclaimed, "Stop following me, good woman! Your responsibility is to return home now and perform the funeral rites for Satyavan. That is your obligation as a wife. You are not entitled to accompany Satyavan's soul on its final journey. Take comfort in the fact that you have done everything that a virtuous wife can do for her beloved husband and lord."

"No, good Yama," Savitri replied. "I know that you are the wise and powerful son of Vivasvat, the sun—and that you are Lord of the Law! Therefore, you must know that, according to the Law, marriage is the best and highest life for a woman. And since that is my life, I must behave as I have been taught—with self-discipline, self-control, loyalty, and generosity of spirit. I must accompany my husband and lord wherever he goes, whether he goes of his own free will or whether he must accompany another.

"I am a virtuous wife, and I do not intend to become a widow. Therefore, as Satyavan's wife, I ask you to permit me to continue to accompany my husband and lord, even now, in his death.

"I have already walked seven steps with you," Savitri continued, "and according to the sages, a person who walks seven steps with another becomes that person's friend. Therefore, I am now your friend, good Yama! As your friend, I would like to talk with you, and as my friend, you are obligated to listen.

"And so, good Yama, I will begin by telling you what I have learned from my husband's father, for he is my spiritual teacher and leader. Dyumatsena has taught me that the righteous—those who practice the Law in the forest—have mastered their souls. For them, the Law is more important than anything else in life and, therefore, they praise you most highly, good Yama, for you are Lord of the Law."

To these words, Yama replied, "Good woman, you must turn back now. However, since your knowledge of the Law pleases me, I will reward you with a blessing! Ask any favor of me—except to restore your husband's life!—and I will grant it!"

"Good Yama, as you may know, Dyumatsena is blind. When he lost his sight, he lost his kingdom as well, and he now lives the life of one of the righteous. He is a pious ascetic in a hermitage in the forest. Therefore, I ask you to restore Dyumatsena's sight so that he may once again become strong and splendid!"

"It will be just as you wish it, lovely princess," Yama replied. "However, now you must return home. To continue will take greater effort than you can give. Turn back, so that your strength will be restored."

To these words, Savitri replied, "Good Yama, I am grateful for your blessing. However, the wife who is near her beloved husband and lord does not become tired, for her path is his, and her fate is his. Therefore, my path will be wherever you lead my husband.

"Moreover, since you are my friend, good Yama, I ask you to listen to what I will tell you," Savitri continued. "Your friendship floods my heart with delight! To encounter one who is righteous is a blessing. To speak with one who is righteous is a greater blessing. And to become a friend of one who is righteous is the greatest of blessings. Therefore, friendship with the righteous is most worthy of praise, and all who are righteous wish to live among them."

To these words, Yama replied, "Wise woman, you must turn back now. However, since your words add to the knowledge of the sages, I will reward you with a second blessing! Ask any favor of me—except to restore your husband's life!—and I will grant it!"

To these words, Savitri replied, "Then, good Yama, I ask you to return the kingdom of Shalwa to my husband's learned and wise father. May Dyumatsena once again lead and protect his people, and may Dyumatsena, who is my own teacher and guide in the ways of righteousness, continue to observe the Law."

"It will be just as you wish it, noble princess," Yama replied. "However, now you must return home. To continue will take greater effort than you can give. Turn back, so that your strength will be restored."

To these words, Savitri replied, "Good Yama, I am grateful for your second blessing, but my response remains the same. The wife who is near her beloved husband and lord does not become tired, for her path is his, and her fate is his. Therefore, I tell you once again that my path will be wherever you lead my husband.

"Moreover, since you are my friend, Good Yama, I ask you to listen to what I will tell you," Savitri continued. "Oh, Lord of the Law, I have learned that everyone must obey your decrees! And I have learned that you take the lives of mortals from them, not because you freely choose to do so—for that is not your wish!—but because Divine Law decrees that you must. Therefore, you are known as Yama, or He Who Rules by Decrees.

"I have also learned that the Law demands kind thoughts, kind words, and kind deeds," Savitri declared, "even toward those who think, speak, and act with evil intent. Those who are righteous love all who live, and they treat even their enemies with kindness and mercy."

To these words, Yama replied, "Pious woman, you must turn back now. However, your words are like water to a mortal whose throat is parched with thirst. Therefore, I will reward you with a third blessing! Ask any favor of me—except to restore your husband's life!—and I will grant it!"

To these words, Savitri replied, "Good Yama, as you may know, Asvapati, my father, has long wished for a son so that he would have a male heir. He had hoped for a son when the goddess Savitri told him that I would be born. My father is a righteous man and a fine king of the Madras. Therefore, I ask you to bless Asvapati with one hundred sons so that his lineage will continue."

"It will be just as you wish it, wise princess," Yama replied. "However, now you must surely return home. You have already come a long way, and you may come no farther. Now turn back, so that your strength will be restored."

To these words, Savitri replied, "Good Yama, I am grateful for your third blessing. However, my response remains the same. The wife who is near her beloved husband and lord does not become tired, for her path is his, and her fate is his. So it is that my body and fatigue are strangers! And for me this journey has been short, not long, since whatever I do with Satyavan eases my task. In fact, my heart chooses to travel even farther and, therefore, my path will continue to be wherever you lead my husband.

"Moreover, since you are my friend, good Yama, I ask you to listen to what I will tell you," Savitri continued, "for my mind leaps far ahead to spiritual matters! You are Lord of Justice, since you treat all people alike. It is your justice that makes it possible for trust—the ability to rely on another's character, strength, and skill—to exist. Everyone tries to win the friendship of the righteous, since their pure hearts inspire confidence and security. In fact, trust in the righteous is more reliable than trust in oneself."

To these words, Yama replied, "Beautiful woman, you must really turn back now! However, I must tell you that you are the first to address me as "good Yama" and to speak to me as a friend. Because I destroy all who live, mortals greet me with dread, not with appreciation and love. And since you are the first to express these ideas—ideas that bring joy to my heart—I will reward you with a fourth blessing! Ask any favor of me—except to restore your husband's life!—and I will grant it!"

To these words, Savitri replied, "Then, good Yama, I will ask you to give me one hundred sons! And may they possess the courage, strength, and skill to make Dyumatsena's lineage shine with the brilliance of the sun!"

"It will be just as you wish it, gentle princess," Yama replied. "Your sons will be as wise as they are powerful, and your lineage will endure for generations. However, once again, I urge you to return home. You have already come too far, and you may come no farther. Now turn back, so that your strength will be restored."

To these words, Savitri replied, "Good Yama, I am grateful for your fourth blessing. However, my response must remain the same. The wife who is near her beloved husband and lord does not become tired, for her path is his, and her fate is his. So it is that my body and fatigue are strangers! And for me this journey continues to be short, not long, since whatever I do with Satyavan eases my task. In fact, my heart chooses to travel still farther and, therefore, my path will continue to be wherever you lead my husband."

"Moreover, since you are my friend, good Yama, I ask you to continue to listen to what I will tell you," Savitri continued, "for my mind still leaps far ahead to spiritual matters! Oh, Lord of the Law, mortals, like the gods, always let the Law rule their lives. The thoughts, words, and deeds of the righteous propel the sun, support the life-giving earth, and protect all who are mortal.

"Upon meeting others like themselves, the righteous have no reason to fear or to despair, for their meeting will bring blessings upon both of them," Savitri continued. "They give to others freely, without expecting any benefit in return, and yet their good deeds are always worthwhile. Such behavior is the chief obligation of the righteous and, therefore, they protect all who walk the earth. Their ways are the path of the past, the path of the present, and the path of the future."

To these words, Yama replied, "Most pious woman, you must surely turn back now. And yet, you have made my journey a most rewarding one. Your knowledge of the Law has slowed my pace and flooded my heart with reverence for your virtue. It is impossible to decide which is greater, your love for the Law or your love for your husband and lord! And therefore, faithful woman, I will reward you with a fifth blessing! Ask a special favor of me, and I will grant it!"

To these words, Savitri replied, "Then, good Yama, Mighty Lord of the Law, since you give me this blessing without any exceptions, I would ask you to restore life to my husband Satyavan, my beloved lord! For I am his faithful wife, and I will have no other lord!

"Without Satyavan, I might as well be dead," Savitri declared, "for without my husband and lord at my side, I have no interest in happiness, or in wealth, or in any worldly matter. You have given me the blessing of one hundred sons, and yet you cannot fulfill your promise unless you restore their father! For I will have only Satyavan! And so I ask you for the life of my husband and lord so that you can honor your own decree!"

"It will be just as you wish it, dear princess," Yama replied. "No one has ever prevailed upon me to restore the dead to life, and I do not expect that another ever will! But your knowledge of the Law and your virtue as a wife have warmed my heart!"

And so it came to pass that Yama, Lord of the Law and Lord of Death, removed his noose from Satyavan's soul.

"Savitri, see how I now release your husband's soul and return it cheerfully to you!" Yama exclaimed. "So return home with this greatest of my blessings! You will see that Satyavan will recover his life and good health.

"Moreover, I decree that these blessings will also be yours," Yama announced. "Disease will never again afflict your husband and lord. You and Satyavan will live together for four hundred years, and both of you will prosper! Satyavan will become renowned for his knowledge of the Law.

"As I have promised you," Yama continued, "Satyavan will become the father of your hundred sons, and your sons will become kings, and their sons and their sons' sons will become kings after them. Your lineage will be famous as long as mortals walk the earth!

"And as I have promised you," Yama continued, "your father and mother will become the parents of one hundred sons, your brothers. And they and their sons and their sons' sons will become a lineage that lives as long as mortals walk the earth."

And it came to pass that, with these words, Yama, Lord of the Law and Lord of Death, turned Savitri back upon the path that they had taken, and he continued his journey, alone, toward his own kingdom.

Savitri took Satyavan's soul and returned along the path to the forest where Satyavan's corpse still lay, cold and pale in death. She lovingly placed her husband's soul upon his body and then resumed her place upon the grass, placing Satyavan's head in her lap as it had been before Yama had arrived to claim him.

In time, it came to pass that Satyavan returned to life. He opened his eyes and lovingly gazed up at his wife as if he had returned to her from a long journey to a strange land.

Then Satyavan remarked, "I have slept too long, my beloved! Why, night has already fallen! Why did you choose to let me sleep?

"I remember that I fell ill while cutting wood, and I think that I fell asleep while you comforted me. But then a terrifying thing occurred, Satyavan!" he continued. "A crowned Dark One emerged from the depths of a horrifying blackness, holding a staff in one hand and a noose in the other! And he dragged me away from you! I am certain that he was real, and yet everything appears to be just as it was before I fell asleep! If this was but a dream, it was surely the strangest dream! My heart floods with dread even to think of it!"

To these words, Savitri replied, "My dearest, it is true that many hours have come and gone with the sun since you fell asleep in my lap. It was Yama, Blessed Lord of the Law and Lord of Death—he who destroys all who live—who came for you! But now he has gone! And your fatigue and illness have gone with him! It is too late to talk about this now, but tomorrow I will explain it all to you.

"Now we must decide how we are going to spend this night," Savitri continued. "If you are able to make the journey, let us return to the hermitage. For with the darkness, the beasts of the forest come to life, and their voices flood my heart with fear! However, if we must, we can remain here. I can see where a tree still burns from a fire, and I can ignite the wood you have collected. That will keep us safe until the sun next brings light to the forest!"

"Ready or not, we must leave here at once, my beloved!" Satyavan declared. "I fear that my parents will think that I have become ill, or that I have died! Then their hearts will flood with such worry and grief that they themselves will die. They have told me that they cannot live without me, for they have but one son to assure their future in life and to honor their souls in death! And I cannot live if I neglect my responsibilities to support and cherish them!" he concluded tearfully.

To these words, Savitri replied, "Just as I now wipe your tears from your cheeks, my beloved, so I hope that my virtue—my devotion to the Law—will keep your parents and you alive and well! Return tomorrow for the fruits and the wood that you have cut. Now, come lean on me, and if you can find the path, my strength will bring you safely home to the hermitage!"

"All is well now, dear one!" Satyavan exclaimed. "Your words have restored my spirit, and the moon now brings light to the forest and shows me the paths that I know so well!"

Meanwhile, it had come to pass that, as Yama had promised Savitri, Dyumatsena had suddenly regained his sight. As Satyavan had foreseen, Dyumatsena and his wife were distraught over their son's unexplained delay, and they proceeded to search the neighboring forests and visit the nearby hermitages. Their neighbors, all sages, returned to their hermitage with them in order to comfort them in their vigil.

"I have lived the life of a righteous man of wisdom!" the greatest of the sages exclaimed. "I have prayed and fasted, and I have performed the proper vows and deeds. I know the future, and I know that Satyavan surely lives!"

"I, too, have lived the life of a righteous man of wisdom!" another of the men exclaimed. "And I know that, because Savitri is Satyavan's wife and her behavior has been virtuous, Satyavan surely lives!"

"I, too, have lived the life of a righteous man of wisdom!" another of the men exclaimed. "And I know that, because of Savitri's period of penance and the sudden return of your sight, Dyumatsena, that Satyavan surely lives!"

"I, too, have lived the life of a righteous man of wisdom!" another of the men exclaimed. "And I know that, because of his virtue, Satyavan surely lives!"

And so it came to pass that Dyumatsena and his wife received hope and comfort from the sages until Savitri happily appeared with Satyavan.

"Dyumatsena, you are triply blessed!" the sages exclaimed. "First, your son has returned. Second, your sight has returned. And third, Savitri has returned with a radiant face! Surely time will bring even more blessings!"

The wise men built up the fire in the fireplace, and they invited everyone present to sit with them. Then they asked Satyavan, "Why have you returned in the middle of the night? What caused such a delay? Everyone here was very worried about you! If you are permitted to reveal it, do tell us what happened!"

To these words Satyavan replied, "I can only tell you that Savitri and I went into the forest to gather fruits and collect wood for the sacrificial fires. Savitri was determined to accompany me, and my father gave her permission to make the journey. Later, while I was cutting wood, an unbearable headache suddenly made it too painful for me to continue working, and I fell asleep. By the time I awakened, it had already become dark. Then I returned as quickly as I could because I knew how worried my parents must be."

"We are questioning you, Satyavan, because of the unusual events that have occurred today," the greatest of the sages responded. "Not only did you have a strange experience in the forest, but your father has suddenly regained his sight. Apparently, you cannot explain this.

"And therefore I now turn to you, Savitri—you who are so like the great goddess whose name you bear!" the great sage exclaimed. "I would ask that you now tell us what you know about both of these events. If you are permitted to reveal it, do tell us what happened!"

To these words, Savitri replied, "I am able to tell you the whole tale, exactly as it happened. Before my marriage, the godlike Narada had told me that Satyavan was destined to die on this particular day. I did my best to prepare myself spiritually for the occasion by praying and fasting, and then I insisted upon accompanying Satyavan on his journey into the forest.

"When Satyavan became very ill and fell asleep, Yama himself came to collect his soul," Savitri continued. "He bound it with his noose and proceeded to carry it off to his kingdom. I praised Yama as Lord of the Law, and he granted me five blessings. First, he promised to restore my father-in-law's eyesight, and then he promised to restore his kingdom. Third, he promised that my father and mother would have one hundred sons in order to continue Asvapati's lineage. Fourth, he promised that Satyavan and I would have one hundred sons in order to continue Dyumatsena's lineage. And, finally, Yama promised to restore Satyavan to a long, healthy, and prosperous life of four hundred years.

"What a blessed end to a day that I had begun with such dread!" Savitri concluded.

To these words, the greatest of the sages responded, "We praise you, noble princess! You are truly a woman of virtue whom the Law blesses. You have rescued your father-in-law, the greatest of kings, from his dark prison, and you have brought light into your own father's life as well! You have won the blessings of good health and prosperity for yourself, your husband, your parents, and all of your descendants!

"We will take leave of you now, since the hour is so late," he concluded. "However, we will return when the sun makes the day light, for we would see what that day, too, will bring!"

And it came to pass that, when the sun next made the day light, ministers arrived at Dyumatsena's hermitage from the kingdom of Shalwa. They announced that the usurper, his family, and his supporters had all been murdered by his chief minister. The army of the evil king had fled as well.

"The people are clamoring for the return of their lawful king!" they declared. "The streets are alive with excitement and joy! 'Whether or not his eyes can see, we want Dyumatsena to lead and protect us!' the people shout. And so, Your Majesty, we have come to escort you back to the palace of your father and your ancestors. The kingdom of Shalwa is yours, as it always has been yours under the Law."

And so it came to pass that Dyumatsena once again became king of the Shalwas. Satyavan returned home with his father to be blessed as the young king and, of course, Savitri accompanied him. In time, Savitri gave birth to one hundred great sons. And, in time, Savitri's mother presented her father, Asvapati, with one hundred great sons as well.

And so gentle Savitri, through her great piety, saved her father-in-law and his dynasty and assured the continuation of her own father's dynasty. Through her great piety, she brought happiness and prosperity to all whom she loved.

Kun and the Great Flood
and **Yu the Great**
and the Great Flood

Historical Background

China's Earliest History

China has one of the world's oldest civilizations. Its recorded history begins with Yao, Shun, and Yu the Great, the three monarchs of the golden age of antiquity. Oral reports attributed to these rulers and their ministers provide the content for the *Book of History* (also known as the *Book of Documents*), which is one of the five Confucian Classics.

The *Book of History* depicts Yu as a great warrior who gains the allegiance of ten thousand states and establishes China's first hereditary dynasty, the Hsia (c. 1994–c. 1523 B.C.). However, no evidence, either archaeological or in other writings, confirms the existence of Yao, Shun, and Yu or their reigns. Consequently, these men are considered to be mythological or, at best, legendary figures.

The Chou Dynasty and Confucius

The Chou dynasty (1027–256 B.C.) left important archaeological evidence and a body of authentic written texts. Most of the surviving ancient literature and much of the content of the Confucian Classics were written during the late Chou dynasty.

In ancient China, religion, literature, and sociopolitical behavior became interconnected through the efforts of Confucius (551–479 B.C.), one of the great men in history. Born K'ung (family name) Ch'iu (personal name), in time he became known as K'ung Fu-tzu (Master Kung), or Confucius (the Latinized form). What we know about his life and philosophy is based on the *Analects*, dialogues and sayings that were probably recorded by his followers and attributed to him.

Confucius lived during a period that was marked by tyranny, instability, and war. Determined to try to bring about a just government, social order and peace, and moral human behavior, he first entered politics, where he was moderately successful as a minor government official. However, he was dissatisfied with his lack of influence and turned to teaching. In this capacity, he was truly gifted. Confucius gained the title of "supreme sage and foremost teacher," and it is said that he had seventy-two personal disciples and three thousand students.

According to the *Analects,* the Chinese people needed to return to virtuous behavior—"human-heartedness"—in their treatment of one another. Noting the power structure that existed in society, Confucius determined that society would function in an orderly, moral way if all people would treat those over whom they had power as they themselves would wish to be treated by those who had power over them.

Moreover, Confucius decided that the study of history and literature could teach moral behavior. If the human behavior depicted in the great works from the past were presented with the proper focus, it could become the principal moral guide that people needed. Then it would become clear that virtuous behavior in the conduct of human affairs is actually in harmony with the natural moral order of the universe.

In the view of Confucius, God Supreme (also known as "Shang-ti" and "Lord on High") is both the supreme ruler and the moral force in the universe, where he watches over human beings and takes a personal interest in their lives. Confucius used the term *Heaven* to signify the same moral force.

Confucius put his beliefs into practice by editing five books that were thought to contain China's ancient religious, literary, and historical heritage. These five books have become known as the Confucian Classics, and it is as an editor of this body of literature—where he interpreted and reshaped China's ancient culture—that Confucius has had the greatest influence on Chinese society.

The Ch'in Dynasty

The Chou dynasty was followed by the short-lived Ch'in dynasty (221–207 B.C.), from which the name "China" is derived. China's first emperor, Shih Huang Ti, united China's states under his rule but, unfortunately, he is as infamous as he is famous.

Determined to create a complete break with China's past, in 213 B.C. Shih Huang Ti commanded that all books except those about medicine, prophecy, farming, and the growing of trees be burned. Outlawed books included two of the Confucian Classics, the revered *Book of Poetry* and

Book of History. Despite the fact that 460 scholars were killed for concealing banned books, many of the old books, including the Confucian Classics, survived the emperor's purge. However, his program and its consequences have made the authenticity of ancient Chinese literature, history, and myth difficult to establish.

The Han Dynasty

During the great Han dynasty (202 B.C.–A.D. 220), the emperors instituted the teaching of Confucius as the state religion and banned the older religious practices that involved nature worship. In the first century B.C., Confucianism became generally accepted, and the five Classics became the curriculum for all educated Chinese people. By the following century, Confucianism had become the official creed of China, and the Classics had become China's official literary heritage.

Under the rule of the Han emperors, scholars reconstructed the old books but, in the process, they rewrote and reinterpreted them—including the great Confucian Classics—to reflect the political and religious climate of their own time. They also wrote books and then gave them "authenticity" by making it appear as if they had been written much earlier.

However, in addition to being editors of and commentators on the ancient texts, the Han scholars were also great collectors. Unlike earlier scholars, who were more aristocratic in their focus, Han scholars collected oral myths, legends, and folktales from the common people. Consequently, some of the material that appeared for the first time during the years of the Han dynasty is actually from an earlier period.

Literary Background

The Chinese have four flood myths. In the first, the water god Kung Kung inadvertently causes one of the sky supports to collapse, causing fire to burn and water to overflow without stopping. In the second, the four supports that hold up the sky collapse, and the goddess Nu Kua, who created human beings, preserves the earth by building dams to control the flood waters. The third and fourth are the following myths about Kun and Yu.

The myths of Kun and Yu can be found in four original sources. First, *The Book of Poetry,* or *The Book of Odes,* originally compiled in about 600 B.C. and later edited by Confucius, contains four poems that praise Yu as the hero who saved the world from the great flood.

Second, "Questions of Heaven," written between 400 B.C. and 300
B.C. and included in the later *Songs of Ch'u,* presents Kun as the hero
who failed to stem the flood and his son Yu as the hero who succeeded.
This poem is the best single source of what is considered to be authentic Chou mythology. It is the most important source of Chinese myth,
since it includes the principal myths of the Chou dynasty, beginning with
the creation of the world, moving on to the deeds of the gods and the
demigods, and concluding with the deeds of the historical kings who ruled
the Chou dynasty before 500 B.C.

Third, *The Book of Mountains and Seas,* compiled between 300 B.C.
and A.D. 100 and including material from a variety of anonymous authors,
also presents Kun as the hero who failed to stem the flood and his son
Yu as the hero who succeeded. This is the second most valuable source
of what is considered to be authentic Chinese mythology. It presents only
fragments of the myths, but it includes a broad range, including several
versions of certain myths.

Finally, *The Book of History*—originally written as early as the early
Chou period (in about 1000 B.C.), then edited by Confucius, with additions throughout the Chou era and revisions in the Han era—contains a
valuable version of the Yu myth, despite severe distortions. Given the
authors' goal of teaching ethical behavior, this source humanizes and
historicizes China's myths, using them as models of human behavior.

In *The Book of History,* both Kun and Yu are depicted as human beings
who are King Yao's subjects and his "masters of public works," or chief
civil engineers. King Yao first commands Kun to control irrigation, which
is flooding the land. Kun tries unsuccessfully for nine years, and finally
Yao is so aggravated by this prolonged disruption of the natural order
that he has Kun put to death for his failure to solve the problem. When
Yao then commands Yu to continue his father's work, Yu employs a different method and is successful.

Although *The Book of History* portrays Kun and Yu as human beings,
the Chinese forms of their names reveal their nonhuman, aquatic, mythological origin. Kun's name contains the symbol for K'un, a gigantic mythical fish, while Yu's name contains the symbol that is associated with
reptiles.

Appeal and Value

The myths of Kun and Yu, two of the oldest Chinese myths, are considered to be the greatest in the Chinese tradition. Depending on the
source, Kun and Yu may be divine or human. However, they are always

the great culture heroes who represent Confucian (and universally respected) values, each devoting his life to making it possible for human beings to survive and prosper.

Throughout the ages, the Chinese have been so appreciative of Yu's sacrifices, so attuned to his values, and so pleased with his success that they have devoted more myths, legends, and folktales to him than to any of their other ancient heroes. In one Chinese source, a nobleman in 540 B.C. is quoted as joking, "If it were not for Yu, we would all be fish!"

The myths of Kun and Yu have the appeal and value of the other great hero myths from around the world. First, they are appealing as stories because they both have an admirable hero and an interesting plot. In addition, they are valued because the nature of their heroes makes them a source of cultural pride, and therefore they are influential within their own culture. Finally, they are valued because both the nature of their heroes and the connections between these myths and the hero myths of other cultures make them universally appealing.

Although Kun is not as well-developed a character as Yu, he is unusually appealing. Not only does he have the courage to take an independent stand among the gods, but he also risks his own life in order to rescue human beings and alleviate the cause of their suffering. Therefore, he takes his place beside the other great benefactors of humankind—found in myths throughout the world—who, often in the role of tricksters, incur divine wrath because of their sympathy for human beings and for the fragility of the human condition.

Yu is a very appealing figure because he possesses qualities that are valued not only by his own culture, but by other cultures as well. Like other traditional heroes, he puts aside his personal life and selflessly performs many labors for the welfare of human society.

Specific details about both Kun's life and Yu's life fit the pattern of the traditional hero and yet are fascinating in their own right. Other details, such as Kun's death, Yu's birth, and the birth of Yu's son Ch'i, reveal that these myths are rooted in the ancient past, a time when both the gods and nature were of major importance. Finally, the relationship between the myth of Kun and the myth of his son Yu reflects the motif of successive generations of gods, with consequences that are echoed in other myths from around the world. ("Yu the Great and the Great Flood" begins on page 406.)

KUN AND THE GREAT FLOOD

Prologue

A great flood has once again settled upon the earth, covering the farmlands like a blanket, burying the hills, and turning the greatest mountains into foothills as it climbs up the rocks and sends its surly, surging waves against the sky. Men and women, grandparents, and grandchildren huddle—shivering and wet—in their small boats as towering waves threaten them. Other, less fortunate, mortals have climbed trees and rest there like birds, only to find that the towering waves all too quickly uproot their trees and toss them into a watery grave.

Who knows who caused this flood? Some blame Shang-ti, Lord on High and God Supreme. They say that Shang-ti was furious with those who walk the earth because they were so cruel to each other. They say that Shang-ti decided to punish these fragile, mortal beings and that he commanded Kung Kung to cause this flood. However, Shang-ti denies this!

Others blame Kung Kung, the Black Dragon, for that warrior is the god of water, and everyone knows that he caused an earlier flood. He was so busy indulging in one of his fights that he carelessly bumped into one of the four mountains that support the sky. One of his horns broke apart that mountain, and without its support, total disorder and disarray enveloped the universe! And the world still has not recovered! From that day to this, the sun, moon, and stars flow westward, while all the rivers flow eastward. However, Kung Kung denies that he caused this flood!

Indeed, it is possible that Kung Kung is not the cause at all! Maybe this flood simply happened. After all, that is how the first flood happened. Long, long ago, the four pillars that support the sky suddenly collapsed. Who knows why they collapsed? They just broke! Then, too, surging, surly flood waters swamped the earth, enjoying their freedom and refusing to be contained. And remember those fires! They too blazed far and wide—wherever there were reeds to consume—refusing to be checked until, finally, they burned themselves out.

However, one good thing came from those fires. Nu Kua, that greatest of goddesses, was able to stem that flood by using the ashes from all of those burned-up reeds to build life-restoring dikes.

Nu Kua had created human beings, and then she had come to their aid.

But where is Nu Kua now? Where is she now, when another great flood has once again settled upon the earth, covering the farmlands like a blanket, burying the hills, and turning the greatest mountains into foothills as it climbs up the rocks and sends its surly, surging waves against the sky? Where is she now, when men and women, grandparents, and grandchildren huddle—shivering and wet—in their small boats as towering waves threaten them? Where is she now, when other, less fortunate, mortals have climbed trees and rest there like birds, only to find that the towering waves all too quickly uproot their trees and toss them into a watery grave?

Now Nu Kua is strangely silent! Now Nu Kua is strangely still! Who knows why? Maybe the great goddess thinks that one flood was enough. Maybe she is tired of rescuing the mortals whom she herself created—those fragile creatures who walk the earth. Maybe Nu Kua no longer cares! After all, Shang-ti does not seem to care either!

But wait! Look! There is hope for human life on earth after all! The god Kun—son of a sky god and great-grandson of Shang-ti, God Supreme himself—hears the heart-rending cries and groans of the people. From the home of the gods in the sky above, he looks down upon the earth, and his heart floods with sorrow and pity! For he sees men and women, grandparents, and grandchildren, all scurrying from the surly, surging waves that are eagerly lapping at their heels as they rush to take what can only be temporary refuge in mountain caves. He sees dragons and serpents welcome their human visitors with the gift of poison and then drive them, dying, from their dens.

Yes, Kun's heart floods with sorrow and pity! For he sees men and women, grandparents, and grandchildren, all scrambling for food that more clever birds and animals easily snatch from their hands. He sees famished, fierce beasts preying on these fragile mortals and feasting upon their fresh, warm flesh. He sees vultures and eagles swooping down upon all those who are too old, too young, or too weak to run. And he sees these birds of prey grab their victims with their claws and carry them off to become their own fresh, warm feast.

• • •

It came to pass that Kun went before each of the other gods with an appeal. He appeared before each of them in his divine form—the form of a white horse. And he exclaimed, "Look below! See the plight of all who walk the earth! See how the flood is swallowing up all who are mortal! See how these fragile creatures have now become prey for the serpents in the caves, the beasts on the mountainsides, and the birds high on the rocky cliffs! See what I see, and let your hearts, like mine, flood with sorrow and pity for their dire fate!"

And Kun asked each of the other gods, "Will you end the flood? Will you restore the land? Will you make it possible for those who walk the earth to cultivate the land so that they can survive?"

Kun asked these questions, but not one among all the gods responded to him. Each was silent. Each was still. When Kun looked into the eyes of each of the gods, they all turned their eyes away. And when Kun looked into the heart of each of the gods, he could find no trace of either sorrow or pity. Even Shang-ti, Lord on High and God Supreme, seemed to have a rock for a heart.

"You make me ashamed to be one of you!" Kun declared to each and every one. "And if you will make no effort to help the fragile creatures whom Nu Kua created, then I myself will save the earth and all who walk upon it!"

And so it then came to pass that Kun went down to earth in his human form and began to build dikes. His heart flooded with hope as he told himself, "After all, Nu Kua did this, and it worked for her! Surely it will also work for me!"

Kun built his dikes, but these flood waters were too surly and too strong to be contained. They surged against Kun's dikes, overwhelming them and collapsing them beneath their pressure.

Then Kun's heart overflowed with sorrow and pity. Worn and weary from his work, and with his head bowed low in defeat, he was returning to his home when he saw that two creatures were approaching him. One was a horned owl, and its companion was a three-footed black tortoise.

"You look awfully worn and weary, Kun!" the owl exclaimed. "It is too bad that your efforts to control the flood were not successful!"

"But you do not need to hang your head in defeat!" the tortoise declared.

"Why not?" Kun asked. "How can you observe my failure and yet say this?"

"We can tell you what we know," the owl responded, "but you must possess great courage if you would take advantage of our knowledge!"

"We can tell you what we know," the tortoise added, "but you must possess great skill if you would take advantage of our knowledge!"

Kun raised his head, and his heart once again flooded with hope. "Tell me what you know," he declared, "and you will see that I possess whatever courage and skill the task will demand!"

"All right, then," the tortoise replied. "You should know that Shang-ti has a secret that is his most valued possession."

"Yes," agreed the owl. "God Supreme possesses a magical soil that can continue to reproduce or recreate itself until the end of time."

"He calls it Ceaselessly Expanding Soil," declared the tortoise. "But you can call it whatever you wish. It does what it does, no matter what it is called. And it is the only substance that will confine these flood waters!"

"However, Kun, if you truly are determined to control the flood, you will have to solve two problems," the owl explained. "Shang-ti keeps his treasure well hidden. And since you cannot ask God Supreme for what you are not supposed to know that he has, first you must contrive to learn where he keeps his magical soil, and then you must contrive to steal it from him!"

"Do you know where Shang-ti has hidden this precious substance?" Kun asked.

"We have no idea," the owl and the tortoise replied together.

"That is why I said that you must possess great courage if you would take advantage of our knowledge!" the owl responded.

"And that is why I said that you must possess great skill if you would take advantage of our knowledge!" the tortoise added.

"Well, then," Kun replied, "as I see it, I have no choice but to steal Shang-ti's magical earth! Since God Supreme possesses the only substance that will confine the flood waters, I will put my courage and my skill to the test. After all, Shang-ti is my great-grandfather—even if he is God Supreme—and he trusts me. Somehow, I will get him to tell me about his secret, and then I will contrive to steal it from him! Just wait, and you will see that my actions are as good as my words!"

And it came to pass that Kun proved that his actions were, indeed, as good as his words. No one knows how, but somehow, Kun secretly managed to steal Shang-ti's Ceaselessly Expanding Soil.

And no one knows how—but somehow—Kun secretly managed

to carry that magical soil down to earth, where once again in his human form, he began to use it to construct new dikes. And as Kun built these dikes, little by little the surly, surging flood waters became confined between life-saving barriers.

Joy and gratitude now flooded the hearts of those who walk the earth! Men and women, grandparents, and grandchildren began to leave their caves and descend from the mountains. Slowly, they began to rebuild their farms, their villages, their towns, and their lives. And they loved and revered Kun as the god to whom they owed their lives!

And it came to pass that, from the home of the gods in the sky above, Shang-ti looked down upon the earth, and he—God Supreme—saw that Kun had stolen his magical soil and that he was using it to control the flood waters. And Shang-ti saw that men and women, grandparents, and grandchildren were all busily at work. They were rebuilding their farms, their villages, their towns, and their lives. And God Supreme saw that they loved and revered Kun for their deliverance.

Then did the heart of God Supreme flood with wrath against Kun! Shang-ti's heart flooded with wrath against Kun even though Kun was his own great-grandson! For Kun had not only stolen his prized possession, but he had tricked him out of it! And then Kun had used this magical soil that he had stolen in order to win the love and reverence of human beings!

And so it came to pass that Shang-ti called his executioner before him and declared, "God of Fire, I command you to find Kun at Feather Mountain and kill him! Leave his corpse there to rot in the wind and snow, for it is only right that it should wither and decay in that dark and barren far-northern place! Then collect my magical soil and bring it back to me!"

God of Fire did as God Supreme commanded and, without the Ceaselessly Expanding Soil to confine them, the great flood waters once again settled upon the earth, covering the farmlands like a blanket, burying the hills, and turning the greatest mountains into foothills as they climbed up the rocks and sent their surly, surging waves against the sky. Once again, men and women, grandparents, and grandchildren sat huddled—shivering and wet—in their small boats as towering waves threatened them. Once again, other, less fortunate, mortals climbed trees and rested there like birds, only to find that the towering waves all too quickly uprooted their trees and tossed them into a watery grave.

It then came to pass that three years of summers and winters came and went like the leaves on the trees. Kun's corpse remained on Feather Mountain without decomposing. Who knows why his body refused to rot? Maybe because Feather Mountain is located in that dark and barren far-northern place. Maybe because Kun is a god, and gods are immortal.

Whatever the reason, when Shang-ti looked down from the home of the gods in the sky, and he saw that Kun's corpse looked alive in death even after three years of summers and winters had come and gone, he sent for one of the gods. No one knows whom God Supreme commanded, but he declared to that nameless immortal, "I command you to take this sword that I now give you and use it to destroy Kun's corpse! But be careful when you handle my weapon! For it is the Sword of Wu, and it will slice through anything that it touches!"

Like God of Fire, this nameless immortal also did as Shang-ti commanded. He traveled to that dark and barren far-northern place, and he found Kun's corpse. He found the body of the god who was the son of a sky god and the great-grandson of Shang-ti, God Supreme himself, just where it had fallen on Feather Mountain. And this nameless immortal sliced into the belly of that corpse with the Sword of Wu.

And it came to pass that, to his amazement, a great dragon—bearing a pair of sharp horns and a pair of powerful wings—suddenly emerged from the opening in the belly of Kun's corpse. It then quickly extended its wings and flew off into the sky. Such was the birth of Kun's son, Yu the Great.

As for the god Kun, he now transformed himself into an animal, threw himself into Feather Gulf, and disappeared. Some say that he took the form of a yellow bear or a yellow dragon. Others say that he took the form of a three-legged tortoise or a black fish. But everyone agrees that the god Kun—he who was the son of a sky god and the great-grandson of Shang-ti, God Supreme himself—took to the water and was never seen again!

YU THE GREAT AND THE GREAT FLOOD

Prologue

Three long years of summers and winters have come and gone like the leaves on the trees since God of Fire obeyed Shang-ti's command and traveled to Feather Mountain—that dark and barren far-northern place—where he killed the god Kun—that god who was the son of a sky god and the great-grandson of Shang-ti, God Supreme himself. Three long years of summers and winters have come and gone since God of Fire retrieved Shang-ti's magical soil and returned it to him.

And so it has come to pass that, for three long years of summers and winters, the great flood has settled upon the earth, covering the farmlands like a blanket, burying the hills, and turning the greatest mountains into foothills as it has climbed up the rocks and sent its surly, surging waves against the sky.

For three long years of summers and winters, men and women, grandparents, and grandchildren have sat huddled—shivering and wet—in their small boats as towering waves have threatened them. For three long years of summers and winters, other, less fortunate, mortals have climbed trees and rested there like birds, only to find that the towering waves have all too quickly uprooted their trees and tossed them into a watery grave.

But wait! Look! Once again, there is hope for human life on earth! For Shang-ti has commanded a nameless immortal to take the Sword of Wu—that sword that slices through anything that it touches!—and destroy Kun's corpse. And that nameless immortal does as Shang-ti commands. He travels to that dark and barren far-northern place and finds Kun's corpse just where it has fallen on Feather Mountain. And when he slices into the belly of that corpse with the Sword of Wu, a great dragon—bearing a pair of sharp horns and a pair of powerful wings—suddenly emerges, quickly extends its wings, and flies off into the sky.

And so it comes to pass that, like his father before him, the god Yu—son of the god Kun and great-great-grandson of Shang-ti, God Supreme himself—hears the heart-rending cries and groans of the people. From the home of the gods in the sky above, he looks down upon the earth, and his heart floods with sorrow and pity! For he sees men and women, grandparents, and grandchildren, all scurrying from the surly, surging waves that are eagerly lapping at their heels as they rush to take what can only be temporary refuge in mountain caves. He sees dragons and serpents welcome their human visitors with the gift of poison and then drive them, dying, from their dens.

Yes, Yu's heart floods with sorrow and pity! For he sees men and women, grandparents, and grandchildren, all scrambling for food that more clever birds and animals easily snatch from their hands. He sees famished, fierce beasts preying on these fragile mortals and feasting upon their fresh, warm flesh. He sees vultures and eagles swooping down upon all those who are too old, too young, or too weak to run. And he sees these birds of prey grab their victims with their claws and carry them off to become their own fresh, warm feast.

• • •

It came to pass that Yu—son of the god Kun and great-great-grandson of Shang-ti, God Supreme himself—went before Shang-ti with an appeal. He appeared before God Supreme in his divine form—the form of a great dragon. And he exclaimed, "Grandfather! Look below! See the plight of all who walk the earth! See how the flood is swallowing up all who are mortal! See how these fragile creatures have now become prey for the serpents in the caves, the beasts on the mountainsides, and the birds high on the rocky cliffs! See what I see, and let your heart, like mine, flood with sorrow and pity for their dire fate!

"Grandfather, I ask you, will you now end the flood? Will you now restore the land? Will you now make it possible for those who walk the earth to cultivate the land so that they can survive? For I would like to take on my father's task, and I need your help if I am to succeed."

And this time, Shang-ti was not silent. God Supreme was not still. And this time, when it was Yu who looked into Shang-ti's eyes, Lord on High did not turn his eyes away. And when it was Yu who looked into Shang-ti's heart, he saw that it was now flooded with sorrow and pity for the plight of those who walk the earth.

Nevertheless, to Yu's surprise, Shang-ti replied, "No, my grandson, I will not end the flood. Not now, not ever. Nor will I restore the land. Not now, not ever. And I will not make it possible for those who walk the earth to cultivate the land so that they can survive. Not now, not ever.

"However, my grandson," Shang-ti—Lord on High and God Supreme—declared, "I will permit you to end the flood. I will permit you to restore the land. And I will permit you to make it possible for those who walk the earth to cultivate the land so that they can survive."

"Then, Grandfather, will you now give me your valued possession, the Ceaselessly Expanding Soil? For I need it if I am going to control the flood and end the suffering of those fragile beings whom Nu Kua created. I ask you openly for your magical soil—that substance that can continue to reproduce or recreate itself until the end of time—for I will not steal it from you as my father did."

"Yes, Grandson, to you I will give that magical soil for which you ask, even though it is my most valued possession. Your father secretly stole that soil from me, and he paid for that theft with his life! But I willingly offer it to you so that you can use it to control the great flood. You have my permission to take as much of it as can be carried upon the shell of the black tortoise that I will send to accompany you.

"And, in addition, Grandson, I will give you the yellow winged dragon who is God of Drought. He is called Dragon Ying, or Responding Dragon, and he will help you by controlling the rainfall as well as in any other way that you choose to use him."

To these words, Yu replied, "My heart floods with gratitude for your help, Grandfather. And because of your kindness and your selfless generosity, the hearts of all of Nu Kua's mortal beings will flood with gratitude as well. And they will love and revere you because you have made it possible for me to restore the earth. Soon men and women, grandparents, and grandchildren will be able to leave their caves and descend from the mountains. Soon they will be able to begin to rebuild their farms, their villages, their towns, and their lives. And they will honor and revere you as the god to whom they owe their lives!"

"If you succeed, in time that may come to be so," Shang-ti replied. "But it is enough for me that Nu Kua's creatures will love and revere you!"

And so it came to pass that Yu placed as much of the green, muddy, Ceaselessly Expanding Soil on the back of the black tortoise as it could carry. Then, together with Dragon Ying, they left the home of the gods and came down to earth in order to resume Kun's work.

Once on earth, Yu assumed his human form. He worked first

with the tortoise, which he commanded to follow him as he traveled around the earth so that the Ceaselessly Expanding Soil would be readily available. Yu used it first to close many of the water sources. Then he used it to rescue those who were in danger of drowning, since whatever pieces of magical soil he dropped into the flood waters quickly expanded into life-saving land. Yu then used the magical soil to build great mountains at the four corners of the earth so that they would anchor the land and keep some areas from flooding. In the process, he built other tall mountains and high hills.

Yu did all this, but the great flood waters still needed to be confined. They needed to be channeled, and they needed to be able to drain into specific areas, or else no lowlands would exist that could be cultivated.

And so it came to pass that Yu began to work with God of Drought. Yu harnessed Dragon Ying and drove him ahead of him through the waters so that the dragon would drag his tail over the ground that lay beneath those waters. In this way, Yu led Dragon Ying to create the deep channels that became the beds of all the great rivers. They would all flow east to the sea because of the tilt of the land caused by Kung Kung's destruction long before.

And everything happened just as Yu planned. The flood waters naturally flowed into these deep ditches, draining the surrounding land. And they formed the great rivers whose waters soon formed the four seas.

Yu then set about preparing the lowlands for cultivation. Once they had properly drained, Yu strode through the marshlands, driving out every dragon and every serpent and sending them into the caves and holes that are their natural dens.

Yu did all this, but areas of great flood waters still remained to be confined. Waters still needed to be channeled, and they needed to be able to flow east into the four seas. However, whole mountain ranges blocked their drainage.

And so it came to pass that Yu began the most difficult of his tasks, digging passageways through the mountains so that the flood waters would have a means to escape and flow east toward the sea. He often transformed himself into a gigantic black bear with mighty claws, because it was in this form that he could remove the enormous boulders that formed the mountains and thus permit the water to drain from the land.

It came to pass that, during these years in the mountains, Yu became thirty years old. And as his work took him into the District of T'u-shan, he said to himself, "So this is the T'u-shan of the popular song! According to the song, he who visits T'u-shan and encounters a nine-tailed fox will surely sit upon a king's throne, for nine tails are the sign of royal power! And he who marries the T'u-shan girl will not only prosper, but his descendants will prosper! Power and wealth will be theirs, for Heaven smiles upon that man!

"No wonder everyone knows this song!" Yu exclaimed to himself. "After all, who among Nu Kua's mortals does not wish to have power and wealth! And who among them would not like to establish a successful family line! Why, the gods, too, value power and family! And both my father's life and my own surely reveal that the gods, too, prosper if they have Shang-ti's good will!

"Now I have lived for thirty years," Yu mused, "and yet I have never considered taking a wife. But, if not now, when? Soon it will be too late! And yet, if this is the time for me to marry, I would like to see some sign that this indeed is so."

And it came to pass that, as if in reply to Yu's thoughts, a nine-tailed white fox emerged from within a group of willow trees and walked across his path.

"Why, this is surely the omen that I seek!" Yu exclaimed to himself. "Today I am wearing a white robe, and here is the nine-tailed fox. Now all I have to do is find the T'u-shan girl and make her my wife!"

It then came to pass that Yu found a beautiful girl of T'u-shan waiting for him. He called her Nu-Chiao, and love called out to both of them! However, Yu was much too busy channeling the flood waters to marry Nu-Chiao then and there. So he continued with his present task, returned to marry Nu-Chiao as soon as he could leave his work, and then quickly returned to his labors.

It was not long before Nu-Chiao became very lonesome for Yu because he was almost always away at his work—busily digging passageways through the mountains—and she seldom saw him. Whenever she could, she pleaded with him to let her accompany him, and it came to pass that Yu finally agreed—although very reluctantly!

Before leaving her for the day, Yu would always say, "Now I want you to stay away from the mountain today, Nu-Chiao! My work is very dangerous, and it is not a safe place for you! I will hang my drum on the side of the mountain near the tunnel that I am digging, and when you hear me beat upon it, it will be safe for you to come to me. If you wish, you may bring me some food."

And so it came to pass that a dreadful accident occurred. If Nu-Chiao had not prevailed upon Yu to let her accompany him, it would never have happened. And if Yu had not transformed himself into a gigantic black bear with mighty claws, it also would never have happened. But she did. And he did. And it did.

Everyone agrees that the accident occurred while Yu was in the process of digging the passageway through the mountain. However, some say that Yu leaped upon a boulder and inadvertently struck it with his foot, making it resound like his drum. Some say that Yu was in the habit of tossing the boulders behind him as he dislodged them, and that one of these boulders bounced upon his drum, causing it to resound from the blow. Others say that Yu inadvertently tripped on a boulder, which then flew out from under his foot and hit his drum, causing it to resound from the blow. Still others say that Yu stumbled against a boulder that made a sound like the sound of his drum.

However Nu-Chiao spent these days, she lived for the sound of Yu's drum. And so it came to pass that when she heard its sound on this particular day, she quickly dropped whatever she had been doing, grabbed the basket of food that she had prepared, and set off for the mountain where Yu was working.

Meanwhile, the accident did not cause Yu to pause in his work. He paid no attention to the sound of his drum or the drumlike sound, since he was busily concentrating on his digging.

And so it came to pass that Nu-Chiao arrived at the mountain at a time when Yu did not expect to see her, and she saw her husband in his bear form. Her heart flooded with horror, terror, and shame. She screamed, dropped her basket, and fled!

Hearing Nu-Chiao's scream, Yu quickly turned from his work, ran out of the tunnel, and pursued his fleeing wife. Being very concerned about her, he forgot that he was in his bear form.

"Nu-Chiao!" he called. "Stop! What is the matter? Let me help you!"

Without stopping, Nu-Chiao looked back and saw that the great bear was chasing after her. She shuddered with horror at the thought of being married to such a beast! She shivered with terror at the thought of what would happen when that bear caught up to her, as he surely would! And she shrank with shame that her husband was not an ordinary man!

The race continued. Both Yu and Nu-Chiao ran ever faster. Yu could not wait to catch up to his wife and learn why she continued to flee.

Nu-Chiao continued to flee from Yu, her heart now flooded with panic—for she knew that her horror and terror of the bear could not sustain her flight much longer! And as she ran, Nu-Chiao's panic began to cause her body to shrivel up and stiffen. The living part of her began to withdraw deep within her, while her body became as hard and round as a rock. By the time that Yu caught up with her, Nu-Chiao had transformed herself into a boulder!

Yu was still too caught up in these events to be conscious of his own form. And his own heart now flooded with terror and rage. He knew that Nu-Chiao was pregnant, and he could not bear the thought that he would lose both his wife and his child.

"Nu-Chiao!" he screamed. "At least give me my child!"

And so it came to pass that, as Yu watched, the north side of the boulder that had been Nu-Chiao split apart, and Yu's infant son tumbled out upon the ground.

Yu quickly picked up the infant and warmed him, saying, "Welcome, little one! I will call you Ch'i ("to open"), for you emerged when a stone cracked open! And when you are grown, you will be the head of our family and a leader of Nu Kua's people!"

Little Ch'i was reared by Nu-Chiao's parents during all the years that Yu continued his work. The boy grew up with stories of his father's heroic exploits, instead of enjoying his father's loving presence.

And it came to pass that, by the time that Yu had brought the great flood under control, he had traveled throughout the entire earth. First, he had traveled as far to the east as the District of the Leaning Tree, with its dense forests and its mountains whose peaks tear into the sky. This journey had taken Yu through the District of Bird Valley, the District of the Green Mound, and the Land of the People with Black Teeth. And Yu had rescued all of the people who lived in these areas from the surly, surging flood waters.

Yu had then turned south and had traveled as far as the Land of Crossed Toes and the District of the Mountains of Nine Brilliances, with their many trees and roaring rivers. This journey had taken Yu through the Land of the Feathered Men, the Land of the Naked People, and the Land of Eternal Life. And Yu had rescued all of the people who lived in these areas from the surly, surging flood waters.

Yu then had turned west and had traveled as far as the Land of the Three Dangers. This journey had taken Yu through the District of the Banked Gold Mountain, the District of the Odd Arm, the District of the One Arm and Three Faces, and the Land of the People Who Sip Air and Drink Dew. And Yu had rescued all of the people who lived in these areas from the surly, surging flood waters.

Finally, Yu had turned north and had traveled as far as the Land of the Dog-Fight. This journey had taken Yu to the Region of Wilderness and to the Region of the Great Rivers and the Rocky Mountains. And Yu had rescued all of the people who lived in these areas from the surly, surging flood waters.

And so it had come to pass that, wherever the land had flooded, Yu had traveled. And he was always as concerned about the poor peasants as he was about the wealthy landowners.

Some say that it took Yu ten years before he had brought all the flood waters under control. Others say that his task took him thirteen years to complete. However, everyone agrees that Yu worked year after year without diversion. For ten years his work sometimes took him near his home in T'u-shan, and yet he was always too busy to stop and visit his family. Even when he heard his son crying, Yu forced himself to continue to concentrate on controlling the flood waters.

Yu worked so hard that his face became as black as pitch from the summer sun and the winter winds. He worked so hard that his hands and feet became hard and stiff from their callouses. He worked so hard that he wore the fingernails off his fingers, and no new nails could grow to replace them. He worked so hard that he wore the hair off his lower legs, and no new hair could grow to replace it.

Yu worked so hard that, in time, he limped because his leg muscles had shriveled up from their long periods of submersion in freezing winter flood waters, and his walk became no more than an unsteady shuffle. He worked so hard that his body shrank to half its size, and he became as thin as a rake.

And yet, Yu worked year after year without taking time for Ch'i, his son. He did not pause until he had brought all the flood waters under control, measured the whole world, and set the boundaries for the Nine Provinces.

And so it came to pass that Yu channeled the flood waters, drained all the lands in the Nine Provinces, and created the Four Seas. With the help of the black tortoise, he created dikes to protect the

Nine Marshes. With the help of Dragon Ying, he deepened the sources of the Nine Rivers. He made it possible for Nu Kua's mortal beings to rebuild their farms, their villages, their towns, and their lives in the Four Quarters. He removed the forests from the Nine Mountains so that that land, also, could be cultivated. Order now replaced chaos, and life on earth could begin anew.

In time it came to pass that Yu established the Hsia dynasty, which he ruled for only eight years—some say because he was very old by then. No one knows what happened to him after that. Some say that Yu died and is buried in a great cave on Mount Hui-chi, the mountain where he married Nu-Chiao, and that birds fly to this cave each year in order to care for the tomb of the hero they honor. Others say that Yu's human body may be buried on earth but that he returned to the home of the gods in his divine form. However, everyone agrees that wherever Yu is, the world is a better place because of him!

Song of the Water Goddess

The following myth about the water goddess originates with a Stone Age people who called themselves the Ainu, which means "human being." This Asiatic people inhabited the Japanese islands until Mongoloid invaders, who became the Japanese, drove them to live on the island of Hokkaido.

For many years, the Ainu were able to remain unaffected by other civilizations—and even unaffected by other Ainu settlements on Hokkaido—because they lived in isolated river valleys that contained a plentiful supply of food for their small population. The Ainu lived by hunting, fishing, and gathering, occupations that sustained their life in small, permanent villages that contained between ten and thirty households. In addition to wild edible plants, deer and salmon provided their principal sources of food. The Ainu had no system of writing, no political organization beyond their small villages, no system of agriculture beyond the cultivation of small plots, and no domesticated animals besides the dog.

The Ainu had little contact with the Japanese until about 1670, and whatever bronze or iron implements they possessed they received from the Japanese in exchange for dried fish, animal pelts, and live hawks. Two hundred more years passed before the Japanese decided to settle the island of Hokkaido, where most of the Ainu lived. Japanese settlement destroyed the traditional Ainu way of life. The Japanese cut down the forests, thus depriving the wild animal population of its food and shelter, and set up permanent fishing nets, which caught most of the fish in the area. Without their traditional occupations of hunting and fishing to support them, the Ainu men had to become migrant farm workers. Alcoholism and disease became part of their new way of life.

Early in the twentieth century, between fifteen thousand and sixteen thousand Ainu still lived on the island of Hokkaido. Many Ainu still knew their oral tradition, and scholars could collect and record the people's oral literature from Ainu storytellers. Most of the Ainu literature that we possess dates from the first three decades of the twentieth century. By the 1940s, although Ainu adults knew their native language as well as

Japanese, their children knew only Japanese. By 1955, fewer than twenty Ainu on the island of Hokkaido could still speak their native language fluently. Finally, in the 1970s, the plight of the Ainu became a public issue and attempts began to preserve the Ainu heritage.

"Song of the Water Goddess" provides a window both into a distant time and into the traditional life of a people who have ancient roots. The myth dates from the early Ainu period (the sixth or seventh century to the tenth century). Whether it is a literary creation or whether it originally served a religious purpose, the myth reveals how the Ainu came to develop rituals in connection with hunting and fishing.

The divinities in this myth are appealing because of their similarity to human beings. Except for the fact that they are divine and possess superhuman powers, they possess the same interests, values, and emotions that human beings possess.

The fact that the Ainu bard speaks in the voice of the water goddess permits listeners and readers to view events through her eyes. This technique reinforces the connection between the performer and the audience, reminding us that, despite individual and cultural differences, human beings continue to have much in common.

SONG OF THE WATER GODDESS

My way of living is to spend my time doing needlework, a task so exacting that I have to keep my eyes on my needle. Day followed day uneventfully until the day came when a large goblet, filled with our sacred drink, dropped down upon my windowsill. A winged, sacred drinking wand leaped this way and that upon the top of the goblet. As soon as my eyes rested upon it, it said the following words to me:

"Great Water-Dwelling Goddess, the god Okikurmi, he who watches over the Ainu and teaches them, has commanded that I bring you this message. The god Okikurmi says to you, 'Famine has come to live in the land of the Ainu. I have been helping my relatives by giving them all the food that I possess, but now I have no more to give them. I have used the last of my grain in order to brew the sacred drink in this goblet so that I could offer it to you as I now invoke your aid. Oh, Water-Dwelling Goddess, please help us!' These are the words of the god Okikurmi."

Having heard the god Okikurmi's message, I set up twelve tubs and emptied the sacred drink in the goblet into all twelve. I then invited four gods to a sacred feast at my home: Owl God, who rules the earth and the Ainu; Game God, who is the master of deer; Fish God, who is the master of salmon; and River-Rapids Goddess. Meanwhile, I spent my time doing needlework, a task so exacting that I have to keep my eyes on my needle. Day followed day uneventfully until the day came when my guests arrived.

I seated them, gave them our sacred drink, and said to them: "I have invited all of you here today in order to tell you that famine has come to live in the land of the Ainu. The god Okikurmi has been helping his relatives by giving them all the food that he possesses, but now he has no more to give them. He has used the last of his grain in order to brew our sacred drink, which he sent to me as a gift along with his prayer to invoke your aid. I, too, pray that you will honor his request."

At first, no one spoke a word. Then Game God said, "I can tell you this. When the deer, who are my relatives, visit the Ainu, the Ainu are not pleased to see the deer. Instead they regard them with contempt. They exclaim, 'Spring deer! No one wants to eat such meat!' They kill them, and then they throw them away. And so my poor relatives return home to me in tears. My heart feels sorrow for my deer and anger toward the Ainu. Therefore, I have confined the souls of all my deer in my storehouse."

Fish God then said, "I can tell you this. When the salmon, who are my relatives, visit the Ainu, the Ainu are not pleased to see the salmon. Instead they regard them with contempt. They exclaim, 'Scrawny fish! No one wants to eat such flesh!' They beat them with rotten wood until they are dead, and then they throw them away. And so my poor relatives return home to me in tears. My heart feels sorrow for my salmon and anger toward the Ainu. Therefore, I have collected the souls of all my salmon in baskets, and I have confined them in my storehouse."

Now, while Game God and Fish God were speaking, River-Rapids Goddess and I were singing and dancing. Meanwhile, Owl God did not speak a word. Instead, he sat very still with closed eyes. My heart told me that his heart was angry toward the Ainu because he thought that he had found a strand of hair from an Ainu woman's head in his sacred drink.

Therefore, I announced, "What a careless goddess I am! A strand of my hair fell into Owl God's sacred drink, and I did not even realize it! And now Owl God is angry at the Ainu because he thinks that the strand of hair belongs to an Ainu woman."

At these words, Owl God opened his eyes and said, "How fortunate! A strand of Water-Dwelling Goddess's beautiful hair has graced my sacred drink. And to think that I assumed that the strand had come from the head of an Ainu woman! I was wrong to have blamed the Ainu!"

While Owl God was speaking, River-Rapids Goddess and I were still singing and dancing. Suddenly my soul left my body and flew off to the home of Game God. It opened the doors of the god's storehouse and freed the souls of all the deer. Herds of large deer and small deer ran down the mountainsides, skipping and jumping with the joy of freedom. Having done this, my soul flew back to me and reentered my body.

Meanwhile, the soul of River-Rapids Goddess left her body and flew off to the home of Fish God. It opened the doors of the god's storehouse, collected the baskets containing the souls of all the salmon, and freed them, distributing them over the river's fishing beds. So many fish swam in the river that it appeared that those on the bottom would surely scrape against the rocks, while those near the water's surface would surely become scorched by the sun. Having done this, the soul of River-Rapids Goddess flew back to her and reentered her body.

Of course, River-Rapids Goddess and I were still singing and dancing, and the other gods smiled as they watched us. In time they learned that we had gone to their homes and had opened their storehouses, freeing their deer and their fish. However, since they could do nothing about it, they did not speak a word. Finally, they graciously offered their gratitude for the sacred feast and returned to their homes.

Thereafter, I spent my time doing needlework, a task so exacting that I have to keep my eyes on my needle. Day followed day uneventfully until the day came when, in a dream, I spoke to the god Okikurmi and told him what I had learned from the gods when I invited them to the sacred feast at my home.

I announced, "When I received your sacred drink and your message, I invited Game God, Fish God, Owl God, and River-Rapids Goddess to a sacred feast. River-Rapids Goddess and I sang and danced, and as the other gods enjoyed themselves, I learned why famine has come to live in the land of your relatives, the Ainu.

"Game God revealed that when the deer, who are his relatives, visit the Ainu, the Ainu are not pleased to see the deer," I explained. "Instead the Ainu regard them with contempt. They exclaim, 'Spring deer! No one wants to eat such meat!' They kill them, and then they throw them away. And so Game God's poor relatives return home to him in tears. His heart feels sorrow for his deer and anger toward the Ainu. Therefore, he has punished the Ainu by confining the souls of all his deer in his storehouse.

"Fish God revealed that when the salmon, who are his relatives, visit the Ainu, the Ainu are not pleased to see the salmon," I explained. "Instead, the Ainu regard them with contempt. They exclaim, 'Scrawny fish! No one wants to eat such flesh!' They beat them with rotten wood until they are dead, and then they throw them away. They apparently do not know that the proper way to kill fish is to make head-beating clubs from willow branches so that the souls of the salmon will be able to return happily to the land of the gods. And so Fish God's poor relatives return home to him in tears. His heart feels sorrow for his salmon and anger toward the Ainu. Therefore, he has collected the souls of all his salmon in baskets and has confined them in his storehouse.

"Meanwhile, River-Rapids Goddess and I were still singing and dancing, and the other gods were enjoying themselves at the sacred feast," I explained to Okikurmi. "Suddenly, my soul left my body and flew off to the home of Game God. It opened the doors of the god's storehouse and freed the souls of all the deer. Herds of large deer and small deer ran down the mountainsides, skipping and jumping with the joy of freedom. Having done this, my soul flew back to me and reentered my body.

"River-Rapids Goddess and I were still singing and dancing, and the other gods were enjoying themselves at the sacred feast," I continued, "when suddenly the soul of River-Rapids Goddess left her body and flew off to the home of Fish God. It opened the doors of the god's storehouse, collected the baskets containing the souls of all the salmon, and freed them, distributing them over the river's fishing beds. So many fish swam in the river that it appeared that those on the bottom would surely scrape against the rocks, while those near the water's surface would surely become scorched by the sun. Having done this, the soul of River-Rapids Goddess flew back to her and reentered her body."

"Therefore," I concluded, "the Ainu now have an abundance of deer and fish, and famine will leave their land. However, you must now command your relatives never to mistreat deer and fish again. And you yourself, on behalf of the Ainu, must thank River-Rapids Goddess for her help and worship her with proper rites. You must also apologize both to Game God and Fish God, and you must worship them with proper rites as well."

After this dream, in which I spoke to the god Okikurmi and told him what I had learned from the other gods when I invited them to the sacred feast at my home, I spent my time doing needlework, a task so exacting that I have to keep my eyes on my needle.

Day followed day uneventfully until the day came when both Game God and Fish God came to my home and thanked me for my help. "Oh, Great Water-Dwelling Goddess! Because of your advice to the god Okikurmi, the Ainu are now treating our relatives, the deer and the fish, in the way that they deserve," they declared.

And now the god Okikurmi worships me! He has offered me our sacred drink and proper rites as a way of showing his gratitude. My way of living is still to spend my time doing needlework, a task so exacting that I have to keep my eyes on my needle. Day still follows day uneventfully. However, my divine glory now sparkles like water when it reflects the dancing flames of the sun!

Taro Urashima, the Young Fisherman

The earliest people known to have inhabited the Japanese islands were Caucasians from northern Asia and Siberia, the people called the Ainu. Although two of the three earliest Japanese accounts of their early history still exist (the *Kojiki: Records of Ancient Matters,* completed in A.D. 712, and the *Nihongi* or *Nihonshoki: Chronicles of Japan from the Earliest Times to* A.D. *697,* completed in A.D. 720), accurate Japanese history is difficult to establish before A.D. 400, and it does not become completely reliable until A.D. 500. The *Kojiki* provides no chronology. According to the *Nihongi,* which attempts to provide historical accounts of Japan's mythical and legendary periods, Japan was founded in 660 B.C.

Scholars think that Mongolian peoples crossed the Korea Strait and settled the Japanese islands during the second and first centuries B.C. They brought with them the knowledge of how to grow rice in flooded fields, how to melt iron and forge it into tools (particularly fishhooks) and weapons (swords, spears, knives), and how to weave cloth. Although these people became islanders, they apparently had little interest in navigation.

The Japanese had no written language until the middle of the sixth century A.D., when the people became interested in Chinese culture. By the end of that century, they were reading and writing in Chinese, and by the early eighth century, they had adapted Chinese written forms to express their own language and ideas.

Early Japanese religion was a type of nature worship called Shintoism. Most of the Shinto deities were beneficent beings who inhabited the local forms and forces of nature. Shinto worship involved revering ancestors and offering prayer and food to the divinities. The *Kojiki* and the *Nihongi* are collections of Shinto records and beliefs.

The tale of Taro Urashima is one of the oldest and most popular Japanese myths. It appears twice in the Nara period (A.D. 710–784), first as a summary in the *Nihongi,* and then as the subject of the poem "The Boy Urashima of Mizunoe," composed by Takahashi Mushimaro and found in the oldest Japanese collection of poetry, the *Man'yoshu* (A.D. 760).

Six other versions of the Urashima myth were written between 794 and 1393, followed by one in Noh drama, one in a book of fairy tales, seven other dramatic versions and, finally, many versions in modern Japanese literature. These versions often emphasize important values of the particular era, such as respect for an ancient myth or legend, veneration for long life and immortality, obedience, and the importance of reciprocating a good deed.

According to scholars, the tortoise or turtle is one of the oldest animals in world mythology. In Japan, it is usually connected with the sea or with a goddess who lives beneath the sea. Urashima may originally have been viewed as God of the Earth, who rode on the back of a tortoise. However, legend has transformed him into an ordinary fisherman who first accepts, and then rejects, immortality. The temple at Kanagawa, located on the Pacific Ocean, displays what are said to be his tomb, the jewels and the lacquer box that he brought back from the land of the Dragon-King, as well as his fishing line.

The Urashima myth has counterparts in other cultures throughout the world. While the plots are always different, the themes are usually the same. For example, Oisin Mac Finn, the poet of the Fianna of Ireland, agrees to go with a goddess to the Land of Youth; he disappears with the goddess across the sea and, when he returns, three hundred years have passed, and Celtic Ireland has become Christian. (The myth about Oisin appears in Part 3 of this book.) In an American version, Rip Van Winkle falls asleep, and when he awakens "the next morning," twenty years have passed, and the American Revolution has occurred. ("Rip Van Winkle" appears in Part 4 of this book).

The Urashima myth addresses the universal human wish to remain eternally alive and young and the fantasy that these would be blessings. Taro Urashima finds that he misses his family. Other such characters miss the companionship of friends, the excitement of challenges and surprises, and the joys of accomplishments. In the end, these characters find that the human world is more appealing than the immortal world, despite the fact that human beings are frail and mortal. Consequently, the Urashima myth can lead us to appreciate that we are human and that our life is a priceless, fleeting treasure that, once gone, cannot be recaptured.

In the following version of this myth, Taro Urashima's name appears in its English order, with his surname last.

TARO URASHIMA, THE YOUNG FISHERMAN

Taro Urashima was a strong, handsome youth who lived in a small fishing village called Midzunoye, in the province of Tango, in Japan. Taro was a fisherman, and the son of a fisherman. Every day, he would row himself out to sea in order to catch fish. Some days, he returned with bream, bonito, or bass. Other days, he returned with carp, trout, or abalone. Other days, he returned with no fish at all.

One day, in the autumn of the year 477, during the reign of Emperor Yuriaku, Taro Urashima chose to row beyond the traditional fishing limits. He had been out for three days and four nights without catching a fish, and he decided that he might fare better if he rowed beyond the slope of the sea. His luck turned, and he caught a beautiful tortoise.

"I have seen a tortoise like this one once before," Taro said to himself. "I remember when a storm washed one ashore upon the beach, where it landed on its back. The village children had discovered it there before I did. And, by the time I came along, they were amusing themselves by prodding its tender belly with their sticks. But I soon put a stop to their game!

"I chased them away, saying, 'Shame on all of you! A tortoise can live for ten thousand years, and it is sacred to the Dragon-King of the Sea! Surely, it deserves your respect!'

"Then I turned the tortoise right-side up. With a prayer to the gods, I sent it off toward the water. And the last I saw of it, the tortoise was swimming safely out to sea," mused Taro.

"This tortoise is as beautiful as that one was!" he then exclaimed to himself. "Its wet back reflects the colors of the rainbow as it shines in the sun! I do not have the heart to take the life of one that has lived for so many years. I will release it so that it can live to the natural end of its days. I still have fresh bait for my hook. And surely I will get another bite before I must return home."

So it came to pass that Taro Urashima—again with a prayer to the gods—set the tortoise free and then settled back in his little boat to wait for another bite. However, the warmth of the sun and the gentle rocking motion of the waves put him to sleep.

It was then that Taro heard someone calling his name. "Taro Urashima! Taro Urashima!" the voice called sweetly.

Taro could not resist the appealing sound of that voice. He stood up in his boat and, to his surprise, he saw the tortoise whose life he had just saved.

Speaking Taro's language, the tortoise announced, "Taro Urashima, because of the kindness and respect that you have shown to me on two occasions, the Dragon-King of the Sea invites you to accompany me to his palace in the Land Where Time Stands Still."

Upon hearing the tortoise's words, the young fisherman thought to himself, "Who would believe that a tortoise has invited me to visit the palace of the great Dragon-King of the Sea! What a special opportunity! What a great honor! I cannot imagine that I have anything to lose by accepting it."

And so it came to pass that Taro Urashima climbed upon the tortoise's back and set forth on this journey. Although the tortoise quickly descended into the depths of the sea, Taro found that he could breathe naturally and that his clothing remained completely dry.

Before he had time to reflect upon this miracle, Taro found himself facing the beautiful palace of the Dragon-King of the Sea. Fashioned of coral and decorated with abalone shell and pearls, it was truly an awesome sight to behold. Moreover, it became clear that he was an expected and welcome guest. As soon as he arrived, flounder, carp, and sole, wearing royal robes, came out to welcome him. Meanwhile, the tortoise disappeared.

The fish took Taro Urashima inside the palace and into a great hall. There swordfish, sea horses, and dolphins proceeded to escort him into an even greater room that was located deeper within the palace. There the Dragon-King's daughter, Princess Otohime, was seated with her attendants, eagerly awaiting the arrival of the young fisherman who was as handsome as he was kind.

Princess Otohime was the most beautiful woman that Taro Urashima had ever seen. Her long black hair flowed down her back to her feet. Her robes were as brilliant as the sun, shimmering with the reds and golds that waves reflect when the sun shines upon them.

And it came to pass that Princess Otohime greeted Taro warmly, saying, "Welcome, kind-hearted young fisherman! I had heard tales of your great heart, and twice I changed myself into the form of a tortoise in order to see for myself whether what I had heard about you was true. Since it is true, I hereby promise to love you until the sun and the moon no longer ride across the heavens to mark the passing of day, night, and the seasons.

"If you will accept my love, Taro Urashima, and if you love me in return," Princess Otohime promised, "you will become my husband. And we will live together here in my father's kingdom, a land where the seasons always smile in natural harmony. Here, day after day, the golden sun shines upon the golden hills, while night after night, the silver moon shines upon the silver hills. Here, flowers never fade and never die.

"Like these flowers, you will find that you will never age and that you will never die. You will find that your heart will be forever happy, for sorrow never enters this land. And you will find that my love for you will remain as strong as the rocks that form the mountains, and that it will always be as pure as spun gold," Princess Otohime declared.

Upon hearing Otohime's words, the young fisherman thought to himself, "Who would believe that the Princess of the Sea, daughter of the great Dragon-King, has asked to marry me! What a special opportunity! What a great honor! She is so beautiful that I cannot resist her love. And I cannot help but love her in return. I cannot imagine that I have anything to lose by accepting her offer."

And so it came to pass that Taro Urashima replied, "Oh, most beautiful princess, of course I will accept your love and will love you in return! I am honored to become your husband and to remain here with you in your father's kingdom! And you will find that my love for you will remain as strong as the rocks that form the mountains, and that it will always be as pure as spun gold."

Once again, swordfish, sea horses, and dolphins appeared before Taro. This time they were wearing long ceremonial robes in honor of the royal wedding, and they were carrying great coral trays that were piled high with the great edible delicacies of the sea. Taro Urashima and Princess Otohime pledged to love one another to the end of time and shared the sacred drink that is part of the traditional marriage ceremony. Meanwhile, the fish of the sea danced on the white sand and sang to the strains of soft music, their silver scales and golden tails reflecting the golden sand and the silvery white pebbles that were strewn upon it.

In time, Princess Otohime showed her husband the wonders of her father's kingdom. And, truly, the land was just as remarkable as she had told him it was! Here, spring reigned eternally in the East. Warblers and nightingales sang lovely songs. Cherry trees and plum trees remained in full bloom, their pink and white blossoms providing nourishment to myriads of bright-winged butterflies that drank their nectar.

Here, summer reigned eternally in the South. The cuckoo sang its song for the blooming iris. Frogs croaked in ponds adorned with floating lilies, and trees remained clothed with leaves that shimmered like emeralds in the light breeze.

Here, autumn reigned eternally in the West. Maple trees remained fully clothed in their leaves of fiery red, and chrysanthemums bloomed continuously in the colors of the setting sun. The stag roamed through the woodlands, and the cries of wild geese filled the air.

And here, winter reigned eternally in the North. Ice-covered ponds reflected the blue-tinted light of the pale sun, while wild ducks took refuge among the reeds. Winter trees gleamed silvery-white with snow, with their berries shining ruby-red and crackling in the frosty breeze.

The wonders of the Land Where Time Stands Still might have been enough for Taro Urashima. However, he found that his marriage was just as remarkable as Princess Otohime had told him that it would be! Happiness always flooded his heart, for sorrow never entered that land. His wife's love for him remained as strong as the rocks that form the mountains. And, indeed, it was as pure as spun gold.

However, it came to pass that in the Land Where Time Stands Still, time nevertheless passed quickly. Taro's heart sensed that three years had passed as if they were but three days in his life. And as happy as he was in his new life, Taro began to think more and more about his parents. He remembered how he had left them suddenly and unexpectedly, without support and without even a loving farewell. Taro's love for the couple who had reared him now fought in his heart with his love for his wife. And his eyes would fill with tears whenever he gazed at the woman he loved.

One day, when Taro could stand the pain no longer, he said to Otohime, "Dear one! As much as love for you floods my heart, I long to see my parents and take my loving farewell of them. Because of how I left them, sorrow must rule their hearts and their lives. So I ask you to let me leave you for just a day. I give you my word that I will return to you tomorrow. And then I will love you alone to the end of time—with a love that, like yours, will remain as strong as the rocks that form the mountains and as pure as spun gold."

To these words, Otohime tearfully replied, "Your desire floods my heart with fear, Taro! I dread your departure, for my heart senses that I will never see you again! So I plead with you, dearest husband, stay with me but one day longer. And then I will send you back to your home!"

But Taro Urashima would not agree. "Dear one! The duty that I owe my parents is forged of unbreakable metal!" he declared. "Just as I spared your life when you appeared to me in the form of a tortoise, so I must respect the life of my parents and leave you for a day in order to look after them.

"I am not breaking the promise that I made to you when we became husband and wife," Taro explained. "I give you my word that I will return to you tomorrow. And then I will love you alone to the end of time—with a love that, like yours, will remain as strong as the rocks that form the mountains and as pure as spun gold."

To these words, Otohime tearfully replied, "Taro, dearest husband, if nothing that I can say or do will dissuade you, then I will return you to your own land. But take this parting gift in memory of our love, and listen well to my parting words.

"I want you to have this beautiful little black-lacquered box as a keepsake," declared Otohime. "However, once you return home, if you still remember me and if you still love me, no matter how much you may wish to do so, you must not untie these red silk tasseled cords and you must not open the box! Instead, if you wish to return to me, just hold the box in your hands and grip it with all your might.

"I must warn you, Taro: If you forget my words, or if you disobey my command, something terrible will happen! And you will never be able to return to my father's kingdom or see me again! So remember, Taro! Never untie these silk cords. And never open this beautiful box!" she concluded.

To these words, Taro Urashima replied, "Lovely Otohime, put your worries to rest. I promise that I will treasure your gift! And I will remember your warning. I will never open your box. In fact, I will never even loosen its silken cords!"

So it came to pass that, after a loving farewell, the tortoise reappeared and quickly carried Taro Urashima back to his own country. Of course, his journey through the sea left him as dry as it had originally.

Taro's heart flooded with joy as the tortoise entered the familiar bay and left him on its beach. His eyes flooded with joy at the sight of his homeland. He quickly went forth to greet his parents. He smiled to see the familiar hills, with the mountains a soft blue in the distance beyond them. He laughed to see the familiar stream that meandered through his village.

However, as he walked along, Taro's smile froze on his face, and his laughter stuck in his throat. He expected to find the old road. However, he found that he was walking on a new road where the old road had been. He expected to find his old village. However, he found a larger, bustling town where his old village had been.

Taro Urashima passed many townsfolk. However, he could not discover one familiar face. And the townspeople, in turn, regarded Taro as a stranger.

Taro Urashima looked for his home. However, he found a large new house where his cottage had been. Nevertheless, he approached this house and knocked on the door.

When a strange woman answered, Taro asked her, "Madam, would you please show me the way to the house of the young fisherman Taro Urashima and his parents? Your house is not their house. But they should be living where your house now stands."

To these words, the woman replied, "Young man, I have never heard of a young fisherman called Taro Urashima, or his family. My own family has lived in this house since the time of my great-grandfather! You will have to ask someone else about those people. I wish you good luck in your search!"

So it came to pass that Taro Urashima continued on his way through the town. He searched every face to see if it was the face of one of his parents—or, at least, the face of a friend or an acquaintance. However, he saw only strange faces where familiar faces had been.

And as Taro walked and walked, he became more and more anxious with each step. Now he stopped each person he met and asked, "Would you please show me the way to the house of the young fisherman Taro Urashima and his parents?"

However, these townspeople simply shook their heads from side to side and continued on their way.

Finally, Taro came upon a very old man, who was slowly hobbling down the road. He was a great-great-grandfather and surely the town elder. Therefore, Taro greeted him and asked, "Most Respected

Grandfather, would you please show me the way to the house of the young fisherman Taro Urashima and his parents?"

To these words, the town elder replied, "Young man, who are you? And where are you from that you ask me such a foolish question? Surely you know that it is now the year 825. The boy you mention, Taro Urashima—and, of course, his family as well—have been dead for well over three hundred years! Therefore, it is foolish to ask where their house is.

"However, if you wish to see their last home, go to the old village burial ground," he advised Taro. "It is just outside the town, near what remains of the old Shinto temple. No one goes there anymore, so the old gravestones are covered with moss and hard to read. Nevertheless, if you look closely, you will find what remains of Taro Urashima and his family.

"Villagers still talked about them when I was a child," the town elder added. "They said that the young Urashima used to row out to sea in order to fish. One day, he was seen heading beyond the traditional fishing limits toward treacherous waters, where he drowned! His parents died of grief soon thereafter."

And with these final words, the old man continued on his way, shaking his head from side to side in wonder as he slowly hobbled down the road.

Taro Urashima stared after the old man in silence. The town elder's words brought to his ears the same message that the sights of the town had brought to his eyes. More than a hundred years in this land had passed as only one year in the sea kingdom of the Dragon-King! Everything in his world as he had known it—and every person he remembered—was long gone!

Taro Urashima easily found the old graveyard because that, at least, was just where it had been. And searching the gravestones for the names of his parents gave Taro the only sense of home that was left for him. For here, at last, in the graveyard, he found the village that he had left behind! Here, at last, he found the names of all the familiar faces that he had hoped to see upon his return. Finally, here, at last, he found his parents. And, buried next to them, he found his own grave. Taro Urashima was alive among the dead, and dead among the living!

Taro then left the graveyard. He turned his back on the town and returned to the sea. Overcome with shock and horror, he ran along the shore, ranting and raving in his sorrow. He waved his arms, stamped his feet, and rolled upon the ground. However, he could not capture Time and bring back the past.

Finally, Taro Urashima lay still upon the sand, his eyes red with weeping and his heart worn thin with despair. The gentle lapping of the waves upon the shore brought the memory of beautiful Otohime and the sea kingdom of the Dragon-King into his mind.

Suddenly, the waves became louder. Taro's ears fastened onto their sound. Did he hear, "Taro Urashima! Taro Urashima!"? Was Otohime once again calling to him in her sweet voice?

Taro rose to his feet and scanned the waves. However, he could not see the tortoise whose life he had saved. And so it came to pass that Taro Urashima remembered his wife's parting gift. He reached into his pocket and withdrew the beautiful black-lacquered box that his beloved had tied with red tasseled cords of silk. He stared at it thoughtfully.

Then Taro Urashima broke the promise that he had made to Otohime. Slowly he untied the cords that sealed the box, and he began to remove the lid. As if it were longing to escape, a cold vapor instantly rushed out of the box. It flew up to Taro's face, where it stopped for a moment. And then it floated out to sea on the wings of the wind as if it were a small white summer cloud. Except for that vapor, the box was empty.

As Taro Urashima watched the cloud of vapor leave him, it seemed to him that it took the shape of his beloved wife. He reached out to the departing cloud and called, "Otohime! Oh, Otohime! Please come back! I am so sorry that I broke my promise to you!"

Taro strained to see when and where the small white cloud had vanished. However, as he searched the horizon, suddenly he began to shiver and shake uncontrollably from head to toe. And suddenly his eyes became too dim to see the cloud.

Taro instinctively stepped toward the waves, as if to follow the cloud to its home in the sea. However, suddenly his body cried out in agonizing protest and refused to obey his wishes. Suddenly his back was no longer able to support him. Instead, it forced him to bend forward until he found that he was staring down at his own feet and the sandy shore on which they rested.

And it came to pass that, as Taro Urashima looked down at his feet, snowy-white hair and a long, snowy-white beard blew across his face on the wings of the wind. And he knew that they belonged to him.

With growing amazement, Taro noticed that his arms had shriveled to mere bones, with only a waxlike, wrinkled covering of skin to protect them. He saw that his legs were now withered and wobbly from the weight of his body. And then, suddenly, they gave way beneath him.

Taro Urashima opened his mouth to cry out, and his teeth dropped upon the sand like seashells. His heart became too weak to beat in anger or in protest. Finally, even the process of beating became too difficult, and his heart, too, collapsed.

The next morning, children found Taro Urashima's body where it had crumpled upon the sand. They had never seen anything like it. And so they ran to tell their parents about the fearsome sight. Even the old ones of the town were awestruck by the sight of such an ancient being. The corpse that lay upon the beach was far older than the town's great-great-grandfather. Its face was shriveled like a dried peach; its hair was whiter than snow; and its limbs were as crooked as the branches of a gnarled tree.

Only the town elder, that great-great-grandfather, thought that he could explain the sight. As he looked at the ancient, withered figure, whose crooked fingers still gripped the top of a beautiful black-lacquered box, he remembered the young stranger and his questions. And then he put the pieces of the puzzling tale into their proper places.

This is the story that the town elder told to the people of Midzunoye, in the year 825. And this is the story that, through generations of storytellers, I have now passed down to you.

The Tiger's Whisker

Korea has long been influenced by its neighbor China. During the period of the Han dynasty in China (202 B.C.–A.D. 220), Korea was a Chinese colony. Several Korean states became united as one country in the seventh century A.D.

Korea came under the control of the Mongolian Chinese in the thirteenth century. Confucianism was the country's official religion from 1392 until Japan annexed Korea in 1910. Based on the teachings of the great Chinese philosopher Confucius (551–479 B.C.), which are known only through the writings of his disciples, the philosophy and religion of Confucianism aimed to establish justice in a time of tyrannical government and peace in a time of war. Confucianism emphasizes "human-heartedness" and includes such principles as responsibility and loyalty to one's family, self-discipline and self-restraint, the appropriate way to relate to other people, and the value of learning. The values to be found within "The Tiger's Whisker" are consistent with these aspects of Confucianism.

"The Tiger's Whisker" has universal appeal and relevance. The plight of the young woman is one that we can apply to our own lives, and what she learns from obtaining the tiger's whisker is valuable to us as well. This short tale contains a lifetime of wisdom—wisdom that continues to enrich the lives of readers long after the tale itself has ended.

THE TIGER'S WHISKER

It came to pass that, as soon as the war came to an end, Yun Ok's husband returned home. However, the war had changed him. In fact, he was so changed that he was now a different man. The young man who had left Yun Ok had loved life, whereas the man who returned now rejected all that he had loved. The young man who had left Yun Ok had been gentle and kind, whereas the man who

432

returned was rough-mannered and mean-spirited. The young man who had left Yun Ok had looked well to the ways of his farm, whereas the man who returned was lazy and idle much of the time.

Months of days and nights had come and gone since the return of Yun Ok's husband. For Yun Ok, each new day had begun with the promise of hope, but each night had brought the despair of failure. Winter had become spring, and spring had become summer. Wildflowers now bloomed in the fields. However, they did not bloom for her husband and, therefore, they did not bloom for Yun Ok.

Yun Ok's first thoughts each morning and her last thoughts each night were the same. "I hate the war!" she would exclaim to herself. "It has taken the man I love from me, and in his place it has given me a stranger! Woe is me! I am so unhappy!"

Finally, it came to pass that Yun Ok was desperate. "I am miserable!" she exclaimed to herself one night. "And there is no end in sight to my misery. But surely there must be someone somewhere who can help me!"

Yun Ok thought and thought, and then she suddenly remembered the learned mountain hermit. "I will find the Sage of the Mountains and tell him my story," she declared to herself. "Once he hears my tale of woe, his heart will surely flood with sorrow and sympathy for my plight, and he surely will know which of his powerful charms or magic potions will restore my loving husband to me. I will set out as soon as the sun makes the land bright."

And so it came to pass that Yun Ok arose as early as the sun and set off for the mountains. The way was long, and the climb was hard, but the well-worn path made Yun Ok confident that her journey would not be in vain.

The sun was high in the sky when Yun Ok finally reached the learned man's mountain hut. She knocked on the door but heard no reply. Finding that the door was unlatched, she opened it and stepped into a dim, firelit room.

A bent old figure sat huddled in front of the fire, staring into its flames. With his back to Yun Ok, and without moving, the Sage of the Mountains asked, "What brings you up this steep mountain path to my door?"

"Oh, renowned sage," Yun Ok replied. "My heart cries out to you in pain. I know that one of your special charms or potions is the only thing that can help me!"

"Go home!" the mountain hermit replied. "I can do nothing for you. You are just like everyone else. You have troubles, and you think that a charm or potion will make them disappear. Well, you are wrong. The whole world is sick, and no charm or potion will cure what is wrong with it! So I repeat, go home! I am sorry that you have made this journey for nothing!"

"Oh, please, learned one! At least hear my story before you send me away empty-handed. You are truly my last resort!"

The Sage of the Mountains gave an audible sigh of resignation, turned toward Yun Ok, and replied, "All right. Tell me, what is troubling you?"

"I have come about my husband," Yun Ok responded. "Three years ago, the man I loved went off to war, and he has returned so different that I no longer know him. He used to smile upon the world and greet everyone in friendship, but now the world no longer makes his heart sing, and he has no interest in talking to anyone, even to me.

"My husband is very dear to my heart, and yet he does not seem to care about me at all! If he speaks to me, his voice is abrupt and harsh. If I speak to him, he is deaf to the sound of my voice. If I feed him a tasty meal, he eats it in silence. If he dislikes what I have cooked, he angrily pushes away the plate and leaves the room. And our farm, which used to be a source of pride to him, now bores him. When there is work to be done in the rice fields, I often see my husband sitting on the hill with his eyes fastened on the sea. He has come home from the war, and yet he is not really home at all!"

"Your story is not unusual, my dear," the Sage of the Mountains replied. "Many wives and mothers see this type of behavior in their men when they return from war. They return with their bodies whole, but their spirits suffer from serious wounds. Is there more to your story?"

"No," Yun Ok responded. "I have told you all that there is to tell. This is why my heart cries out in pain! I want you to make my husband become the man that he used to be. I want him to be kind, and loving, and interested in our life together. His heart has frozen. Surely you have something to give me that can warm the human heart!"

"The potion for the human heart is not a simple matter!" the

Sage of the Mountains exclaimed. "You obviously know nothing about what you ask! Such a potion calls for special ingredients, and I will need to give the matter serious thought. I will need three days and three nights. Now, if you are willing to return to me when those days and nights have come and gone, then we will be able to discuss what is necessary."

With these words, the Sage of the Mountains turned his back on Yun Ok and once again sat staring into the flames of his fire.

"I will do as you ask," Yun Ok declared.

The young woman returned home to her husband, and it came to pass that, when three days and nights had come and gone, she once again returned to the learned mountain hermit. He was sitting just as she had left him, staring into the flames of his fire.

"As you have requested, I have waited for three days and nights, and now I have returned to you," Yun Ok announced. "Have you found that you can help me?" she asked.

As soon as he heard Yun Ok's words, the Sage of the Mountains turned away from the fire's flames and toward Yun Ok. "Young woman, I am certain that I can help you if you are willing to help me!" he declared. "I have every ingredient that your potion requires except for the most important one—a whisker from a living tiger! Now, if you can bring me that whisker, then I will be able to give you the potion that will warm your husband's heart."

"A whisker from a living tiger!" Yun Ok exclaimed in disbelief. "Surely you know what you are asking of me! And surely you know that I cannot possibly get that for you! The tiger is the most savage of beasts! If no other whisker will do, can you not get a tiger's whisker for yourself?"

"No, I cannot," responded the mountain hermit. "You must do your part to make the potion. And if you care enough to have it, then you will find that you will be able to get the whisker that I need."

With these words, the Sage of the Mountains turned his back on Yun Ok and once again stared into the flames of his fire.

Yun Ok returned home to her husband. Many days and nights came and went while she thought about her love for her husband and considered how she might acquire a whisker from a living tiger. Finally, she decided to appeal to the tiger's appetite by bringing it a bowl of tasty rice and meat sauce.

So it came to pass that, one moonlit night, after her husband had fallen asleep, Yun Ok stealthily crept first from their bed and then from their house and, with only her need for the potion to sustain her, she fearfully made her way up into the mountains to the cave where she had heard that a tiger had made its den. As soon as she entered the clearing and saw in the distance the blackness that marked the entrance to the cave, Yun Ok called out in a soft, trembling voice, "Tiger! Tiger! Come forth from your den! I have brought you tasty rice and meat. So, Tiger! Tiger! Come forth now and eat!"

Nothing happened. Yun Ok could hear no sound at all. And she could see no sign of the tiger. So she took the tasty rice and meat sauce from her bowl and emptied it on the ground at her feet. Then she turned, made her way back down the mountainside, and returned home to her sleeping husband.

And it came to pass that Yun Ok made that journey one moonlit night after another as soon as her husband had fallen asleep. Night after night, she would stealthily slip away first from their bed and then from their house and make her way up into the mountains to the clearing that revealed the cave where the tiger made its den. Now that her journey was becoming more familiar, Yun Ok was no longer afraid. And now she knew that a tiger did, in fact, live in the mountain cave, for each night when she arrived at the clearing, she noticed that her food offering from the previous night had disappeared without a trace.

And each night, when Yun Ok came into the clearing, she thought of her love for her husband, gathered her courage, and moved a step or two closer to the mouth of the tiger's cave than she had been the night before. Then, in a voice that also grew stronger with each night, she called out, "Tiger! Tiger! Come forth from your den! I have brought you tasty rice and meat. So, Tiger! Tiger! Come forth now and eat!"

However, still nothing happened. Still Yun Ok could hear no sound at all. And still she could see no sign of the tiger. So she would take the tasty rice and meat sauce from her bowl and empty it on the ground at her feet. Then she would turn, make her way back down the mountainside, and return home to her sleeping husband.

And so it came to pass that Yun Ok continued to make her journey one night after another, now, even on the nights when the moon had turned its face away from the earth. Two months of nights came and went, and still Yun took her bowl of tasty rice and meat sauce and went forth into the mountains to the clearing that revealed the tiger's cave. There, night after night, she would step ever closer to the mouth of the tiger's cave and call out, "Tiger! Tiger! Come forth from your den! I have brought you tasty rice and meat. So, Tiger! Tiger! Come forth now and eat!"

However, still Yun Ok could hear no sound at all. But now, she could see a pair of shining eyes staring out at her from the mouth of the cave. So she would take the tasty rice and meat sauce from her bowl and empty it on the ground at her feet. Then she would turn, make her way back down the mountainside, and return home to her sleeping husband.

And it came to pass that two more months of nights came and went like the others before them. Still Yun took her bowl of tasty rice and meat sauce and went forth into the mountains to the clearing that revealed the tiger's cave. There, night after night, she would step ever closer to the mouth of the tiger's cave and call out, "Tiger! Tiger! Come forth from your den! I have brought you tasty rice and meat. So, Tiger! Tiger! Come forth now and eat!"

It now came to pass that the night came when Yun Ok still heard no sound, but she saw the pair of shining eyes moving slowly out of the cave and into the moonlight of the clearing in which she was standing. Gathering her courage, Yun Ok forced herself to think only of her love for her husband and stood her ground. She continued to stand breathlessly still until it came to pass that she was looking directly into the tiger's shining eyes. That night, as always, Yun Ok took the tasty rice and meat sauce from her bowl and placed it on the ground at her feet for the tiger to eat. The tiger was still standing silently in front of the food when Yun Ok silently turned, made her way back down the mountainside, and returned home to her sleeping husband.

And then it came to pass that the night came when the tiger met Yun Ok outside its cave even before she would have called, "Tiger! Tiger! Come forth from your den! I've brought you tasty rice and meat. So, Tiger! Tiger! Come forth now and eat!"

And then it came to pass that the night came when the tiger ate the food that Yun Ok had placed on the ground at her feet while she stood facing it.

And then it came to pass that the night came when the tiger ate the food out of the bowl that Yun Ok held out to it.

And, in this way, it came to pass that two more months of nights came and went like the others before them. Yun Ok would come up the mountain and enter the clearing to find that the tiger was always waiting outside its den for her. And now the tiger would always eat the tasty rice and meat sauce from the bowl that she held in her hand. And Yun Ok began to reward the tiger by gently caressing its head while speaking soft words to it to reassure it as she touched it.

It came to pass that the tiger continued to behave as if it were a large, tame house cat rather than the most savage of beasts. And Yun Ok knew that now, at long last, she could hope to get one of the tiger's whiskers for the learned hermit.

On the following night, after the tiger had eaten and had received his caresses, Yun Ok said to it softly, "Tiger! Tiger! Do not be angry with me, but I need a whisker, please. Tiger! Tiger! If you would stand quietly while I snip just one, I will be grateful to you now and always!"

As she calmly spoke these words, Yun Ok slowly raised her hand and clipped one of the tiger's whiskers. To her surprise, the tiger continued to stand patiently in front of her. She rewarded it by rubbing its head. Then she turned, made her way back down the mountain, and returned home to her sleeping husband. She almost skipped along the trail that she had made during the course of these six months, for her heart was flooded with the joy of her hard-won triumph.

And so it came to pass that Yun Ok arose as early as the sun and set off once again for the mountains and the hut of the learned hermit. The treasured whisker that she carried clutched in her hand now made the way seem short and the climb up the well-worn path seem easy. However, as always, the sun was high in the sky when Yun Ok finally reached the learned hermit's mountain hut.

Once again, when Yun Ok knocked on the door, she heard no reply. And, once again, finding that the door was unlatched, she opened it and stepped into the dim, firelit room. As she expected, the familiar bent old figure still sat huddled in front of the fire, staring into its flames. His back was to Yun Ok, and without moving, the Sage of the Mountains asked, "What brings you up this steep mountain path to my door?"

To these words, Yun Ok replied, "Oh, renowned sage, it is I, Yun Ok. And I have brought you the special ingredient that you requested. Here is a whisker from a living tiger! So now you can make the potion that will warm my husband's heart!"

Upon hearing these words, the Sage of the Mountains turned from his fire and looked at his visitor. Without a word, he then took the tiger's whisker from Yun Ok's outstretched hand and carefully examined it.

"It is just as you say, Yun Ok," he declared. "This is indeed a whisker from a living tiger!"

And with these words, the learned hermit turned and cast the tiger's whisker into the flames of his fire.

"Oh! Oh! What have you done!" Yun Ok cried. "Surely you know how hard I worked to get that whisker for you!"

As if he were deaf to her words, the learned man commanded, "Now, tell me, Yun Ok, just how did you manage to acquire a whisker from a living tiger?"

"Well, most wise one, I thought long and hard about the problem. Finally, I decided to try to win the tiger's confidence with offerings of tasty food. So every night, as soon as my husband had fallen asleep, I would quietly leave our bed and our house, and then make my way up into the mountains to the tiger's den. Every night, when I reached the clearing in front of his cave, I would call out, 'Tiger! Tiger! Come forth from your den! I have brought you tasty rice and meat. So, Tiger! Tiger! Come forth now and eat!'

"At first, I only set forth when the moon could show me the way. And I was terrified of the savage beast, so when I reached the clearing, I stood as far away from its cave as I could. However, when night followed night and still I did not see the tiger, I gradually became more confident and moved ever closer to the mouth of the cave. By this time, my path up the mountainside was very familiar, and I never missed a night. Each night, before returning to my sleeping husband, I would empty my bowl of rice and meat sauce on the ground and leave it there for the tiger to eat if it chose. It appeared that the tiger always ate my food, for I never saw any sign of it when I returned on the following night. However, I never saw the tiger.

"Then, after two months of nights had come and gone, the time came when I could see the tiger's pair of shining eyes staring at me from within the cave. Two more months of nights came and went before the tiger trusted me enough to leave its den and meet me in the clearing in front of its cave. There, I would place its food on the ground, and the tiger would eat it while I stood by and watched.

"Then I tried to hold the bowl up to the tiger's head before I put it on the ground to see if it would take the food from my hands.

Eventually, the time came when the tiger would eat from my bowl while I held the bowl up to its mouth. And then I began to reward the tiger by gently caressing its head while speaking soft words to it to reassure it as I touched it. In this way, two more months of nights came and went.

"And so it came to pass that, last night, the tiger let me clip one of its whiskers so that I could bring it to you as you had asked. And this I have now done."

To these words, the Sage of the Mountain replied, "Yun Ok, I can see that you have worked long, and hard, and well, to accomplish your task. Now I ask you to remember what I also said to you the last time that we talked together. I told you that I could help you if you were willing to help me. You see, there are actually many different types of potions. You used one of your own making when you spoke kind words to the tiger and brought it a tasty dinner night after night for six months. Slowly and carefully you earned the confidence and affection of a savage beast, and you even tamed it to the point where it permitted you to cut off one of its whiskers."

"Yes, I did," Yun Ok replied. "And I had hoped that you would use that whisker to give me the potion that I need, just as you had told me you that you would. But you have only taken my hard-won whisker and tossed it into the flames of your fire! I cannot bear to think of all the time and effort that I have wasted on your silly request! Once again, my heart cries out in pain! But now I have nowhere to turn for help!"

To these words, the Sage of the Mountains replied, "Yun Ok, I see that you still do not understand. You have not wasted any of your time, nor have you wasted any of your efforts. I did not send you off with a silly request. I tossed the tiger's whisker into the flames because now that you have acquired it, neither you nor I need it any longer!

"Now tell me, Yun Ok," the learned hermit continued, "who is more savage, a tiger or a man? And who is easier to tame? And who is more worthy of your efforts? You decided that it was worth six months of soft words and good food in order to bring me a whisker from a living tiger, the animal that is known to be the most savage of all beasts. Surely, your husband—whom you love enough to have conquered your fear of the tiger and to have gone to all of this trouble—is worth even more of your thought, and more of your effort, and more of your patience!

"Thought, effort, and patience are, in fact, the most important ingredients in the potion that you seek," the Sage of the Mountains continued. "And the ingredients for this potion are not within my mind. You yourself have them within your own heart. Surely you, as well as I, must realize that your taming of the tiger reveals that you already possess the power to heal your husband! So return to your husband and use that potion. And you will see that it will surely warm his heart!"

With these words, the Sage of the Mountains turned his back on Yun Ok and once again sat staring into the flames of his fire. Meanwhile, in stunned silence, Yun Ok continued to stand in the firelit room, letting the words of the wise man sink into her mind and into her heart.

Yun Ok made her way back down the mountain slowly, the wise words of the hermit echoing in her mind and reechoing in her heart. The sun was setting as she finally walked up the path to her home. Seeing that her husband had returned before her, she gave him a bright smile and declared, "We will eat in just a few minutes, dear one! What do you think of having rice and meat sauce for dinner?"

Kerta's Sacrifice

The myth of Kerta originates on the island of Java, which is part of Indonesia. With its tropical climate and its rich volcanic soil, Java's hospitable environment supports a dense population. Its rubber, spices, and sugar have long been prized by other countries, and its history includes centuries of foreign domination by India and, later, Holland.

Through the ages, the people of Java have prized the nests of small swifts (swallowlike birds) because instead of building them from materials like stems and leaves, the swifts form them from their own saliva. Consequently, a swift's nest is edible, and it makes a soup that is popular in many areas of the Far East, including China. The swifts build their nests in caves that are within the rocky cliffs that line the south shore of Java and that are lashed by waves of the Indian Ocean.

This fertility myth is rooted in the indigenous culture of Java. Those who gathered the nests of the swifts, as well as those who depended in other ways on the sea, traditionally have respected Roro Kidul, the Javanese goddess of the "South Sea," the Javanese name for the Indian Ocean. Whenever anyone drowned, Roro Kidul was always to blame.

"Kerta's Sacrifice" is an example of a myth that has acquired aspects of a folktale. In its original setting and oral form, it both reflects the society that created it and represents a type of myth that is universal in its generic plot, its theme, and its purpose. As is common in myths, the plot begins with a human being who dishonors a divinity. The god then retaliates with a punishment that is so terrifying that it motivates all who hear the myth to remember to respect and honor their divinities.

However, the folktale elements that are present in "Kerta's Sacrifice" soften the harshness of the basic myth. In the original myth, the offending human being would be depicted as an accomplished but arrogant young adult, whereas here he is a boy who is disrespectful because he has not yet learned to have the proper respect for the gods. Moreover, the original myth would focus on the relationship between the offending individual and the divinity, and the way in which the punishment would work itself out. In contrast, this version of the myth focuses on the relationships among the members of one human family, and it relegates the divinity to the background.

"Kerta's Sacrifice" is particularly appealing because it combines the power that divinity wields in a myth with the more human-centered world of a folktale. Kerta is both very heroic in his accomplishments and very human in his personality. The issues of why he brings the wrath of the goddess upon himself and how he handles her vengeance create a story that contains both suspense and psychological interest.

Moreover, "Kerta's Sacrifice" is unusually powerful because it examines the relationship between human beings and the powers upon which they depend for their survival. It reminds us of the wonder and terror that we, too, feel whenever the forces of nature attack us and our technology can do little to protect us.

KERTA'S SACRIFICE

In a time long past, Kerta's father, Pak Miam, was a swift's-nest gatherer. Such a man had to possess great strength, greater courage, and even greater judgment in order to succeed at this dangerous task. Therefore, everyone in his community respected and honored him for his skills. And he in turn respected and honored Roro Kidul, Goddess of the Sea, above all the other gods, for his life and well-being depended on her goodwill.

Kerta could hardly wait to become a swift's-nest gatherer so that everyone would give him the admiration and respect that they gave to his father. This had been his dream ever since he could remember. And now it would not be long before he could take his place as a man among the other men in his village.

So it came to pass that the day came when Kerta said to Pak Miam, "Father, I think that I am now old enough to become a swift's-nest gatherer! I will soon become a man among the other men of our village. I am already brave, strong, and quick, and I do not fear the sea!"

"You are not ready yet, Kerta," his father replied. "Strong as you are, and as sure of foot, you must be a man before you can test your courage and your skill. And above all, you must have a man's respect for the power of Roro Kidul! Without that, all of your courage, strength, and skill—no matter how great they are—will not help you!"

"Surely you know, Kerta, that the swifts make their nests within the rocky cliffs that line the south shore of our island, and that those cliffs face the great South Sea," his mother added.

"Of course, Mother! Every child in our village knows that!" Kerta replied.

"And you know, Kerta, that Roro Kidul rules that sea!" his father exclaimed.

"Of course, Father! Every child knows that, too!" Kerta replied.

"And that is the trouble, Kerta!" Pak Miam responded. "You are about to become a man among the other men in our village—yet you see Roro Kidul with the eyes of a child! We swift's-nest gatherers respect and fear her power! We hear her angry voice in the fierce howling of the wind that is always lashing the cliffs with great waves. And whenever she is displeased, we fear the great storms that she suddenly sends upon us.

"Therefore, Kerta," Pak Miam declared, "if you wish to become a swift's-nest gatherer, it is good that you know that you must be stout of heart, strong of hand, and quick of mind. However, my son, I tell you—once again—that you must fear the sea. You cannot become a swift's-nest gatherer unless you understand this. You must fear and respect Roro Kidul as a man fears and respects her—for no matter how great your courage, strength, and skill, your life will always be in Roro Kidul's hands!"

To these words, Kerta responded, "I think that you are wrong, Father! I will soon become a man among the other men of our village. So surely I am not too young to test my courage and my skill! Just take me with you, and I will show you how great a swift's-nest gatherer I will be!"

"Do not listen to our son, my husband!" Kerta's mother exclaimed. "I do not want him to go anywhere near those cliffs! As old as he is, he really has no idea of how dangerous it is to gather a swift's nest. And I do not want him to die before he has had a chance to live!"

"Your mother is right, Kerta," Pak Miam declared. "You have the strength and skill of a young man, but you think and speak like a hot-headed youth! A swift's-nest gatherer faces great danger! You have never seen what he does, so you cannot really know the challenges that he faces! Let me try to describe the process to you so carefully that you will be able to appreciate what his work entails. Then you may understand why a swift's-nest gatherer both fears and respects Roro Kidul!

"First, he must find a strong tree near the edge of the cliff and carefully tie to it one of the ropes that you have helped me weave from the fibers of the palm tree. When he is certain that it is completely secure, he must grasp that rope and slowly and carefully lower himself over the top of the high, steep cliff," Pak Miam explained.

"He must continue to move slowly and carefully, for he must climb down the slick, wet face of the cliff to the slippery ledges that are just above the raging waves of the great South Sea. Despite the fierce wind, he must keep his grasp on the swaying rope, and he must use his feet to keep his balance on the wet rock. He must never forget—even for an instant—that Roro Kidul is always watching him. He must never forget—even for an instant—that if she chooses, Roro Kidul will shake him loose from the cliff!" Pak Miam exclaimed.

"I already know that!" Kerta exclaimed impatiently.

"Once he has safely landed on these ledges, he continues to be in great danger," Pak Miam continued calmly. "He is right above the cave in which the swifts have made their nests. However, he can enter that cave only by riding on the crest of a great wave. Otherwise, he is too far above the sea to jump into it safely. And even if he should succeed in entering the cave, the floor is too far below the nests for him to be able to reach them. Therefore, he must keep his balance on the slick rock while the angry wind and waves constantly attack him. And he must wait patiently there until a wave of the right size lashes the cliff."

"How does he know which wave is the right wave?" Kerta asked.

"He learns by watching the other men," Pak Miam replied. "A swift's-nest gatherer cannot afford to act rashly!

"Then he must quickly drop his rope and jump into the water, letting the swell of the great wave carry him back into the dark depths of the cave," Pak Miam explained, continuing with his description of the process. "There, he must carefully climb from one wet and slippery ledge to another in the dim light—always being sure to keep his balance as he gathers the nests from beneath each ledge and puts them into his bag. Meanwhile, he continues to hear Roro Kidul's angry voice in the fierce howling of the wind outside—and in the splashing of the angry waves against the rock walls inside the cave.

They remind him that Roro Kidul is watching him—and that she holds his life in her hands!

"The swift's-nest gatherer must work very quickly," Pak Miam continued, "for when the next great wave washes into the cave, he cannot let it shake him loose from the rock and swallow him up! Instead, he must prepare to let the swell of the wave carry him out of the cave and back up toward his rope—for without that rope he cannot climb to the top of the cliff. This is the most dangerous part of his task because it is the most difficult. He has but a moment to catch his rope!"

"What happens if he reaches for the rope, but he misses it, Father?" Kerta asked.

"If he misses it, the waves will either slam him against the cliff or sweep him out to sea. Roro Kidul does not give him a second chance!

"Of course, once he has caught hold of his rope, he is still in great danger!" Pak Miam concluded. "For he still hears Roro Kidul's angry voice in the fierce howling of the wind, and that wind continues to lash the cliff with great waves. He knows that Roro Kidul is still watching him. He knows that if she chooses, Roro Kidul can still shake him loose—first from the slippery ledges that are just above the raging waves, and then from the wet, slick rock as he makes his slow and careful ascent of the cliff."

"Father, now that I have heard your description, I am certain that I am ready to test my courage and my skill!" Kerta declared. "Just take me with you, and I will show you how great a swift's-nest gatherer I will be!"

"Kerta, I am not a sapling palm that your words, like the wind, can bend me!" Pak Miam exclaimed sternly. "However, if you wish, when the first day of the swift's-nest-gathering season arrives—because you will soon take your place as a man among the other men of our village—you may carry my sacrifice to the priests of Roro Kidul. Do not look lightly upon this task, for these priests pray to the great goddess and ask her to look kindly upon me as I gather each swift's nest. Then you can help me prepare my bag and my rope and watch as I begin my descent."

"That would be a great honor for you, Kerta, since your father's life depends on that offering!" his mother declared. "And I, too, will do my part! I will prepare a special meal of chicken and rice for the great goddess!"

"All right then, Father," Kerta declared. "This year, I will carry the sacrifice. And next year, I will gather the nests!"

"If that is what you agree to do, then I am sure to receive Roro Kidul's blessing!" Pak Miam exclaimed. "For your mother knows how to please the goddess, and her offering will travel in good hands!"

Finally, it came to pass that the first day of the swift's-nest-gathering season arrived. Just as the sun made the day light, Pak Miam and Kerta set out for the palm forest with all the other swift's-nest gatherers. There, Roro Kidul's priests would be waiting to receive the sacrifices to the great goddess. Kerta, as planned, was carrying his father's sacrificial offering. It was the custom that, out of respect for the goddess, the swift's-nest gatherers would refrain from eating until the priests had presented Roro Kidul with their special offering of food.

The journey was long and hot. Kerta found that all he could think about was the tempting food that he was carrying and the fact that his father would not permit him to eat any of it. "I am so hungry, Father, that I cannot continue our journey without something to eat!" he complained.

"I am truly sorry about that, Kerta!" Pak Miam replied. "However, today you have the responsibility of a man. And you must take that responsibility seriously. No matter how hungry you are, you must respect Roro Kidul and not eat before she does—or you will anger her, and she will punish both of us! I promise to get you some food as soon as you deliver our offering to the priests. However, if you wish, you can give the offering to me and return home."

"That will take just as long!" Kerta exclaimed. "I will stay with you."

So it came to pass that as Kerta and his father traveled to see the priests, Kerta began to drag his feet. "I am so hungry!" he said to himself. "And Mother's chicken and rice smell too good to resist! Since the dish is covered with a cloth, I am sure that no one will notice if a small piece is missing."

These thoughts drummed inside Kerta's head like the rain on the roof of his house in monsoon season. He was now walking more slowly than his father. And he could see that if he was very quiet about it, his father would not be aware of his behavior. So it came to pass that Kerta slowly lifted a corner of the cloth, reached in for some food, and put a small portion of the sacrificial offering into his mouth.

"This tastes even better than I expected!" he exclaimed to himself. "But now, I am even hungrier than I was before! I am sure that no one will know the difference if I take another bite!"

So it came to pass that Kerta took one bite after another as he and his father continued on their way. Since the bowl was covered, Kerta could not see how much he was eating—and he remained certain that no one would discover what he had done.

When Kerta and his father finally arrived at their destination, Pak Miam announced, "Kerta, uncover the sacrificial offering and hand it to a priest. Meanwhile, I will get us something to eat."

Kerta did as his father directed. "Now that I see it, my father's offering is very small!" Kerta exclaimed to himself. "And everyone else's is much larger! Fortunately, either the priest does not notice—or he does not care! I would really be in trouble if he did!"

When the time came to prepare for the descent, Pak Miam let Kerta help him. Then he said, "You may stay here and wait for me, my son, or you may return home. However, if you choose to stay, do not go too near the edge of the cliff. It is a long, straight drop down to the sea, and jagged rocks lie awake beneath the angry waves!"

Kerta decided to wait for his father's return. However, after a while, he found nothing to do. Feeling hot and tired, he lay down in the shade of two palm trees and fell asleep. He was awakened by the sharp sounds of a stranger's voice.

"Get up, my boy, and quickly return home—for a great storm is coming! Surely you hear Roro Kidul's angry voice in the fierce howling of the wind and in the raging waves that are lashing the base of the cliffs!" exclaimed the stranger.

"Where is Pak Miam, my father?" Kerta asked.

"I do not know. He must already have returned to your village with the other men," the stranger replied. "I am sure that you will find that he is waiting for you at home."

So it came to pass that Kerta returned home without his father. Pak Miam had not returned, but Kerta's mother was not worried. Therefore, Kerta ate his dinner and went happily to sleep.

Suddenly, an ugly old woman appeared before Kerta. Her green robe was dripping with foamy seawater. Long eel-like fingers, green with slimy seaweed, hung from her hands. Small fish, caught like insects in a spider's web, hung amid the strands of her uncombed hair. Through the unkempt strands that partly covered her face, Kerta could see that a pair of watery red eyes were glaring accusingly at him. His heart flooded with terror—for he knew that this was the great goddess Roro Kidul!

"You had no right to eat my food, Kerta, and you know it!" declared the goddess. "Therefore, your father now belongs to me! He is trapped in the Cave of the Octopi, where he will die! And you are now going to be mine as well!"

Kerta screamed in terror and woke up. Although it was the middle of the night, his mother was watchfully waiting because his father still had not returned home. Kerta went to his mother and confessed that he had eaten most of Roro Kidul's food. Then he told his mother about his dream.

Her heart flooded first with fury, then with terror, and finally, with resignation. "Try to get a good night's sleep, Kerta," advised his mother. "Tomorrow, we are going to do what we can to appease Roro Kidul's anger. If the goddess has not killed your father by then, I hope that we can convince her to relent and let him return home!"

Once again, Kerta went to sleep. And once again, Roro Kidul appeared before him. This time, however, the sea goddess looked beautiful! Her long golden hair was adorned with strands of pearls. Her neck and her long fingers were graced with beautiful coral jewelry, and her green satin gown was heavily embroidered with abalone flowers.

"Your father is still alive, Kerta," the great goddess declared. "And if you have the courage, the skill, and the strength, I will permit you to rescue him!" she continued. "First, you must descend the cliff and enter the outer cave on the crest of a great wave. There one of my servants will help you enter the inner Cave of the Octopi. Then you must search for your father and contrive to bring him out."

And so it came to pass that as soon as the sun made the next day light, Kerta arose, told his mother about his second dream, and announced that he was setting out to rescue his father.

His mother responded, "Kerta, despite the danger, I will make no effort to discourage you. It is only right that you do your best to rescue your father since it was your behavior that angered the great goddess and led her to take your father from us."

She then added, "I remember the day, not very long ago, when you pleaded with your father to become a swift's-nest gatherer. Even though you are not yet a man, you were certain, then, that you already possess the necessary courage, strength, and skill. Well, you have heard your father's description of the demands and the dangers. This is your chance to prove yourself! And it appears from your dream that Roro Kidul is going to help you! We are indeed fortunate!"

Kerta returned to the cliff from which his father had descended. Although he had brought one of his father's ropes with him, he saw that the rope that his father had used on the prior day was still in its place.

"I had better be cautious and replace my father's rope with this fresh one," Kerta said to himself.

Then, before grasping the rope and beginning his descent, Kerta stood for a few minutes at the top of the cliff. For the first time in his life, he could hear Roro Kidul's angry voice in the fierce howling of the wind that was lashing the cliff with great waves.

"Now I know just how a swift's-nest gatherer feels!" he said to himself. "Well, the time has finally come for me to prove my courage, strength, and skill. And I had better begin before Roro Kidul steals my courage!"

So it came to pass that Kerta slowly and carefully lowered himself over the top of the high, steep cliff and began his descent down the vertical wall. In his ear, his father's voice reminded him of just what to do and how to do it.

"Kerta, you must slowly and carefully make your way down the slick, wet face of the cliff to the slippery ledges that are just above the raging waves of the great South Sea," Pak Miam's voice directed. "Despite the fierce wind, you must keep your grasp on the swaying rope and keep your balance with your feet. For Roro Kidul is watching you! She is testing your courage, your strength, and your skill. And if Roro Kidul chooses, she will shake you loose from the cliff!"

Kerta listened carefully to his father's voice and let it guide him down the slick face of the cliff. Once he had reached the slippery ledges that were just above the raging waves of the great South Sea, the voice of Pak Miam spoke to him again.

"Wait here carefully, Kerta, until I tell you to jump," Pak Miam's voice commanded. "It is very hard to keep your balance on this slick rock while the wind and waves constantly attack you. However, you must do it. Then you must wait patiently here until a wave of the right size lashes the cliff. Remember, I will tell you when you should be prepared to jump."

Kerta waited patiently.

"Are you ready?" asked Pak Miam's voice.

"I am ready!" Kerta replied.

"All right, then. As soon as I say 'jump,' let go of the rope," directed the voice. "Now—*jump!*"

Kerta dropped the rope and jumped into the wave, letting it carry him back into the depths of the outer cave. Once he was inside, it was as dark as his father had said it would be. Meanwhile, he continued to hear Roro Kidul's angry voice in the fierce howling of the wind outside—and in the splashing of the angry waves against the rock walls inside the cave. They reminded him that Roro Kidul was watching him—and that she was holding his life in her hands.

"Kerta!" shouted the voice of Pak Miam, jolting Kerta to attention. "Quickly look for a protected area on one of the high ledges in this cave! Otherwise, when the next great wave washes into the cave, it will shake you loose from the rock and swallow you up!"

Kerta once again listened to his father's voice and took refuge on a high ledge toward the back of the cave. "This is certainly far from a safe place!" he exclaimed to himself. "The spray from the waves has made this rock just as slick underfoot as the other rocks are. But at least, here, Roro Kidul cannot send a great wave to sweep me off my feet!

"I wonder where the entrance to the Cave of the Octopi is," Kerta said to himself as he stood looking around him. "That cave should be right behind this one. If it is, I do not see any way to enter it."

Suddenly, Kerta noticed a narrow crack in the back wall of the cave. "Could the entrance be through that crevice?" he wondered, his heart flooding with despair. "If it is, I will never be able to rescue my father! For no human being—not even the smallest child—could squeeze through that opening!"

It then came to pass that while Kerta was staring at the crack, a patch of brightness suddenly appeared right in front of it. Upon looking more closely, he saw that the brightness was the glasslike figure of a bearded old man. To his amazement, the figure immediately noticed him as well and began to approach him.

As soon as he had come close enough to be heard above the roar of the wind and the waves, the glasslike man asked, "What can I do for you, my boy?"

"The goddess Roro Kidul said that she would send one of her servants to help me, and surely you are he!" Kerta exclaimed. "At least, I hope that that is who you are—for then you can tell me how I can rescue my father!" Kerta declared.

"Because I ate Roro Kidul's food before the priests could offer it to her, the goddess has imprisoned my father in the Cave of the Octopi. I have been searching for the entrance to that cave. And, if it is that narrow crevice that you came through, then my task is surely hopeless!" Kerta exclaimed.

"Without my help, your task is hopeless, indeed!" the glasslike old man replied. "I have served the goddess ever since I, myself, angered her. And that was hundreds of years ago! My tomb is within those rocks that you can see near the entrance to this cave. Once every hundred years, from one sunrise to the next, Roro Kidul returns me to life so that I can help someone. Today, you are that fortunate person, my boy!

"I will make it possible for you to enter the Cave of the Octopi," announced the old man. "However, you must return to this outer cave before the sun next makes the day light. Therefore, you have only as long as this night lasts in order to rescue your father. If you tarry longer than that, I will no longer be able to help you—for I will have returned to my tomb!"

With these words, the eyes of the glasslike old man suddenly became as bright as two suns. And as he stared into Kerta's eyes, Kerta shivered and shook beneath his gaze.

Suddenly, Kerta's heart flooded with terror. He could see that—while he watched—his body was stretching farther away from his head. And it was becoming too weak to support him in an upright position. He could see that—while he watched—his arms and legs were shrinking into four small feet. He could see that—while he watched—his tongue was becoming so long and thin that he could watch it flick in and out repeatedly as if he were terribly thirsty and could not get enough to drink.

By this time, Kerta was stretched out on the rock ledge. Slowly and fearfully, he gathered the courage to turn his head and examine his body. He saw that—like his tongue—it also had become very long and thin. And it was now completely covered with a scaly, hidelike skin. He saw that if he raised his head as high as he could, he could see the long tail that swept the ground behind his back legs.

"Why, that glasslike old man has transformed me into a lizard!" Kerta exclaimed to himself. "Now I can crawl through that crevice and rescue my father in the Cave of the Octopi!"

So it came to pass that Kerta crawled through the passageway and into the rear cave in search of his father. Once again, his heart flooded with despair. "This cave is so large and so crowded with giant sea creatures that I cannot see my father anywhere!" he cried to himself. "And Roro Kidul's voice seems to be getting angrier! Even in here, I can hear that the wind is howling more fiercely. And the waves are raging more furiously as they lash the cliff outside the front cave. Although she sent the glasslike old man to help me, the goddess may not want me to succeed after all!"

Nevertheless, Kerta gathered his courage and slowly crawled over the floor of the cave, moving between and around many hundreds of giant sea creatures. However, he could not find his father. Kerta then slowly crawled up one of the sides of the cave and wandered back and forth across its roof so that he could get a better view of the scene below. However, he still could not find his father. Kerta then slowly began to examine each and every crack that lined the four walls of the cave, in case one was a crevice in which Pak Miam was hiding. However, even then he could not find his father.

By this time it seemed to Kerta that the hours were passing like minutes. He felt as if his heart had turned to stone and that it was slowly cracking apart under the strain.

"I cannot believe that even with the help of Roro Kidul's servant I cannot rescue my father! And I certainly cannot rescue him if I cannot even find him! If I had not met that glasslike old man—and if he had not turned me into a lizard—I would believe that my second dream was meaningless. And I would give up the search right now. However, I did meet him—and I am a lizard! Therefore, I had better start looking all over again!" Kerta declared.

So it came to pass that, even more slowly and more carefully, Kerta began to search the floor of the cave once again. He had no idea how late in the night it was. However, he knew that many, many hours must have passed by now.

"Roro Kidul's voice continues to become angrier and angrier!" Kerta said to himself. "I can hear that the wind is howling even more fiercely. And the waves are raging even more furiously as they lash the cliff outside the front cave. The goddess surely does not want me to succeed in my task!"

Kerta had covered the entire floor of the cave for the second time when, suddenly, at the very back of the cave, he spied a human foot that was encircled by one of the great arms of a giant octopus. "That has to be my father's foot!" he cried. "However, the giant octopus may have already crushed him to death!"

As quickly as he could, Kerta crawled over to his father's foot. As soon as he touched it with his tongue, he transformed Pak Miam into another lizard. Kerta climbed all over this lizard's body. However, he could not get him to move. Finally, Kerta leaned his head against the lizard to see if he could hear a heartbeat.

"I do feel a pulse. However, it is very weak!" Kerta exclaimed to himself. "Father! Father!" he called. "Wake up! Wake up! I have come to rescue you! But you must help me!"

However, Pak Miam could not hear his son's voice. The larger lizard lay stretched out, senseless, within the encircling arms of the giant octopus.

"My poor father must have worn himself out trying to escape from this giant octopus and from this frightful cave," Kerta thought to himself. "I can see that if I am going to rescue him I am going to have to do it without his help. We may be close to the same size, but my father—even in the form of a lizard—is much heavier than I am. And he has now become a dead weight. It is going to be quite a task to drag his body across the cave to the entrance! In fact, it may well be impossible! Oh, how I wish that I were back in my human form! I do not see how I will ever be able to do this. However, I must try."

And so it came to pass that every nearby octopus who cared to look saw a smaller lizard slowly begin to drag and push a larger lizard out from the coiled arm of a giant octopus. The larger lizard was so much heavier than the smaller lizard that the task seemed hopeless. Yet the smaller lizard persevered. The harder Kerta worked, the longer he needed to rest. Consequently, as he grew more tired, Kerta's rest periods became longer and longer, while his efforts to drag and push his father across the floor of the cave became shorter and shorter.

"These giant sea creatures flood my heart with terror!" Kerta exclaimed to himself. "Yet even though they stir menacingly as I pass them, they have not hurt me! I had better not think about them, or Roro Kidul will succeed in stealing my courage!

"And Roro Kidul's voice continues to become angrier and angrier!" Kerta thought. "I can hear that the wind is howling ever more fiercely. And the waves are raging ever more furiously as they lash the cliff outside the front cave. The goddess surely is trying to prevent me from saving my father! However, I must succeed!

"I must have very little time left before the sun makes the day light. Somehow, I have to get my father to the entrance to this cave. If only he had collapsed at the front of the cave instead of at the rear!" Kerta exclaimed to himself.

In this way, one hour slowly followed another until it finally came to pass that Kerta—now by dragging, and now by pushing—had succeeded in bringing Pak Miam to the crevice that connected the two caves.

"Can you hear me, servant of Roro Kidul?" he shouted into the passageway. "I need your help with my father! I do hope that you are still alive!"

In response to these words, the glasslike old man immediately reappeared. He picked up the lizard that was Pak Miam and carried him through the passageway. Once they were in the outer cave, he transformed Kerta's father back into his human form.

Meanwhile, Kerta had totally exhausted his own strength. With a final effort, he lurched into the entrance to the passageway and collapsed. Roro Kidul's voice suddenly became calm. The fierce howling of the wind suddenly quieted. And the fury of the waves as they struck the cliff outside the cave suddenly subsided.

"Hurry! Hurry, my boy!" cried the glasslike old man. "I would like to help you! However, the sun has just begun to make the new day light—and so I must now return to my tomb! My sight and my strength are failing fast! Hurry through the passageway so that I can return you to your human form before I must leave you!"

"Kerta! Kerta!" Pak Miam called. "Hear my voice, my son! And let it give you the strength to come to me!"

However, Kerta could not hear their voices. The smaller lizard lay stretched out, senseless, at the entrance to the passageway between the two caves. And so it came to pass that the glasslike old man reentered his tomb, where he would spend the next hundred years.

Pak Miam crouched on the slick rock ledge in the outer cave and wept. "Oh, my son, my son! You have saved me, only to lose your own life! What a pity that you die so young!"

However, in time it came to pass that, while Pak Miam remained in the cave, mourning the loss of his son, a little lizard crawled through the passageway, out of the crevice, and across the slick rock ledge to the sorrowing man.

"Do not grieve too long for me, Father," declared Kerta consolingly. "It was I who did not respect Roro Kidul. Therefore, it is only proper that I—and not you—should be her sacrifice. I am only sorry that you suffered as much as you did because of my selfishness!"

And with these words, the little lizard left his father and crawled back toward the inner cave.

In time it came to pass that while Pak Miam continued to remain in the cave, still mourning the loss of his son, a great wave lashed the outside cliff and washed into the cave. Pak Miam lifted his head and automatically waited for just the right moment to jump in and ride out on the receding swell.

As Pak Miam left the darkness of the cave, the morning sun of the new day was shining brightly, and a brisk wind was blowing the waves of the South Sea toward the cliff. The swell of the great wave carried him to within reach of the dangling rope. At the right moment, he quickly caught hold of the rope and began his careful ascent up the slick, wet face of the cliff.

No one ever saw Kerta again. However, no one ever forgot him. The people of Java remembered Kerta whenever the wind howled fiercely and great waves lashed their cliffs. They remembered Kerta—and they remembered always to fear and respect the great goddess of the South Sea, Roro Kidul.

NOTES

For each selection, the following notes provide the titles and publishers of my principal sources as well as information about the original source of this material. I have also supplied supplementary information that will enhance your reading pleasure, such as the content of alternative versions and additional historical information.

The introduction to each selection discusses pertinent historical, religious, and literary background as well as the selection's appeal and value. The Selected Bibliography, which follows these notes, provides a detailed listing of all sources mentioned in the notes.

For each selection, I have used authoritative English translations of original material, and my sources have provided information about their own sources. Wherever possible, my version is based on a minimum of two different sources.

My goal has been to tell a good story in the way that a professional storyteller might tell it. In each story, I have made an effort to adhere faithfully to the original plot and to the personalities of the principal characters. Wherever the style has been appealing, I have tried to capture the flavor of the original in translation. However, the style of each of these selections is my own. I have tried to reflect the cadences of spoken language, and I have used repetition and figurative language, which are characteristic of oral tales. Where applicable, the following notes reveal the specific ways in which I have changed the material.

Part I Africa

The Creation of Human Beings

James George Frazer relates this myth in "The Creation of Man," in *Folklore in the Old Testament* (a Hart reprint of Macmillan, 1918). Frazer's source is W. Hofmayr's "Die Religion des Schilluk" (*Anthropos* VI, 1911).

Mircea Eliade, in *Gods, Goddesses, and Myths of Creation* (Harper Row, 1974), and Theodor H. Gaster, in "Adam and Eve," in *Myth, Legend, and Custom in the Old Testament* (Harper Row, 1975), have reprinted Frazer's version.

I have added a few details from the version in Richard Cavendish's "Central and Southern Africa: Myths of Origins," in *Mythology* (London: Orbis, 1980). It is not clear which of the works listed in Cavendish's bibliography is the source for his version of this myth.

Although I have expanded a few of the details, the spirit of my version of the myth is true to Frazer's version. However, I have changed the style of the myth considerably. I have reversed the order, and I have created a first paragraph that functions as a concluding paragraph as well.

Anansi, the Clever One

Peggy Appiah relates this tale, which she calls "How Death Came to Mankind," in *Tales of an Ashanti Father* (Beacon, 1967, 1989). According to Appiah, these tales were collected orally in Ghana by adults and children, since the Ashanti have no written language. Appiah's husband has told many of these tales to their children (hence, the book's title).

The tale itself is unusual in that it is not included in the well-known collections of African folklore that include Ashanti tales of Anansi. One possible reason for this is that popularity breeds popularity, and some collectors choose to include the most frequently anthologized material. Another possible reason may be that this tale is not representative of the genre because of its powerful subject. Anansi stories are popular children's stories. Obviously, this tale is more serious; it is too powerful to be simply amusing.

The content of the tale is Appiah's, with the exception of the Ashanti proverb that appears at the end. "No sensible person leaves a stream to drink from a pool" is one of many Ashanti proverbs that Harold Courlander includes in *A Treasury of African Folklore* (Crown, 1975). Courlander's sources include a compilation by Daniel A. Osei-Cobbina.

The language and the repetitive style of the tale are my own.

The Woman with One Hand

Harold Scheub relates this tale, which he calls "The Girl with One Hand," in *The African Storyteller* (Kendall/Hunt, 1990). Scheub's source is Edward Steere's *Swahili Tales As Told by Natives of Zanzibar* (London: Society for Promoting Christian Knowledge, 1869).

In addition to changing the title, I have made two other changes in Scheub's version of this tale. First, I have removed Christian and contemporary references. For example, in Scheub's version, the snake calls the young woman "Child of Adam," and his father gives her his ring with God's blessing. Also, at the end of Scheub's version of the tale, the young woman views the king and his companions through a telescope.

Second, I have changed certain details because they are not necessary to the tale. For example, I have deleted the fact that the snake's mother also gives an important gift—a casket—to the young woman because the tale does not mention anything else about it. Moreover, in Scheub's version the young woman spends years undiscovered in her large house on the outskirts of the capital town. This does not seem believable.

The Roamer-of-the-Plain

Paul Radin relates this tale, which he calls "The Wonder-Worker of the Plains," in *African Folktales* (Schocken, 1983), which is a reprint from *African Folktales and Sculpture* (Princeton Univ. Press, 1952). Harold Scheub calls the tale "The Gamboler-of-the-Plain" and includes it in *The African Storyteller* (Kendall/Hunt, 1990). In *The African Saga* (Payson and Clarke, 1927), Blaise Cendrars includes Margery Bianco's translation of the same tale, which she calls "The Roamer-of-the-Plain." All three translations are nearly identical.

Radin's source is Henri A. Junod's *Les Ba-Ronga* (Paul Attinger, 1898). The tale was later reprinted in Volume 2 of Junod's *The Life of a South African Tribe* [the Thonga] (Macmillan, 1927). Scheub's source is also Junod. Bianco's source is *L'Anthologie Nègre* (1921).

Susan Feldmann reprints Radin's version in *African Myths and Tales* (Dell, 1963).

The language and style of my version, although very close to those of the other translations, are my own.

The Crocodile and His Son

In *The African Saga* (Payson and Clarke, 1927), Blaise Cendrars includes Margery Bianco's translation of this tale, which she calls

"Ngurangurane, the Crocodile's Son." Bianco's source is *L'Anthologie Nègre* (1921).

The style of the legend is my own. I have emphasized the repetitive aspect of the tale, since it is characteristic of African tales as well as all other tales in the oral tradition.

Part 2 The Middle East

Enki, Lord of the Earth and the Waters of Life and Adapa

My version of the Enki myth "Enki, Lord of the Earth and the Waters of Life," combines the related aspects of three Enki myths: (1) "Enki and the World Order: The Organization of the Earth and Its Cultural Processes" (later called "Enki and Inanna: The Organization of the Earth and Its Cultural Processes"); (2) "Inanna and Enki: The Transfer of the Arts of Civilization from Eridu to Erech"; and (3) "Enki and Eridu: The Journey of the Water-God to Nippur."

Based on original tablets, Samuel Noah Kramer translates the earliest versions of all three Enki myths for "Myths of Origins," in *Sumerian Mythology* (Univ. of Pennsylvania Press, revised, 1961). He then translates the first complete version of "Enki and the World Order" for "Literature: The Sumerian *Belles-Lettres*," in *The Sumerians* (Univ. of Chicago Press, 1963). Finally, he and John Maier present the most-current versions of these myths in their *Myths of Enki* (Oxford Univ. Press, 1989).

The Kramer and Maier edition, which is part translation and part summary, contains more current and complete translations of the three Enki myths. "Enki and Inanna: The Organization of the Earth and Its Cultural Processes" is based on Carlos Benito's 1970 edition and translation. "Inanna and Enki: The Transfer of the Arts of Civilization from Eridu to Erech" is based on Gertrud Farber Flugge's 1971 edition and translation. "Enki and Eridu: The Journey of the Water-God to Nippur" is based on A. A. Al-Fouadi's 1969 edition and translation.

E. A. Speiser translates the myth of Adapa from the original tablets for "Akkadian Myths and Epics," in *Ancient Near Eastern Texts* (Princeton Univ. Press, 1969). Stephanie Dalley also translates this myth from the original tablets, in *Myths from Mesopotamia* (Oxford Univ. Press, 1990). Wherever possible, she fills in missing sections with probable material.

Other fine versions of "Adapa" include (1) Theodor Gaster's "The Lost Chance," in *The Oldest Stories in the World* (Beacon, 1958), an embellished story; (2) S. H. Hooke's "Adapa," in *Middle Eastern Mythology* (Penguin, 1976), a narrative; (3) Thorkild Jacobsen's version in *The Treasures of Darkness* (Yale Univ. Press, 1976), a narrative; (4) Samuel Noah Kramer's version in *Mythologies of the Ancient World* (Anchor, 1961), a narrative; (5) L. W. King's version in *Babylonian Religion and Mythology* (Kegan Paul, Trench, Trübner, 1899), a narrative; (6) Stephen Herbert Langdon's version in *Semitic Mythology* (Cooper Square, 1964), part translation, part summary; (7) Henrietta McCall's "Adapa," in *Mesopotamian Myths* (British Museum and Univ. of Texas Press, 1990), part translation, part summary; and (8) A. Leo Oppenheim's version in *Ancient Mesopotamia* (Univ. of Chicago Press, 1972), a summary.

With regard to the introduction to the myths of Enki and Adapa, Jack Finegan, in *Light from the Ancient Past* (Princeton Univ. Press, 1974), quotes Ashurbanipal's inscription about writing. The quotation about reading appears in Time-Life's *The Birth of Writing* (1974). Hammurabi's quotation appears in "The Rising Sun of Babylon," in Time-Life's *Mesopotamia: The Mighty Kings* (1995). Kramer and Maier, in *Myths of Enki* (Oxford Univ. Press, 1989), provide the quotation about the fish bones at Eridu and the quotation about King Sennacherib's fish sacrifice. Time-Life's *Sumer: Cities of Eden* (1993) presents current information on the archaeology of Eridu.

Although as written languages Sumerian and Akkadian are approximately equal in age, they are very different languages that were spoken by rival peoples. Sumerian bears some relationship to the language of the Turks, the Finns, and the Hungarians (having a Uralic and Altaic base), whereas Akkadian was the Semitic language spoken by the Babylonians and the Assyrians.

Sumerian ceased to be a spoken language by about 2000 B.C. However, between about 1600 and 1300 B.C., it came to be taught as standard curriculum in schools for scribes that were located in Anatolia (the western part of Asian Turkey), Palestine (Israel), and Egypt, as well as in Mesopotamia. Therefore, many Sumerian texts were preserved and modernized enough for copies to have withstood the ravages of time.

Between about 1900 and 1300 B.C., the Babylonians and, to a lesser extent, the Assyrians also produced fine literature. Often

Sumerian writings were reworked and expanded in effective ways. However, other famous literary works are original.

From about 1500 to 500 B.C., Akkadian became the language of diplomacy in Egypt, Anatolia, and Persia as well as in Mesopotamia. Fortunately, during this period scribes practiced on Akkadian literary texts, once again creating copies and thereby helping to preserve the original texts.

In the "Adapa" myth, the god Dumuzi is better known as Tammuz, and Gishzida is usually called Ningishzida. Both gods are usually associated with the cycle of fertility, and they alternate between time on earth during the growing season and time in the underworld during the dry season. In this myth, of course, they are in the kingdom of heaven. Although current scholars do not view the myth as performing a role in a religious ritual, the myth does blame Adapa and not the gods for the human condition. The myth may also have been used to summon the goddess of healing.

Publication dates are very important in this area of study. Dalley's work and the volume by Kramer and Maier reflect the latest discoveries and scholarship, but Speiser's work includes translations of tablets that do not appear in the works by Dalley or Kramer and Maier. The introduction to the Kramer and Maier work alerts the reader to the fact that Langdon's conclusions are untrustworthy and misleading due to very limited source material and the serious linguistic problems that existed at the time that he was writing. This problem may apply to other scholars in the field as well.

Because the beginning of "Adapa" is missing and its conclusion is only partly discernible, scholars are in great disagreement as to what the events in the myth signify. For example, it is not clear who or what Adapa represents. According to Gaster, Ea fashioned Adapa as a prank, creating a creature who is neither mortal nor immortal. (It is surprising that, given his knowledge of mythology, Gaster does not consider the many heroes who are demigods, having received superhuman power from their divine parent and mortality from their mortal parent.) According to Hooke and Kramer, Adapa is First Man. Had he acquired immortality for himself, all mortals would have become immortal as well.

Scholars also disagree as to whether Ea, the god who cares most about mortals and who teaches Adapa (his son in some translations) how to win Anu's sympathy, purposely misleads Adapa into rejecting Anu's offer of the food and water that confer immortality.

King and Kramer interpret Ea's advice as reflecting his fear that Anu would try to kill Adapa for his presumption and transgression. Gaster, Jacobsen, Langdon, and Oppenheim interpret Ea's behavior as reflecting his jealousy that Adapa might become immortal and, consequently, that he would then lose his servant. Langdon points out that Ea's attitude is not surprising, since Ea also withheld immortality from Adapa when he created him.

Finally, it is unclear whether Adapa returns to earth with Anu's blessing or as his punishment. Speiser's translation reflects that the original tablet is both cryptic and fragmentary. (His ellipses signify missing or illegible material.) Therefore, it actually reads as follows: ". . . as for Adapa, the human offspring, (who . . .), lord-like, broke the south wind's wing, went up to heaven—and so forth—(. . .) what ill he has brought upon mankind, (and) the disease that he brought upon the bodies of men, these Ninkarrak will allay. (Let) malady be lifted, let disease turn aside. (Upon) this (. . .) let horror fall, let him (in) sweet sleep not lie down, (. . .) . . . joy of human heart(s)."

Dalley states that it is possible that Anu punishes Adapa because he has disobeyed the laws of hospitality by refusing the food and drink that are offered to him as Anu's guest. Gaster interprets the myth to reveal that Anu gives Adapa the gift of immunity from the diseases and other ills that plague mortals, since the goddess of healing will always be at his side.

Hooke and Langdon decide that Adapa's fate is a mixed blessing: Adapa brings sorrow and pain (disease) into the life of mortals, which will be tempered by the goddess of healing; and the priesthood of Eridu will gain an eternally privileged status. King holds the view that Anu pardons Adapa.

Kramer holds the view that mortals already were the victims of disease, but that now Anu rewards Adapa by sending the goddess of healing to help them. McCall and Oppenheim state that Anu rewards Adapa by making him the wisest of men (although the tablets state that Ea had already given him this gift). Oppenheim adds that Anu gives Adapa magic powers against disease, and that disease existed prior to Anu's journey up to heaven.

I have interpreted the available material in a way that makes sense to me, given Adapa's situation, the nature of his religion, and the human condition.

Although the content of my versions of "Enki" and "Adapa" relies on the available translations of primary material, the style in which I have written these myths is my own. I have made an effort to adopt the repetition that is characteristic of the Mesopotamian myths and, wherever possible, to use language structure that is reminiscent of the epic of *Gilgamesh*.

The Craftsman's Wife

Micha bin Gorion relates this tale in *Mimekor Yisrael: Classical Jewish Folktales* and *Mimekor Yisrael: Selected Classical Jewish Folktales* (both from Indiana Univ. Press, 1990). H. M. Nahmad relates it in *"A Portion in Paradise" and Other Jewish Folktales* (Schocken, 1974), as does Angelo Rappoport, under the title "The Master and His Faithful Wife," in *Ancient Israel: Myths and Legends* (Bonanza, 1987).

Rappoport and bin Gorion both cite Israel ben Sasson's *Likkutei Ma'asiyyot* (Jerusalem, 1909) as their source of the tale. This forty-four-page booklet was reprinted in 1967 and, like the original, is available only in Hebrew. The story is called "Ma'aseh Shel Shlomo Ha-Melech" ("Story of Solomon the King," pages 11b–15a).

Possibly the earliest surviving written source of this version of the tale appears as #69 in the *Gesta Romanorum*. The similar tale in the *Thousand and One Nights* is told on the Tenth Night. An analogous version also appears in Giovanni Boccaccio's *Decameron*, where it is the eighth tale on the Eighth Day. (However, in my opinion, the relationship between this tale and Boccaccio's tale is not close.)

The style of the bin Gorion version is more authentic in its use of language and more repetitive in its structure than the other versions. However, these attributes also make bin Gorion's version longer. None of the versions mentions what gift King Solomon gave the craftsman's wife; however, it was "worthy of a king" or "costly."

The information about King Solomon that appears in the introduction to this tale appears in the First Book of Kings in the Bible. Solomon's acquisition of an understanding heart in order to be able to discern between good and evil and rule with justice appears in I Kings 3:7–13. The tale of the contested infant appears in 3:16–27. Solomon's wisdom appears in 4:29–31.

Unfortunately, I have had to retell this tale in a way that is more compact than Bin Gorion's delightful style.

Rostam, Shield of Persia and The Tragedy of Sohrab

The principal English sources of Ferdowsi's *Shahnameh* (*The Book of Kings*) are (1) Matthew Arnold's poem "Sohrab and Rustem" (1853), which is based on John Malcolm's summary in *History of Persia* (1815) and Atkinson's 1832 translation of the *Shahnameh*; (2) James Atkinson's abridged version in prose and verse, *The Shah Nameh of the Persian Poet Firdausi* (Routledge, 1832); (3) Helen Zimmern's abridged prose version, *The Epic of Kings* (a 1926 Macmillan reprint of the original 1882 text, which is based on Jules Mohl's French version; (4) Jerome Clinton's modern translation of the Sohrab and Rostam legend, *The Tragedy of Sohrab and Rostam* (Univ. of Washington Press, 1987); (5) Reuben Levy's abridged modern prose version, *The Epic of the Kings* (Arkana/Viking Penguin, 1990); and (6) Barbara Leonie Picard's abridged modern prose version, *Tales of Ancient Persia* (Oxford Univ. Press, 1993).

Ferdowsi wrote the *Shahnameh* in rhymed couplets. My prose versions of the legends of Rostam and Sohrab are based primarily on Atkinson and Zimmern, supported by the modern, scholarly renditions of Clinton and Levy. I have also relied on two old, charming editions written for adolescents, Elizabeth Renninger's *The Story of Rustem* (Scribner's, 1909) and Wilmot-Buxton's *Stories of Persian Heroes* (Crowell, 1908). I chose the content of Zimmern and the two modern, scholarly sources (Clinton and Levy) in preference to Atkinson's content if theirs appeared to be more accurate. However, wherever Atkinson included material that I could not find in Zimmern, Clinton, or Levy, I relied on Atkinson.

With regard to the legend of Sohrab, there are major differences between Atkinson and Arnold on the one hand, and Zimmern and the two modern sources on the other. These include the questions of (1) whether Tahmineh reveals to Rostam that Sohrab is a boy (in Atkinson and Arnold, she tells him it's a girl); (2) whether Tahmineh arranges to have Rakhsh stolen (Atkinson says yes; Zimmern, Clinton, and Levy are unclear); (3) whether the Tatar warrior whom Rostam kills before the battle is Tahmineh's brother (most agree that he is); and (4) whether Sohrab fathers a son named Barzu—an amazing feat for one who is clearly under the age of twelve, and usually about a ten-year-old! (Atkinson says yes; Zimmern and Levy make no mention of Barzu and the episodes in which he is involved.)

Before Ferdowsi chose to feature Rostam in his version of the *Shahnameh*, Rostam was a favorite hero among the Persians. In fact, tales about Rostam also existed in oral traditions with which Ferdowsi was not familiar. For example, Central Asian stories about Rostam that have not appeared in any epic poetry exist in the Middle Persian language.

The legends of Rostam and the Persian kings reflect aspects of the earlier Scythian inhabitants of Persia, particularly their style of warfare and their treatment of their enemies.

It is also possible that, because of its age, the Rostam legend reflects aspects of an earlier matriarchal society. Potter's *Sohrab and Rostam* (1902) is a published Harvard University thesis. The author finds the roots of father-son conflicts in the matriarchal society, where children remained with and were reared by their mothers and their uncles, thereby creating situations where fathers and sons did not know each other. The thesis examines these societies as they existed throughout the world. However, better sources on matriarchal culture are two books by Marija Gimbutas: *The Language of the Goddess* (Harper Row, 1989) and *The Goddesses and Gods of Old Europe: 6500–3500 B.C.* (Univ. of California Press, 1982).

Stylistically, I have made two changes in the epic. First, I have repeated particular descriptions word for word throughout the story in a manner that is consistent with the oral epic tradition throughout the world. Such repeated patterns both made it easier for the bard to remember the material and unified the epic. Second, I have reworked Ferdowsi's similes and metaphors so that they read like a shortened form of Homer's similes.

I have also chosen to use "Persia," the English name for Iran until 1935, when the Shah of Iran announced that his country should be called Iran. The use of "Persia" is consistent with the age of the epic and its translation into English.

Aspects of the *Shahnameh* have much in common with the Greek myths of Heracles and Theseus, the legends of Britain's King Arthur, and the *Iliad*. First, Rostam is like Heracles and Theseus in that he takes dangerous journeys in which he kills a succession of monsters and evil beings. Second, the king of Persia's collection of noble warriors is similar to Arthur's Knights of the Round Table in that both groups of warriors make names for themselves in individual feats of strength and skill. Third, it is possible to compare many of the characters in the *Shahnameh* with those in the *Iliad*, particularly the relationship between Kay Kavus and Rostam with that between Agamemnon and Achilles.

The best secondary sources in English appear to be Atkinson's and Clinton's introduction and notes; Levy's introduction; and William Hanaway Jr.'s "The Iranian Epics," in Felix J. Oinas's *Heroic Epic and Saga* (Indiana Univ. Press, 1978), which is superb.

Part 3 Europe

Prometheus, the Fire-Bringer

The three principal sources of the Prometheus myth are the versions told by the ancient Greek poet Hesiod (c. 700 B.C.) in *Theogony* and *Works and Days*; the ancient Greek dramatist Aeschylus (525–456 B.C.) in *Prometheus Bound* (c. 450 B.C.); and the ancient Roman mythographer Hyginus, in *Fabulae* and *Poetica Astronomica* (c. A.D. 205).

My first source is Hesiod's *Theogony* and *Works and Days*, as translated by (1) Apostolos N. Athanassakis (Johns Hopkins Univ. Press, 1983); (2) H. G. Evelyn-White (Harvard Univ. Press, 1977); (3) Richmond Lattimore (Univ. of Michigan Press, 1973); and (4) M. L. West (Oxford Univ. Press, 1989). Second, I used Aeschylus's *Prometheus Bound* as translated by (1) David Grene (Univ. of Chicago Press, 1959); (2) Paul Elmer More (Random House, 1938); (3) James Scully and C. John Herington (Oxford Univ. Press, 1975); and (4) Herbert Weir Smyth (Harvard Univ. Press, 1988). My third source is Hyginus's *Fabulae* and *Poetica Astronomica* as translated by Mary Grant (Univ. of Kansas Press, 1960).

In addition to Aeschylus's *Prometheus Bound*, the myth of Prometheus has also provided the inspiration for George Gordon Lord Byron's "Prometheus" and *Prophecy of Dante*; Pedro Calderón de la Barca's *The Statue of Prometheus*; Johann Wolfgang von Goethe's poem "Prometheus"; Victor Hugo's *The Genius: Odes and Ballads* (IV, 6) and *God* (4, *The Vulture*); and Percy Bysshe Shelley's *Prometheus Unbound*.

Given that Hesiod wrote in poetry and Aeschylus was a dramatist, the style of the myth is my own. I took most of the Homeric similes from the *Iliad* and the *Odyssey*, as translated by A. T. Murray (Harvard Univ. Press, 1976, 1978, 1980).

Oisin Mac Finn, Poet of the Fianna

My version of this myth is based on the following sources:
(1) Michael Comyn's "Lay of Oisin in the Land of Youth" (Trans-
actions of the Ossianic Society #4, 1859); (2) John O'Daly's *Fenian
Poems* (Comyn, above); (3) William Butler Yeats's "The Wanderings
of Oisin" (1889) in *The Poems: A New Edition* (Macmillan, 1983);
(4) Lady Isabella Augusta Gregory's *Gods and Fighting Men* (a Colin
Smythe reprint of John Murray, 1904); (5) Thomas W. Rolleston's
"Tales of the Ossianic Cycle," in *Myths and Legends of the Celtic
Race* (a Schocken reprint of Harrap, 1911) and *Celtic Myths and
Legends* (a Dover reprint of Harrap, 1917); and (6) James Stephens's
"Oisin's Mother," in *Irish Fairy Tales* (a Macmillan reprint of the
1920 edition).

Other significant versions include (1) Jeremiah Curtin's "Oisin in
Tir na n-Og," in *Myths and Folk Tales of Ireland* (a Dover reprint of
Myths and Folk-Lore of Ireland) (Little Brown, 1890), an alternative
but somewhat similar version from an ancient tradition; (2) Charles
Squire's *Celtic Myth and Legend* (a Newcastle reprint of the 1905 and
191– editions); (3) P. W. Joyce's "Oisin in Tir Na nOg or The Last of
the Fena," in Mary McGarry's *Great Folk Tales of Ireland* (Muller,
1980); (4) Frank Delaney's "Oisin and the Land of Youth," in
Legends of the Celts (Sterling, 1992), an embellished version; and
(5) Marie Heaney's "Oisin in the Land of Youth," in *Over Nine
Waves* (Faber & Faber, 1994), taken from P. W. Joyce's version
(above).

Excellent secondary sources include (1) Nora Chadwick's *The
Celts* (Penguin, 1977); (2) Lady Gregory's notes to *Gods and Fighting
Men* (above); (3) J. A. MacCulloch's *Celtic Mythology* (Dorset, 1992);
(4) explanatory materials in O'Daly's *Fenian Poems* (above); and
(5) notes in Yeats's *The Poems* (above).

The English spelling of Gaelic words varies from Scotland to
Ireland, and varies among the Irish versions themselves.

The various versions of the Oisin legend are remarkably similar,
with the notable exception of Jeremiah Curtin's version, in which
champions compete for the throne of Tir na nOg every seventh year.
The king learns from his druid that only his son-in-law can take his
place, so he orders the druid to cast a spell upon his daughter and
give her a pig's head so that no one will want to marry her. However, the druid tells the princess that she will break the spell if she
can succeed in marrying one of Finn Mac Cumhal's sons. She meets
Oisin, who can see that she is beautiful despite her head. When he

hears her tale, he marries her, returns with her to Tir na nOg, wins the racing contest for kingship, and reigns uncontested for years. Finally, overcome with longing for his father and his friends, Oisin returns to Ireland. Oisin becomes a blind old man when he falls from his horse as he helps a herdsman to overturn a great stone, under which the Fianna have hidden the great horn with which they would summon their band from throughout Ireland.

It is worth noting that this particular version has the following ancient, matriarchal overtones: (1) kingship for a limited period of seven years; (2) a contest of skill to determine the new king; (3) the important role of the druid; (4) selection of a mate by the woman; and possibly (5) the use of the pig's head.

In another Irish version, related by O'Daly, Oisin enters a cave, where he lives with a beautiful woman for what he thinks is a few days but is really three hundred years. Returning to Ireland with the same admonition that appears in the version in this book, he becomes a blind old man when he falls from the woman's horse as he attempts to help a man by lifting a heavy bag of sand from the man's upset cart.

According to MacCulloch, a Scottish version from the eighteenth century (related by J. F. Campbell) states that Oisin, in his old age, meets a beautiful woman who implies that she is his mother and invites him to accompany her. When Oisin agrees, she opens a door in a rock. Oisin thinks that he remains with her for a week, but in fact he has stayed for centuries, and, when he wishes to return to the Fianna, the woman tells him that they are all dead. MacCulloch also states that it is typical for mortals in Celtic tales to become tired of their life with the divine women who woo them.

Oisin leaves Ireland shortly after the battle of Gabhra, at the end of the third century, and he returns in the time of Saint Patrick, probably in the mid-fifth century. Therefore, it is probable that Oisin actually returns to Ireland after an absence of about one hundred fifty years, rather than after his mythical absence of three hundred years. Versions vary in their treatment of Oisin's response to Saint Patrick. In most versions, Oisin rejects Christian beliefs and chooses to die a pagan. However, in a few later versions, St. Patrick converts and baptizes Oisin.

Although Oisin is renowned as the poet of the Fianna, the other members of the Fianna were poets as well. In another myth about Finn and the Fianna, Caoilte (Oisin's cousin and companion) enters a hill occupied by the Tuatha Dé Danaan (the people of the goddess Danu), where he is healed of his wounds. Caoilte emerges in the time of Saint Patrick, whom he finds before Oisin arrives, and it is Caoilte who first relates the legends of the Fianna to Patrick, who has his scribe record them. Versions differ as to whether Caoilte is present when Oisin arrives at Saint Patrick's and performs the same function, and others do not mention Caoilte at all.

Saga of Gunnlaug Serpent-Tongue

Alan Boucher translates this legend, which he calls the *Saga of Gunnlaug Snake-Tongue* (Iceland Review, 1983). Gwynn Jones also translates this legend, which she calls *Gunnlaug Wormtongue*, in *Eirik the Red and Other Icelandic Sagas* (Oxford Univ. Press, 1991).

Egil's Saga (Penguin, 1982) contains additional information about Thorstein Egilsson, who was Egil's son. Good secondary sources include Peter Hallberg's *The Icelandic Saga* (Univ. of Nebraska Press, 1962) and Jónas Kristjánsson's *Eddas and Sagas* (Reykjavík: Hid íslenska bókmenntafélag, 1988).

I have made the following changes in Boucher's version. First, I have retold the legend to focus on plot and characterization and to clarify and enhance them. Therefore, I have omitted material that I do not consider essential, and I have amplified conversations that I think enrich the story.

Second, I have omitted the poetry recited by Gunnlaug and Hrafn because the poems' complex style makes them very difficult to rewrite appropriately and, often, very difficult to understand as well. In contrast to the saga's poetry, the saga's prose is much simpler in structure, a contrast that is characteristic of saga style.

Third, I have also used kennings—the hyphenated, metaphorical compound words that are characteristic of Old Norse and Old English poetic language—throughout my version of the saga. Egil uses kennings in his poetry in *Egil's Saga*. Gunnlaug and Hrafn express themselves poetically in this style and since they were poets, it is logical to assume that a somewhat poetic use of language was part of their ordinary speech as well. Moreover, kennings are a characteristic of *Beowulf*—written in Anglo-Saxon in about the year 1000—the period in which the events in the *Saga of Gunnlaug* occur.

Fourth, I have reorganized the section that includes Gunnlaug's travels to make the chronology clearer, since the timing of Gunnlaug's return is a major element in the saga.

Fifth, I have also moved the saga writer's mention of the conversion of Iceland to Christianity to the time in the epic when, given the timing of the other events, it must actually have occurred.

In my version, I have included the substance of the conversations very much as they exist in Boucher's version. However, I have made the following exceptions: Occasionally, two characters converse, but the saga writer does not reveal the content of their conversation. In such situations, I have expanded a character's remarks; however, I have always tried to keep my additions consistent with that character's other remarks. In addition, I have developed King Ethelred's conversations with Gunnlaug so that they explain the political situation that motivates Ethelred to keep Gunnlaug in London for an additional year.

Egil's Saga, which is closely related to the later *Saga of Gunnlaug Serpent-Tongue*, provides details of setting, plot, and character that are consistent with those found in the later saga. Scholars think that this biography of Egil—who was Gunnlaug's grandfather—was probably written in c. 1230 by Snorri Sturluson (1179–1241), Iceland's most famous literary figure. Snorri spent most of his adult years in the district of Borgarfjord, in western Iceland, and he actually lived for a period of time at Borg, the home of Egil, Thorstein, and Gunnlaug. Given Snorri's reputation as a scholar and writer, and given his access to oral and written literature about Egil's family, he undoubtedly presents this material as it existed two centuries after the events in *Egil's Saga* occurred.

Egil's Saga describes how Egil left his farm at Borg to his son, Thorstein. It states that after Thorstein married Jofrid (in the year 972), they had ten children (eight sons and two daughters). Their first daughter was Helga the Fair, who was named after Jofrid's mother. The saga also states that Thorstein Egilsson and his daughter, Helga the Fair, were two of the four best-looking people ever to have been born in Iceland, and it mentions the quarrel between Gunnlaug Serpent-Tongue and Poet-Hrafn over Helga the Fair that is the central event in the *Saga of Gunnlaug Serpent-Tongue*.

My sources for the historical information about the courts Gunnlaug visited—set forth in the following paragraphs—include Alan Boucher's and Gwyn Jones's notes to Gunnlaug's saga; Winston Churchill's *A History of the English-Speaking Peoples* (Volume One: *The Birth of Britain*); the *Cambridge Biographical Dictionary*; the *Dictionary of National Biography*; and *Webster's Biographical Dictionary*.

Sources vary as to the spelling of names and, occasionally, as to particular dates.

Earl Hakon the Great of Norway freed Norway from Danish political domination. He was overthrown in the year 995 by Olaf Tryggvason. Earl Hakon had been a champion of paganism, whereas Olaf Tryggvason began to convert Norway to Christianity.

According to the *Heimskringla, Olaf Tryggvason's Saga* (chapter 49), Earl Hakon's thrall (slave) murdered his master in order to earn the reward of wealth and honor promised by Olaf Tryggvason to anyone who harmed Earl Hakon. The thrall slit the earl's throat, cut off his head, and took it to King Olaf. King Olaf rewarded the thrall by having him beheaded. Olaf then hung both heads from a gallows so that warriors could throw stones at them.

Five years later, in 1000, Earl Eirik Hakonarson, son of Earl Hakon the Great of Norway, allied himself with King Olaf Skötkonung ("the Swedish") and King Svein of Denmark (who was his brother), and their combined fleet overthrew Olaf Tryggvason. Then, from the year 1000 until 1014 (the year of King Svein's death) or 1016 (according to other sources), Earl Eirik ruled Norway as a feudal estate of the Danish king.

To complete this legend with later history: Olaf Haraldsson, known as Saint Olaf, seized the Norwegian throne from Earl Eirik Hakonarson in either the year 1014 or 1016. Olaf is the patron saint of Norway and its national hero. During his reign, he completed Norway's conversion to Christianity. However, when lesser Norwegian kings rebelled against his rule, in 1028, they asked King Svein's youngest son, Knut (known as Knut Sveinsson the Great, and spelled "Canute" by the English), for help. Knut Sveinsson helped them, Olaf fled the country, and Knut became king of Norway in that year. Olaf never succeeded in recovering his crown.

At this time, England was ruled by King Ethelred II (978–1016), called "the Unready" (as in "ill-counseled"), or "the Redeless," who succeeded his murdered half-brother, Edward the Martyr, as king of England. The people of eastern England were Danish in heritage and spoke Anglo-Saxon. Meanwhile, King Svein of Denmark coveted the English crown. Ethelred preferred buying peace to fighting war. However, as the years passed, although he paid the Danish king more money, the Danish threat became more serious.

Ethelred suspected that a group of Danish mercenary soldiers—who were being employed to defend England against invasions by their own king—were planning to kill him. Consequently, in the year 1002, Ethelred, being terrified of this plot, executed a plan to slaughter all of the Danes who were presently living in southern England, including those who were not in his service but were simply living peacefully on English soil. One of those murdered was the sister of King Svein of Denmark.

King Svein vowed to avenge Ethelred's despicable deed, and thereafter Ethelred spent much of his reign defending England against Danish invasions that were led first by King Svein and then, after Svein's death in the year 1014, by King Knut (Canute) Sveinsson the Great. Both Danes coveted the English crown, and both succeeded in winning it. Svein was proclaimed king in 1013, when he and Knut conquered most of England with the notable exception of London. Not long after Ethelred's death in 1016, Knut (Canute) conquered London, giving all of England a Danish king, and he ruled until the year 1035.

Dublin was a Norse kingdom founded in the year 840. King Sigtrygg Silk-Beard had been ruling Dublin for a short time when the Irish Confederation, led by Brian Boru, defeated the alliance that Sigtrygg supported at the battle of Clontarf in the year 1014. Sigtrygg's ally, Earl Sigurd Hlödvisson ("the Stout"), who ruled Orkney from the year 980 to 1014, was killed in this battle. However, Sigtrygg himself did not take part in it. He continued to fight the Irish until he left his kingdom in the year 1035, probably to enter religious retirement.

The "Southern Isles" that Earl Sigurd Hlödvisson and Gunnlaug raided are the Hebrides.

King Olaf Skötkonung ("the Swedish") ruled from c. 995 to c. 1021. He was Sweden's first Christian king. The clergy brought schools, writing, and their interest in the arts to Sweden.

Aucassin and Nicolette

Andrew Lang's translation of this tale can be found in *Medieval Romances* (edited by Roger Sherman Loomis and Laura Hibbard Loomis, and published by Random House, 1957). Eugene Mason's translation appears in *"Aucassin and Nicolette" and Other Mediaeval Romances and Legends* (Dutton, 1958). The original tale is written in a dialect that was spoken in northeastern France early in the thirteenth century.

D. D. R. Owen gives a detailed summary of the tale in the chapter, "The Comedy of Love," in his *Noble Lovers* (New York Univ. Press, 1975).

The quotation by Andreas Capellanus that appears in the Introduction can be found in *The Portable Medieval Reader* (Viking, 1969), edited by James Bruce Ross and Mary Martin McLaughlin.

Frederick Joseph Harvey Darton relates a prose version of "Floris and Blanchefleur," the tale that might have influenced the author of "Aucassin and Nicolette," in *Stories of Romance from the Age of Chivalry* (Arlington House/Crown, 1984, and a reprint of *A Wonder Book of Old Romance*, published by F. A. Stokes, 1907). Darton's source is the metrical version of the tale, written in Middle English, in the East Midlands dialect. The English version is based upon the French source of the tale.

"Floris and Blanchefleur" is a traditional rendition of this type of tale in that the male is the hero. He espouses traditional values, takes the risks, and rescues the heroine, who is a passive victim. In contrast, the author of "Aucassin and Nicolette" has reversed these elements of the plot.

My version of "Aucassin and Nicolette" is consistent with the versions given by Lang, Mason, and Owen. However, I have deleted all of the verse passages and have integrated their ideas into the narrative instead. It is worth noting that Lang and Mason translated the verse passages quite differently. Often, only wisps of a theme connect them.

Doctor Faust

The earliest surviving English versions of this legend appear in three sources: first, *The Historie of the Damnable Life and Deserved Death of Doctor John Faustus*, also known as the English *Faust-Book*, translated by P. F. Gent(leman) in 1592 (edited by William Rose, and published by Univ. of Notre Dame Press in 1963 as a reprint of the Dutton 1925 edition); second, in Christopher Marlowe's *The Tragicall History of Doctor Faustus*, probably performed by 1589; and third, in John Ashton's chapbooks of the eighteenth century, published in 1882.

Marlowe's source for *Doctor Faustus* was either the contemporary version of the English *Faust-Book* or an earlier, now-lost version. James Foster's source for his version of "Doctor Faustus," in *The World's Great Folktales* (Galahad, 1994), was the Ashton chapbooks.

In the introduction, I have omitted the fact that Theophilus consults a Jewish magician. (In its original form, the Faust legend fostered anti-Semitism.) Walter Kaufmann relates the two quotations in his introduction to Goethe's *Faust* (Doubleday, 1961). William Rose relates the anecdote about Homer's heroes and Polyphemus in his introduction to the English *Faust-Book*.

I have taken my version of the legend primarily from the English *Faust-Book*, where Mephistopheles simply functions as Faust's means to achieve his goals. In contrast, in Marlowe's version, Mephistopheles becomes a more complex personality in that he is clearly unhappy with his own fate.

However, I have taken details about Doctor Faust's goals from Marlowe's version. In the English *Faust-Book*, Faust is interested in wine, food, women, and tourism as ends in themselves. It is Marlowe who gives Faust his interest in acquiring knowledge and power. However, even under Marlowe's pen, Faust is nothing more than a glorified tourist, and he does nothing with the information that he gains. I have also taken some details about Hell from Marlowe's version as well as Faust's welcome of Helen and his speech about his impending death.

I have taken part of Doctor Faust's tour of Hell as well as his adventures as Cupid and with the pigs from James Foster's version of the legend.

I have also made the following changes in the legend: I have rearranged certain incidents in order to make the legend more cohesive. I have deleted Faust's servant, Wagner, as well as conversations with Mephistopheles about God. Moreover, I have deleted incidents that reflect the obvious anti-Catholic bias of both the German *Faust-Book*—which was written by an anonymous, presumably Lutheran, author—and its English version. In both, Mephistopheles always appears before Faust dressed in the attire of a Franciscan monk. Faust also has encounters with the pope that reflect his disrespect for Catholicism.

In addition to Christopher Marlowe's *The Tragicall History of Doctor Faustus*, the Faust legend has also provided the inspiration for Honoré de Balzac's *Lost Illusions* and *Melmoth Reconciled* (a parody); Robert Browning's *Paracelsus*; George Gordon Lord Byron's *The Deformed Transformed* (unfinished) and *Manfred*; Johann Wolfgang von Goethe's *Faust*; Nathaniel Hawthorne's "Ethan Brand"; and Thomas Mann's *Doctor Faustus*.

In "Ethan Brand," Hawthorne uses the Faust legend to portray a man who, being intellectually curious about the nature of the one unpardonable sin, evokes and converses with Satan, who appears within the flames of Brand's lime kiln. Brand then proceeds to search for this sin by traversing the world and studying the hidden recesses of every human soul. He discovers that his own amoral intellectual curiosity is the very sin—that greatest of sins—for which he has been searching in vain.

An extensive but abridged version of the *Faust-Book*'s sixty-three chapters appears appended to Marlowe's *Doctor Faustus* (NAL Signet, 1969). "Folklore," in Jeffrey Burton Russell's *Lucifer: The Devil in the Middle Ages* (Cornell Univ. Press, 1988) and "The Reformed Devil," in Russell's *Mephistopheles: The Devil in the Modern World* (Cornell Univ. Press, 1986), are superb secondary sources for the Faust legend.

Part 4   The Americas

Botoque, Bringer of Fire

Claude Lévi-Strauss relates this myth in "Ge Variations," in *The Raw and the Cooked* (Univ. of Chicago Press, 1983), where he provides six versions that he collected.

Peter G. Roe, in *The Cosmic Zygote* (Rutgers Univ. Press, 1982), and "The Ancestral Forest: Origin Myths of the Forest Peoples" in *World Mythology*, edited by Roy Willis (Henry Holt, 1993), provide additional material.

The principal version of this myth, as given by Claude Lévi-Strauss, also appears in "Tropical South America: When Men Received Fire," in *Mythology*, edited by Richard Cavendish (London: Orbis, 1980).

The six myths from related Ge tribes in central Brazil and the Amazon Basin are very similar, and yet they differ in significant respects. I decided that the story would be more interesting if I took the basic Kayapo myth, which is logical in its construction, and added additional details from some of the other versions.

In the process, I followed the Kayapo version in the following respects: First, Botoque kills Jaguar's wife; he does not wound her (alternative version). Also, Botoque steals fire and other possessions from Jaguar; Jaguar does not choose to give them to Botoque (alternative version). The Kayapo version places the origin of Jaguar's animosity toward human beings on Botoque's decision to lead his people back to Jaguar's house in order to steal fire and Jaguar's other possessions.

In the Kayapo version, Botoque tosses down two macaw eggs, which turn into rocks that wound his brother-in-law. However, I chose the version in which Botoque is afraid to capture the chicks because this version makes more sense. I chose to imply that Jaguar gives Botoque permission to kill his wife. In the Kayapo version, Jaguar openly gives this permission; in other versions, Botoque kills her on his own initiative. I also chose to have the animals themselves offer to help Botoque transport fire back to the village because that is consistent with Botoque's theft. (The animals have no part in the Kayapo version; in an alternative version, Jaguar organizes the animals.)

I have rearranged and included Botoque's journey through the forest and his experience with the ogre (not in the Kayapo version) because they explain the origin of human mortality.

In versions of the myth told by Lévi-Strauss, the raccoon and the alligator are actually their relatives the coati and the caiman, respectively.

The Little Frog

Yolando Pino-Saavedra relates this tale in *Folktales of Chile* (Univ. of Chicago Press, 1967). It was taken from a three-volume Spanish collection, *Cuentos folklóricos de Chile* (*Chilean Folk Tales*) (1960–1963). Pino-Saavedra recorded the tale on tape on April 21, 1962, in Parral, Linares, as told by a country woman named Amelia Quiroz, who was born in 1889.

This tale appears in numerous versions throughout the West. The banquet with the bones occurs in eleven of the thirty versions from the Iberian Peninsula, Brazil, and Spanish America. Although the Spanish versions feature a frog, a toad, or a monkey, other European versions feature other animals.

In Pino-Saavedra's version, the frog is ugliest for the second son and least ugly for the youngest son. Since the frog's appearance changes from one son to the next, I changed the sequence so as to make the frog progressively uglier. In my opinion, this provided a pattern for the frog's changes in appearance, and it made the youngest son more courageous in his acceptance of the frog.

The Journey beneath the Earth

Harold Courlander relates this tale, which he calls "The Voyage below the Water," in *"The Piece of Fire" and Other Haitian Tales* (Harcourt, Brace, and World, 1941). His version is based on that of a Haitian narrator. Although Courlander lists his sources, he does not specify who is responsible for each tale.

This tale also appears in *A Treasury of Afro-American Folklore* (Crown, 1976), where Courlander connects it with its related African (Mbundu) version, which he calls "The Voyage below the Water: A Mbundu Version."

The Mbundu version also appears in *A Treasury of African Folklore* (Crown, 1975), where Courlander calls it "King Kitamba kia Xiba." Geoffrey Parrinder, in "The World Beyond," in *African Mythology* (Hamlyn, 1982), provides a briefer version of the same Mbundu tale.

Courlander's source for the Mbundu tale is Heli Chatelain's translation, "King Kitamba kia Xiba," in *Folk-Tales of Angola* (*American Folk-Lore Society Memoirs*. Stechert, 1894). It is not clear which of Parrinder's sources contains this tale.

In Courlander's reprint of Chatelain's notes, King Kitamba is the twentieth king of Kasanji; yet the tale says that he founded the village.

Courlander's notes to the Haitian tale indicate that some Haitians believe that when human beings die, their spirits take a freshwater road (such as a spring, river, or waterfall) down to a land below the water, where they continue to live as they lived on earth. The living can communicate with the dead by holding special rites that involve a cult priest. In a number of Haitian tales, living beings travel to the land below the water for this purpose.

The two versions of the tale are remarkably similar. Characterization, plot, and theme are identical. Only details vary. I have combined the two tales by substituting and adding specific details from the more elaborate Mbundu version.

In the Haitian tale, the mourner is a wealthy countryman (not a king) by the name of Bordeau. Bordeau is a farmer, but he refuses to work in his fields. A Vodoun priest (not a medicine man) goes beneath the water (not beneath the earth) to find the Land of the Dead and Bordeau's wife. There he finds her in the marketplace selling coffee beans (not weaving a basket). However, he does not find Bordeau there. Bordeau's wife gives the priest one of her gold earrings (not her arm ring) to give to her husband.

In Courlander's Mbundu version, the shaman is called a medicine man. He receives a gun as a calling gift and two slaves as his payment. The medicine man takes his child with him into the underworld. Because, in my opinion, these points contribute nothing to the tale, I have changed the slaves to servants and deleted the rest.

Finally, I have told the tale in my own style.

El Bizarrón and the Devil

Dorothy Sharp Carter relates this tale, which she calls "How El Bizarrón Fooled the Devil," in *Greedy Mariani and Other Folktales of the Antilles* (Atheneum, 1974). Her source is Samuel Feijoo's *Cuentos Populares Cubanos* (*Popular Cuban Stories*, 1960).

Joanna Cole (*Best-Loved Folktales.* Doubleday, 1982) and Jane Yolen (*Favorite Folktales.* Pantheon, 1986) reprint Carter's version of this tale in their respective anthologies.

I have made the following changes in my version of this tale: I have given the Devil many of his traditional physical characteristics, but I have also given him the ability to know "what evil lurks" in the hearts of human beings, which is consistent with his nature.

I have also increased the presence of the Devil's wife in the tale because in Carter's version she appears only at the very end of the tale, where she sneers at her husband's gullibility and goads him into recovering his property. I have tried to keep my additions consistent with both her personality and her role in the tale.

Wiley and the Hairy Man

B. A. Botkin relates this tale in *A Treasury of American Folklore* (Bonanza, 1983). He attributes his version to Donnell Van de Voort's Manuscripts of the Federal Writers' Project of the Works Progress Administration for the State of Alabama (N.D.).

Harold Courlander reprints Botkin's version in *A Treasury of Afro-American Folklore* (Crown, 1976) and suggests that Van de Voort imposed his own style on this traditional tale.

Virginia Haviland also relates this tale in *The Faber Book of North American Legends* (Faber & Faber, 1979). Jane Yolen reprints Haviland's version in *Favorite Folktales* (Pantheon, 1986). However, both Haviland and Yolen omit Van de Voort's ending.

Information on the Hairy Man can be found in Jeffrey Burton Russell's *Lucifer* (Cornell Univ. Press, 1988).

I have made the following changes in my version of the tale. First, I have changed the style so that it can represent any country area in the United States. In this process, I have changed "Mammy" and "Pappy" to "Mama" and "Daddy."

Like Haviland and Yolen, I have deleted the original ending. There Wiley takes out his father's liquor and says that he is now going to become "hog-drunk and chicken-wild." His mother tells him that she will join him, saying that it's nice that Wiley's father was so "no-count" that he kept liquor in the house.

The Shepherd Who Understood Animal Speech

Rudolfo A. Anaya includes his translation of José Griego y Maestas's "The Shepherd Who Knew the Language of the Animals" in their *Cuentos: Tales from the Hispanic Southwest* (Museum of New Mexico, 1980). Juan B. Rael collected the tale in New Mexico in 1929, and it appears in the unabridged Spanish anthology *Cuentos Espanoles de Colorado y Nuevo México* (*Spanish Tales from Colorado and New Mexico*) (Museum of New Mexico, 1977).

The tale originates in India and appears in the *Ramayana*. Geza Roheim relates it in *Fire in the Dragon* (Princeton Univ. Press, 1992); Stith Thompson summarizes it in *The Folktale* (Univ. of California Press, 1977); and the Brothers Grimm include a version of it, entitled "The White Snake" (*The Complete Grimm's Fairy Tales*. Pantheon, 1944; and *The Grimms' German Folk Tales*. Southern Illinois Univ. Press, 1960).

I have followed Anaya's version of this tale, although the style is my own.

Rip Van Winkle

Washington Irving tells the famous American version of this tale in *The Sketch Book of Geoffrey Crayon, Gent.* (BOMC 1993 reprint from the 1820 edition). According to Francis Lee Utley, in his Introduction to Max Luthi's *Once Upon a Time* (Indiana Univ. Press, 1976), Irving took the idea for "Rip Van Winkle" from a German *volkssage* (folk-legend) by Johann Carl Cristoph Nachtigall, entitled "Peter Klaus the Goatherd," which is associated with the mountain known as the Kyffhauser. Stith Thompson, in *The Folktale* (Univ. of California Press, 1977), also associates "Rip Van Winkle" with the Kyffhauser legend. Daniel Hoffman (*American Literature to 1900*. St. Martin's/Macmillan, 1980) gives Irving's source as Otmar's *Volkssagen*. Otmar's remarkably similar rendition appears in Milton

Rugoff's *A Harvest of World Folk Tales* (Viking, 1949). Rugoff uses Thomas Roscoe's translation of "Peter Klaus" (included in *The German Novelists*, London: N. P., 1826).

Irving added the Hudson River valley setting, the connection between the ancient men and Hendrick Hudson, the characterization of Rip and his wife, and the fact that Rip slept through an important historical period. Irving's version contains wonderful detail and more difficult language than either Otmar's version or my own.

In contrast, I have presented the tale as it might be told in an oral tradition, emphasizing plot rather than description and using language and phrasing that appeal to the ear.

Giant, the Fire-Bringer

Franz Boas relates this myth, which he calls "The Origin of Fire," in "Tsimshian Mythology," published in the *Thirty-First Annual Report of the Bureau of American Ethnology 1909–1910* (1916). His version is based on texts recorded by Henry W. Tate, and he includes many variants of this myth in the notes that complete his paper.

The Tsimshian, Tlingit, and Haida peoples tell most of the Raven myths. The Tsimshian relate thirty-two of the forty-five principal Raven tales listed by Boas in his major work on Tsimshian ethnography (above). Peter Goodchild's *Raven Tales* (Chicago Review, 1991) is superb. However, he does not include the Tsimshian version of the theft of fire.

Certain aspects of the content of Boas's version are open to question. The role of Giant's father in refusing to give Giant fire is not clear. Also, it is not clear who, if anyone, is human, and who are animal people. It is possible that every character is both human and animal, and since the blurring of the distinction between animals and humans is a very important aspect of this myth, I have made no attempt to clarify it.

Finally, based on other Tsimshian myths, I have added cormorants and cranes to the list of visitors.

Part 5   The Far East

Savitri

J. A. B. van Buitenen translates this myth in its most complete form in *The Book of the Forest*, in Vol. 2 of *The Mahabharata* (Univ. of Chicago Press, 1981).

The versions told by Donald A. Mackenzie in *India: Myths and Legends* (London: Bracken, 1985) and by R. K. Narayan in *Gods, Demons, and Others* (Bantam, 1986) are shorter, but basically the same. The version by Ananda K. Coomaraswamy and Sister Nivedita (Dover, 1967) is also accurate, but is considerably shorter. Madhur Jaffrey's version, which she calls "Savitri and Satyavan," in *Seasons of Splendour* (Atheneum, 1985), has been transformed into a tale that will appeal to children.

An excellent secondary source is Stuart H. Blackburn's *Oral Epics in India* (Univ. of California Press, 1989).

I have retold van Buitenen's version in a style that attempts to preserve the charming aspects of the *Mahabharata*.

Kun and the Great Flood and
Yu the Great and the Great Flood

Anne Birrell relates the myths of Kun and Yu in "Saviors: Kun and the Flood; and Yu Controls the Flood," and "Myths of Yu the Great," in *Chinese Mythology* (Johns Hopkins, 1993). Derk Bodde also relates the myths in "Myths of Ancient China," in *Mythologies of the Ancient World*, edited by Samuel Noah Kramer (Doubleday/ Anchor, 1961). Both Birrell and Bodde give superb introductions to Chinese mythology, and Birrell includes quotations from original sources as she presents the two myths.

In *The World of Myth* (Oxford Univ. Press, 1990), David Adams Leeming includes material based on Derk Bodde's versions of these two myths. These myths are also well told by Anthony Christie in "The Useful Arts: Yao and Gun; and Yu, Master of Floods," in *Chinese Mythology* (Hamlyn/Newnes, 1983); by Cyril Birch in "The Quellers of the Flood," in *Chinese Myths and Fantasies* (Oxford Univ. Press, 1992); by Tao Tao Liu Sanders in "Yu Controls the Flood," in *Dragons, Gods, and Spirits* (Schocken, 1980); and by Jan Walls and Yvonne Walls in "Yu Drives Away Gong Gong" and "The Bear and the Rock," in *Classical Chinese Myths* (Beijing: Joint, 1984). An interesting but somewhat divergent version is given by Yuan Ke in *Dragons and Dynasties* (Penguin, 1993).

According to Anne Birrell, four major and two lesser primary sources are important with regard to the myths of Kun and Yu. Two sources, the *Book of Poetry* and the *Book of History*, are Confucian classics. Information about these six sources and their relevance to the myths of Kun and Yu follows.

The first of the four principal primary sources is the Confucian classic *The Book of Poetry,* or *The Book of Odes* (*Shih ching*), which was compiled in about 600 B.C., during the early Eastern Chou period. It contains 305 poems; some were created by aristocrats and others are folksongs. All of these poems were supposedly selected and edited by Confucius. Four poems (#210, #244, #301, and #304) give valuable poetic versions of the myth of Yu, and in all four, Yu is praised as the hero who saved the world from a great flood.

Birrell provides an excerpt from the second of the principal primary sources, "Questions of Heaven" (*T'ien wen*), composed in about the fourth century B.C. (late Eastern Chou era) and included as Chapter 3 in the *Songs of Ch'u* (*Ch'u Tz'u*). This source provides excellent information about Kun and Yu and their handling of the flood. It is the richest single source of Chou mythology and, because of its authenticity, it is the most valuable source of Chinese myth. Based on ancient Chou mythology, it reflects a single system of beliefs and a single cultural tradition in its systematic discussion of the creation of the world, the actions of gods and demigods and, finally, the deeds of historical Chou kings in the late sixth century B.C.

The *Songs of Ch'u,* in which "Questions of Heaven" appears, is an anthology of seventeen Chou and Han poems that was compiled in the second century A.D. Scholars think that its anonymous author was a culturally well-educated official who was a member of the Ch'u court (in central China) during the Warring States Period of the late Eastern Chou era. Traditionally, Chü Yuan has been considered the author, but today scholars view him as an adapter of a priestly textual tradition rather than as the author of the anthology.

The third of the principal primary sources of the myths of Kun and Yu is *The Book of Mountains and Seas* (*Shan hai ching*), composed by various anonymous authors from the late Eastern Chou era (third century B.C.) to the late Han era (first century A.D.). This work contains many myths about various parts of China and is the second most valuable source of Chinese myth. These versions are recorded in a fragmentary manner. They were compiled from earlier source material and may represent several, sometimes contradictory, versions of certain myths. Scholars consider the versions of the myths that deal with Kun and Yu and their handling of the flood to be authentic.

The fourth of the principal primary sources of Chinese myth, including the myths of Kun and Yu, is the Confucian classic *The Book of History*, or *The Book of Documents* (*Shu ching*), which is also called *Ancient History* (*Shang shu*). This work claims to be a genuine account of the period that begins with the monarch Yao and ends with the early Chou dynasty. It contains oral reports from Yao, Shun, and Yu (the three great monarchs of China's golden age of antiquity) and their ministers. However, aside from this book, scholars have found no reliable evidence confirming either the existence of any of these three men or the period in which they ruled.

Supposedly edited by Confucius, *The Book of History* was actually composed by various anonymous authors from the Chou era to the Han era, which ended in the third century A.D. Scholars consider the content written during the earlier part of the Chou era to be more authentic than that written later in the Chou era. The material from the later Han era—which, in some instances, has been forged—is the least reliable.

By the Han era, *The Book of History* was viewed as the true version of historical events and as the ideal way to depict ancient history. However, the authors of the book transformed the existing myths, including that of Yu and the flood, into history. In this version of the flood myth, Kun and Yu are not divinities but real people who function as the subjects of Yao and Shun. However, despite this type of distortion, *The Book of History*'s versions of the myths contain valuable material.

Birrell provides an excerpt from "The Tribute of Yu" in *The Book of History*, which lists Yü's geographical accomplishments (each beginning with the number nine). Scholars currently place the writing of the "Tribute" sometime during the fourth to the third centuries B.C., although the source of its content is much older. It presents the mythic geography of the world as it was known to the Chinese in the Chou dynasty, either firsthand or through hearsay.

Finally, Birrell provides excerpts from two other primary sources that deal with the myth of Yu. The first is *Shih Tzu* (no English title given), a short text written in the fourth century B.C., which describes Yu's unselfish devotion to his task and the personal toll that it takes. The second is the *Spring and Autumn Annals of Master Lu* (*Lu Shih ch'un-ch'iu*), attributed to Lu Pu-wei, who was the prime minister of the state of Ch'in in 249 B.C. This work contains philosophy, literature, and mythology, including the mythical geography that Yu encounters as he explores the four directions.

According to Birrell, the legend of the birth of Yü's son Ch'i first appears in the seventh century A.D., but the event is mentioned as early as 111 B.C.

The source of the quotation from 540 B.C., "Were it not for Yu, we would indeed be fish!" is the history book *Chronicle of Tso* (*Tso chuan*, or *Chao kung*, First Year, Corvreur, 1914). This joke is attributed to Duke Ting, Prince of Lu, and it is quoted by Birrell (p. 147).

According to Confucian tradition, thirty is the proper age for a man to marry. This may be why Yu is thirty years old when he decides that it is time to think about marriage.

While the above sources provide the content of these myths, I have created the style of the version in this text.

Song of the Water Goddess

Donald L. Philippi relates this myth in poetic form in *Songs of Gods, Songs of Humans* (Princeton Univ. Press, 1979). He took the text for this song from Kamui Yukar 81 in Itsuhiko Kubodera's *Ainu jojishi: Shin'yo, seiden no kenkyu*. Kubodera (1902–1971) was a native of Hokkaido who collected Ainu texts directly from Ainu sources. Kubodera's primary source for this song was Hiraga Etenoa, a resident of the Saru area of Hidaka. She spent from August of 1932 until April of 1933 working with Kubodera in his home in Tokyo. Etenoa sang the "Song of the Water Goddess" on September 19, 1932, so that Kubodera could record it in writing.

Kunimatsu Nitani (1888–1960), who lived with Kubodera early in 1935, and Kanunmore Hiramura, both also from the Saru area, provided Kubodera with other versions of this song.

I have changed Philippi's style into a narrative. However, I have kept the repetition and the first-person narrator because they are characteristic of Ainu style.

Taro Urashima, the Young Fisherman

In creating the version of "Urashima," I used the following five sources: (1) W. G. Aston's translation of the *Nihongi* (also called the *Nihonshoki*) (Tuttle, 1980); (2) and (3) two translations of Takahashi Mushimaro's poem, "Urashima of Mizunoe" in the *Man'yoshu* (A.D. 760): (a) the Nippon Gakujutsu translation (Columbia Univ. Press, 1969); and (b) Hiroaki Sato and Burton

Watson's translation, in *From the Country of Eight Islands* (Columbia Univ. Press, 1986); (4) F. Hadland Davis's "Urashima," in *Myths and Legends of Japan* (a Graham Brash reprint of the 1913 edition); and (5) Lafcadio Hearn's "Urashima," in *Out of the East* (Houghton Mifflin, 1895).

In the introduction, the information about the tortoise in world mythology is attributed by Kawai Hayao, in *The Japanese Psyche* (Spring Publications, 1988), to the Hungarian classicist Karl Kerenyi. Kawai provides the connection between the tortoise/turtle and the ocean or the woman who lives beneath the sea, and it is Kawai who states that it was the god of land who originally rode on a tortoise's back and that Urashima's rides on the tortoise's back were added to the myth at the end of the eighteenth century.

Because the dates of Urashima's departure and return are documented in the *Nihongi*, this myth is also considered to be a legend.

Many different versions of this myth are available. It is included in (1) Joanna Cole's *Best-Loved Folktales* (Doubleday, 1982); (2) F. Hadland Davis's *Myths and Legends of Japan* (above); (3) Lafcadio Hearn's *Out of the East* (above); (4) Grace James's *Green Willow* (Avenel, 1987); (5) Margaret Mayo's *Magical Tales from Many Lands* (Dutton, 1993), where it is called "The Kingdom under the Sea"; (6) Helen and William McAlpine's *Japanese Tales and Legends* (Oxford Univ. Press, 1990); (7) Yei Ozaki's *The Japanese Fairy Book* (a Dover reprint of the 1903 edition); (8) Juliet Piggott's *Japanese Mythology* (Bedrick, 1982); (9) Dale Saunders's "Japanese Mythology," in Samuel Kramer's *Mythologies of the Ancient World* (Anchor/Doubleday, 1961); (10) Royall Tyler's *Japanese Tales* (Pantheon, 1987); and (11) Jane Yolen's *Favorite Folktales* (Pantheon, 1986).

The myth usually begins in two different ways, and I have chosen to combine them in my version. However, in still another version (Tyler; Yolen)—taken from the *Tango Fudoki* (*Account of the Province of Tango*), a fragment dated at A.D. 713 and written in archaic Japanese—Urashima is taken by a sky goddess to an eternal mountain on an island. At the end of this version, he neither ages nor dies, but longs for the goddess and grieves for himself.

Other variations include later changes. For example, in Cole's version, the goddess enters the boat and, in the end, Urashima returns to the water. In James's version, the goddess keeps Urashima against his will for one night. In Mayo's version, Urashima becomes a crane and flies off into the sky, whereas in McAlpine's version, in the end a sorrowful Urashima continues to live.

The Urashima myth also has counterparts in other cultures throughout the world. Indries Shah, in *World Tales* (Harcourt Brace Jovanovich, 1979), retells a similar version from Romania, which he calls "The Land Where Time Stood Still." Tao Tao Liu Sanders, in *Dragons, Gods and Spirits* (Schocken, 1980), retells a Chinese version, which she calls "Liu Yi and the Dragon King of Lake Dongting." Katherine Briggs, in *British Folktales* (Pantheon, 1977), relates the tale of King Herla.

The Tiger's Whisker

Harold Courlander relates this tale in *"The Tiger's Whisker" and Other Tales and Legends from Asia and the Pacific* (Harcourt Brace, 1959). He recorded it from a Korean seaman named Lee Bok, who recited it to him.

Joanna Cole, in *Best-Loved Folktales* (Doubleday, 1982), reprints Courlander's version.

I have made one change in the content of Courlander's version of the tale. He ends the tale with Yun Ok's thinking about the sage's wisdom, whereas I have continued the tale to the point where Yun Ok returns home and suggests to her husband that they eat rice and meat sauce for dinner. My addition provides one more indication that Yun Ok will now apply the lessons that she learned through taming the tiger to her experience with her husband. It also adds an element of humor in providing a tangible connection between Yun Ok's taming of the tiger and her healing of her husband.

Kerta's Sacrifice

Jan Knappert relates this myth, called "The Son Who Sinned," in *Myths and Legends of Indonesia* (Singapore: Heinemann, 1977). Alice M. Terada bases her version, which she calls "Kerta's Sin," in *"The Magic Crocodile" and Other Folktales from Indonesia* (Univ. of Hawaii Press, 1994) on Knappert's version.

I have used both versions to create the version in the text. Although Terada's more detailed version reads like a folktale, rather than like a myth, the basic plot is identical to Knappert's.

I have made the following changes in the plot: First, I have changed Kerta's age from about ten years to almost an adult in his community. It is not clear what Kerta's age would have been in the original myth. He could even have been an adult. Adapters of myth change details like this in order to appeal to a particular audience.

Second, I have enhanced Pak Miam's attitude about Roro Kidul, the goddess of the South Sea, and his desire to communicate this attitude of respect and honor to Kerta. My intent has been to restore some of the power of the original myth and give the proper weight to Kerta's offense and his attempt to atone.

Third, I have combined the details about the profession of swift's-nest gatherer from various parts of Terada's version and from her notes and have had Pak Miam relate them to Kerta. This enables the readers of this tale to understand the attitudes of the characters toward this profession as well as toward the goddess of the sea. It also enabled me to use the details as a type of psychological realism, in the form of Pak Miam's guiding voice, in order to help Kerta succeed with the first part of his heroic task.

I have also made the following minor changes in the tale. I have used the name Roro Kidul instead of Ratu Lara Kidul for the goddess of the South Sea. I have also called the Cave of Squids the Cave of the Octopi, since that is a more familiar term. Finally, I have had the glasslike man use his eyes, rather than his glass hand across Kerta's eyes, in order to transform Kerta into a lizard.

SELECTED BIBLIOGRAPHY

Part I Africa

The Creation of Human Beings

Cavendish, Richard, ed. "Central and Southern Africa: Myths of Origins." *Mythology: An Illustrated Encyclopedia.* London: Orbis, 1980.

Eliade, Mircea. *Gods, Goddesses, and Myths of Creation: From Primitives to Zen.* (Part I) New York: Harper Row, 1974.

Frazer, James George. "The Creation of Man." *Folklore in the Old Testament: Studies in Comparative Religion, Legend, and Law.* New York: Hart, 1975. Reprint of London: Macmillan, 1918.

Gaster, Theodor H. "Adam and Eve." *Myth, Legend, and Custom in the Old Testament: A Comparative Study with Chapters from Sir James G. Frazer's* Folklore in the Old Testament. Vol. I. New York: Harper Row, 1975.

Anansi, the Clever One

Appiah, Peggy. "How Death Came to Mankind." *Tales of an Ashanti Father.* Boston: Beacon, 1989.

The Woman with One Hand

Scheub, Harold, ed. "The Girl with One Hand." *The African Story-teller: Stories from African Oral Traditions.* Trans. Edward Steere. Dubuque, IA: Kendall/Hunt, 1990.

Steere, Edward, ed. and trans. *Swahili Tales as Told by Natives of Zanzibar.* London: Society for Promoting Christian Knowledge, 1869.

The Roamer-of-the-Plain

Cendrars, Blaise. "The Roamer-of-the-Plain." *The African Saga.* Trans. Margery Bianco. From *L'Anthologie Nègre,* 1921. New York: Payson & Clarke, 1927.

Feldmann, Susan, ed. "The Wonder Worker of the Plains." Trans. Paul Radin. *African Myths and Tales.* New York: Dell, 1963.

Junod, Henri A. *Les Ba-Rongas.* Neuchatel: Paul Attinger, 1898.

———. *The Life of a South African Tribe.* (Thonga) Vol. 2. London: Macmillan, 1927.

Radin, Paul, ed. and trans. "The Wonder-Worker of the Plains." *African Folktales.* New York: Schocken, 1983.

——— and J. Sweeney. *African Folktales and Sculpture.* New York: Bollingen Foundation, 1952.

Scheub, Harold, trans. "The Gamboler-of-the-Plain." *The African Storyteller: Stories from African Oral Traditions.* Dubuque, IA: Kendall/Hunt, 1990.

The Crocodile and His Son

Cendrars, Blaise. "Ngurangurane, the Crocodile's Son." *The African Saga.* Trans. Margery Bianco. From *L'Anthologie Nègre* (1921). New York: Payson & Clarke, 1927.

Part 2   The Middle East

Enki, Lord of the Earth and the Waters of Life and Adapa

Bonnefoy, Yves, ed. *Mythologies.* Vol. I. Trans. Wendy Doniger. Chicago: Univ. of Chicago Press, 1991.

Dalley, Stephanie. "Adapa." *Myths from Mesopotamia.* New York: Oxford Univ. Press, 1990.

Finegan, Jack. *Light from the Ancient Past: Archaeological Background of Judaism and Christianity.* Vol. 1. Princeton: Princeton Univ. Press, 1974.

Gaster, Theodor H. "The Lost Chance." *The Oldest Stories in the World.* Boston: Beacon, 1958.

Hooke, S. H. "The Myth of Creation." "The Myth of Adapa." *Middle Eastern Mythology.* New York: Penguin, 1976.

Jacobsen, Thorkild. *The Treasures of Darkness: A History of Mesopotamian Religion.* New Haven: Yale Univ. Press, 1976.

King, L. W. *Babylonian Religion and Mythology.* London: Kegan, Paul, Trench, Trübner, 1899.

Kramer, Samuel Noah. "Mythology of Sumer and Akkad." Ed. Samuel Noah Kramer. *Mythologies of the Ancient World.* New York: Anchor, 1961.

————. "Myths of Origins." *Sumerian Mythology.* Philadelphia: Univ. of Pennsylvania Press, 1972.

————. "Literature: The Sumerian *Belles-Lettres.*" *The Sumerians: Their History, Culture, and Character.* Chicago: Univ. of Chicago Press, 1963.

———— and John Maier. "Enki and Inanna: The Organization of the Earth and Its Cultural Processes." "Inanna and Enki: The Transfer of the Arts of Civilization from Eridu to Erech." "Enki and Eridu: The Journey of the Water-God to Nippur." *Myths of Enki, the Crafty God.* New York: Oxford Univ. Press, 1989.

Langdon, Stephen Herbert. *Semitic Mythology.* Vol. V. Ed. Canon John Arnott MacCulloch. *The Mythology of All Races.* New York: Cooper Square, 1964.

Mackenzie, Donald A. *Myths of Babylonia and Assyria.* London: Gresham, N.D.

McCall, Henrietta. "Adapa." *Mesopotamian Myths.* Austin: British Museum and Univ. of Texas Press, 1990.

Oppenheim, A. Leo. *Ancient Mesopotamia: Portrait of a Dead Civilization.* Chicago: Univ. of Chicago Press, 1972.

Speiser, E. A. "Adapa." "Akkadian Myths and Epics." *Ancient Near Eastern Texts Relating to the Old Testament.* Third ed. with Supplement. Ed. James B. Pritchard. Princeton: Princeton Univ. Press, 1969.

Time-Life Books, eds. *Mesopotamia: The Mighty Kings.* Alexandria, VA: Time-Life, 1995.

————. *Sumer: Cities of Eden.* Alexandria, VA: Time-Life, 1993.

The Craftsman's Wife

bin Gorion, Micha J. and Emanuel bin Gorion. "The Craftsman's Wife." *Mimekor Yisrael: Classical Jewish Folktales: Abridged and Annotated Edition.* Trans. I. M. Lask. Bloomington: Indiana Univ. Press, 1990.

————. "The Craftsman's Wife." Mimekor Yisrael: *Selected Classical Jewish Folktales.* Trans. I. M. Lask. Bloomington: Indiana Univ. Press, 1990.

Gesta Romanorum (1595). "Tale #69." Delmar, NY: Scholars' Facsimiles and Reprints, 1973.

Gesta Romanonum or Entertaining Moral Stories Invented by the Monks. "Tale #69." Ed. Wynnard Hooper. Trans. Charles Swan. Bohn's Antiquarian Library. New York: AMS, 1970. Reprint of London, 1894.

Nahmad, H. M., ed. "The Craftsman's Wife." "*A Portion in Paradise*" *and Other Jewish Folktales.* New York: Schocken, 1974.

Rappaport, Angelo. "The Master and His Faithful Wife." *Ancient Israel: Myths and Legends.* New York: Bonanza, 1987.

Rostam, Shield of Persia and The Tragedy of Sohrab

Arnold, Matthew. "Sohrab and Rustem" (1853). *Prose and Poetry.* New York: Scribner's, 1927.

Atkinson, James, trans. *The Shah Nameh of the Persian Poet Firdausi.* New York: Routledge, N.D. (Preface: 1832.)

Cavendish, Richard. "The Valiant Rustom." *Legends of the World.* London: Orbis, 1982.

Clinton, Jerome W., trans. *The Tragedy of Sohrab and Rostam: From the Persian National Epic, The Shahname of Abol-Qasem Ferdowsi.* Seattle: Univ. of Washington Press, 1987.

Curtis, Vesta S. "The Family of Rustam." "The Stories of Rustam." *Persian Myths.* Austin: British Museum Press/Univ. Texas Press, 1993.

Goodrich, Norma Lorre. "The Coming of Rustam." "Rustam and Kai-Kaus." "Rustam and Suhrab." *Myths of the Hero.* New York: Orion, 1962.

Hanaway, William L., Jr. "The Iranian Epics." Felix J. Oinas, ed. *Heroic Epic and Saga: An Introduction to the World's Great Folk Epics.* Bloomington: Indiana Univ. Press, 1978.

Levy, Reuben, trans. *The Epic of the Kings: Shah-Nama, the National Epic of Persia, by Abol-Qasem Ferdowsi.* Rev. by Amin Banani. New York: Arkana/Viking Penguin, 1990.

Picard, Barbara Leonie. (Numerous Chapters) *Tales of Ancient Persia: Retold from the Shah-Nama of Firdausi.* New York: Oxford Univ. Press, 1993.

Potter, Murray A. *Sohrab and Rustem: The Epic Theme of a Combat between Father and Son: A Study of Its Genesis and Use in Literature and Popular Tradition.* London: David Nutt, 1902.

Puhvel, Jaan. *Comparative Mythology.* Baltimore: Johns Hopkins Univ. Press, 1987.

Renninger, Elizabeth D. *The Story of Rustem & Other Persian Hero Tales from Firdusi.* New York: Scribner's, 1909.

Warner, Arthur G., and Edmond Warner. *The Shahnama of Abol-Qasem Ferdowsi.* (9 Vols.) London: Kegan, Paul, 1905–1925.

Wilmot-Buxton, E. M. *Stories of Persian Heroes.* New York: Crowell, 1908.

Zimmern, Helen. *The Epic of Kings: Hero Tales of Ancient Persia. Retold from Firdusi's Shah-Nameh.* New York: Macmillan, 1926. Reprint of New York: Macmillan, 1882.

Part 3   Europe

Prometheus, the Fire-Bringer

Aeschylus. *Prometheus Bound.* Trans. David Grene. *The Complete Greek Tragedies.* Vol. 1. Chicago: Univ. of Chicago Press, 1959.

———. *Prometheus Bound.* Trans. Paul Elmer More. *The Complete Greek Drama.* Vol. 1. New York: Random House, 1938.

———. *Prometheus Bound.* Trans. James Scully and C. John Herington. New York: Oxford Univ. Press, 1975.

———. *Prometheus Bound.* Trans. Herbert Weir Smyth. Cambridge: Harvard Univ. Press, 1988.

Apollodorus. *The Library.* Vol. 1. Trans. Sir James G. Frazer. Cambridge: Harvard Univ. Press, 1976.

Bonnefoy, Yves, ed. *Mythologies.* Vol. 1. Trans. Wendy Doniger. Chicago: Univ. of Chicago Press, 1991.

Burn, Andrew Robert. *The World of Hesiod: A Study of the Greek Middle Ages c. 900–7 B.C.* New York: Benjamin Blom, 1966.

Evelyn-White, H. G., trans. Hesiod. *The Homeric Hymns and Homerica.* Cambridge: Harvard Univ. Press, 1977.

Havelock, E. A. *Prometheus, with* Prometheus Bound. Seattle: Univ. of Washington Press, 1968.

Hesiod. *Theogony; Works and Days; The Shield of Herakles.* Trans. Apostolos N. Athanassakis. Baltimore: Johns Hopkins Univ. Press, 1983.

———. *The Works and Days; Theogony; The Shield of Herakles.* Trans. Richmond Lattimore. Ann Arbor: Univ. of Michigan Press, 1973.

———. *Theogony; The Works and Days.* Trans. M. L. West. New York: Oxford Univ. Press, 1989.

Hyginus. *The Myths: Fabulae and Poetica Astronomica.* Trans. Mary Grant. Lawrence: Univ. of Kansas Press, 1960.

Oisin Mac Finn, Poet of the Fianna

Bonnefoy, Yves, ed. *Mythologies.* Vol. 1. Trans. Wendy Doniger. Chicago: Univ. of Chicago Press, 1991.

Chadwick, Nora. *The Celts.* New York: Penguin, 1977.

Comyn, Michael. "Lay of Oisin in the Land of Youth." Ed. and trans. Bryan O'Looney. *Fenian Poems.* Ed. John O'Daley. Transactions of the Ossianic Society for the year 1856. (No. 4.) N.P., 1859.

Curtin, Jeremiah. "Oisin in Tir na n-Og." *Myths and Folk Tales of Ireland.* New York: Dover, 1975. Reprint of *Myths and Folk-Lore of Ireland.* Boston: Little, Brown, 1890.

Delaney, Frank. "Oisin and the Land of Youth." *Legends of the Celts.* New York: Sterling, 1992.

Gregory, Lady Isabella Augusta. *Gods and Fighting Men: The Story of the Tuatha De Danaan and of the Fianna of Ireland.* Gerrards Cross, Buckinghamshire, G.B.: Colin Smythe, 1993. Reprint of London: John Murray, 1904.

———. "Usheen's Return to Ireland." Ed. Henry Glassie. *Irish Folk Tales.* New York: Pantheon, 1985. Reprint from *The Kiltarian History Book.* Galway, Ireland: N.P., 1926.

Heaney, Marie. "Oisin in the Land of Youth." *Over Nine Waves: A Book of Irish Legends.* Boston: Faber & Faber, 1994.

Herm, Gerhard. *The Celts.* New York: St. Martin's, 1975.

Hubert, Henri. *The Rise of the Celts.* London: Constable, 1987. Reprint of London: Kegan, Paul, Trench, and Trübner, 1934.

Joyce, P. W. "Oisin in Tir Na nOg or The Last of the Fena." Ed. Mary McGarry. *Great Folk Tales of Ireland.* London: Frederick Muller, 1980.

Llywelyn, Morgan. *Finn MacCool.* New York: Doherty, 1994.

MacCulloch, J. A. "The Heroic Myths: Fionn and the Féinn." *Celtic Mythology.* New York: Dorset, 1992. Reprint of Scotland: N.P., 1916.

O'Daly, John, ed. "Dialogues of Oisin and Patrick." *Fenian Poems.* Transactions of the Ossianic Society. No. 4., 1859.

Rolleston, Thomas William. "Tales of the Ossianic Cycle." *Myths and Legends of the Celtic Race.* New York: Schocken, 1986. Reprint of London: George G. Harrap, 1911.

———. "Tales of the Ossianic Cycle." *Celtic Myths and Legends.* New York: Dover, 1990. Reprint of *Myths and Legends of the Celtic Race.* Revised. London: George G. Harrap, 1917.

Rutherford, Ward. *Celtic Mythology: The Nature and Influence of Celtic Myth from Druidism to Arthurian Legend.* New York: Sterling, 1990.

Squire, Charles. *Celtic Myth and Legend*. Hollywood, CA: Newcastle, 1975. Reprint of London: Gresham, 191-. Reprint of *The Mythology of the British Islands*. N.P., 1905.

Stephens, James. "Oisin's Mother." *Irish Fairy Tales*. New York: Macmillan, 1968. Reprint of New York: Macmillan, 1920.

Time-Life Books, ed. *The Celts: Europe's People of Iron*. Alexandria, VA: Time-Life, 1994.

Williamson, Robin. "The Dialogue of Ossian and St. Patrick." *The Wise and Foolish Tongue: Celtic Stories*. San Francisco: Chronicle, 1991.

Willis, Roy, ed. "Finn and His Warriors: The Fenian Myths." *World Mythology*. New York: Henry Holt, 1993.

Yeats, William Butler. "The Wanderings of Oisin." *The Poems: A New Edition*. Ed. Richard J. Finneran. New York: Macmillan, 1983.

———. *Prefaces and Introductions*. *The Collected Works of W. B. Yeats*. Vol. VI. Ed. William H. O'Donnell. New York: Macmillan, 1989.

Saga of Gunnlaug Serpent-Tongue

Boucher, Alan, trans. *Saga of Gunnlaug Snake-Tongue*. Reykjavík: Iceland Review, 1983.

Hallberg, Peter. *The Icelandic Saga*. Trans. Paul Schach. Lincoln: Univ. of Nebraska Press, 1962.

Jones, Gwyn. *Gunnlaug Wormtongue*. *Eirik the Red and Other Icelandic Sagas*. New York: Oxford Univ. Press, 1991.

Kristjánsson, Jonas. *Eddas and Sagas: Iceland's Medieval Literature*. Trans. Peter Foote. Reykjavík: Hid íslenska bókmenntafélag, 1988.

Sturluson, Snorri (?). *Egil's Saga*. Trans. Hermann Palsson and Paul Edwards. New York: Penguin, 1982.

Aucassin and Nicolette

Capellanus, Andreas. "The Rules of Courtly Love." *The Portable Medieval Reader*. James Bruce Ross and Mary Martin McLaughlin, eds. New York: Viking, 1969.

Lang, Andrew, trans. "Aucassin and Nicolette." *Medieval Romances*. Roger Sherman Loomis and Laura Hibbard Loomis, eds. New York: Random House, 1957.

Mason, Eugene, trans. *"Aucassin and Nicolette" and Other Mediaeval Romances and Legends*. New York: Dutton, 1958.

Matarasso, Pauline, trans. "Aucassin and Nicolette." New York: Penguin, 1971.

Owen, D. D. R. "The Comedy of Love." *Noble Lovers.* New York: New York Univ. Press, 1975.

Doctor Faust

Cavendish, Richard, ed. "Legendary Magicians." *Legends of the World.* London: Orbis, 1982.

Foster, James R., ed. "Doctor Faustus." *The World's Great Folktales.* New York: Galahad, 1994.

Marlowe, Christopher. *Doctor Faustus.* New York: New American Library, 1969. (includes abridgment of the English *Faust-Book,* 1592)

Rose, William, ed. *The Historie of the Damnable Life and Deserved Death of Doctor John Faustus.* Trans. and ed. P. F. Gent., 1592. Notre Dame, IN: Univ. of Notre Dame Press, 1963. Reprint of New York: E. P. Dutton, 1925.

Russell, Jeffrey Burton. "Folklore." *Lucifer: The Devil in the Middle Ages.* Ithaca: Cornell Univ. Press, 1988.

———. "The Reformed Devil." *Mephistopheles: The Devil in the Modern World.* Ithaca: Cornell Univ. Press, 1986.

Part 4   The Americas

Botoque, Bringer of Fire

Cavendish, Richard, ed. "Tropical South America: When Men Received Fire." *Mythology: An Illustrated Encyclopedia.* London: Orbis, 1980.

Lévi-Strauss, Claude. "Ge Variations: Six Arias Followed by a Recitative." *The Raw and the Cooked.* Chicago: Univ. of Chicago Press, 1983.

Roe, Peter G. *The Cosmic Zygote: Cosmology in the Amazon Basin.* New Brunswick: Rutgers Univ. Press, 1982.

Willis, Roy, ed. "The Ancestral Forest: Origin Myths of the Forest Peoples." *World Mythology.* New York: Henry Holt, 1993.

The Little Frog

Pino-Saavedra, Yolando, ed. "The Little Frog." *Folktales of Chile.* Trans. Rockwell Gray. Chicago: Univ. of Chicago Press, 1967.

The Journey beneath the Earth

Chatelain, Heli, trans. "King Kitamba kia Xiba." *Folk-Tales of Angola. American Folk-Lore Society Memoirs.* New York: Stechert, 1894.

Courlander, Harold, ed. "King Kitamba kia Xiba." *A Treasury of African Folklore.* Trans. Heli Chatelain. New York: Crown, 1975.

———. "The Voyage below the Water." *"The Piece of Fire" and Other Haitian Tales.* New York: Harcourt Brace and World, 1941; 1964.

———. "The Voyage below the Water." *A Treasury of Afro-American Folklore.* New York: Crown, 1976.

———. "The Voyage below the Water: A Mbundu Version." *A Treasury of Afro-American Folklore.* Appendix V. New York: Crown, 1976.

Parrinder, Geoffrey. "The World Beyond." *African Mythology.* London: Hamlyn, 1982.

El Bizarrón and the Devil

Carter, Dorothy Sharp. "How El Bizarrón Fooled the Devil." *Greedy Mariani and Other Folktales of the Antilles.* New York: Atheneum, 1974.

Cole, Joanna, ed. "How El Bizarrón Fooled the Devil." *Best-Loved Folktales of the World.* Garden City, NY: Doubleday, 1982.

Yolen, Jane, ed. "How El Bizarrón Fooled the Devil." *Favorite Folktales from Around the World.* New York: Pantheon, 1986.

Wiley and the Hairy Man

Botkin, B. A., ed. "Wiley and the Hairy Man." *A Treasury of American Folklore.* New York: Bonanza, 1983.

Courlander, Harold, ed. "Wiley and the Hairy Man." *A Treasury of Afro-American Folklore.* New York: Crown, 1976.

Haviland, Virginia, ed. "Wiley and the Hairy Man." *The Faber Book of North American Legends.* Boston: Faber & Faber, 1979.

Russell, Jeffrey Burton. "Folklore." *Lucifer: The Devil in the Middle Ages.* Ithaca: Cornell Univ. Press, 1988.

Van de Voort, Donnell. "Wiley and the Hairy Man." Manuscript of the Federal Writers' Project for the Works Progress Administration for the State of Alabama. N.D.

Yolen, Jane, ed. "Wiley and the Hairy Man." *Favorite Folktales from Around the World.* New York: Pantheon, 1986.

The Shepherd Who Understood Animal Speech

Griego y Maestas, José, and Rudolfo A. Anaya. "The Shepherd Who Knew the Language of the Animals." *Cuentos: Tales from the Hispanic Southwest.* Santa Fe: Museum of New Mexico Press, 1980.

Grimm, Jacob, and Wilhelm Grimm. "The White Snake." *The Complete Grimm's Fairy Tales.* New York: Pantheon, 1944.

———. "The White Snake." *Grimms' Fairy Tales.* Trans. Mrs. E. V. Lucas, Lucy Crane, and Marian Edwardes. New York: Grosset & Dunlap, 1945.

———. "The White Snake." *The Grimms' German Folk Tales.* Trans. Francis P. Magoun, Jr., and Alexander H. Krappe. Carbondale: Southern Illinois Univ. Press, 1960.

Roheim, Geza. "The Language of Birds." *"Fire in the Dragon" and Other Psychoanalytic Essays on Folklore.* Princeton: Princeton Univ. Press, 1992.

Thompson, Stith. "Knowledge of Animal Speech." *The Folktale.* Berkeley: Univ. of California Press, 1977.

Rip Van Winkle

Irving, Washington. *Rip Van Winkle.* Philadelphia: J. B. Lippincott, N.D.

———. *Rip Van Winkle.* New York: Morrow, 1987.

———. *Rip Van Winkle and The Legend of Sleepy Hollow.* New York: Mayflower, 1980. Reprint of New York: Macmillan, 1893.

———. *Three Tales from The Sketch Book: The Legend of Sleepy Hollow; Rip Van Winkle; The Spectre Bridegroom.* New York: Book-of-the-Month Club, 1993. Reprint from *The Sketch Book of Geoffrey Crayon, Gent.* N.P., 1820.

Otmar. "Peter Klaus." Trans. Thomas Roscoe. *The German Novelists.* London: N. P., 1826.

Rugoff, Milton. "Peter Klaus." Trans. Thomas Roscoe. *A Harvest of World Folk Tales.* New York: Viking, 1949.

Giant, the Fire-Bringer

Boas, Franz. "Tsimshian Mythology: Origin of Fire." *Thirty-First Annual Report of the Bureau of American Ethnology 1909–1910.* Washington, DC: Government Printing Office, 1916.

Goodchild, Peter, ed. *Raven Tales: Traditional Stories of Native Peoples.* Chicago: Chicago Review Press, 1991. (Other Raven tales)

Hays, H. R. "The Epic of Raven." *Children of the Raven: The Seven Indian Nations of the Northwest Coast.* New York: McGraw-Hill, 1975.

Part 5   The Far East

Savitri

Bierlein, J. F. "Savitri." *Parallel Myths.* Ballantine/Random House, 1994.

Blackburn, Stuart H., Peter J. Claus, Joyce B. Flueckiger, and Susan S. Wadley. *Oral Epics in India.* Berkeley: Univ. of California Press, 1989.

Coomaraswamy, Ananda K., and Sister Nivedita. "Savitri." *Myths of the Hindus and Buddhists.* New York: Dover, 1967. Reprint of London: George G. Harrap, 1913.

Jaffrey, Madhur. "Savitri and Satyavan." *Seasons of Splendour: Tales, Myths, and Legends of India.* New York: Atheneum, 1985.

Mackenzie, Donald A. *India: Myths and Legends.* London: Bracken, 1985. Reprint of London: Gresham, N.D.

Narayan, R. K. "Savitri." *Gods, Demons, and Others.* New York: Bantam, 1986.

van Buitenen, J. A. B., trans. "Savitri." *The Book of the Forest. The Mahabharata.* Vol. 2. Chicago: Univ. of Chicago Press, 1981.

Kun and the Great Flood and
Yu the Great and the Great Flood

Birch, Cyril. "The Quellers of the Flood." *Chinese Myths and Fantasies.* New York: Oxford Univ. Press, 1992.

Birrell, Anne. "Saviors: Kun and the Flood; and Yu Controls the Flood." "Myths of Yu the Great." *Chinese Mythology: An Introduction.* Baltimore: Johns Hopkins Univ. Press, 1993.

Bodde, Derk. "Myths of Ancient China." Ed. Samuel Noah Kramer. *Mythologies of the Ancient World.* Garden City, NY: Doubleday/Anchor, 1961.

Bonnefoy, Yves, ed. *Mythologies.* Vol. 2. Trans. Wendy Doniger. Chicago: Univ. of Chicago Press, 1991.

Cavendish, Richard. "Myths of Asia: The Control of Nature." *Mythology: An Illustrated Encyclopedia*. London: Orbis, 1980.

Christie, Anthony. "The Useful Arts: Yao and Gun; and Yu, Master of Floods." *Chinese Mythology*. Rushden, Northants, London: Hamlyn/Newnes, 1983.

Leeming, David Adams. "The Flood: Chinese: Yu." *The World of Myth*. New York: Oxford Univ. Press, 1990.

Mackenzie, Donald A. *Myths of China and Japan*. London: Gresham, N.D.

Sanders, Tao Tao Liu. "Yu Controls the Flood." *Dragons, Gods, and Spirits from Chinese Mythology*. New York: Schocken, 1980.

Walls, Jan, and Yvonne Walls, ed. and trans. "Yu Drives Away Gong Gong." "The Bear and the Rock." *Classical Chinese Myths*. Beijing: Joint, 1984.

Willis, Roy, ed. "Yu the Great." *World Mythology*. New York: Holt, 1993.

Yuan Ke. "Divine Heroes: Gun Battles the Great Flood; Yu Conquers the Flood." *Dragons and Dynasties: An Introduction to Chinese Mythology*. Ed. and trans. Kim Echlin and Nie Zhixiong. New York: Penguin, 1993.

Song of the Water Goddess

Philippi, Donald L. "Song of the Fire Goddess." "Song of the Water Goddess." *Songs of Gods, Songs of Humans: The Epic Tradition of the Ainu*. Princeton: Princeton Univ. Press, 1979.

Taro Urashima, the Young Fisherman

Briggs, Katherine. "King Herla." *British Folktales*. New York: Pantheon, 1977.

Cole, Joanna, ed. "Urashima." *Best-Loved Folktales of the World*. Garden City, NY: Doubleday, 1982.

Davis, F. Hadland. "Urashima." *Myths and Legends of Japan*. Singapore: Graham Brash, 1989. Reprint of N.P., 1913.

Hearn, Lafcadio. "Urashima." *Out of the East: Reveries and Studies in New Japan*. Boston: Houghton, Mifflin, 1895.

James, Grace. "Urashima." *Green Willow and Other Japanese Fairy Tales*. New York: Avenel, 1987.

Kawai, Hayao. *The Japanese Psyche*. Dallas: Spring, 1988.

Mayo, Margaret. "The Kingdom under the Sea." *Magical Tales from Many Lands*. New York: Dutton, 1993.

McAlpine, Helen, and William McAlpine. "The Young Urashima."
  Japanese Tales and Legends. New York: Oxford Univ. Press, 1990.
Nihongi: Chronicles of Japan from the Earliest Times to A.D. *697.* Trans.
  W. G. Aston. Rutland, VT: Tuttle, 1980.
Ozaki, Yei Theodora. "The Story of Urashima Taro, the Fisher Lad."
  The Japanese Fairy Book. New York: Dover, 1967. Reprint of
  Tokyo: Archibald Constable, 1903.
Piggott, Juliet. "Urashima." *Japanese Mythology.* New York: Bedrick,
  1982.
Sanders, Tao Tao Liu. "Liu Yi and the Dragon King." *Dragons, Gods
  and Spirits from Chinese Mythology.* New York: Schocken, 1980.
Saunders, E. Dale. "Urashima of Mizunoe." "Japanese Mythology."
  In Samuel Noah Kramer, ed. *Mythologies of the Ancient World.*
  Garden City, NY: Anchor/Doubleday, 1961.
Shah, Indries. "The Land Where Time Stood Still." *World Tales.* New
  York: Harcourt Brace Jovanovich, 1979.
Takahashi Mushimaro. "The Boy Urashima of Mizunoe." *From the
  Country of Eight Islands: An Anthology of Japanese Poetry.* Trans.
  and ed. Hiroaki Sato and Burton Watson. New York: Columbia
  Univ. Press, 1986.
  . "Urashima of Mizunoe." *The Man'yoshu.* Trans. Nippon
  Gakujutsu Shinkokai. New York: Columbia Univ. Press, 1969.
Tyler, Royall. "Urashima the Fisherman." *Japanese Tales.* New York:
  Pantheon, 1987.
Yolen, Jane, ed. "Urashima the Fisherman." *Favorite Folktales from
  around the World.* New York: Pantheon, 1986.

The Tiger's Whisker

Cole, Joanna, ed. "The Tiger's Whisker." *Best-Loved Folktales of the
  World.* Garden City, NY: Doubleday, 1982.
Courlander, Harold. *"The Tiger's Whisker" and Other Tales and Legends
  from Asia and the Pacific.* New York: Harcourt Brace, 1959.

Kerta's Sacrifice

Knappert, Jan. "The Son Who Sinned." *Myths and Legends of Indone-
  sia.* Singapore: Heinemann Educational Books (Asia), 1977.
Terada, Alice M. "Kerta's Sin." *"The Magic Crocodile" and Other
  Folktales from Indonesia.* Honolulu: Univ. of Hawaii Press, 1994.

General Folklore, Mythology, and Legend

Bachofen, J. J. *Myth, Religion, and Mother Right.* Princeton: Princeton Univ. Press, 1967.

Bettelheim, Bruno. *The Uses of Enchantment: The Meaning and Importance of Fairy Tales.* New York: Knopf, 1976.

Bierlein, John Francis. *Parallel Myths.* Ballantine/Random House, 1994.

Bonnefoy, Yves. *Mythologies.* 2 vols. Trans. and ed. Wendy Doniger. Chicago: Univ. of Chicago Press, 1991.

Bottigheimer, Ruth B., ed. *Fairy Tales and Society: Illusion, Allusion, and Paradigm.* Philadelphia: Univ. of Pennsylvania Press, 1989.

Burrows, David, Frederick Lapides, and John Shawcross. *Myths and Motifs in Literature.* New York: Free Press, 1973.

Campbell, Joseph. *The Flight of the Wild Gander: Explorations in the Mythological Dimensions of Fairy Tales, Legends, and Symbols.* New York: HarperCollins, 1990.

———. *The Masks of God.* 4 vols. New York: Viking Penguin, 1991.

———. *Transformations of Myth Through Time.* New York: Harper and Row, 1990.

———, with Bill Moyers. *The Power of Myth.* New York: Doubleday, 1988.

Cavendish, Richard, ed. *Legends of the World.* London: Orbis, 1982.

———. *Mythology: An Illustrated Encyclopedia.* London: Orbis, 1980.

Cole, Joanna. *Best-Loved Folktales of the World.* Garden City, NY: Doubleday, 1982.

Doty, William G. *Mythography: The Study of Myths and Rituals.* Tuscaloosa: Univ. of Alabama Press, 1991.

Downing, Christine. *The Goddess: Mythological Images of the Feminine.* New York: Crossroads, 1984.

Dundes, Alan, ed. *Folklore Matters.* Knoxville: Univ. of Tennessee Press, 1989.

———. *Interpreting Folklore.* Bloomington: Univ. of Indiana Press, 1980.

———. *Sacred Narrative: Readings in the Theory of Myth.* Berkeley: Univ. of California Press, 1984.

Eliade, Mircea. *Gods, Goddesses, and Myths of Creation: From Primitives to Zen.* (Part I) New York: Harper and Row, 1974.

———. *Myths, Rites, Symbols: A Mircea Eliade Reader.* 2 vols. Ed. Wendell C. Beane and William C. Doty. New York: Harper and Row, 1975.

Frazer, Sir James George. *The Golden Bough: The Roots of Religion and Folklore.* New York: Avenel/Crown, 1981. Reprint of *The Golden Bough: A Study in Comparative Religion.* 2 vols. London: Macmillan, 1890.

Freud, Sigmund. "The Interpretation of Dreams." "Totem and Taboo." *The Basic Writings of Sigmund Freud.* Trans. A. A. Brill. New York: Random House, 1938.

———. *The Interpretation of Dreams.* Trans. James Strachey. New York: Random House, 1978.

Frye, Northrop. *Anatomy of Criticism.* New York: Atheneum, 1968.

Gaster, Theodor, ed. *The New Golden Bough: A New Abridgment of the Classic Work by Sir James George Frazer.* New York: Phillips, 1972.

Gimbutas, Marija. *Goddesses and Gods of Old Europe, 7000–3500 B.C.: Myths, Legends, and Cult Images.* Rev. Ed. Berkeley: Univ. of California Press, 1982.

———. *Language of the Goddess.* San Francisco: Harper, 1991.

Jung, Carl G. *The Archetypes and the Collective Unconscious.* Princeton: Princeton Univ. Press, 1969.

———. *The Essential Jung.* Ed. Anthony Storr. Princeton: Princeton Univ. Press, 1983.

Kane, Sean. *Wisdom of the Mythtellers.* New York: Broadview, 1994.

Kirk, G. S. *Myth: Its Meaning and Functions in Ancient and Other Cultures.* Berkeley: Univ. of California Press, 1970.

Leach, Maria, ed. *Funk & Wagnall's Dictionary of Folklore, Mythology, and Legend.* San Francisco: Harper and Row, 1984.

Leeming, David Adams. *The World of Myth.* New York: Oxford Univ. Press, 1990.

Lévi-Strauss, Claude. *Myth and Meaning.* New York: Schocken, 1987.

———. *Structural Anthropology.* Trans. Claire Jacobson and Brooke Grundfest Schoepf. New York: Basic Books, 1963.

Luthi, Max. *The European Folktale: Form and Nature.* Trans. John D. Niles. Philadelphia: Institute for the Study of Human Issues, 1982.

———. *The Fairy Tale as Art Form and Portrait of Man.* Trans. Jon Erickson. Bloomington: Indiana Univ. Press, 1987.

———. *Once Upon a Time: On the Nature of Fairy Tales.* Trans. Lee Chadeayne and Paul Gottwald. Bloomington: Indiana Univ. Press, 1976.

Miller, Lucien. Introduction to *South of the Clouds: Tales from Yunnan.* Seattle: Univ. of Washington Press, 1994.

Murdock, George Peter. *Africa: Its Peoples and Their Culture History.* New York: McGraw-Hill, 1959.

Neumann, Erich. *The Great Mother: An Analysis of the Archetype.* Princeton: Princeton Univ. Press, 1964.

O'Flaherty, Wendy Doniger. *Other Peoples' Myths: The Cave of Echoes.* New York: Macmillan, 1988.

Propp, Vladimir. *Theory and History of Folklore.* Trans. Ariadna Y. Martin and Richard P. Martin. Minneapolis: Univ. of Minnesota Press, 1985.

Rabkin, Eric S. *The Fantastic in Literature.* Princeton: Princeton Univ. Press, 1977.

Radin, Paul. *Primitive Man as Philosopher.* Rev. Ed. New York: Dover, 1957.

———. *Primitive Religion: Its Nature and Origin.* New York: Dover, 1937.

Raglan, FitzRoy. *The Hero: A Study in Tradition, Myth, and Drama.* New York: New American Library, 1979.

Rank, Otto; FitzRoy Raglan; and Alan Dundes. *In Quest of the Hero.* Princeton: Princeton Univ. Press, 1990.

Róheim, Géza. *Fire in the Dragon and Other Psychoanalytic Essays on Folklore.* Princeton: Princeton Univ. Press, 1992.

Schlobin, Roger C., ed. *The Aesthetics of Fantasy, Literature, and Art.* Notre Dame: Univ. of Notre Dame Press, 1982.

Shah, Indries. *World Tales.* New York: Harcourt Brace Jovanovich, 1979.

Thompson, Stith. *The Folktale.* Berkeley: Univ. of California Press, 1977.

von Franz, Marie-Louise. *An Introduction to the Interpretation of Fairy Tales.* Dallas: Spring, 1982.

———. *Shadow and Evil in Fairy Tales.* Dallas: Spring, 1980.

Willis, Roy, ed. *World Mythology.* New York: Holt, 1993.

Yolen, Jane, ed. *Favorite Folktales from Around the World.* New York: Pantheon, 1986.

PRONUNCIATION GUIDE

Folklore, Myths, and Legends contains selections from many different cultures, each with its own language and dialect. Most of these languages are unfamiliar to English-speaking readers. Some of the languages are so old that scholars know little about how they were pronounced in ancient times. The sounds of many other languages are different from those in English, so that no exact English equivalents exist for these sounds.

Scholars deal with this problem in a variety of ways. While some scholars offer pronunciation guides, their spelling and pronunciation often differ from those offered by other scholars in the same field. Some scholars suggest using the International Phonetic Alphabet, which they provide along with American English pronunciation. Most scholars refuse to offer any guide because of its inherent inaccuracy.

In order to facilitate pronunciation, some authors who publish myths, legends, and folktales for the general reading public present a character's name in its English equivalent. Other authors replace a character's original name with an English one.

The following list provides the Anglicized pronunciation of characters' names in cases where scholars have provided guidance. For all the other characters, it is acceptable to pronounce their names as they would be pronounced in your own language.

Part I Africa
The Creation of Human Beings
    Culture: Shilluk (shee'-luke)
    Character: Juok (ju'-ohk)

Anansi, the Clever One
    Culture: Ashanti (ah-shahn'-tee)
    Country: Ghana (gah'-nuh)
    Character: Anansi (ah-nahn'-see)

The Woman with One Hand
   Culture: Swahili (swah-hee'-lee)
   Countries: Kenya (kayn'-yuh); Tanzania (tahn-zahn-ee'-uh);
      Zaire (zah-eer')
The Roamer-of-the-Plain
   Culture: Ronga/Baronga (rohn'-gah/bah-rohn'-gah)
The Crocodile and His Son
   Culture: Fan (fahn)
   Character: Ombure (ohm'-bu-ray)

Part 2   The Middle East

Rostam, Shield of Persia
The Tragedy of Sohrab
   Epic: Shahnameh (shah-nah-meh')
   Characters: Afrasyab (ah-frah-see-yahb')
      Ahriman (ah-ree-mahn')
      Akvan (ahk-vahn')
      Arjasp (ahr-jahsp')
      Aulad (ah-u-lahd')
      Bizhan (beez-hahn')
      Dastan (dahs-tahn')
      Faramarz (fah-rah-mahrz')
      Giv (geev)
      Gordafarid (gor-dah-fah-reed')
      Gudarz (gu-dahrz')
      Hojir (hah-jeer')
      Human (hu-mahn')
      Kavus (kah-voos')
      Khosrow (khahs-raw')
      Kobad (kah-bahd')
      Manizha (mah-neez-hah')
      Manuchehr (ma-nu-chehr')
      Nariman (nah-ree-mahn')
      Rakhsh (rahk-ish)
      Rostam (rahs-tahm')
      Rudabeh (ru-dah-beh')
      Sam (sahm)
      Shaghad (shahg-hahd')

Simurgh (see-murg')
Sohrab (sah-rahb')
Tahamtan (tah-hahm-tahn')
Tahmineh (tah-mee-neh')
Urmazd (ur-mahzd')
Zal (zahl)
Zavareh (zah-vah-reh')
Zhende (zhen-deh')
Places: Hamaveran (hah-mah-veh-rahn')
Kabul/Kabulestan (kah-bool'/kah-bu-les-tahn')
Mazanderan (mah-zahn-deh-rahn')
Samengan (sah-men-gahn')
Seistan (sees-tahn')
Turan (tu-rahn')

Part 3   Europe

Prometheus, the Fire-Bringer
Characters: Cronus (kro'-nus)
Deucalion (du-kay'-lee-un)
Hephaestus (hee-fes'-tus)
Helius (hee'-lee-us)
Heracles (her'-uh-kleez)
Pandora (pan-doh'-ruh)
Poseidon (puh-si'-dn)
Prometheus (proh-mee'-thoos)
Selene (see-lee'-nee)
Themis (thee'-mis)
Zeus (Zoos)

Oisin Mac Finn, Poet of the Fianna
Characters: Fianna (fee'-an-nuh)
Finn Mac Cumhal (koo'-ul)
Niamh (nee'-am)
Oisin (Ireland: ush-een'; Scotland: ahs'-see-un)
Sadbh (sahv)
Tuatha De Danaan (thoo'-ah-haw day dah-nawn')
Places: Almhuin (all'-oon)
Erin (eer'in)
Gabhra (gau'-ruh)

Saga of Gunnlaug Serpent-Tongue
  Characters: Thorstein Egilsson (thohr'-tayn ay'-gee-lohn)
    Ethelred (eth'-l-red)
    Hakon (hah'-kohn)
    Eirik Hakonarson (ay'-rik hah'-kohn-ah-rohn)
    Thorkel Hallkelsson (thor'kl hahl'-kay-lohn)
    Sigurd Hlodvisson (ee'-goord huh-lahd'-vee-ohn)
    Illugi (ee'-loo-gee)
    Gunnlaug Illugason (goon'-loug ee'-lu-gah-ohn)
    Hermund Illugason (hayr'-moond ee'-lu-gah-ohn)
    Jofrid (joh'-freed)
    Olaf (oh'-lahf)
    Onund (oh'-noond)
    Hrafn Onundarson (huh-rahf'-n oh'-noond-dah-rohn)
    Sigtrygg (eeg'-troog)
    Olaf Skötkonung (oh'-lahf koht'kohn-noong)
    Knut Sveinsson (kuh-nute' vay'-nohn)
    Helga Thorsteinsdottir (hayl'-guh thohr'-tayn-doh-teer)
  Places: Althing (awl'-theeng)
    Borgarfjord (bohr'-gahr-fee-ohrd)
    Gautland (gout'-lahnd)
Aucassin and Nicolette
  Characters: Aucassin (oh-kuh-san')
    Garin (ga-ran')
    Nicolette (nee-ko-let')
  Places: Beaucaire (bo-care')
    Torelore (toh-ray-lor')
Doctor Faust
  Characters: Astaroth (as'-tuh-roth)
    Beelzebub (bee-el'-zi-bub)
    Belial (bee'lee-l)
    Faust (fowst)
    Lucifer (lu'-sih-fer)
    Mephistopheles (meh-fis-tahf'-uh-leez)

Part 4   The Americas

Botoque, Bringer of Fire
  Character: Botoque (boh-toh'kay)

The Little Frog
    Countries: Chile (chee'-lay); Argentina (ar-hen-tee'-nah);
       Mexico (may'-hee-koh)
    Characters: Diego (dee-ay'-goh)
       Juan (wahn)
       Pedro (pay'-droh)

The Journey beneath the Earth
    Culture: Mbundu (muh-boon'-du)
    Characters: Kitamba (kee-tahm'-bah)
       Muhongo (mu-hohn'-goh)
       Kalunga-ngombe (kah-loon'-gah nuh-gohm'-bay)
    Places: Kalunga (kah-loon'-gah)
       Kasanji (kah-sahn'-jee)

El Bizarrón and the Devil
    Character: El Bizarrón (el bee-zahr-rohn')

Part 5 The Far East

Savitri
    Epic: Mahabharata (muh-hah-bah'-ruh-tuh)
    Characters: Asvapati (ahsh-wah-pah'-tee)
       Dyumatsena (dyoo-mut-say'-nuh)
       Narada (nah-ruh'-duh)
       Satyavan (sut'-yuh-wun)
       Savitri (sah-wee'-tree)
       Yama (yuh'-muh)

Kun and the Great Flood
    Characters: Kung Kung (gung gung)
       Kun (gun)
       Nu Kua (nu wah')

Yu the Great and the Great Flood
    Characters: Ch'i (jee)
       Nu-Chiao (nu-jow')
    Dynasty: Hsia (shee-ah')

INDEX OF TITLES

A

Adapa, xxv, 63–64, 65–72, 74–85,
460–464
Anansi, the Clever One, xxi, xxv, 1–
2, 7–16, 458
Aucassin and Nicolette, xxii, xxiii,
160, 236–253, 473–474

B

Botoque, Bringer of Fire, xxv, 283,
286–299, 476–477

C

Craftsman's Wife, The, xxi, xxii,
xxiii, 63–64, 86–93, 464
Creation of Human Beings, The,
xxv, 1, 4–6, 457–458
Crocodile and His Son, The, xxi,
xxv, 2–3, 43–61, 459–460

D

Doctor Faust, xxvii, 160, 254–281,
474–476

E

El Bizarrón and the Devil, xxi, 284,
321–332, 479
Enki, Lord of the Earth and the
Waters of Life, xxv, 63–64, 65–74,
460–464

G

Giant, the Fire-Bringer, xxv, 285,
364–370, 481

J

Journey beneath the Earth, The, xxv,
284, 314–320, 478–479

K

Kerta's Sacrifice, xxv, 372, 442–456,
487–488
Kun and the Great Flood, xxv, 371,
395–405, 482–485

L

Little Frog, The, xxi, xxii, 283–284,
300–313, 477

O

Oisin Mac Finn, Poet of the Fianna,
xxv, xxvii, 159–160, 178–203,
468–470

P

Prometheus, the Fire-Bringer, xxv,
159, 161–177, 467

R

Rip Van Winkle, xxvii, 284, 354–
363, 423, 480–481
Roamer-of-the-Plain, The, xxv, 2–3,
28–42, 459
Rostam, Shield of Persia, xxvii, 63–
64, 94–131, 465–467

S

Saga of Gunnlaug Serpent-Tongue,
xxvii, 160, 204–235, 470–473
Savitri, xxv, xxvii, 371, 373–394,
481–482
Shepherd Who Understood Animal
Speech, The, xxii, 284, 347–353,
480
Song of the Water Goddess, The,
xxv, 371–372, 415–420, 485

T

Taro Urashima, the Young Fisherman, xxv, xxvii, 372, 421–431,
485–487
Tiger's Whisker, The, xxii, 372, 432–
441, 487
Tragedy of Sohrab, The, xxvii, 63–
64, 94–106, 131–157, 465–467

W

Wiley and the Hairy Man, xxi, 284,
321–323, 332–346, 479–480
Woman with One Hand, The, xxi–
xxii, xxiii, 2–3, 17–27, 458–459

#

Yu the Great and the Great Flood,
xxv, 371, 395–399, 406–414,
482–485

QUESTIONS FOR RESPONSE, DISCUSSION, AND ANALYSIS

Part I   Africa

The Creation of Human Beings (page 5)

1. How does this creation myth reflect the culture to which it belongs?
2. How does this myth view human beings and their purpose?
3. When Juok's human beings need tongues in order to dance, what does this reveal?

Anansi, the Clever One (page 8)

1. In what ways is Anansi like a human being? Give examples to support your ideas. Why have the tellers of tales made Anansi so human?
2. What makes Anansi such a popular character?
3. How does the saying "Only a person who has no sense will choose to drink from a pool when a stream is close by" apply to this tale? What would lead a person to choose the pool? Why would such a choice be unwise? What connection exists between the saying and Anansi's behavior? To what extent, if any, is Anansi wise to avoid thinking about this connection?
4. What gives this story its power?
5. Repetition is characteristic of the African folktale. What does it contribute to this tale?

The Woman with One Hand (page 18)

1. Given that the sister is both younger than her brother and female, to what extent, if any, does she have a choice of gift from her parents?

2. What does this tale say about the comparative value of personal property and being blessed?

3. Why is the brother so cruel to his sister?

4. What qualities does the young woman possess that enable her to survive? Give examples to support your ideas.

5. What does this tale reveal about human nature? Give examples to support your ideas.

6. What attitude does this tale reveal about animals and their relationship to human beings?

7. To what extent, if any, do the brother's and sister's choices of inheritance actually determine their destiny? How does this relate to the possible purpose of this tale?

8. To what extent, if any, is the sister being kind when she asks only that her brother be sent away from the capital?

The Roamer-of-the-Plain (page 29)

1. If it is the custom for parents to choose a mate for their children, why do the young man's parents permit him to choose his own wife? Why do the young woman's parents permit her to marry a stranger from a strange people?

2. Given the importance of buffalo to her people: (a) Why does the young woman ask for the Roamer-of-the-Plain? (b) Why do her parents allow her to take the buffalo?

3. Why does the young woman not tell her husband about the buffalo?

4. Why does the young woman not find a way to feed the buffalo? After the buffalo has destroyed the crops, why does the young woman not anticipate the demand for watchmen?

5. Examine the young woman's incantation. What might it reveal about the buffalo? What characteristics does it possess that might make it effective in restoring the buffalo to life? Why do the presence of the husband and his mother destroy

the buffalo's restoration? Why do the restoration ceremonies occur at night, and why does the buffalo die once the new day arrives?

6. Why do the buffalo's hunger and lack of strength affect the villagers to whom he is connected? When he is killed, why do those villagers not die along with him?

7. Why does the young woman return to her village in order to reveal that its buffalo has died? What would have happened had she not returned? What might she have thought would happen if she did not return?

8. Why do the young woman's people kill themselves? Why do they not kill the young man who killed their buffalo?

9. A cautionary tale, by the nature of its consequences, is designed to discourage a particular attitude or activity by a member of the family or group. What does this tale teach?

10. Consider the following characters: (a) the young man's parents; (b) the young man; (c) the young woman's parents; (d) the young woman. Explain the extent to which each is responsible for what happens in this tale. Who is most responsible? Give reasons to support your point of view.

11. In Greek mythology, the hero Meleager lives only as long as the log to which his life is attached does not burn. When it finally burns, Meleager burns up and dies, even though he is far from the log. How would such an ending have affected the nature of this tale?

12. The ethnologist Paul Radin thinks that a group's shaman (medicine man) creates myths that terrify the people, and that he then designs related religious practices that act on that feeling of terror—all in such a way that he will have emotional power over the people and gain economic reward as well. To what extent, if any, does this tale support Radin's view?

13. From what point of view is this tale told? Consider which people and which age group would perpetuate the tales.

14. What themes might the communal suicide symbolize?

15. What gives this tale its power? What effect would a happy ending have?

The Crocodile and His Son (page 44)

1. In what ways is the crocodile like a divinity?
2. In what ways is the crocodile like a human being?
3. In what ways is Son-of-the-Crocodile a traditional hero? In what way is he a culture hero?
4. What enables the crocodile to wield such power over the Fan people?
5. What does the death of the crocodile represent?
6. What is the role of magic in this legend?
7. Describe the nature of the universe in which the Fan people live.
8. Why is the crocodile depicted as having a scaly skin that is invulnerable to weapons?
9. Why do the Fan respect the crocodile, both in life and in death?

Part 2   The Middle East

Enki, Lord of the Earth and the Waters of Life (page 72)

1. Describe Enki's nature as it is depicted in this myth. What view of the universe does this depiction of Enki reflect?
2. What does this myth about Enki reveal about Sumerian society?
3. How does the depiction of Enki as a creator-god in this myth differ from the depiction of him in the myth about Adapa? To what extent, if any, is it helpful to know both myths?

Adapa (page 74)

1. To what extent, if any, does this myth present a modern view of the parent-child relationship?
2. What does this myth reveal about the relationship between the Akkadians, Babylonians, and/or Assyrians and their gods? What does it reveal about their view of the world in which they live?

3. To what extent, if any, is each of the following to blame for Adapa's punishment: (a) Adapa; (b) South Wind; (c) Ea; (d) Anu?

4. Why does Ea tell Adapa that Anu will offer him the food and water of death? When we are told that Ea knows everything and that nothing can be hidden from him, does this mean that Ea was purposely tricking Adapa into remaining mortal? Why, then, does Ea tell Adapa how to win the sympathy and support of Anu's sentries?

5. Why does Anu offer Adapa the food and water of life? Does Anu feel that Ea's gifts to his son have left him no choice, or is Anu purposely tricking Adapa as to the true nature of the food and water?

6. To what extent, if any, is Adapa tricked by Anu? To the extent that Adapa is tricked, why does this occur?

7. Why does Anu show Adapa the kingdom of Heaven?

8. How does Anu feel about Ea's interference with his own importance when Ea gives Adapa godlike gifts? Why does Anu reward Ea's temple-city of Eridu and Ea's priests?

9. Does Anu forgive Adapa? Why does Anu, who claimed to offer Adapa the gift of everlasting life, then punish Adapa by making him the bearer of disease to humankind? To what extent, if any, might Anu's reaction be due to Adapa's discourteous response to Anu's hospitality?

10. To what extent, if any, does Anu reward Adapa?

11. What aspects of life does this myth explain?

12. What lesson or lessons does this myth teach?

The Craftsman's Wife (page 88)

1. To what extent, if any, is the craftsman justified in worrying about his wife's fidelity?

2. What argument most influences King Solomon's decision with regard to how to treat the craftsman's wife?

3. Based on her behavior, does the craftsman's wife believe her explanation about the colored eggs? To what extent, if any, do you agree with her explanation?

4. Choose four adjectives that describe the character of the craftsman's wife, and support each with an example from the story.

5. What characteristics does the craftsman's wife share with the typical trickster figure in myth and folklore?

6. What enables the craftsman's wife to succeed in tricking King Solomon? What knowledge does she possess, and how does she use it?

7. In what ways is the craftsman's wife a role model for the women of her time? In what ways can she be a role model for the women of today?

Rostam, Shield of Persia (page 107)

1. What do Zal's birth and marriage contribute to the Rostam legend?

2. What do Rostam's remarkable birth and youth contribute to his legend?

3. What function do Rostam's Seven Stages perform in the legend? What, if anything, do any of them reveal about Rostam's personality?

4. What do Kavus's adventures reveal about him? What do Rostam's rescues reveal about him?

5. Rostam's experience with the Demon Akvan is one of the most popular stories in the *Shahnameh*. What makes it so appealing?

6. Afrasyab's daughter is considered to be a great heroine because of her treatment of her father and Bizhan. What admirable qualities does she possess? What is your opinion of her behavior?

7. Why does Zal neither abandon nor kill Shaghad once he hears the dire prophecy about him?

8. To what extent, if any, are the following responsible for Rostam's death? Who is most responsible? (a) Rostam; (b) Rakhsh; (c) Shaghad; (d) the king of Kabul

9. In some versions of this legend, Rostam and Rakhsh plunge into and out of seven pits. What, if anything, do the seven pits add to the plot?

10. What does Rakhsh contribute to this legend?

11. In this legend, why are Persia's enemies often depicted as Demons?

The Tragedy of Sohrab (page 131)

1. To what extent, if any, is Tahmineh's behavior believable?

2. What do Sohrab's remarkable infancy and childhood contribute to his legend?

3. In some versions of this legend, no relationship exists between the theft of Rakhsh and Tahmineh's desire to meet Rostam. What does each version contribute to the plot?

4. Why is Rostam so quick to leave Tahmineh in Samengan, since his father brought his mother to Seistan? Why do you think that Rostam keeps his marriage to Tahmineh a secret? How would it have affected the plot if he had not done so?

5. In some versions, Tahmineh tells Rostam that he is the father of a daughter. Why might she do that? Why, in this version, does she choose to tell Rostam the truth?

6. How does Rostam's knowledge of the sex of his child affect the plot? Evaluate the difference between Rostam's having a daughter and having a son. Why, given the information he receives from those who have seen Sohrab, does it never occur to Rostam that Sohrab is his son?

7. What does Sohrab's threat, if Tahmineh does not reveal his father's name, reveal about Sohrab?

8. Why does this legend have Sohrab go to war at the age of ten or twelve, when it is clear from the reactions of Rostam and the other warriors that this is much too early an age? To what extent, if any, do Sohrab's reasons for going to war reflect the thinking of a child, rather than the thinking of an adult? What other options does Sohrab have with regard to finding his father? Why does Tahmineh not suggest other options?

9. What does Gordafarid contribute to this legend?

10. What does the argument between Kay Kavus and Rostam contribute to the plot? What does it contribute to the characterizations of these two leaders?

11. What does Rostam's spying expedition contribute to the plot of this legend? What does it contribute to Rostam's characterization? Do you think that Rostam recognizes Zhende? If not, why not? If so, why does he kill him?

12. What does the scene in which Hojir identifies the Persians for Sohrab contribute to this legend?

13. Why does Sohrab choose not to tell Hojir that Rostam is his father, when Sohrab is so eager to find him? What, if anything, does Sohrab have to lose? If Sohrab had told Hojir the truth, do you think that Hojir would have believed him? Would Hojir then have told Sohrab the truth? Explain.

14. Why does Sohrab accept without question Human's lie about Rostam when Human is under Afrasyab's command and his mother has warned him about Afrasyab? Compare this with his response to Hojir. To what extent, if any, do you think it is relevant that Human is Turanian, whereas Hojir is Persian?

15. Why does Sohrab insist on fighting Rostam on the first day, when Rostam is reluctant to fight him? Why, at the end of the afternoon, does he then let Rostam leave the field when he could have vanquished him?

16. Why does Rostam distrust Sohrab's offer of a truce at the start of the second day's combat?

17. To what extent, if any, do you think that Sohrab really believes Rostam's ruse? Give reasons to support your point of view.

18. In some versions of this legend, Rostam chooses to fight Sohrab in unmarked armor in order to look like the slave that he claims he is. How does this change affect the plot? How should Sohrab have been able to recognize Rostam despite the fact that no one would identify him? Name four identifying factors.

19. Why does Sohrab never tell Rostam that Rostam is his father? What, if anything, does Sohrab have to lose by revealing this fact?

20. Why does Sohrab wear Rostam's signet arm ring inside his armor where no one can see it, particularly when he knows that it is an object of identification? What, if anything, does Sohrab have to gain by concealing it?

21. When Gudarz is unsuccessful in getting Kay Kavus to give

Sohrab his salve, should Rostam have gone after it? In your opinion, would Rostam rather have been attempting to get the salve, or would he rather have been sitting with Sohrab when he died?

22.   In another version of this legend, Sohrab does not die. How would this affect the plot? If Rostam does not die either, how would you end their combat?

23.   In another version of this legend, Rostam always shouts "Rostam" as he charges forth against his foe. Therefore, he automatically reveals his name as he makes his final effort to defeat Sohrab. Sohrab, in amazement, drops his weapon, and Rostam kills an unarmed foe. What effect does this change have on the plot? How does it affect the depiction of both Rostam and Sohrab?

24.   To what extent, if any, is it rational of Kay Kavus to withhold the life-saving salve from Sohrab? Consider whether Kay Kavus lets Sohrab die because of what Rostam said to Kavus in the course of their argument.

25.   How do you react to the scene in which Rostam burns his most treasured war gear? To what extent, if any, does this act seem plausible to you?

26.   To what extent, if any, do you think Tahmineh eventually believes that it was a mistake to have married Rostam? Do you think she made a mistake? To what extent, if any, is this situation a blemish on Rostam's character?

27.   To what extent, if any, does Sohrab's goal to kill Kay Kavus and put his father on the throne justify Sohrab's death? Consider whether Sohrab would have had this goal if he had been the usual age of a young warrior.

28.   Matthew Arnold has the dying Sohrab ask his father to hold him and tell him of his love. Then Sohrab asks Rostam to live for him and perform the deeds that he will never have the opportunity to perform himself. In your opinion, would Sohrab be more likely to react like this, or with anger, as he does in the traditional versions? Which is more consistent with Sohrab's age? Which is more consistent with his personality?

29.   To what extent, if any, are the following responsible for Sohrab's death? Who is most responsible? (a) Sohrab

himself; (b) Rostam; (c) Tahmineh; (d) Sohrab's grandfather; (e) Hojir; (f) Afrasyab; (g) Human; (h) Kay Kavus

30.   Tragic heroes are good human beings whose greatest strength becomes their greatest weakness in that it leads them to act imprudently, without thinking of the consequences of their actions. Often, they belatedly realize how their own attitudes and actions brought their tragic fate upon themselves.

What characteristics, if any, does Rostam possess that cause his tragic experience with Sohrab? To what extent, if any, is Rostam a tragic hero?

31.   What role does Fate play in this legend?

32.   The reader knows the relationship between Sohrab and Rostam when they themselves do not. What does this type of irony contribute to this legend?

Part 3   Europe

Prometheus, the Fire-Bringer (page 165)

1.   The name Prometheus means "forethought." To what extent, if any, does Prometheus exercise forethought?

Irony is the recognition of a discrepancy or an incongruity between apparent meaning and real meaning. Therefore, given Prometheus's behavior, to what extent, if any, is the meaning of his name ironic?

In a paradox, two opposite or seemingly contradictory conditions exist. Given the nature of forethought, to what extent is the meaning of Prometheus's name paradoxical?

2.   What heroic qualities does Prometheus possess that account for his lasting fame? To what extent, if any, is he less of a hero because he is immortal? In what ways can Prometheus be considered a criminal? Considering his personality and his actions, how do you view him?

3.   What does this myth reveal about the nature of divinities? The nature of the universe? The place of human beings in the universe? The causes of good and evil?

4.   Since Prometheus helped Zeus become the ruler of the universe, why have the two divinities become enemies? What

does Prometheus object to in Zeus? What does Zeus object to in Prometheus? Which of the two is a more sympathetic character? Explain your choice.

5. The ancient Greeks believed that it was important to be moderate in all things. Apply the motto Nothing in Excess to the behavior of both Prometheus and Zeus. How would the situation have changed if Zeus and Prometheus had behaved with moderation? Explain the ways in which the situation would then have been better or worse.

6. The ancient Greeks observed a self-destructive pattern of attitude and behavior in which a person who was unusually gifted in a particular way (called *aretē*) could easily succumb to feelings of excessive pride (called *hubris*). Such excessive pride then led the person to act in an imprudent manner, without thought to personal boundaries and the consequences of these actions (called *atē*) . Finally, such rash behavior would result in retributive punishment (called *nemesis*).

    Apply this pattern to both Zeus and Prometheus. To what extent, if any, do both divinities experience all four stages of the pattern?

7. Why would Zeus wish to destroy the mortal men whom Prometheus created? What type of human being would Zeus create in their place?

8. To what extent, if any, are Zeus's attitudes and actions related to the fact that he has only recently become Lord of Olympus? How might his attitudes and actions change over time? Why?

9. If Zeus suspects that Prometheus is tricking him, why does he proceed to make the obvious choice? What other options does he have?

10. Why does Zeus put Hope into Pandora's jar, and why is it left there in Hesiod's version? To what extent, if any, is hope an evil as well as a blessing?

11. Why is the myth about Prometheus often considered to be the greatest Greek myth? Which aspects make it so important?

Oisin Mac Finn, Poet of the Fianna (page 183)

1. What aspects of this myth make Oisin a hero? Consider (a) his birth, (b) his life, and (c) his last years.

2. How do you regard Oisin? To what extent, if any, do you admire him? To what extent, if any, do you pity him?

3. To what extent does Oisin bring his fate upon himself, and to what extent is he the victim of circumstance?

4. What does the myth of Oisin reveal about (a) illusion and reality, (b) love, and (c) life and death?

5. To what extent, if any, do you think Oisin would have been better off if he had not been captivated by Niamh's beauty and her world?

6. In a later version of the Oisin myth, Saint Patrick is able to convince Oisin to convert to Christianity. To what extent, if any, is this consistent with Oisin's character?

7. Why did those who created this myth place Oisin's heroic deeds with the Fianna in the background? What do magic and transformation contribute to the tone of this myth?

8. What human needs and fantasies does the myth of Oisin address that might explain its popularity?

9. What historical purpose does the myth of Oisin address that might explain its creation?

10. What aspects of the myth do you think motivated William Butler Yeats to write a poem about the journey of Oisin to the Land of Youth?

11. Find a copy of William Butler Yeats's poem "The Wanderings of Oisin" in the library and share it with your classmates. Discuss what Yeats's treatment of the subject contributes to the myth.

Saga of Gunnlaug Serpent-Tongue (page 209)

1. Why does this saga begin with Helga's birth and end with her death? What role does she play in the saga?

2. Given the importance of Helga and Hrafn in the saga, why did the saga writer name the saga after Gunnlaug?

3. Explain the extent to which each of the following people is to

blame for Gunnlaug's inability to marry Helga. In your opinion, who is most to blame: (a) Gunnlaug, (b) King Ethelred, (c) Thorstein, (d) Illugi, (e) Hrafn, or (f) the farm-youth?

4. Why does Thorstein Egilsson make marriage arrangements for Helga without consulting her? What does this saga reveal about the role of women in Icelandic society in the year 1000?

5. Why does Gunnlaug accept the farm-youth's wrestling challenge when he is already late in arriving home?

6. Why does Hrafn take Helga to live at Borg with her family once Gunnlaug returns?

7. Why does Gunnlaug trust Hrafn's response about the drink when he distrusts him enough to question his honor?

8. To what extent, if any, does the saga reveal whether Gunnlaug or Hrafn is the better man? Consider (a) the ship-master's tale about Hrafn; (b) Helga's attitude toward Hrafn; (c) Gunnlaug's comments to and about Hrafn; (d) Gunnlaug's behavior; and (e) Hrafn's behavior.

9. What role do dreams play in this saga?

10. What role does Fate play in this saga?

11. What effect do Gunnlaug's following personality traits have upon his fate: (a) courage, (b) arrogance, (c) loyalty, (d) self-confidence, (e) ambition, and (f) inflexibility ?

12. To what extent, if any, is Gunnlaug a tragic hero? In what ways is this a tragic story?

13. To what extent, if any, do Gunnlaug, Hrafn, Thorstein, and Helga think and act like "real" people?

14. Since the principal characters are historical figures, and since the fight over Helga actually occurred, what do you think the saga writer added to the historical version?

15. Explain the extent to which this saga is (a) the story of a love triangle; (b) the story of a blood-feud; and (c) the biography of Gunnlaug Serpent-Tongue. In your opinion, which is the saga's primary focus?

Aucassin and Nicolette (page 237)

1. "Aucassin and Nicolette" contains many surprises in that characters do not speak and act as we might expect. What reversals occur in this tale? What do they contribute to the tale?

2. Describe the character of both Aucassin and Nicolette. To what extent, if any, are they believable?

3. What is the tone of "Aucassin and Nicolette"? To what extent, if any, is it humorous? Satiric?

4. What examples of contrast do you find in this tale? What do they contribute? How do you explain the inclusion of Aucassin's encounter with the farmhand? To what extent, if any, would the tale have been better without it?

5. Since the author of "Aucassin and Nicolette" is anonymous, the tale could have been written by a female rather than by a male. What aspects of the tale support the possibility of a female author? What factors support the possibility of a male author?

6. What aspects of "Aucassin and Nicolette" account for its great popularity? Consider the nature of the conflict and its resolution, the personalities of the characters, and the manner in which the author keeps the audience engaged.

7. What elements made adolescent love such a popular literary subject in the Middle Ages? To what extent, if any, do these reasons continue to exist today?

Doctor Faust (page 258)

1. Faust blames his envy, his ambition, his disdain, and his stubborn will for his destiny. Explain how each contributes to his destiny.

2. To what extent, if any, does a conflict exist in this legend? Evaluate the role of Mephistopheles.

3. What does Faust hope to gain from his bargain with the Devil? What, in fact, does he gain from this bargain?

4. What is the nature of the knowledge that Faust gains? How useful to others is it? Why does he not value it in the end?

5. Why does Faust give up the practice of medicine and other deeds that benefit society after his tour of Hell?

6. Explain who is to blame when Faust tells the buyer of the horse not to ride it through water, and the buyer disregards his warning.

7. What is the nature of Cupid (the Roman name for the Greek god Eros) that the author compares Faust to him?

8. To what extent, if any, is Faust wrong (a) to want more knowledge than society possessed? (b) to want to experience all earthly pleasures?

9. What would Faust have needed to do in order to repent before God? Why does he not repent after his neighbor causes him to evaluate his life? To what extent, if any, could he have canceled his first contract and refused to create a second?

10. Psychologists such as Sigmund Freud and Carl Jung were interested in the legend of Faust, and people throughout the centuries have responded sympathetically to Faust's "identity crisis." What identity crisis does he experience? What, if anything, does his experience reveal about human nature?

11. To what extent, if any, can Faust be viewed as a rebel? A hero? A villain? A fool?

12. In what ways could Faust have better used Mephistopheles?

13. What does the author accomplish (a) by depicting Faust as he does? (b) by including such graphic descriptions of Hell and its Devils? How do these aspects relate to each other and to the legend's theme, tone, and purpose?

14. To what extent, if any, is it wrong for people or nations to do whatever they want to do? What factors cause some people to restrain themselves? What goals might people sacrifice in order to achieve other goals? How do people's values affect their decisions?

15. To what do you attribute the extensive and lasting power and influence of this legend in folklore and literature?

16. The phrase "Faustian bargain" is a common allusion in writing, even today. Discuss an example of a Faustian bargain.

Part 4   The Americas

Botoque, Bringer of Fire (page 287)

1. What aspects of Kayapo life does this myth reflect and explain?

2. What aspects of the jaguar might motivate a shaman to create this myth?

3. In another version of this myth, Botoque uses deception with regard to the macaws. What does his cowardice, which is present in other versions, contribute to the myth?

4. In another version of this myth, Jaguar gives Botoque permission to kill his wife if necessary. However, Botoque still flees in terror because of his deed. What effect does Jaguar's permission have on this myth?

5. Why does Botoque kill Jaguar's wife in this version of the myth? In other versions, he only wounds her. To what extent, if any, does it affect the characterization of Botoque?

6. Why does Botoque steal fire from Jaguar in this version of the myth? In other versions, despite the fact that Botoque kills Jaguar's wife, Jaguar offers Botoque fire. What difference does this change create in the myth?

7. The part of the myth that deals with Botoque's journey back to his village is not part of another version of the myth. What does this version gain by including it?

8. Botoque is the culture hero of the Kayapo people. What qualities does he possess that are heroic? What qualities does he possess that make him human? To what extent, if any, is it possible to justify his theft of fire? In the end, how do you react to his character? Explain.

The Little Frog (page 301)

1. From whose point of view is this folktale told? What evidence in the tale supports your view? Consider the depiction of the various characters.

2. What distinguishes the youngest prince from his two older brothers in his attitude toward the little frog?

3. What, if anything, is unusual about the characterization of the two older brothers? What does their characterization contribute to the tale?

4. (a) Aside from her ability to perform magic, what important qualities does the little frog possess? (b) Why does the frog become uglier for each prince? (c) Why is it important that the princess was born a frog rather than a human being? (d) Why does the release of the frog from the magic spell occur when it does?

5. When the king and queen come to live with Juan at the end of the tale, what meaning does this have for him? What meaning might their decision have for the listener or reader?

6. What is the role of magic in this tale?

7. To what extent, if any, does the narrator contribute to the tale by adding personal comments?

8. What moral(s) or theme(s) does this tale contain?

The Journey beneath the Earth (page 315)

1. Why is King Kitamba in the Village of the Ancestors before he has died?

2. What purpose does this tale serve?

3. How well does this tale achieve its purpose? What elements make it effective?

El Bizarrón and the Devil (page 323)

1. Why does El Bizarrón choose to work for the Devil after he hears about the risk?

2. What is El Bizarrón's goal? How does he achieve it? How does he fool the Devil?

3. Why is El Bizarrón able to fool the Devil?

4. What aspects of this tale are humorous?

5. What function does the Devil's wife perform in the tale?

6. To what extent, if any, is this tale realistic? What does its realism achieve?

7. To what extent, if any, does the Devil learn from his experiences with El Bizarrón? Will another clever person be able to fool him? Explain.

8. Why is the Devil such a popular victim in trickster tales?

Wiley and the Hairy Man (page 332)

1. What qualities make Wiley an appealing character?

2. What role does Wiley's mother play in the folktale? What qualities does she possess that enable her to trick the Hairy Man? What does Wiley learn from her?

3. Why does Mama think that the Hairy Man will try to catch Wiley? What do you think she means when she tells Wiley to be careful?

4. It is clear from the Hairy Man's hair, eyes, and cloven hoofs that he is the Devil. What does he appear to be doing in the swamp with his bag? How does the tale depict him? Why does he keep calling Wiley "boy"? How do you think Wiley reacts to this? Why?

5. What qualities does the Hairy Man possess that make it possible for Wiley and his mother to trick him?

6. What is appealing about the fact that Mama and Wiley are able to trick the Hairy Man? How does this fact affect the traditional concept of the Devil?

7. The Hairy Man is tricked three times in this tale. To what extent, if any, does he learn from these experiences?

8. What is the tone of this tale? What factors contribute to its tone?

9. This tale is usually told by a narrator who is not a participant in the events. What does a first-person narrator contribute to the tale?

The Shepherd Who Understood Animal Speech (page 348)

1. What appears to be the purpose of this tale?

2. Describe the tone of the tale. Why is tone important here?

3. To what extent, if any, is the message of this tale limited to a particular time and place?

4.   To what extent, if any, does this tale express a man's rather than a woman's point of view?

Rip Van Winkle (page 355)

1.   How does Rip appear to feel about the loss of twenty years of his life? If he found himself in the company of Hendrick Hudson and his men again, do you think that he would once again choose to drink their mysterious beverage? Why or why not?

2.   What is the tone of this tale, and how does the author achieve it?

3.   How does the author use irony? What is its purpose?

4.   Why is this legend so famous? What human needs and fantasies does it address?

5.   Which periods of life, if any, might a person wish to sleep through today? Do you think that it would be more interesting to wake up years earlier or years later? Why? If a person were to wake up years earlier, to what extent, if any, do you think that he or she could and would make different decisions?

Giant, the Fire-Bringer (page 365)

1.   What might the fact that the chief gives his son, Giant, a Raven blanket reveal about the raven in Tsimshian society?

2.   Why might Giant, in the form of Raven, be given the role of populating the earth with fruits and fish?

3.   To what extent, if any, is it clear which characters in this myth are human and which are animals? What does this depiction reveal about the environment in which the Tsimshian people have traditionally lived and their values?

4.   What is the relationship between the setting of this myth and the events that occur in it?

5.   What makes Giant such an appealing figure that so many myths and tales are told about him?

6.   What purposes might this myth serve in its culture?

Part 5   The Far East

Savitri (page 377)

1. What does the myth of Savitri reveal about family relation-ships? What does it reveal about the role of women in Hindu society?

2. What role does religion play in the daily lives of these charac-ters?

3. What does the myth of Savitri reveal about the universe in which its characters live? What does it reveal about the Hindu divinities?

4. How does Savitri manage to conquer Yama?

5. How does the goddess Savitri grant Asvapati's wish for sons? What view of life does this fact reveal?

6. The concept of *dharma* refers to a person's sacred obligation to live life in a virtuous way, given one's particular social situation and stage in life. Consequently, *dharma* differs from one person to the next. What does the myth of Savitri reveal about the *dharma* of a wife?

7. In what ways is Savitri a model for other women in her culture?

8. What characteristics of a hero does Savitri possess? Give examples from the myth to support your choices.

9. The concept of *karma* refers to the belief that the ethical nature of one's actions determines the consequences of those actions. How does *karma* function in the myth of Savitri?

10. What values does the myth of Savitri teach?

11. What qualities does the ideal wife possess in your own culture? To what extent, if any, would Savitri be viewed as the ideal wife in that culture? In order to become ideal, how would she have to change?

Kun and the Great Flood (page 400)

1. What events in Kun's life are unusual? Why is the traditional hero's life often characterized by the occurrence of unusual events?

2. What type of universe does the myth of Kun reflect? What does it reflect about the natural world? What does Shang-ti's character reveal about the divine world and the human world?

3. Kun is one of the great rebels in mythology. What heroic qualities does he possess? To what extent, if any, does his rebellion contribute to his heroic image?

Yu the Great and the Great Flood (page 406)

1. What events in Yu's life are unusual? Why is the traditional hero's life often characterized by the occurrence of unusual events?

2. Why does Yu choose not to steal the magic soil from Shang-ti?

3. What type of universe does the myth of Yu reflect? What does it reflect about the natural world? What does Shang-ti's character reveal about the divine world and the human world?

4. Why does Shang-ti tell Yu that he will not end the flood, but that he will permit Yu to end it?

5. What heroic qualities does Yu possess? To what extent, if any, is he a Confucian hero?

6. Why does Shang-ti grant to Yu what he denied to Yu's father, Kun? In what ways is Yu favored by Shang-ti? What could be the basis for this depiction of the situation?

7. What relationship exists between the flood myth of the father and that of the son? What do these myths accomplish through the father-son relationship? Who is the greater hero, Kun or Yu? Explain the reasons for your choice.

8. What is the role of Nu-Chiao in the myth of Yu?

Song of the Water Goddess (page 416)

1. The Ainu divinities in this myth possess human attributes. What anthropomorphic qualities does the Water-Dwelling Goddess possess? What qualities set her apart from mortals?

2. What does the depiction of the Ainu divinities in the "Song of the Water Goddess" reveal about the divine world of the Ainu? What does it reveal about the life of Ainu people?

3. What can we learn from the "Song of the Water Goddess"?

4. What does the perspective of a first-person narrator contribute to this myth?

Taro Urashima, the Young Fisherman (page 423)

1. Why does Taro Urashima decide to open Princess Otohime's box instead of gripping it tightly? What do you think comes out of that box?

2. How does Taro feel at the end of the myth?

3. Who is more responsible for Taro Urashima's fate, Taro himself or Princess Otohime?

4. How do you regard Taro Urashima? To what extent, if any, do you pity him? Why did the Japanese build a shrine to him?

5. What does the myth of Taro Urashima reveal about (a) illusion and reality, (b) love, and (c) life and death?

6. To what extent, if any, do you think that Taro would have been better off if he had rejected the tortoise's invitation?

7. One popular Japanese version of the Urashima myth depicts the tortoise princess as a sky goddess who lives on an eternal mountain. Her form leaves the box and returns to the sky. Taro remains alive, longing for her and grieving for himself as punishment for his disobedience.

    To what extent are the following versions of parts of the myth superior or inferior to the version in the text?

    (a) Otohime is a sky goddess who lives on a mountain.

    (b) Otohime is confined within the box she gives Taro.

    (c) Taro remains alive at the end of the myth.

    (d) Taro does not age.

    (e) The point of this version is that Taro disobeys the goddess and therefore is punished by losing her.

8. In another Japanese version of the myth, the Daughter of the Deep Sea captures Taro and casts a spell on him. Taro wants

to return to his wife and children even though the goddess would make him king of the Deep Sea. He finally succumbs to her tears and agrees to remain with her for one night. When he returns, the rest of the myth is the same as that in the text.

Explain the effect on the myth of having the goddess capture Taro and keep him against his will, finally using her tears to soften his heart.

9. A Chinese version of the Urashima myth is set in the T'ang dynasty (seventh to tenth centuries A.D.) and called "Liu Yi and the Dragon King." A student rescues the youngest daughter of the Dragon King of Lake Dongting from a bad marriage and falls in love with her. However, he cautiously refuses to marry a goddess and returns to life on earth. Later, the goddess returns to earth in disguise and marries him. In time, he recognizes her and they live happily ever after, first on earth, where he never ages, and then in the underwater palace of the Dragon King.

How does this reversal of the Urashima myth compare with the Japanese version in the text? Which is a better myth? Why?

10. What human needs and fantasies does the myth of Urashima address that might explain its popularity in Japan as well as its universality?

The Tiger's Whisker (page 432)

1. Why does Yun Ok assume that she needs the Sage of the Mountains to create a potion for her?

2. Why does the learned hermit tell Yun Ok that she has to supply the tiger's whisker for the potion that he will give her? Why does he insist that the whisker must come from a living tiger?

3. What gives Yun Ok the ability to face the tiger and the motivation to spend so many months attempting to tame it?

4. Why does Yun Ok still think she needs the learned hermit's potion after she has returned with the tiger's whisker? The term *irony* describes a contrast between appearance and reality. What is ironic about Yun Ok's situation? Consider

how she views her situation, and what the reality of her situation is.

5. Why does the learned hermit ask Yun Ok to describe how she acquired the tiger's whisker?

6. In the traditional folktale, the hero or heroine often must pass a test in order to gain a reward. What test, if any, must Yun Ok pass? What, if anything, is her reward?

7. What role does the learned hermit perform in this tale? To what extent, if any, do you think he deserves his reputation for wisdom?

8. What themes do you find in this tale? In what ways are they relevant to human lives around the world and through time?

Kerta's Sacrifice (page 443)

1. Why does Kerta ignore his father's statements about Roro Kidul?

2. What factors influence Kerta's decision to eat Roro Kidul's food?

3. Why does Roro Kidul appear before Kerta twice, each time with a different personality?

4. Why does Roro Kidul punish Pak Miam when it is Kerta who ate her food? What would have happened if Kerta had not decided to rescue his father?

5. What factors motivate Kerta to rescue his father?

6. Why does Kerta hear his father's voice? What determines when he hears it?

7. How does Kerta maintain the courage that he needs in order to perform his task?

8. What does the detailed description of swift's-nest gathering contribute to the myth?

9. What is the function of magic in this myth?

10. What gives this myth its power?